REGIONAL APPROACHES TO SOCIETY AND COMPLEXITY

Monographs in Mediterranean Archaeology
Series Editor: A. Bernard Knapp, University of Glasgow and Cyprus American Archaeological Research Institute

Aimed at the international archaeological community, *Monographs in Mediterranean Archaeology* (*MMA*) seeks significant new contributions from the multicultural world of Mediterranean archaeology, publishing problem-oriented studies that present a solid, extensive corpus of archaeological data within a sound theoretical and/or methodological framework. *MMA* volumes deal with major archaeological issues related to the islands and lands or regions that border (or impact on) the Mediterranean Sea. No constraints are placed on the period of focus, from Palaeolithic through early Modern. We encourage contributions that treat the social, politico-economic and ideological aspects of local or regional production and development; issues related to social interaction and change or exchange; or more specific and contemporary issues such as gender, agency, identity, representation, phenomenology and landscape.

Published volumes:

Mortuary Ritual and Society in Bronze Age Cyprus
(Volume 9)
Priscilla Keswani

Debating Orientalization: Multidisciplinary Approaches to Change in the Ancient Mediterranean
(Volume 10, Volume Editor: John F. Cherry)
Edited by Corinna Riva and Nicholas C. Vella

Rural Landscapes of the Punic World
(Volume 11)
Peter van Dommelen and Carlos Gómez Bellard

The Power of Technology in the Bronze Age Eastern Mediterranean: The Case of the Painted Plaster
(Volume 12)
Ann Brysbaert

Citadel and Cemetery in Early Bronze Age Anatolia
(Volume 13)
Christoph Bachhuber

The Archaeology of Nuragic Sardinia
(Volume 14)
Gary S. Webster

Regional Approaches to Society and Complexity

Studies in Honor of John F. Cherry

Edited by
Alex R. Knodell and Thomas P. Leppard

eQuInOx

SHEFFIELD uk   BRISTOL ct

Published by Equinox Publishing Ltd.

UK: Office 415, The Workstation, 15 Paternoster Row, Sheffield, South Yorkshire, S1 2BX
USA: ISD, 70 Enterprise Drive, Bristol, CT 06010

www.equinoxpub.com

First published 2018

British Library Cataloguing-in-Publication Data

A catalogue record for this book is available from the British Library.

ISBN-13   978-1-78179-739-6   (hardback)
          978-1-78179-527-9   (paperback)

Library of Congress Cataloging-in-Publication Data

Names: Knodell, Alex R., editor. | Leppard, Thomas P., editor. | Cherry, John F., honouree.
Title: Regional approaches to society and complexity / edited by Alex R. Knodell and Thomas P. Leppard.
Description: Sheffield, UK ; Bristol, CT : Equinox Publishing Ltd, 2018. | Series: Monographs in Mediterranean archaeology ; volume 15 | Includes bibliographical references and index. | Description based on print version record and CIP data provided by publisher; resource not viewed.
Identifiers: LCCN 2016055122 (print) | LCCN 2017019990 (ebook) | ISBN 9781781795859 (ePDF) | ISBN 9781781797396 (hb)
Subjects: LCSH: Social archaeology--Case studies. | Social archaeology--Methodology--Case studies. | Mediterranean Region--Antiquities.
Classification: LCC CC72.4 (ebook) | LCC CC72.4 .R45 2018 (print) | DDC 930.1--dc23
LC record available at https://lccn.loc.gov/2016055122

Typeset by ISB Typesetting, Sheffield
www.sheffieldtypesetting.com

Printed and bound by Lightning Source Inc. (La Vergne, TN), Lightning Source UK Ltd. (Milton Keynes), Lightning Source AU Pty. (Scoresby, Victoria)

Contents

List of Figures and Tables

Figures

Foreword

Colin Renfrew

A key task of the archaeologist and historian is to understand the processes of culture change as they have worked in the past, and indeed as they work right up to the present day. That task may be attempted in tight focus at a local scale, or in a very broad optic at a global level. Yet it is the regional approach, undertaken at an intermediate or meso-scale, which permits the consideration of specific data (as the global scale may not), while offering the hope of discerning patterns or regularities whose recognition and analysis may make the observed changes intelligible and in a sense meaningful to the researcher and the historian. Here the value of the regional approach becomes very clear.

This remarkable collection of well-focused studies reveals how the very nature of the task has changed over the past half century of archaeological fieldwork, and specifically of field survey. The key to the transformation lies only partly in the new technologies of GPS and GIS, of digital recording, and of online publication, as reviewed here. It lies more specifically in the self-critical approach, and in the theoretical awareness both of the problems of emerging social complexity and of the praxis of regional survey, as represented so well in the fieldwork, the teaching, and the publications of John F. Cherry, to whom this volume is dedicated. Most of the general problems which underlie the analysis of emerging social complexity, not least the phenomenon of state formation, have been addressed by him in a series of seminal papers over the past 40 years. This volume, written in response to his work by those who have been his students and his other admirers, gives a fresh and clear overview of the challenges of regional survey, of data analysis, synthesis, and interpretation.

I am very happy to have the opportunity of writing a few preliminary words, since in earlier years I have had the benefit of working in the field with John Cherry, and of admiring his calm and methodical approach, always applying a sampling strategy which addresses the central problems under investigation, while realistically appraising the available resources of time and energy. I have reason to be grateful for his application of these qualities in our fieldwork, first in Orkney and then in Melos. And I have admired the clarity of his more theoretical writing, not least in the field of state formation and of island archaeology.

In their Introduction, the editors firmly set the agenda for the papers which follow, very effectively advocating the value of the meso-scale regional approach taken by all the papers here. As they point out: 'It is relatively rare to encounter regional studies with an explicitly comparative agenda', and they rightly acknowledge that the initiative can be traced back to two leading figures in the archaeology of the mid-twentieth century,

Gordon Willey and Robert Braidwood. They situate the papers which follow against the background of their work and of the pioneering systematic surveys of Robert Adams in Mesopotamia and of the Teotihuacan survey and other early initiatives in Mesoamerica and Peru.

The volume begins, in Part I, with the problems surrounding the rise of social complexity and the formation of state societies in the prehistoric Aegean. Issues of wider control and local agency are then discussed. The role of prestige goods imported from afar is considered, and of the new localized meanings which they acquired. The limited role of monumentality and the absence of representations of rulers in the early Aegean are considered in relation to the specific functions of writing.

Then the temporal and geographical scale widens to the later Mediterranean and beyond. Issues in island archaeology, illuminated by Cherry's early papers, are addressed in the west Mediterranean as well as in the Aegean, and then in the Caribbean. Insularity has been one of the most coherently explored issues in recent archaeological theory, and island environments bring out well the conflicting themes of isolation and interaction.

The more abstract and explicitly comparative concerns which are addressed in the papers which follow draw upon theoretical constructs which Cherry has pioneered, such as peer polity interaction. The authors demonstrate well how the techniques of regional survey, when informed by a self-critical theoretical approach, can be applied as effectively to the political territories of the ancient Maya as to the city states of Ancient Greece or the polities of prehistoric Crete. They grapple also with the contemporary concerns with the notion of agency, and whether material things can themselves have agency.

In their concluding Retrospect and Prospect the editors offer a perceptive overview of current trends in world archaeology, where the 'material turn' associated with what they identify as the 'new materialisms' has to be integrated with the biophysical and environmental considerations which underlie regional settlement systems. They wisely endorse the increasingly divergent range of theoretical approaches applied.

John Cherry, it should be remembered, undertook the non-trivial task of co-editing what became Lewis Binford's most readable collection of writings, *In Pursuit of the Past*. In his work he has consistently sought both the firm reliance upon good data and robust analysis to reveal significant patterning in the working of culture process to which Binford aspired. All the papers here have benefitted from the lucidity and the reflexive attention to method which Cherry has consistently applied and promoted. It is because this volume exemplifies those qualities so effectively, as well as advocating them so coherently, that it will become a landmark publication in the advocacy of good, theoretically robust archaeology, with a respectful approach to the collection and analysis of data.

In 2004, John was the co-editor of the *Festschrift* presented to me on my retirement as Disney Professor of Archaeology in Cambridge, and in 2011 he kindly wrote the Foreword to the reprint of my *The Emergence of Civilisation*, first published in 1972. As the supervisor of his doctoral dissertation at the University of Southampton, initiated more than 40 years ago, I am very happy to reciprocate in writing this Foreword to his *Festschrift*, and in wishing him many more years of innovative research and publication.

About the Author

Colin Renfrew (Lord Renfrew of Kaimsthorn) is Disney Professor of Archaeology Emeritus at the University of Cambridge, and former Director of the McDonald Institute for Archaeological Research, where he is currently a Senior Fellow. He is a preeminent figure in world archaeology, known for his work on radiocarbon dating, archaeogenetics, and Aegean Prehistory, and his efforts to prevent looting and quell the illegal antiquities trade. His recent publications include *The Cambridge World Prehistory* (Cambridge, 2013) and a reissue of *The Emergence of Civilisation: The Cyclades and Aegean in the Third Millennium BC* (Oxbow Books, 2011, with Foreword by John F. Cherry). E-mail: acr10@cam.ac.uk

Preface

Alex R. Knodell and Thomas P. Leppard

This volume presents a group of studies in honor of John F. Cherry, Joukowsky Family Professor of Archaeology at the Joukowsky Institute for Archaeology and the Ancient World at Brown University. The papers herein consider regional approaches to complex societies from a variety of perspectives and on a global scale. John Cherry has been a key figure in regional-scale inquiry throughout his career, producing, mentoring, and inspiring a remarkably eclectic body of work, which nevertheless remains oriented around this central theme. We explore this core concern of regional approaches to society and complexity in a broad, comparative sense, largely reflecting the wide-ranging interests of the honorand. We begin in the Aegean, then branch out to the wider Mediterranean and to the New World, and finally reflect on issues of concern to all archaeologists working at levels above the site.

Let us begin with some context. On 4 and 5 December 2015, a two-part conference was held to honor the long, productive, and very much ongoing career of John Cherry, the intellectual content of which forms the foundation for this volume. John's research, teaching, and mentorship have been widely influential in the field of archaeology, especially of the Mediterranean world. His scholarly career has included fieldwork on three continents (in Great Britain, Texas, Greece, Albania, Armenia, and Montserrat). He has served on numerous editorial boards and as co-editor of *World Archaeology* and the *Journal of Mediterranean Archaeology*; he is also the founder and Series Editor for the Joukowsky Institute Publication series. His own scholarly production (at time of writing) includes some 14 books and well over 150 journal articles, book chapters, and book reviews. But it is perhaps as a teacher, mentor, and director of graduate programs that his impact on the field has been most widely felt. After beginning his career at Sheffield, he has held teaching positions and directed graduate programs at the University of Cambridge, the University of Michigan, and Brown University, where he continues to serve as Director of Graduate Studies at the Joukowsky Institute for Archaeology and the Ancient World. Many of his graduate students (including several contributors to this book) have gone on to become major scholars and leaders in their respective fields, which is perhaps the truest testament of all to John's care for and devotion to thoughtful and rigorous research and training.

The aforementioned conference, therefore, was an assembly of John's current and former students, colleagues, friends, and family, featuring some lighthearted reminiscences on Friday evening, followed by an academic program on Saturday oriented around the theme of Regional Approaches to Society and Complexity. Presentations on both days were delivered to a full house, as colleagues and former students—many not involved in the formal program and having traveled across the country (or Atlantic) to attend—packed into the lecture hall and atrium of the Joukowsky Institute to honor and celebrate John's myriad contributions to the field.

In the course of organizing the conference we composed a letter to invite participants and to explain the goals and scope of the event and intended volume. In it we quoted the well-known parable of Archilochus, 'The fox knows many things, but the hedgehog knows one big thing', which has been used by several later writers to divide thinkers into those whose work is built around a single great idea (hedgehogs) and those who draw on and engage with a multiplicity of concepts (foxes). Isaiah Berlin famously employed this device to describe Leo Tolstoy, arguing that while Tolstoy seemed to be a fox, he was at heart a hedgehog, his varied intellectual approaches unable to conceal a fundamental belief in the limitations of a rational approach to the world. We suggested such a comparison for John Cherry, whose diverse contributions to our field make him appear to be a fox, but whose core, fundamental interests in regional-scale inquiry and its contribution to understanding the organization of societies suggest he has also the best attributes of the hedgehog.

Cherry's career has at its core focused on the challenge of integrating the social and spatial organization of human communities: on understanding societies and behavior at the level of a readily-graspable and meaningful territorial framework, via the distribution and analysis of material culture. Beneath the ebb and flow of theoretical and terminological tides, we as archaeologists are still fundamentally concerned with these two types of organization, how they drive each other, and how we can track change through deep time. Archaeology conducted beyond the site (regional survey or landscape archaeology) is uniquely positioned to contribute to these questions.

This volume brings together leading scholars, from research contexts in the Mediterranean and well beyond, whose work has focused on connecting the diachronic distribution of material culture over the landscape with the growth (and decay) of social systems. In particular, attention is paid to the following questions: How and why did people organize themselves, or become organized, socially and spatially? How do social and spatial organization relate? What are the best methods for understanding the emergence, operation, and decline of complex social systems? How can we make meaningful comparisons of such processes in different cultural contexts? How do we understand and explain past social change at a regional scale? The varied yet clustering contributions to answering these questions provide a *tour d'horizon* of archaeology above the level of the site.

There are many people to thank for their roles in staging the conference at Brown and in putting together this volume. The conference and volume have been a pleasure to organize at every step along the way, not least due to the support with which we were met at every turn. Sue Alcock, Cyprian Broodbank, Jack Davis, and Bernard Knapp were brought into our planning from a very early stage, and offered much careful guidance throughout the process. Peter van Dommelen became Director of the Joukowsky Institute during the course of the organization, and eagerly supported what we and Sue Alcock had already begun to put in place. We are very grateful to the Joukowsky Institute for generously sponsoring the December 2015 event, and especially to Sarah Sharpe and Jess Porter for handling so expertly all of the many logistical and administrative arrangements that go into such a gathering.

We are of course grateful to all of the contributors to this volume for their papers and enthusiastic participation, even in the face of narrow deadlines. We regret that some participants were not able to contribute to the volume in the end, for various reasons: Sue Alcock, Bryan Burns, Lori Khatchadourian, and Laurie Talalay were nonetheless invaluable participants in the foregoing conference and discussion. Bernard Knapp provided sage advice and expertise on putting the volume together, along with his support as Series Editor of Monographs in Mediterranean Archaeology. Richard Bartholomew was an indispensable copy editor and Ayla Çevik prepared the index. Evan Levine produced several of the maps and Chris Cloke brought to light the images used for the cover, frontispiece, and afterword (from the archives of the Nemea Valley Archaeological Project, courtesy of the Department of Classics, University of Cincinnati). Many thanks go also to Bob Chapman and Tom Tartaron for reviewing and commenting on the volume in its entirety. Finally, we are most grateful to John Cherry for bringing this group together and for the years of teaching, mentorship, friendship, and inspiration that made such a book possible.

Participants in the December 2015 conference at the Joukowsky Institute (left to right): Tom Leppard, Sue Alcock, Sturt Manning, Cyprian Broodbank, Brad Sekedat, Camilla MacKay, Lori Khatchadourian, Bryan Burns, Scott Fitzpatrick, Alex Smith, Mike Galaty, Sylvian Fachard, John Cherry, Tom Garrison, Bill Parkinson, Jack Davis, Krysta Ryzewski, Bernard Knapp, Laurie Talalay, Chris Witmore, Peter van Dommelen, Alex Knodell (photograph by Sarah Sharpe).

1 Regional Approaches to Society and Complexity: Setting an Agenda

Alex R. Knodell and Thomas P. Leppard

Introduction

This book examines the archaeology of complex societies. It is concerned with how such societies are constituted, how they are maintained, how they break down, and how they are studied and understood on a variety of spatial and conceptual scales. The papers in this volume approach complex societies, then, from the view offered by regional approaches to the archaeological record, rather than the perspective of the individual site. The capacity of regional archaeology to elucidate how and in what terms human social and spatial organization changed over time is not a new theme, especially in the case of Mediterranean archaeology. It is relatively rarer, however, to encounter regional studies with an explicitly comparative agenda— one that aims toward methodological and theoretical relevance beyond the sub-disciplines of archaeology in which individual studies tend to be situated, and where environmentally based methodological discussions and regionally specific research concerns predominate. By regional archaeology we are concerned here less with a series of methods and more with an integrative, synthesizing approach that takes geographically coherent parts or wholes of ancient and historical polities to be useful scales of study. We recognize, moreover, that a 'region' and thus 'regional approaches' can well refer to multiple geographical and analytical scales, from microregions (see Horden and Purcell 2000; Broodbank 2013) to whole islands (e.g., Bevan and Conolly 2013; Manning, this volume), to the Mediterranean as a whole, for example under the Roman empire. In the context of this volume all of these scales of regionality obtain, depending on the geographical and political definitions of territory relevant to the studies at hand. We are therefore not so concerned with developing strict definitions of regions or prescriptions for regional studies as we are in forwarding approaches that are theoretically transparent, broadly relevant to other scholars, and acknowledge the multi-scalar nature of regional dynamics.

Complexity is used here to refer to archaeological studies of sociopolitical organization, with a particular interest in the creation, maintenance, and change of power relationships over time (e.g., Renfrew and Cherry 1986; Chapman 1990; 2003; Knapp 1993). This volume builds on recent approaches to regional interaction, politics, and social complexity (e.g., Kohring and Wynne-Jones 2007; Schoep *et al.* 2012; Knappett 2013) in its insistence (1) that regional archaeology in the Mediterranean can speak to archaeology outside of the Mediterranean, (2) that surface survey has useful things to say to single-site excavation, and (3) that prehistorians and those archaeologists who work with documentary evidence need not be divided by method or the structure of the academy. Individually the chapters in this book provide case studies, theoretical perspectives, and disciplinary outlooks concerning regional approaches to the study of past social groups. As a whole, they aim to build more robust and cross-culturally relevant models for the study of complex societies, which we define as social groups that are variously hierarchical, specialized, and urban or centralized, with often radically skewed distributions of actual and symbolic capital.

It seems appropriate, if somewhat presumptuous, that a book of studies assembled in honor of John F. Cherry should begin with an aspirational Cherry-esque essay discussing the 'state of the field' for regional archaeology (Cherry 1983b; 1994; 2003; 2005; Alcock and Cherry 2004). It has been over a decade, however, since Cherry's last trenchant assessment (although see comments in Alcock and Cherry 2013 for some more recent views). The timing seems generally right for an update, and the context even more so.

In this chapter, as a means of both framing and introducing the subsequent contributions, we provide an overview of where things stand in terms of our two key concerns—regional studies and the archaeology of complex societies—and propose an agenda for moving them forward in an increasingly varied disciplinary landscape. While some of the ideas and concepts presented here will be familiar to many readers, we hope to offer (here and in the concluding chapter of this volume) the sort of retrospect and prospect necessary for some thoughtful consideration of the context of the current volume and the work of its honorand. Here we follow the model of the volume as a whole, with emphasis on a broad region—the Aegean (especially) and the wider Mediterranean—but including examples from other world archaeologies, prioritizing a comparative agenda as a productive way forward in individual regional studies, anthropological comparisons, and macroregional syntheses. We conclude with a cautiously optimistic agenda, which we believe to be well represented in the papers of this volume.

Critical Moments in the Archaeology of Regions

Understanding the current state of regional archaeology depends, to a considerable extent, on appreciating its intellectual origins and trajectories. Our goal here is not to provide a comprehensive review from protohistory to the present, but rather to identify some key points, some of which have not been emphasized by previous scholarship on the subject (e.g., Bennet and Galaty 1997; Cherry 2003; Tartaron 2008). In particular, we emphasize articulations between the Mediterranean world and other world archaeologies, maintaining an approach that is at once Mediterranean-focused and yet conceptually comparative.

Regional studies of past human activity can be traced back to Herodotus, Thucydides, and perhaps even Homer, who, in the 'Catalog of Ships' (*Iliad* 2.494-759), aimed to describe the political geography of the (to him) semi-legendary Bronze Age. A particular focus on documenting the past through its material remains is first seen in the travel writers of the Roman period, such as Strabo and Pausanias, who provide a convenient starting point for materially oriented studies of regions (e.g., Cherry 2001; Fachard, this volume). This genre of travel writing remained the primary venue for the publication of archaeological sites and landscapes for the bulk of recorded history, with highlights in the Mediterranean including Cyriac of Ancona (early fifteenth century AD) and later wealthy Europeans on various versions of the Grand Tour from the eighteenth to twentieth centuries (see, e.g., Pajor 2006: 50-53 for an extensive list). A similar trend in travel writing emerged in the New World following its 'discovery' by Europeans. Out of these accounts, which combined elements of what we would now describe as amateur archaeology, geography, and ethnography, came specific—if not systematic—studies of the past production of material culture at regional and macroregional scales.

More orderly accounts appeared in the nineteenth century, for example in the work of Colonel William Martin Leake in Greece, who published extensive summaries of the topography and monuments of Athens (Leake 1821), the Peloponnese (Leake 1830), and northern Greece (Leake 1835), among dozens of other volumes and articles (Wagstaff 2001; Witmore 2004; Witmore and Buttrey 2008). This era also saw the birth of multi-disciplinary regional studies in Greece, with the French Expédition Scientifique de Morée (Blouet 1831), set up in the wake of Napoleon's scientific expedition to Egypt, which was published as the multi-volume *Description de l'Égypte*. The multi-field, scientific approach of such projects provided inspiration for later archaeological efforts, but at this point remained largely descriptive, with an archaeological component operating as one of several largely independent scientific efforts.

Accounts similar to Leake's followed shortly after in the New World (Stephens 1841; 1843), indeed involving some of the same adventurer-scholars, such as John Lloyd Stephens and Frederick Catherwood, who had previously undertaken similar work in the Old World, most notably at sites such as Petra (Stephens 1837; 1838). This semi-systematic scholarly documentation continued as a popular endeavor through a long legacy of explorer-archaeologists (Ashmore and Willey 1981: 5), remaining the primary mode of regional archaeological fieldwork even after the advent of long-term excavation projects in the late nineteenth and early twentieth centuries. Such studies form an essential backdrop of much contemporary regional work. In some cases they laid the groundwork for other forms of inquiry, such as long-term excavation projects, and provided a base for intensive site-oriented studies associated with the early professionalization of archaeology; in nearly every case they record an archaeological landscape that has transformed dramatically over the last two centuries. These early accounts are too often overlooked as colonial curiosities, when in fact they form an essential, and still relevant, part of disciplinary, archaeological, and ethnographic history.

The middle of the twentieth century marks a critical juncture in the development of regional studies in archaeology on a global scale, in which priorities shifted from cataloging and describing sites to explaining and understanding their distribution in a broader context. Following the path-breaking work of Gordon Willey's Virú Valley Project (carried out in 1946), regional archaeology gradually became more structured through the lens of settlement pattern studies (Willey 1953). Roughly contemporary was Braidwood's Prehistoric Project (1947–1955) in Mesopotamia, with Adams's Diyala Basin Archaeological Project (1957–1958) beginning shortly thereafter (Braidwood and Howe 1960; Adams 1965). In Mesoamerica, Willey's work in the Belize Valley (1954–1956) began immediately after the publication of the Virú Valley Project, followed closely by Sanders's Teotihuacán Valley Project in 1960–1964 and MacNeish's contemporary work in the Tehuacan Valley (Sanders 1965; Willey *et al.* 1965; Byers 1968; see also Garrison 2007 for a historical review of Maya settlement pattern studies). This early stage of systematic regional fieldwork coincided with Adams's *Evolution of Urban Society* (1966), which remains one of the more interesting and important Old World / New World comparative studies to this day.

In the Aegean, the oft-cited progenitor of systematic, multidisciplinary survey in the Mediterranean, the University of Minnesota Messenia Expedition (UMME), carried out fieldwork in the 1950s and 1960s (McDonald and Rapp 1972). The coincident publication of UMME and Renfrew's *Emergence of Civilisation* (1972)— along with insurgent works such as Clarke's *Models in Archaeology* (1972; see also Clarke 1968) and Binford's *An Archaeological Perspective* (1972)—all functioned, as Cherry has put it, to 'kick-start' regional studies in the Aegean (Cherry 2003: 141). The English translation of Braudel's (1972) landmark work on Mediterranean history spurred further interest in human–environmental interactions, landscape, and the very long term (Bintliff 1991; Knapp 1992). The groundwork for Mediterranean regional studies was thus fairly well established by the early 1970s, and in line with wider developments in world archaeology.

The origins of this movement, however, seem more serendipitous. UMME's initial motivation was the recovery of Homeric and Bronze Age topography in the southwest Peloponnese, informed by the tradition of classical topography (going back to Pausanias). Recognition quickly followed, however, that any detailed survey of the landscape involved encounters with remains from many different periods, necessitating a diachronic range, if not equal precision, of recording. While UMME can be said to have looked to projects from both Old and New World contexts, Cherry (2003: 142) cogently observed that this influence seems to have been present more in the ultimate publication than in the actual fieldwork. Nevertheless, it remains the case that the Aegean followed closely the aforementioned trends in global archaeology, after which there was a massive boom in research whose goals were to study the distribution of human settlement across the landscape on a regional scale.

Around the same time as the gestational period of systematic regional survey in the 1950s–1960s, Julian Steward (1960)—a long-time colleague of Willey who was involved in the initial planning of the Virú Valley Project—described the region as the most meaningful scale of analysis in the social sciences in general. By the time Willey went to Peru, he was in many ways out to deploy Steward's theories concerning regions in an archaeological context. Binford (1964), in turn, argued in one of the New Archaeology's foundational texts that regions, rather than sites, represented the most important units of analysis in archaeology. An increasingly explicit shift toward problem orientation, methodological transparency, and sampling were all part of what Clarke (1973) referred to as archaeology's 'loss of innocence' and led to practical and theoretical discussions of regional research design becoming increasingly important for both the documentation and interpretation of the archaeological record (e.g., Redman 1973; 1987; Plog *et al.* 1978; Schiffer *et al.* 1978). Survey also emerged as a more economically viable (low-cost) alternative to lengthy excavations and (early on, at least) was not subject to many of the permitting regulations of excavations, thus representing a sort of democratization of the field in parts of the world with long-standing fieldwork traditions oriented around excavation. Many of these conversations took form in North American archaeology long before they had made waves across the Atlantic, coinciding with the early, US-based graduate career of John Cherry, one element that may partially explain his leading role in pioneering developments in Aegean regional survey in the 1970s and 1980s.

Periodic accounts of the development of archaeological survey in Greece (Cherry 1983b; 1994; 2003; Fotiadis 1995; Bennet and Galaty 1997; Tartaron 2008) describe a 'new wave' of survey projects in terms of methodological explicitness, increasing intensity, and systematic sampling. The wave included several roughly contemporary projects running from the mid-1970s to mid-1980s: the Melos Survey (Cherry 1982), the Argolid Exploration Project (Jameson *et al.* 1994), the Cambridge/Bradford Boeotia Expedition (Bintliff and Snodgrass 1985), and the Keos Archaeological Survey (Cherry *et al.* 1991). These projects and their successors all (1) emphasized the importance of regions over the individual site, making strong cases for survey as a stand-alone endeavor, (2) began to incorporate off-site data into archaeological research questions, (3) sought to synthesize diachronic regional datasets to answer questions of historical and anthropological importance, and (4) were committed to the continual incorporation of multiple methods and new techniques. The use of increasingly intensive methods—where intensity is measured by amount of person hours/days invested per square kilometer—followed the maxim that greater intensity of investigation results in the discovery of more sites and the acquisition of more data (Cherry 1983b: 390-91). Parkinson (this volume) argues that these developments have been carried even further in recent years, describing a new 'new wave' of microregional studies. This movement, while originating in the Mediterranean, has spread increasingly far afield, as witnessed by the work of several contributors to this volume in the Middle East, Europe, and the New World (e.g., Parkinson and Gyucha 2012; Ryzewski and Cherry 2016; Knodell *et al.* 2017).

While the discussion above prioritizes Aegean archaeology, it seems fair to characterize two general phases in the development of regional archaeology globally during the mid- to late-twentieth century. First, an 'awakening' that involved systematization of fieldwork and research design, which rested upon a new appreciation of what the most mundane materials can tell us. Many of the key debates that would follow hinged upon how to interpret surface materials and other such run-of-the-mill remains. Second, a 'new wave' of projects generally embodied and then intensified attention to these principles, both methodologically and theoretically. With increasing attention to theory and modes of interpretation came a diversification of interpretative frameworks, again paralleling broad, 'postprocessual' trends in world archaeology. We might identify here a third phase of regional studies, often under the banner of 'landscape' archaeology (e.g., Ashmore and Knapp 1999; David and Thomas 2008), although there is remarkable variation in how this term is deployed. While these phases may be seen as global trends, Mediterranean archaeology has demonstrated a long-standing interest in the explicit integration of long-term historical perspectives with the 'processual' achievements of the 'new wave' and the more interpretative approaches that followed (e.g., Cherry *et al.* 1991; Given and Knapp 2003; Given 2013). Finally, we suggest that developments in technologies of data acquisition, management, and analysis have ushered in a fourth phase of regional archaeology, witnessed across the globe. In recent years the proliferation of spatial and database technologies has dramatically changed the ways in which archaeologists gather, analyze, and curate information, substantially enough to usher in a new era of research production and design. Such advances may appear at face value to be strictly technical, but it would be a mistake to think that they have not reshaped conceptual and interpretative frameworks as well, as new types of analysis become more widespread and accessible, and are utilized with increasingly large and diverse datasets.

Geographic Information Systems (GIS) and spatial data collection and analysis have played a role in regional archaeology for a long time, but exponential change in how they are deployed in recent years has made these technologies more widely available and accessible than ever before, not to mention much more powerful (McCoy and Ladefoged 2009). Compare, for example, the vast differences between books on GIS in archaeology published over the last 20 years (Aldenderfer and Maschner 1996; Conolly and Lake 2006; Bevan and Lake 2013), and in its use in individual studies (Gaffney and Stancic 1996; Bevan and Conolly 2013). Commercial and open-access GIS applications, along with the rest of the 'tech' world, are becoming cheaper, more user-friendly, more mobile, and more powerful every year. Most data recording necessary for an archaeological survey project can now be carried out on a tablet or cellphone, from mapping and notation to photography and drawing. Many projects have fully embraced 'going digital' and rely on mobile systems for spatial and the bulk of other data recording (e.g., Fachard *et al.* 2015; Roosevelt *et al.* 2015), although not without caution concerning the potential of data loss and the need for careful curation.

Remotely sensed data—and especially its public availability—represents another rapidly expanding zone of opportunity. High-resolution satellite imagery is now a *sine qua non* for regional archaeology, whether from open-source repositories such as Google Earth or any number of commercial vendors such as DigitalGlobe. At its most basic level, the view from above offered by high-resolution satellite imagery is essential, and researchers are already leveraging—and grappling with the ethical implications of—the potential of Google Earth in the location and description of archaeological remains (Myers 2010; Kennedy and Bishop 2011). Multi-spectral imagery offers its own analytical values in its capacity to draw 'highlights', 'hot spots', or other anomalies out of hundreds or even thousands of square kilometers in a relatively short amount of time (Parcak 2009; Garrison 2010; Garrison *et al.* 2011). One of the most promising (if depressing) applications of such analysis is in monitoring damage or destruction to threatened landscapes over time (Parcak *et al.* 2016). It remains to be seen how new efforts in crowd-sourcing the remote examination of archaeological landscapes play out. Certain aspects of imagery analysis remain highly subjective and dependent on the personal experience of researchers. There is not currently, nor is there ever likely to be, a magic button for unequivocally identifying archaeological remains from space. Nevertheless, people can be trained, and such efforts toward outreach and engagement hold great potential. Even more potentially field-shaping is the use and increasing availability of LiDAR data, especially in regions in which surface survey and other forms of remote sensing are hampered by thick vegetation (Chase *et al.* 2012; Opitz *et al.* 2015). Finally, in the last five years alone, the rapidly decreasing costs of drone-based aerial photography and photogrammetry have made such practices nearly standard on archaeological projects (Sapirstein and Murray 2017).

Data-sharing technologies have also fundamentally changed the way archaeologists do work in and out of the field. From server-based, mobile data collection systems to data-sharing and syncing applications like Dropbox or Google Drive, collaboration across continents is easier and faster than ever before. Such changes in collaborative knowledge production affect not only the ways in which data are made available, but also how datasets are created. One of the major challenges of archaeology in the twenty-first century is the problem of long-term curation of digital datasets (Shanks 2007). Solutions are by no means straightforward, and the optimistically anticipated potentials of the digital age (e.g., Cherry 1983b; 1994; 2003) for the most part have yet to be realized (MacKay, this volume), at least in terms of large-scale processing and comparison of diverse archaeological information.

Rapidly expanding opportunities for data acquisition and analysis do not necessarily represent some kind of unqualified good, but to the contrary raise serious questions about how to deal with this 'data deluge' critically and responsibly (Bevan 2015). Technological advances in data recording certainly do not represent a cure-all, and spatial and information-sharing technologies are as susceptible to the pitfalls of a 'black box' approach as any other. Nevertheless, they have fundamentally changed the way we undertake and interpret regional archaeology. This by no means suggests that the 'tried and true' ways of doing things are obsolete: hand drawings in the field are in most cases superior to anything produced on a tablet, GPS points do not provide a sense of landscape context, and databases do not provide the meaningful interpretations that come with deep thought and familiarity with particular landscapes or materials. In these terms critical approaches to the media of engagement are more important than ever (Ryzewski 2009). But there is no going back from what can only be described as an ongoing, even intensifying, digital revolution. We turn next to issues of interpretation.

The Order of Things, Questions of Scale: Making Sense of Social Complexity

This volume is concerned with what questions we ask of the archaeological record on regional scales. The papers that follow examine issues of social complexity, namely its development over time, its relation to landscape, and the role of archaeological materials—things—in its constitution. We must also ask how we can put the results of diversely conducted archaeological fieldwork into dialogue—within and across regions, across cultures, integrating multiple types of archaeological data—and how we can make our results more broadly relevant to researchers working in different areas with often divergent research traditions.

This is no small matter, for it affects directly just how we can, beyond the geographical bounds of individual projects, ask questions concerning the social and spatial organization of human societies. This concern with archaeology beyond the site, social structures at multiple scales, and how best to access and reconstruct their dynamics is the great taproot of this volume, largely inspired by Cherry's work on island archaeology (e.g., Cherry 1982), Minoan and Mycenaean states (e.g., Cherry 1977; 1983a; 1986; Cherry and Davis 2001; 2007), and his fieldwork on three continents (e.g., Cherry 1982; Wright *et al.* 1990; Cherry *et al.* 1991; 2010; 2012). The broader questions raised herein require not only the comparison of different types of survey data, but the integration of disparate artifactual, excavation, and environmental evidence, often across a range of geographical scales.

Data comparability between projects has been seen increasingly as a thorny issue, and one requiring significant attention (Alcock and Cherry 2004). Intensive survey undertaken by the 'new wave' of Mediterranean projects, mentioned above, has come under criticism from both outside the Mediterranean and within. Some researchers argue that the intensive coverage of small areas results in problems of data comparability and overall regional coverage (Blanton 2001; Terranato 2004). Blanton's (2001) review of the POPULUS volumes, which published over 100 articles on Mediterranean survey (Barker and Mattingly 1999–2000), is one of the better-known critiques. The increasingly narrow foci of Mediterranean projects, he argues, has resulted in datasets with little meaningful to say about regional social organization, and the focus on ever more intensive and environmentally driven methods has led to Mediterranean practice becoming 'a kind of anthropological geomorphology' (Blanton 2001: 629). Tartaron

(2008: 89-93) answers this critique by explaining that (1) national antiquities laws, permit structures, and environmental circumstances dramatically affect the research conditions and results of archaeological projects in different areas; and (2) that the 'full-coverage' survey advocated by some New World archaeologists (Fish and Kowalewski 1990; Kowalewski 2008), which claims complete coverage of areas that are often of over several hundred kilometers, is not in reality an actionable or useful concept. As Clarke (1973) observed long ago, all archaeology involves a hierarchy of sampling, and if 'full-coverage' survey 'entails neither inspection of nor even interest in the totality of the surface of a given region ... this is sampling by another name' (Tartaron 2008: 91). Nonetheless, Blanton does make some resonant points concerning a need for greater dialogue between projects and between regions (Cherry 2002), a theme to which we return in the conclusions of this volume.

Arguments over intensity versus breadth of coverage strike us as more illustrative of differences in priorities than indicating good or bad methodologies. Whatever our views are on how we *should* be doing survey, the fact of the matter is that archaeological data—at least in parts of the world with long traditions of archaeological fieldwork—have been collected using a variety of intensive and extensive methods in regions that are often contiguous or overlapping. It is as important to ask how we may deal with and integrate existing datasets as it is to debate methods of acquiring new data. Moreover, at least in the case of most of the Mediterranean world, excavations of some kind have been conducted in nearly any region that is the target of archaeological survey work, posing another front for data integration. Methodological debates rarely emphasize the large amount of regional work conducted using less systematic, more extensive methods, or the variety of excavations (research, rescue, illegal, salvage) that have taken place within these regions (and are often ignored completely). This archaeological hodgepodge—comprised of unsystematic surveys, sporadic excavations, and scattered reports—remains the only documentation we have for the vast majority of many archaeological landscapes.

We believe that it is still fair, or at least realistic, to say that no set of 'best practices' for archaeological surveys is forthcoming, or even desirable, in terms of facilitating comparisons (Alcock and Cherry 2004: 6; Millett in Francovich *et al.* 2000: 93). This point is well supported by the fact that the 'Manual of Best Practice', intended as the final result of the five-volume POPULUS project on Mediterranean landscape archaeology (Barker and Mattingly 1999–2001: vii), never appeared. Good practice is another matter entirely, and in our view does not assume that one approach tops all.

In terms of comparison, responses to Alcock and Cherry's (2004) call for viewing survey data 'side-by-side' have been occasional and varied in success. The most useful, or at least most widely cited, examples of integrating survey data from different projects have focused on particular problems or issues concerning social change on a macroregional scale (Alcock 1993; 1994; Halstead 1994; Bintliff 1997). But using regional datasets to answer questions concerning social complexity requires us to shift our attention from developing some kind of *ideal* survey to (1) issues of transparency in data production, (2) innovation in the meaningful analysis of existing datasets, and (3) clarity of articulation when it comes to research goals. This requires us to cross media, cross scales, and be somewhat flexible—which is not to say uncritical—in our consideration of regional archaeology.

Studies of social complexity must also operate on multiple scales, even if our primary focus is on one particular region, due to simple (or not-so-simple) facts of how human societies extend themselves, socially and spatially. For example, face-to-face interactions on the level of a community (Goffman 1967; Counts *et al.* 2013; Westgate 2015) must be considered in light of local and regional interactions between settlements such as alliances, marriage relationships, or social storage (Halstead 1989; Broodbank 2000: 84), which in turn are impacted by longer-distance or inter-cultural relationships and processes (Parkinson and Galaty 2010; Broodbank 2013). It is also important to note that inter-scalar relationships should not be dependent on a strict progression from one proximity-based scale to the next. For example, long-distance interactions can be relevant to face-to-face interactions without immediately including an intermediate scale of regional relationships (see Manning, this volume, on locally constituted meanings of imports). This crossing of scales, at least spatially, is an issue archaeologists are increasingly willing to grapple with in recent years, not least through the expanding capabilities of GIS and database technologies (Bevan and Conolly 2006; Lock and Molyneaux 2006; Parkinson 2010; Knodell 2013).

The constitution of scales, however, is not uncomplicated, as is clear from the diversity of multi-scalar approaches in this volume (e.g., papers by Parkinson, Sekedat, Garrison). On the one hand, studies of social complexity are interested in conceptions of territory and regionality in the ancient world, which we might think of in terms of local, regional, and macroregional scales, largely based on notions of distance. On the other hand, there are scales of household, community, polity, and culture that overlap and complement more spatial conceptions. Such classificatory schemes are unavoidable in archaeological attempts to understand the organization of societies, whose objects of study are artifacts, sites, landscapes, culture areas, and geographical zones. Again, we see no prescription of best practices, other than terminological and methodological transparency. If our goal, as here, is to achieve some understanding of the organization of societies and how they change over time, and to do this in a meaningful way beyond the bounds of one particular society, comparison is a desirable way forward. But it cannot be expected that approaches, descriptions, or interpretations relevant to one region apply to another, and of course intra-regional or intra-societal comparisons are also necessary.

Cross-cultural analysis is an inviting, albeit challenging, framework in which to pursue the study of the past. Yet it is also here that we see an opportunity for regional studies to make their most original contributions to the archaeology of complex societies. Comparing the development of complex societies has a long-standing tradition in archaeology. Much of this, however, happens on a cultural or civilizational scale, or in terms of the comparison between principal sites. Chang's settlement archaeology (Chang 1968; Fletcher 1986), Trigger's (2003) comparative approach to early civilizations, and Yoffee's (2005) work on early cities, states, and civilizations all fall into this mold, as do several other explicitly comparative volumes of studies (e.g., Feinman and Marcus 1998; M.L. Smith 2003). Even recent work on comparative archaeology that foregrounds 'regional trajectories' in a global context—comparing the Indus Valley, Mesopotamia, North China, etc.—operates on a very large, civilizational scale (Peterson and Drennan 2012). Meso-scales of analysis, driven by regional datasets, are much rarer in comparative projects, although A.T. Smith's (2003) study of political landscapes predicted the value of such endeavors. Much archaeological attention now seems to have narrowed its focus following the 'material turn' to examine the role of things in the constitution of complex polities (Smith 2015; Khatchadourian 2016; Witmore, this volume; cf. Knapp, this volume). Between things and assemblages, political territories and culture areas, there thus seems opportunity for the types of regional approaches to society and complexity espoused here to make a real contribution.

The papers included in this volume, then, represent a set of regional studies from the Aegean, the wider Mediterranean, the Caribbean, and Mesoamerica, and at the same time articulate theoretical orientations and perspectives which, we argue, are much more broadly relevant to the study of complex societies from a comparative perspective. By explicitly engaging such 'meso-scale' case studies in order to examine the regional dynamics of polities, the chapters aim to build upon the tradition of John Cherry's own contributions to studies of ancient polities and interactions between them.

Some Disciplinary Concerns: Persistent Divides

While a comparative agenda in the study of complex societies has broad appeal, especially in recent years, serious impediments remain. Theoretical and methodological priorities within archaeology vary widely, due to deep and long-standing divisions between different sub-fields. Comparisons involving the Mediterranean world are particularly challenging, due to its particular disciplinary history. Calls to break down such divides have long been articulated by leading voices in the field, including some contributors to this volume (Renfrew 1980; Snodgrass 1987; Dyson 1993; Morris 1994; Davis 2001; Papadopoulos and Levanthal 2003; Galaty and Parkinson 2007). Nevertheless, structural divisions within the academy, as well as national and continental trends, remain problematic, as do more general scholarly concerns such as increasing 'hyper-specialization', the rapid growth in the bibliographical corpus for any given sub-field, and a sort of myopia of expertise that develops as a result. At the event in which the papers in this volume were first presented, Jack Davis commented that not long ago it was possible to stay reasonably 'on top of' most of the literature published in the field of Aegean Prehistory. It is now difficult to keep up with literature relevant to the island of Crete. Such growth in archaeological literature is equally apparent in other parts of the world. A recently published review article on Teotihuacan boasts a bibliography of over 800 references for this site alone (Nichols 2016). Periodicals such as the *Journal of Archaeological Research*, *Journal of World Prehistory*, and *Annual Review of Anthropology* do a great service by publishing such articles that review recent literature on specialized topics of potentially broader relevance.

Beyond such practical challenges, archaeologists of different backgrounds are simply trained differently, especially in North America. While independent institutes and graduate programs in archaeology are becoming increasingly common, most academic archaeologists in the United States operate (as either faculty or students) in departments of anthropology, while Mediterraneanists are much more likely to be found in departments of classics, art history, or occasionally history. Anthropological comparison is thus much more the exception than the norm, despite the widely cited work of several Mediterranean archaeologists in comparative studies (e.g., Renfrew 1972; Renfrew and Cherry 1986; Broodbank 2000). Academic archaeologies in other parts of the world face equally challenging environments for comparison. The national and regional archaeologies prevalent in Europe prioritize material-based, often period-specific specializations, rather than broad themes that lend themselves to comparative analysis (but cf., for example, the discussion article 'Is archaeology still the project of nation states?' and following responses in *Archaeological Dialogues* 23 [2016]).

We echo here Renfrew's (1980) call—of nearly 40 years ago—that data-rich traditions, such as those of the classical world, have a tremendous amount to offer comparative studies. Time has told that comparisons bear fruit, but that historical archaeologies nevertheless remain most resistant to comparative endeavors, albeit with growing numbers of exceptions. This might be explained by the trend that historical archaeologies as sub-disciplines tend to be culturally specific with voluminous datasets, long traditions, deep bibliographies, and an inclination toward self-perpetuation. More data mean more capacity for analysis, attracting more researchers, projects, and students. This has certainly been the case for classical archaeology and is increasingly so for Maya archaeology, to name one further example. So what Renfrew suggested concerning the richness of the classical tradition now equally applies to other intensively researched, multifaceted datasets around the world.

Despite the broad trends noted above, many Mediterraneanists, especially those represented in this volume, have worked throughout their careers to present aspects of the 'great tradition' in anthropological light. Indeed, the classical world is inescapable when considering the archaeology of city-states (e.g., Hansen 2000) or empires (Alcock *et al.* 2001). Even in comparative studies, however, the aforementioned divide remains visible, as many monographs or edited volumes focus on the 'ancient world', referring almost exclusively to the circum-Mediterranean lands (e.g., Gates 2011). Nonetheless, anthropological archaeologists interested in comparison, but not working in the Mediterranean, advance global, anthropological perspectives (Nichols and Charlton 1997; Richards and Van Buren 2000; Yoffee 2015) that sometimes, but not always, include nods to the classical world (Morris 1997; Small 1997; Alcock 2000; Morris and Knodell 2015), usually limited to Greek city-states or the Roman empire. Some of the most interesting recent work on comparative approaches to complex societies includes little or no discussion of the Mediterranean (e.g., M.L. Smith 2003; Smith 2012; Drennan *et al.* 2015).

Such omissions are not necessarily problematic—we need not all be included in everything—but this volume seeks somewhat to flip these trends, focusing mostly on the Aegean and wider Mediterranean, but aiming to include broader perspectives of relevance to the theme at hand. While we do not suggest that this represents some kind of groundbreaking solution to lamentable disciplinary division, we hope it can serve as a worthwhile example of another way to expand comparative dialogues.

Conclusions

We believe that the contributions assembled in this book, in honor of one of the leading proponents of regional studies in archaeology, offer exciting ways forward. They use regional archaeological data, and the integration of such data across a range of scales, to answer questions concerning the development of complex societies. We stress that all of these papers have intended relevance beyond the sociocultural circumstances they seek to address. A comparative agenda, however, is not simply a matter of putting papers from different regions side-by-side, but rather is necessary in the design, articulation, and argument of individual studies. Some chapters in this volume lend themselves to external comparison more easily than others, but all presented here provide models and frameworks adaptable to other cultural contexts. In these papers, then, and in particular in those conceptual spaces in which they overlap (whether in agreement or dissonance), we suggest that there may be found the kernel of an agenda for the regional archaeology of complex societies as it continues to develop.

To that end, Part I of this volume examines pathways to social complexity in the eastern Mediterranean Bronze Age, with case studies concerning the local and long-distance dynamics of state formation (Manning), the role of prestige goods and systems of signification in social structure and interaction (Galaty, Bennet), and the need to integrate datasets across geographical scales (Parkinson). Part II comprises papers spanning the entire Mediterranean in historical periods, and necessarily integrates regional studies with the macrogeographical machinations of imperial and colonial powers. These papers include a text-driven GIS approach to examining the political geography of Roman Greece (Fachard), an examination of industrial landscapes in the Roman East (Sekedat), and a discussion of island traditions in the western Mediterranean (Smith and van Dommelen). The final section of the book presents comparative views on regional approaches to society and complexity grounded in American historical archaeology (Ryzewski), Mesoamerican archaeology (Garrison), and comparative island archaeology (Broodbank, Fitzpatrick). This section also explores issues of concern to all archaeologists—namely by offering different viewpoints on the 'new materialisms' in archaeological thought and the role of things in human relationships and social change (Witmore, Knapp), as well as changes in the modes of archaeological publication and their impact on how we present, encounter, and redeploy regional archaeological datasets (MacKay).

For our part, an agenda for regional archaeology necessarily involves crossing intellectual boundaries and working across conceptual scales. We emphasize the need for diversity, specificity, and dialogue between subdisciplines of archaeology, along with deeply critical, engaged approaches to individual regions, datasets, and projects. These are agendas that John Cherry has pushed throughout his career, even if not as explicitly as we advocate here. He has embodied such ideas in his scholarship, in his teaching, and in his mentorship of graduate students. We hope that the papers assembled here form a fitting tribute to carry this agenda forward.

Acknowledgments

We are very grateful to all of the contributors to this volume, whose long-standing interests in the subjects at hand have informed and inspired this book and its introduction. We are most grateful, of course, to John Cherry for providing the motivation, opportunity, and inspiration behind much of the foregoing text. We also wish to thank Sue Alcock, Michelle Berenfeld, Bernard Knapp, Peter van Dommelen, and Chris Witmore for their thoughtful feedback on various drafts of this introduction.

About the Authors

Alex R. Knodell is Assistant Professor of Classics and Co-Director of the Archaeology Program at Carleton College, Northfield, Minnesota. He currently co-directs the Mazi Archaeological Project (northwest Attica, Greece) and previously served as Field Director of the Brown University Petra Archaeological Project (Petra, Jordan). Other research interests include the development of complex societies in the Late Bronze Age and Early Iron Age Mediterranean, especially in relation to the Euboean Gulf of Greece. Recent articles have appeared in the *American Journal of Archaeology*, *Antike Kunst*, the *Journal of Archaeological Science*, the *Journal of Field Archaeology*, and *World Archaeology*. E-mail: aknodell@carleton.edu

Thomas P. Leppard is Renfrew Fellow in the McDonald Institute for Archaeological Research at the University of Cambridge. His research concerns the comparative archaeology of island societies in the Mediterranean, Caribbean, and Pacific, especially issues of colonization, mobility, and emergent social complexity. Recent articles on these subjects have appeared in *Human Ecology*, the *Cambridge Archaeological Journal*, *Current Anthropology*, the *Journal of Island and Coastal Archaeology*, the *Journal of*

Mediterranean Archaeology, and *World Archaeology*. He currently conducts fieldwork in Micronesia and Sardinia. E-mail: tpl26@cam.ac.uk

Classical Authors and Texts

Homer, *Iliad*.
Pausanias, *Description of Greece*.
Strabo, *Geography*.

References

Adams, R. McC.
1965 *Land Behind Baghdad: A History of Settlement in the Diyala Plains*. Chicago: University of Chicago Press.
1966 *The Evolution of Urban Society: Early Mesopotamia and Prehispanic Mexico*. Chicago: Aldine.

Alcock, S.E.
1993 *Graecia Capta: The Landscapes of Roman Greece*. Cambridge: Cambridge University Press.
1994 Breaking up the Hellenistic world: survey and society. In I. Morris (ed.), *Classical Greece: Ancient Histories and Modern Archaeologies*, 171-90. Cambridge: Cambridge University Press.
2000 Classical order, alternative orders, and the uses of nostalgia. In J. Richards and M. Van Buren (eds.), *Order, Legitimacy, and Wealth in Ancient States*, 110-19. Cambridge: Cambridge University Press.

Alcock, S.E., and J.F. Cherry
2004 Introduction. In S.E. Alcock and J.F. Cherry (eds.), *Side-by-Side Survey: Comparative Regional Studies in the Mediterranean World*, 1-12. Oxford: Oxbow Books.
2013 Susan E. Alcock and John F. Cherry, with Michael Shanks and Christopher Witmore. In W.L. Rathje, M. Shanks, and C. Witmore (eds.), *Archaeology in the Making: Conversations Through a Discipline*, 229-47. London and New York: Routledge.

Alcock, S.E., T.E. D'Altroy, K.D. Morrison and C.M. Sinopoli (eds.)
2001 *Empires: Perspectives from Archaeology and History*. Cambridge: Cambridge University Press.

Aldenderfer, M.S., and H.D.G. Maschner (eds.)
1996 *Anthropology, Space, and Geographic Information Systems*. Oxford: Oxford University Press.

Ashmore, W.A., and A.B. Knapp (eds.)
1999 *Archaeologies of Landscape: Contemporary Perspectives*. Malden, Massachusetts: Blackwell.

Ashmore, W.A., and G.R. Willey
1981 A historical introduction to the study of lowland Maya settlement patterns. In W.A. Ashmore (ed.), *Lowland Maya Settlement Patterns*, 3-18. Albuquerque: University of New Mexico Press.

Barker, G., and D. Mattingly (series eds.)
1999–2001 *The Archaeology of Mediterranean Landscapes*. 5 vols. Oxford: Oxbow Books.

Bennet, J., and M. Galaty
1997 Ancient Greece: recent developments in Aegean archaeology and regional studies. *Journal of Archaeological Research* 5: 75-120. https://doi.org/10.1007/BF02229031

Bevan, A.
2015 The data deluge. *Antiquity* 89: 1473-84. https://doi.org/10.15184/aqy.2015.102

Bevan, A., and J. Conolly
2006 Multiscalar approaches to settlement

pattern analysis. In G. Lock and B. Molyneaux (eds.), *Confronting Scale in Archaeology: Issues of Theory and Practice*, 217-34. New York: Springer.

2013 *Mediterranean Islands, Fragile Communities and Persistent Landscapes: Antikythera in Long-Term Perspective.* Cambridge: Cambridge University Press. https://doi.org/10.1017/CBO9781139519748

Bevan, A., and M. Lake (eds.)
2013 *Computational Approaches to Archaeological Spaces.* Walnut Creek, California: Left Coast Press.

Binford, L.R.
1964 A consideration of archaeological research design. *American Antiquity* 29: 425-41. https://doi.org/10.2307/277978
1972 *An Archaeological Perspective.* New York and London: Seminar Press.

Bintliff, J.L.
1991 (ed.) *The Annales School and Archaeology.* Leicester: Leicester University Press.
1997 Regional survey, demography, and the rise of complex societies in the ancient Aegean: core-periphery, neo-Malthusian and other interpretive models. *Journal of Field Archaeology* 24: 1-38. https://doi.org/10.1179/jfa.1997.24.1.1

Bintliff, J.L., and A.M. Snodgrass
1985 The Cambridge/Bradford Boeotian Expedition: the first four years. *Journal of Field Archaeology* 12: 123-61. https://doi.org/10.1179/009346985791169490

Blanton, R.
2001 Mediterranean myopia. *Antiquity* 75: 627-29. https://doi.org/10.1017/S0003598X00088918

Blouet, A.
1831 *Expédition Scientifique de Morée.* 2 vols. Paris: Firmin Didot.

Braidwood, R.J., and B. Howe
1960 *Prehistoric Investigations in Iraqi Kurdistan.* Studies in Ancient Civilization 30. Chicago: University of Chicago Press.

Braudel, F.
1972 *The Mediterranean and the Mediterranean World in the Age of Phillip II.* New York: Harper and Row.

Broodbank, C.
2000 *An Island Archaeology of the Early Cyclades.* Cambridge: Cambridge University Press.
2013 *The Making of the Middle Sea: A History of the Mediterranean from the Beginning to the Classical Age.* London: Thames and Hudson.

Byers, D.S. (ed.)
1968 *The Prehistory of the Tehuacan Valley* I. *Environment and Subsistence.* Austin: University of Texas Press.

Chang, K.C.
1968 *Settlement Archaeology.* Palo Alto, California: National Press Books.

Chapman, R.
1990 *Emerging Complexity: The Later Prehistory of South-East Spain, Iberia, and the West Mediterranean.* Cambridge: Cambridge University Press. https://doi.org/10.1017/CBO9780511735486
2003 *Archaeologies of Complexity.* London and New York: Routledge. https://doi.org/10.4324/9780203451779

Chase, A.F., D.Z. Chase, C.T. Fisher, S.J. Leisz and J.F. Weishampel
2012 Geospatial revolution and remote sensing LiDAR in Mesoamerican archaeology. *Proceedings of the National Academy of Sciences of the United States of America* 109: 12916-21. https://doi.org/10.1073/pnas.1205198109

Cherry, J.F.
1977 Investigating the political geography of an early state by multidimensional scaling of Linear B tablet data. In J. Bintliff (ed.), *Mycenaean Geography: Proceedings of the Cambridge Colloquium, September 1976*, 76-83. Cambridge: British Association for Mycenaean Studies.
1982 A preliminary definition of site distribution on Melos. In C. Renfrew and M. Wagstaff (eds.), *An Island Polity: The Archaeology of Exploitation in Melos*, 10-23. Cambridge: Cambridge University Press.

1983a Evolution, revolution, and the origins of complex society in Minoan Crete. In O. Krzyszkowska and L. Nixon (eds.), *Minoan Society: Proceedings of the Cambridge Colloquium 1981*, 33-45. Bristol: Bristol Classical Press.

1983b Frogs round the pond: perspectives in current archaeological survey projects in the Mediterranean region. In D. Keller and D. Rupp (eds.), *Archaeological Survey in the Mediterranean Area*. British Archaeological Reports, International Series 155: 375-416. Oxford: Archaeopress.

1986 Palaces and polities: some problems in Minoan state formation. In C. Renfrew and J.F. Cherry (eds.), *Peer Polity Interaction and Socio-Political Change*, 19-45. Cambridge: Cambridge University Press.

1994 Regional survey in the Aegean: the 'new wave' (and after). In P.N. Kardulias (ed.), *Beyond the Site: Regional Studies in the Aegean Area*, 91-112. Lanham, Maryland: University Press of America.

2001 Travel, nostalgia, and Pausanias's giant. In S.E. Alcock, J.F. Cherry and J. Elsner (eds.), *Pausanias: Travel and Memory in Roman Greece*, 247-55. Oxford: Oxford University Press.

2002 Vox POPULI? Landscape archaeology in Mediterranean Europe. Review of G. Barker and D. Mattingly (general eds.), *The Archaeology of Mediterranean Landscapes*, 5 vols. (Oxford, 1999-2000). *Journal of Roman Archaeology* 15: 561-73. https://doi.org/10.1017/S1047759400014409

2003 Archaeology beyond the site: regional survey and its future. In J.K. Papadopoulos and R. Levanthal (eds.), *Theory and Practice in Mediterranean Archaeology: Old World and New World Perspectives*. Cotsen Advanced Seminars 1: 137-59. Los Angeles: Cotsen Institute of Archaeology.

2005 Chapter 14 revisited: sites, settlement and population in the prehistoric Aegean since *The Emergence of Civilisation*. In J. Barrett and P. Halstead (eds.), *The Emergence of Civilisation Revisited*. Sheffield Studies in Aegean Archaeology 6: 1-20. Oxford: Oxbow Books.

Cherry, J.F., and J.L. Davis
2001 'Under the scepter of Agamemnon': the view from the hinterlands of Mycenae. In K. Branigan (ed.), *Urbanism in the Aegean Bronze Age*. Sheffield Studies in Aegean Archaeology 4: 141-59. Sheffield: Sheffield Academic Press.

2007 An archaeological homily. In M.L. Galaty and W.A. Parkinson (eds.), *Rethinking Mycenaean Palaces II: Revised and Expanded Second Edition*. Monograph 60: 118-27. Los Angeles: Cotsen Institute of Archaeology.

Cherry, J.F., J.L. Davis and E. Mantzourani
1991 *Landscape Archaeology as Long-Term History: Northern Keos in the Cycladic Islands from Earliest Settlement until Modern Times*. Monumenta Archaeologica 16. Los Angeles: UCLA Institute of Archaeology.

Cherry, J.F., E. Faro and L. Minc
2010 Field survey and geochemical characterization of the southern Armenian obsidian sources. *Journal of Field Archaeology* 35: 147-63. https://doi.org/10.1179/009346910X12707321520639

Cherry, J.F., K. Ryzewski and T.P. Leppard
2012 Multi-period landscape survey and site risk assessment on Montserrat, West Indies. *Journal of Island and Coastal Archaeology* 7: 282-302. https://doi.org/10.1080/15564894.2011.611857

Clarke, D.L.
1968 *Analytical Archaeology*. London: Methuen.

1972 *Models in Archaeology*. London: Methuen.

1973 Archaeology: the loss of innocence. *Antiquity* 47: 6-18. https://doi.org/10.1017/S0003598X0003461X

Conolly, J., and M. Lake
2006 *Geographical Information Systems in Archaeology*. Cambridge: Cambridge

University Press. https://doi.org/
10.1017/CBO9780511807459

Counts, D., E. Cova, P.N. Kardulias and M.K.
Toumazou
  2013   Fitting in: archaeology and commu-
          nity in Athienou, Cyprus. *Near Eastern
          Archaeology* 76: 166-77. https://doi.
          org/10.5615/neareastarch.76.3.0166

David, B., and J. Thomas
  2008   *Handbook of Landscape Archaeology*.
          Walnut Creek, California: Left Coast
          Press.

Davis, J.L.
  2001   Classical archaeology and anthropo-
          logical archaeology in North America:
          a meeting of minds at the millenium?
          In G.M. Feinman and T.D. Price
          (eds.), *Archaeology at the Millennium:
          A Sourcebook*, 415-37. New York: Klu-
          wer Academic / Plenum Publishers.

Drennan, R.D., C.A. Berrey and C.E. Peterson
  2015   *Regional Settlement Demography in
          Archaeology*. New York: Eliot Werner
          Publications.

Dyson, S.L.
  1993   From new to new age archaeology:
          archaeological theory and classical
          archaeology—a 1990s perspective.
          American Journal of Archaeology 97:
          195-206.

Fachard, S., A.R. Knodell and E. Banou
  2015   The 2014 Mazi Archaeological Pro-
          ject (Attica). *Antike Kunst* 58: 178-86.

Feinman, G., and J. Marcus (eds.)
  1998   *Archaic States*. Santa Fe, New Mexico:
          School for Advanced Research Press.

Fish, S.K., and S.A. Kowalewski
  1990   *The Archaeology of Regions: The Case
          for Full-Coverage Survey*. Washington,
          DC: Smithsonian Institution Press.

Fletcher, R.
  1986   Settlement archaeology: world-wide
          comparisons. *World Archaeology* 18:
          59-83.

Fotiadis, M.
  1995   Modernity and the past-still-present:
          politics of time in the birth of regional
          archaeological projects in Greece.
          American Journal of Archaeology 99:
          59-78.

Francovich, R., H. Patterson and G. Barker (eds.)
  2000   *Extracting Meaning from Ploughsoil
          Assemblages*. The Archaeology of
          Mediterranean Landscapes 5. Oxford:
          Oxbow Books.

Gaffney, V.L., and Z. Stancic
  1996   *GIS Approaches to Regional Analysis: A
          Case Study of the Island of Hvar*. Lju-
          bljana: Znanstveni Institut Filozofske
          Fakultete.

Galaty, M.L., and W.A. Parkinson (eds.)
  2007   *Rethinking Mycenaean Palaces II:
          Revised and Expanded Second Edition*.
          Monograph 60. Los Angeles: Cotsen
          Institute of Archaeology.

Garrison, T.G.
  2007   Ancient Maya territories, adaptive
          regions, and alliances: contextualizing
          the San Bartolo-Xultun intersite sur-
          vey. Unpublished PhD dissertation,
          Harvard University, Cambridge, Mas-
          sachusetts.
  2010   Remote sensing ancient Maya rural
          populations using QuickBird satel-
          lite imagery. *International Journal of
          Remote Sensing* 31: 213-31.

Garrison, T.G., B.D. Chapman, S.D. Houston
and E. Román
  2011   Discovering ancient Maya settlements
          using Airborne Radar Elevation Data.
          Journal of Archaeological Science 38:
          1655-62.

Gates, C.
  2011   *Ancient Cities: The Archaeology of
          Urban Life in the Ancient Near East
          and Egypt, Greece, and Rome*. 2nd edn.
          London and New York: Routledge.

Given, M.
  2013   Commotion, collaboration, convivial-
          ity: Mediterranean survey and the
          interpretation of landscape. *Journal of
          Mediterranean Archaeology* 26: 3-26.

Given, M., and A.B. Knapp
  2003   *The Sydney-Cyprus Survey Project:
          Social Approaches to Regional Archaeo-
          logical Survey*. Monumenta Archaeo-
          logica 21. Los Angeles: Cotsen
          Institute of Archaeology.

Goffman, E.
  1967   *Interaction Ritual: Essays on Face-to-*

Face Behavior. New York: Anchor Books.

Halstead, P.
1989 The economy has a normal surplus: economic stability and social change among early farming communities of Thessaly, Greece. In P. Halstead and J. O'Shea (eds.), *Bad Year Economics*, 68-80. Cambridge: Cambridge University Press.
1994 The north-south divide: regional paths to complexity in prehistoric Greece. In C. Mathers and S. Stoddart (eds.), *Development and Decline in the Mediterranean Bronze Age*. Sheffield Archaeological Monographs 8: 195-219. Sheffield: J.R. Collis Publications.

Hansen, M.H. (ed.)
2000 *A Comparative Study of Thirty City-State Cultures: An Investigation Conducted by the Copenhagen Polis Centre*. Copenhagen: Royal Danish Academy of Sciences and Letters.

Horden, P., and N. Purcell
2000 *The Corrupting Sea: A Study of Mediterranean History*. Malden, Massachusetts: Blackwell.

Jameson, M.H., C.N. Runnels and T.H. van Andel
1994 *A Greek Countryside: The Southern Argolid from Prehistory to the Present Day*. Stanford, California: Stanford University Press.

Kennedy, D., and M.C. Bishop
2011 Google Earth and the archaeology of Saudi Arabia: a case study from the Jeddah area. *Journal of Archaeological Science* 38: 1284-93.

Khatchadourian, L.
2016 *Imperial Matter: Ancient Persia and the Archaeology of Empires*. Berkeley: University of California Press.

Knapp, A.B.
1992 (ed.) *Archaeology, Annales and Ethnohistory*. Cambridge: Cambridge University Press.
1993 Social complexity: incipience, emergence and development on prehistoric Cyprus. *Bulletin of the American Schools of Oriental Research* 292: 85-106.

Knappett, C.
2013 *Network Analysis in Archaeology: New Approaches to Regional Interaction*. Oxford: Oxford University Press

Knodell, A.R.
2013 Small-World Networks and Mediterranean Dynamics in the Euboean Gulf: An Archaeology of Complexity in Late Bronze Age and Early Iron Age Greece. Unpublished PhD Dissertation, Brown University, Providence, Rhode Island.

Knodell, A.R., S.E. Alcock, C. Tuttle, C.F. Cloke, T. Erickson-Gini, C. Feldman, G.O. Rollefson, M. Sinibaldi, and C. Vella
2017 The Brown University Petra Archaeological Project: Landscape Archaeology in the Northern Hinterland of Petra, Jordan. *American Journal of Archaeology* 121(4): 621–683.

Kohring, S., and S. Wynne-Jones (eds.)
2007 *Socialising Complexity: Structure, Interaction and Power in Archaeological Discourse*. Oxford: Oxbow Books.

Kowalewski, S.
2008 Regional settlement pattern studies. *Journal of Archaeological Research* 16: 225-85.

Leake, W.M.
1821 *The Topography of Athens: With Some Remarks upon its Antiquities*. London: John Murray.
1830 *Travels in the Morea*. 3 vols. London: John Murray.
1835 *Travels in Northern Greece*. 4 vols. London: J. Rodwell.

Lock, G., and B. Molyneaux (eds.)
2006 *Confronting Scale in Archaeology: Issues of Theory and Practice*. New York: Springer

McCoy, M.D., and T.N. Ladefoged
2009 New developments in the use of spatial technology in archaeology. *Journal of Archaeological Research* 17: 263-95.

McDonald, W., and G.R. Rapp, Jr. (eds.)
1972 *The Minnesota Messenia Expedition: Reconstructing a Bronze Age Regional Environment*. Minneapolis: University of Minnesota Press.

Morris, I.
1994 (ed.) *Classical Greece: Ancient Histories and Modern Archaeologies*, Cambridge: Cambridge University Press.
1997 An archaeology of equalities? The Greek city-states. In D.L. Nichols and T. Charlton (eds.), *The Archaeology of City-States: Cross-Cultural Approaches*, 91-105. Washington, DC: Smithsonian Institution Press.

Morris, I., and A.R. Knodell
2015 Greek cities in the first millennium BCE. In N. Yoffee (ed.), *The Cambridge World History* III. *Early Cities in Comparative Perspective, 4000 BCE–CE 1200*, 343-63. Cambridge: Cambridge University Press.

Myers, A.
2010 Camp Delta, Google Earth and the ethics of remote sensing in archaeology. *World Archaeology* 42: 455-67.

Nichols, D.L.
2016 Teotihuacan. *Journal of Archaeological Research* 24: 1-74.

Nichols, D.L., and T. Charlton (eds.)
1997 *The Archaeology of City-States: Cross-Cultural Approaches*. Washington, DC: Smithsonian Institution Press.

Opitz, R.S., K. Ryzewski, J.F. Cherry and B. Moloney
2015 Using airborne LiDAR survey to explore Historic-era archaeological landscapes of Montserrat in the Eastern Caribbean. *Journal of Field Archaeology* 40: 523-41.

Pajor, F.
2006 *Eretria—Nea Psara: Eine klassizistische Stadtanlage über der antiken Polis*. 2 vols. Eretria fouilles et recherches 15. Gollion, Switzerland: Ecole Suisse d'archéologie en Grèce.

Papadopoulos, J.K., and R.M. Leventhal (eds.)
2003 *Theory and Practice in Mediterranean Archaeology: Old World and New World Perspectives*. Cotsen Advanced Seminars 1. Los Angeles: Cotsen Institute of Archaeology.

Parcak, S.H.
2009 *Satellite Remote Sensing for Archaeology*. London and New York: Routledge.

Parcak, S., D. Gathings, C. Childs, G. Mumford and E. Cline
2016 Satellite evidence of archaeological site looting in Egypt: 2002-2013. *Antiquity* 90: 188-205.

Parkinson, W.A.
2010 Beyond the peer: social interaction and political evolution in the Bronze Age Aegean. In D. Pullen (ed.), *Political Economies of the Aegean Bronze Age*, 11-34. Oxford: Oxbow Books.

Parkinson, W.A., and M.L. Galaty (eds.)
2010 *Archaic State Interaction: The Eastern Mediterranean in the Bronze Age*. Santa Fe, New Mexico: School for Advanced Research Press.

Parkinson, W.A., and A. Gyucha
2012 Tells in perspective: long-term patterns of settlement nucleation and dispersal in central and southeast Europe. In R. Hoffman, F.-K. Moetz and J. Müller (eds.), *Tells: Social and Environmental Space*. Universitätsforschungen zur prähistorischen Archäologie 207: 105-16. Bonn: Verlag Dr. Rudolf Habelt.

Peterson, C.E., and R.D. Drennan
2012 Patterned variation in regional trajectories of community growth. In M.E. Smith (ed.), *The Comparative Archaeology of Complex Societies*, 88-137. Cambridge: Cambridge University Press.

Plog, S., F. Plog and W. Wait
1978 Decision making in modern surveys. *Advances in Archaeological Method and Theory* 1: 383-421.

Redman, C.L.
1973 Multistage fieldwork and analytical techniques. *American Antiquity* 38: 61-79.
1987 Surface collection, sampling, and research design: a retrospective. *American Antiquity* 52: 249-65.

Renfrew, C.
1972 *The Emergence of Civilisation*. London: Methuen.
1980 The great tradition versus the great divide: archaeology as anthropology?

American Journal of Archaeology 84: 287-98.

Renfrew, C., and J.F. Cherry (eds.)
1986   *Peer Polity Interaction and Socio-Political Change.* Cambridge: Cambridge University Press.

Richards, J., and M. Van Buren (eds.)
2000   *Order, Legitimacy, and Wealth in Ancient States.* Cambridge: Cambridge University Press.

Roosevelt, C.H., P. Cobb, E. Moss, B.R. Olson and S. Ünlüsoy.
2015   Excavation is ~~destruction~~ digitization: advances in archaeological practice. *Journal of Field Archaeology* 40: 325-46.

Ryzewski, K.
2009   Seven interventions with the flatlands: archaeology and its modes of engagement. Contributions from the WAC-6 Session, 'Experience, Modes of Engagement, Archaeology'. *Archaeologies* 5: 361-88.

Ryzewski, K., and J.F. Cherry
2016   Surveying a long term settlement on Potato Hill, Montserrat. In L. Bates, J.M. Chenoweth and J.A. Delle (eds.), *Archaeologies of Slavery and Freedom in the Caribbean: Exploring the Places In Between*, 258-308. Gainesville: University of Florida Press.

Sanders, W.T.
1965   *The Cultural Ecology of the Teotihuacán Valley.* University Park: Department of Sociology and Anthropology, Pennsylvania State University.

Sapirstein, P., and S. Murray
2017   Establishing best practices for photogrammetry during archaeological fieldwork. *Journal of Field Archaeology* 42: 337-50.

Schiffer, M.B., A.P. Sullivan and T.C. Klinger
1978   The design of archaeological surveys. *World Archaeology* 10: 1-28.

Schoep, I., P. Tomkins and J. Driessen (eds.)
2012   *Back to the Beginning: Reassessing Social and Political Complexity on Crete during the Early and Middle Bronze Age.* Oxford: Oxbow Books.

Shanks, M.
2007   Digital media, agile design, and the politics of archaeological authorship. In M. Brittain and T. Clack (eds.), *Archaeology and the Media*, 273-89. Walnut Creek, California: Left Coast Press.

Small, D.
1997   City-state dynamics through a Greek lens. In D.L. Nichols and T. Charlton (eds.), *The Archaeology of City-States: Cross-Cultural Approaches*, 107-18. Washington, DC: Smithsonian Institution Press.

Smith, A.T.
2003   *The Political Landscape: Constellations of Authority in Early Complex Polities.* Berkeley: University of California Press.
2015   *The Political Machine: Assembling Sovereignty in the Bronze Age Caucasus.* Princeton, New Jersey: Princeton University Press.

Smith, M.E. (ed.)
2012   *The Comparative Archaeology of Complex Societies.* Cambridge: Cambridge University Press.

Smith, M.L. (ed.)
2003   *Social Construction of Ancient Cities.* Washington, DC: Smithsonian Institution Press.

Snodgrass, A.M.
1987   *An Archaeology of Greece: The Present State and Future Scope of a Discipline.* Berkeley: University of California Press.

Stephens, J.L.
1837   *Incidents of Travel in Egypt, Arabia Petraea, and the Holy Land.* 2 vols. New York: Harper and Brothers.
1938   *Incidents of Travel in Greece, Turkey, Russia and Poland.* 2 vols. New York: Harper and Brothers.
1841   *Incidents of Travel in Central America, Chiapas and Yucatan.* 2 vols. New York: Harper and Brothers.
1843   *Incidents of Travel in Yucatan.* 2 vols. New York: Harper and Brothers.

Steward, J.H.
1960   Evolutionary principles and social types. In S. Tax (ed.), *The Evolution of Man: Mind, Culture and Society*, 169-

86. Chicago: University of Chicago Press.

Tartaron, T.F.
2008 Aegean prehistory as world archaeology: recent trends in the archaeology of Bronze Age Greece. *Journal of Archaeological Research* 16: 83-161.

Terrenato, N.
2004 Sample size matters! The paradox of global trends and local surveys. In S.E. Alcock and J.F. Cherry (eds.), *Side-by-Side Survey: Comparative Regional Studies in the Mediterranean World*, 36-48. Oxford: Oxbow Books.

Trigger, B.G.
2003 *Understanding Early Civilizations: A Comparative Study*. Cambridge: Cambridge University Press.

Wagstaff, J.M.
2001 Pausanias and the topographers: the case of Colonel Leake. In S.E. Alcock, J.F. Cherry and J. Elsner (eds.), *Pausanias: Travel and Memory in Roman Greece*, 190-206. Oxford: Oxford University Press.

Westgate, R.
2015 Space and social complexity in Greece from the Early Iron Age to the Classical period. *Hesperia* 84: 47-95.

Willey, G.R.
1953 *Prehistoric Settlement Patterns in the Virú Valley, Peru*. Bureau of American Ethnology Bulletin 155. Washington, DC: Smithsonian Institution Press.

Willey, G.R., W.R. Bullard, Jr., J.B. Glass and J.C. Gifford
1965 *Prehistoric Maya Settlements in the Belize Valley*. Papers of the Peabody Museum of Archaeology and Ethnology 54. Cambridge, Massachusetts: Harvard University.

Witmore, C.
2004 On multiple fields: between the material world and media. Two cases from the Peloponnesus, Greece. *Archaeological Dialogues* 11: 133-64.

Witmore, C., and T.V. Buttrey
2008 William Martin Leake: a contemporary of P.O. Brøndsted, in Greece and in London. In B.B. Rasmussen, J.S. Jenson, J. Lund and M. Märcher (eds.), *P.O. Brøndsted (1780-1842)—A Danish Classicist in his European Context*, 15-34. Copenhagen: Royal Danish Academy of Sciences and Letters.

Wright, J.C., J.F. Cherry, J.L. Davis, E. Mantzourani, S.B. Sutton and R.F. Sutton, Jr.
1990 The Nemea Valley Archaeological Project: a preliminary report. *Hesperia* 59: 479-559.

Yoffee, N.
2005 *Myths of the Archaic State: Evolution of the Earliest Cities, States, and Civilizations*. Cambridge: Cambridge University Press.
2015 (ed.) *The Cambridge World History* III. *Early Cities in Comparative Perspective, 4000 BCE–CE 1200*. Cambridge: Cambridge University Press.

Part I

Pathways to Complexity in the Prehistoric Aegean

Introduction to Part I: Pathways to Complexity in the Prehistoric Aegean

Alex R. Knodell and Thomas P. Leppard

The four papers that comprise the first part of this volume examine aspects of the development of social complexity in the prehistoric Aegean. The Aegean basin has long been an attractor of complexity studies, beginning with Colin Renfrew's *Emergence of Civilisation* (1972). Following this foundational text, Aegean prehistorians increasingly turned their attention away from the long-standing material- and sequence-based preoccupations of classical archaeology and toward themes more engaged with contemporary developments in North American anthropological archaeology. John Cherry's work on the archaeology of early Aegean states, begun as a PhD student under Renfrew's supervision, has been particularly influential and surprisingly broad: his contributions range from the application of multidimensional scaling of Linear B tablet data in a study of the political geography of Mycenaean Pylos (Cherry 1977) to seminal papers concerning state formation on Minoan Crete (Cherry 1983; 1986), with numerous further contributions between and beyond. The lasting influence of both Renfrew and Cherry on the archaeology of complex societies, and especially the role of cross-cultural comparison, is highlighted in the continued relevance of their co-edited volume, *Peer Polity Interaction and Socio-Political Change* (*PPI*) (Renfrew and Cherry 1986).

Perennial debates in the archaeology of social complexity in the Aegean have revolved around evolution versus revolution in the development of the state, as well as endogenous development versus exogenous influence, especially with respect to the particular situation of 'secondary states' (Cherry 1983; 2010; Parkinson and Galaty 2007; Watrous 2012). *PPI* aimed to articulate a middle ground, but still reflected an attitude supporting a mostly endogenous, relatively rapid model of sociopolitical development. Cherry and others have compared this to theories of punctuated equilibria in evolutionary biology (Eldredge and Gould 1972).

This model has been met with general agreement by many Aegeanists, especially those engaged in comparative research (e.g., Manning 2008; Whitelaw 2012; Legarra Herrero 2016). Other recent approaches to the development of social complexity in the Aegean have taken a different tone, instead returning to longer-term models and external influence by other eastern Mediterranean states (Schoep *et al.* 2012). What is interesting in these studies, however, is an emphasis on architectural elaboration at particular central places, while less attention is paid to evidence from local or regional surveys and island-wide syntheses. Meanwhile Knappett (2011; 2013) has been particularly active as a proponent for network analysis in examining material culture approaches to workshops, communities of practice, and macroregions (the southern Aegean), while Bevan (2010), like the contributors to this volume, has focused more on regional interactions and political dynamics within the island of Crete.

The papers in this section reflect the range of questions that can be asked of regional datasets concerning pathways to complexity in the prehistoric Aegean. Manning provides a masterful summary and appraisal of the state of debates concerning the first European states in Crete, and looks to the interplay between climate, chronology, inter-cultural interactions, and local practices in the emergence of leadership and social complexity around 2200 BC. This study complements well other recent work on the decline of Bronze Age societies in the eastern Mediterranean (Knapp and Manning 2016). As increasingly nuanced and comparative perspectives have been offered concerning environmental discourses on collapse (e.g., Middleton 2012), Manning suggests we pay more attention to finding balance between wider climatic contexts, external stimuli, and local agency.

Bennet builds upon the broad stage set by Manning's paper to examine the specific role of media (images and text) in the emergence of leadership in complex regional polities, using examples from both Minoan Crete and the Mycenaean world. He addresses the absence of monumental iconography and labeling in Aegean writing systems, a major departure from the Aegean's eastern Mediterranean neighbors. Yet at the same time, writing and image were used in particular to project—even perform—power in space through technologies first learned through Minoan–Near Eastern interfaces, which were dramatically transformed over time and eventually passed on to Mycenaean contexts. It is particularly significant that images and architecture were in dialogue much more with landscape features than with writing, monumentalizing connections between palaces and the surrounding ritual and agricultural landscapes.

Galaty and Parkinson both adopt comparative perspectives, examining case studies related to Minoan and Mycenaean state formation side-by-side with ethnographic and archaeological parallels in Albania and Hungary, respectively. Like Bennet, Galaty addresses questions of external influence through prestige-goods networks, building upon Parkinson's (2010) quantification and restudy of Cline's (1994) catalog of imports. He draws upon Cherry's (2010) reassessment of the role of imports in Minoan state formation and Burns's (2010) and Murray's (2013; 2017) studies of imports to the Mycenaean mainland to suggest that Mycenaean (but not Minoan) society may have relied on ideological systems that were similar to those of modern Albanian tribes.

In both Bennet's and Galaty's papers there seems to be a suggestion that while contacts with the wider world provided important stimuli for the development of sociopolitical complexity in the form of writing technologies and aspects of 'elite' material culture, these cultural elements were redeployed in their new, Aegean contexts with major departures from how they were used in their 'parent' civilizations. This pattern reinforces the idea that while external agencies certainly played a role in the development of Aegean complexity, the ways in which they were used in the longer term were largely an effect of endogenous forces. (It does not escape us that, given the context of this volume, this is a somewhat predictable sense of agreement with positions Cherry has articulated in the past.)

Environmental shifts, long-distance interactions, and emergent leadership were experienced in drastically varied ways in different parts of the Aegean and its eastern European and Mediterranean surroundings. It is precisely for this reason that there is a need to articulate comparisons between regions, and across scales, as Parkinson argues in the final chapter of this section. He discusses the history of regional studies in the Carpathian Basin and in the Aegean in light of his own recent work in both areas to demonstrate how remarkably rich archaeological records reveal dramatically different trajectories of change through the Neolithic and Bronze Age, which nevertheless serve to illuminate each case in new ways.

The papers in this section examine themes of core interest to regional studies broadly, and on the scales of islands, polities, and microregions. Each contributes to specific questions of interest to Aegean prehistorians and also has utility and intended relevance well beyond the particular case studies it presents.

About the Authors

Alex R. Knodell is Assistant Professor of Classics and Co-Director of the Archaeology Program at Carleton College, Northfield, Minnesota. He currently co-directs the Mazi Archaeological Project (northwest Attica, Greece) and previously served as Field Director of the Brown University Petra Archaeological Project (Petra, Jordan). Other research interests include the development of complex societies in the Late Bronze Age and Early Iron Age Mediterranean, especially in relation to the Euboean Gulf of Greece. Recent articles have appeared in the *American Journal of Archaeology*, *Antike Kunst*, the *Journal of Archaeological Science*, the *Journal of Field Archaeology*, and *World Archaeology*. E-mail: aknodell@carleton.edu

Thomas P. Leppard is Renfrew Fellow in the McDonald Institute for Archaeological Research at the University of Cambridge. His research concerns the comparative archaeology of island societies in the Mediterranean, Caribbean, and Pacific, especially issues of colonization, mobility, and emergent social complexity. Recent articles on these subjects have appeared in *Human Ecology*, the *Cambridge Archaeological Journal*, *Current Anthropology*, the *Journal of Island and Coastal Archaeology*, the *Journal of Mediterranean Archaeology*, and *World Archaeology*. He currently conducts fieldwork in Micronesia and Sardinia. E-mail: tpl26@cam.ac.uk

References

Bevan, A.
2010 Political geography and palatial Crete. *Journal of Mediterranean Archaeology* 23: 27-54. https://doi.org/10.1558/jmea. v23i1.27

Burns, B.E.
2010 *Mycenaean Greece, Mediterranean Commerce, and the Formation of Identity*. Cambridge: Cambridge University Press.

Cherry, J.F.
1977 Investigating the political geography of an early state by multidimensional scaling of Linear B tablet data. In J. Bintliff (ed.), *Mycenaean Geography*, 76-83. Cambridge: British Association for Mycenaean Studies.

1983 Evolution, revolution, and the origins of complex society in Minoan Crete. In O. Krzyszkowska and L. Nixon (eds.), *Minoan Society: Proceedings of the Cambridge Colloquium 1981*, 33-45. Bristol: Bristol Classical Press.

1986 Palaces and polities: some problems in Minoan state formation. In C. Renfrew and J.F. Cherry (eds.), *Peer Polity Interaction and Socio-Political Change*, 19-45. Cambridge: Cambridge University Press.

2010 Sorting out Crete's Prepalatial off-island interactions. In W.A. Parkinson and M.L. Galaty (eds.), *Archaic State Interaction: The Eastern Mediterranean in the Bronze Age*, 107-40. Santa Fe, New Mexico: School for Advanced Research Press.

Cline, E.H.
1994 *Sailing the Wine-Dark Sea: International Trade and the Late Bronze Age Aegean*. British Archaeological Reports, International Series 591. Oxford: British Archaeological Reports.

Eldredge, N., and S.J. Gould
1972 Punctuated equilibria: an alternative to phyletic gradualism. In T.J.M. Schopf (ed.), *Models in Palaeobiology*, San Francisco: Freeman Cooper.

Knapp, A.B., and S. Manning
2016 Crisis in context: the end of the Late Bronze Age in the eastern Mediterranean. *American Journal of Archaeology* 120: 99-149. https://doi.org/10.3764/ aja.120.1.0099

Knappett, C.
2011 *An Archaeology of Interaction: Network Perspectives on Material Culture and Society*. Oxford: Oxford University Press. https://doi.org/10.1093/acprof: osobl/9780199215454.001.0001

2013 *Network Analysis in Archaeology: New Approaches to Regional Interaction*. Oxford: Oxford University Press. https://doi.org/10.1093/acprof:oso/ 9780199697090.001.0001

Legarra Herrero, B.
2016 Primary state formation processes on Bronze Age Crete: a social approach to change in early complex societies. *Cambridge Archaeological Journal* 26: 349-67. https://doi.org/10.1017/ S0959774315000529

Manning, S.W.
2008 Protopalatial Crete: formation of the palaces. In C.W. Shelmerdine (ed.), *The Cambridge Companion to the Aegean Bronze Age*, 105-20. Cambridge: Cambridge University Press. https://doi. org/10.1017/CCOL9780521814447. 005

Middleton, G.D.
2012 Nothing lasts forever: environmental discourses on the collapse of past societies. *Journal of Archaeological Research* 20: 257-307. https://doi.org/10.1007/ s10814-011-9054-1

Murray, S.C.
2013 Trade, Imports, and Society in Early Greece: 1300-900 B.C.E. Unpublished PhD Dissertation, Stanford University, Stanford, California.

2017 *The Collapse of the Mycenaean Economy: Imports, Trade, and Institutions 1300-700 BCE*. Cambridge: Cambridge University Press. https://doi. org/10.1017/9781316890424

Parkinson, W.A.

2010   Beyond the peer: social interaction and political evolution in the Bronze Age Aegean. In D. Pullen (ed.), *Political Economies of the Aegean Bronze Age*, 11-34. Oxford: Oxbow Books.

Parkinson, W.A., and M.L. Galaty

2007   Secondary states in perspective: an integrated approach to state formation in the prehistoric Aegean. *American Anthropologist* 109: 113-29. https://doi.org/10.1525/aa.2007.109.1.113

Renfrew, C.

1972   *The Emergence of Civilisation.* London: Methuen.

Renfrew, C., and J.F. Cherry (eds.)

1986   *Peer Polity Interaction and Socio-Political Change.* Cambridge: Cambridge University Press.

Schoep, I., P. Tomkins and J. Driessen (eds.)

2012   *Back to the Beginning: Reassessing Social and Political Complexity on Crete during the Early and Middle Bronze Age.* Oxford: Oxbow Books.

Watrous, L.V.

2012   An overview of secondary state formation on Crete: the Mirabello region during the Bronze Age. In E. Mantzourani and P.P. Betancourt (eds.), *Philistor: Studies in Honor of Costis Davaras.* Prehistory Monographs 36: 273-82. Philadelphia: INSTAP Academic Press.

Whitelaw, T.M.

2012   The urbanisation of prehistoric Crete: settlement perspectives on Minoan state formation. In I. Schoep, T. Tomkins and J. Driessen (eds.), *Back to the Beginning: Reassessing Social and Political Complexity on Crete during the Early and Middle Bronze Age*, 11476. Oxford: Oxbow Books.

2 The Development of Complex Society on Crete: The Balance between Wider Context and Local Agency

Sturt W. Manning

The Development of Complex Society and the First States in the Aegean

The island of Crete is noted for the development of some large settlements of an urban character, focused around monumentalized open-court-centered compounds (palaces), which form the apex of several respective regional settlement hierarchies and routes of communication from around 2000 BC. This phenomenon—allied with evidence of large-scale storage, specialized craft production, long-distance contacts, and widespread employment of seals and sealings—has led to this civilization being deemed to be more or less 'state'-level (Renfrew 1972: 369; Cherry 1978; 1984; 1986; 2010; Dabney 1995; Knappett 1999; Manning 2008a; Legarra Herrero 2016). Cretan urban civilization was usually understood as a 'lineal descendant' of the primary old world urban civilizations (Childe 1950). Whether seen as the bridgehead by which older, Near Eastern state-level civilization entered Europe (e.g., Childe 1925), or merely as Europe's first state-level civilization, Crete has been deemed fundamental to the history of the Aegean region (Figure 2.1), and more widely to anywhere in the Mediterranean world.

This topic area is now (2017) a venerable and indeed reflective scholarly field at Time (T) + 44/45 years from the R^2 combination of Radiocarbon and Renfrew (1972; 1973). Indeed, it is a topic that has to some extent gone out of fashion of late, but is important and deserving of attention (Cherry 2010: 108; Legarra Herrero 2016). After the moon-shot kick-start of Renfrew (1972), the real scholarly coming of age, and consequent echoes, came to be defined by John Cherry in a set of elegant articles published in rapid series in the 1980s (Cherry 1983; 1984; 1986). Cherry critiqued and demanded explanation, condemning the prevailing non-explanatory framework based on an 'infinite regress of causation' (Cherry 1984: 20).

The deep historiography of scholarship on the development of complex society and the 'state' on Crete and in the Aegean is well known and comprises the following five main stages:

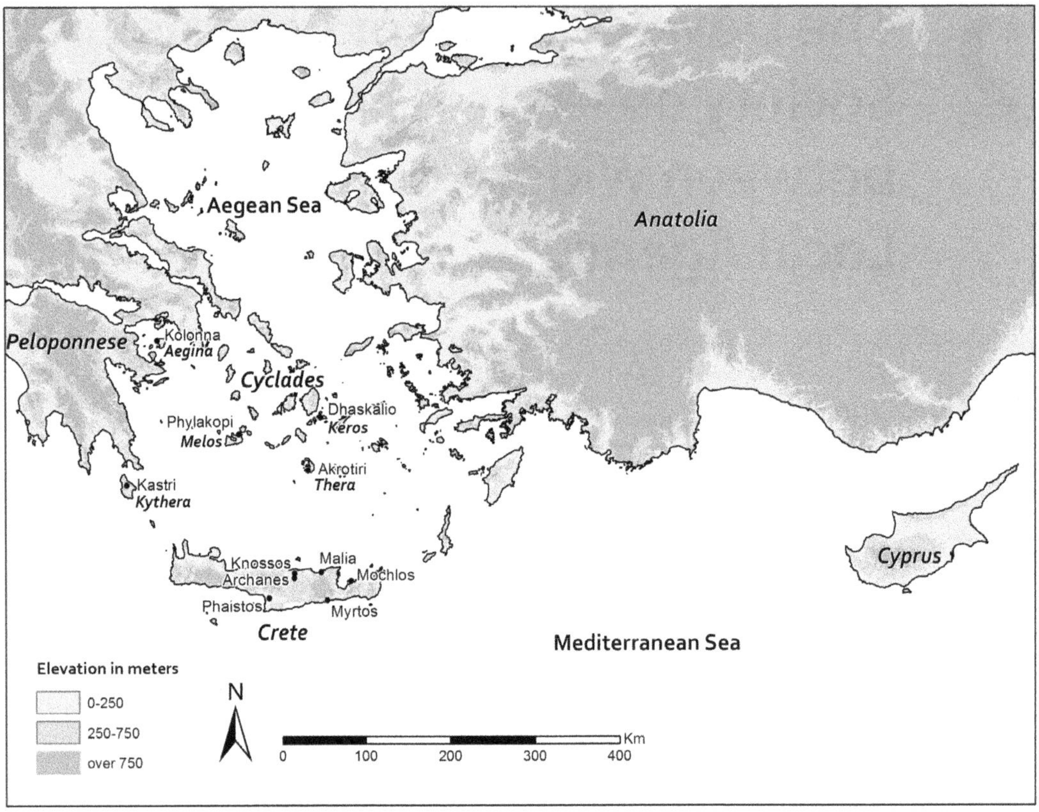

Figure 2.1   Sites and regions mentioned in the text (map by Evan Levine).

(1)   Before R²: There was a general culture-history approach where diffusion—whether of things, ideas, and/or people—offered a characterization and (largely non-explicit) explanation for changes and developments emanating outwards from the most ancient Near East. Overlooking his material-Marxist phase, Childe is usually cited as the definitive scholar of this earlier phase (e.g., Childe 1925). Childe restricted such contacts and movement to the spread of technological innovations (Childe 1930), but others went further and considered movements of people (e.g., Wace 1923: 591). Evans (1921: 13, 16-17; 1928: 45, 47) wondered about immigrants from the Nile Delta to Crete around the start of Dynasty I in Egypt and later, although he was mainly determined to see the Minoans as essentially independent—taking what they wanted from the diffusionary influences of Egypt and the Near East, but remaining free (Evans 1921: 19).

(2)   Renfrew (1972) created a new paradigm and field. The construction and development of complex society was an important topic and required explanation. The diffusionist model was dead (with rare subsequent exceptions: e.g., Watrous 1987). A local Aegean answer was necessary, based in the interactions of the social, economic, and ideational systems that could be defined

and summarized. Anthropological archaeology was now at last relevant to the Bronze Age Aegean, ending archaeology's previously subservient status as merely illustrating history/texts (e.g., Lorimer 1950). Aegean prehistory started to reshape classical archaeology and end its designation as a 'handmaiden of history' (Renfrew 1980; Snodgrass 1987: 37; Morris 1994: 15).

(3)   The R^2+ generation, dominated by Renfrew's graduate students, followed into a field that now required attention. The most important scholar was John Cherry. A series of papers in the 1980s addressed Minoan and Aegean state formation; two papers briskly critiqued previous work and articulated and delineated the topic (Cherry 1983; 1984), dismissing the gradualist perspective for the development of Aegean civilization. There was a long (millennium-scale) pre-palatial Early Bronze Age which appeared largely irrelevant to the dramatic changes that occurred in the period of a couple of centuries either side of 2000 BC. A third paper (Cherry 1986) synthesized the state of evidence and offered an explanatory description: the peer polity model that sought also to 'break out of the sometimes sterile dichotomy between "diffusion" and "independent invention"' (Renfrew 1993: 8).

(4)   A post-R^2 generation writing from the 1990s onward started to critique models that were solely local and regional. Instead, developments in the Aegean began (again) to be seen as the local products of interaction, especially with the east (Sherratt and Sherratt 1991; Sherratt 2010). It was argued that even limited extra-Aegean contacts and influences from the east Mediterranean and Anatolia were critical in stimulating, structuring, shaping, and forcing new development trajectories on Crete and in the Aegean—internally among the societies and constituent groupings in the Aegean and in terms of the actions of agents and followers within the existing local sociopolitical processes and structures (e.g., Manning 1994; 1997; 2008a; Schoep 2006; Colburn 2008).

This work was starting to consider the social value and life of things, ethnography, agent and object encounters, entanglements, and how all these could affect existing social, economic, and political structures and practice (Mauss 1954; Bourdieu 1977; Appadurai 1986; Helms 1988). These sorts of discussions were seen in diametrical contrast with (although in fact they are largely complementary to) the quantified logic of Renfrew (1972), which is that lots of X and lots of Y, especially multiplied together, can potentially explain Z. This is exemplified in Renfrew's (1994: 8, 10) critical comments on Manning's (1994) study, questioning the importance of a 'few foreign knick-knacks', and wondering 'whether such study brings us very often to the nexus between power and elite status'. Renfrew here subscribed to the somewhat anachronistic economic view of Johnson (1988–89: 602) that 'we tend to overrate the importance of rare, pretty and preserved "exotics"'. The countervailing assessment, as Sherratt (1995: 12-13) observed, is the general pattern that 'it is the trade in "knick-knacks" that precedes the serious business of rationalisation of production: sixteenth-century Europeans turned the world upside down in pursuit of pepper. This desire for exotics is what motivates the generation of the surplus' (see also Sherratt and Sherratt 1991; Sherratt 2000).

(5)   A 'millennial' reflective, maturing phase has critiqued cultural evolutionary approaches and has generally sought to avoid claims for any particular theory or answer. Instead, it has invested considerable effort and time into developing the amount, complexity, and nuances of the available evidence—highlighting especially the varying development trajectories across Crete (e.g., Legarra Herrero 2009; 2014). In particular, scholarship has critiqued previous orthodoxies and supposed certainties. Such rethinking includes reassessment of questions such as: were there, and if so from when, 'states' on Crete? Or what exactly is a 'palace'? (And should the term be avoided?) Studies have also queried an assumed role for the palaces as (primarily) the residences of institutionalized rulers or ideational figures, versus, for example, as places of congregation and performance (Driessen 2002). These studies have questioned the assumption of a unitary hierarchical model of society, versus, say, a more heterarchical structure, or other looser, less comprehensive models (Knappett 1999; Haggis 2002; Schoep 2002; 2006). Other developments have included questioning when court-centered complex architectural compounds (palaces or their ilk) first exist on Crete and challenging our assumed evolutionary model, rethinking interpretation of ceramics to inform about contemporary society, and rethinking settlement scale and history on Crete and in the Aegean—suggesting a lack of evidence of necessarily centralized bureaucratic systems and controls, and so on—in a fairly comprehensive re-boot. In general, there has been a new emphasis on social approaches, phenomenology, and memory, and a turn toward emphasis on the internal versus the external (Driessen *et al.* 2002; Hamilakis 2002; 2014; Barrett and Halstead 2004; Schoep *et al.* 2012). Legarra Herrero (2016) offers the most recent assessment, seeking to turn away from external factors or influences. Instead, he proposes that 'the development of state formation on Crete was mainly due to internal decisions and an idiosyncratic cultural configuration that enabled innovations to become stable' (Legarra Herrero 2016: 350).

Moving to the present and looking forward, and maintaining a broad perspective, there remain some rather obvious, related points of tension in current discussions of Crete in the Prepalatial (third millennium BC) to Protopalatial periods (early second millennium BC). Contention largely centers around (1) timescale/process, (2) scale/analysis, and (3) the question of the balance between internal versus external stimuli and the nature of the encounter between agency (human and material) and context. I reflect on these issues below.

Timescale/Process

Long or short, gradual or rapid, was any particular moment/period especially significant? One position (exemplified by Sherratt 2010: 92-93) envisages the development of complex societies in the Aegean as a long, gradual, multi-faceted process building from at least the middle of the fourth millennium BC onward (see also Rahmstorf 2006; 2015). In contrast, Cherry (1983; 2010) advocates a punctuated evolutionary model: he argues that most significant change that led to an entirely different level of sociopolitical complexity and form (the palaces) occurred in a relatively short period from the last few centuries of the third millennium BC into the first century of the second millennium BC, and he critiques the lack of evidence to sustain a much longer and gradual viewpoint.

This dichotomy returns us to a debate many thought ended. The long-term, gradualist, position (e.g., Branigan 1970) seemed vanquished a generation ago (Cherry 1983; 1984), but it has made a striking new return through the work especially of Tomkins and collaborators (e.g., 2008; 2012; 2014; Papadatos and Tomkins 2013; 2014). Tompkins suggests that key structural features of the later (Middle Minoan) palaces date back to the Early Minoan (EM) II period or earlier—arguing for example that the Knossos palace seems to have antecedents in a series of precursor structures from the Final Neolithic (FN) onward. Papadatos and Tomkins (2013; 2014) have meanwhile pushed back evidence of longboats, trade, and interaction in the southern Aegean from the well-known Early Bronze (EB) II phase highlighted by Broodbank (1989; 2000) into the fourth millennium BC.

Two issues stand out: (1) relevant timescale (really a discussion about scale and analysis); and (2) whether we can resolve any key period of change late in the third millennium BC. First, the absolute timescale is now reasonably clear, despite an embarrassing lack of high-quality chronometric evidence for much of the Aegean and especially Crete. Recent data, especially from the Cyclades, confirm (Renfrew *et al.* 2012), as Cherry (2010: 112-13) previously summarized, that the overall Prepalatial or EM period occupied around a millennium or so (e.g., Manning 1995). Hence 'when we refer (often somewhat cavalierly) to "the prepalatial period", we should remember that this now refers to a vast span of some 1,200 years, far too long to constitute an era about which any meaningful generalizations are possible' (Cherry 2010: 112). The issue then of what constitutes *significant* change, influence, or stimulus, and gradual versus punctuated, episodic change, is foregrounded—and I discuss this in the next section. However, as concerns timescale and process, the second issue is key, and here recent evidence complicates the previously assumed situation and raises questions about the relevance of an episode of arid climate change around 2200 BC—affecting lower latitudes in particular—which has become a focus of much discussion (e.g., Dalfes *et al.* 1997; Manning *et al.* 2014; Meller *et al.* 2015). What happened in the later third millennium BC? And is the 2200 BC (or 4200 BP) episode relevant to the Cretan case?

The standard position until recently held that the later EB II period seemed to end in the Aegean in the twenty-third century BC or around about 2200 BC. In Crete,

EM III followed to about 2000 BC and the Middle Minoan (MM) IA from then (Manning 1995: 217). The close of EB II by around 2200 BC seemed to offer the possibility of some form of association with the climate change episode observed from around this time (considered of wider relevance after Weiss *et al.* 1993; Dalfes *et al.* 1997; Meller *et al.* 2015). Manning (1997) largely downplayed the apparent *direct* effects on Crete, given evidence then available, but nonetheless argued for the broader relevance of this climate episode and its effects. The EB II 'system' in Anatolia and Mesopotamia—Renfrew's (1972) 'International Spirit', subsequently named the Anatolian Trade Network (ATN: Şahoğlu 2005)—stretched west into the Aegean, which was consequently affected when (whether due to climate change and/or other factors) this system collapsed or retrenched from around 2200 BC (e.g., Forsén 1992). This set of circumstances left relatively peripheral Crete less affected both directly and indirectly—at that time, Crete had only limited contact with the east Mediterranean, and the island was comparatively less hierarchical, with less apparent dependence on prestige-good networks via the rest of the Aegean or ATN, and with a highly variegated geography minimizing climate change impacts versus other areas with little geographic variation. However, with a vacuum to fill and a major opportunity in the southern Aegean, Crete thus found itself in a strong and favourable position to develop rapidly. Moody (2009) subsequently made a reasonable case for Crete being impacted to some extent by the 2200 BC arid climate change episode, and she suggests that there may be a reflection in the changes in religious practices observed on the island from the EM III period, but this if anything only reinforces EM III as an opportunity for dynamic internal change on Crete.

Elsewhere in the east Mediterranean-Near East, several cases of archaeometric dating in the last few years have suggested instances of change and reorientation in the period around 2200 BC in a number of areas, and especially in those susceptible to arid conditions (e.g., at Tell Leilan in northern Syria [Weiss *et al.* 2012], or the transition from the Philia Phase to the Early Cypriot in Cyprus [Manning 2013]). There has unfortunately been little modern radiocarbon work for Crete, but the venerable series of radiocarbon dates from Myrtos (Warren 1972) again place the close of EM IIB destruction around 2200 BC (Figures 2.2a and 2.2b; see also Manning 2017: 461, 464-65). This might also support the theory that the change from EM II to EM III has some potential association with the 2200 BC episode and therefore with the collapse of the ATN and wider east Mediterranean trading systems.

However, it has been argued recently that radiocarbon dates suggest that the post-EB II period on the mainland, Early Helladic (EH) III, and in the Cycladic Islands, actually started before 2200 BC, which would mean that the 2200 BC climate change episode was not responsible after all (e.g., Renfrew *et al.* 2012; Jung and Weninger 2015). The two key sets of dates and sites are the suite of radiocarbon dates published by Wild *et al.* (2010) from Kolonna, Aegina, and the dates from Dhaskalio, Keros (Renfrew *et al.* 2012).

The first well-dated context at Kolonna is the early EH III destruction of Phase E. Rerunning the sequence of Wild *et al.* (2010) with IntCal13 (Reimer *et al.* 2013),

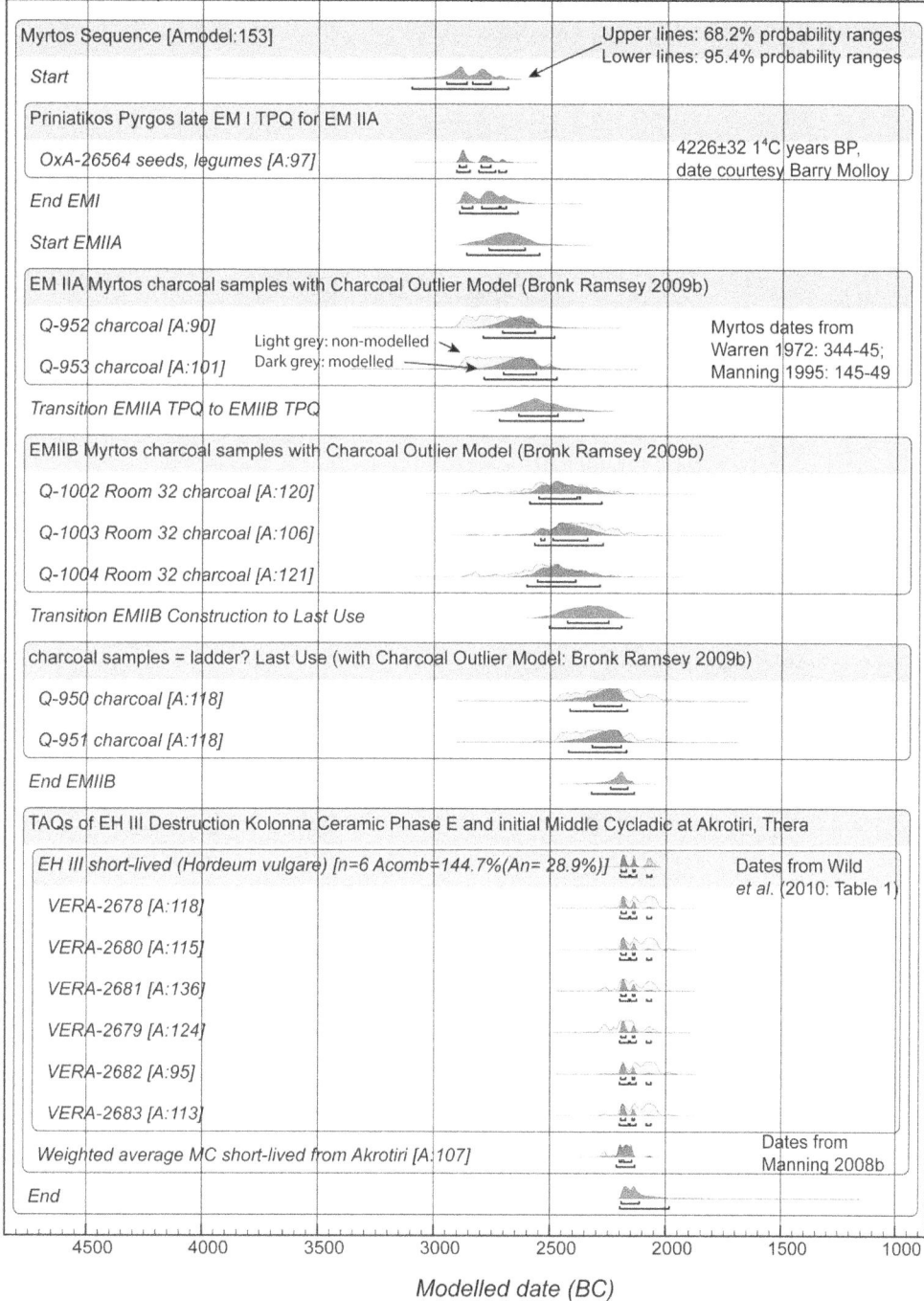

OxCal v4.2.4 Bronk Ramsey (version 2013; for software, see Bronk Ramsey 2009a); IntCal13 atmospheric curve (Reimer et al 2013), resolution 5 years

Figure 2.2a   Sequence analysis of the ¹⁴C dates on charcoal from EM IIA and EM IIB Myrtos, Crete, with additional constraints from dates from contexts before and after Myrtos.

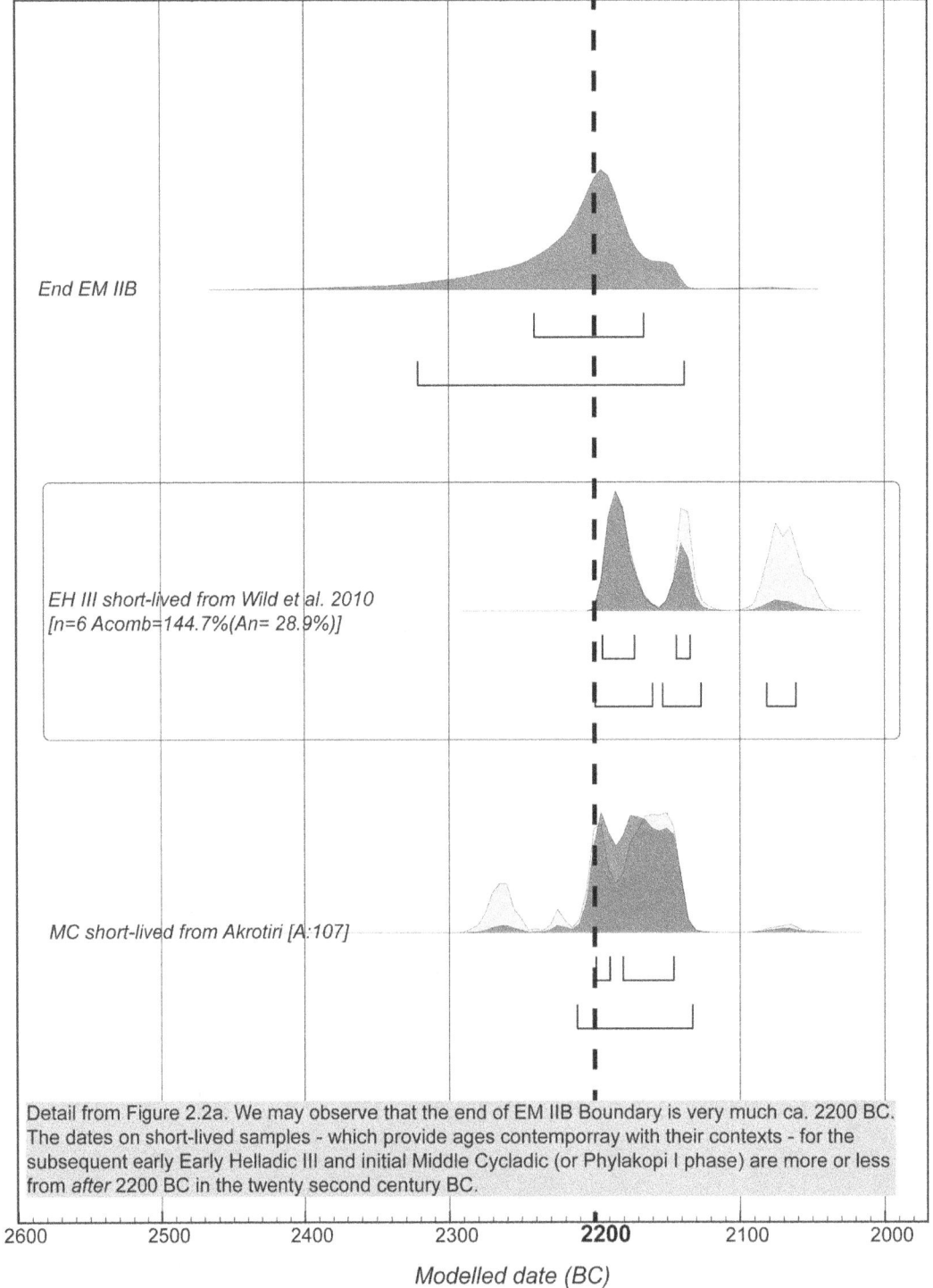

OxCal v4.2.4 Bronk Ramsey (version 2013; for software, see Bronk Ramsey 2009a); r:5 IntCal13 atmospheric curve (Reimer et al. 2013)

End EM IIB

EH III short-lived from Wild et al. 2010
[n=6 Acomb=144.7%(An= 28.9%)]

MC short-lived from Akrotiri [A:107]

Detail from Figure 2.2a. We may observe that the end of EM IIB Boundary is very much ca. 2200 BC. The dates on short-lived samples - which provide ages contemporray with their contexts - for the subsequent early Early Helladic III and initial Middle Cycladic (or Phylakopi I phase) are more or less from *after* 2200 BC in the twenty second century BC.

2600   2500   2400   2300   **2200**   2100   2000

Modelled date (BC)

Figure 2.2b   Detail from Figure 2.2a.

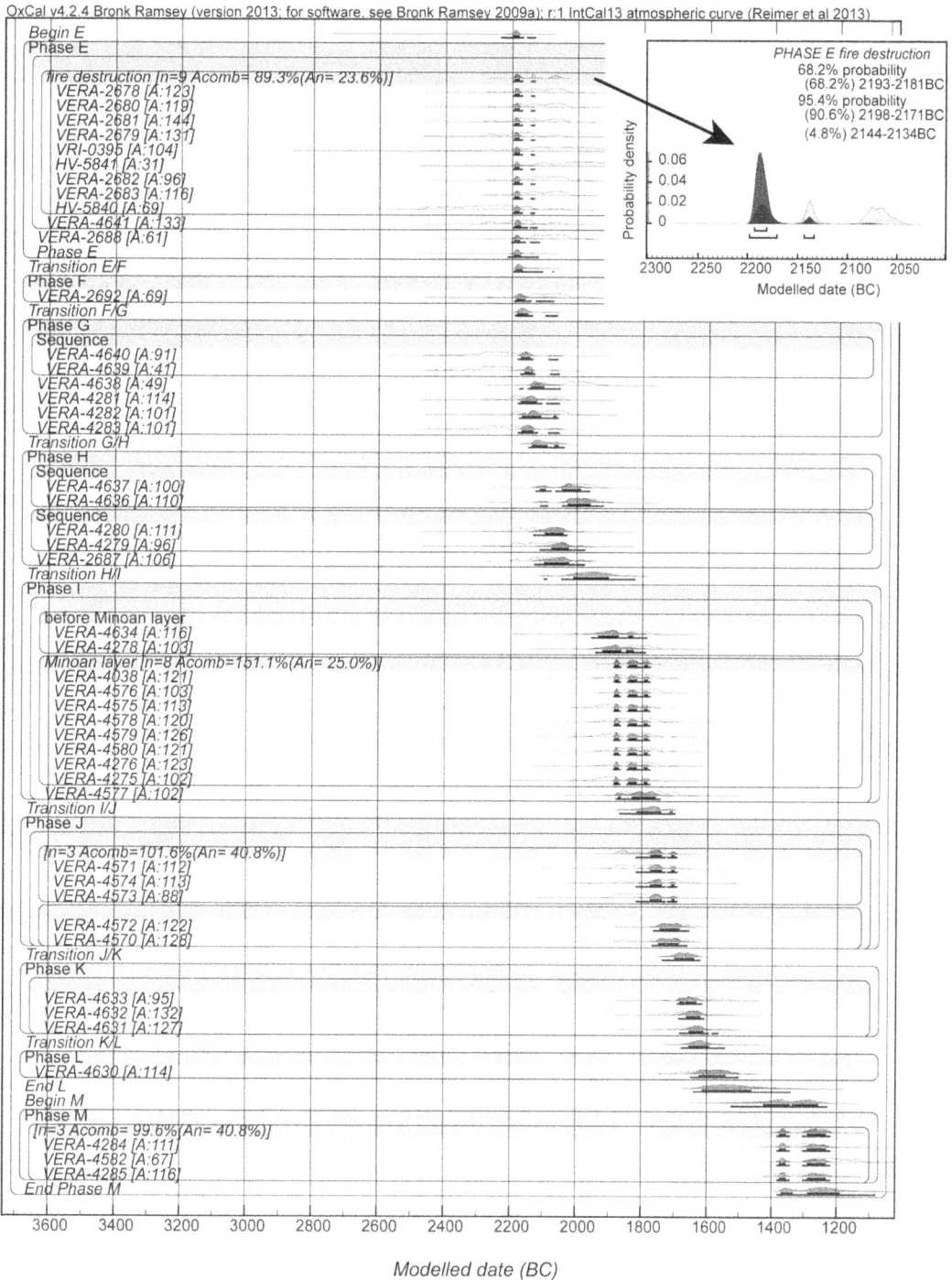

Figure 2.3   The Kolonna, Aegina, radiocarbon sequence of Wild *et al.* (2010) rerun employing IntCal13 (Reimer *et al.* 2013) with curve resolution modelled at one calendar year.

the date range for the close of Phase E fire destruction is 2193–2181 BC (68.2% probability), 2198–2177 BC (90.6%), and 2144–2134 (4.8%) (95.4% probability): see Figure 2.3. The time span of Phase E thus lies before: the early EH III period at the site—depending on how long this was—likely ran from somewhere in the (mid to later) twenty-third century BC to the first two to three decades of the twenty-second century BC. If early EH III was not a long temporal interval at Kolonna, then the end of EH II and start of EH III might well correspond with the date for the climate change event (Meller *et al.* 2015).

There are two issues relevant to the dates from Dhaskalio: (1) whether it is correct to all but discount the effect of in-built age (so old tree rings) when analyzing the dates in this set on potentially long-lived wood charcoal (Jung and Weninger 2015: 215-17; Manning 2017: 459-61); and (2) whether there is a 'gap' in the Cycladic sequence after Dhaskalio and before the initial MBA in the Cyclades (the so-called Rutter gap).

As regards the first point, the key Dhaskalio samples are all charcoal. Potentially long-lived species are used: *Olea europaea*, *Juniperus* sp., *Pistacia* sp., and some shorter-lived cases, notably *Hedera helix* (R7, OxA-22746) and Ericaceae (R51, OxA-22760). Renfrew *et al.* (2012: 149, 151) admit that the olive wood samples might be from roof timbers (and so could be instances of use of long-lived wood), but otherwise they suggest that the wood charcoal derives from branches and twigs. Indeed, it is noticeable that there is a range of ages in the radiocarbon dates for each phase, and especially that the date of the Ericaceae sample is the most recent for Phase C (Renfrew *et al.* 2012: table 4) and that the date for the *Hedera helix* sample is the second-most recent for Phase B but, most obviously, over 100 ^{14}C years more recent than the two oldest dates in this set (R4, OxA-22745 and R8, OxA-22747).

On the second point, the potential of a gap (Rutter 1983), Renfrew *et al.* (2012) specifically exclude this possibility. They argue that 'the evidence of Dhaskalio indicates a striking continuity between the successive phases there, with no suggestion of a gap' (Renfrew *et al.* 2012: 157). However, this misses the point. If a gap exists it is *after* the Dhaskalio sequence ends and *before* the initial Middle Cycladic—and in particular *before* the initial Middle Cycladic radiocarbon dates from Akrotiri on Thera employed by Renfrew *et al.* (2012: 155, fig. 9). Such a gap in the material culture of the Cyclades after the Kastri Group (late/end EB II) and before the Middle Cycladic of the Phylakopi I group still seems real in the evidence we have (Rutter 2013: 593; see also Brogan 2013).

If we rerun the Dhaskalio sequence allowing for some in-built age for the samples on wood charcoal and for such a 'Rutter Gap', then a somewhat different picture emerges (Manning 2017: 459-61; contra Renfrew *et al.* 2012): see Figures 2.4a and 2.4b. Dhaskalio Phase C likely ends even a little earlier than Renfrew *et al.* (2012) suggest—in the late twenty-fourth century BC. A possible Rutter Gap lies mainly in the twenty-third century BC, and the Middle Cycladic period does not start until around or indeed likely *after* 2200 BC. Thus, in the Cycladic Islands, significant cultural change seems to begin in

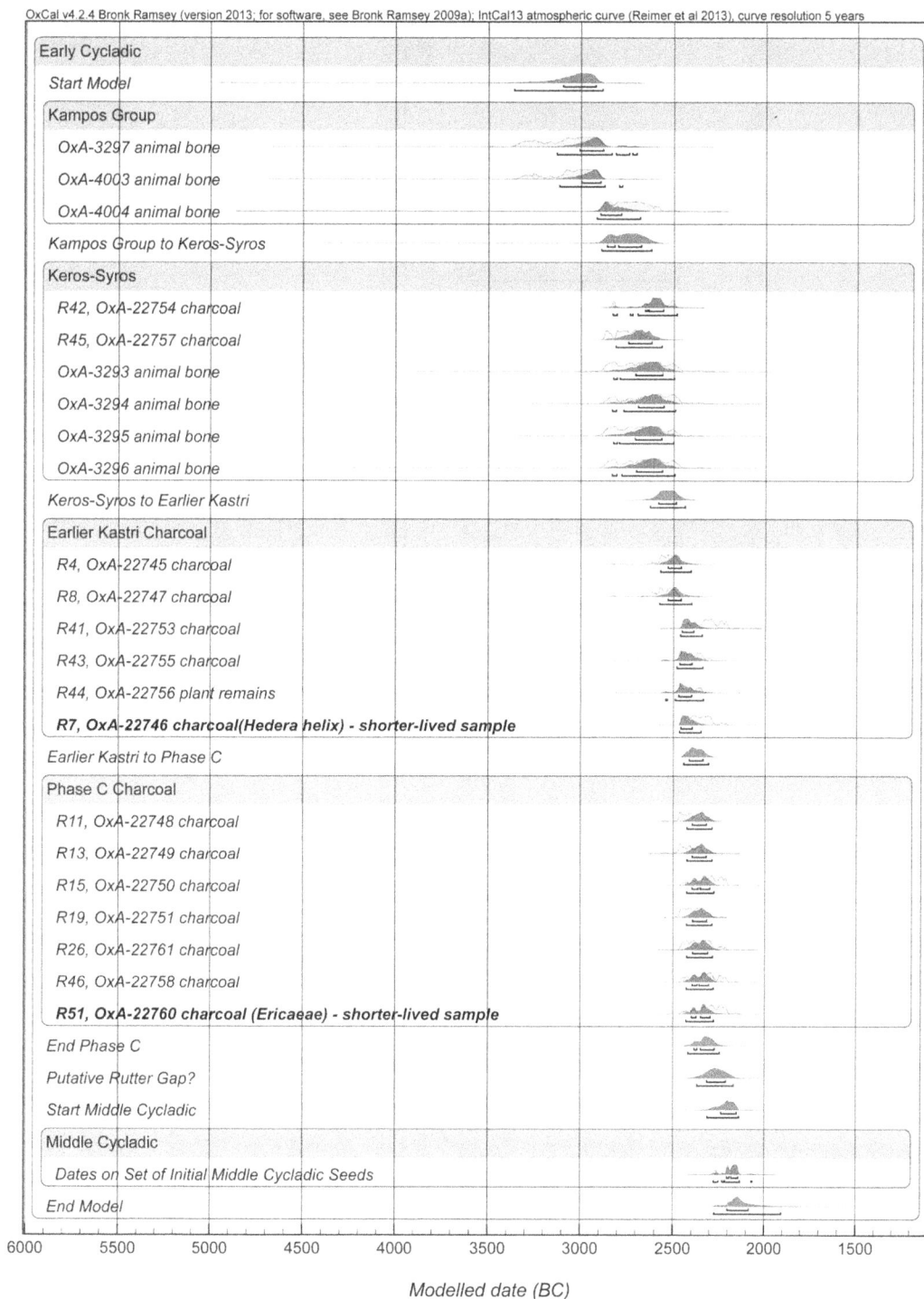

OxCal v4.2.4 Bronk Ramsey (version 2013; for software, see Bronk Ramsey 2009a); IntCal13 atmospheric curve (Reimer et al 2013), curve resolution 5 years

Modelled date (BC)

Figure 2.4a   Renfrew *et al.* (2012) Early Cycladic sequence rerun with the Charcoal Outlier model applied to non-short/shorter-lived charcoal samples and the General Outlier model applied to the other dates (Bronk Ramsey 2009b), and including asking for the length of a possible Rutter Gap phase (interval) between the end of Phase C and the start of the Middle Cycladic period.

OxCal v4.2.4 Bronk Ramsey (version 2013; for software, see Bronk Ramsey 2009a); r:5 IntCal13 atmospheric curve (Reimer et al 2013)

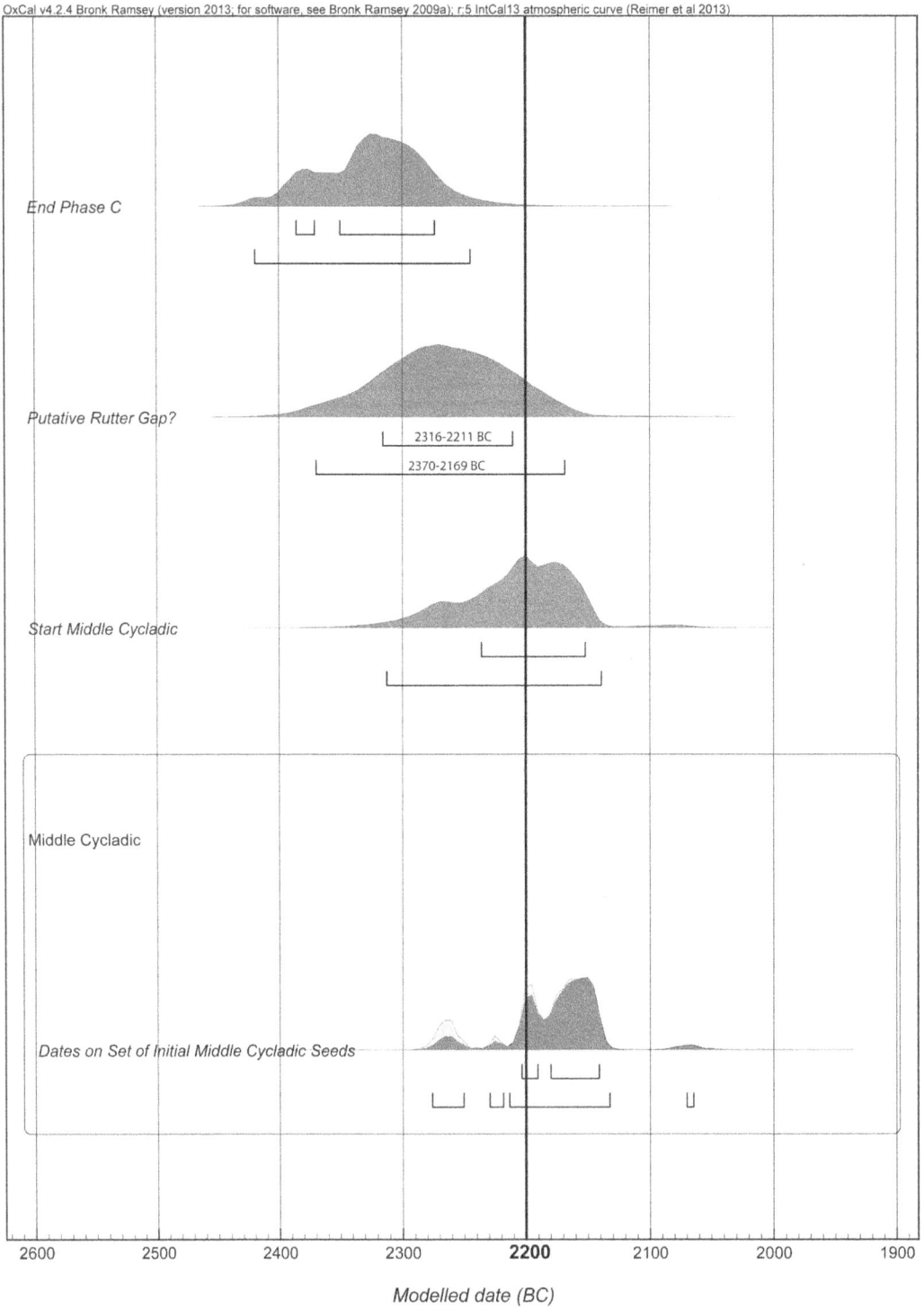

Figure 2.4b   Detail from Figure 2.4a showing the End of Phase C, Possible Rutter Gap, and Start of Middle Cycladic.

the twenty-third century BC (post-Kastri Group and post-ATN—or as the latter ends/collapses), and a new *status quo* (Middle Cycladic) starts from around or *after* ca. 2200 BC. This seems in fact rather compatible with the wider east Mediterranean scenario of a period of challenge and change developing in the later twenty-third century BC and from 2200 BC—directly affecting marginal areas and indirectly affecting others—associated with the effects of a (more arid, cooler) climate change (Meller *et al.* 2015).

In terms of chronology alone, what happens on Crete in EM III and MM IA appears temporally separate from the third-millennium BC cycle of development, linked to and likely stimulated by the ATN, and leading up to the forms of emergent complex society observed widely in the later EB II Aegean and in western Anatolia. This cycle and boom ended—a major bust—over much of the region (seemingly variously in the later twenty-fourth through twenty-third centuries BC). What happened next was both different and separate.

Scale/Analysis

We know what happens next: the (MM) palaces of Crete. But the correct questions concerning their origins and development remain debated. It is clear that there was a dramatic demographic, infrastructural, and societal transformation in terms of scale and complexity at Knossos (and to a lesser extent at some other large sites on Crete) in the period from during EM III and especially in MM I (Whitelaw 2012). The key requisite agrarian support systems (Whitelaw 2004) must have seen significant increases in technology and scale (including the developed secondary products revolution), with the advent of the peak sanctuaries at this same time likely indicating new larger, integrated, territorial entities (states) (Haggis 1999). Despite Tomkins's reservations (Tomkins 2008), no one has challenged the extraordinary 'take-off' and a change in settlement size by a factor of three to six after the EM II period in EM III and especially MM IA (Whitelaw 2012, esp. figs. 4.12-4.14) (Figure 2.5). How and why did this occur? Some see 'proto' and 'early' indications of later entities and push meaningful structural changes in society back toward early dates; others do the opposite.

There were undoubtedly multiple episodes of social change through time at Knossos (and in other communities on Crete)—as in most societies and areas. Tomkins (2008; 2012) is correct to point to earlier processes and organizational changes, especially in FN, EM I, and EM II on Crete, and at Knossos in particular (see also Wilson 1994). The question, looking at the bigger picture and the period leading to the palaces, is whether there is one key developmental threshold/episode, or, rather, a series of steps. Whitelaw's (2012) research on the settlement history of Knossos suggests the former. Indeed, this almost appears to be a generalization for initial urbanization—Fletcher's (1986) cross-cultural review of settlement size history at primate sites finds a 'take-off' inflection to be typical.

The next question is when these key changes occur. The settlement history (and chronology) of Whitelaw (2012) as summarized in Figure 2.5 indicates that one

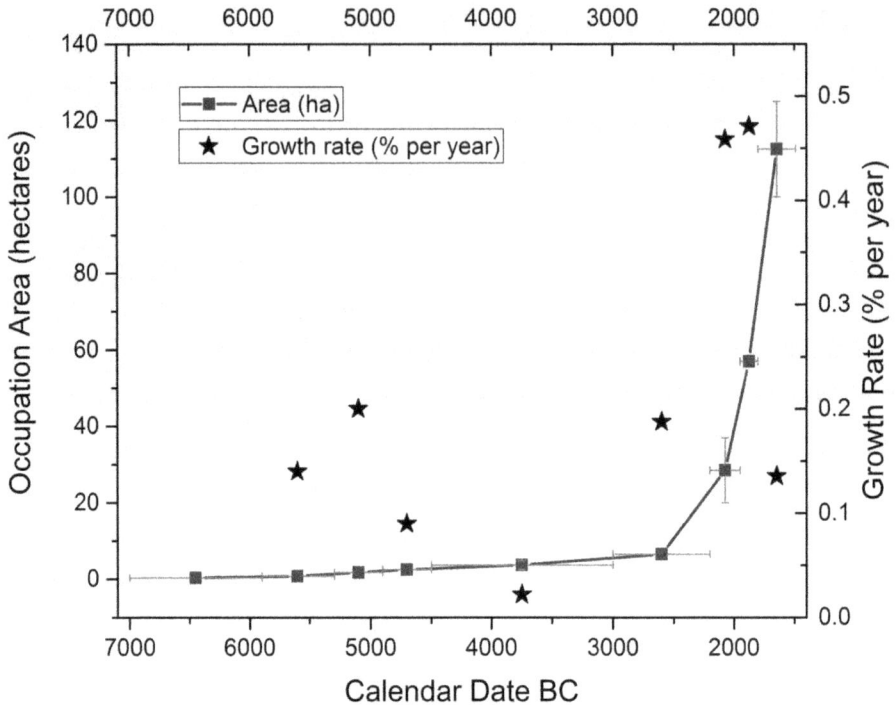

Figure 2.5   Knossos occupation area (squares, with range indicated by vertical grey bars) against the chronology (horizontal grey bars) and estimate of growth rate (stars) taken from the estimates provided in Whitelaw (2012: table 4.1; see also his fig. 4.12). Here occupation area estimate is placed in the center of the time interval for which it is an estimate; contrast with Figure 2.6, where the estimate for EMI–II is placed at the end of the time period (see Tomkins 2008: esp. fig. 3.4).

might seem to place the start of an inflection in the EM I–II period and dramatic take-off in EM III–MM IA—these are the time intervals captured by Whitelaw in this figure—but of course the EM I–II unit (settlement at Knossos ca. 6.5 ha) covers a period of 800 years. The EM III-MM IA unit (settlement ca. 20–37 ha) covers 250 years. In contrast, Tomkins (2008: fig. 3.4) regards the change in settlement size during EM I–II as during EM II and plots a peak settlement size of ca. 5 ha at the *end* of EM II. If we adjust Figure 2.5 following Tomkins and place the maximum EM I–II settlement size at the end of EM II we come up with Figure 2.6. Now the clear inflection point is after EM II and in the EM III–MM IA interval (indicated by the grey box in Figure 2.6). Whitelaw's (2012: fig.4.14) graph of population estimates for Knossos, Phaistos, and Malia emphasizes the same view—major inflection or take-off after about 2200 BC (or from the start of EM III).

In terms of time and space, what happens on Crete in EM III and afterward is entirely separate from the EB II International Spirit of the Aegean and the ATN. As reviewed in the previous section, the Cycladic later EB II-ATN world seems to conclude around or even before 2300 BC, whereas EM IIB seems not to end until nearer 2200 BC.

If we consider the even more peripheral connection of Crete to the east Mediterranean, noted above, we also can detect no pattern or link of significance

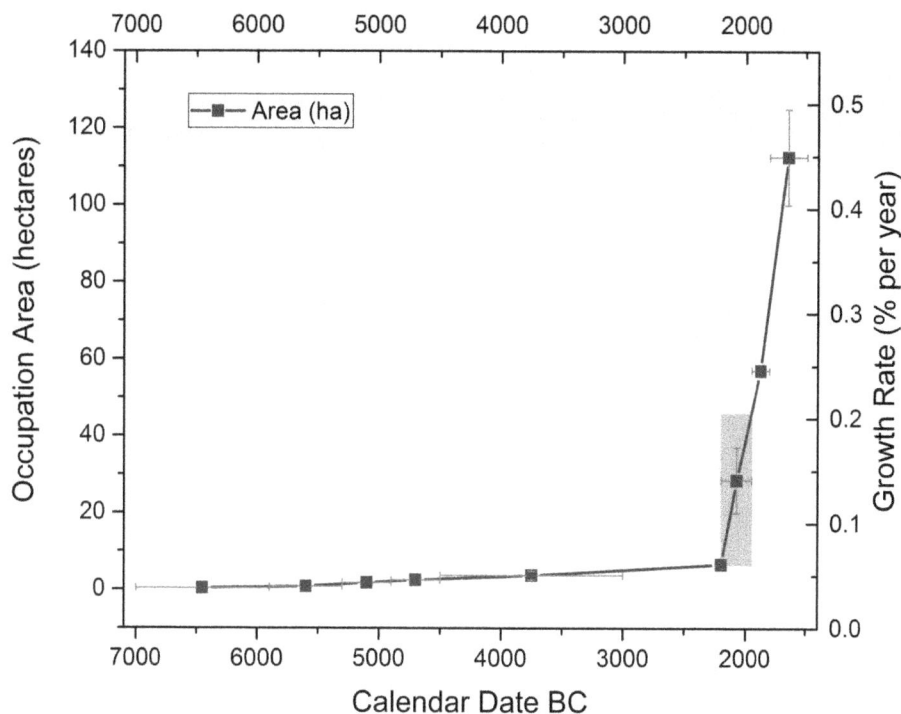

Figure 2.6   Occupation area at Knossos from Figure 2.5 but modified to place the estimate for EMI–II at the end of the time period in line with the discussion of Tomkins (2008) and his summary (Tomkins 2008: fig. 3.4), where the greatest area of EM I–II occupation is only deemed as occurring at the end of EM II.

before the late third millennium BC, and quite possibility not until around 2000 BC. The mere existence of such a connection is distinctive and important for Crete (as opposed to elsewhere in the Aegean or further west in the Mediterranean) and is widely recognized as part of the answer to Lewthwaite's (1983) question of 'why Crete?' (and why civilization did not emerge more often and elsewhere). Nonetheless, despite the geographic proximity, Cherry (2010) observed that the secure evidence for contacts between Crete and the east Mediterranean before the late third millennium BC comprised in total just one silver Syrian cylinder seal from Tomb I at Mochlos. Thus, arguments for substantive EM II contact appear exaggerated (a handful of other items *may* have arrived around then but are in fact likely to derive from later EM III and especially MM I contexts—Cherry 2010: 118-20). If east Mediterranean / Near Eastern direct contacts are important to the development of palatial Crete, it seems this period of transformative engagement and subsequent entanglement was at the earliest EM III and quite possibly MM I—very separate in time from whatever happened in the Aegean in the EB I–II periods.

The internal history on Crete must also be considered. Tomkins (2012) has drawn attention to a long history of incipient complexity on Crete and at Knossos especially. We may assume this repeated confluence of habitual interaction and social practices over time led to a community with its own identity, and one in which individuals associated themselves and their history with a sense of place (Feld and Basso 1996; Canuto and Yaeger 2000). Such repeated and reproduced place-making and memory inscription at the larger and long-lived settlements (especially Knossos and Phaistos), and at communal tomb centers (Hamilakis 2014), would have created forms of social history and capital potentially exploitable by later actors and groups. There are several indicators of developing complex society during EM I–II, including: specialized crafting; trade within and beyond Crete; larger, proto-urban settlements (Knossos, Phaistos, Malia), and at Knossos indications of central place-making (the court area) and associated monumental construction; special-purpose structures; the development of a representational and perhaps bureaucratic system involving seals and sealings; and perhaps evidence of warfare (Muhly 2004; Betancourt 2008; 2013; Tomkins 2012). There were also central and increasingly complex, elaborate, and regionally varied mortuary practices through EM I–II, indicating different groupings and social formations (Legarra Herrero 2009; 2014).

This evidence provides something of a recalibration from the general dismissal of EM Crete as largely egalitarian in scholarly writing from a generation ago, but it is also easy to lose perspective. This evidence on Crete is highly *un*impressive in terms of scale and complexity in comparison with the proto-urban and urban developments of the fourth and third millennia in Anatolia (e.g., Horejs and Mehofer 2014; Fidan *et al.* 2015) and in the Aegean in the EB II period (e.g., Konsola 1990; Broodbank 2013: 320-23). It is also very different than what is found on Crete from the MM I period onward, also in terms of practice and human–object relations. For example, Knappett (2011: 84-91) observes changes in the *matériel* of storage and of drinking at the very beginning of the Protopalatial period. Thus, even though Tomkins (2012: 74-75) suggests that he regards a key social-civilization transformation on Crete as occurring perhaps as early as EM IIA (if not as far back as FN), he nonetheless accepts that the EM II changes 'did not directly drive' the 'dramatic later demographic growth during EM III and MM I'. We must also remember the temporal dimension and avoid infinite regression as causation: Tomkins (2012: 74-75) ends by suggesting that 'the EM II changes in turn made possible' the 'dramatic later demographic growth during EM III and MM I' but—and especially since he states that 'it is in EM IIA that one sees clear evidence for a qualitative change in social organization and social relations'—we need to remember that we are now talking about a period of around 400 to 600 years (from during EM IIA to during EM III or MM IA).

Although we now have a much better and fuller picture of EM Crete, and see that some incipient forms of complex society developed during the EM I–II period, there remains little satisfactory argument to explain the very different and dramatic changes that occur on Crete in EM III and especially MM I. What is important, however, and different from the view of a generation ago of a largely egalitarian EM period, is that, while EM II Crete was peripheral and small-scale versus other polities in the Aegean, Anatolia, and farther east, there was an established emergent elite and some hierarchy in several long-formed, larger, communities. This nexus comprised people, built space/

infrastructure, and capital, but also sets of shared social practices and perceptions. There were thus the bases and ingredients that could provide a platform from which a dramatic social, economic, and political 'take-off' could occur, especially at some larger sites based in productive and favorable agricultural areas, allied with developments in production and trade and the beginnings of social organization and community gathering (for example at courts and court-centered monumental compounds and communal tombs). Such developments were in stark contrast with most of the rest of the Aegean and Anatolia after the widespread horizon of late EB II reorientation and collapse—where the potential had at that point been lost for several centuries.

As noted above, Crete appears to have escaped the boom and bust elsewhere in the third millennium BC Aegean. This may be due in part to its relative isolation, peripheral position, variegated and thus flexible geography and subsistence base, and scale—all factors that together make the island a 'mini-continent' (Rackham and Moody 1996) and so better able to weather the climate downturn around 2200 BC. Moreover, Crete was peripheral to both the ATN and the east Mediterranean. Its elite was thus powerfully connected, stimulating and supporting possibilities and potentials, but was not structurally reliant on these networks. Embedded histories at the key sites also offered potential power beyond any direct memory through key ancestors, genealogies, and associations. And the continental status of the island provided sufficient scale and diversity to sustain growth internally. In this situation various sets of elites were able to benefit from and use, but also control and monopolize, limited external contacts as part of building what became a long-term and eventually permanent social, political, and economic system with sustained internal (agrarian) bases and an exploitable southern-Aegean periphery. This platform, and the general rise of 'voyaging' and connectivity through the third millennium BC in the Aegean and whole Mediterranean (Broodbank 2013: 325-29), provided and supported the idea and ability—after the EB II collapse—for the several ambitious leaders and their groups on Crete to enter, engage with, and fill what had become something of a vacuum, both north and east, to dramatic effect.

Internal and External Stimuli and Enabling Encounters

Legarra Herrero (2016: 352-53), critiquing previous analyses based on what he terms the 'prestige model', advocates a bottom-up reconsideration. He concludes that 'this review of the data cannot identify a single instance where the "prestige" model's expectations of high-value materials in wealthy exclusive burials can be clearly identified in the archaeological record' (Legarra Herrero 2016: 358). Downplaying the importance of new widespread but limited occurrences of imported or emulating material (primarily Egyptian and Egyptianizing) as merely part of the same deposition logic as local products, he notes the lack of clear evidence for leadership in the funerary (or other) record from Crete at this period, and challenges suggestions made previously for the rise of a more individual ethos from the increased use of burial containers. Instead, he argues for an analysis centered around the community and group, primarily internal to Crete, concluding that 'mechanisms of internal change, such as individualized conspicuous consumption and the symbolic role of exotica in creating differentiation, cannot be easily recognized in the evidence presented' (Legarra Herrero 2016: 359). His corrective sharpens our focus.

At the same time, I wonder if we need to consider the evidence from Crete differently: is the tomb itself the place to focus on, or rather the performative, transitional process? A similar suggestion can be made regarding the palaces: that the focus should be on the activities and performance and not the built structures—the mere stage. The palaces, tombs, and peak sanctuaries of Crete seem to be about regional- and community-integrating processional routes, social gatherings and the entwined performances. In each case some form of large-scale drinking/feasting is associated. Is the assertion, production, and reproduction of roles and status on Crete—including potentially of leading individuals and the missing 'elite'/leaders—primarily occurring within these recurring, dynamic, fluid, and non-permanent sociopolitical processes? And, therefore, may they not be well represented in the built, iconographic, or interred material record?

For example, Egyptian or Egyptianizing stone vessels and scarabs and scaraboids are found in small quantities at a number of collective tombs (Legarra Herrero 2016: fig. 5b-c). Legarra Herrero (2016: 357-58) thus downplays their significance, observing a similar deposition logic as local products, and instead suggests a focus on concentrations of overall sets of objects at some tombs. But the palimpsest conundrum appears to apply; and, perhaps, we also lose sight of the power of particular things to afford significance as part of a 'political machine' (Smith 2015). It is true that the overall pattern is a massive increase in the numbers of stone vessels and seals from EM II to MM I contexts (Legarra Herrero 2016: fig. 5a), but within this bigger picture we do not know that the local and rarer imported/emulating objects were used, displayed, or deployed exactly as equivalents. Their repeated and widespread presence, but conspicuous relative rarity, would rather suggest the reverse, and could well indicate that in the context of social gatherings and performances they afforded and created key graduations of status and power to just a few restricted persons or small groups within a larger community. The value of rare exotic imports within a society should never be underestimated (Helms 1988). Which persons held and consumed from the imported vessels (perhaps with further important local biographies), versus the emulating vessels, versus the local products? Who wore the imported scarabs, as opposed to scaraboids, and in contrast to those displaying local seals? It is easy to undervalue how in such small but key markers and details a specific human body and person are transformed into authoritative and sociopolitically central entities, and how, via such items, status and roles are embodied, reproduced, and potentially enhanced (note also instances of wear and repair—Colburn 2008: 214-19).

Legarra Herrero (2016: 358) writes:

> The off-island connections of certain sealstones and stone vessels may express nuances within this pattern … It seems clear that this material was not mainly related to elite

identities as is sometimes assumed, but was a component in the complex set of multi-level relationships that were enacted and materialized at the cemeteries.

I would actually argue that the opposite is more likely the case: these rare items might very well express key nuances (i.e., social status). Moreover, these rare elements might specifically afford elite identities and comprise key elements demarcating and reproducing them during the 'complex set of multi-level relationships that were enacted and materialized at the cemeteries'.

In particular, building and maintaining recognized social centrality is fundamental to successful and sustained leadership of groups, especially those of a pre-institutionalized character (Roscoe 1993). This typically involves regular performance and reinforcing of social and economic benefits to followers and the group as a whole. Providing feasts or other events that benefit both individuals and the group, and create social ties and obligations, can afford and produce power and status (e.g., Hayden 2001). Such collective, public events are also those where status is displayed, negotiated, recognized, and reproduced. We might therefore speculate, revising Legarra Herrero (2016), that the relatively rare, various 'eastern'/Egyptian objects and influences evident on Crete at this time provided these valued and increasingly essential status signifiers. Situations would include feasting events and funerary processions and ceremonies, especially when associated with the creation and then use of increasingly elaborate venues, whether central court compound areas (as emerge progressively at the sites of the future Protopalatial palaces: e.g., Tomkins 2004: 43-45; 2012) or funerary complexes (Legarra Herrero 2016: 354-57—especially for example the monumental Chrysolakos Tomb at Malia or Tholos B at Archanes-Phourni).

As time passes, and if social, political, and economic roles become more permanent (versus merely achieved), these signifiers and their associated genealogies become in themselves tokens of office. In conditions of sustainable, intensifiable competition— which seems to be present in several of the larger settlements on Crete with available agricultural bases in EM III–MM IA—these sets of circumstances would mean that larger and larger groups would likely evolve through individuals selecting for group membership in order to maximize the overall success for each individual, which in turn benefits the larger groups (Kosse 1994). The effects of the more arid, cooler, 2200 BC climate episode on Crete might have further exacerbated this circumstance in EM III, with people in the more marginal areas of Crete tending to migrate to the more favorable agricultural areas and so further fueling demographic growth at the larger centers. These processes and the likely associated settlement nucleation then promote political centralization to maintain group efficiency (Roscoe 1993), and other new forms of social integration. Suggestions that the observed material culture regionalism of the Protopalatial period started in EM III (Cadogan 1990) are consistent, as larger, inherently self-defining groups and thence proto-polities emerged.

Larger groups inherently challenge previous small-scale and direct personal communication methods because of the practicalities of time and space. Modes of communication are necessary that are more efficient through use of technologies:

clothes, symbols, signs, objects, smells, and sounds that enable meanings to be conveyed to multiple persons even in the absence of direct interpersonal communication (see Bennet, this volume). Again, recognized prestige goods (signifiers) that are seen being used, consumed from, worn, displayed, burnt (incense), or sounded (sistra) could all form key resources for the emerging state-level elite of Crete in the late Prepalatial to Protopalatial periods.

The issue that is less satisfactory is the relevance of the off-island associations for the imported and/or emulating items. Wengrow (2010) correctly highlights that we have little idea whether or how the original meanings and associations of the—originally not high-status—Egyptian objects were transferred or transformed in(to) the Cretan setting (see also Cherry 2010: 135-37). Equally, his initial suggestion that the association with Egypt or the East was 'not so much as a particular territory, but rather as a spatial locus of time immemorial, closely associated with the ancestral status of powerful individuals and accessible through particular types of material culture' (Wengrow 2010: 146), might be as or might be most relevant as the primary interpretative framework for these objects on Crete. The relationship was not about space or place, but genealogical, with these exotic items interpreted as supernaturally important, closer to key, higher powers, and not just part of the everyday world. Their personal associations in use or wear, their long-term curation, and their occasional modification would conform to such a model. Neither the lack of original special status in their place of origin, nor the issue of the transfer of original meanings and roles, are then especially important. Wengrow (2010: 147) further expresses concern that the earliest known Egyptian imports to Crete are not especially obvious prestige goods, because 'glazed scarab seals and stone vessels would have been recognizable as exotic variants of existing types of material culture'. But, again, the reverse logic is that this formed their very possibility of affording social efficacy: they were familiar and similar enough that they could be incorporated into the existing social *habitus*, and yet distinctive, rare, and exotic enough to empower and afford extended and new meanings, definitions, and associations beyond those pre-existing.

It is noticeable that later Prepalatial Mochlos shows evidence of significant external links and trade both north and to the east. Broodbank (2000) speculates that this site began its own voyaging tradition around this time, and a settlement with strong Minoan associations is also established in this period at Kastri on Kythera. In general, we may observe a change in the direction of interaction in the Aegean after EB II. Some southern Aegean centers become initiators in EB III to MB I, notably Phylakopi on Melos, and especially some sites on Crete. This represents a shift from Anatolia and the east Aegean acting as the main source and ultimate driver, and Crete forming merely the end or periphery of a wider Aegean interaction zone. This may partly reflect a filling of the gap left by the collapse of the ATN, and the wider opportunity presented by the travails of more marginal agricultural areas created by the period of climate change from the twenty-third century BC onward. While secure evidence is scarce, we see traces of such new southern Aegean networks from EM III, with the find of a Cycladic, probably Melian or Theran, handle at Knossos, along with other Cycladic vessels (Momigliano and Wilson 1996: 44, pls. 8, 58; Momigliano 2007: 94). Moreover, either Cretan activity or the new Cycladic network is probably evident in the use of Cycladic metals at EM III Chrysakamino (Betancourt 2006).

An observation in all this that is clearly fundamental is that the funerary record of Crete in EM IIB and into the earlier part of EM III seems 'to have gone relatively quiet' (Legarra Herrero 2016: 353) and some changes in funerary practice are widely evident (Legarra Herrero 2009; 2012; 2014). This situation and change might reflect the decline of the previous external Cycladic traders arriving at numerous locations on Crete under a scenario of relatively open access to certain valued resources (like metals), which was not particularly controlled (or controllable) by EM I–II Cretan elites. Instead, whether because of external changes (collapse of the ATN and linked Cycladic system), or also because of internal processes, we might posit the beginnings of greater control enforced by some Cretan elites seen in the reduction in volume and restriction in supply and availability of imports and key resources to just a few sites on Crete. Acquisition was perhaps now largely restricted to proactive and direct activities (voyaging) by only some Cretan groups at and from these few sites. Assuming the EM I–IIA imports were mainly brought by external agents, such as Cycladic traders, the reduction in contacts *into* Crete in EM IIB and earlier EM III, and thus the restricted supply and limited circulation of authoritative goods on Crete, may also have permitted more successful monopolization of these resources on peripheral Crete by those now engaged in the voyaging out from Crete. This would explain the absence of authoritative goods in many tomb deposits of this period, since the usual prestige-goods logic of inflation and destruction of value (Gregory 1982) did not apply. Further, since Crete previously avoided the inflationary boom and bust cycle observed elsewhere in later EB II due to its relatively peripheral location and limited supply potential, circumstances may have enabled the Cretan elites to successfully build and maintain (monopolize) their position unchallenged by the usual plural and inflationary pressures afflicting prestige goods economies. This could have facilitated the incipient elite of earlier EM II at major sites on Crete to become a more permanent and rarefied elite through EM III (Manning 1997).

In these circumstances, and empowered now as established leaders, some groups at a few sites on Crete clearly began to be proactive, developing capacity on Crete and starting to seek external links at some point from EM IIB–III. The funerary record from Mochlos is suggestive, but currently unique—and what dates to EM IIB or rather EM III–MM IA is not settled. There was apparently intense competition there by at least some families or groupings involving off-island material in what looks like a prestige-goods political economy model. Whether some other sites, such as Knossos, engaged in similar activities in EM IIB–EM III, while yet other sites were not able to, is not evident from the available evidence, but this might be assumed. Outside Crete, some similar proactive and likely rival expansionary enterprises are evident in the form of the Phylakopi I culture network (Broodbank 2000: 351-56). One or more centers on Crete, led in each case by one or more prominent individuals or families or other groupings, appear to have expanded trade and other activities, perhaps even by force (Broodbank 2000: 359-60), into the southern Aegean during MM IA, and direct contact and trade seems likely to begin in this same period with the east Mediterranean. Such trade was based (for the first time) on exports from Crete into the east Mediterranean as well as a number of imports and imitations of east Mediterranean items to Crete (e.g., Warren 1995; Watrous 1998).

The fundamental and enabling (but specialist and capital intensive) technology appears to be the deep-hulled sailing ship—itself an import or imitation from the east Mediterranean (Broodbank 2000: 341-47). The organization around the development and use of this technology is of a fundamentally different scale versus longboats and the previous EB II world. It requires sustained leadership, control of substantive capital, and control of substantive labor: a pre-existing hierarchy and political machine. Whether characterized as palatial or other (Schoep 2006), such elites at the several larger settlements on Crete must have come into being by/before MM IA. Their status and power were undoubtedly built from developing central roles in their communities and as centers of increasingly larger groups within wider communities. Shared performative practices focused at the main venues for social gatherings likely formed the principal vectors (Legarra Herrero 2016: 359-62). However, an association with the 'East', via a genealogical model, was articulated through the use, display, and presentation of some exotic items linked to commensality, feasting, and the bodies of key persons. This was, I suggest, an essential power resource as the 'state' formed on Crete, and this connection of internal and external should remain vital and central to accounts of the development of the state on Crete.

Conclusions

A tension between a gradualist versus revolutionary perspective on Minoan state formation has long hung over Aegean prehistory. John Cherry has rightly criticized infinite regression as causation, and highlighted the millennial scale even of the Prepalatial EBA period, let alone the combined later Neolithic through EBA period, which negates the usefulness of either as analytical units. Nonetheless, the siren call of origins and conflating centuries and millennia into apparent processes seems irresistible to many. Similarly, there has been a long-running divide over the importance and timing of off-island and especially extra-Aegean contacts and influences, and how to assess the appropriate degree of critical specificity required to establish relevance and causal connection. Clearly subsequent Protopalatial Crete exhibits the adoption and transformation of at least some aspects of Near Eastern / Egyptian administrative practice, iconography, and beliefs, but it remains debated how initial contacts and influences stimulated social, political, and ideological practice in the late Prepalatial period. For just one fundamental example: whereas some see the administrative system of the MM II palaces as a Near Eastern import (e.g., Weingarten 1990), others argue for local development, even if influenced (Schoep 1999), but with very little actual evidence closely linking the earlier administrative practices of the EB II Aegean and EM II Crete with the (very different) sophisticated systems of the early palatial (MM) period. Cherry's insistence on a rigorously critical reading of the available evidence dramatically changed discussion in the 1980s, but there has been something of a retreat and watering down over the last two decades. An evidence-based critical analysis continues to suggest that the key transformation of Crete into a state-level society occurred within a relatively brief period, and that extra-Aegean resources, contacts, and influences were critical in this process.

Acknowledgments

I thank Alex Knodell and Tom Leppard for organizing the splendid event at the Joukowsky Institute, and also for their patience. The currently in-progress writing of John Cherry will undoubtedly demarcate the next phase of the Minoan field for another generation. Thus an interregnum discussion which seeks to raise and discuss just a few points of interest seems appropriate for a paper in his honor. This return to a field first entered under his influence and supervision at Cambridge allows me to express my many thanks to John for helping start and support my career. I also absolve him from any responsibility (both from this particular paper, and otherwise). I thank Alex, Tom, John, and Tom Tartaron for comments.

About the Author

Sturt W. Manning is Goldwin Smith Professor of Classical Archaeology and Chair of the Department of Classics at Cornell University in Ithaca, New York, where he also directs the Cornell Tree Ring Laboratory. His research interests include Aegean, Cypriot, and east Mediterranean archaeology, along with the archaeology of complex societies, dendrochronology, radiocarbon dating, and archaeological science. Recent publications include *A Test of Time and A Test of Time Revisited: The Volcano of Thera and the Chronology and History of the Aegean and East Mediterranean in the Mid-Second Millennium BC* (Oxbow Books, 2014), and *Tree-Rings, Kings and Old World Archaeology and Environment: Papers Presented in Honor of Peter Ian Kuniholm* (Oxbow Books, 2009). E-mail: sm456@cornell.edu

References

Appadurai, A.
  1986 Introduction: commodities and the politics of value. In A. Appadurai (ed.), *The Social Life of Things: Com-modities in Cultural Perspective*, 3-63. Cambridge: Cambridge University Press. https://doi.org/10.1017/cbo9780511819582.003

Barrett, J., and P. Halstead (eds.)
2004   *The Emergence of Civilisation Revisited*. Oxford: Oxbow Books.

Betancourt, P.P.
2006   *The Chrysokamino Metallurgy Workshop and Its Territory*. Hesperia Supplement 36. Princeton, New Jersey: American School of Classical Studies in Athens.
2008   *The Bronze Age Begins: The Ceramics Revolution of Early Minoan I and the New Forms of Wealth that Transformed Prehistoric Society*. Philadelphia: INSTAP Academic Press.
2013   *Aphrodite's Kephali: An Early Minoan I Defensive Site in Eastern Crete*. Philadelphia: INSTAP Academic Press.

Bourdieu, P.
1977   *Outline of a Theory of Practice*. Trans. R. Nice. Cambridge: Cambridge University Press. https://doi.org/10.1017/CBO9780511812507

Branigan, K.
1970   *The Foundations of Palatial Crete*. London: Routledge and Kegan Paul.

Brogan, T.M.
2013   'Minding the gap': reexamining the Early Cycladic III 'gap' from the perspective of Crete: a regional approach to relative chronology, networks, and complexity in the Late Prepalatial Period. *American Journal of Archaeology* 117: 55567.

Bronk Ramsey, C.
2009a Bayesian analysis of radiocarbon dates. *Radiocarbon* 51: 337-60. https://doi.org/10.1017/S0033822200033865
2009b Dealing with outliers and offsets in radiocarbon dating. *Radiocarbon* 51: 1023-45. https://doi.org/10.1017/S0033822200034093

Broodbank, C.
1989   The longboat and society in the Cyclades in the Keros-Syros culture. *American Journal of Archaeology* 93: 319-37. https://doi.org/10.2307/505584
2000   *An Island Archaeology of the Early Cyclades*. Cambridge: Cambridge University Press.

2013   *The Making of the Middle Sea: A History of the Mediterranean from the Beginning to the Emergence of the Classical World*. London: Thames & Hudson.

Cadogan, G.
1990   Lasithi in the Old Palace period. *Bulletin of the Institute of Classical Studies* 37: 172-74.

Canuto, M.A., and J. Yaeger (eds.)
2000   *Archaeology of Communities: A New World Perspective*. London and New York: Routledge.

Cherry, J.F.
1978   Generalization and the archaeology of the state. In D.R. Green, C.C. Haselgrove and M.J.T. Spriggs (eds.), *Social Organisation and Settlement: Contributions from Anthropology, Archaeology and Geography*. British Archaeological Reports, Supplementary Series 47: 411-37. Oxford: British Archaeological Reports.
1983   Evolution, revolution, and the origins of complex society in Minoan Crete. In O. Krzyszkowska and L. Nixon (eds.), *Minoan Society: Proceedings of the Cambridge Colloquium 1981*, 33-45. Bristol: Bristol Classical Press.
1984   The emergence of the state in the prehistoric Aegean. *Proceedings of the Cambridge Philological Society* 30: 18-48. https://doi.org/10.1017/S0068673500004600
1986   Polities and palaces: some problems in Minoan state formation. In C. Renfrew and J.F. Cherry (eds.), *Peer Polity Interaction and Socio-Political Change*, 19-45. Cambridge: Cambridge University Press.
2010   Sorting out Crete's Prepalatial off-island interactions. In W. A Parkinson and M.L. Galaty (eds.), *Archaic State Interaction: The Eastern Mediterranean in the Bronze Age*, 107-40. Santa Fe, New Mexico: School for Advanced Research Press.

Childe, V.G.
1925   *The Dawn of European Civilization*. London: Kegan Paul.

1930 *The Bronze Age.* Cambridge: Cambridge University Press.
1950 The urban revolution. *Town Planning Review* 21: 3-17. https://doi.org/10.3828/tpr.21.1.k853061t614q42qh

Colburn, C.S.
2008 Exotica and the Early Minoan elite: eastern imports in Prepalatial Crete. *American Journal of Archaeology* 112: 203-24. https://doi.org/10.3764/aja.112.2.203

Dabney, M.K.
1995 The later stages of state formation in palatial Crete. In R. Laffineur and W.-D. Niemeier (eds.), *Politeia: Society and State in the Aegean Bronze Age.* Aegaeum 12: 43-47. Liège and Austin: Université de Liège and University of Texas at Austin.

Dalfes, H.N., G. Kukla and H. Weiss (eds.)
1997 *Third Millennium BC Climate Change and Old World Collapse.* NATO ASI Series I, 49. Berlin: Springer.

Driessen, J.
2002 'The king must die': some observations on the use of Minoan court compounds. In J. Driessen, I. Schoep and R. Laffineur (eds.), *Monuments of Minos: Rethinking the Minoan Palaces.* Aegaeum 23: 1-14. Liège and Austin: Université de Liège and University of Texas at Austin.

Driessen, J., I. Schoep and R. Laffineur (eds.)
2002 *Monuments of Minos: Rethinking the Minoan Palaces.* Aegaeum 23. Liège and Austin: Université de Liège and University of Texas at Austin.

Evans, A.J.
1921 *The Palace of Minos at Knossos* I. *The Neolithic and Early and Middle Minoan Ages.* London: Macmillan.
1928 *The Palace of Minos at Knossos* II.1. *Fresh Lights on Origins and External Relations.* London: Macmillan.

Feld, S., and K.H. Basso (eds.)
1996 *Senses of Place.* Santa Fe, New Mexico: School for Advanced Research Press.

Fidan, E., D. Sari and M. Türkteki
2015 An overview of the western Anatolian Early Bronze Age. *European Journal of Archaeology* 18: 60-89. https://doi.org/10.1179/1461957114Y.0000000070

Fletcher, R.
1986 Settlement archaeology: world-wide comparisons. *World Archaeology* 18: 59-83. https://doi.org/10.1080/00438243.1986.9979989

Forsén, J.
1992 *The Twilight of the Early Helladics: A Study of the Disturbances in East-Central and Southern Greece Towards the End of the Early Bronze Age.* Studies in Mediterranean Archaeology and Literature Pocket-book 116. Jonsered: Paul Åströms Förlag.

Gregory, C.A.
1982 *Gifts and Commodities.* London: Academic Press.

Haggis, D.C.
1999 Staple finance, peak sanctuaries, and economic complexity in Late Prepalatial Crete. In A. Chaniotis (ed.), *From Minoan Farmers to Roman Traders: Sidelights on the Economy of Ancient Crete*, 5385. Heidelberger althistorische Beiträge und epigraphische Studien 29. Stuttgart: Franz Steiner.
2002 Integration and complexity in the Late Pre-Palatial period: a view from the countryside in eastern Crete. In Y. Hamilakis (ed.), *Labyrinth Revisited: Rethinking 'Minoan' Archaeology*: 120-42. Oxford: Oxbow Books.

Hamilakis, Y.
2002 (ed.) *Labyrinth Revisited: Rethinking 'Minoan' Archaeology.* Oxford: Oxbow Books.
2014 Sensuous memory, materiality and history: rethinking the 'rise of the palaces' on Bronze Age Crete. In A.B. Knapp and P. Van Dommelen (eds.), *The Cambridge Prehistory of the Bronze and Iron Age Mediterranean*, 320-36. New York: Cambridge University Press.

Hayden, B.
2001 Fabulous feasts: a prolegomenon to the importance of feasting. In M. Dietler and B. Hayden (eds.), *Feasts: Archaeo-*

logical and Ethnographic Perspectives on Food, Politics, and Power, 23-64. Washington, DC: Smithsonian Institution Press.

Helms, M.W.
1988   *Ulysses' Sail: An Ethnographic Odyssey of Power, Knowledge, and Geographical Distance.* Princeton, New Jersey: Princeton University Press. https://doi.org/10.1515/9781400859542

Horejs, B., and M. Mehofer (eds.)
2014   *Western Anatolia before Troy: Proto-Urbanism in the 4th Millennium BC?* Vienna: Austrian Academy of Sciences Press.

Johnson, G.A.
1988–89   Late Uruk in greater Mesopotamia: expansion or collapse? *Origini* 14: 595-611.

Jung, R., and B. Weninger
2015   Archaeological and environmental impact of the 4.2 ka cal BP event in the central and eastern Mediterranean. In H. Meller, H.W. Arx, R. Jung and R. Risch (eds.), *2200 BC—Ein Klimasturz als Ursache für den Zerfall der Alten Welt?/2200 BC—A climatic Breakdown as a Cause for the Collapse of the Old World?*, 205-34. Halle, Germany: Landesmuseum für Vorgeschichte.

Knappett, C.
1999   Assessing a polity in Protopalatial Crete: the Malia-Lasithi state. *American Journal of Archaeology* 103: 615-39. https://doi.org/10.2307/507075
2011   *An Archaeology of Interaction: Network Perspectives on Material Culture and Society.* Oxford: Oxford University Press. https://doi.org/10.1093/acprof:osobl/9780199215454.001.0001

Konsola, D.
1990   Settlement size and the beginning of urbanization. In P. Darcque and R. Treuil (eds.), *L'habitat Égéen préhistorique.* Bulletin de correspondance hellénique supplément 19: 463-71. Paris: de Boccard.

Kosse, K.
1994   The evolution of large, complex groups:

a hypothesis. *Journal of Anthropological Archaeology* 13: 35-50. https://doi.org/10.1006/jaar.1994.1003

Legarra Herrero, B.
2009   The Minoan fallacy: cultural diversity and mortuary behaviour on Crete at the beginning of the Bronze Age. *Oxford Journal of Archaeology* 29: 29-57. https://doi.org/10.1111/j.1468-0092.2008.00318.x
2012   The construction, deconstruction and non-construction of hierarchies in the funerary record of prepalatial Crete. In I. Schoep, P. Tomkins and J. Driessen (eds.), *Back to the Beginning: Reassessing Social and Political Complexity on Crete during the Early and Middle Bronze Age*, 325-57. Oxford: Oxbow Books.
2014   *Mortuary Behaviour and Social Trajectories in Pre- and Protopalatial Crete.* Philadelphia: INSTAP Academic Press.
2016   Primary state formation processes on Bronze Age Crete: a social approach to change in early complex societies. *Cambridge Archaeological Journal* 26: 349-67. https://doi.org/10.1017/S0959774315000529

Lewthwaite, J.
1983   Why did civilization not emerge more often? A comparative approach to the development of Minoan Crete. In O. Krzyszkowska and L. Nixon (eds.), *Minoan Society: Proceedings of the Cambridge Colloquium 1981*, 171-83. Bristol: Bristol Classical Press.

Lorimer, H.L.
1950   *Homer and the Monuments.* London: Macmillan.

Manning, S.W.
1994   The emergence of divergence: development and decline on Bronze Age Crete and the Cyclades. In C. Mathers and S. Stoddart (eds.), *Development and Decline in the Mediterranean Bronze Age*, 221-70. Sheffield: John Collis.
1995   *The Absolute Chronology of the Aegean*

Early Bronze Age: Archaeology, History and Radiocarbon. Monographs in Mediterranean Archaeology 1. Sheffield: Sheffield Academic Press.

1997 Cultural change in the Aegean c. 2200 BC. In H.N. Dalfes, G. Kukla and H. Weiss (eds.), *Third Millennium BC Climate Change and Old World Collapse.* NATO ASI Series I, 49: 149-71. Berlin: Springer.

2008a Protopalatial Crete: formation of the palaces. In C.W. Shelmerdine (ed.), *The Cambridge Companion to the Aegean Bronze Age*, 105-20. Cambridge: Cambridge University Press. https://doi.org/10.1017/CCOL9780521814447.005

2008b Some initial wobbly steps towards a Late Neolithic to Early Bronze III radiocarbon chronology for the Cyclades. In N.J. Brodie, J. Doole, G. Gavalas and C. Renfrew (eds.), Ὁρίζων: *A colloquium on the prehistory of the Cyclades*, 55-59. Cambridge: McDonald Institute for Archaeological Research.

2013 Cyprus at 2200 BC: rethinking the chronology of the Cypriot Early Bronze Age. In A.B. Knapp, J.M. Webb and A. McCarthy (eds.), *J.R.B. Stewart: An Archaeological Legacy.* Studies in Mediterranean Archaeology 139: 1-21. Uppsala: Åströms Förlag.

2017 Comments on climate, intra-regional variations, chronology, the 2200 BC horizon of change in the east Mediterranean region, and socio-political change on Crete. In F. Höflmayer (ed.), *The Early/Middle Bronze Age Transition in the Ancient Near East: Chronology, C14, and Climate Change*, 451-90. Chicago: Oriental Institute.

Manning, S.W., M.W. Dee, E.M. Wild, C. Bronk Ramsey, K. Bandy, P.P. Creasman, C.B. Griggs, C.L. Pearson, A.J. Shortland and P. Steier

2014 High-precision dendro-^{14}C dating of two cedar wood sequences from First Intermediate Period and Middle Kingdom Egypt and a small regional climate-related ^{14}C divergence. *Journal of Archaeological Science* 46: 401-16. https://doi.org/10.1016/j.jas.2014.03.003

Mauss, M.

1954 *The Gift: The Form and Reason for Exchange in Archaic Societies.* Trans. I. Cunnison. London: Routledge.

Meller, H., H.W. Arx, R. Jung and R. Risch (eds.)

2015 *2200 BC—Ein Klimasturz als Ursache für den Zerfall der Alten Welt?/2200 BC—A Climatic Breakdown as a Cause for the Collapse of the Old World?* Halle, Germany: Landesmuseum für Vorgeschichte.

Momigliano, N.

2007 Late Prepalatial (EM III–MM IA): South Front House foundation trench, Upper East Well and House C/Royal Road South fill groups. In N. Momigliano (ed.), *Knossos Pottery Handbook: Neolithic and Bronze Age (Minoan).* British School at Athens Studies 14: 79-103. London: British School at Athens.

Momigliano, N., and D.E. Wilson

1996 Knossos 1993: excavations outside the south front of the palace. *Annual of the British School of at Athens* 91: 1-57. https://doi.org/10.1017/S0068245400016385

Moody, J.

2009 Environmental change and Minoan sacred landscapes. In A.L. D'Agata and A. Van de Moortel (eds.), *Archaeologies of Cult: Essays on Ritual and Cult in Crete in Honor of Geraldine C. Gesell.* Hesperia Supplement 42: 241-49. Princeton, New Jersey: American School of Classical Studies at Athens.

Morris, I.

1994 Archaeologies of Greece. In I. Morris (ed.), *Classical Greece: Ancient Histories and Modern Archaeologies*, 8-47. Cambridge: Cambridge University Press.

Muhly, J.D.

2004 Chrysokamino and the beginnings of metal technology on Crete and in the Aegean. In L.P. Day, M.S. Mook and J.D. Muhly (eds.), *Crete Beyond the Palaces*, 283-89. Philadelphia: INSTAP Academic Press.

Papadatos, Y., and P. Tomkins

2013   Trading, the longboat, and cultural interaction in the Aegean during the late fourth millennium B.C.E.: the view from Kephala Petras, East Crete. *American Journal of Archaeology* 117: 353-81. https://doi.org/10.3764/aja.117.3.0353

2014   The emergence of trade and the integration of Crete into the wider Aegean in the late 4th Millennium: new evidence and implications. In B. Horejs and M. Mehofer (eds.), *Western Anatolia before Troy: Proto-Urbanism in the 4th Millennium BC?*, 329-43. Vienna: Austrian Academy of Sciences Press.

Rackham, O., and J. Moody

1996   *The Making of the Cretan Landscape.* Manchester: Manchester University Press.

Rahmstorf, L.

2006   Zur Ausbreitung vorderasiatischer Innovationen in die frühbronzezeitliche Ägäis. *Praehistorische Zeitschrift* 81: 49-96.

2015   The Aegean before and after c. 2200 BC between Europe and Asia: trade as a prime mover of cultural change. In H. Meller, H.W. Arx, R. Jung and R. Risch (eds.), *2200 BC—Ein Klimasturz als Ursache für den Zerfall der Alten Welt?/2200 BC—A Climatic Breakdown as a Cause for the Collapse of the Old World?*, 149-80. Halle, Germany: Landesmuseum für Vorgeschichte.

Reimer, P.J., E. Bard, A. Bayliss, J.W. Beck, P.G. Blackwell, C. Bronk Ramsey, C.E. Buck, H. Cheng, R.L. Edwards, M. Friedrich, P.M. Grootes, T.P. Guilderson, H. Haflidason, I. Hajdas, C. Hatté, T.J. Heaton, D.L. Hoffmann, A.G. Hogg, K.A. Hughen, K.F. Kaiser, B. Kromer, S.W. Manning, M. Niu, R.W. Reimer, D.A. Richards, E.M. Scott, J.R. Southon, R.A. Staff, C.S.M. Turney and J. van der Plicht

2013   IntCal13 and Marine13 radiocar-bon age calibration curves 0-50,000 Years Cal BP. *Radiocarbon* 55: 1869-87. https://doi.org/10.2458/azu_js_rc.55.16947

Renfrew, C.

1972   *The Emergence of Civilisation: The Cyclades and the Aegean in the Third Millennium B.C.* London: Methuen.

1973   *Before Civilization: The Radiocarbon Revolution and Prehistoric Europe.* London: Jonathan Cape.

1980   The great tradition versus the great divide: archaeology as anthropology? *American Journal of Archaeology* 84: 287-98. https://doi.org/10.2307/504703

1993   Trade beyond the material. In C. Scarre and F. Healy (eds.), *Trade and Exchange in Prehistoric Europe*, 5-16. Oxford: Oxbow Books.

1994   Preface. In C. Mathers and S. Stoddart (eds.), *Development and Decline in the Mediterranean Bronze Age*, 5-11. Sheffield: J.R. Collis Publications.

Renfrew, C., M. Boyd and C. Bronk Ramsey

2012   The oldest maritime sanctuary? Dating the sanctuary at Keros and the Cycladic Early Bronze Age. *Antiquity* 86: 144-60. https://doi.org/10.1017/S0003598X00062517

Roscoe, P.B.

1993   Practice and political centralisation: a new approach to political evolution. *Current Anthropology* 34: 111-40. https://doi.org/10.1086/204149

Rutter, J.B.

1983   Some observations on the Cyclades in the later third and early second millennia BC. *American Journal of Archaeology* 87: 69-76. https://doi.org/10.2307/504665

2013   'Minding the gap': from filling archaeological gaps to accounting for cultural breaks. A 2013 perspective on a continuing story. *American Journal of Archaeology* 117: 593-97. https://doi.org/10.3764/aja.117.4.0593

Şahoğlu, V.

2005   The Anatolian trade network and the Izmir region during the Early Bronze

Age. *Oxford Journal of Archaeology* 24: 339-61. https://doi.org/10.1111/j.1468-0092.2005.00240.x

Schoep, I.
1999 The origins of writing and administration on Crete. *Oxford Journal of Archaeology* 18: 265-76. https://doi.org/10.1111/1468-0092.00083

2002 Social and political organization on Crete in the Proto-Palatial period: the case of Middle Minoan II Malia. *Journal of Mediterranean Archaeology* 15: 101-32. https://doi.org/10.1558/jmea.v15i1.101

2006 Looking beyond the first palaces: elites and the agency of power in EM III–MM II Crete. *American Journal of Archaeology* 110: 37-64. https://doi.org/10.3764/aja.110.1.37

Schoep, I., P. Tomkins and J. Driessen (eds.)
2012 *Back to the Beginning: Reassessing Social and Political Complexity on Crete during the Early and Middle Bronze Age.* Oxford: Oxbow Books.

Sherratt, A.
1995 Reviving the grand narrative: archaeology and long-term change. *Journal of European Archaeology* 3: 1-32. https://doi.org/10.1179/096576695800688223

2000 Envisioning global change: a long-term perspective. In R.A. Denemark, J. Friedman, B.K. Gills and G. Modelski (eds.), *World Systems History: The Social Science of Long-Term Change*, 115-32. London and New York: Routledge.

Sherratt, A., and S. Sherratt
1991 From luxuries to commodities: the nature of Mediterranean Bronze Age trading systems. In N.H. Gale (ed.), *Bronze Age Trade in the Mediterranean.* Studies in Mediterranean Archaeology 90: 351-86. Jonsered: Paul Åströms Förlag.

Sherratt, S.
2010 The Aegean and the wider world: some thoughts on a World-Systems perspective. In W.A. Parkinson and M.L. Galaty (eds.), *Archaic State Inter-*

action: *The Eastern Mediterranean in the Bronze Age*, 81-106. Santa Fe, New Mexico: School for Advanced Research Press.

Smith, A.T.
2015 *The Political Machine: Assembling Sovereignty in the Bronze Age Caucasus.* Princeton, New Jersey: Princeton University Press. https://doi.org/10.1515/9781400866502

Snodgrass, A.M.
1987 *An Archaeology of Greece: The Present State and Future Scope of a Discipline.* Berkeley: University of California Press.

Tomkins, P.
2004 Filling in the 'Neolithic background': social life and social transformation in the Aegean before the Bronze Age. In J.C. Barrett and P. Halstead (eds.), *The Emergence of Civilisation Revisited*, 38-63. Oxford: Oxbow Books.

2008 Time, space and the reinvention of the Cretan Neolithic. In V. Isaakidou and P. Tomkins (eds.), *Escaping the Labyrinth: The Cretan Neolithic in Context*, 21-48. Oxford: Oxbow Books.

2012 Behind the horizon: reconsidering the genesis and function of the 'First Palace' at Knossos (Final Neolithic IV–Middle Minoan IB). In I. Schoep, P. Tomkins and J. Driessen (eds.), *Back to the Beginning: Reassessing Social and Political Complexity on Crete during the Early and Middle Bronze Age*, 32-80. Oxford: Oxbow Books.

2014 Tracing complexity in 'the missing millennium': an overview of recent research into the Final Neolithic Period on Crete. In B. Horejs and M. Mehofer (eds.), *Western Anatolia before Troy: Proto-Urbanism in the 4th Millennium BC?*, 345-64. Vienna: Austrian Academy of Sciences Press.

Wace, A.J.B.
1923 Early Aegean civilization. In J.B. Bury, S.A. Cook and F.E. Adcock (eds.), *The Cambridge Ancient History*

I. *Egypt and Babylonia to 1580 B.C.*: 589-615. Cambridge: Cambridge University Press.

Warren, P.
1972 *Myrtos: An Early Bronze Age Settlement in Crete.* London: British School at Athens.
1995 Minoan Crete and Pharaonic Egypt. In W.V. Davies and L. Schofield (eds.), *Egypt, the Aegean and the Levant: Interconnections in the Second Millennium BC*, 1-18. London: British Museum Publications.

Watrous, L.V.
1987 The role of the Near East in the rise of the Cretan palaces. In R. Hägg and N. Marinatos (eds.), *The Function of the Minoan Palaces.* Skrifter Utgivna av Svenska Institutet i Athen, 4.XXXV: 65-70. Stockholm: Paul Åströms Förlag.
1998 Egypt and Crete in the early Middle Bronze Age: a case of trade and cultural diffusion. In E.H. Cline and D. Harris-Cline (eds.), *The Aegean and the Orient in the Second Millennium.* Aegaeum 18: 19-27. Liège and Austin: Université de Liège and University of Texas at Austin.

Weingarten, J.
1990 Three upheavals in Minoan sealing administration: evidence for radical change. In T.G. Palaima (ed.), *Aegean Seals, Sealings and Administration.* Aegaeum 5: 105-14. Liège and Austin: Université de Liège and University of Texas at Austin.

Weiss, H., M.-A. Courty, W. Wetterstrom, F. Guichard, L. Senior, R. Meadow and A. Curnow
1993 The genesis and collapse of third millennium north Mesopotamian civilization. *Science* 261: 995-1004. https://doi.org/10.1126/science.261.5124.995

Weiss, H., S.W. Manning, L. Ristvet, L. Mori, M. Besonen, A. McCarthy, P. Quenet, A. Smith and Z. Bahrani
2012 Tell Leilan Akkadian imperialization, collapse and short-lived reoccupation defined by high-resolution radiocarbon dating. In H. Weiss (ed.), *Seven Generations Since the Fall of Akkad.* Studia Chaburensia 3: 163-92. Wiesbaden: Harrassowitz Verlag.

Wengrow, D.
2010 The voyages of Europe: ritual and trade in the eastern Mediterranean circa 2300-1850 BC. In W. A Parkinson and M.L. Galaty (eds.), *Archaic State Interaction: The Eastern Mediterranean in the Bronze Age*, 141-60. Santa Fe, New Mexico: School for Advanced Research Press.

Whitelaw, T.M.
2004 Alternative pathways to complexity in the southern Aegean. In J.C. Barrett and P. Halstead (eds.), *The Emergence of Civilisation Revisited*, 232-56. Oxford: Oxbow Books.
2012 The urbanisation of prehistoric Crete: settlement perspectives on Minoan state formation. In I. Schoep, T. Tomkins and J. Driessen (eds.), *Back to the Beginning: Reassessing Social and Political Complexity on Crete during the Early and Middle Bronze Age*, 114-76. Oxford: Oxbow Books.

Wild, E.M, W. Gauß, G. Forstenpointner, M. Lindblom, R. Smetana, P. Steier, U. Thanheiser and F. Weninger
2010 ^{14}C dating of the Early to Late Bronze Age stratigraphic sequence of Aegina Kolonna, Greece. *Nuclear Instruments and Methods in Physics Research B* 268: 1013-21. https://doi.org/10.1016/j.nimb.2009.10.086

Wilson, D.E.
1994 Knossos before the palaces: an overview of the Early Bronze Age (EM I–III). In D. Evely, H. Hughes-Brock and N. Momigliano (eds.), *Knossos: A Labyrinth of History: Papers in Honour of Sinclair Hood*, 23-44. Oxford: British School at Athens.

3 Gelb and Gell in the Aegean: Thoughts on the Relations between 'Writing' and 'Art'

John Bennet

Introduction

John Cherry is one of the few Aegean prehistorians explicitly to engage—albeit critically—with Morellian attribution studies à la Beazley (although see also Morris 1993). He concludes his paper in the *Aegaeum* volume *EIKΩN*, published in 1992, with these words: 'I recommend in future work some healthy servings of explicit methodology and larger doses of social archaeology, the results to be taken with regular pinches of salt' (Cherry 1992: 144). With characteristic breadth of knowledge, his paper on that occasion began with Australian rock art (appropriate to the location of the conference in Tasmania), moved through a review and critique of Beazley's and others' use of attribution studies, to a consideration of their deployment in Bronze Age examples, including the identification of scribal hands in Linear B and of 'master' sculptors in the corpus of Cycladic marble 'idols'. The quotation above is the final sentence of his contribution to that volume and I start with it because I am interested in both 'writing' and 'art', and because I would like to suggest that they are interlinked in quite interesting ways in the Minoan-Mycenaean Aegean. My thinking on writing has been influenced (negatively) by Gelb's synthesis (Gelb 1963) and on art (positively) by Gell's posthumous study (Gell 1998), but I do not offer here 'servings of explicit methodology' (despite the reference to both in my title), nor necessarily 'doses of social archaeology'. But I do expect the reader to take this with 'regular pinches of salt'.

I start with a seemingly simple question: knowing the comparative significance of image and text in the formation, maintenance, and manipulation of power in complex societies, why did objects like the Victory Stele of Naram-Sin (ca. 2230 BC; Louvre Museum Sb4; height 2 m) or Yaxchilán Lintel 24 (709 AD; British Museum Am1923, Maud.4; height 1.09 m) apparently not exist in the complex polities of the Bronze Age Aegean? That is, why do we not have in the Aegean large-scale depictions of rulers or members of the elite engaged in significant actions (conquest, in the case of Naram-Sin; ritual in the case of King Shield Jaguar II and Lady Xook in the Maya example) *and* captioned with text that identifies the particular actor(s) and the occasion? Four possible answers suggest themselves:

(1)   Such forms require the *existence* of writing, while writing appeared relatively late in the Aegean—an explanation based on timing;

(2)   There is (almost) no surviving monumental art in the Aegean (the Lion Gate at Mycenae, a late example belonging to the thirteenth century BC, is so far unique)—an explanation based on medium;

(3)   There is no explicit 'third party' ruler iconography, the sort of artistic production around which such combined visual and textual narratives might have formed—again, an explanation based on medium;

(4)   There is (arguably) no narrative art, to which a text might become attached—an explanation based partly on medium and partly on content.

Of these, the first is indisputable: the appearance of writing in the Aegean is much later—by over a millennium—than it is in either Mesopotamia or Egypt. The remaining points, however, are all debatable.

Image and text are inextricably linked in the history of writing. Since the nineteenth century AD, at least, the idea has been current that writing evolved from pictures (e.g., Tylor 1865: 83-106; Gelb 1963), while objects like those cited above combined writing and image in the same field. Instances of pictorially rich writing systems (like Egyptian hieroglyphs or Maya glyphs) confused decipherers: was the content behind the writing system to be read through the images or were they merely conventional signs denoting the phonetic components of a language? Gelb (1963: 51-59) even denied that the Maya glyphs constituted a writing system. Arthur Evans himself was led to Crete by the identification of decorations carved on miniature sealstones as a 'pictographic' writing system (e.g., Evans 1894: 274-88).

It is with those early examples that I start this contribution, before exploring how writing and image became separated in the Bronze Age Aegean. I argue that people in the complex societies of the second millennium Aegean (see Manning, this volume) developed what we might term an interactive relationship with objects and their built environment that required their co-presence. Such co-presence—of people and objects and/or spaces—functioned in a similar manner to the juxtaposition of image and text in other regional-scale polities and groups of polities: rulers (and other significant actors) 'activated' spaces and iconographic compositions by their presence, while narratives were generated orally in response to static representations at small to miniature scale. Within this frame the removal of seal-generated written texts—achievable without the need to be literate—made writing on clay (and on ephemeral media, such as parchment or papyrus) an activity that also required the presence of the writer. Similar transactions were materialized—without the necessary intervention of text at all—through various sealing practices that again required the presence of (minimally) a single seal-owner to press the seal into damp clay. Exceptions to this rule were the small numbers of objects to which writing was applied, not as *caption* (to give specificity to a potentially generic scene), but as *comment*, conveying some specific property or properties of the object to potential readers, mortal or immortal.

Second, I consider monumentality, arguing that architecture can be considered the only monumental Aegean form (itself linked, at least in Crete, to the 'monumentality' of landscape) and how variations in scale were exploited in relation to human interaction with objects and depictions, notably in the area of wall-painting. Third, this leads to a summary of ideas developed elsewhere of the complementary performance of certain individuals (rulers?), who were presented in 'framed' positions, thus emphasizing their presence as powerful individuals, while in nearby contexts 'narrative' featured in oral performance. Given the situation of such practices at the center of Mycenaean polities, I argue that these are elements of what might be described as court behavior, and thus that elite behavior in the states of the Aegean Late Bronze Age combined not only textual literacy (in the form of documents produced to mark transactions carried out by palatial authority), but also visual and performance 'literacy'. This element of oral performance was sustained around centers of regional power across the so-called Dark Age (Late Helladic IIIC to Late Geometric, in ceramic terms), in which large-scale representational forms and monumental architecture were largely lost. Ultimately, when narratives reappeared in visual format (i.e., in the eighth century BC), they came quite quickly (later seventh century BC) to be anchored by the addition of text in the recently adapted Greek alphabet.

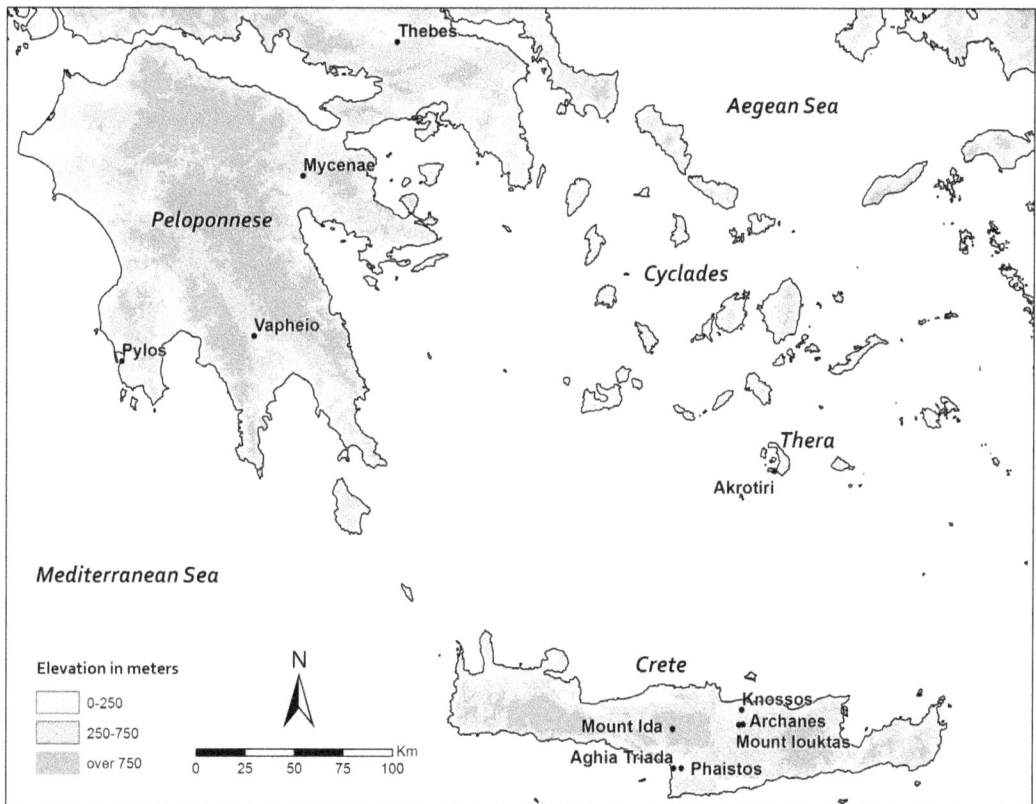

Figure 3.1   Map, showing places mentioned in the text (map by Evan Levine).

Text and Image in the Bronze Age Aegean

The first writing in the Bronze Age Aegean is generally recognized to be the 'Archanes script', so called after the site (Figure 3.1) at which several examples were found (Sakellarakis and Sapouna-Sakellaraki 1997: 326-30; see also Godart and Olivier 1996: 18, n. 59; Krzyszkowska 2005: 70-72). These include a segmented 14-sided bone bar or 'baton' recovered from Building 6 in the Fourni cemetery, on which two faces (I, H: Godart and Olivier 1996: 290-91 #315; Sakellarakis and Sapouna-Sakellaraki 1997: 328, fig. 284) contain a plausible inscription, also found in other examples. As Cherry (2010: 120-25) has himself pointed out, the archaeological contexts on Crete of such objects (as well as the imported Egyptian scarabs that must have inspired them) are problematic, spanning quite long periods from Early Minoan (EM) III to Middle Minoan (MM) IA. Building 6 at Archanes raises similar chronological issues, since it is said to date to the EM III–MM IB period (Sakellarakis and Sakellaraki 1997: 202). Potentially, however, these objects with writing pre-date the construction of the earliest monumental structures traditionally called palaces, thus refuting the argument that writing is only required when a certain level of social complexity is reached. (This is to leave aside the question of whether social changes that might be termed 'palatial' had already commenced earlier in the third millennium BC: e.g., Tomkins 2012: 72-75; cf. Manning, this volume.) Whether such objects ever formed part of an administrative system and were used to impress damp clay cannot be determined; in the absence of appropriate contemporary burnt deposits, we cannot exclude their use in this way.

At the very least, however, the Archanes seals' context in high-status burials, among other objects of value, suggests that writing was one of a set of 'responses' to contacts with polities and peoples in the eastern Mediterranean, accelerated and augmented by the introduction of sail-propelled craft late in the third millennium BC (e.g., Sherratt 2000: 18-20; Broodbank 2013: 353-55). Hippopotamus ivory, scarabs, and stone vessels point to an Egyptian connection, most likely through Byblos, as Bevan and others have suggested (Bevan 2003: 57-65; 2007: 95-96; Schoep 2006: 54-55). It is not irrelevant that Byblos possessed a syllabic writing system in this period (Dunand 1945; Daniels and Bright 1996: 29-30). On the other hand, neither cuneiform writing nor cylinder seals were adopted, although it is possible that multi-faceted Minoan seals, common among those inscribed with the script conventionally known as 'Cretan Hieroglyphic', were inspired by cylinder seals, a small number of which are attested in similar early contexts on Crete (e.g., Krzyszkowska 2005: 98).

By the time writing on clay is preserved in contexts available archaeologically and in the Cretan Hieroglyphic script, it is striking that elements of the glyptic realization of signs, notably points made with a drill on seals, are repeated—skeuomorphically—in their inscribed clay form, hinting at least that the script had its origins in glyptic, not in clay inscription. This is particularly clear in signs 031, 034, 049, 063, 070, and 092 (Godart and Olivier 1996: 100-101 #049, 108-109 #056, 142-43 #091 [on clay]; 254-55 #257, 286-87 #308 [on stone]). It is possible, at least, that the glyptic form of the script had priority over later manifestations inscribed on clay. The earliest inscribed seals, then, combine image and text in the same field, something that led Evans to imagine that, even though he understood the script to be phonetic, the images still functioned to convey meaning, almost as Tylorian relics of an earlier evolutionary stage of writing (Evans 1909: 263-70; cf. Tylor 1865: 1-2; 1871 I: 63-144).

During the period of use of Cretan Hieroglyphic, then, text and image combine on miniature objects, and the production of texts with seals happens in a single action, without the need to inscribe, and identical in form and content on each occasion. The generation of the text itself was removed in time from any of the multiple potential impressions of the text that did not depend on the presence of an actual writer. By the early Neopalatial period, when Linear A is in exclusive use as a script, text is no longer applied *alongside* image on seal faces, but the two are *exclusive*. A striking example is the gold ring found in Tomb IX of the Mavrospilio cemetery at Knossos, which bears a spiral inscription comprising 19 signs in Linear A on its bezel (Godart and Olivier 1982: 152-53 [KN Zf 13]), but no image, in contrast to the number of gold ring bezels known on Crete in the same period with (often complex) imagery, but no writing (e.g., Krzyszkowska 2005: 126-31). Writing presumably substitutes for image, conveying analogous information, perhaps, but not modifying or interacting with an image in the same field. In addition to objects created simply to bear an inscribed text—mostly clay tablets—Linear A was applied to a range of objects and media (like the gold ring just mentioned), again presumably conveying some specific property or properties of the object to others or making them special in some way.

We need, however, again to be wary of reading the surviving archaeological material too literally. Differential contexts and preservation mean that we might easily over- or underestimate the frequency of different types of written media. Figure 3.2 is a diagram designed to suggest how unrepresentative the *preserved* sample of

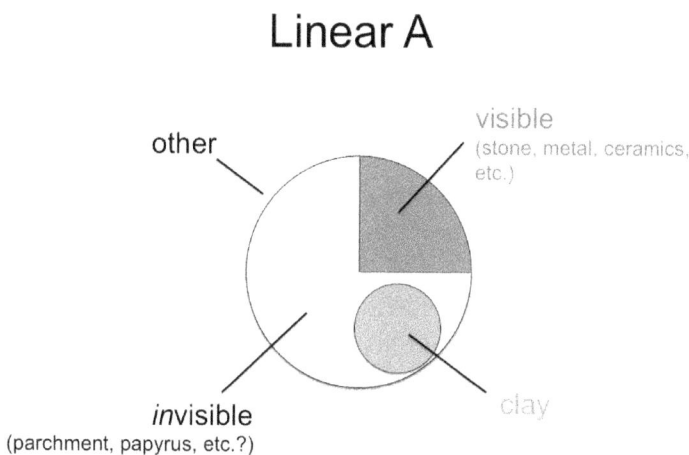

Figure 3.2   Diagram to suggest impressionistically the relative visibility and potential recoverability of materials inscribed with Linear A script in Neopalatial Crete. The large circle represents the totality of written materials produced, distinguished into 'clay' versus 'other' and 'visible' (12 o'clock to 3 o'clock) versus 'invisible' (3 o'clock to 12 o'clock).

Linear B

invisible
(parchment, papyrus, etc. ???)

other

visible
(stone, ceramics,
etc.?)

clay

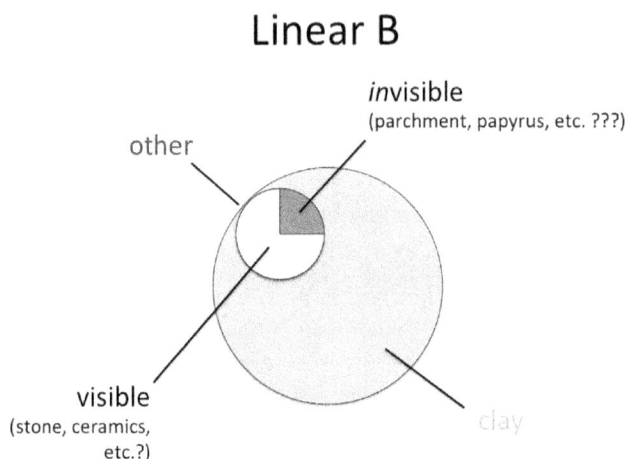

Figure 3.3   Diagram to suggest impressionistically the relative visibility and potential recoverability of materials inscribed with Linear B script in LM III Crete and LH III mainland Greece. The large circle here represents the predominance of 'clay' versus 'other' written materials; among 'other' materials, the majority are 'visible' (3 o'clock to 12 o'clock) versus 'invisible' (12 o'clock to 3 o'clock).

written materials might be in relation to the totality of past products: clay inscriptions might have been in a minority, while inscriptions on parchment or papyrus are now completely lost to us.

We can compare a similar diagram for the later Linear B script (Figure 3.3), where in the likely absence of ephemeral materials, like parchment or papyrus, surviving clay documents might reflect a greater proportion of textual output, although subject themselves to selective preservation through taphonomic and administrative factors (see also Bennet and Halstead 2014: 274-77).

Returning to the question posed at the beginning of this contribution, the absence of monumental (life-size or larger) representational fields in Minoan Crete during the first half of the second millennium BC meant that there was no opportunity to attach texts to such representations. The separation by the mid-second millennium BC of the active practice of writing from that of stamping using seals moved writing into a situation where it was normally practiced in the moment, requiring the presence of a writer. Beyond that moment of creation it was either ephemeral (as seems most likely for the Linear A tablets) or was carefully controlled (by the application of secure sealing, as in the case of the so-called 'flat-based nodules': Hallager 1996: 135-58; Krzyszkowska 2005: 155-58) or acted as a comment on certain objects (rings, pins, or—most commonly attested—stone 'libation tables').

Could Bronze Age Cretan writers have captioned images, though? That this was possible is suggested by a number of practices. First, the use of certain forms of sealing which were attached to objects without actually sealing them (so-called 'crescents' in Cretan Hieroglyphic: e.g., Krzyszkowska 2005: 101-102; or 'two-holed hanging nodules' in both Linear A and Linear B: e.g., Hallager 1996: 159-61; Krzyszkowska 2005: 160-61; Panagiotopoulos 2014: 108-13, 119-21) implies a notion of text *complementing* an object, creating a hybrid syntax of object plus written information (cf. Baines 2004: 165), with or without the addition of information conveyed by a seal impression. Second, application of text to a member of a class of objects more normally found without text (jewelry, stone vessels, for example) again implies a *complementary* relationship: that the text distinguishes that particular object with specific properties—it effectively 'comments on' the object to which it is applied. Without being able to understand the *content* of such text written in an undeciphered script, we cannot be certain *how* the inscription changed the object, but possibilities are simple statements of ownership or associations to a particular narrative in which the object was implicated, such as the dedicator, the dedicatee, and/or the place of dedication (as has been argued, for example, for the sometimes quite long inscriptions on 'libation tables': see most recently Davis 2014 for a systematic study of the corpus of 49 such vessels). A similar phenomenon might be the so-called inscribed transport stirrup jars of the Late Helladic (LH) / Late Minoan (LM) IIIA2-B period (van Alfen 2008; Haskell *et al.* 2011), on which inscriptions, made before the vessels were fired, appear to implicate the object in an administrative or productive chain.

A third example, however, is the use of images as so-called 'ideograms' or 'logograms' in Linear A and Linear B texts (Melena 2014: 17-21, 128-63; see also Knappett 2002; Barrett 2013: 6-8). In some cases, these are accompanied by a text that specifies the particular item concerned. Duhoux (2000–2001) has suggested this for a list of vessels on a Linear A tablet (HT 31) from Aghia Triada, while there are a number of examples in Linear B, such as Knossos K 778, Ld(1) 573, and Sd 4403. In each instance an image (conventionally described as an ideogram or logogram) provides a visual representation of an object or objects (respectively stirrup jars, pieces of cloth, and chariot chassis) that are also notated in phonetic signs elsewhere on the document (again respectively *ka-ra-re-we*, *pa-we-a*, and *i-qi-ja*). One could take this *either* as a general indication of a perceived link between text and image, manifested more generally as oral text and large-scale image, *or* as another indication of the need to restrict and maintain the mechanisms embodied in the use of writing within a circumscribed central entity. Either way, the combination only occurred within a restricted domain, image and text both created 'in the moment'.

Framing Performance

One can argue that truly monumental art was missing in both Minoan and Mycenaean culture. In Crete there is perhaps a sense in which landscape acted as a monumental art form. This is particularly clear in the way in which palaces stand in relation to landscape features, notably peak sanctuaries (e.g., Cherry 1978: 429-31; 1986: 31-32), such as Mt. Iouktas dominating the skyline south of the palace at Knossos, or caves, like the Kamares cave, visible from the palace at Phaistos on the upper slopes of Mt. Ida, which itself has the appearance of a twin-peaked mountain from that perspective.

Goodison (2004) and others have also argued that palaces might perhaps have been situated to capture solar or celestial phenomena.

It is within these monumental structures that large-scale (life-size or close to life-size) representations are incorporated for the first time at the beginning of the Neopalatial period in the form of wall-paintings, either flat or in relief (Immerwahr 1990: 39-75). In the special case of relief wall-paintings, the figures almost seem trapped within the walls of the monumental structures. Human bodies are by this period rendered in three ways (Figure 3.4): two-dimensional (in wall-paintings, for example); three-dimensional (mostly at a small scale, and therefore portable, such as clay figurines); and in 2.5 dimensions in relief (at multiple different scales, carved in ivory, for example, or in relief wall-paintings). If we imagine a 1.6-m tall 'hypothetical Minoan viewer' (or HMV: cf. Flannery 1976; 1982) interacting with these different types of representation, then we can think further of scale in two ways: scale *within* the scene represented, in which size can be manipulated for effect and figures interact *within* the scene; and absolute scale in which the HMV interacts with *the object or scene itself.*

There is much of interest in the use of scale *within* scenes, but insufficient space to explore in detail here, except to note one instance: the way in which relative scale can be attributed to a fictitious or imaginary animal. On the well-known Late Helladic seal representation from Vapheio (Xenaki-Sakellariou 1964: no. 223) showing a robed

Scales of (bodily) representation

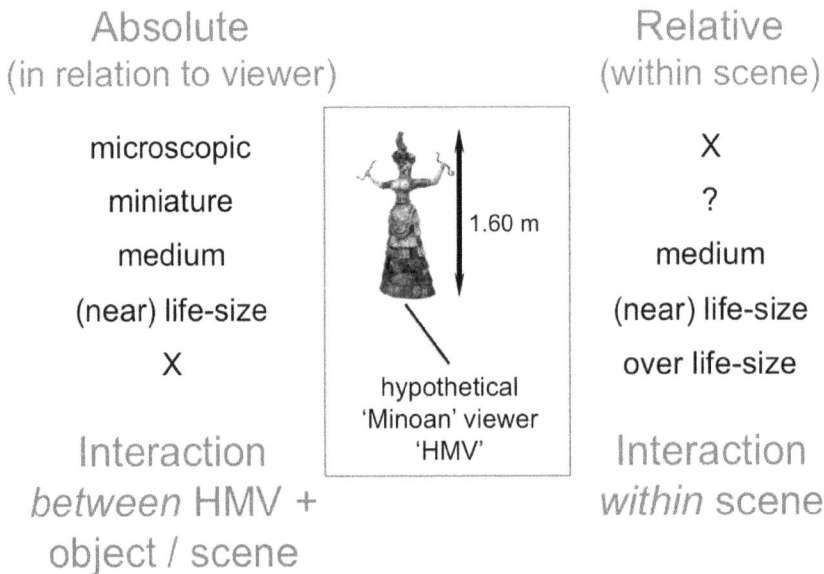

Absolute (in relation to viewer)		Relative (within scene)
microscopic		X
miniature	1.60 m	?
medium		medium
(near) life-size		(near) life-size
X		over life-size
	hypothetical 'Minoan' viewer 'HMV'	
Interaction *between* HMV + object / scene		Interaction *within* scene

Figure 3.4   Diagram representing the different scales at which the human body is represented in (predominantly) Minoan art, distinguishing between scale *within* a particular scene and *absolute* scale. The height of a 'hypothetical Minoan viewer' (1.6 m) is suggested on the basis of stature measurements derived from osteological samples..

male figure holding a griffin by a leash, within the relative scale of the image the griffin is clearly large in relation to the human, its shoulder reaching the male figure's upper chest. Similar scales for griffins are implied in other representations, such as the famous image in House Xeste 3 at Akrotiri, in which a griffin accompanies a seated 'goddess', who, if she were to stand up, would clearly tower over the standing female human figure and monkey that approach her: again relative scale is used to distinguish her from the humans who interact with her (e.g., Doumas 1992: 158-59). This does, however, perhaps raise the vexing question: how big is a life-size griffin?

Returning to absolute scale, I and others (Bennet 2007: 3-4; 2015: 29-31; cf. Palyvou 2000: 418-20; 2012: 12-13; Renfrew 2000: 140-43) have discussed the way in which HMVs interact with wall-painting scenes on different scales. Figures in such representations range from life-size down to very small (1.59 m to 0.05 m). For life-size figures, it is possible to think of those present in the room *interacting* with them, as vividly illustrated in a computer-generated reconstruction of Room 5 in the West House at Thera, showing how the boys holding fish appear to emerge from the wall, converging on an individual in the center of the room (Palyvou 2012: 13, figs 5-6). We are also familiar with the use of life-size figures mimicking (we imagine) the actions of human actors in certain spaces, such as processions, where humans are guided along a parallel plane to the image (e.g., Evely 1999: 228-32 [Knossos Procession Fresco], 252-53 [Knossos Grand Staircase]). I have described such a relationship as 'participatory' (Bennet 2007: 3; cf. Renfrew 2000: 140, who uses the term 'inclusive space'). Similar examples are known on the mainland at Thebes and Pylos (e.g., Immerwahr 1990: 115-18).

A special variant of this participatory practice is the frame created by placing a seat, facing out of the wall, surrounded by antithetically placed figures—a well-attested motif particularly in miniature on seals, but also in the only surviving example of Mycenaean monumental sculpture, the Lion Gate at Mycenae. Probably the two best-known examples in the Aegean are the Throne Room at Knossos and Room 6, the main megaron, at Pylos, in both of which griffins are depicted antithetically on the wall either side of an elaborate seat, or throne. As Hiller (1996) noted, the Pylos megaron appears to echo the Knossos Throne Room, despite their being as many as 200 years apart, perhaps in a form of Gellian 'retention' (Gell 1998: 232-42, 251-58). The effect of this framing in these (and other) instances is to generate a 2.5-dimensional composition: the human actor *becomes part* of the scene and so participates in the relative scale of the scene, thus (in Peircean terms: cf. Knappett 2002; Barrett 2013: 6-8) the image is not only *iconic* (it depicts griffins), but also both *symbolic* (it symbolizes the griffin's and, by association, the human actor's power) and *indexical* (it implicates the human figure with the *size* of griffins, which, as we saw above, are conceived as large beings). Effectively, without an explicitly attached textual narrative, this scene achieves what text- and scale-based ruler imagery achieve in other places in the ancient Old World. It is, as I have described it (Bennet 2007: 12-13; 2015: 27-28), 'first-person ruler representation'—'I am the ruler and here I am!'

The other type of representation I have termed 'panoptic' (Renfrew uses the term 'detached observer space': Renfrew 2000: 139), meaning that the images are designed to be seen as a whole, from outside the scene. In many cases, these seem to be the kinds of scene that imply a narrative—the most famous being the long miniature fresco in the West House at Thera (e.g., Doumas 1992: 58-85), but there are many other examples and they are not limited to wall-paintings. I have in mind here some of the scenes on gold signets from the Shaft Graves (e.g., Xenaki-Sakellariou 1964: nos. 9, 15, 16) or Neopalatial gold signets with probable ritual scenes (e.g., Cain 2001). Without captions, it follows (or so I would argue) that the interaction between human actors and panoptic scenes invites the development of an oral narrative (cf. Bennet 2004: 98-99).

It is such a relationship that Davis and I proposed some years ago for the way in which oral poetic performance was implicated in episodes of feasting at Bronze Age Pylos (Davis and Bennet 1999). I do not belabor those points here, since they have been well rehearsed elsewhere (e.g., Davis and Bennet 1999; Bennet 2007), but the key points are that at Pylos the participatory and the panoptic are both deeply implicated. The performance of the *wanax* (king) in situating himself on the throne in the main megaron (Room 6) required his co-presence, while the processional scenes that lead through the porch and ante-room (Rooms 4-5) to the main megaron mirrored the actions of humans moving through that space. Both instances reflect the participatory. The panoptic, on the other hand, is exemplified by the representations of humans in conflict and of military and naval materiel in Room 64, with their narrative content, mediated by oral performance that enlivened the scenes and gave them specific meaning on each occasion (on the extent and content of these narrative scenes, see, e.g., Brecoulaki *et al.* 2008; 2015). The scene of feasting with the 'lyre player' in the main megaron (Room 6) at Pylos (e.g., Immerwahr 1990: 133-34, 198) clearly falls in to the panoptic category, given its scale, but one could argue that its location, in close association with the seat of the ruler and in a room perhaps only accessible to the highest-ranking members of Pylian society (Bendall 2004: 122-24), allowed its interpretation as a commentary on events elsewhere in the palatial complex. The presence of a bird (or griffin?) flying away from the player, who is in fact depicted holding, not playing, his lyre (Younger 1998: 69) might suggest the oral nature of his utterances (see also Bennet 2007: 17-18).

The multi-sensorial palatial performance thus choreographed a complex set of sensory representations—sound, sight, smell, taste—brought to bear on a single occasion, generating bodily memories in the participants of the palace as a special place. There is, however, no place for writing within either the oral poetic performance or the bodily performance of the *wanax*. The co-presence of both ruler and performer, *and* audience, is required in the moment; the juxtaposition of image, performer, and audience are all necessary for the 'scenario' to be effective. There are suggestions that the elements of such a performance were commemorated in the form of animal bones of certain species apparently retained in the so-called Archives Complex (Room 7) or specifically deposited as refuse in particular locations (Isaakidou *et al.* 2002; Stocker and Davis 2004: 181-88). A similar practice seems to have governed fragmentary wall-paintings: once removed from the palace walls, these were placed in specific dumps in the immediate vicinity of the palace (Lang 1969: 5-6, 32).

Writing was, however, implicated in palatial performances and events, but only in the background, so to speak. Pylos tablet Un 2 lists the ingredients for a substantial event associated with the *wanax*, possibly his coronation (Palaima 1998–99: 221), while the Ta series from Pylos represents an inventory of elaborate furniture and equipment for a sacrificial banquet on another specific occasion, this time commemorating an action of the *wanax* (Killen 1998; Palaima 2004; more generally, Palaima 2000). Tablet Pylos Un 718 documents *future* contributions to a festival for Poseidon from key individuals within the Pylian polity (Nakassis 2012: esp. 3-5), coincidentally exemplifying an important aspect of textual documentation: the possibility of recording *hypothetical* events that are yet to take place (and might never have taken place, since the documents were preserved in the palace's destruction deposits). Only in the minds of those who wrote the tablets concerned could these remotely be defined as 'captions' to the events; these documents belong within the restricted sphere of administrative literacy. It was in this restricted literate environment that the 'captioning' of ideograms or logograms referred to above took place.

Conclusions

To conclude, then, at the turn of the third and second millennia BC in the Aegean, writing combined image and text and, indeed, writing might have emerged in a non-administrative, non-functionalist context, alerting us to the possibility that writing was something other than the way it is conceived of in the modern world (potentially underscoring different pathways to various types of literacy in complex regional polities). Creation of the text was glyptic in the earliest surviving examples, allowing text to be impressed, without the need to compose and generate an inscribed text on each occasion. A polar opposition between image and text appeared by the Minoan Neopalatial period and beyond, the same period in which large-scale wall-painting representations of human figures (and other beings) appeared. From then on, writing on clay was, across the southern Aegean, only carried out 'in the moment', with the writer present. This might imply a close relation to speech—writing capturing the oral nature of a transaction and fixing it, hence its restricted usage, especially by the latest Late Bronze Age on the mainland. Writing, however, was *only a part* of a much wider cultural literacy among the Aegean elite, that comprised visual, textual, and performative elements, such as etiquette, etc.—for which perhaps the best term is *decorum* (*sensu* Baines and Yoffee 1998).

In this contribution I hope to have made a convincing case that both 'art' and 'writing' formed complementary, not overlapping, aspects of a broader high-status cultural literacy in the Aegean Bronze Age that also encompassed archaeologically intangible practices of performance. Viewed in this way, I would suggest that the absence of captioned images, particularly of rulers *vel sim.*, and of life-size or larger three-dimensional representations, becomes explicable. Further, with the loss—in the years around 1200 BC—of the frames within which such performances took place, the continuity of practice that is ultimately embodied in (written versions of) oral poetry from ca. 700 BC appears more comprehensible (Bennet 2004: 92, fig. 5.1; 2014: 220). Similarly, the deployment (one might say a millennium and a half too late) of writing in the recently adapted alphabet to give specificity to visual representations reveals a radically different social context for literacy that comes to characterize the Greco-Roman world.

Acknowledgments

I would like to thank the editors for their invitation to the original event at which this paper was presented and for their patience in awaiting the written version's arrival, as well as the two reviewers, whose comments helped clarify some points. Needless to say, any remaining infelicities are my own responsibility. Jack Davis kindly delivered the paper on the day in his inimitable style (immortalized on Brown University's YouTube channel). Some of the ideas on scale included here were presented first at, but did not make it into the publication of, a conference organized by Maria Mina, Yiannis Papadatos, and Sevi Triantaphyllou in Nicosia, Cyprus in April 2012 entitled 'Embodied Identities in the Prehistoric Eastern Aegean: Convergence of Theory and Practice'. I am grateful to them for the opportunity to air those ideas on that pleasant occasion.

About the Author

John Bennet is Director of the British School at Athens and Professor of Aegean Archaeology at the University of Sheffield. His research interests lie in early writing and administrative systems (especially Linear B), and the integration of material and textual data to understand past complex societies. He has applied this approach to the Minoan and Mycenaean cultures of the Bronze Age Aegean, as well as to the Venetian and Ottoman periods of Greece. His recent books include *The Disappearance of Writing Systems: Perspectives on Literacy and Communication* (Equinox, 2008), co-edited with John Baines and Stephen Houston, and *ΑΘΥΡΜΑΤΑ: Critical Essays on the Archaeology of the Eastern Mediterranean in Honour of E. Susan Sherratt* (Archaeopress, 2014), co-edited with Yannis Galanakis and Toby Wilkinson. E-mail: d.j.bennet@sheffield.ac.uk

References

Baines, J.
  2004 The earliest Egyptian writing. In S.D. Houston (ed.), *The First Writing: Script Invention as History and Process*, 150-89. Cambridge: Cambridge University Press.

Baines, J., and N. Yoffee
  1998 Order, legitimacy, and wealth in ancient

Egypt and Mesopotamia. In G.M. Feinman and J. Marcus (eds.), *Archaic States*, 199-260. Santa Fe, New Mexico: School of American Research Press.

Barrett, J.C.

2013 The archaeology of mind: it's not what you think. *Cambridge Archaeological Journal* 23: 1-17. https://doi.org/10.1017/S0959774313000012

Bendall, L.M.

2004 Fit for a king? Hierarchy, exclusion, aspiration and desire in the social structure of Mycenaean banqueting. In P. Halstead and J. Barrett (eds.), *Food, Cuisine and Society in Prehistoric Greece*, 105-35. Sheffield Studies in Aegean Archaeology 5. Oxford: Oxbow Books.

Bennet, J.

2004 Iconographies of value: words, people and things in the Late Bronze Age Aegean. In J.C. Barrett and P. Halstead (eds.), *The Emergence of Civilisation Revisited*, 90-106. Sheffield Studies in Aegean Archaeology 6. Oxford: Oxbow Books.

2007 Representations of power in Mycenaean Pylos: script, orality, iconography. In F. Lang, C. Reinholdt and J. Weilhartner (eds.), *ΣΤΕΦΑΝΟΣ ΑΡΙΣΤΕΙΟΣ: Archäologische Forschungen zwischen Nil und Istros: Festschrift für Stefan Hiller zum 65. Geburtstag*, 11-22, Vienna: Phoibos.

2014 Linear B and Homer. In Y. Duhoux and A. Morpurgo Davies (eds.), *A Companion to Linear B: Mycenaean Greek Texts and their World* 3. Bibliothèque des Cahiers de l'Institut de Linguistique de Louvain 133: 187-233. Bibliothèque des Cahiers de l'Institut de Linguistique de Louvain 133. Louvain-la-Neuve: Peeters.

2015 Telltale depictions: a contextual view of Mycenaean wall-paintings. In H. Brecoulaki, J.L. Davis and S.R. Stocker (eds.), *Mycenaean Wall Painting in Context: New Discoveries, Old Finds*

Reconsidered. Meletemata 72: 21-34. Athens: National Hellenic Research Foundation.

Bennet, J., and P. Halstead

2014 O-no! Writing and righting redistribution. In D. Nakassis, J. Gulizio and S.A. James (eds.), *Ke-ra-me-ja: Studies Presented to Cynthia Shelmerdine*, 271-82. Philadelphia: INSTAP Academic Press.

Bevan, A.

2003 Reconstructing the role of Egyptian culture in the value regimes of the Bronze Age Aegean: stone vessels and their social context. In R. Matthews and C. Roemer (eds.), *Ancient perspectives on Egypt*, 57-73. London: UCL Press.

2007 *Stone Vessels and Values in the Bronze Age Mediterranean*. Cambridge: Cambridge University Press. https://doi.org/10.1017/CBO9780511499678

Brecoulaki, H., S.R. Stocker, J.L. Davis and E.C. Egan

2015 An unprecedented naval scene from Pylos: first considerations. In H. Brecoulaki, J.L. Davis and S.R. Stocker (eds.), *Mycenaean Wall Painting in Context: New Discoveries, Old Finds Reconsidered*. Meletemata 72: 260-91. Athens: National Hellenic Research Foundation.

Brecoulaki, H., C. Zaitoun, S.R. Stocker and J.L. Davis

2008 An archer from the Palace of Nestor: a new wall-painting fragment in the Chora Museum. *Hesperia* 77: 363-97. https://doi.org/10.2972/hesp.77.3.363

Broodbank, C.

2013 *The Making of the Middle Sea: A History of the Mediterranean from the Beginning to the Emergence of the Classical World*. London: Thames & Hudson.

Cain, C.D.

2001 Dancing in the dark: deconstructing a narrative of epiphany on the Isopata ring. *American Journal of Archaeology*

105: 27-49. https://doi.org/10.2307/507325

Cherry, J.F.

1978   Generalization and the archaeology of the state. In D. Green, C. Haselgrove and M. Spriggs (eds.), *Social Organisation and Settlement: Contributions from Anthropology, Archaeology and Geography*. British Archaeological Reports, International Series 47: 411-37. Oxford: British Archaeological Reports.

1986   Polities and palaces: some problems in Minoan state formation. In C. Renfrew and J.F. Cherry (eds.), *Peer Polity Interaction and Socio-Political Change*, 19-45. Cambridge: Cambridge University Press.

1992   Beazley in the Bronze Age? Reflections on attribution studies in Aegean prehistory. In R. Laffineur and J.L. Crowley (eds.), *EIKΩN. Aegean Bronze Age Iconography: Shaping a Methodology*. Aegaeum 8: 123-44. Liège: Université de Liège.

2010   Sorting out Crete's Prepalatial off-island interactions. In W.A. Parkinson and M.L. Galaty (eds.), *Archaic State Interaction: The Eastern Mediterranean in the Bronze Age*, 107-40. Santa Fe, New Mexico: School for Advanced Research Press.

Daniels, P.T., and W. Bright

1996   *The World's Writing Systems*. Oxford: Oxford University Press.

Davis, B.

2014   *Minoan Stone Vessels with Linear A Inscriptions*. Aegaeum 36. Leuven: Peeters.

Davis, J.L., and J. Bennet

1999   Making Mycenaeans: warfare, territorial expansion, and representations of the other in the Pylian Kingdom. In R. Laffineur (ed.), *POLEMOS: Le contexte guerrier en Égée á l'âge du Bronze. Actes de la 7ᵉ Rencontre égéenne internationale Université de Liège, 14-17 avril 1998*. Aegaeum 19: 105-20. Liège and Austin: Université de Liège and University of Texas at Austin.

Doumas, C.

1992   *The Wall-Paintings of Thera*. Athens: Thera Foundation.

Duhoux, Y.

2000–2001 Un inventaire linéaire A de vases: la tablette HT 31. *Minos* 35-36: 31-62.

Dunand, M.

1945   *Byblia grammata: documents et recherches sur le développement de l'écriture en Phénicie*. Beirut: Imprimerie catholique.

Evans, A.J.

1894   Primitive pictographs and a Prae-Phoenician script, from Crete and the Peloponnese. *Journal of Hellenic Studies* 14: 270-372. https://doi.org/10.2307/623973

1909   *Scripta Minoa: The Written Documents of Minoan Crete with Special Reference to the Archives of Knossos* I. *The Hieroglyphic and Primitive Linear Classes*. Oxford: Clarendon Press.

Evely, D.

1999   *Fresco: A Passport into the Past. Minoan Crete through the Eyes of Mark Cameron*. Athens: British School at Athens; N.P. Goulandris Foundation—Museum of Cycladic Art.

Flannery, K.V.

1976   (ed.) *The Early Mesoamerican Village*. New York: Academic Press.

1982   The Golden Marshalltown: a parable for the archeology of the 1980s. *American Anthropologist* 84: 265-78. https://doi.org/10.1525/aa.1982.84.2.02a00010

Gelb, I.J.

1963   *A Study of Writing*. 2nd edn. Chicago: University of Chicago Press.

Gell, A.

1998   *Art and Agency: An Anthropological Theory*. Oxford: Clarendon.

Godart, L., and J.-P. Olivier

1982   *Recueil des inscriptions en Linéaire A IV. Autres documents*. Études Crétoises 21. Paul Geuthner, Paris.

1996   (eds.) *Corpus Hieroglyphicarum Inscriptionum Cretae*. Études Crétoises 31. Paris: de Boccard.

Goodison, L.
  2004   From tholos tomb to Throne Room: some considerations of dawn light and directionality in Minoan buildings. In G. Cadogan, E. Hatzaki and A. Vasilakis (eds.), *Knossos: Palace, City, State.* BSA Studies 12: 339-50. London: British School at Athens.

Hallager, E.
  1996   *The Minoan Roundel and other Sealed Documents in the Neopalatial Linear A Administration.* Aegaeum 14. Liège: Université de Liège.

Haskell, H.W., R.E. Jones, P.M. Day and J.T. Killen
  2011   *Transport Stirrup Jars of the Bronze Age Aegean and East Mediterranean.* Prehistory Monographs 33. Philadelphia: INSTAP Academic Press.

Hiller, S.
  1996   Knossos and Pylos: a case of special relationship? *Cretan Studies* 5: 73-83.

Immerwahr, S.
  1990   *Aegean Painting in the Bronze Age.* University Park, Pennsylvania: Penn State University Press.

Isaakidou, V., P. Halstead, J.L. Davis and S.R. Stocker
  2002   Burnt animal sacrifice at the Mycenaean 'Palace of Nestor', Pylos. *Antiquity* 76: 86-92. https://doi.org/10.1017/S0003598X00089833

Killen, J.T.
  1998   The Pylos Ta tablets revisited. *Bulletin de correspondance hellénique* 122: 421-22.

Knappett, C.
  2002   Photographs, skeuomorphs and marionettes: some thoughts on mind, agency and object. *Journal of Material Culture* 7: 97-117. https://doi.org/10.1177/1359183502007001307

Krzyszkowska, O.H.
  2005   *Aegean Seals: An Introduction.* BICS Supplement 85. London: Institute of Classical Studies.

Lang, M.L.
  1969   *The Palace of Nestor at Pylos in Western Messenia* II. *The Frescoes.*

Princeton, New Jersey: Princeton University Press. https://doi.org/10.1515/9781400878383

Melena, J.L.
  2014   Mycenaean writing. In Y. Duhoux and A. Morpurgo Davies (eds.), *A Companion to Linear B: Mycenaean Greek Texts and their World* III. Bibliothèque des Cahiers de l'Institut de Linguistique de Louvain 133. Louvain-la-Neuve: Peeters.

Morris, C.
  1993   Hands up for the individual! The role of attribution studies in Aegean prehistory. *Cambridge Archaeological Journal* 3: 41-66. https://doi.org/10.1017/S0959774300000718

Nakassis, D.
  2012   Prestige and interest: feasting and the king at Mycenaean Pylos. *Hesperia* 81: 1-30. https://doi.org/10.2972/hesperia.81.1.0001

Palaima, T.G.
  1998–99 Special vs. normal Mycenaean: hand 24 and writing in the service of the king? In J. Bennet and J. Driessen (eds.), *A-NA-QO-TA: Studies Presented to J.T. Killen, Minos* 33-34: 205-21.
  2000   The Pylos Ta series: from Michael Ventris to the new millennium. *Bulletin of the Institute of Classical Studies* 44: 236-37.
  2004   Sacrificial feasting in the Linear B documents. *Hesperia* 73: 217-46. https://doi.org/10.2972/hesp.2004.73.2.217

Palyvou, C.
  2000   Concepts of space in Aegean Bronze Age art and architecture. In S. Sherratt (ed.), *The Wall Paintings of Thera* I, 413-36. Athens: Petros M. Nomikos and the Thera Foundation.
  2012   Wall painting and architecture in the Aegean Bronze Age: connections between illusionary space and built realities. In D. Panagiotopoulos and U. Günkel-Maschek (eds.), *Minoan Realities: Approaches to Images, Architecture, and Society in the Aegean*

Bronze Age, 9-26. Louvain-la-Neuve: Presses Universitaires de Louvain.

Panagiotopoulos, D.

2014   *Mykenische Siegelpraxis: Funktion, Kontext und administrative Verwendung mykenischer Tonplomben aus dem griechischen Festland und Kreta.* Athenaia 5. Munich: Hirmer.

Renfrew, C.

2000   *Locus iste*: modes of representation and the vision of Thera. In S. Sherratt (ed.), *The Wall Paintings of Thera* I, 135-58. Athens: Petros M. Nomikos and the Thera Foundation.

Sakellarakis, J.A., and E. Sapouna-Sakellaraki

1997   *Archanes: Minoan Crete in a New Light.* Athens: Ammos.

Schoep, I.

2006   Looking beyond the first palaces: elites and the agency of power in EMIII-MMII Crete. *American Journal of Archaeology* 110: 37-64. https://doi.org/10.3764/aja.110.1.37

Sherratt, E.S.

2000   *Catalogue of Cycladic Antiquities in the Ashmolean Museum: The Captive Spirit.* Oxford: Oxford University Press.

Stocker, S.R., and J.L. Davis

2004   Animal sacrifice, archives and feasting at the Palace of Nestor. *Hesperia* 73: 179-95. https://doi.org/10.2972/hesp.2004.73.2.179

Tomkins, P.

2012   Behind the horizon: reconsidering the genesis and function of the 'First Palace' at Knossos (Final Neolithic IV–Middle Minoan IB). In I. Schoep, P. Tomkins and J. Driessen (eds.), *Back to the Beginning: Reassessing Social and Political Complexity on Crete during the Early and Middle Bronze Age*, 32-80. Oxford: Oxbow Books.

Tylor, E.B.

1865   *Researches into the Early History of Mankind and the Development of Civilization.* London: John Murray.

1871   *Primitive Culture: Researches into the Development of Mythology, Philosophy, Religion, Art, and Custom.* London: John Murray.

van Alfen, P.G.

2008   The Linear B inscribed vases. In Y. Duhoux and A. Morpurgo Davies (eds.), *A Companion to Linear B: Mycenaean Greek Texts and their World* I. Bibliothèque des cahiers de l'Institut de Linguistique de Louvain 120: 235-42. Louvain-la-Neuve: Peeters.

Xenaki-Sakellariou, A.

1964   *Corpus der minoischen und mykenischen Siegel* I. *Die minoischen und mykenischen Siegel des National-Museums in Athen.* Berlin: Mann.

Younger, J.G.

1998   *Music in the Aegean Bronze Age.* Studies in Mediterranean Archaeology and Literature Pocket-Book 144. Jonsered: Paul Åströms Förlag.

4 Prestige-Goods Economies: The Prehistoric Aegean and Modern Northern Highland Albania Compared

Michael L. Galaty

> The tabulation of imports is a work in progress, of course, but relatively little attention has been paid to *what* was being imported and what such items signified in the parent culture. (Cherry 2010: 136, italics in original)

Introduction

Prestige goods have a checkered history in archaeology. Once they were in (e.g., Friedman and Rowlands 1977; Helms 1979; 1988; 1993; Clark 1986) and now they are out (but see Plourde 2008; 2009), and the term itself was never very well defined (Trubitt 2003: 245-50). What constitutes a prestige good? Answering this question depends to some large degree on whether or not we can determine how particular goods were valued by an archaeological society (Bevan 2007; Papadopoulos and Urton 2012) and what symbolic meanings they might have carried. This is a difficult task, of course, compounded when a prestige good was imported from a distant, dissimilar society, e.g., from Egypt to the Bronze Age Aegean. Even if we think we know what a prestige good, such as a scarab, meant at the point of origin, we typically do not know how it was received by the importing culture and subsequently invested with meaning.

If the concept of prestige-goods exchange is to be useful to the study of prehistoric political economies, then we must address this question of meaning and value. I will do so in this chapter with reference to the origin and evolution of exchange networks in modern highland northern Albania. Northern Albania is the only place in Europe where 'tribal' societies—with chiefs, oral law codes, and blood feuds—survived into the twentieth century. The tribal political economies of northern Albania were highly dependent on imported prestige goods, which were acquired in Ottoman territories and shared between families during periodic displays of ritual hospitality (Galaty *et al.* 2013). Such displays reinforced local power structures by signaling the capacity of a household, and its patriarch, to operate in the wider world (Galaty *et al.* 2016). However, to the extent possible, my aim is to use modern highland northern Albania's prestige-goods exchange network as a comparative analogy for investigating the trade in prestige goods in Minoan and Mycenaean societies (Figure 4.1).

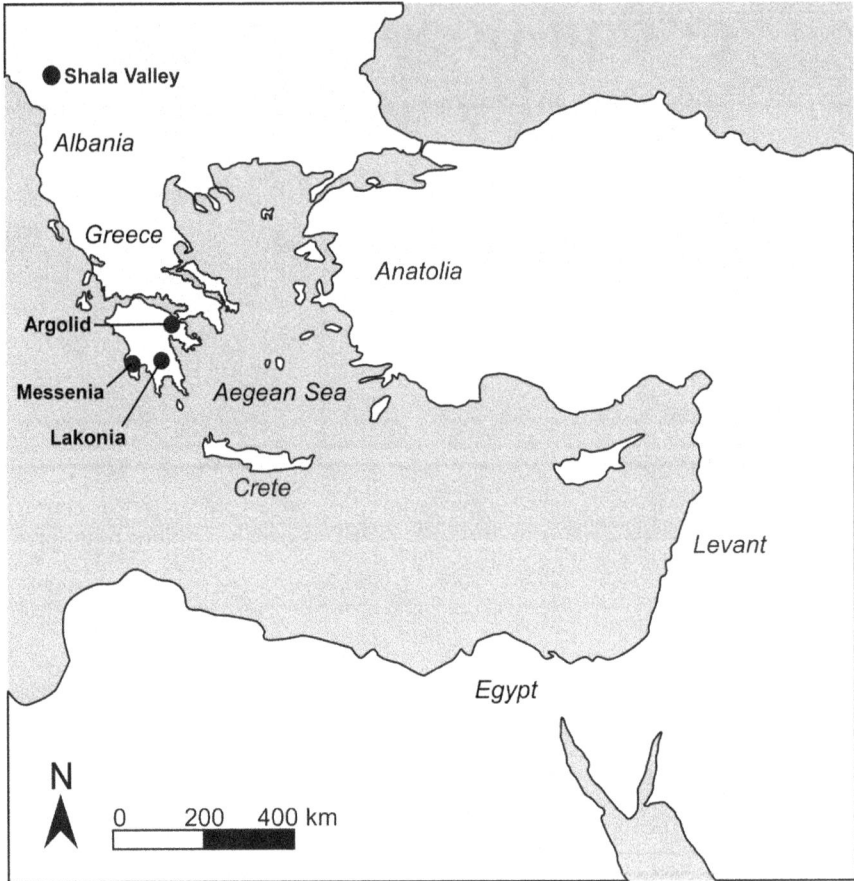

Figure 4.1   Map of the eastern Mediterranean showing regions mentioned in the text.

Surprisingly little systematic work has been done on foreign imports to Bronze Age Greece in terms of their origin and find contexts: i.e., there are many lists and catalogs of imports, but rarely do authors consider how objects were used *both* at the source and where they were ultimately deposited (though see, e.g., Watrous 1998; Burns 2010; Murray 2013; 2017), which is the key to determining what value and meanings objects might have held for their owners. It is important therefore to look at context. This task was made easier for me because Parkinson (2010) has entered all the data from Cline's (2009) catalog into a searchable database, including find spots, which is not publically available but which he was good enough to share with me. For the purposes of this paper, I focus on Late Bronze Age (LBA; ca. 1700–1050 BC) Egyptian imports only. The results I have gathered are interesting. But in true Cherry fashion I approach them with some skepticism and take a minimalist approach. Like Parkinson (2010; *contra* Cline, who tends to take a 'maximalist' approach; see, e.g., Cline 2010), Cherry (e.g., 2010) has consistently and repeatedly pointed to the relatively small numbers of goods imported into Minoan and Mycenaean Greece from the Near East and Egypt over very long stretches of time. With regard to Cline (2009), he writes: '[T]he entire corpus amounts to the exchange of only 0.5 objects annually from the entire Aegean over the six centuries in question' (Cherry 2010: 112). Given the small number of items involved, we are right to ask, therefore, whether their import could have had meaningful impacts at all, let alone stimulate state-formation processes. I approach this question in this chapter by looking carefully at those contexts in the Aegean in which Egyptian goods were used and deposited, and I interpret results by analogy to a similar, albeit modern, context: that of the northern Albanian mountains.

Table 4.1   Distribution of Egyptian artifacts from mainland Greece and Crete.

	Tombs		Settlements		Total	
Mainland	69	73%	25	27%	94	100%
Crete	37	28%	95	72%	132	100%

Late Bronze Age Egyptian Imports in the Aegean

Of the 1119 artifacts in the Cline-Parkinson database, 94 are Egyptian from secure mainland contexts (Table 4.1). Of those 94, 69 (73%) are from tombs and 25 (27%) are from settlements. Conversely, of the 1119 artifacts in the database, 132 are Egyptian from secure contexts on Crete. Of those 132, 37 (28%) are from tombs and 95 (72%) are from settlements. This analysis is quick and dirty, and there are biases (e.g., a similar analysis of *all* foreign imports to the Aegean might reveal different patterns: see Murray 2013: 459), but something meaningful seems to be going on here. I would argue that Egyptian imports are being deposited differently in Crete versus the mainland because they held very different meanings and were used differently in both places. And moreover, such varied meaning and use reflects two very different, underlying sociopolitical systems. A closer look at the data reveals additional interesting patterns.

Mainland Greece

Egyptian imports into mainland Greece are relatively equally divided between Late Helladic (LH) I–II, LH IIIA–B, and LH IIIC (Table 4.2, Figure 4.2). Those from LH I–II are from a diverse array of sites (n = 6) in the Argolid, Laconia, and Messenia. By contrast, the vast majority (73%) of the LH IIIA–B Egyptian imports are from Mycenae (a pattern previously noted by Cline 2007). All but one of the LH IIIC Egyptian imports are from the Perati cemetery. This would appear to indicate a tightening of access over the course of the LBA, culminating in a single LH IIIC 'contact,' to use Parkinson's (2010) terminology, at Perati. This pattern seems to fit expectations of the traditional 'prestige goods' model, whereby elite members of society import exotic goods for their own conspicuous consumption, many of which end up in graves. That being the case, the original symbolic meaning of these goods was probably not maintained, or considering their primary function—as status markers—was less important than their obviously foreign origin and material value. Looking at the range

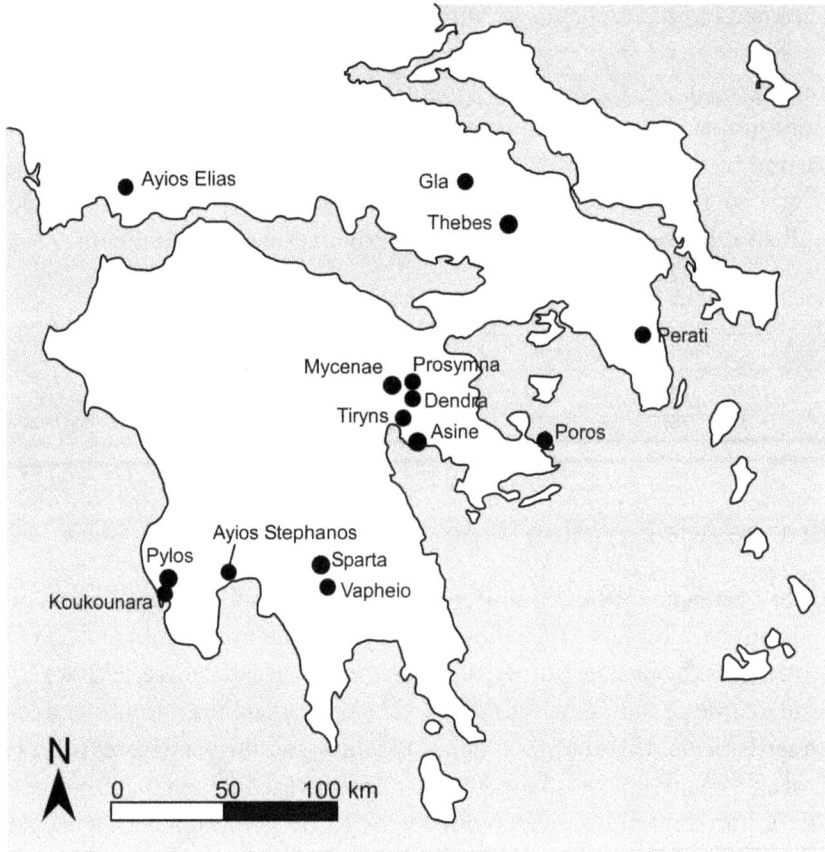

Figure 4.2   Map of Greece showing sites mentioned in the text.

of items imported can help clarify whether or not original symbolic meanings might have been retained and mattered.

Of the 69 Egyptian imports from mainland graves, ten are figurines or amulets (seven of which are from Perati, all from Tomb 30), two are cartouches (both from Perati), and 16 are scarabs (10 of which are from Perati, from five different tombs) (Table 4.3) (see Murray 2013: 402-409). There are two silver spoons, from Dendra and Vapheio, and five ostrich shell rhyta, four of which are from shaft graves at Mycenae. And, last but not least, there are 40,000 faience beads from Dendra, probably from a cloak (and therefore for the purposes of this analysis counted as a single import). The rest are 33 vessels of various kinds: only one is ceramic, 15 are alabaster, the rest are faience, porphyrite, diorite, stone, glass (possibly locally made in imitation of an Egyptian glass vessel), and ivory. Leaving aside the beads, spoons, and rhyta (which carry particularly Aegean symbolic meanings and functions), we can separate the remaining items into two groups: figurines/amulets/scarabs/cartouches (n = 28) and vessels (n = 33). The former had very specific symbolic meanings and functions in Egypt. Three of the figurines were of Bes, a deity worshipped as a protector of households; one was of Taweret, goddess of fertility. Such figurines were typically used in and are recovered from Egyptian domestic contexts, whereas the Mycenaeans deposited them in graves. The amulets are all animals—a monkey, crocodiles, and a hippopotamus—with one exception: an Aoh amulet from Asine, which, according to Cline (2009: 136), 'is used to call upon the protection of the moon god against evil and witchery'. Scarabs were multi-functional, but generally symbolized rebirth. Finally, the two cartouches are dedicated to Ramses II and are pierced vertically for hanging or wearing.

Table 4.2   Egyptian artifacts from mainland Greek sites.

	LH I–II	LH IIIA–B	LH IIIC	'LH III'	Indeterminate	Total
Tiryns	0	1	0	0	0	1
Ayios Elias	0	0	0	0	2	2
Asine	0	1	0	0	2	3
Prosymna	0	0	0	2	0	2
Dendra	0	3	0	2	0	5
Koukounara	1	0	0	0	0	1
Caulauria (Poros)	0	0	0	0	1	1
Vapheio	4	0	0	0	0	4
Chalkis (Euboea)	0	0	0	1	0	1
Argive Heraion	2	0	0	0	0	2
Nauplion	0	1	0	1	0	2
Pylos	0	1	0	0	0	1
Osmanaga	1	0	0	0	0	1
Thebes	0	0	0	1	0	1
Gla	0	1	0	0	0	1
Ayios Stephanos	0	0	0	0	1	1
Kakavatos	1	0	0	0	0	1
Sparta	0	0	0	0	1	1
Mycenae	9	22	1	6	5	43
Perati	0	0	20	0	0	20
Total	18	30	21	13	12	94

Nineteen (68%) of the figurines/amulets/scarabs/cartouches are from the Perati tombs, including all of the figurines and most of the amulets and scarabs. It seems likely that these represent a single mass shipment of low-weight, high-value exotics sometime in the LH IIIC. They post-date the Palatial period and probably do not represent sustained contact leading to adoption of Egyptian religious beliefs. An intriguing, alternative suggestion made by Murray (2013: 461-62) is that Perati's exotic goods mark graves of Cypriot or Italian sailors, who may well have possessed some appreciation of the original symbolic values of the items with which they were buried. Either way, that leaves nine objects from five sites spanning LH I to LH IIIC: Ayios Elias in Aetolia (n = 2; monkey amulet and scarab), Asine (n = 1; Aoh amulet), Prosymna (n = 2; hippo amulet and scarab), Koukounara near Pylos (n = 1; scarab), and Mycenae (n = 3; scarabs). I would argue that nine objects imported across Greece over the course of 500 years probably did not stimulate widespread adoption, or even knowledge, of Egyptian religious beliefs. Rather, these items were personal items—prestige goods—that went into graves with the bodies of their elite owners.

Table 4.3   Egyptian artifacts from mainland Greek grave contexts.

	Figurines/ Amulets	Cartouches	Scarabs	Spoons	Ostrich shell rhyta	Beads	Vessels	Total
Perati	7	2	10	0	0	0	1	20
Mycenae	0	0	3	0	4	0	17	24
Dendra	0	0	0	1	1	1	2	5
Vapheio	0	0	0	1	0	0	3	4
Ayios Elias	1	0	1	0	0	0	0	2
Asine	1	0	0	0	0	0	2	3
Prosymna	1	0	1	0	0	0	0	2
Koukounara	0	0	1	0	0	0	0	1
Chalkis (Euboea)	0	0	0	0	0	0	1	1
Argive Heraion	0	0	0	0	0	0	2	2
Nauplion	0	0	0	0	0	0	2	2
Osmanaga	0	0	0	0	0	0	1	1
Thebes	0	0	0	0	0	0	1	1
Kakavatos	0	0	0	0	0	0	1	1
Total	10	2	16	2	5	1	33	69

What of the 33 vessels from mainland tombs? They are from 11 different sites, from all phases of the LBA. Seventeen (52%) are from Mycenae. Only one, though, is LH IIIC, from Perati. Clearly, stone vessels went out of fashion during the Postpalatial period or were not worth importing—or, more likely, access to them via Crete was lost (as argued by Warren 1969). Egyptian stone vessels, including alabastra and pyxides, were used for a variety of purposes, including but not limited to the storage and preparation of cosmetics, unguents, and oils (Bevan 2007: 134-35). When found in Aegean graves, they may have been used in preparation of the body for burial but more probably were personal items that belonged to the deceased (Bevan 2007: 189-91). The stone vessels from Mycenaean graves represent prestige imports that arrived in mainland Greece via Crete, where there was a very long history of stone vessel use and manufacture. The Mycenaeans, however, do not appear to have 'fetishized' antique Egyptian stone bowls, unlike the Minoans who copied and modified them, and sometimes inherited them as heirlooms (Bevan 2007: 124).

There are only 25 Egyptian imports from mainland LBA settlement contexts (Table 4.4). Of these, 19 (76%) are from Mycenae and most are LH IIIB. The others, one each, are from Tiryns, Poros, Pylos, Gla, Ayios Stephanos, and Sparta. The range of imports is similar to that from tombs: figurines, plaques, and scarabs (n = 9), ostrich shell rhyta (n = 4), and 12 vessels, mostly stone. The rhyta and stone vessels are all from 'secular' contexts, like houses, and probably fulfilled 'utilitarian' rather than ritual functions, as described above, having served as containers. The figurines, plaques, and scarabs are also mostly from 'secular' contexts, with three exceptions: one faience plaque and two scarabs, all heirlooms found in the Cult Center at Mycenae. These items do not point to widespread Mycenaean adoption of Egyptian religious beliefs; rather, they appear to have been left as part of a foundation deposit (Murray 2013: 383).

Table 4.4   Egyptian artifacts from mainland Greek settlement contexts.

	Figurines/ Amulets	Plaques	Scarabs	Spoons	Ostrich shell rhyta	Beads	Vessels	Total
Mycenae	1	3	2	0	2	0	11	19
Tiryns	1	0	0	0	0	0	0	1
Caulauria (Poros)	0	0	1	0	0	0	0	1
Pylos	0	0	0	0	0	0	1	1
Gla	0	0	0	0	1	0	0	1
Ayios Stephanos	0	0	0	0	1	0	0	1
Sparta	0	0	1	0	0	0	0	1
Total	2	3	4	0	4	0	12	25

In sum, mainland Greek access to Egyptian prestige goods appears to have narrowed over the course of the LBA, from six sites during LH I–II, to Mycenae during LH IIIA–B, to the Perati cemetery in LH IIIC. In fact, as suggested by Cline (2007: 194; see also Knodell 2013: 154-55), during LH IIIB Mycenae may have enjoyed a special relationship with Egypt, thereby explaining why other large, palatial centers with international trade connections, such as Thebes, produced very few or no Egyptian artifacts. Given the very small numbers of objects involved (94 over the course of 500 years) and given their very limited distribution (20 sites—of which 11 produced only a single object and two, Mycenae and Perati, accounted for 67% [n = 63] of the total), it seems highly unlikely that most Mycenaeans had any understanding of the original symbolic meanings of the items imported. The majority ended up in tombs, signaling their primary function as status markers. The exceptions that prove the rule are the faience plaques and scarabs from the Cult Center at Mycenae, which were disposed of in proper Egyptian fashion: in a foundation deposit. Thus if anyone appreciated Egyptian beliefs and practices, it was the cult specialists at Mycenae, but not Mycenaean elite generally—who appear to have been most attracted to Egyptian stone vessels, used to hold cosmetics—and certainly not the rank and file.

Minoan Crete

The situation in Mycenaean Greece can be contrasted to that of LBA Crete. Only 37 LBA Egyptian imports into Crete are from tomb contexts (Table 4.5, Figure 4.3). Seventeen (46%) are from the Late Minoan (LM) II Royal Tomb at Isopata. Only two are from Knossos and the rest are from eight different sites. Most date to the LM IIIA. There are two amulets, a monkey and frog, both from Isopata; lapis lazuli beads, also

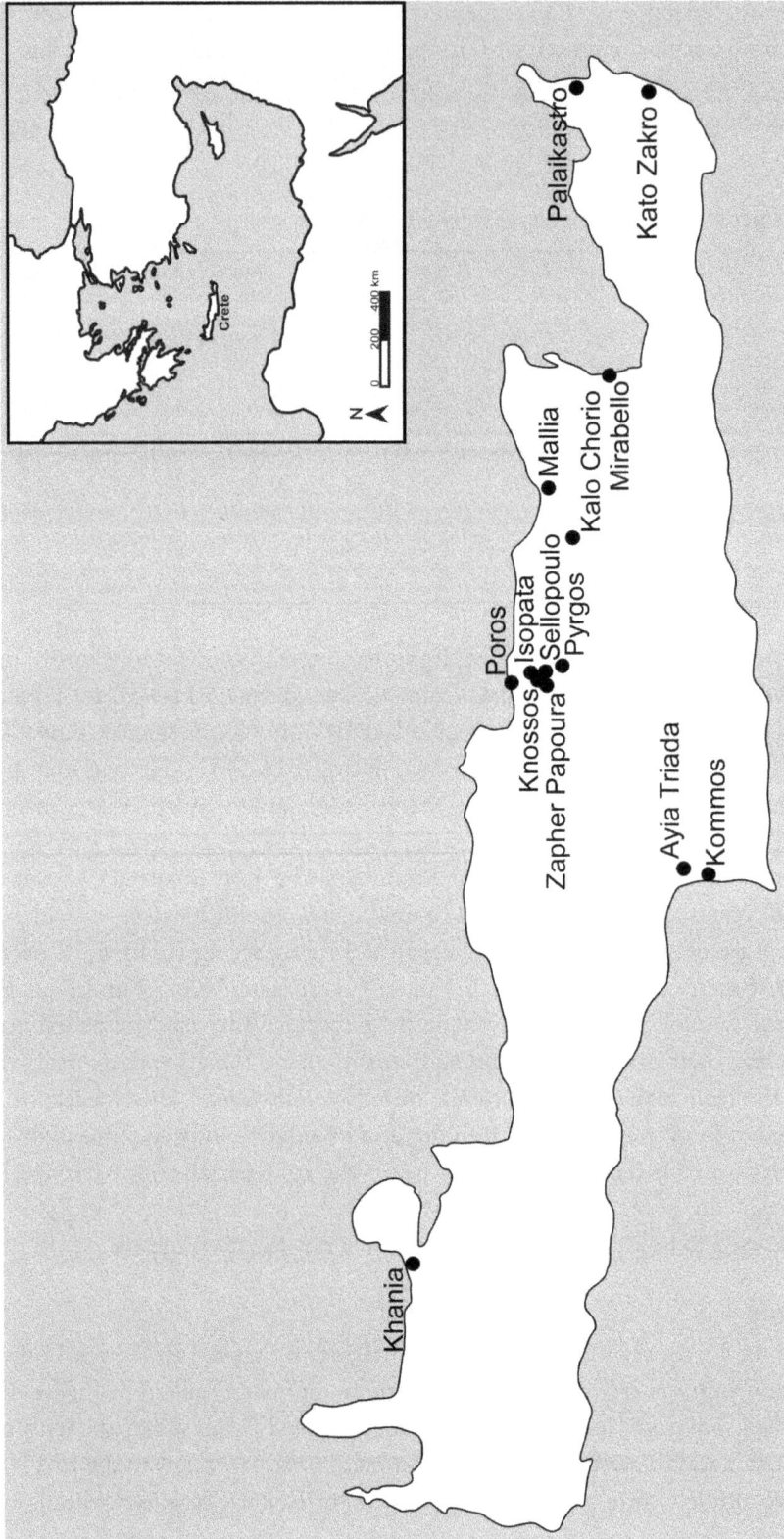

Figure 4.3   Map of Crete showing regions mentioned in the text.

from Isopata; an uninscribed stone plaque from Kalo Chorio, Mirabello; and three scarabs, from Sellopoulo (Knossos), Aghia Triada, and Zapher Papoura. There are 30 vessels, of which 16 are alabaster. Almost half (n = 14) are from Isopata. As compared to Mycenaean Greece, the prestige-goods economy of LBA Crete, as represented in tombs, seems far less dependent on Egyptian exotics (though see also discussion in Manning, this volume). Instead, most Egyptian imports appear to have been used and discarded in settlement contexts.

Ninety-five Egyptian imports to LBA Crete were recovered from settlement contexts (Table 4.6). Of these, a whopping 88 (93%) are vessels, mostly stone, but also

Table 4.5   Egyptian artifacts from Minoan grave contexts.

	Figurines/ Amulets	Plaques	Scarabs	Spoons	Ostrich shell rhyta	Beads	Vessels	Total
Isopata	2	0	0	0	0	1	14	17
Knossos	0	0	0	0	0	0	1	1
Kalo Chorio	0	1	0	0	0	0	0	1
Sellopoulo (Knossos)	0	0	1	0	0	0	0	1
Ayia Triada	0	0	1	0	0	0	1	2
Zapher Papoura	0	0	1	0	0	0	2	3
Kalyvia	0	0	0	0	0	0	4	4
Katsamba	0	0	0	0	0	0	4	4
Archanes	0	0	0	0	0	0	1	1
Ayios Fanourios	0	0	0	0	0	0	2	2
Khania	0	0	0	0	0	0	1	1
Total	2	1	3	0	0	1	30	37

Table 4.6   Egyptian artifacts from Minoan settlement contexts.

	Figurines/ Amulets	Plaques	Scarabs	Spoons	Ostrich shell rhyta	Beads	Vessels	Total
Knossos	0	0	2	0	1	0	48	51
Kommos	0	0	0	0	0	0	27	27
Ayia Triadha	0	0	0	0	0	0	1	1
Mallia	1	0	0	0	0	0	1	2
Kato Zakro	0	0	0	0	2	0	5	7
Palaiakastro	0	0	0	0	0	0	2	2
Pyrgos	0	0	0	0	0	0	1	1
Isopata	1	0	0	0	0	0	0	1
Pyrgos	1	0	0	0	0	0	0	1
Khania	0	0	1	0	0	0	0	1
Poros (Heraklion)	0	0	1	0	0	0	0	1
Total	3	0	4	0	3	0	85	95

three ostrich shell rhyta. Twenty-six vessels are ceramic, all (with an LM I exception) from LM III Kommos. Forty-eight of the 88 vessels are from Knossos, from a wide variety of phases and contexts, none of which are overtly sacred; most are domestic. The rest (n = 11) are from six different sites and are mostly LM I from palatial or domestic contexts: Aghia Triada (n = 1, LM I), Mallia (n = 1, LM IB), Kato Zakro (n = 5, LM IA–B), Palaiakastro (n = 2, LM I), Pyrgos (n = 1, LM IB), and Kommos (n = 1, a glass vessel, LM IIIA1–2). In addition to the vessels, there is one figurine (a sphinx), two amulets (one amorphous, the other a monkey), and four scarabs (one Amenhotep III, one Horemheb, two generic) from six different sites: Knossos (n = 2), Mallia, Isopata, Pyrgos, Khania, and Poros (Heraklion). All are from palatial or domestic contexts spanning LM I to LM IIIB. As with Mycenaean Greece, seven imports from six sites spanning 500 years probably does not indicate a deep appreciation for Egyptian symbolism in LBA Crete. Moreover, the stone vessel distribution at Knossos would seem to indicate that these particular objects—both foreign and locally made—had been fully integrated into the domestic economy and scarcely counted as prestige goods, thus explaining their scarcity in Late Minoan tombs.

To sum up, unlike mainland Greece, where Egyptian goods were prestige goods, Egyptian imports to Crete, the majority of which were stone vessels (many of them heirlooms), had been fully adopted into the utilitarian repertoire of elite households. Likewise, there was likely very little appreciation during the LBA, amongst both Neopalatial and Postpalatial Minoans (and Mycenaean occupiers), for the specific Egyptian meanings of Egyptian imports. A brief, more explicit comparison of mainland Greece to Minoan Crete in terms of Egyptian imports helps elucidate this point.

Comparing Mainland Greece to Minoan Crete

The preceding analysis of Egyptian imports to LBA Greece reveals several important factors when it comes to answering the question of whether or not objects held their symbolic value when removed from a parent culture and brought to the Aegean. Mainland Greece and Crete did not differ overly much in terms of what kinds of Egyptian objects were acquired. They did differ in terms of where these objects were deposited, in tombs versus settlements. They may well have differed in terms of what Egyptian goods meant and how they functioned within the respective political economies. Wengrow (2010: 151) has made the interesting argument that Egyptian items imported into late Pre- and Protopalatial Crete arrived as part of a package, including stone cosmetic jars and amulets, related to 'the aesthetic care and symbolic protection of [women's] bodies'. This would also explain the early Minoan interest in the goddess Tawaret, who was transformed into the Minoan genius (Weingarten 1991), unlike Bes, whose Egyptian symbolism as a 'snake-killer' did not translate and was therefore dropped from the Minoan repertoire (Weingarten 2015: 192). It may also explain the presence of *sistra*, which in Egypt were linked to female sexuality and played by women (Wengrow 2010: 151). If Wengrow is correct, then the *earliest* Egyptian imports into Crete did in fact hold their symbolic values, but were not integrated into elite island-wide prestige-goods exchange networks. By the LBA, though, these packages had broken down, Egyptian imports were few and had lost their prior meanings, and a fascination with stone vessels in general, at Knossos in particular, was all that remained. A very different set of circumstances characterized the mainland Mycenaean experience of Egyptian imports. The earliest imports, which date to the earliest phases of the LBA, did not arrive as a package, but rather entered Greece from Crete in very small numbers as prestige goods and were mostly deposited in graves as personal possessions. By LH IIIA–B, the majority of Egyptian imports to the mainland went to Mycenae, and only three of those were recovered from religious contexts. The vast majority of Egyptian imports to Mycenae, including stone vessels, were prestige goods that circulated through a strongly wealth-financed political economy.

The careful analysis of exotic imports to Mycenaean Greece undertaken by Burns (2010) is relevant to the above comparison. According to Burns (2010: 29-36), the original symbolic meaning of luxury imports was unimportant (or unknown) to Aegean consumers, as was perhaps their exact origin. Much more important was how they were received by consumers, put to use, imbued with local meanings, and finally deposited. At the basic level, exotic goods would have stimulated wonder, not least because of the unique materials with which they were made (Burns 2010: 71-72). For example, Burns (2010: 2-3), following Rehak (1994), notes that extremely large eggs imported to the Aegean from afar (often used to make rhyta, as described above) likely evoked awe not because they were laid by ostriches, an animal with which most Mycenaeans were unfamiliar, but rather because they could be associated with griffins, which had royal connotations. Given this approach to prestige goods, we can assume that during the LBA, the small numbers of Egyptian goods imported to Greece were used (in life and in death) by some few Mycenaeans, primarily at Mycenae, to buttress systems of status competition that depended on broad, very complex, relatively unstable networks of political economy: i.e., they were one small piece of a much larger puzzle. However, as Burns (2010: 192) describes, and as the following northern Albanian analogy reinforces, while small and limited in number, prestige goods may play outsized roles in stabilizing and changing political-economic systems, in particular when granted important, new symbolic associations, as they were by LBA Mycenaeans.

Modern Highland Northern Albania

Now what, if anything, can a discussion of prestige-goods exchange in modern highland northern Albania add to the previous analysis? Because northern Albania is the only place in modern Europe where systems of prestige-goods exchange continued to function into the twentieth century, it may serve as a convenient, accessible analog for systems of LBA prestige-goods exchange. The Shala Valley Project (SVP), which I directed in northern Albania from 2004 to 2008 (Galaty *et al.* 2013), employed participant-observation ethnography, interviews with tribal elders (many of whom took part in and remembered well the pre-World War II tribal system, including the prestige-goods trade), and archival historical research to document the functioning of the tribal political economy. Large houses led by patriarchs, some occupied by joint families of 50+ members, competed with one another for access to resources, including land, which was privately owned (Galaty *et al.* 2013: 107-28), and women, who were acquired as brides in endogamous patrilocal marriage exchange systems (Galaty *et al.* 2013: 85-106). These houses also cooperated with one another, sharing labor, for instance, and conducting joint military operations (Galaty 2013). These relationships, which underpinned middle-range systems of political economy, were regulated by oral customary law (e.g., the *Kanuni i Lekë Dukagjinit*, which was not written down until the 1930s: see Gjeçov 1989), enforced by a tribal council. Albanian oral customary law was (and still is) built around the concept of honor (*nder*). Honor was highly symbolized, of course, but also materialized in interesting ways: it had substance and could be measured. A man might possess more or less of it, and therefore be judged more or less honorable. Such dynamics were particularly relevant when a man was 'in blood' (*ne gjak*), i.e., involved in a feud to which he owed blood, or when men from different households shared reciprocal hospitality (*mikpritja*). Hospitality laws required that various prestige goods, including white flour, coffee, sugar, and tobacco, which could only be acquired in Ottoman market towns, be provided by a host and consumed during ritualized feasts (Figure 4.4). A host who did not produce such goods in quantity was dishonored. Thus, there was an ideological component to the northern Albanian trade in and use of prestige goods: they symbolized honor or a lack thereof, and a man would (literally) rather die than be dishonored. Importantly, the symbolic meanings held by these items in Ottoman culture were not critical to their functioning in Albanian tribal culture (see Jezernik 2004: 147-69 regarding coffee).

The Ottoman hospitality package adopted by northern Albanians is similar to the Egyptian fertility package adopted into Pre- and Protopalatial Crete: in both cases the symbolic connotations were roughly understood, even though the importing cultures were quite different from the exporting cultures. The early Mycenaeans appear to have skipped this step, perhaps because they occupied highly competitive tertiary states and imported Egyptian goods via Minoan Crete (Parkinson and Galaty 2007). These then circulated through wealth-financed political economies, mostly ending up in graves. In fact, northern Albanians also acquired various other, non-perishable prestige goods from the Ottomans, the most important of which were guns and ammunition (Figure 4.5a). Guns were essential to the proper functioning of feuds and, therefore, the system of honor, which fueled the tribal political economy. Guns were symbolically loaded: e.g., a man's sons are referred to as 'guns' in the language of the *kanun*. They were, however, inalienable possessions—upon his death, a man's gun passed to his oldest son—and served as important markers of status, carried by men everywhere they went. Likewise, foreign prestige goods like coins were incorporated by women into local dress, symbolizing a woman's marital status, but the meaning of the coins as coins was irrelevant (Figure 4.5b). Thus, foreign prestige goods were symbolically meaningful for LBA Minoans and Mycenaeans, and for northern Albanians—indicative of status,

Figure 4.4   Group of mountain men at Sofras, From Theth in the Dukagjin, by S. Pici, 1938 (used by permission of the Fototeka Kombëtare Marubi, Shkodra, Albania).

for example—but their original connotations, including their iconography, seem to have been largely lost (as in the case of Bes or the Egyptian fertility package imported into Pre- and Protopalatial Crete) or ignored (as in the case of the Mycenaeans and northern Albanians).

The northern Albanian tribes were largely Catholic and appear to have arrived in the high mountains sometime after the Ottoman occupation (Galaty *et al.* 2013: 53-59). Like many frontier cultures, they supported highly syncretic religious systems and undertook various crypto-religious practices. Most were nominally Catholic, but were directly influenced by other Christian sects, such as the Bogomils, and adopted various Muslim beliefs and behaviors. The SVP identified many good ethnohistoric and ethnographic examples of syncretic and crypto-Christian religious practices undertaken during both the Ottoman and Communist periods (Galaty *et al.* 2013: 149-62). Generally speaking, foreign religious beliefs do not appear to have been easily understood and assimilated by northern Albanians, even when taught to tribesmen by religious specialists. For instance, SVP research in the Secret Archives of the Vatican revealed this excerpt from a letter written by the Bishop of Scutari in the late eighteenth century:

> In these parts, it has always been practiced that, when the sown portion of fields is infested with worms or locusts, or other harmful insects, the priests are summoned, and prayers are said. When these priests recite these prayers, they use a certain book entitled *Collection of Ancient and Holy Blessings*. In the course of their prayers,

Figure 4.5   (a) Young men of Shala, by K. Marubi, 1900–1915; (b) costume of a mountain woman from Puka, by P. Marubi, 1885–1903 (used by permission of the Fototeka Kombëtare Marubi, Shkodra, Albania).

all they do is repeat, 'I exorcize you, pestiferous worm, and I abjure you, and render you anathema'. I cannot excuse this method of exorcizing unreasoning creatures of the charge of *superstitio*, and we would like to know whether this procedure should continue to be allowed in such grave cases, or forbidden; and what rule ought to apply, if it is forbidden.

(*Archivio Segreto Vaticano Fondo Missioni, busta* no. 105, folio 5v, trans. M. Lubin)

Clearly, northern Albanians continued to perform various non-Christian rites even though they were Christians and had been for centuries. An appreciation for pagan beliefs is reflected in the symbols carved into houses, which we documented throughout Shala (Galaty *et al.* 2013: 149-62). In addition to Christian iconography, like crosses, there are also sun and moon symbols, wheels, stars, various geometric shapes, abstract caves and mountains, weapons, hands, and raised knobs. Finally, our work with the records of Carleton Coon, a Harvard physical anthropologist who measured heads in Shala in the 1920s (Coon 1950), stored in the Anthropological Archives of the Smithsonian, revealed that several men from Catholic Shala took multiple wives. One had as many as five; he seems to have had all female children, but wanted a son, and did not recognize that the 'problem' was his, not that of his wives. Polygamy in Catholic Shala probably betrays some degree of Muslim influence. In fact, it was not uncommon for whole northern Albanian tribes to convert *en masse* to Islam in order to gain more favorable terms from the Ottomans, including more favorable access to prestige goods. In short, although fiercely Catholic, the northern Albanians do not seem to have known much about Catholic doctrine, nor were they unwilling to convert to Islam if and when it served their needs. While nominally Muslim, tribesmen often kept secret Christian names and practiced Catholicism covertly.

Like the modern northern Albanians, the Minoans appear to have created a mildly syncretic religious system, transforming and assimilating several Egyptian religious symbols: the goddess Taweret became the Minoan genius (Weingarten 1991); the Minoan *sistrum* appears to have been used, by men, in harvest festivals (Wengrow 2010: 151); and Minoan Horns of Consecration may also have Egyptian origins (Watrous 1998). The Mycenaeans, however, do not appear to have adopted Egyptian religious beliefs and practices to any great extent. Nevertheless, we should not underestimate the social power and importance of foreign prestige goods, which almost always possess ideological, if not religious, force.

When the Albanian federal government formed in 1912, it did not attack northern Albanian religious practices; when it came to religion, the northern tribes were too malleable, even ambivalent. Instead, the authorities went after the prestige-goods trade. They closed borders, restricting access to market towns, and thereby disrupted the prestige-goods economy. Without access to prestige goods, including guns, and systems of reciprocal hospitality, feuding (and therefore economic practices based upon it) faltered. The role of prestige-goods in the operation and then collapse of northern Albanian tribal social systems was not techno-functional; it was ideological, framed in emic terms by mountaineers as a failure of honor. Something similar may have happened to the Minoans, though my analysis indicates that their political economy seems to have been less dependent on prestige-goods exchange, and those goods they did import had by the LBA lost their symbolic resonance. The Mycenaeans, on the other hand, appear to have operated political economies that were directly dependent on prestige-goods exchanges, including of foreign imports. These exchanges likely had symbolic importance in networks of reciprocal obligation that bound Mycenaean individuals one to the other. When the eastern Mediterranean trade system faltered at the end of the LBA, the Mycenaean states collapsed. Loss of access to prestige goods likely had something to do with their demise.

Conclusion

To conclude, I would assert that careful study of extant prestige-goods exchange systems, like those of northern Albania, can elucidate features of archaeological prestige-goods exchange systems, like those of the Minoans and Mycenaeans, by circumscribing issues of theoretical importance. For example, it is quite clear that foreign prestige goods imported into northern Albania generally lost their symbolic, including religious, and iconographic associations, but gained new, localized meanings in ways similar to those described by Burns (2010) for the Mycenaeans. In northern Albania, prestige-goods exchange was strongly tied to systems of political economy built on concepts of honor.

A similar process of meaning-making may have characterized the acquisition and assimilation of Egyptian goods by some Mycenaeans, who used such goods in competitions linked to building and augmenting social status (see Murray 2013). Given the results of my analysis, the Minoan response to Egyptian exotica appears to have been distinctly different, characterized by the adoption of religious iconography (if not religious syncretism) in the Pre- and Protopalatial periods. This may have been the result of more immediate access on the part of Minoans to Egypt and Egyptians, as compared to Mycenaeans, who may have interacted with Egypt mostly or only via Minoan intermediaries. By the Neo- and Postpalatial Periods, Egyptian prestige-goods, the vast majority of which were vessels, had been incorporated into Minoan (or Mycenean-Minoan) daily life and normalized, carrying no identifiable, overtly Egyptian meanings. Loss of access to foreign prestige-goods did not bring down the Minoan palaces, 'old' or 'new'; Minoan corporate political economies were too mature, too resilient for that to have been the case. But loss of access to foreign prestige-goods might well have contributed to the fall of the Mycenaean palaces. As noted by Knodell (2013: 160), with regard to the Mycenaeans,

> consumption of particular exotica was certainly in the domain of the elite, and was carefully controlled to project exclusivity … Tensions caused by this exclusivity, among other things, may have contributed to the ultimate collapse and rejection of the Mycenaean palace system.

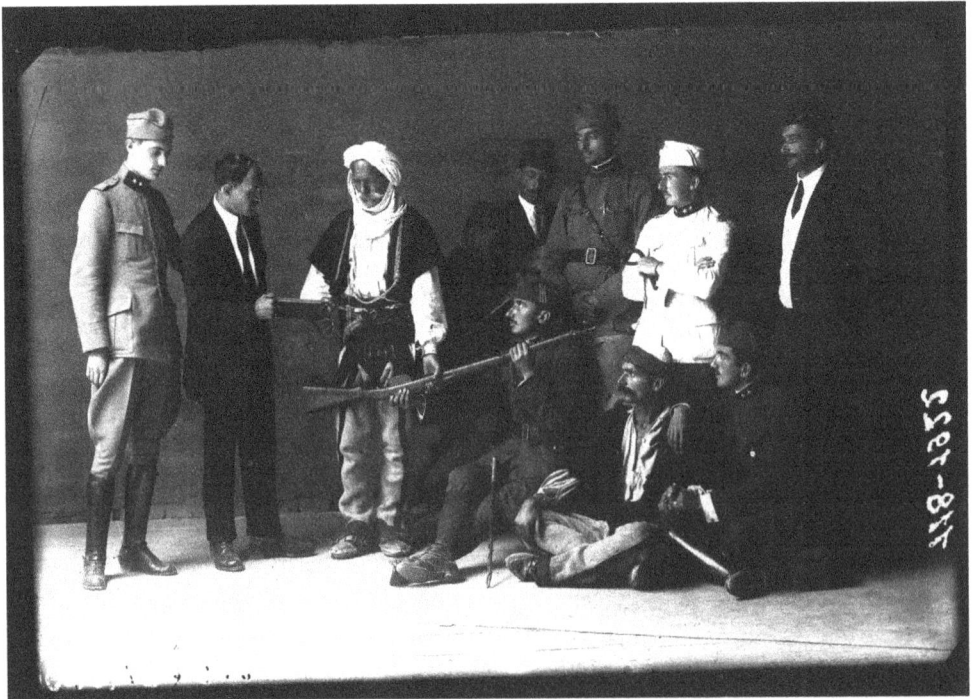

Figure 4.6   The last war chief of the Shala surrenders his gun to representatives of the new Albanian state, by P. Marubi, 1922 (used by permission of the Fototeka Kombëtare Marubi, Shkodra, Albania).

This statement could just as easily have been applied to northern Albania ca. 1912, when guns were taken from the hands of the chiefs and their followers, honor failed, and the tribal system collapsed (Figure 4.6).

Acknowledgments

I would like to thank Alex Knodell and Tom Leppard for inviting me to participate in Cherry-fest 2015. It was an event I will not soon forget. I would like also to thank Bill Parkinson for providing database access. SVP historian Matthew Lubin provided the quote from the Bishop of Scutari and an English translation. Finally, thanks are due John: for inspiring excellent archaeology in the Aegean and elsewhere throughout the world, but more importantly, for cold beer, good conversation, and friendship.

About the Author

Michael L. Galaty is Professor of Anthropology at the University of Michigan, where he is Director and Curator of European and Mediterranean Archaeology at the Museum of Anthropological Archaeology. He conducts field research in Albania and Greece, in Shkodër and Mani respectively, with a focus on the origins of complexity. The final publication of the Shala Valley Project, *Light and Shadow: Isolation and Interaction in the Shala Valley of Northern Albania* (Cotsen Institute of Archaeology Press, 2013) won the Society for American Archaeology's 2014 Book Award. E-mail: mgalaty@umich.edu

References

Bevan, A.
  2007   *Stone Vessels and Values in the Bronze Age Mediterranean.* Cambridge: Cambridge University Press. https://doi.org/10.1017/CBO9780511499678

Burns, B.E.
  2010   *Mycenaean Greece, Mediterranean Commerce, and the Formation of Identity.* Cambridge: Cambridge University Press.

Cherry, J.F.
  2010   Sorting out Crete's Prepalatial off-island interactions. In W.A. Parkinson and M.L. Galaty (eds.), *Archaic State Interaction: The Eastern Mediterranean in the Bronze Age*, 107-40. Santa Fe, New Mexico: School for Advanced Research Press.

Clark, G.
  1986   *Symbols of Excellence.* Cambridge: Cambridge University Press.

Cline, E.H.
  2007   Rethinking Mycenaean international trade with Egypt and the Near East. In W.A. Parkinson and M.L. Galaty (eds.), *Rethinking Mycenaean Palaces II: Revised and Expanded Second Edition.* Monograph 60: 190-200. Los Angeles: Cotsen Institute of Archaeology.
  2009   *Sailing the Wine-Dark Sea: International Trade and the Late Bronze Age Aegean.* 2nd edn. British Archaeo-

logical Reports, International Series 591. Oxford: British Archaeological Reports.

2010   Bronze Age interactions between the Aegean and the eastern Mediterranean revisited: mainstream, periphery, or margin? In W.A. Parkinson and M.L. Galaty (eds.), *Archaic State Interaction: The Eastern Mediterranean in the Bronze Age*, 161-80. Santa Fe, New Mexico: School for Advanced Research Press.

Coon, C.
1950   *The Mountains of Giants: A Racial and Cultural Study of the North Albanian Mountain Ghegs*. Papers of the Peabody Museum of American Archaeology and Ethnology, Harvard University 23.3. Cambridge, Massachusetts: Peabody Museum.

Friedman J., and M.J. Rowlands
1977   Notes towards an epigenetic model of the evolution of 'civilization'. In J. Friedman and M.J. Rowlands (eds.), *The Evolution of Social Systems*, 201-76. London: Duckworth.

Galaty, M.L.
2013   'An offense to honor is never forgiven…': violence and landscape archaeology in highland northern Albania. In S. Ralph (ed.), *The Archaeology of Violence: Interdisciplinary Approaches*, 143-57. Albany, New York: SUNY Press.

Galaty, M.L., O. Lafe, W. Lee and Z. Tafilica
2013   *Light and Shadow: Isolation and Interaction in the Shala Valley of Northern Albania*. Monumenta Archaeologica 28. Los Angeles: Cotsen Institute of Archaeology Press.

Galaty, M.L., D. Nakassis and W. Parkinson
2016   Reciprocity in Aegean palatial societies: gifts, debt, and the foundations of economic exchange. *Journal of Mediterranean Archaeology* 29: 61-132. https://doi.org/10.1558/jmea.v29i1.31013

Gjeçov, S.
1989   *Kanuni i Lekë Dukagjinit* [The Code of Lekë Dukagjini]. Translated by M. Fox. New York: Gjonlekaj Publishing.

Helms, M.
1979   *Ancient Panama: Chiefs in Search of Power*. Austin: University of Texas Press.

1988   *Ulysses' Sail: An Ethnographic Odyssey of Power, Knowledge, and Geographical Distance*. Austin: University of Texas Press. https://doi.org/10.1515/9781400859542

1993   *Craft and the Kingly Ideal: Art, Trade and Power*. Austin: University of Texas Press.

Jezernik, B.
2004   *Wild Europe: The Balkans in the Gaze of Western Travellers*. London: SAQI Books.

Knodell, A.R.
2013   Small-World Networks and Mediterranean Dynamics in the Euboean Gulf: An Archaeology of Complexity in Late Bronze Age and Early Iron Age Greece. Unpublished PhD dissertation, Brown University, Providence, Rhode Island.

Murray, S.C.
2013   Trade, Imports, and Society in Early Greece: 1300-900 B.C.E. Unpublished PhD dissertation, Stanford University, Stanford, California.

2017   *The Collapse of the Mycenaean Economy: Imports, Trade, and Institutions 1300-700 BCE*. Cambridge: Cambridge University Press. https://doi.org/10.1017/9781316890424

Parkinson, W.A.
2010   Beyond the peer: social interaction and political evolution in the Bronze Age Aegean. In D. Pullen (ed.), *Political Economies of the Aegean Bronze Age*, 11-34. Oxford: Oxbow Books.

Parkinson, W.A., and M.L. Galaty
2007   Secondary states in perspective: an integrated approach to state formation in the prehistoric Aegean. *American Anthropologist* 109: 113-29. https://doi.org/10.1525/aa.2007.109.1.113

Papadopoulos, J.K., and G. Urton (eds.)
2012   *The Construction of Value in the Ancient World*. Cotsen Advanced Seminar 5.

Los Angeles: Cotsen Institute of Archaeology Press.

Plourde, A.M.

2008 The origins of prestige goods as honest signals of skill and knowledge. *Human Nature* 19: 374-88. https://doi.org/10.1007/s12110-008-9050-4

2009 Prestige goods and the formation of political hierarchy: a costly signaling model. In S. Shennan (ed.), *Pattern and Process in Cultural Evolution*, 265-76. Berkeley: University of California Press.

Rehak, P.

1994 The Aegean 'priest' on CMS I.223. *Kadmos* 33: 76-84. https://doi.org/10.1515/kadm.1994.33.1.76

Trubitt, M.B.D.

2003 The production and exchange of marine shell prestige goods. *Journal of Archaeological Research* 11: 243-77. https://doi.org/10.1023/A:1025028814962

Warren, P.

1969 *Minoan Stone Vases*. Cambridge: Cambridge University Press.

Watrous, L.V.

1998 Egypt and Crete in the early Middle Bronze Age: a case of trade and cultural diffusion. In E.H. Cline and D. Harris-Cline (eds.), *The Aegean and the Orient in the Second Millennium*, 19-28. Aegaeum 18. Liège: Université de Liège.

Weingarten, J.

1991 Late Bronze Age trade within Crete: the evidence of seals and sealings. In N.H. Gale (ed.), *Bronze Age Trade in the Mediterranean*. Studies in Mediterranean Archaeology 90: 303-24. Jonsered: Paul Åströms Förlag.

2015 The arrival of Bes[et] on Middle Minoan Crete. In J. Mynárová, P. Onderka and P. Pavúk (eds.), *There and Back Again – The Crossroads* II: 181-96. Prague: Charles University in Prague, Faculty of Arts.

Wengrow, D.

2010 The voyages of Europa: ritual and trade in the eastern Mediterranean, circa 2300-1850 BC. In W.A. Parkinson and M.L. Galaty (eds.), *Archaic State Interaction: The Eastern Mediterranean in the Bronze Age*, 141-60. Santa Fe, New Mexico: School for Advanced Research Press.

5 Continent, Region, Microregion, Site: Settlement Nucleation in the European Neolithic

William A. Parkinson

Introduction

Of John Cherry's various significant contributions to archaeology, his commitment to analysis at the regional scale has had the most direct influence on how I have come to practice archaeology. Building upon the (then) revolutionary paradigm of the New Archaeology, which was itself a call for approaching culture as a regional phenomenon (Binford 1964), Cherry's pioneering survey work led eventually to an explosion not only in archaeological surface surveys throughout the Mediterranean (Cherry 1983), but also to the creation of a new multi-regional dataset that permitted archaeologists to think about the past in an entirely new way. The proliferation of regional surveys throughout the eastern Mediterranean allowed, for the first time, the comparison of regional cultural trajectories within a broad, diachronic framework (Alcock and Cherry 2004).

This chapter looks specifically at the role of microregional approaches in the study of settlement nucleation in the Neolithic of southeastern Europe. I hope to make two points. First, that although regional-scale studies have become commonplace in European archaeology, due in large part to Cherry's influence, they are seldom integrated into macro-scale syntheses (Galaty *et al.* 2014); and second, that in the same way that regional datasets are necessary for keeping larger-scale syntheses 'honest', the detailed examination of sites and their immediate vicinities at the microregional scale can now be helpful in interpreting patterns at the regional scale.

The Grand Synthesis and Regional Studies

European archaeology is historically schizophrenic. The tradition of writing grand narratives that attempt to synthesize the prehistory of the entire European continent has been a favorite pastime of European prehistorians (e.g., Lubbock 1865). That tradition—which is a good one, an important one—continues today (e.g., Whittle 1996; Gamble 1999; Kristiansen and Larsson 2005), but the vast majority of our knowledge of European prehistory still derives from information about individual sites. As a result, most continental-scale syntheses do not take adequate account of the regional variability that has emerged as a result of the various survey projects that have been conducted over the last several decades (see Galaty *et al.* 2014 for discussion).

The explosion of regional survey projects across Europe since the 1970s has led to a more nuanced understanding of the European past, especially in the Mediterranean. Social changes that previously seemed to occur more-or-less simultaneously across the continent have given way to a more variable archaeological landscape within which individual regions underwent different changes as they adapted to their changing places in the world. The development of regional surveys coincided with the widespread adoption of radiocarbon dating, adding a chronological dimension to this variability (Yerkes *et al.* 2009). The chronological and regional patterning of social change in European prehistory has taken on a subtler form that archaeologists now must face head-on.

But grand, continental-scale syntheses continue to be written, and most either gloss—or conveniently ignore—the vast quantities of information that have been generated from different regional studies across the continent.

Take, for example, the recent synthesis by Kristiansen and Larsson (2005), which attributes the emergence of Bronze Age hierarchies in northern Europe ultimately to the long-distance diffusion of ideas and people from Mesopotamia and Anatolia through the Aegean and into central and northern Europe. Instead of bolstering their model with archaeological evidence for interregional interaction between these far-flung regions, Kristiansen and Larsson fall back on a much more tenuous iconographic argument based on the adoption of symbols of leadership, such as hats and helmets, which they trace from the Hittites through the Mycenaeans and into northern Europe (e.g., Kristiansen and Larsson 2005: fig. 24). While there is extensive archaeological evidence for contact between the Mycenaeans and their contemporaries in the Near East and Anatolia, this macro-scalar iconographic argument ignores the lack of direct evidence of contact between the Mycenaeans and central Europe. When Galaty, Tomas, and I addressed this previously, we concluded that 'precisely during the time that Mycenaean states were in the best position to transmit Near Eastern Objects, symbols, and ideas to Europe via the eastern Adriatic (during the Late Helladic IIIA-B), *they had no, or very few, northern contacts*' (Galaty *et al.* 2014: 169, emphasis in original). The contacts that did occur during that time focused primarily on ceramics, not material culture related to warfare and hierarchy.

As we noted, Kristiansen and Larsson's (2005) book is intended as a synthesis, not an analysis, and the glossing of regional variation is a necessary evil if we are to continue to synthesize our understanding of the past at broad geographic and chronological scales—a task that is incumbent upon archaeologists for communicating the results of our work to non-specialists and the general public. Nevertheless, there is much to be gained by integrating examples of archaeology beyond the site to such larger-scale endeavors.

Multi-Scalar Research and Microregional Studies

One lesson that has emerged from the last few decades of regional survey projects is that we need to adopt a perspective that approaches the investigation of social processes at multiple temporal and geographic scales (Knodell and Leppard, this volume). Only a multi-scalar perspective will elucidate the more subtle, nuanced, regional variation that now characterizes the archaeological record of Europe. If we are going to write grand syntheses that address continental-scale processes like the Neolithization of Europe or the origins of Bronze Age elites it is important to be specific about how those macro-scale processes relate to regional processes.

Similarly, our regional models also stand to be informed from microregional studies, which can help bridge the gap between regional-scale models and information derived from research at specific sites (Figure 5.1). Due to recent advances in geophysics (Sarris

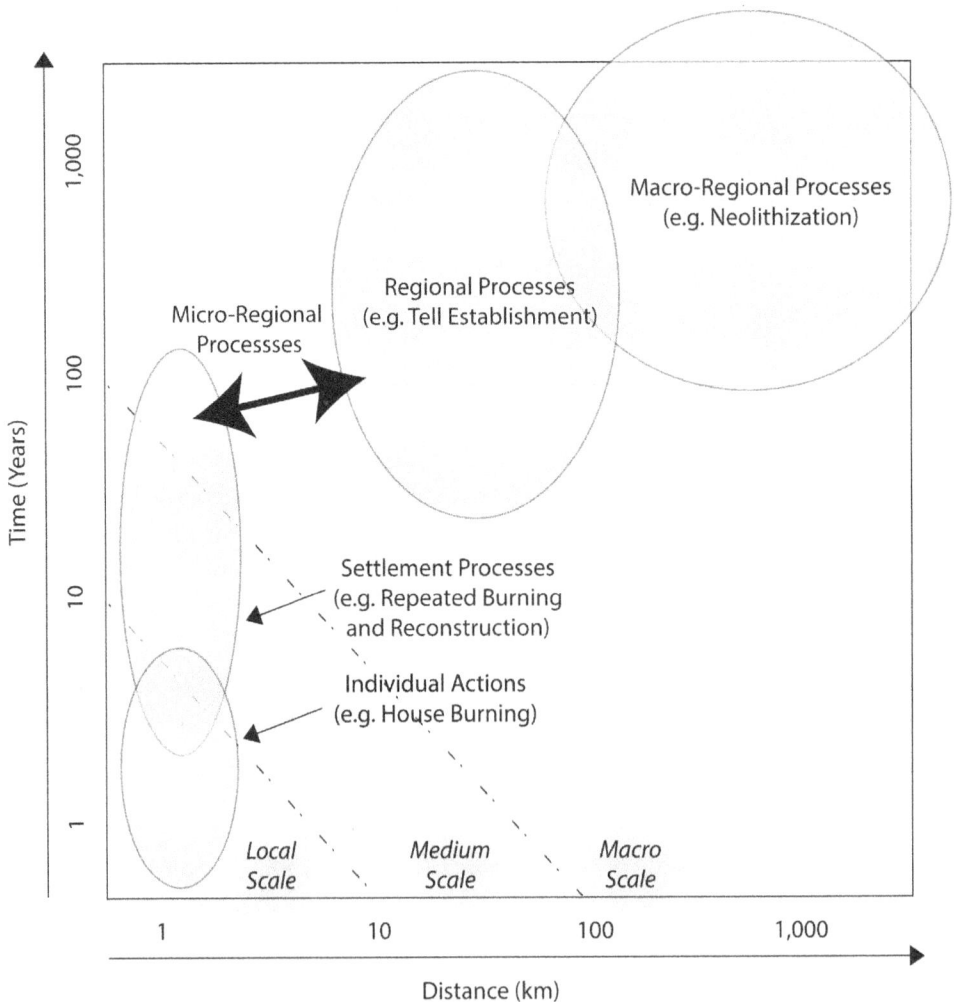

Figure 5.1   Social processes at different geographic and temporal scales (based on Parkinson and Galaty 2010: fig. 1.2; illustration by Rebecca Seifried, modified by W.A. Parkinson).

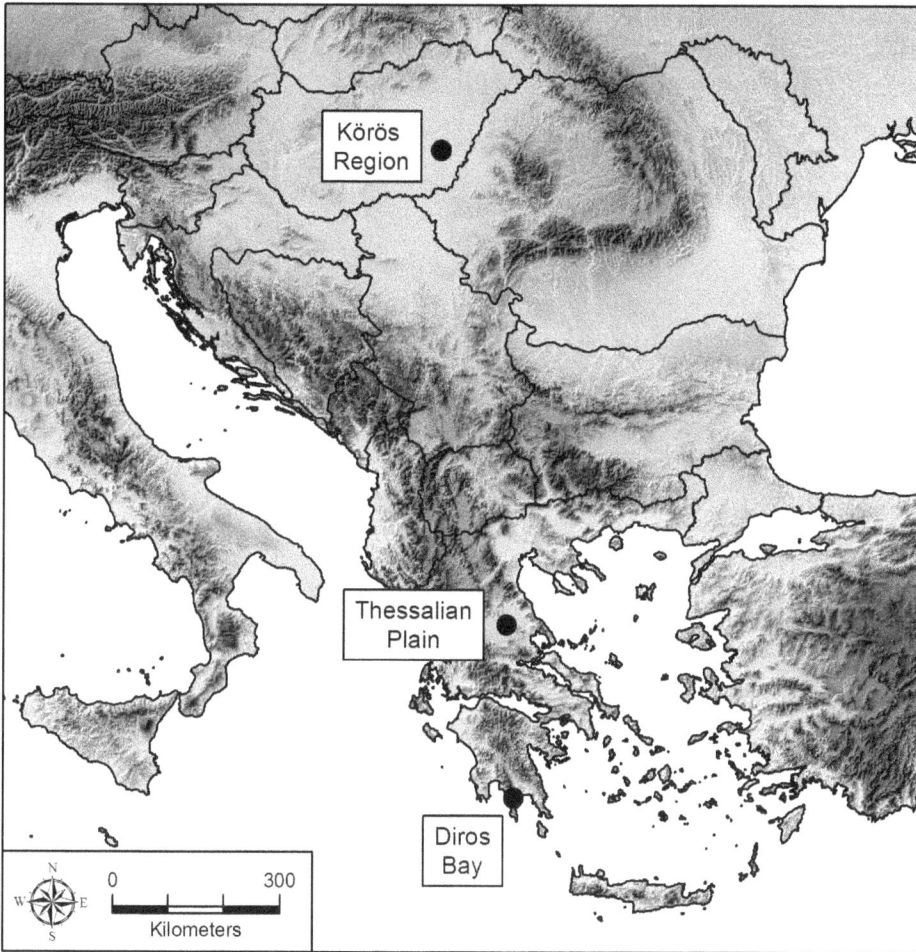

Figure 5.2   Map of southeastern Europe showing the location of the Körös Region on the Great Hungarian Plain in the Carpathian Basin, the Thessalian Plain in Greece, and Diros Bay in Greece (map by Rebecca Seifried, elevation data from the USGS Earth Resources Observation and Science Center).

et al. 2013), geochemistry (Sarris *et al.* 2004), and even in the cost and precision of real-time topographic equipment, it is now possible to reveal details about a site within its immediate, local, microenvironmental context that can be critical for making sense of regional patterns (Gyucha *et al.* 2015).

Here I present two examples from my own research. The first comes from the Carpathian Basin in central Europe and the other from Diros Bay on the Mani peninsula of the southern Greek mainland (Figure 5.2).

The Körös Region on the Great Hungarian Plain
The first example comes from the Körös region on the Great Hungarian Plain, where my colleague Attila Gyucha and I have been investigating the emergence of tell sites at the end of the sixth millennium BC (Parkinson *et al.* 2010; Parkinson and Gyucha 2012).

Unlike most of the Neolithic tells in the central and southern Balkans, which, like their Near Eastern counterparts, were created from the recurrent construction of settlements on the same spot, tells on the Great Hungarian Plain were almost always discrete special activity areas within larger settlement complexes that also incorporated so-called 'flat' or horizontal settlements. Not only were the Neolithic tells on the Great Hungarian Plain created by different social processes than the settlement tells of the central and southern Balkans, they also had a different chronological genesis (Parkinson and Gyucha 2012). Unlike the tells in eastern Thessaly, for example, which were established during the Early Neolithic (EN) period, probably within a few generations of the earliest Neolithic populations in the region, the tells on the Great Hungarian Plain were not established until nearly a thousand years after the earliest agricultural populations in that region. Also unlike the Thessalian tells, which in many cases persisted throughout the Neolithic for thousands of years, the later Neolithic tells in eastern Hungary seldom were used for more than a few hundred years, and they were all abandoned at the beginning of the Copper Age. These two very different regional trajectories both led to the formation of tell sites, but the tells themselves were very different archaeological artifacts because the social processes that brought them about were quite different (Figure 5.3).

In our investigation of the process of tell formation in the Körös region of the Great Hungarian Plain, we sought to examine the origin of two tells located near the modern town of Vésztő. Working from detailed settlement pattern maps generated during the course of the Archaeological Topography of Hungary project, we focused on the sites of Vésztő-Mágor and Szeghalom-Kovácshalom, located about 7 km apart on the same river system along the edge of a huge marsh. Both sites had been excavated previously, and like most later Neolithic tells on the Great Hungarian Plain they were established at the end of the Middle Neolithic period, around the middle of the sixth millennium BC. We focused on these two sites because they seemed to be incorporated into different settlement patterns. The site of Vésztő-Mágor stood alone, with no other contemporaneous settlements in its immediate vicinity. The site of Szeghalom-Kovácshalom, by contrast, was surrounded by several contemporaneous sites (Figure 5.4).

Using methods derived from Mediterranean survey projects, we initiated micro-regional projects around both sites, including intensive gridded surface collections, geochemical studies, and a wide array of geophysical surveys. At the site of Vésztő-Mágor, which is the largest Neolithic tell on the Great Hungarian Plain, covering about 4 ha, our research largely reinforced the results of the Hungarian regional surface survey. The site was a stand-alone settlement with no contemporaneous settlements nearby and no 'flat' or horizontal settlement surrounding the tell (Figure 5.5). Our excavations at the site confirmed the chronological breadth of the Neolithic layers at the site—from around 5300 to 4900 BC—although micromorphology suggested that there may have been an even earlier settlement nearby that was incorporated into the lowermost levels of the tell.

Just downstream at the site of Szeghalom-Kovácshalom, we found a completely different situation (Figure 5.6). Here, Hungarian survey teams had identified several sites located around the Kovácshalom tell. As we began to investigate these outlying

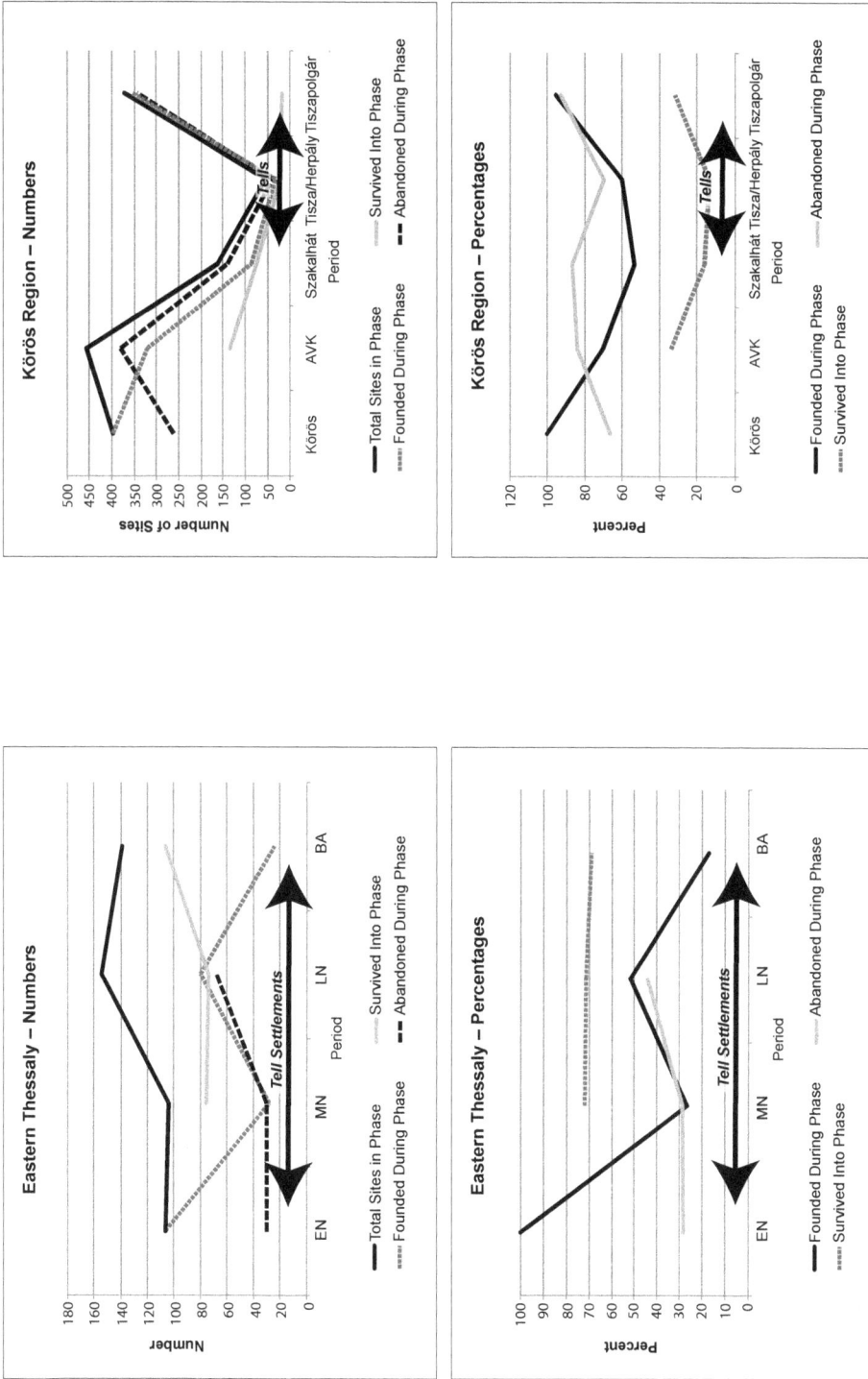

Figure 5.3   The long-term trajectory of Neolithic settlement patterns in eastern Thessaly, Greece, and the Körös Region of the Great Hungarian Plain, eastern Hungary (based on Parkinson and Gyucha 2012: fig. 4; data from Ecsedy *et al.* 1982; Jankovich *et al.* 1989; Gallis 1992; van Andel *et al.* 1994; van Andel and Runnels 1995: table 4; Jankovich *et al.* 1998; Gyucha 2015). (A) Raw numbers; (B) frequencies (original illustration by Jill Seagard, modified by W.A. Parkinson).

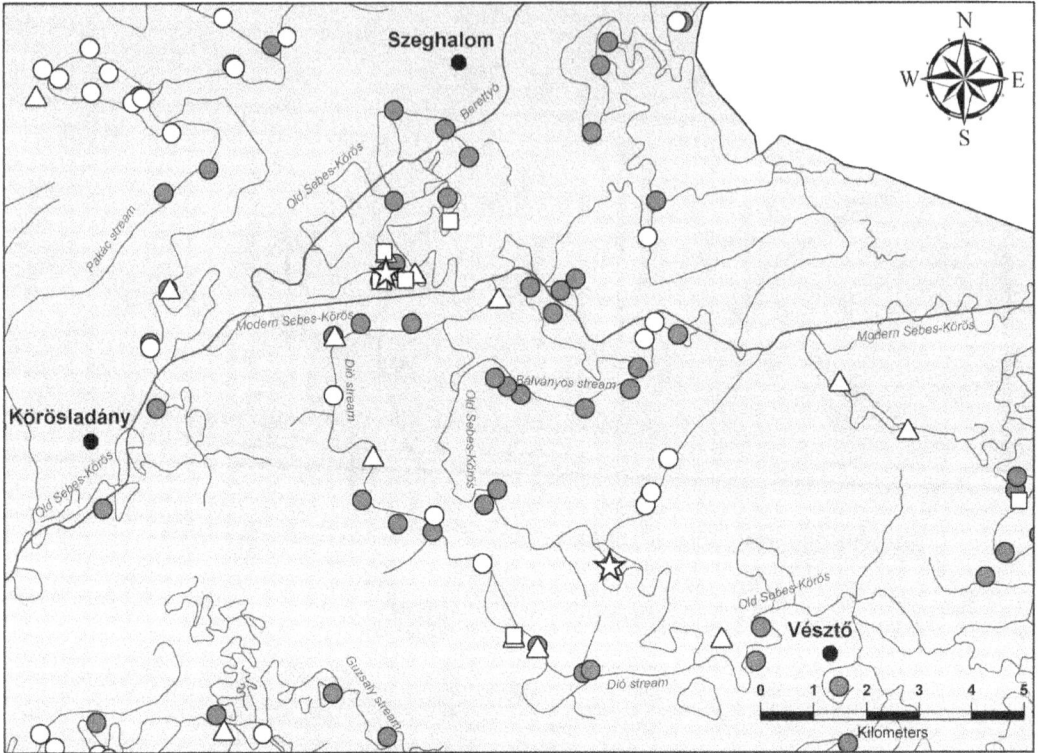

Figure 5.4   Map of the location of Szeghalom-Kovácshalom, Vésztő-Mágor, and other prehistoric sites in their immediate vicinity. Fine lines: ancient paleochannels; dark lines: postregulation canals; dark stars: Neolithic tell sites; dark circles: earlier Middle Neolithic (Alföld Linear Pottery Phase) sites; dark triangles: later Middle Neolithic (Szakálhát Phase); dark squares: Late Neolithic (Tisza Culture); light circles: Early Copper Age (Tiszapolgár Culture) sites; black circles: modern towns (illustration by A. Gyucha, based on information from Ecsedy *et al.* 1982).

settlements we noticed that there were several burnt daub scatters interspersed throughout the microregion, and we decided to conduct intensive gridded surface collections over the entire microregion. We also conducted geochemical studies and geophysical surveys throughout the microregion. Our results yielded a complicated picture of a small tell—less than 1 ha—surrounded by a massive contemporaneous settlement that extends in an area over 100 ha. The tell itself does not have fortifications like those at Vésztő-Mágor, but it was surrounded by a natural bend in the river that likely was modified to form a moat. There is a settlement zone immediately surrounding that with deeper deposits that was occupied for a longer amount of time, and beyond that there are clusters of longhouses that were inhabited for considerably shorter amounts of time.

Excavations at the tell verified the absolute chronology, which is similar to that at Vésztő-Mágor, and test excavations in other parts of the site verified our suspicions from the surface collections that although the tell was occupied from the end of the Middle Neolithic, the flat settlement around the tell expanded during the Late Neolithic (LN) and—like Vésztő-Mágor—the site was abandoned at the beginning of the Copper Age.

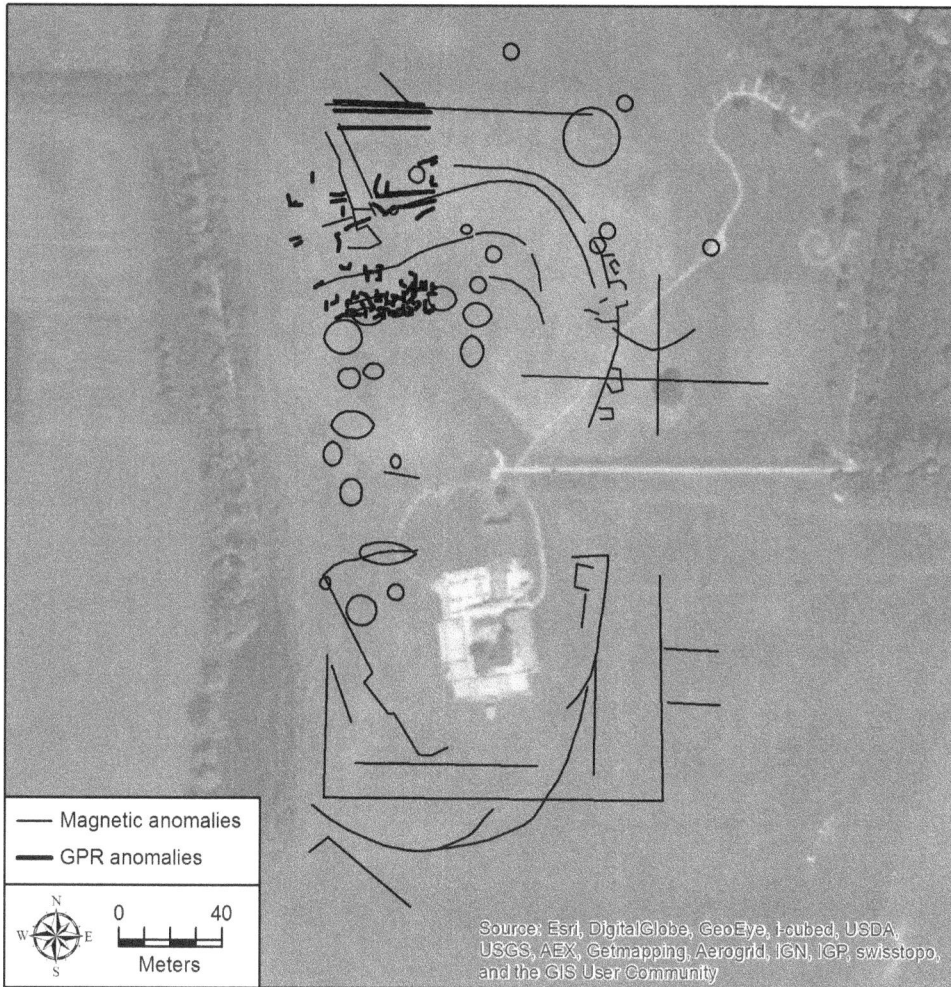

Figure 5.5   Map of Vésztő-Mágor showing geophysical anomalies (map by Rebecca Seifried, based on Sarris *et al.* 2013: fig. 10; background imagery from Esri ArcGIS Online World Imagery Basemap).

The picture that emerges from these microregional studies, which relate to local communities, puts flesh on the bones of the patterns derived from regional surveys, which include many communities (Figure 5.1). Even before we started our work in the Körös Region, thanks to our Hungarian predecessors, we knew that the LN was characterized by a tendency toward nucleation onto tell sites, but now we have a much better understanding of how that process of nucleation occurred on the ground and how it played out at different sites within their local topographies.

The Diros Project in Southern Greece

The second example comes from my work on the Diros Project on the Mani Peninsula of southern Greece. In collaboration with our colleagues Anastasia Papathanasiou of the Ephorate of Palaeoanthropology and Speleology and Takis Karkanas, Director

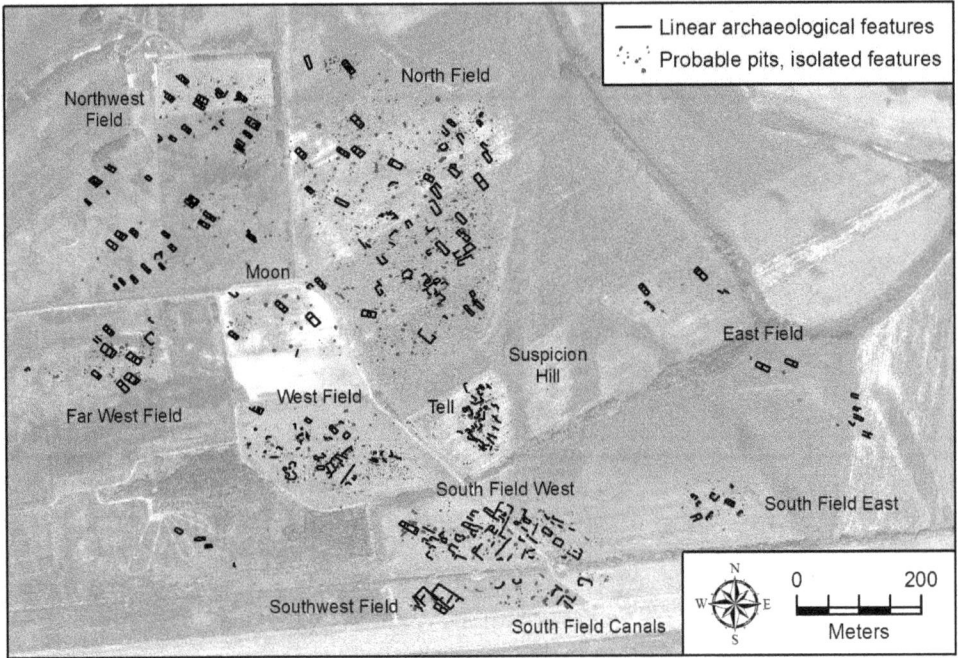

Figure 5.6 Map of Szeghalom-Kovácshalom showing geophysical anomalies (map by Rebecca Seifried, based on Gyucha *et al.* 2015: fig. 6).

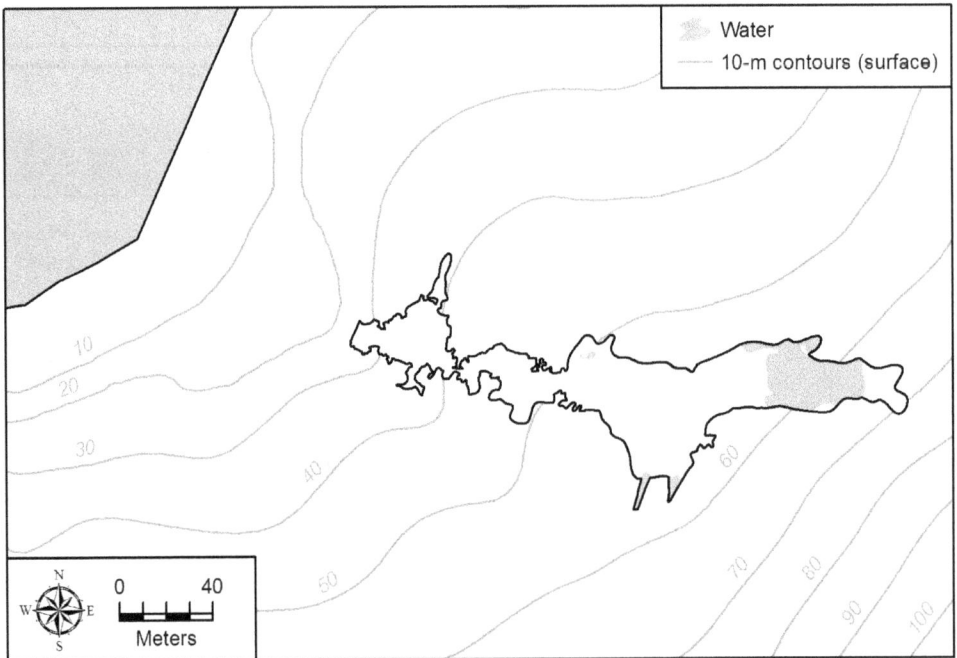

Figure 5.7 Map of Diros Bay showing the location and extent of Alepotrypa Cave (outlined in black), which opens toward the sea on the western end (map by Rebecca Seifried, elevation data from the National Cadastre & Mapping Agency S.A.).

of the Malcolm H. Wiener Laboratory for Archaeological Science at the American School of Classical Studies at Athens, Michael Galaty, Daniel Pullen, and I have been working to place the Neolithic site of Alepotrypa Cave into a regional context. Alepotrypa is a massive cave that was discovered in 1958, and it has been excavated by Giorgos Papathanassopoulos, now Honorary Ephor of Antiquities and Director of Excavations, since the late 1970s (Papathanassopoulos 1971a; 1971b; 1971c; 1983; 1996; see also Lambert 1971; 1972; Papathanasiou 1999; 2001; 2003; 2005; Papathanasiou *et al.* 2000). Our recent work in Diros has focused on (1) facilitating the analysis and publication of the materials that have been excavated from inside the cave, (2) conducting an intensive survey around Diros Bay in an attempt to identify other sites in the immediate vicinity of the cave, and (3) excavating a previously known site on the promontory in front of the mouth of the cave.

In most publications Alepotrypa is referred to as a Late and Final Neolithic (FN) site, but we now have the entire Neolithic sequence represented in many parts of the cave (Figure 5.7). The nearly 5-m deep sounding at the entrance, Trench B1, now has an absolute sequence that extends from the EN to the end of the FN. Some of the ossuaries in the cave also appear to have been used, if not continuously, then at least repeatedly, for thousands of years. There also is an area in the middle of the cave with stratified layers of burnt sheep dung that has yielded dates that extend from the end of the sixth millennium to the fourth millennium BC. Throughout the Neolithic, the center and back of the cave appears to have been used primarily for ritual activities, as indicated by the stratified burned deposits, burials, ossuaries, and dispersed fragmentary human bone. Although the front of the cave, too, has significant evidence for ritual activities—including ossuaries and burials—it also seems to have been used for more domestic tasks, as indicated by the distribution of faunal remains, lithics, and ceramic assemblages.

Our survey of the bay indicated that other than Alepotrypa Cave and the open-air site immediately outside its entrance on Ksagounaki Promontory, there was no substantial Neolithic habitation elsewhere in Diros Bay. To investigate the open-air site on Ksagounaki Promontory (Figure 5.8), located just north of the cave entrance, we conducted intensive gridded surface collections, geochemical studies, and geophysical surveys. We then initiated test excavations on the dilapidated modern terraces to expose the preserved Neolithic deposits. In one of our excavation blocks we identified the corner of a stone-built structure that dated to the beginning of the fourth millennium BC. The recent terrace fill and the intact Neolithic levels are loaded with fauna, ceramics, lithics, and small finds that indicate that there was a substantial settlement on the promontory during the FN.

In the other excavation unit we identified many overlapping burials, including a double baby burial, a burial of a couple buried in a 'spooning' position, and the burial of a half of a neonate that was placed inside a wall. All of these dated to the FN, within a few hundred years of 4000 BC. These burials were placed inside parallel linear terraces that were built with massive stones along the promontory. These Neolithic

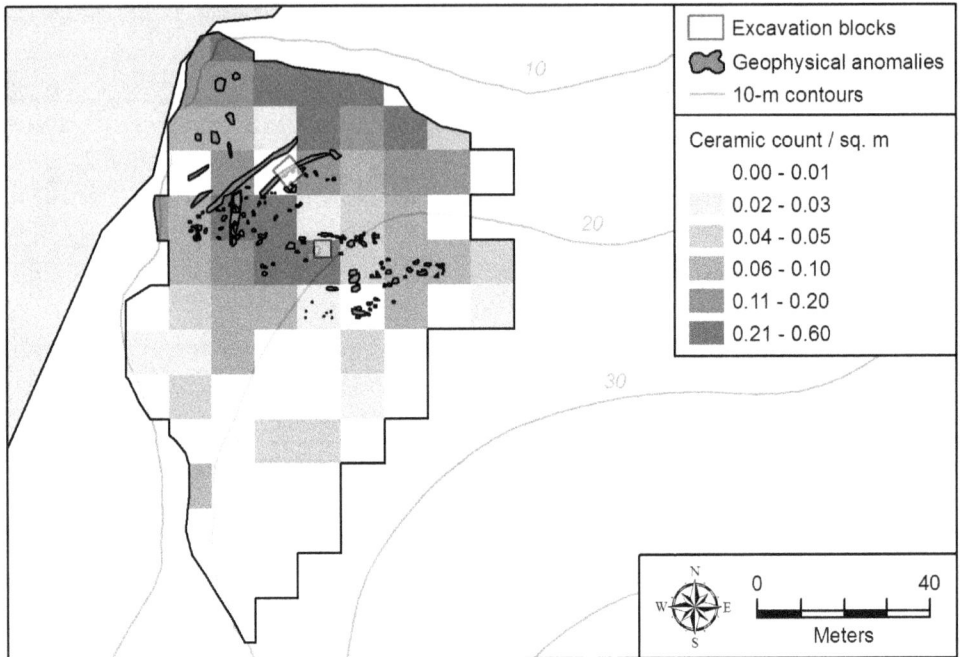

Figure 5.8   Map of Ksagounaki Promontory showing geophysical anomalies, intensively collected gridded surface units, and excavation blocks (map by Rebecca Seifried, elevation data from the National Cadastre & Mapping Agency S.A.).

architectural terraces are distinguishable from the more recent agricultural terraces, which are wider and follow the natural topography of the hill, and were made with much smaller rubble walls.

Our microregional research in Diros Bay has given us a much better understanding of how the settlement evolved over time. The cave had been used for thousands of years for burials and other rituals, but it was not until the FN that the site expanded onto Ksagounaki Promontory. Both the cave and the open-air site were abandoned at the end of the Neolithic, sometime around 3000 BC, and other than a small scatter of Early Helladic pottery at one site, the entire bay appears to have been abandoned until the Mycenaeans came back and built an ossuary directly on top of the Neolithic burials on the promontory, suggesting an intimate knowledge of the location.

Conclusions: The New 'New Wave' of Microregional Studies

Continental-scale syntheses are important for archaeology. If we archaeologists do not write syntheses ourselves, non-specialists will (and there are good and bad examples). But synthetic works must be kept honest by taking into account the vast amount of regional variation that has emerged in the last few decades, thanks in large part to the hard work of John Cherry and his like-minded colleagues. In the same way that regional studies can inform macro-scale syntheses, they in turn can benefit from microregional studies that help explain and flesh out the patterns that emerge at broader chronological and geographic scales.

In the examples discussed here, for example, we have been able to model how regional-scale patterns played out at the local, microregional scale. Our detailed investigations revealed in each case that the phenomenon of settlement nucleation occurred only after the long-term use of the site. In Neolithic Hungary, both sites were used for several hundred years from the Middle Neolithic period but then exploded in size during the LN. Yet, despite the regional tendency toward nucleation and increased site size, the microregional trajectory of each site was considerably different. In the case of Vésztő-Mágor, this resulted in a large, nucleated, fortified tell settlement with no surrounding horizontal settlement. In the case of Szeghalom-Kovácshalom, the tell did not grow substantially but the site exploded, with several groups of longhouses covering a massive area around the small tell. In Diros, Alepotrypa Cave had been the focus of funerary rituals and other activities for thousands of years before the establishment of the single-component FN site on Ksagounaki Promontory. In each case, the sites were used for generations before they began to attract people in significant quantities. When the sites began to grow, they seem to have grown quickly. Similarly, when they were abandoned, they seem to have been abandoned quickly. These microregional patterns have implications with regards to the causal models we use to explain the regional patterns that occurred within these different Neolithic social trajectories. Whereas some have attributed the evolution of nucleated settlements to the need for defense in other Neolithic contexts (see, for example, Runnels *et al.* 2009), in the cases discussed here people seem to have been pulled to these centers for different economic or religious reasons.

These microregional studies build upon a long history of similar work in the Mediterranean. Early examples of this approach include the investigation of Neolithic (Cherry *et al.* 1988) and classical (Alcock 1991) sites in Nemea, albeit without the benefit of geophysical data. Davis and his colleagues carried out similar microregional studies in Messenia to understand Mycenaean settlements (Davis *et al.* 1997; see also Bennet 1999). The integration of geophysics and soil chemistry, along with aerial and satellite imagery, has taken microregional studies to an unprecedented level in recent years (e.g., Sarris *et al.* 2004; Parkinson *et al.* 2012; Sarris *et al.* 2013).

The detailed analysis of the microregion is in some ways the brave new world of regional studies, made possible through developments not only in survey methodology, but also in archaeological geophysics and soil chemistry. Combined with a theoretical perspective that approaches the archaeological landscape at multiple temporal and geographic scales, microregional studies promise to be the next 'new wave' of archaeological research.

Acknowledgments

This chapter builds upon a paper I presented at the 2012 Society for American Archaeology Annual Meeting in Memphis that was co-authored with Attila Gyucha, Paul Duffy, and Rick Yerkes and focused on our archaeological research in the Carpathian

Basin (Parkinson *et al.* 2012). Fittingly, that paper was presented in a session that Tom Leppard, Brad Sekedat, and Parker VanValkenburgh co-organized to celebrate the 30th anniversary of John Cherry's (1983) 'Frogs round the pond' article. It was a real honor to be invited to participate in Cherry-fest (as it came to be known) and to contribute to this volume. I thank Alex Knodell and Tom Leppard for putting this all together; I am also grateful to Rebecca Seifried for her assistance with maps. I first learned about the legend of John Cherry when I was taking an undergraduate class with Jack Davis at the University of Illinois at Chicago. John's work on the evolution of Minoan states was required reading. Jack was in the process of leaving UIC for the Blegen Professorship at Cincinnati and he encouraged me to go work with John, who had just arrived at the University of Michigan, where I was entering into the graduate program in Anthropology. John served on my dissertation committee and over the last two decades I have gotten to know John as a mentor, a colleague, a drinking buddy, and a friend. I am thrilled to have been a part of this much deserved celebration of his research.

About the Author

William A. Parkinson is Associate Curator of Eurasian Anthropology at the Field Museum of Natural History and Adjunct Associate Professor of Anthropology at the University of Illinois at Chicago. His research interests include the evolution of agricultural villages in the Neolithic and the emergence of bureaucratic states in the Bronze Age. He co-directs the Körös Regional Archaeological Project in Hungary and the Diros Project in Greece. His publications include *Archaic State Interaction* (SAR, 2010) and *Rethinking Mycenaean Palaces* (Cotsen, 2007), both co-edited with Michael Galaty, as well as recent articles in the *Journal of Archaeological Science*, *Hesperia*, and the *American Journal of Archaeology*. E-mail: wparkinson@fieldmuseum.org

References

Alcock, S.E.
  1991   Urban survey and the polis of Phlius. *Hesperia* 60: 421-63.
Alcock, S.E., and J.F. Cherry
  2004   Introduction. In S.E. Alcock and J.F. Cherry (eds.), *Side-by-Side Survey: Comparative Regional Studies in the Mediterranean World*, 1-12. Oxford: Oxbow Books.
Bennet, J.
  1999   Pylos: the expansion of Mycenaean palatial center. In M.L. Galaty and W.A. Parkinson (eds.), *Rethinking Mycenaean Palaces: New Interpreta-* *tions of an Old Idea*. Monograph 41: 9-18. Los Angeles: Cotsen Institute of Archaeology.
Binford, L.
  1964   A consideration of archaeological research design. *American Antiquity* 29: 425-41.
Cherry, J.F.
  1983   Frogs around the pond: perspectives on current archaeological survey projects in the Mediterranean region. In D. Keller and D. Rupp (eds.), *Archaeological Survey in the Mediterranean Area*. British Archaeological

Reports, International Series 155: 375-415. Oxford: British Archaeological Reports.

Cherry, J.F., J.L. Davis, A. Demitrack, E. Mantzourani, T.F. Strasser and L.E. Talalay
  1988 Archaeological survey in an artifact-rich landscape: a Middle Neolithic example from Nemea, Greece. *American Journal of Archaeology* 92: 159-76.

Davis, J.L., S. Alcock, J. Bennet, Y. Lolos and C. Shelmerdine
  1997 The Pylos Regional Archaeological Project. Part I: overview and the archaeological survey. *Hesperia* 66: 391-494.

Ecsedy, I., L. Kovács, B. Maráz and I. Torma
  1982 *Magyarország Régészeti Topográfiája* VI. *Békés Megye Régészeti Topográfiája: A Szeghalmi Járás* IV/1. Budapest: Akademiai Kiadó.

Galaty, M.L., H. Tomas and W.A. Parkinson
  2014 Bronze Age European elites: from the Aegean to the Adriatic and back again. In A.B. Knapp and P. van Dommelen (eds.), *The Cambridge Prehistory of the Bronze and Iron Age Mediterranean*, 157-77. New York: Cambridge University Press.

Gallis, I.K.
  1992 *Ἄτλας προϊστορικῶν οικισμῶν τῆς Ανατολικῆς Θεσσαλικῆς πεδιάδας.* Larisa: Society of Historical Research of Thessaly.

Gamble, C.
  1999 *The Palaeolithic Societies of Europe.* Cambridge: Cambridge University Press.

Gyucha, A.
  2015 *Prehistoric Village Social Dynamics: The Early Copper Age in the Körös Region.* Prehistoric Research in the Körös Region 2. Budapest: Archaeolingua Publishing.

Gyucha, A., R.W. Yerkes, W.A. Parkinson, N. Papodopoulos, A. Sarris, P.R. Duffy and R.B. Salisbury
  2015 Settlement nucleation in the Neolithic: a preliminary report of the Körös Regional Archaeological Project's investigations at Szeghalom-Kovácsh-

alom and Vésztő-Mágor. In S. Hansen, P. Raczky, A. Anders and A. Reingruber (eds.), *Neolithic and Copper Age Between the Carpathians and the Aegean Sea: Chronologies and Technologies from the 6th to the 4th Millennium BCE. International Workshop Budapest 2012.* Archäologie in Eurasien 31: 129-42. Bonn, Germany: Verlag Dr. Rudolf Habelt.

Jankovich, D., J. Makkay and B.M. Szőke (eds.)
  1989 *Magyarország Régészeti Topográfiája* VIII. *Békés Megye Régészeti Topográfiája: A Szarvasi Járás* IV/2. Budapest: Akadémiai Kiadó.

Jankovich, D., P. Medgyesi, E. Nikolin, I. Szatmári and I. Torma (eds.)
  1998 *Magyarország Régészeti Topográfiája* X. *Békés és Békéscsaba* IV/3. Budapest: Akadémiai Kiadó.

Kristiansen, K., and T. Larsson
  2005 *The Rise of Bronze Age Society: Travels, Transmissions, and Transformations.* Cambridge: Cambridge University Press.

Lambert, N.
  1971 Fouilles Franco-Helléniques a la grotte d'Aléopetrypa. *Athens Annals of Archaeology* 4: 199-202.
  1972 Grotte d'Aléopetrypa (Magne). *Bulletin du Correspondence Helléniques* 96: 845-71.

Lubbock, J.
  1865 *Pre-Historic Times, as Illustrated by Ancient Remains and the Manners and Customs of Modern Savages.* London: Williams and Norgate.

Papathanasiou, A.
  1999 A Bioarchaeological Analysis of Health, Subsistence, and Funerary Behavior in the Eastern Mediterranean Basin: A Case Study from Alepotrypa Cave, Greece. Unpublished PhD dissertation, University of Iowa, Des Moines, Iowa.
  2001 *A Bioarchaeological Analysis of Neolithic Alepotrypa Cave, Greece.* British Archaeological Reports, International Series 961. Oxford: British Archaeological Reports.

2003 Stable isotope analysis in Neolithic Greece and possible implications on human health. *International Journal of Osteoarchaeology* 13: 314-24.

2005 Health status of the Neolithic population of Alepotrypa Cave, Greece. *American Journal of Physical Anthropology* 126: 377-90.

Papathanasiou, A., C.S. Larsen and L. Norr

2000 Bioarchaeological inferences from a Neolithic ossuary from Alepotrypa Cave, Diros, Greece. *International Journal of Osteoarchaeology* 10: 210-28.

Papathanassopoulos, G.A.

1971a Σπήλαια Διρού, 1971. *Athens Annals of Archaeology* 4: 289-303.

1971b Σπήλαια Διρού, 1971 (αι ανασκαφαί του 1970-1971). *Athens Annals of Archaeology* 4: 12-26.

1971c Σπήλαια Διρού, 1971 (εκ των ανασκαφών της Αλεπότρυπας). *Athens Annals of Archaeology* 4: 149-54.

1983 Ο ναυτικός χαρακτήρας του νεολιθικού Διρού. In *Proceedings of the First Local Conference of Laconic Studies*, 221-24. Athens: Peloponnesian Studies Society.

1996 (ed.) *Neolithic Civilization in Greece*. Athens: Goulandris Foundation.

Parkinson, W.A., and M.L. Galaty

2010 Introduction: interaction and ancient societies. In W.A. Parkinson and M.L. Galaty (eds.), *Archaic State Interaction: The Eastern Mediterranean in the Bronze Age*, 3-28. Santa Fe, New Mexico: School for Advanced Research Press.

Parkinson, W.A., and A. Gyucha

2012 Tells in perspective: long-term patterns of settlement nucleation and dispersal in central and southeast Europe. In R. Hoffman, F.-K. Moetz and J. Müller (eds.), *Tells: Social and Environmental Space*, 105-16. Bonn, Germany: Verlag Dr. Rudolf Habelt.

Parkinson, W.A., A. Gyucha, P.R. Duffy and R.W. Yerkes

2012 On the shoulders of giants: regional and micro-regional studies in the prehistoric Carpathian Basin. Paper presented at the Society for American Archaeology Annual Meeting, Memphis, Tennessee.

Parkinson, W.A., A. Gyucha, R.W. Yerkes, M.R. Morris, A. Sarris and R.B. Salisbury

2010 Early Copper Age settlements in the Körös region of the Great Hungarian Plain. *Journal of Field Archaeology* 35: 164-83.

Runnels, C.N., C. Payne, N. Rifkind, C. White, N.P. Wolff and S. LeBlanc

2009 Warfare in Neolithic Thessaly: a case study. *Hesperia* 78: 165-94.

Sarris, A., M. Galaty, R. Yerkes, W.A. Parkinson, A. Gyucha, D. Billingsley and R. Tate

2004 Geophysical prospection and soil chemistry at the Early Copper Age settlement of Vésztő-Bikeri, southeastern Hungary. *Journal of Archaeological Science* 31: 927-39.

Sarris, A., N. Papadopoulos, A. Agapiou, M.C. Salvi, D.G. Hadjimitsis, W.A. Parkinson, R.W. Yerkes, A. Gyucha and P.R. Duffy

2013 Integration of geophysical surveys, ground hyperspectral measurements, aerial and satellite imagery for archaeological prospection of prehistoric sites: the case study of Vésztő-Mágor tell, Hungary. *Journal of Archaeological Science* 40: 1454-70.

van Andel, T.H., K. Gallis and G. Toufexis

1994 Early Neolithic farming in a Thessalian river landscape, Greece. In J. Lewin, M.G. Macklin and J.C. Woodward (eds.), *Mediterranean Quaternary River Environments*, 131-43. Rotterdam: A.A. Balkema.

van Andel, T.H., and C.N. Runnels

1995 The earliest farmers in Europe. *Antiquity* 69: 481-500.

Whittle, A.

1996 *Europe in the Neolithic: The Creation of New Worlds*. Cambridge: Cambridge University Press.

Yerkes, R.W., A. Gyucha and W.A. Parkinson

2009 A multi-scalar approach to modeling the end of the Neolithic on the Great Hungarian Plain using calibrated radiocarbon dates. *Radiocarbon* 51: 1071-109.

Part II

Crossing Scales in the Later Mediterranean

Introduction to Part II: Crossing Scales in the Later Mediterranean

Alex R. Knodell and Thomas P. Leppard

The Aegean is in many ways a microcosm of the wider Mediterranean, not only in its fractal geography, but also in the social and cultural processes that are built on this geography. There is a natural progression, then, from papers that deal with the emergence and structure of complex societies in the Bronze Age Aegean to a wider remit concerning the historical Mediterranean, especially interactions between the Mediterranean super-polity of Rome and the societies and geographies it would eventually encompass, namely in Greece, Turkey, and the Mediterranean islands. The chapters in this section—by Fachard, Sekedat, and Smith and van Dommelen—reflect John Cherry's own broader interest in the archaeology of the Mediterranean writ large.

Two magisterial studies have defined what a truly Mediterranean story might look like for archaeologists working in the region in the twenty-first century. Horden and Purcell's *The Corrupting Sea* (2000) and Broodbank's *The Making of the Middle Sea* (2013) can be understood as part of a broader burgeoning of interest in 'big history'; they serve to validate the usefulness of attempting truly large-scale studies of human social, political, and economic organization in Mediterranean Eurasia and Africa. In building upon such large-scale histories, we detect a growing need to cross regional scales, or rather to articulate between the geographical parameters of archaeological studies in ways that address meaningfully how human societies range from the local to the continental and beyond. The papers in this section do precisely this, all having in common local and regional responses to broader Mediterranean phenomena, especially (for Fachard and Sekedat) the specter of Rome, following in part a tone set by Alcock's *Graecia Capta* (1993).

Sekedat's paper begins with a review of the role of survey archaeology in studies of the Roman empire, arguing that while comparative regional studies have been in decline in recent years, the growing number of datasets from across the empire makes such studies timelier (and more necessary) than ever, especially if oriented around new questions that incorporate recent theoretical work on imperial dynamics. He then takes a multi-scalar approach to make inferences about the large-scale organization of the Roman economy from the locally exploited marble quarries of eastern Turkey, drawing in also examples from elsewhere to examine an industry that spanned the Roman empire (and Mediterranean basin).

Boundaries—their creation, iteration, and also transgression, whether drawn by incipient democracies, Hellenistic dynasts, or archaeologists—are another Mediterranean theme. Fachard explores the social and physical manifestation of boundaries through Pausanias's *Description of Greece*, as part of a growing interest in territoriality and liminality. Border studies have long been of interest to historians and anthropologists (e.g., Rosler and Wendl 1999; Lee and North 2016), but they are a topic of increasing interest for archaeologists as well, as we explore how best to study physical definitions of territory and polity when written explication and demarcation is not forthcoming (e.g., Lightfoot and Martinez 1995; Naum 2010; Osborne and Van Valkenburgh 2013). We reflect more generally on the dynamic relationship between the environment and human action in Chatper 16, but speculate here that the repeated appearance of lines on conceptual maps of the Mediterranean—crossed Rubicons, the boundary stones of the Peloponnese, Thiessen polygons drawn around Neolithic villages—derives in part from the fractured nature of the Mediterranean, time and again fitting cycling, emergent complex social forms into similar geographic molds.

Smith and van Dommelen turn their attention earlier, as they consider the long use-lives of monumental architecture on Menorca and Sardinia. They examine how the archaeological imagination has become fixed within certain periods and places for certain monuments in attempting a west Mediterranean—rather than a Sardinian or a Menorcan—archaeology. A deeper homology between these two and between the new pan-Mediterraneanism, however, is their focus on parts of the Mediterranean littoral that might be considered, at best, less-than-central places and, at worst, parochial, at least from the perspective of urban, literate elites. Southern Menorca, the hill country north of Marmara Gölü, and the Campidano have arguably never been enormously important; in this sense, then, they are probably very *good* places to start building archaeologies that focus not on exceptions, but on Mediterranean commonalities. Braudel's (1972) timeless Mediterranean peasant does not need resurrection, but looking intensely at how local conditions specified and framed human responses—and how these responses can be generalized from the local to the regional and beyond—is surely a good foundation for Mediterranean archaeology.

We note in the introduction to this volume that it has long been recognized that Mediterranean archaeologists are an essential part of conversations concerning the comparative archaeology of states and empires (e.g., Cherry 1992; Alcock *et al.* 2003). The papers in this section use case studies from Turkey, Greece, and the western Mediterranean to demonstrate the need to cross scales and integrate specific studies of localities and regions in articulations of macroregional, colonial, and imperial dynamics. These papers also highlight the diversity of approaches and datasets relevant to regional archaeology. Comparative archaeological survey data is applied to a study of the Roman industrial economy (Sekedat); a textual analysis of Pausanias is translated into a geopolitical study of territory and liminality in Roman Greece (Fachard); and a study of the life of monuments illuminates local/colonial dynamics in the landscapes of two western Mediterranean islands (Smith and van Dommelen). We should embrace such diversity in approaches to understanding how societies operate and interact on regional scales and beyond. Further need for comparison, as well as criticality, specificity, and articulation are explored in the final part of this volume.

About the Authors

Alex R. Knodell is Assistant Professor of Classics and Co-Director of the Archaeology Program at Carleton College, Northfield, Minnesota. He currently co-directs the Mazi Archaeological Project (northwest Attica, Greece) and previously served as Field Director of the Brown University Petra Archaeological Project (Petra, Jordan). Other research interests include the development of complex societies in the Late Bronze Age and Early Iron Age Mediterranean, especially in relation to the Euboean Gulf of Greece. Recent articles have appeared in the *American Journal of Archaeology*, *Antike Kunst*, the *Journal of Archaeological Science*, the *Journal of Field Archaeology*, and *World Archaeology*. E-mail: aknodell@carleton.edu

Thomas P. Leppard is Renfrew Fellow in the McDonald Institute for Archaeological Research at the University of Cambridge. His research concerns the comparative archaeology of island societies in the Mediterranean, Caribbean, and Pacific, especially issues of colonization, mobility, and emergent social complexity. Recent articles on these subjects have appeared in *Human Ecology*, the *Cambridge Archaeological Journal*, *Current Anthropology*, the *Journal of Island and Coastal Archaeology*, the *Journal of Mediterranean Archaeology*, and *World Archaeology*. He currently conducts fieldwork in Micronesia and Sardinia. E-mail: tpl26@cam.ac.uk

References

Alcock, S.E.
   1993   *Graecia Capta: The Landscapes of Roman Greece*. Cambridge: Cambridge University Press.
Alcock, S.E., T.E. D'Altroy, K.D. Morrison and C.M. Sinopoli (eds.)
   2003   *Empires: Perspectives from Archaeology and History*. Cambridge: Cambridge University Press.
Braudel, F.
   1972   *The Mediterranean and the Mediterranean World in the Age of Phillip II*. New York: Harper and Row.
Broodbank, C.
   2013   *The Making of the Middle Sea: A History of the Mediterranean from the Beginning to the Classical Age*. London: Thames and Hudson.
Cherry, J.F. (ed.)
   1992   *The Archaeology of Empires*. Special issue of *World Archaeology* 23(3).
Horden, P., and N. Purcell
   2000   *The Corrupting Sea: A Study of Mediterranean History*. Malden, Massachusetts: Blackwell.
Lee, J.W.I., and M. North (eds.)
   2016   *Globalizing Borderlands Studies in Europe and North America*. Lincoln: University of Nebraska Press.
Lightfoot, K.G., and A. Martinez
   1995   Frontiers and boundaries in archaeological perspective. *Annual Review of*

Anthropology 24: 471-92. https://doi.org/10.1146/annurev.an.24.100195.002351

Naum, M.
2010 Re-emerging frontiers: postcolonial theory and historical archaeology of the borderlands. *Journal of Archaeological Method and Theory* 17: 101-31. https://doi.org/10.1007/s10816-010-9077-9

Osborne, J.F., and P. Van Valkenburgh (eds.)
2013 *Territoriality in Archaeology.* Special issue of *Archaeological Papers of the American Anthropological Association* 22.

Rösler, M., and T. Wendl
1999 *Frontiers and Borderlands: Anthropological Perspectives.* New York: Peter Lang.

6 Industrial Landscapes, Spatial Politics, and Settlement Change in the Roman East

Bradley M. Sekedat

Introduction

The scope of this paper deals somewhat broadly with the trajectory of survey archaeology as a comparative project for studies of the Roman Mediterranean. In particular, I aim to develop two primary threads of discussion, based on preliminary observations of industrial landscapes in the central and eastern empire. The first thread suggests that efforts to create large-scale syntheses of survey projects have given way to more isolated applications of survey methodologies, to the detriment of research questions that depend on comparative datasets. The second thread aims to show that new research questions in studies of the Roman economy, with a particular emphasis on landscapes of production, offer suitable ways to reinsert site types as a mechanism for understanding changing settlement dynamics in response to the expansion of the Roman empire. I argue that although the comparison of survey data has become more complicated in the light of an ever-increasing set of surveys, we are able to better understand changing social dynamics in the Roman world by asking, and answering, different questions of our comparative data. By focusing on regions with industrial-scale stone quarries that were active during the Roman imperial period, I demonstrate that survey data is not merely the product of local variability, but that variability corresponds to changing access to social and economic opportunities.

Developments in Survey Archaeology

In his seminal paper entitled 'Frogs round the pond' (1983), John Cherry discussed some of the strengths and weaknesses of archaeological survey. Among a list of five limitations was a comment that survey data had not been particularly useful in determining site function or variation within sites. Quite obviously, this is because of the way subsurface assemblages become plowsoil assemblages—an often messy process that mixes stuff up in conditions that are also susceptible to movement, slippage, slumping, etc. The kinds of stuff we tend to get from survey therefore are not always great at telling us about what people were doing on the ground during times of active habitation at those sites.

In the face of these conditions, many archaeologists have taken up the cause of trying to do more with the data they have. In practice, this has taken many forms, including the application of geophysical and geochemical testing alongside survey, as well as an ever-increasing level of intensity. The former is exemplified by survey work in Laconia (Cavanagh *et al.* 2005), the latter by a host of projects that aim to ramp up site coverage all over the Mediterranean and beyond, including those in Turkey, with which I am most familiar (see also, in this volume, Knodell and Leppard; Parkinson). The Central Lydia Archaeological Survey, for instance, applied what it called 'hyper-intensive' survey to both a set of marble quarries and several known fortified Bronze Age sites, trying to parse out some spatial patterns in short-lived settlements (Roosevelt and Luke 2008; 2009; 2010; 2011; 2012). Although these projects have met with some success, the refinement of conclusions based on survey data is still something we grapple with today, especially as they relate to large-scale (in this case imperial) social processes.

This shift toward greater intensity within survey practice parallels developments in classical and Mediterranean Archaeology more generally. Over the last 30 years, for instance, scholars have taken great strides in pushing beyond the '-izations' that long ruled macrolevel and microlevel interpretations of culture change. These include Romanization, Hellenization, and so on. Books such as Mattingly's (1997) edited volume on discrepant experience, Hingley's (2005) text on Roman identity, alongside other theoretical changes brought about during the postprocessual, postcolonial, and postmodern period have all gone some way toward establishing the significance of multivocality and individual response to external changes as the primary goal of a contextual interpretation of the material record.

These changes, of course, have been welcome developments in the face of an interpretative model that had been far too top-down in orientation. Individual agency has brought the discipline into conversation with new developments in other fields in ways that had been lacking before, in particular by giving voice to the nuanced understandings of political and social dynamics that were necessarily ignored under the previous regime. Diversity is now embraced as a natural aspect of the ancient world, and intensive survey projects have contributed to the growth in significance of local response to supra-regional changes.

This shift in thinking, it turns out, is partly the inevitable byproduct of the simple act of doing more research. As more sites of more variety were uncovered throughout the Roman empire, the diversity of materials, manufacturing techniques, and evident signs of local significance have been marshaled to erect a Roman empire that was less homogenous than ever before thought. Such work includes Murphy and Poblome's (2012) study of local craft production techniques, but also the sheer plurality of material styles that pervade ceramic assemblages from across the empire. The center-out spread of ideas and things is dead—at least by comparison to its former appearance.

This affected the survey world by diminishing interest in producing comparative studies from different regions of the Mediterranean and beyond. This strikes me as somewhat unusual, given the great effort invested during the 1990s and early 2000s to argue in favor of the comparability of survey data in spite of variation in survey design, environmental conditions, or collection techniques. The POPULUS volumes (especially Francovich *et al.* 2000), as well as Alcock and Cherry's (2004) edited volume on *Side-by-Side Survey* put forth compelling arguments that spoke to the necessity of survey design to respond to local conditions, while still facilitating trans-regional analysis of broader trends. These, of course, followed Alcock's studies of survey data within Achaia (Alcock 1993) and throughout the Hellenistic world (Alcock 1994), which effectively demonstrated the success of comparative projects. Some attempts still persist, such as Witcher's (2008) reanalysis of survey in parts of central Italy, but survey has taken an unexpected turn of sorts.

Just as much of Roman archaeology turned toward renewed interest in the merits of local responses to local circumstances, so too did survey begin a more inward trajectory that was partly the product of more data. The number of survey projects, and the range of modern countries in which Mediterranean-style survey is practiced, has increased tremendously over the past 30–40 years. Nevertheless, although we have a few examples of attempts to generalize survey trends in certain places, such as Turkey (Doonan 2012), the aim is seldom to compare datasets, but to show the breadth and diversity of projects. Scholars are appropriately identifying internal motivations for the patterns they see on the ground, which is, on the one hand, necessary. On the other hand, I would argue that this also limits the scope of the conversations we are able to have. We should be able to have a conversation about responses to broad changes in sociopolitical circumstances while maintaining regional (and subregional) individuality.

Superficially, the move away from broad-scale comparisons stems from the difficulty we have comparing data collected in different regions under different conditions. But it seems to have more to do with the fact that some of the questions we traditionally ask of survey data no longer work in the face of increasing regional variation. If, however, we asked different questions, the data might once again lend themselves to comparative goals. Asking how social life changed in response to Roman expansion is simply too broad to capture the multi-scalar nature of the Roman world. The question should be rephrased to assume variability yet also facilitate comparability.

Developments in Studies of the Roman Economy

One of the places where such grappling with multi-scalar networks is most visible in the Roman world is in studies of the economy. Here, one of the topics within Roman history and archaeology that receives the most attention is whether Rome can be characterized as a market economy. This question has persisted, in fact, for roughly a century, taking on various shapes and labels with each iteration of the debate. Ranging from formalist versus functionalist issues to concerns about the appropriateness of gauging an ancient economy while using modern terminology, and to the current and more subtle contention surrounding the degree of interconnectivity and whether economies that take place in markets equate to market-based economies, a tremendous amount of time and energy has been invested in understanding the nature of Rome's economy.

The reason this question has received so much attention is that the outcome of the debate has ramifications for how the empire itself is understood. Indeed, many debates surrounding the efficacy of the Roman state, the extent of its hegemony, and the extent of its cultural influence, if not exactly dependent on questions of economy, at least have a shared interest in the results of economic studies. Explorations of Roman politics, religion, governance, trade, industry, culture, language, and so on require information about how systems operate on a scale as large as the entirety of the Roman empire. Economy has the benefit of being one of the more available and abundant forms of evidence, with its fingers seemingly in every pot. The intersections between economy and all aspects of Roman society (and non-Roman societies) are innumerable and are capable of bridging the yawning gap between a highly centralized imperial apparatus and the households that such an empire comprises—a gap that is similar to the shift reflected in survey developments described above.

Archaeological studies have contributed a great deal in this regard, though the evidence can often appear contradictory. Wilson (2009; see also Wilson *et al.* 2012), for example, enumerates an impressive array of archaeological data that positively correlate with economic growth and an expansive and integrated economy. He includes in his summary such material as marble, amphorae and their associated contents (many of which are assumed rather than positively identified and include olive oil, grain, wine, and fish products), and fine table wares (Wilson *et al.* 2012). More critical to Wilson's argument is the notion that this trade is long-distance in nature, including material from throughout the empire. The increasing availability of goods from far-away places during the imperial period, and in the abundance attested archaeologically, is indeed a strong indicator of a robust and far-reaching infrastructure for the distribution of goods.

As Bang (2011) points out, however, and as others have pointed out also (e.g., de Ligt 1993; Mitchell 2005), there are potentially serious problems with the correlation Wilson draws between robust long-distance trade and a pervasive market economy. Bang notes that more than 50% of the population living within the boundaries of the Roman empire should be classified as 'peasants', for whom integration into a Mediterranean-wide economic structure was unlikely and who provide little to no indication of such active market roles. Studies in Anatolia, for instance, demonstrate that although there is growth in agricultural productivity, there is still little evidence for integration into a hegemonic economic structure, save the use of a centralized system of coinage (de Ligt 1993; Mitchell and Katsari 2005). Uniform coinage is not, however, the same thing as a highly integrated economic system that governs the actions and motivations of the majority of people within a political entity—Lydia, Athens, and even the modern examples of many Latin American states are examples of this. Instead, Roman imperial-period evidence is equally robust for small-scale systems as it is for the kinds of empire-wide trade that Wilson (2009) and Wilson *et al.* (2012) discuss, and evidence for long-distance trade of goods from different regions in the empire is therefore not a suitable proxy for a pervasive economic system within the empire.

There is an unfortunate blending of issues: economic growth (for which there is an irrefutable amount of evidence) and a pervasive economic system are occasionally taken to be one and the same thing. What complicates this more is that a substantial amount of evidence for economic growth during the Roman imperial period comes from the very geographic locations where the peasantry predominates. As mentioned above, agricultural output grew in many areas of the empire, and in several ways. On the one hand is the evidence for growth in terms of agricultural yield in already productive regions, signaling an increase in intensive farming. Another kind of growth, however, is seen in the long-discussed push into the semi-arid desert of North Africa, where marginal lands were cultivated for the exportation of olive oil (Barker 1996). This growth, although certainly more intensive than previous agricultural patterns in semi-arid zones, also represents an expansion of agriculturally productive areas and, in some cases, the production of new markets for trade as a by-product. Indeed, several of the imperially owned quarries that were newly 'opened' during the imperial period (those in Egypt and Tunisia foremost among them) were located in marginal landscapes, indicating that this phenomenon was not limited to grain, oil, and wine.

Scholarship by Smith (1989) and Russell (2009; 2013) on the significance of stone in the Roman economy has clear contributions to make in this debate. The notion of consumer-driven artistic practices in Roman imperial sculpture is established by Russell's (2009) important demonstration that some quarries yielded stone that was particularly sought after by consumers as well, bridging the gap between artisans and resources, and suggesting that at least a portion of the Roman economy is not redistributive in character. This last point is critical, offering as it does evidence for the integration of different industries—a necessary component of a market-based economy. The acquisition of stone to provide for private sculptural programs occurred when market conditions (i.e., a buyer was in place) accommodated it.

From the producer end of the equation, however, the issue becomes murkier, with contradictory and conflicting evidence. Cuvigny (1996) and others (e.g., Fant 1988; 1989a; Hirt 2010) provide evidence for at least some form of centralized oversight of the imperially owned quarries in the form of standard payments, titles, and perhaps block sizes (see Ward Perkins 1973), while Maxfield (2000; 2002) and Maxfield and Peacock (2001) demonstrate some military oversight of imperial quarries in some portions of the empire. What is unfortunately not known is the degree to which this kind of oversight extends to the range of quarries that existed in the imperial period, including the very small quarries that are most numerous throughout and the quarries associated with major urban centers (Sekedat 2016). These smaller, less well-documented or studied quarries are often overlooked because of the more secure documentary evidence from large imperial quarries that regrettably come to stand in for the whole, neglecting a substantial amount of information that can shed light on important issues relating to the nature of the Roman economy. Russell's commendable list of quarries throughout the Roman empire and the amount of evidence for sculptural production are revealing in this regard; that is, the quantity of stone traded and utilized for architectural and sculptural programs in the empire does not come close to accounting for the amount of stone quarried during this period, suggesting that both the redistributive model for absolute centralized control and the consumer-driven model are limited in their reach. In Spain and Turkey, for instance, careful documentation of the several smaller-scale quarries has revealed variation in standards of measurement and in the tools used to extract marble (Gutiérrez Garcia-Moreno and Rodà de Lanza 2012).

Two issues present themselves here. First, these data, though still robust, do not overturn the mounting evidence for limited networks in the countryside that prevail in other parts of the Mediterranean (Mitchell and Katsari 2005). And second, rather than providing support for the presence of a widespread economic system that incorporates all aspects of Roman society, this instead seems to support an alternative model whereby the Roman state makes its presence felt in some areas, while leaving others to operate in a less formal, yet equally viable, manner. De Ligt's (1993) study of different marketplaces in the empire demonstrates this aptly. Different scales of market exist, serving in some ways as proxies for connectivity, while simultaneously upholding local networks. When phrased in the terminology of network analysis, empire-wide Roman markets are served by a few, strong, long-distance ties, though predominantly comprised of strong local ties and very weak long-distance ties. Furthermore, although modern comparisons have their limitations, similar (not identical) systems have long been the target of economic studies of undeveloped and developing nations, wherein multiple economic systems exist side-by-side, often in a symbiotic relationship (frequently called 'informal' or 'shadow' economies: Smith 1989). In the face of data that support a pervasive economic system as derived from a few instances of well-documented villas, the evidence for local networks seems strong, and the rarity of such places as Vindolanda seems significant; rather than assuming that a preponderance of the Roman world followed similar systems, we should combine such data with those produced by such examples as de Ligt's (1993) work on markets.

The larger, more integrated, and rational a system, the greater the expectation for rules governing practice, and the greater the expectation for uniformity of those practices over the span of a political entity. Or, if it truly is a market-driven economy, then we should expect evidence of finance-driven ingenuity to drive increased profits. Since marble was one of the products that appealed to the imperial regime, urban centers, benefactors, and wealthy individual collectors, the stone industry should yield evidence for the kind of overarching system within which it operated. Evidence abounds for both types, suggesting that the expression of a Roman economy was not limited in scope to the security of either finances or resources, central as these are.

An Argument for New Questions

Given the ability of the economic data to contribute to expansive discussions of multi-scalar systems at work within the empire at the same time, the reticence to compare survey projects of late is problematic. Instead of exploring how a given location is at one and the same time connected and distinct from broader trends, and instead of asking how landscapes in different parts of the empire negotiated their role in a complex political system, surveys are increasingly reliant on local social and landscape conditions as the primary explanatory models. Surely this is part of the answer, and it is important to note that recognizing local conditions appropriately responds to what often were overly coarse definitions of cultural processes in years past. But an interregional, comparative approach within the empire, when tied to the political economy, may prove instructive, too.

For scholarship on the Roman empire, the relationship between people and the landscape has never been more critical. New research emphasizes the role of space and spatial practices in establishing new political relationships—a topic right at home in the context of expanding Roman political hegemony throughout the Mediterranean and beyond. Identifying how and where the Roman political and economic apparatus intersected with local populations, and in which ways this resulted in any kind of noticeable change, remains hugely significant for understanding how the empire operated at its basic level. Moreover, imperial things, such as quarries, mines, and monuments, become significant not just as indicators of economic and political change, but as the potential means by which the empire constituted itself in its vast territorial expanse. In essence, we can further contextualize survey data within a very high level notion of site function and, in particular, imperially owned industrial sites. Because I am most familiar with this in terms of imperial quarries, I restrict my focus to these.

This, I argue, is where a merging of distinct research trajectories can be particularly informative. Survey data have helped in the characterization of settlement trends as local responses to higher-level changes, while economic studies have provided persuasive evidence for the persistence of multiple scales of interaction. Exploring the survey data in areas that have traditionally fallen under the umbrella of economic studies might, in this regard, prove useful—we can explore the extent to which these broad trends really do reflect these changing scales. Thus, instead of asking generally how people throughout the Mediterranean responded to a new and expanding Roman presence, we can ask whether specific, new, Roman things, such as enormous imperial quarries or mines, acted to reorient social life in the regions where they operated. In other words, does social life around imperial quarries change in the Roman period, and are these changes distinct from settlement patterns that prevail elsewhere in a given region?

The Landscapes around Quarries

The traditional allure of studying things like marble stems from the material's connection to questions of power, economy, and labor. As such, imperial quarries tend to straddle the divide between economy and political intent. Marble quarries, and quarries for rare stones especially, have long indicated the presence of both economic growth and conspicuous (imperial) consumption. They traditionally represent the ability to control resources and are thus a symbol of the material manifestation of power. For example, Hirt (2010: 368) suggests for the city of Rome itself that:

> [T]he supply of Rome with marbles from different corners of its empire was, in comparison, a costly affair and seemingly not always subjected to an entrepreneurial rationale. The use of marble in the display of imperial wealth and power was the main reason for its extraction. In other words, the emperors had remote quarries worked not for the profit of the treasury, but simply because they had the capability to do so.

For other cities in other places, the local aristocracy was perhaps participating in conspicuous consumption, too. Russell (2013) and Smith (1989) argue just such a thing in noting that most statuary from Aphrodisias and other cities in Asia Minor was produced by local artisans for local patrons using local stone. Russell (2013) in particular demonstrates the strength of local ties by comparing the ratio of local marble used in Asia Minor versus non-local marbles used. The cost of transportation apparently was prohibitive in the vast majority of cases, resulting in wealthy individuals driving production of goods that met local customs and preferences.

Underneath this conspicuous consumption, however, and underneath the signs of power and economic prowess, are other social indicators of change that are subtler in nature and perhaps more meaningful for the communities in marble-rich regions.

The first question is: what is happening socially around quarries in the eastern Roman empire? Frustratingly, the number of intensive survey projects in the vicinity of imperially owned marble quarries is comparatively rare (Figure 6.1). In only a few cases do scholars specifically target them to better understand settlement dynamics (see Tankosić and Chidiroglou 2010). Instead, several projects have targeted the inner workings of stone-cutting operations. At several large-scale marble sources on Euboea, for example, detailed surveys were conducted on the size of quarries, the kinds of tool marks used for extraction, and related infrastructure—such as roads, wells for draft animals, surveillance areas, etc.—within and surrounding the quarry complex (e.g., Vanhove 1996). The evidence points to a complex and integrated series of operations and materials connecting the quarry to the surrounding landscape, with a proliferation of infrastructural elements in the Roman period.

In the eastern desert of Egypt we see again signs of change and increased intensity, including newly founded villages, outposts, and roads, all connected to the extractive operations. The same with Simitthus in North Africa, at Dokimeion in Turkey, and to a lesser degree at Teos, where Fant (1989b) documented signs of internal coordination, record keeping, and so forth—all indications of interest in the coordination of labor and technical aspects of marble extraction.

We do have some survey evidence from areas near major quarries, even though the presence of a major stone source was not the impetus for the location of the survey in those regions. Leaving behind the eastern Mediterranean briefly, an early example comes from Luna in northern Italy. Here, survey conducted around the ancient city and in the foothills, approximately 7–10 km from the sources of Carrara marble,

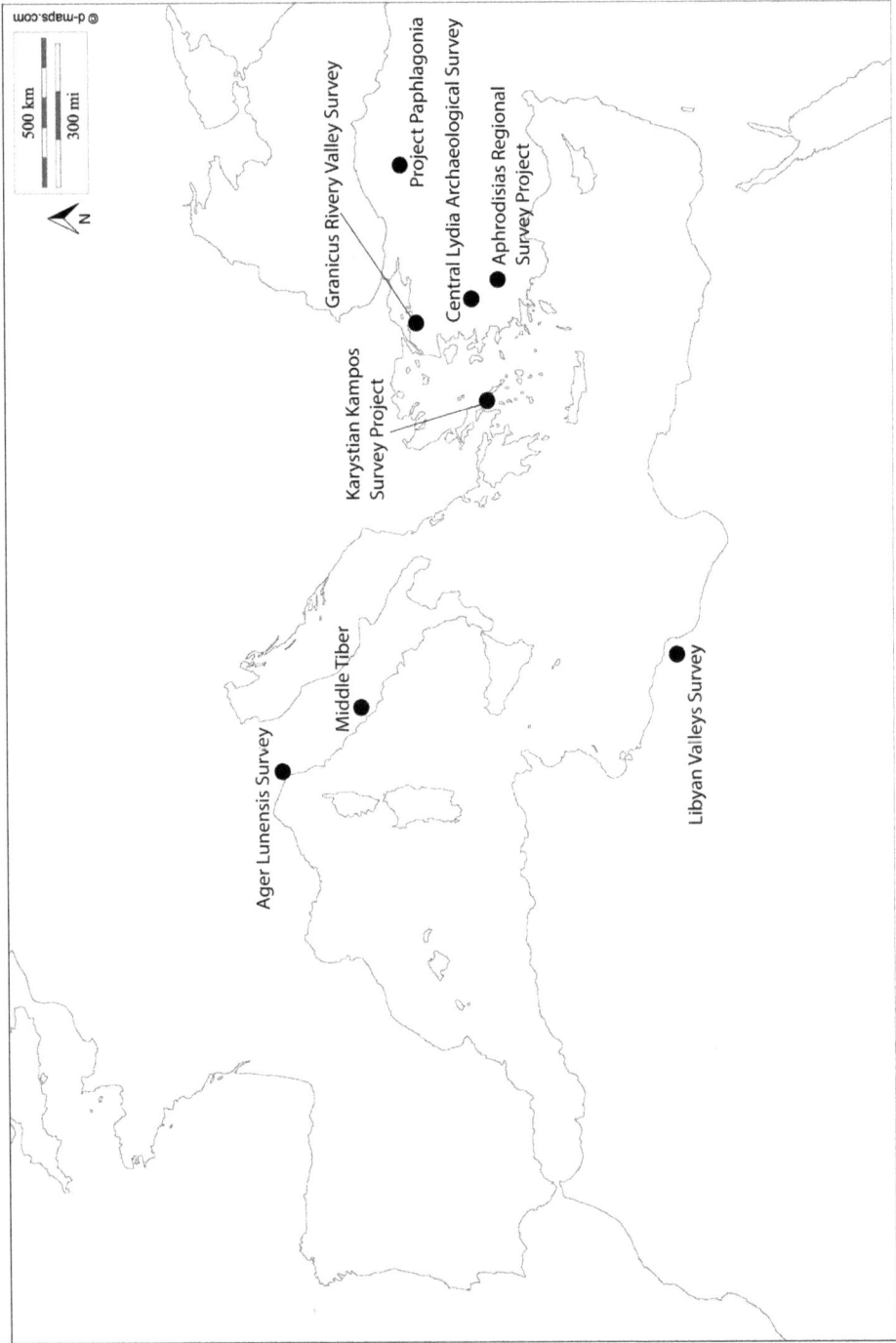

Figure 6.1   Location of survey projects discussed in the text.

revealed a pattern of probable demographic growth during the late republic without corresponding increases in agricultural sites (Delano Smith *et al.* 1986). Directors there interpret these data as indicative of growth related to alternative forms of economic success (Delano Smith *et al.* 1986). Likewise, on Euboea, the early Roman period saw higher aggregate site numbers in the vicinity of Karystos and Marmari, which occurred at a time corresponding to a significant increase in stone-cutting operations (Tankosić and Chidiroglou 2010). At Proconnesus in northwestern Turkey, new settlement structures are indicated, though available maps are poor and it is not fully understood whether these correspond to habitation, industry, or both (Asgari 1973). At Dokimeion, the source of the famous Pavanazetto marble, which has a purplish hue, the quarry operations are hard to study due to continued extraction of marble from ancient branches, but a number of settlements arose in the immediate environment of the Upper Tembris river valley that were frequently related to military outposts and other new settlement foundations (Mitchell 1993).

The data are even more compelling around the cities of Asia Minor. The countryside surrounding Sardis and Aphrodisias, for example, both reveal major upticks in site numbers during the Roman period as well as the opening of more than a dozen quarries in each region (Roosevelt and Luke 2008; 2012; 2013; Ratté and De Staebler 2012).

Lest we think that this is an indication of an overall trend in Roman-period land use intensity, it is worth comparing these patterns to those of other surveys in Greece and Turkey. Although I cannot present a comprehensive discussion here, there are clear signs that the growth in site numbers during the Roman period is not universally the case. Numerous regions of Greece, for example, yield evidence for nucleation and aggregate site reduction that differ from Euboean evidence (Alcock 1993). In Anatolia, the Granicus River valley near Troy yields the same (Rose *et al.* 2007), as did Project Paphlagonia further east (Matthews and Glatz 2009). Roman expansion did not, therefore, mean ubiquitous expansion of settlement intensity in Anatolia, a conclusion already well known for Greece from Alcock (1993).

Interpreting the variation between surveys is not, however, a straightforward endeavor. By this I mean that it likely is not as simple as quarries = growth, and non-industrial zones do not. Instead, a complex interplay likely exists between settlement change, industrial opportunities, and other factors. The fact that cities and quarries tend to go hand in hand shows the reciprocal nature of these things. It is difficult to draw definite conclusions, but the patterns do speak to something more complicated than uniform change in settlement throughout any given region in response to Rome's arrival. Rome's influence was felt unevenly, often through major acts of spatial intervention that reinforced the social and political changes in a given region.

Most of the quarries that were imperially owned existed prior to the Roman period. Their output, however, expanded. Classical- and Hellenistic-period stone extraction is best characterized as project-by-project, on an as-needed basis for both monumental construction and small-scale local projects. These same quarries were used in the

Roman period for export. Roman-period extraction therefore did not appear *ex nihilo*, but built on traditions, knowledge, and expertise already present in new territorial acquisitions. Indeed, there was almost certainly a sharing of knowledge among skilled laborers of the pre-imperial Roman period. Greek and Lydian stonemasons, the latter especially famous for their skill, are known to have interacted, and Rome certainly took advantage of itinerant labor as well. Roman-period quarrying did, however, happen on a considerably larger scale (Figure 6.2).

The Bacakale quarries at Dokimeion, for instance, yielded on the order of 500,000 cu m of marble during a 90-year period from 90–180 AD (Russell 2009). The marble quarries at Proconessos, on the island of Marmara, must also have yielded several hundred thousand cubic meters of marble, and other imperial quarries yielded similar volumes of stone (Russell 2009). Another way to conceptualize this is in terms of horizontal coverage. Teos, a source of green marble in western Turkey, was relatively small at 0.25 sq km, while one branch at Dokimeion called Bacakale was nearly 0.5 sq km in area (Hirt 2010). The quarries at Simitthus in North Africa, sitting on an urban zone, covered more than 1 sq km (Hirt 2010). Mons Claudianus in Egypt is considerably larger, with 130 open cast quarries covering several square kilometers (Maxfield and Peacock 2001). This increase in the scale of extractive operations is important for understanding economy and trade, but it also signals a change in relations between governing bodies, populations, and the material world.

This is in part because of proximity, since quarries tended to be located close to settled areas. This issue remains challenging, however, since the few instances of ancient authors who mention quarries indicate some kind of separation. In the *Natural History*, for example, Pliny the Elder (36.24) implies that those privy to industrial landscapes saw fanciful things, like the regrowth of marble. The reality on the ground, however, is that it was quite common for imperial quarries, and quarries generally, to be located near towns of somewhat prominent size. At Dokimeion, Proconnesus, Teos, Karystos, Styra, Marmarion, Luna (Carrara), Paros, Corduba, Ephesos, Aphrodisias, and so on, towns existed in the immediate vicinity of the imperial quarry, often supplying the labor needed for them. Moreover, the quarries were well connected to surrounding regions and to regional emporia via the Roman network of roads. The communities that lived near the quarries engaged with tangible cues that indicated a reorientation of social and material relationships in the region, both in the form of the quarryscapes themselves and in the form of the infrastructure associated with the movement of stone and other goods.

There were also broader changes to settlement and society in the countryside that were significant for industrial landscapes. The overall settlement dynamic of the eastern Roman provinces, for instance, shifted away from the countryside toward nucleated settlements, partly a result of early imperial Roman laws designed to change the land tenure system. This resulted in the countryside of the Roman East becoming seeming sparsely populated compared to earlier periods, because a system of small farmsteads inhabiting the area surrounding the owner's fields was replaced by a system of fewer

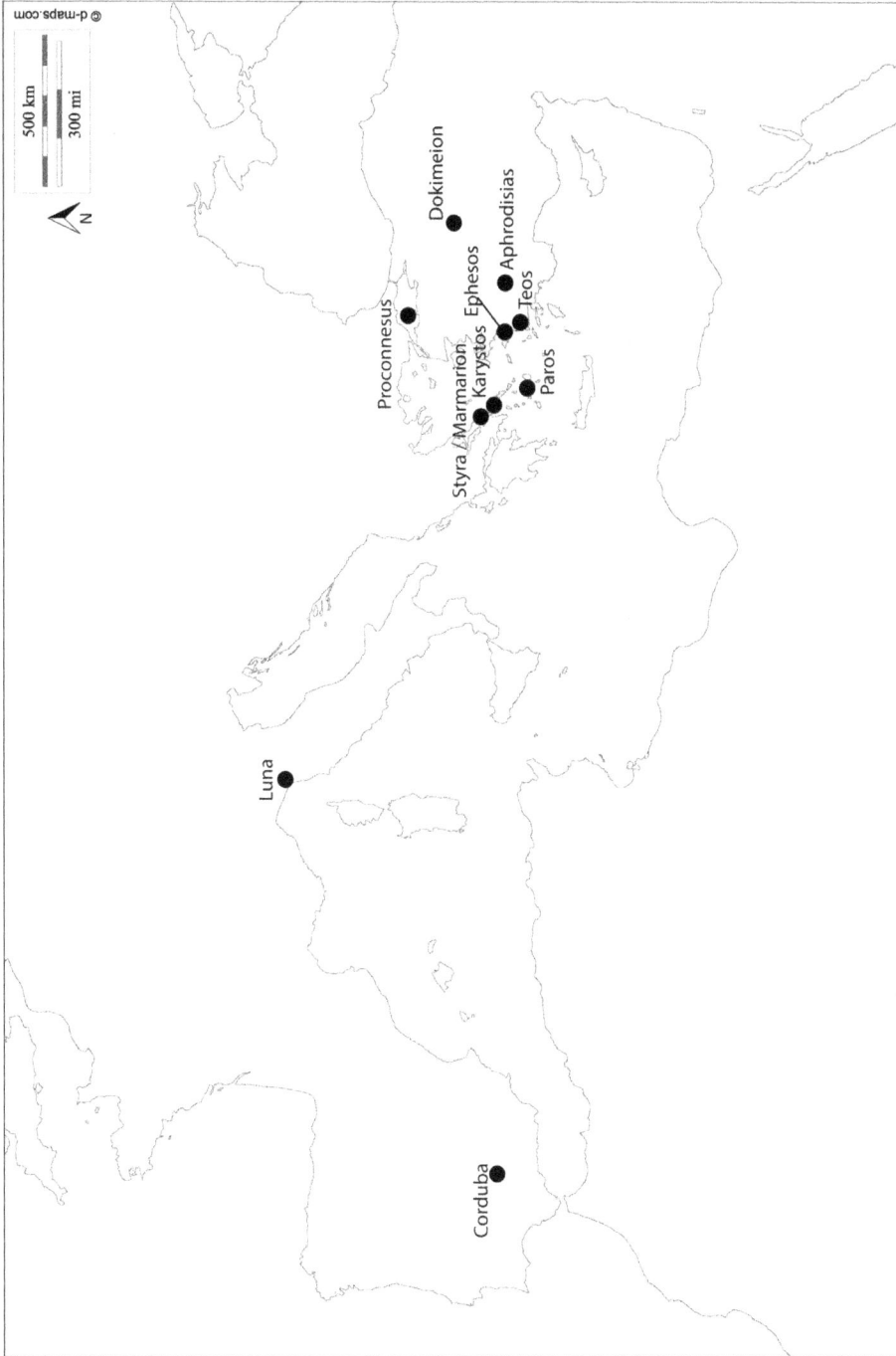

Figure 6.2   Location of major quarries mentioned in the text.

but larger estates, with people living in towns and villages 'commuting' to work each day. The trend is visible in Roman Greece and Asia Minor, though in modern Turkey, Hellenistic-period settlement was also low due to different geopolitical circumstances and a preference for elevated sites (Alcock 1993; Rose *et al.* 2007).

However, there are indications that this shift was not as clear-cut as a simple preference for urban sites in the principate. In some areas, even in regions generally characterized by nucleation, settlement numbers did climb. For example, the Southern Euboea Exploration Project, on the island of Euboea just off the coast of Attica in Greece, covered an area between the marble-rich districts of Marmarion and Karystos, where they identified a growth in the number of rural sites during the Roman period, although a detailed discussion of these sites is still lacking (but see Tankosić and Chidiroglou 2010). The *Ager Lunensis* near the town of Luni, outside of Carrara, Italy, has also been surveyed intensively (Delano Smith *et al.* 1986). Luni lies on the Tyrrhenian Sea, some 7 km from Carrara, whose quarries were active during the empire as well. Here, too, settlement numbers grew during the imperial period, to the point that agricultural production could not sustain the local population (Delano Smith *et al.* 1986). The surveys around Mons Claudianus and Mons Porphyrites also show growth, but their location in the desert makes them exceptional cases.

We therefore have two major developments from a landscape perspective. First, the quarries that became imperial possessions exhibit the intensification of existing stone-working practices. Second, settlement and social organization in the provinces change in varying ways, including nucleation as a general trend in the east alongside some indications that industrial regions witnessed increased levels of settlement and land use. This does not strike me as all that surprising, due to potentially positive associations between industrial operations and personal gain. Participation in quarry operations contributed positively toward upward mobility on the part of the lower rungs of the Roman aristocracy.

Additionally, laborers were often wage earners, a fact that flies in the face of the prevailing assumption that stone was extracted by slaves and prisoners. There were, in short, benefits to living near industrial operations, which are borne out in the textual evidence and the archaeological data. But what is the link between settlement preference and empire? How does this factor into a discussion of spatial politics?

First, the extractive processes, which are firmly rooted in material landscapes, compel a fundamentally different relationship between provincial inhabitants and their environment. The marble-yielding landscapes were seldom the main consumers of stone in the imperial period. The settlements near Proconnesos, for example, yield little evidence for the use of marble during the principate. Instead, the majority of the stone was sent first to Nicomedia, then redistributed to ports throughout the eastern and central Mediterranean. A similar pattern emerges for the quarries at Dokimeion, where the quarries that yielded the especially rare type of marble called *pavonazzetto* were cut for the export market (Waelkens 1985; Fant 1989a). This material appears in many of the major urban centers of Asia Minor, such as the so-called Terrace Houses at Ephesos, where the stone is found as wall veneer and as *opus sectile* floor tiles. From a very basic level, the social relations surrounding the extraction of marble in the Roman period differ from pre-Roman contexts, both in terms of scale and in terms of use. Substantially more stone is produced, but its use changes from local projects to almost exclusively non-local projects. Work also shifts from project-by-project production to one of 'full-time' production at quarries by people who might never see the fruits of their labor in any local architectural examples.

The two most commonly cited explanations for military involvement—that the army protected the supply from theft, damage, raiding, etc., and that the army enforced slave or convict labor—are too restrictive (Hirt 2010). Evidence for theft is absent from the ancient sources, save the example of the Eastern Desert in Egypt, for which a system of roads and forts was constructed, and epigraphic evidence points to a wage labor system with only periodic instances of convict labor. Hirt's (2010) study reveals a plurality of administrative practices at quarries that defy simplistic understandings of military involvement or labor practices. There surely was keen interest in placement of the military near valuable resource sites, but a strictly functional approach does not capture the rationale adequately.

I suggest that during the early imperial period, when Rome was attempting to enact political authority in new places, landscape modification played a critical role. The type of intensive state presence in regions of imperial quarries is not a consistent feature of Roman provincial administration. Instead, what we see are places where the empire is highly active, connected to other places by large-scale networks that run alongside a series of smaller networks. If we were to expand this study to the many thousands of comparatively tiny quarries active during the Roman period, we would, for instance, see that the signs of imperial involvement are not there: tool technologies are different, and the use of stone varies tremendously, including in the construction of dams, roads, and other more mundane things.

From the perspective of relational space, then, the changes to the scale of operations, to the pattern of consumption, and to the proximity of quarries to settlements, along with rural change in general and around industrial sites in particular, and to the presence of the military, all indicate a reconfiguration of relationships between provincial populations, political authorities, and local landscapes during the imperial period. Because these changes entail both coercive and contextual elements, they are necessarily part of the social and political aspects of spatial relations and, to my mind, compel us to think beyond intrinsic value or elite display. The punctuated pattern of imperial involvement in quarries reflects the broader trend of the early Roman empire to be present enough to demonstrate authority and political superiority in far away places—a technique of governance designed to reorient social practices through specific and large-scale interactions with the physical landscape.

The proliferation of survey projects throughout the eastern Mediterranean naturally brings with it projects that identify internally significant patterns of settlement density, material consumption, and social interactions with the landscape. This is obviously a very good thing, since it emphasizes that local responses change. But I think we can retain some of the individuality of each region while also pointing to emerging trends that bring them into communication with each other. Here, one emerging trend appears to be that industrial sites, cities, and harbors facilitated new economic and social practices in the early Roman empire. These were, to some extent, reflected in the choice of where to live during this period, which actually corresponds quite well to new scholarship on the Roman economy, which is similarly stuck trying to straddle the divide between local practices and broad-scale trends. Major quarries are one of the features in the landscape that seem to pull activity toward them, just as they distribute their material outwards.

Conclusions

To conclude, I offer a brief reflection on what this means for the overall story of the Roman polity. To begin with, the data beg for more research. Three regions are not enough to convincingly argue for a pattern within an empire the size of Rome. I would argue, however, that this speaks to pre-existing preferences among scholars for the hinterland of various cities as the starting point for survey design, while pointing to new potentially informative areas. To a certain extent, this entails a new set of questions more suitable to a comparison of survey evidence. Indeed, demonstrating what major landscape interventions on the part of the Roman state mean for local populations in the various places of the empire where they occur demands a comparative approach. The evidence presented here does point to industrial landscapes changing in distinct ways throughout the Roman imperial period.

Moreover, the available evidence suggests that Rome was aware of the political ramifications of spatial practices, often deliberately playing with them as a means of reconfiguring sovereignty throughout the empire. The quarries that yielded special or rare stones were, naturally, few in number. They nevertheless operated in more ways than one. To clarify, this argument does not require replacing the economic models of stone extraction or marble consumption with a new model, but it does indicate that quarries played a much more profound role in the landscape. Instead of providing for the state merely because the state could have what it wanted, or because the consumer elite could compel activity, quarries also served, in some cases, as the center of new landscape patterns that modified the social networks so prevalent in economic discussions.

Acknowledgments

Many thanks to Tom Leppard and Alex Knodell for the invitation to participate in the conference and resulting volume. And special thanks, of course, to John Cherry for his profound influence on the field and on my way of thinking.

About the Author

Bradley M. Sekedat is a Lecturer at the University of California, Davis. His research explores survey methodology and industrial practices in the eastern Roman empire. He is Assistant Director for Survey of the Central Lydia Archaeological Project. Recent articles have appeared in the *Oxford Journal of Archaeology*, the *Journal of Roman Archaeology*, and *Archaeolog*. E-mail: bsekedat@ucdavis.edu

Classical Authors and Texts

Pliny the Elder, *Natural History*.

References

Alcock, S.E.
  1993 *Graecia Capta: The Landscapes of Roman Greece*. Cambridge: Cambridge University Press.
  1994 Breaking up the Hellenistic world: survey and society. In I. Morris (ed.), *Classical Greece: Ancient Histories and Modern Archaeologies*, 171-90. Cambridge: Cambridge University Press.
Alcock, S.E., and J.F. Cherry (eds.)
  2004 *Side-by-Side Survey: Comparative Regional Studies in the Mediteranean World*. Oxford: Oxbow Books.
Asgari, N.
  1973 Roman and early Byzantine marble quarries of Proconnesus. In E. Akurgal (ed.), *Proceedings of the Xth International Congress of Classical Archaeology*, 467-80. Ankara: Türk Tarih Kurumu Basimevi.
Bang, P.
  2011 *The Roman Bazaar: A Comparative Study of Trade and Markets in a Tributary Empire*. Cambridge: Cambridge University Press.
Barker, G. (ed.)
  1996 *Farming the Desert: The UNESCO Libyan Valleys Archaeological Survey*. Ann Arbor: University of Michigan Press.
Cavanagh, W., C. Mee and P. James
  2005 *The Laconia Rural Sites Project*. British School at Athens Supplementary Volume 36. London: British School at Athens.
Cherry, J.F.
  1983 Frogs round the pond: perspectives in current archaeological survey projects in the Mediterranean region. In D. Keller and D. Rupp (eds.), *Archaeological Survey in the Mediterranean Area*. British Archaeological Reports, International Series 155: 375-416. Oxford: Archaeopress.
Cuvigny, H.
  1996 The amount paid to the quarry-workers at Mons Claudianus. *Journal of Roman Studies* 86: 139-45. https://doi.org/10.2307/300426
de Ligt, L.
  1993 *Fairs and Markets in the Roman Empire: Economic and Social Aspects of Periodic Trade in a Pre-Industrial Society*. Amsterdam: J.C. Gieben.
Delano Smith, C., D. Gadd, N. Mills and B. Ward-Perkins
  1986 Luni and the *Ager Lunensis*: the rise and fall of a Roman town and its territory. *Papers of the British School at Rome* 54: 81-146. https://doi.org/10.1017/S0068246200008862
Doonan, O.
  2012 Surveying landscapes: some thoughts on the state of survey archaeoogy in Anatolia. *Backdirt* (2012): 118-36.

Fant, J.C.

1988 The Roman emperors in the marble business: capitalists, middlemen or philanthropists? In N. Herz and M. Waelkens (eds.), *Classical Marble: Geochemistry, Technology, Trade*, 147-58. Dordrecht and Boston: Kluwer Academic Publishers. https://doi.org/10.1007/978-94-015-7795-3_16

1989a *'Cavum Antrum Phrygiae': The Organization and Operations of the Roman Imperial Marble Quarries in Phrygia*. British Archaeological Reports, International Series 482. Oxford: Archaeopress.

1989b *'Poikiloi Lithoi'*: the anomalous economics of the Roman imperial marble quarry at Teos. In S. Walker and A. Cameron (eds.), *The Greek Renaissance in the Roman Empire: Papers from the Tenth British Museum Classical Colloquium*, 206-18. London: Institute of Classical Studies.

Francovich, R., H. Patterson and G. Barker (eds.)

2000 *The Archaeology of Mediterranean Landscapes 5. Extracting Meaning from Ploughsoil Assemblages*. Oxford: Oxbow Books.

Gutiérrez Garcia-Moreno, A., and I. Rodà de Llanza

2012 El mármol de Luni-Carrara en la fachada Mediterránea de Hispania. In S. Keay (ed.), *Rome, Portus and the Mediterranean*, 293-312. London: British School at Rome.

Hingley, R.

2005 *Globalizing Roman Culture: Unity, Diversity and Empire*. London and New York: Routledge.

Hirt, A.M.

2010 *Imperial Mines and Quarries in the Roman World: Organizational Aspects 27 BC–AD 235*. Oxford: Oxford University Press. https://doi.org/10.1093/acprof:oso/9780199572878.001.0001

Matthews, R., and C. Glatz (eds.)

2009 *At Empire's Edge: Project Paphlagonia Regional Survey in North-Central Turkey*. London: British Institute at Ankara.

Mattingly, D.J. (ed.)

1997 *Dialogues in Roman Imperialism: Power, Discourse and Discrepant Experience in the Roman Empire*. Journal of Roman Archaeology Supplementary Series 23. Ann Arbor, Michigan: Journal of Roman Archaeology.

Maxfield, V.

2000 The deployment of the Roman auxilia in Upper Egypt and the Eastern Desert during the principate. In G. Alfoldy, B. Dobson and W. Eck (eds.), *Kaiser, Heer und Gesellschaft in der Römischen Kaiserzeit*, 407-44. Stuttgart: Franz Steiner Verlag.

2002 Armies and quarries: a preliminary look at the evidence from Roman Egypt. In P.R. Hill (ed.), *Polybius to Vegetius: Essays on the Roman Army and Hardrian's Wall Presented to Brian Dobson to Mark his 70th Birthday*, 69-81. Durham: Hadrianic Society.

Maxfield, V., and D. Peacock

2001 *The Roman Imperial Quarries: Survey and Excavation at Mons Porphyrites, 1994-1998 I. Topography and Quarries*. London: Egyptian Exploration Society.

Mitchell, S.

1993 *Anatolia: Land, Men, and Gods in Asia Minor I. The Celts and the Impact of Roman Rule*. Oxford: Clarendon Press.

2005 Olive cultivation in the economy of Roman Asia Minor. In S. Mitchell and C. Katsari (eds.), *Patterns in the Economy of Roman Asia Minor*, 83-113. Swansea: Classical Press of Wales.

Mitchell, S., and C. Katsari

2005 Introduction: the economy of Roman Asia Minor. In S. Mitchell and C. Katsari (eds.), *Patterns in the Economy of Roman Asia Minor*, xiii-xxxii. Swansea: Classical Press of Wales.

Murphy, E., and J. Poblome

2012 Technical and social considerations of tools from Roman-period ceramic workshops at Sagalassos (southwest Turkey): not just tools of the trade?

Journal of Mediterranean Archaeology 25: 197-217.

Ratté, C., and P. De Staebler (eds.)
2012 *The Aphrodisias Regional Survey.* Aphrodisias 5. Darmstadt: Philipp von Zabern.

Rose, B., B. Tekkök, R. Körpe *et al.*
2007 The Granicus River Valley Archaeological Survey Project, 2004-2005. *Studia Troica* 17: 65-150.

Roosevelt, C.H., and C. Luke
2008 Central Lydia Archaeological Survey: 2006 results. *Araştırma Sonuçları Toplantısı* 25(3): 305-26.

2009 Central Lydia Archaeological Survey: 2007 results. *Araştırma Sonuçları Toplantısı* 26(2): 433-50.

2010 Central Lydia Archaeological Survey: 2008 results. *Araştırma Sonuçları Toplantısı* 27(2): 1-24.

2011 Central Lydia Archaeological Survey: 2009 results. *Araştırma Sonuçları Toplantısı* 28(3): 55-74.

2012 Central Lydia Archaeological Survey: 2010 results. *Araştırma Sonuçları Toplantısı* 29(1): 383-400.

2013 Central Lydia Archaeological Survey: 2011 Work at Kaymakçı and in the Marmara Lake Basin. *Araştırma Sonuçları Toplantısı* 30(1): 237-54.

Russell, B.
2009 Sculpted Stone and the Roman Economy, 100 BC–AD 300. Unpublished PhD dissertation, University of Oxford, Oxford, United Kingdom.

2013 *The Economics of the Roman Stone Trade.* Oxford: Oxford University Press. https://doi.org/10.1093/acprof:oso/9780199656394.001.0001

Sekedat, B.M.
2016 X-ray fluorescence and stable isotope analysis of marble in central Lydia, western Turkey. *Oxford Journal of Archaeology* 35: 359-78. https://doi.org/10.1111/ojoa.12094

Smith, M.E.
1989 The informal economy. In S. Plattner (ed.), *Economic Anthropology*, 292-317. Stanford, California: Stanford University Press.

Tankosić, Ž., and M. Chidiroglou
2010 The Karystian Kampos Survey Project: methods and preliminary results. *Mediterranean Archaeology and Archaeometry* 10: 11-17.

Vanhove, D.
1996 *Roman Marble Quarries in Southern Euboea and the Associated Road Systems.* Leiden: E.J. Brill.

Waelkens, M.
1985 From a Phrygian quarry: the provenance of the statues of the Dacian prisoners in Trajan's Forum at Rome. *American Journal of Archaeology* 89: 641-53. https://doi.org/10.2307/504205

Ward Perkins, J.B.
1973 Quarrying in antiquity: technology, tradition and social change. *Proceedings of the British Academy* 57: 137-58.

Wilson, A.I.
2009 Approaches to quantifying Roman trade. In A. Bowman and A.I. Wilson (eds.), *Quantifying the Roman Economy: Methods and Problems*, 213-49. Oxford: Oxford University Press. https://doi.org/10.1093/acprof:oso/9780199562596.003.0009

Wilson, A.I., K. Schörle and C. Rice
2012 Roman ports and Mediterranean connectivity. In S. Keay (ed.), *Rome, Portus and the Mediterranean*, 367-91. London: British School at Rome.

Witcher, R.E.
2008 The Middle Tiber Valley in the Imperial period. In F. Coarelli and H. Patterson (eds.), *Mercator Placidissimus: The Tiber Valley in Antiquity. New Research in the Upper and Middle River Valley*, 467-96. Rome: Quasar.

7 Political Borders in Pausanias's Greece

Sylvian Fachard

In no land, which has been depopulated, is it easy to discover the truth about the boundaries. (Pausanias, *Description of Greece* 2.28.2)

Introduction

In the course of his long tour of the province of Achaia, Pausanias crossed dozens of political borders separating Greek *poleis*. His record of these in his *Description of Greece* provides us with a rare insight into the geography of borders and borderlands in the second century AD—no other Greek author offers such an account of the position and nature of political limits. Arguably, he is also the only one looking for them in the landscape. While other authors use a variety of words and compounds to describe the notion of border, Pausanias is among the few to distinguish himself for his lexical clarity, as ὅρος and μεθόριος are the commonest words used to designate political borders and borderlands, with over 60 instances. This may seem modest as a number. But Pausanias uses the word ὅρος more often than Herodotus and Thucydides combined.

Pausanias's interest in borders has been previously highlighted (Alcock 1993; Hutton 2005). However, as is often the case in Pausanian studies, relevant passages have been cherry-picked instead of thoroughly and systematically analyzed. In this chapter, I establish an exhaustive catalog of occurrences for ὅρος and μεθόριος, entering and mapping each one into a Geographic Information Systems (GIS) database and classifying each border-crossing according to the nature of the border landmark. The primary objective of this paper is to present the evidence and attempt to answer three related questions: (1) What can we learn from Pausanias about the nature of Greek borders in his time, and how does this vision relate to the available epigraphic evidence? (2) Were the borders of Greek *poleis* under Roman rule radically different from their Classical and Hellenistic predecessors? (3) How can we explain Pausanias's unique interest in borders and borderlands? A vital motive behind these questions is to understand how the *polis*, as a regional political entity braced by centuries of peer polity interaction, responded to the macrogeographical phenomenon of Roman ascendancy over the land it progressively controlled throughout the Mediterranean, and, in turn, how the empire assimilated these regional cells into its 'world system'. Pausanias should be considered an important source for studying such issues.

Expressing the Notion of Border in Ancient Greek and in Pausanias

Before focusing on Pausanias's description of borders, a few introductory remarks on the Greek vocabulary of borders and borderlands provides some necessary context. The variety of terms that express the concept of 'border' in ancient Greek is stunning, as the miscellany found in Table 7.1 attests, and no term is exclusively predestined to express the notion of 'border' (Casevitz 1993), here understood as the limits of a polity in space. In other words, the notion was never rigorously defined or rigidly fixed.

Table 7.1   Select vocabulary of borders.

A	ἀγχιτέρμων ('near the border'); ἄπειρος ('infinite', 'without boundaries'); ἄντορος, ὁ ('opposite boundary'); ἀτερμων ('without limits').
Δ	διαβατήρια, τά ('border-crossing rituals').
E	ἐσχατιά, ἡ; ἐσχατιαί ('extreme limit', 'extremity', 'boundary'; in Attica land found on sloppy and more rocky ground at the outskirts of plains).
M	μεθόριος ('bordering', 'marking the boundary or limit'); μέσσορος, ὁ ('boundary stone'); μεθόρια, τὰ ('border').
O	ὅμορος ('bordering', 'neighboring'); ὅριον, τό ('boundary', 'limit'); ὅρια, τά ('border region', perhaps of Mycenaean origin); ὁρία, ἡ ('boundary'); ὅρισμα, τό ('boundary', 'limit'); ὁρισμος, ὁ ('marking out by boundaries'); ὁριαῖος ('marking the boundary'); ὅριος (epithet: Apollo Horios at Ermione, Zeus Horios and Athena Horia at Eleusis); ὅρος, τό ('boundary', 'limit'; 'boundary marker'; 'pillar'); ὁροθεσία, ἡ ('settling of limits'); ὁριστης, ὁ ('one who marks the boundaries').
Π	προσορέω ('to border on'); προσορίζω ('include within boundaries'); πέρας, τό ('limit', 'end'); πολυπείρων ('with vast borders'); περατόω ('to delimit').
T	τέρμα, τό ('limit'); τέρμων, ὁ ('boundary'); τερμιευς ('guardian of boundaries', epithet for Zeus); τερμάζω and τερμᾰτίζω ('to mark the limits'); τερμονίζω (with *chora*, 'to fix the boundaries of the territory'); τερμονισμός, ὁ ('marking of boundaries'); τερμαστῆρες 'boundary commissioners'); τέτρωρον, τό ('ground marked by four boundaries').
Y	ὑπερόριος ('beyond the border'); ὑπεροπία, ἡ ('the land beyond one's own border').

Such variety, albeit more restricted, is also found in other languages. French has a rich border vocabulary, with words and verbs such as *marche, terme, confins, délimitations, démarcations, frontière(s), limites, borne, bornage, borner, aborner*, etc; English has *limits, borders, borderlands*, and *frontier*. The notion also keeps evolving: the increasing theorization of borders and concern with changing networks of mobility across contemporary Europe has added terms such as *hard borders, networked borders, dynamics of bordering, debordering*, and *rebordering* (Rumford 2006). Such lexical complexity should not surprise us; a more limited set of words would suggest a consensus that does not exist in reality. Nordman, following Lucien Febvre, shows how such variety exposes the weight of the notion and its development, as well as significant variations in languages and cultures (Nordman 1998: 23). Inasmuch as the ability of each state to exercise sovereignty is highly variable (Cherry 1987; 2010: 107) the ways and methods of defining, marking, and naming them can alternate through time. Greek *poleis* had different types of borders (linear, zonal, undefined), various ways of marking them on the ground (delimitation versus demarcation), and perhaps even fluctuating attention toward them in the long term. The variety of words belonging to the vocabulary of Greek borders reflects such complexity.

Overall, the most tangible word for expressing 'border' in Greek is the masculine ὅρος (*horos*, plural ὅροι). This word, with a rough breathing, must not be confused with the neuter ὄρος (*oros*, with smooth breathing, plural ὄρη), meaning 'mountain' or 'hill'.[1] A common origin for both words has been hypothesized: mountains notoriously delimit microregions in the Greek landscape and appear as the most common natural boundary markers in inscriptions. Casevitz wondered whether the breathing might be a secondary intervention resulting from a need to differentiate borders from mountains more formally (Casevitz 1993: 18). However, the two words have different etymologies: ὅρος ('boundary', 'limit') seems to originate from the Indo-European *veru-* ('draw'), probably connected with the Greek ἐρύω ('draw'); while ὄρος (mountain) originates from the Indo-European $h_{3}er$ ('rise'), ὄρνυμι 'rise' (Chantraine 1999; Beekes 2010).

The word ὅρος appears in Linear B tablets from Pylos (*wo-wo*) as a topographical term meaning 'boundary' or 'boundary district' (Chadwick and Baumbach 1963; Aura Jorro and Rodríguez Adrados 1999). In Ionic, we find the form οὖρος. In the *Iliad* (12.421, 21.405) it refers to stones used as boundary markers in cultivated fields. The neuter οὖρον can mean the 'distance' plowed by mules, and the 'plow' itself (*Iliad* 10.351, 23.431; *Odyssey* 8.124). According to Casevitz, the word belongs to the agricultural world, indicating, 'furrow', thus the line that delimits, and by extension 'limit', 'boundary', and 'border'. It can be connected with the Latin *urvare*, 'to mark out a boundary with a furrow' (Beekes 2010), reminiscent of the legend of Romulus delimiting the limits of Rome with the plow (Chantraine 1999). The word ὅρος also means 'pillar' (inscribed or not), the pillar or marker which can be set up on a mortgaged property, or a boundary stone marking the limits of sacred, public, or private land.[2] In some cases, the polysemy of ὅρος can be challenging.

Pausanias uses the word ὅρος in some 65 instances and μεθόριος twice. In only two passages, ὅρος does not refer to political borders, but instead to the limits of sacred groves (2.27.1; 2.37). The word ὅρος can be accompanied by χώρα (*chora*) in the genitive (2.20.1: μένειν ἐπὶ τοῖς καθεστηκόσιν ἐξ ἀρχῆς ὅροις τῆς χώρας: 'forced them to stay within the original boundaries of their territory'), or by the name of the territory (2.34.6: ἐν ὅροις τῆς Ἑρμιονίδος: 'on/in the borders/borderlands of the Hermionis'), or ethnic (3.24.8: ἐν ὅροις Σπαρτιατῶν: 'on/in the borders/borderlands of the Spartans'). With the preposition ἐν followed by the dative plural, it is difficult to know if Pausanias refers to the 'line' of the border or the wider borderlands, understood as an area encompassing a border zone of several kilometers next to the borders/borderline. Here context may provide some insight. When Pausanias writes that the town of Iasos is ἐν ὅροις μὲν χώρας τῆς Λακωνικῆς, it is perhaps best to translate 'in the borderlands of Laconia' (4.27.7) since no town could stand on a borderline. The same can be said of Lousoi, situated 'in the borderlands of Kleitor' (8.18.17). More generally in Greek, the plural ἐν ὅροις can mean 'in the territory of', thus 'in the zone of political jurisdiction' similar to the plural *fines* in Latin.

The infrequent use of μεθόριος ('lying between as a boundary') is intriguing. Is it a simple synonym for ὅρος? Alternatively, does it point to something more specific? The plural μεθόρια is found in Greek prose (Thucydides 2.18, 5.3.5), literally meaning 'between the boundaries' and suggesting the existence of a sort of no man's land or zone of mutual exploitation between two *poleis* (Ober 1995: 111-14). However, we should not translate the word too literally, as it could express simply the notion of borderlands. Pausanias (3.2.6) mentions a sanctuary built ἐν μεθορίῳ τῆς τε Λακωνικῆς καὶ τῆς Μεσσηνίας. Is the sanctuary, and the region/locality called Limnai, built 'in the border zone between Laconia and Messenia' or 'in the Laconian–Messenian borderlands'? Later (Pausanias 8.35.2), μεθόριος could be a synonym for ὅρος, used to avoid the repetition of the latter, found in the same passage.

Pausanias also uses the adjective ὅμορος to denote contiguous territories, sharing a common border; however, since such passages seldom provide any information about the nature of the border, I have not included the adjective in the present corpus. Finally, Pausanias often employs the word πέρας for expressing the notion of 'end' or 'extremity', as for the 'end of a road' (5.25.7; 10.34.7). In only two cases does he use the word for expressing the notion of political borders (5.8.6; 8.26.4). Both refer to the grave of Koroibos situated on the *horoi* of Elis (8.26.3; see also Table 7.2).

Overall, Pausanias almost exclusively employs ὅρος when mentioning a political border. His use of the word is consistent and straightforward, and he rarely feels compelled to use synonyms. However, I will argue that behind this apparent simplicity lies a remarkable eye for borders, characterized by a peculiar sensibility toward their historical, political, cultural and religious meaning.

Relying on topographical developments, I have mapped 60 different landmarks delimiting political borders (Figure 7.1). Each border entry was mapped in GIS, entered into a database and analyzed using three criteria: (1) the type of landmark used in the delimitation of the border (mountain, river, etc.); (2) the nature of the landmark (natural or anthropic); and (3) the reasons motivating its mention (Table 7.2). While GIS here is used mainly for thematic cartography, it also offers powerful tools of spatial analysis for studying ancient borders and limits, for example through site catchment analyses or cost-surface allocation (Conolly and Lake 2006: 224-25; Bevan 2010; Knodell 2013; Fachard 2016).

A first observation concerns the distribution of the evidence throughout Achaia as well as throughout Pausanias. It is important to underline that Pausanias is not exhaustive in his treatment of borders, as he does not methodically report them whenever he crosses them. There are conspicuous omissions, such as the historically charged borders between Athens and Megara, as well as between the Corinthia and the Argolid. Overall, 83% of the borders mentioned in Table 7.2 involve the Peloponnese, 15% Attica and Boeotia, and 2% Phokis. Among the Peloponnesian borders, 46% of

Table 7.2 Catalog of 60 political borders recorded by Pausanias using the words ὅρος and μεθόριος (the latter indicated by *).

Key: b. = border; TP = topographical-descriptive, meaning a mention of the border as a geographical and political landmark of the *polis*; MA = mythological account

Reference	Poleis	Landmark	Nature of landmark	Reasons for citing borders'
1.29.6	Eleon–Tanagra	n/d	n/d	ref. to b. conflict
1.38.1	Eleusis–Attica	stretch of water (Rheitoi)	natural	old division between E. and A.
1.38.8	Attica–Boeotia	town (Eleutherai)	anthropic	historical evolution of the b.
1.38.8	Attica–Boeotia	mountain (Mt Kithairon)	natural	historical evolution of the b.
1.44.10	Megarid–Corinthia	n/d (site of a duel)	n/d	TD + stage of a mythical combat
2.20.1 (7.11.2)	Sparta–Argos	n/d	n/d	ref. to b. conflict
2.28.2	Argos–Asine	tree (twisted olive tree on Mt Koryphon)	natural	MA + difficulty regarding the localization of b.
2.34.6, 2.34.12	Hermione–Troizen	sanctuary (Demeter Thermasia)	anthropic	TD
2.35.2	Hermione	n/d	n/d	ref. to b. conflict
2.38.7	Sparta–Argos–Tegea	mountain (Mt Parnon)	natural	TD
2.38.7	Sparta–Argos–Tegea	stone Hermai (Jost 1985: 453–54)	anthropic	monuments on the b.
3.2.6*	Laconia–Messenia	sanctuary (Artemis at Limnai)	anthropic	TD
3.2.6	Laconia–Messenia	χωρίον (locality of Limnai)	n/d	TD
3.23.2	Boiai	χωρίον (locality of Epidelion)	anthropic	TD
3.24.8	Sparta	χωρίον (locality of Hypsa)	anthropic?	TD
3.24.8	Sparta	sanctuary (Asklepios and Artemis Daphnaia)	anthropic	TD
4.1.1	Messenia–Laconia	valley (Choirios)	natural	TD, historical, ethnic, MA
4.4.2	Messenia–Laconia	sanctuary (Artemis Limnatis)	anthropic	TD, religious, historical, MA
4.22.7	Arcadia	n/d	n/d	expulsion of a cursed body
4.36.7 (5.6.3)	Messenia–Elis	river (Neda)	natural	TD
6.16.8	Elis–Arcadia	n/d	n/d	ref. to b. conflict
6.21.3-4	Elis–Arcadia (prev. Elis–Pisa)	river (Diagón)	natural	TD, ref. to older division
6.21.5	Pisa	river (Alpheios)	natural	TD
6.26.10	Elis –Achaea	river (Larisos)	natural	TD, ref. to older division
6.26.10	Elis–Achaea	cape (Araxos)	natural	TD, ref. to older division
7.11.2 (2.20.1)	Sparta–Argos	n/d	n/d	ref. to b. conflict
7.13.7	Laconia–Achaea	town (Iasos, πόλισμα)	anthropic	TD, ref. to older division
7.17.5	Achaea–Elis	river (Larisos)	natural	TD
7.27.12	Pellene–Sikyon	river (Sythas)	natural	TD
8.1.2	Elis–Messenia	n/d (ref. to the Neda river, see 4.36.7, etc.)	natural	TD
8.5.11	Orchomenos–Mantinea	sanctuary (Artemis Hymnia)	anthropic	TD, excursus on the cult
8.6.6	Argos–Mantinea	river (Inachos)	natural	TD

Passage	Border	Landmark / description	Type	Reason
8.11.1	Mantinea–Tegea	altar (βωμός)	anthropic	TD
8.12.4	Megalopolis–Mantinea	χωρίον (Petrosaka), inhabited (Jost 1998: 184)	anthropic?	TD
8.12.9	Mantinea–Orchomenos	mountain (Anchisia-i)	natural	TD
8.13.6	Orchomenos–Pheneos –Kaphyas	mountain (Kaphyatic rock [πέτρα])	natural	TD
8.15.8	Pheneos–Pellene	river (Porinas)	natural	TD
8.15.8	Pheneos–Aigeira	region? (protected by Artemis? see Jost 1998: 194)	natural?	TD
8.16.1; 8.22.1	Pheneos–Stymphalos	mountain (Mt Geronteion)	natural	TD
8.17.5	Pheneos–Pellene	mountain (Mt Chelydorea)	natural	TD + mention of MA
8.18.7	Pheneos–Kleitor	mountain (Aroanian chain); the former polis of Lousoi now belongs to Kleitor (Jost 1998: 197)	natural	TD + mention of MA
8.19.4	Pheneos–Kleitor	χωρίον (Lykouria); topographic landmark?	natural?	TD
8.23.9	Kleitor–Psophis	topographic landmark? village? (Seirai)	natural?	TD
8.25.1	Psophis–Thelpousa	stele	anthropic	TD
8.25.3	Thelpousa–Kleitor	sanctuary (Demeter Eleusinia)	anthropic	TD
8.25.12	Thelpousa–Heraia	river valley of Touthoa (also called Pedion)	natural	TD
8.26.3	Heraia–Elis	river (Erymanthos) for the Arcadians (Jost 1998: 215)	natural	TD + reference to the disputed landmark
8.26.3	Heraia–Elis	grave of Koroibos for the people of Elis (Jost 1998: 215). See 5.8.6 and 8.26.4	anthropic	TD + reference to the disputed landmark
8.26.8, 8.27.17	Heraia–Megalopolis	river (springs of the Bouphagos)	natural	TD + MA regarding the river
8.34.6	Messene–Megalopolis	sanctuary (Hermaion; also Hermes on a stele); border was perhaps located on the saddle closing the Xerilas valley (Jost 1985: 219)	anthropic	TD
8.35.2*	Messene–Megalopolis	sanctuary (Hermaion on the side of Despoina)	anthropic	TD + hypothesis regarding a MA
8.36.4	Megalopolis–Orchomenos–Kaphyai	n/d but perhaps mountains (Jost 1985: 109)	natural?	TD
8.44.5	Megalopis–Tegea–Pallantion	dyke (Jost 1998: 268)	anthropic	TD
8.44.7	Tegea–Megalopolis	plain (or dyke?)	anthropic/ natural	TD
8.54.1	Tegea–Sparta	river (Alpheios)	natural	TD + geographical excursus
8.54.7	Tegea–Argos	mountains, but cultivated land	natural with human presence	TD
9.6.1	Plataea–Thebes	n/d (but probably the Asopos river, from Herodotus, *Histories*, 6.108)	natural?	ref. to b. conflict
9.25.8	Thebes	n/d	n/d	MA
9.40.12	Chaeroncia–Panopeus	n/d	n/d	MA
10.4.1	Panopeus	n/d	n/d	TD + reflection on borders

NB: A detailed analysis of the reasons for mentioning the border in each passage is subject to debate and deserves a study in its own right. Here, I give only the *main* incentive for mentioning the border (several may be intertwined), in order to provide context for the reader.

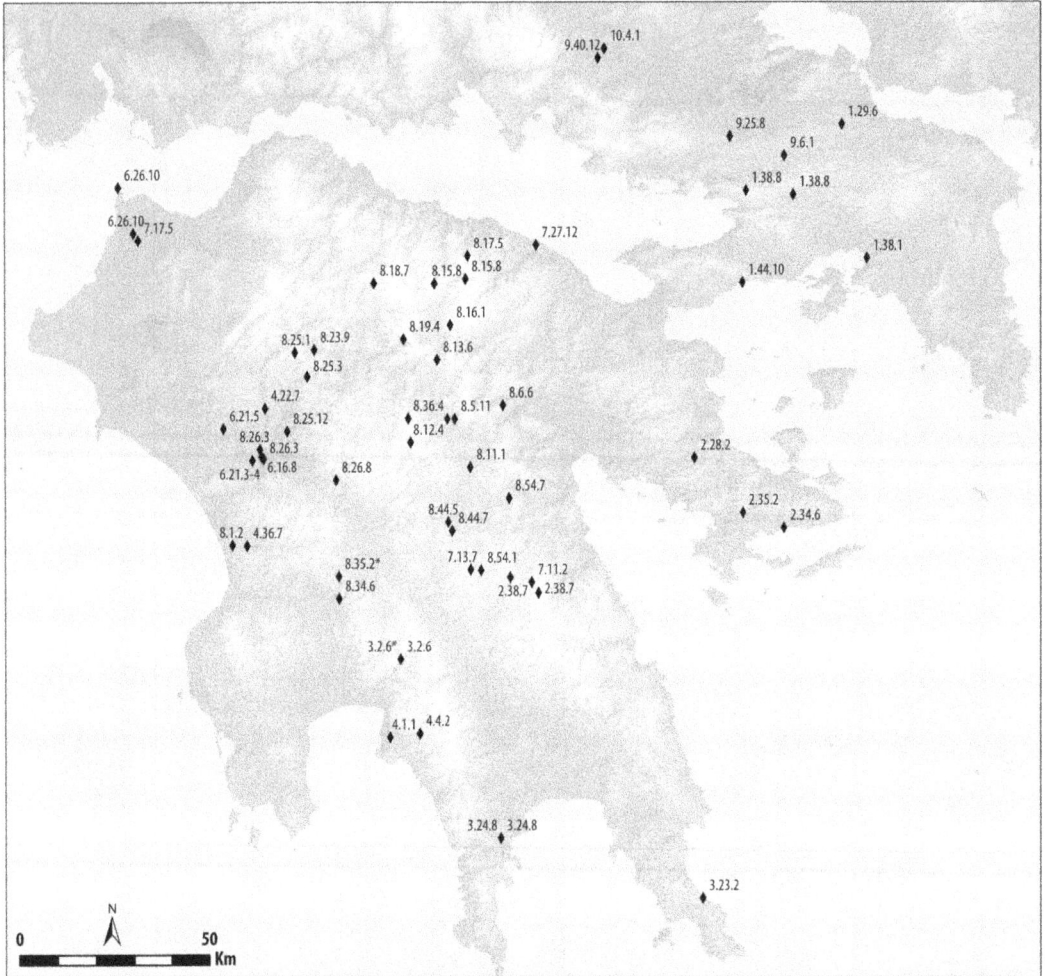

Figure 7.1   Map showing the distribution of border landmarks recorded by Pausanias. The labels refer to the passages in Pausanias.

the evidence concerns Arcadia only (Figure 7.2). The evidence is regularly dispatched, with four to five occurrences per book, until he reaches Arcadia, where he mentions and describes borders on 27 occasions. How can we explain this cluster? I do not think that the region's relative scarcity of monuments and statues, compared with Olympia or Athens, compelled him to describe mountains and rivers to fill in space. Arcadia is among the regions he visited last and by then I suggest that Pausanias had reached a new level of experience in reading the Greek landscape. His descriptive skills are much more acute in Arcadia than they are in Boeotia, a region he may have visited after Attica (Knoepfler 2004). This does not concern borders exclusively, as Book 8 also contains more geographical information than any of the other books (Hutton 2005: 81). This Arcadian emphasis on borders goes along with a trained eye for spotting them, as well as a mature experience in reading the landscape. In Book 8, Pausanias has reached his mature phase as an observer and writer.

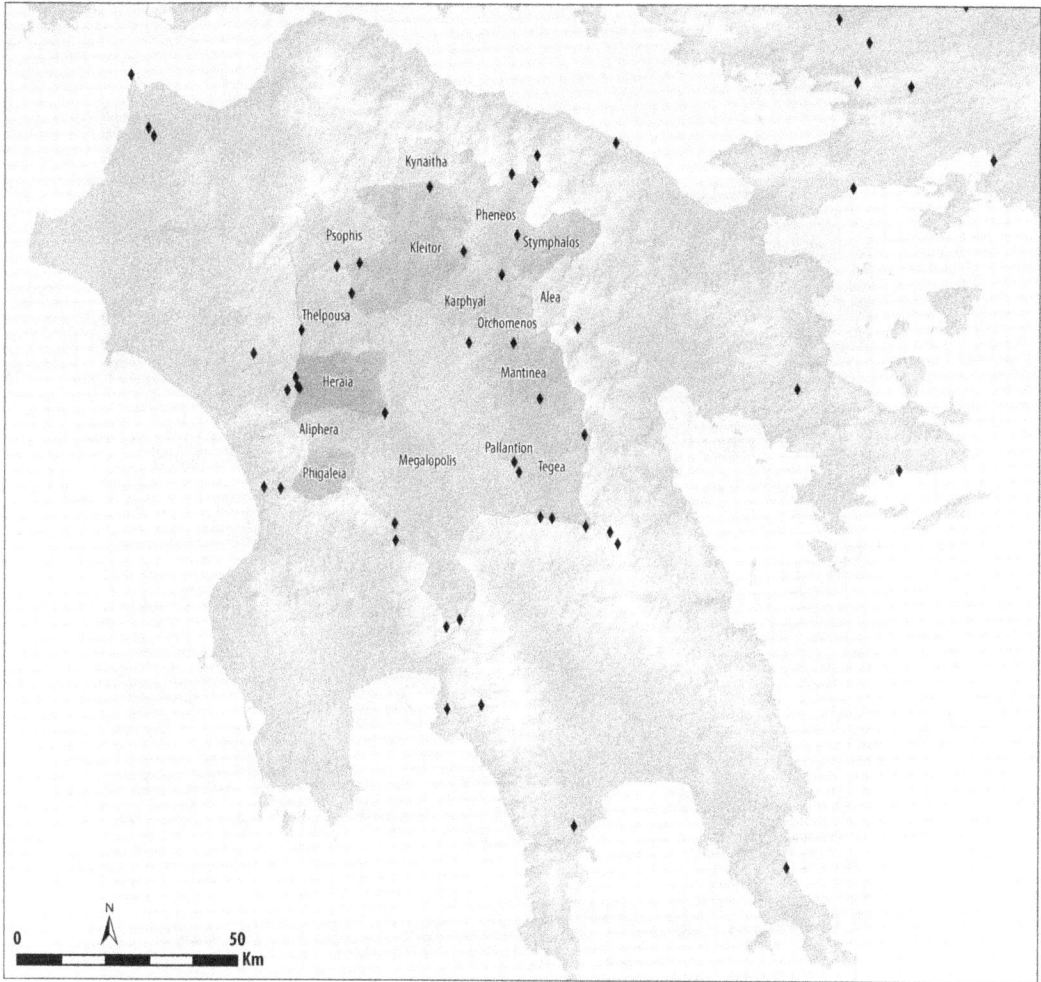

Figure 7.2   Map showing the distribution of border landmarks among the *poleis* of Arcadia (borders mapped according to Jost 1985: pl. A, with slight modifications by S. Fachard).

A second remark concerns the nature of the evidence, and serves as both a reminder and a warning. Pausanias never describes the entire border of a city-state, but only a section of it, most often the one he crosses along his route. This, of course, qualifies him as a direct observer, but not as an omniscient authority. For example, he mentions four times the borders between Messenia and Laconia; the border landmarks he reports are the sanctuary of Artemis Limnatis and the Choirios Valley. Under the reign of Vespasian, rupestral *horoi* were carved on the ridge of Mt Taygetos (Figure 7.3; Koursoumis and Kosmopoulos 2013). Did Pausanias see or know about the *horoi*? At any rate, he decided to mention the sanctuary as a border landmark.

So if Pausanias reports a tree as a boundary marker, it could be the tree that hides the forest. In other words, if Pausanias mentions a mountain as a dividing marker, this does not mean that inscribed markers or other categories of landmarks were not present on the entire stretch of the border. Should such a limitation restrain the scope of this

Figure 7.3   A rupestral *horos* on Mt Taygetos (Voidolakkoula, alt. 1732 m) belonging to the border delimitation of 78 AD (courtesy of S. Koursoumis).

inquiry? Yes and no. Yes, because the marker Pausanias selects is not representative of an entire border; no, because our available evidence hardly ever concerns an entire border to begin with, and we know that the demarcations themselves were patchy, incomplete, and based on intermittent landmarks. Indeed, in the epigraphic record only two documents describe the entire border of a city-state (Rousset 1994: 114). It should be no surprise that our evidence is selective, and that Pausanias's evidence is limited to what he tells us, and not to what he omits.

The Nature of Greek Borders in Pausanias

Pausanias delimits borders by citing landmarks shown to him as being dividing markers. Thus his inquiry is reminiscent of those undertaken by arbitrators hired by Greek *poleis* to delimit contested borders in the landscape. Judges became acquainted with the terrain via local guides and residents who showed them a contested area or the landmarks acting as dividers (Rousset 1994; 2002). A rich corpus of inscriptions echoes such procedures, including decisions regarding the definition of a border, which can be either *demarcated*, involving the physical construction of landmarks in the landscape, or, more commonly and simply, *delimited*, in which existing landmarks are selected and listed. In his pivotal study of borders in the epigraphic record, Rousset has gathered a list of 77 delimitations recording over 400 landmarks, from rocky peaks to green oak trees, rivers, and salt marshes (Rousset 1994). Such landmarks do not mark a continuous line in the landscape: they form intermediary points linked up by a visual dividing line that formally acts as the border. Consequently, border landmarks provide us with a picture of the landscape cut across by notional divisions connecting particular nodes. Rousset's 'geography of borders' (*géographie des frontières*) found in the epigraphic corpus revealed, among other things, the predominance of natural landmarks and the rarity of inscribed markers and boundary stones. By analyzing the landmarks mentioned by Pausanias using the words ὅρος and μεθόριος, I reconstruct the border landscapes he indirectly describes and compare these with the border geography extracted from epigraphy.

Natural features such as rivers/streams and mountains can be identified as embodying just over half (possibly up to 52%) of the border landmarks in Pausanias, while some 30% are clearly anthropic (Figure 7.4; Table 7.2); for the rest (18%), the nature of the borderland cannot be determined. This accords with the epigraphic evidence, where over 60% of landmarks used in border delimitations are natural.[3] In particular, mountains and streams constitute 36% of overall landmarks in Pausanias, compared to ca. 38% in inscriptions. Pausanias's testimony is not based on random observations, and it reflects a now well-established reality of Greek borders as being essentially geographical in nature and most conveniently embodied by mountains and streams. This is a very old practice, already attested from Linear B administration in the Late Bronze Age. And Roman land surveyors, when describing territorial limits between cities (*territoria inter civitates*) cite streams and ridges first (Siculus Flaccus 4.51).

What about the famous border sanctuaries? Scholars recurrently cite a handful of passages to illustrate the crucial role of sanctuaries in the definition of boundaries (Sartre 1979). In Arcadia, Pausanias mentions a Hermaion 'on the side of Despoina' forming a boundary between Messenia and Megalopolis (8.35.2). On the borders between Sparta, Argos, and Tegea are found the *Hermai* (2.38.7), which are three cairns representing the three *poleis*.[4] Although sanctuaries and small mountain shrines rank among the best-represented border landmarks found in Pausanias, they only represent 16% of the total. In border delimitations, sanctuaries form ca. 7% of the

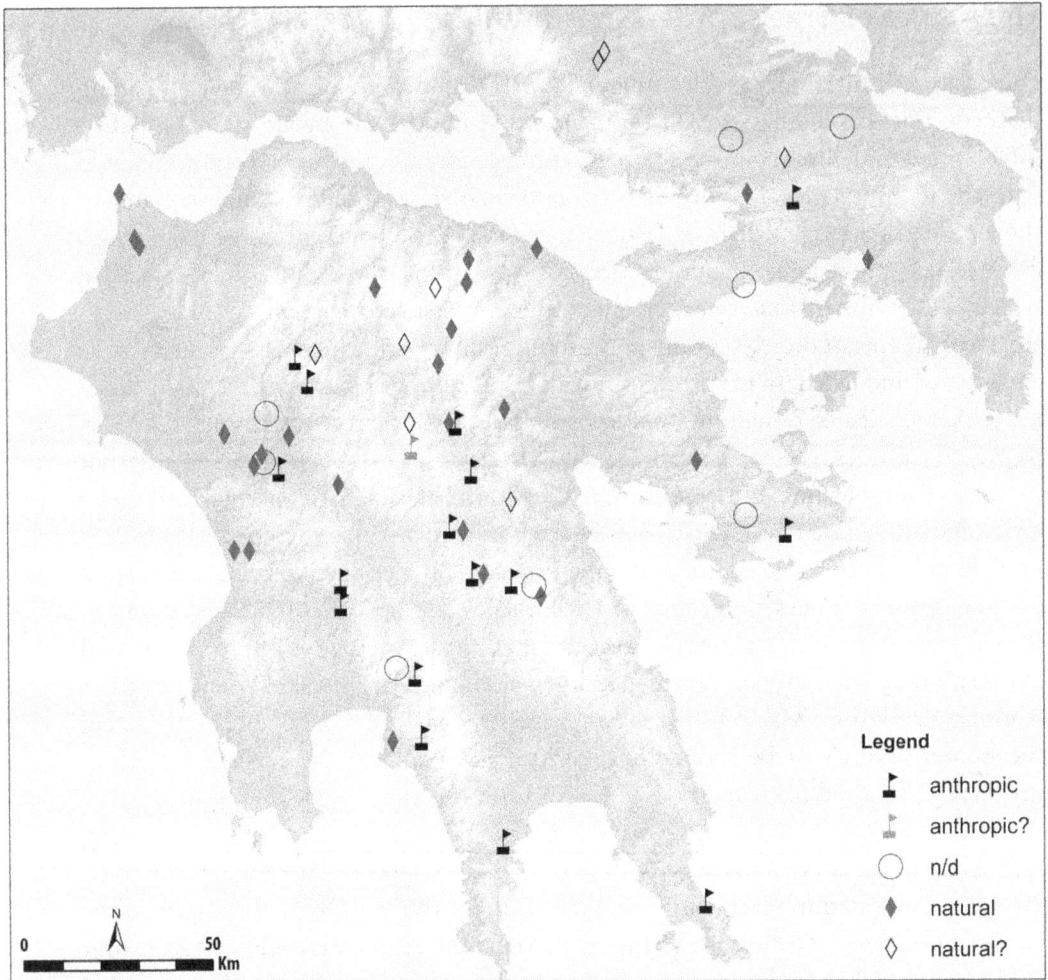

Figure 7.4   Map showing the distribution of border landmarks according to their nature.

total, but half of the total anthropic landmarks (Rousset 1994: 120). In Table 7.2 nine out of the 18 anthropic landmarks are shrines, a similar ratio of sanctuaries among anthropic landmarks. The majority of sanctuaries are found on the eastern border of Messenia (Figure 7.5).

For inscribed boundary landmarks, such as *stelai* or rupestral *horoi*, to my knowledge there is only one case of an inscribed stele as the sole marker of a border in Pausanias. It is found on the borders between Thelpousa and Psophis in Arcadia and consists of a stele inscribed with 'old letters' (ἀρχαῖα γράμματα), stating the following: 'The borders for the people of Psophis toward the chora of Thelpousa' (ὄροι Ψωφιδίοις πρὸς τὴν Θελπουσίαν χώραν). Unlike the *horoi* found inside the *chora*—often carved on limestone outcrops and delimiting religious, public, or private property—only very few *horoi* have been found at the borders of *poleis*. In fact, only 53 polis *horoi* are attested for the entire Greek world, and in many cases more than one will refer to the

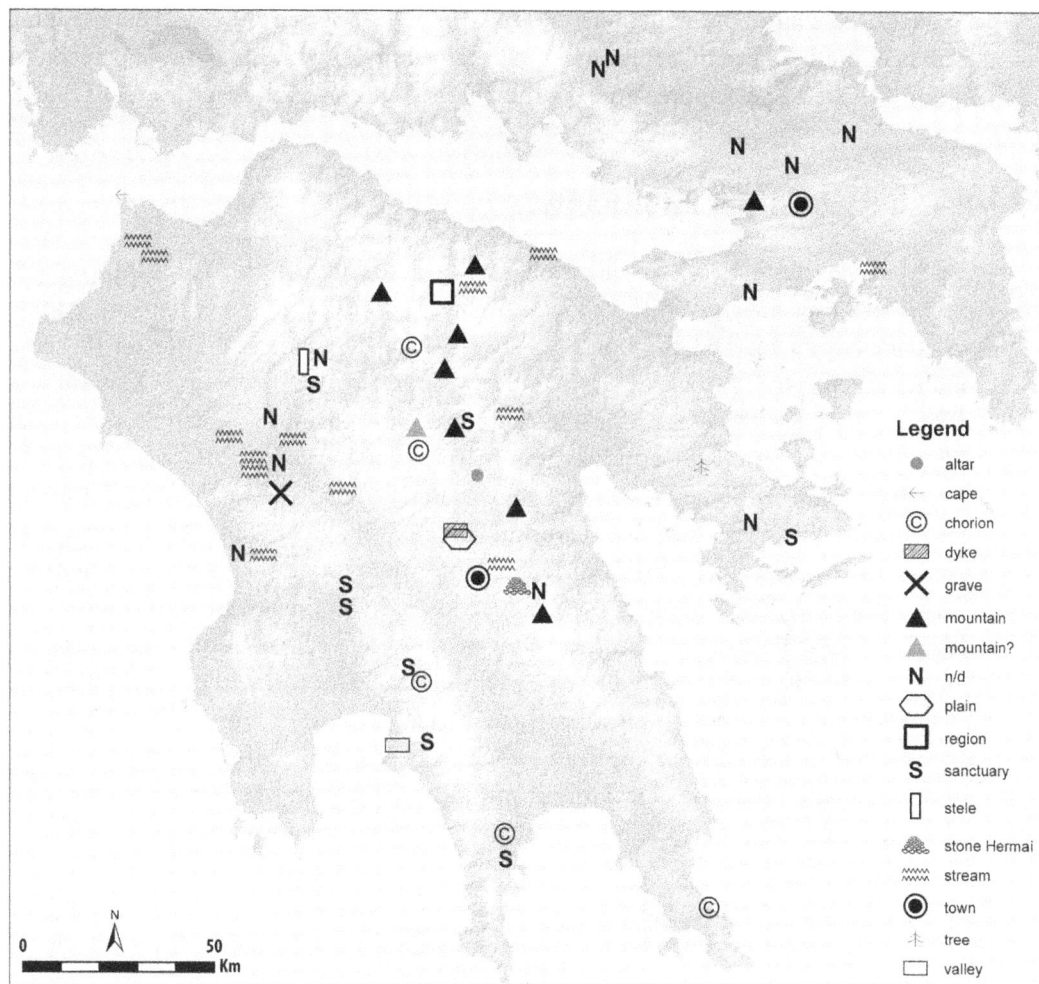

Legend

- ● altar
- ← cape
- ⓒ chorion
- ▨ dyke
- ✕ grave
- ▲ mountain
- ▲ mountain?
- N n/d
- ⬡ plain
- ☐ region
- S sanctuary
- ▯ stele
- 🝙 stone Hermai
- ∿ stream
- ◉ town
- ⊥ tree
- ▭ valley

Figure 7.5   Map showing the distribution of border landmarks by types.

same border—for example, seven *horoi* delimit the 79 AD border between Sparta and Messene (Rousset 1994: 110). Inscribed *horoi* represent only 2% of total landmarks found in Table 7.2 compared to ca. 6% in the corpus of border inscriptions. The idea of a border ringed by boundary marks, derived from a few ancient texts and erroneous assumptions in modern scholarship, is clearly a wrong one.

The nature of borders as described by Pausanias is thus in accordance with epigraphic documents, which are 'the only systematic descriptions of borders' (Rousset 1994: 112). Mountains and rivers dominate the border landscape, dotted with a few sanctuaries and including some disputed microregions. Habicht has persuasively demonstrated that 'when Pausanias speaks as an eyewitness, he can be trusted' (Habicht 1998: 63). The extent of his recourse to inscriptions is remarkable (Zizza 2006), and I would suggest that his treatment of borders should be included among the various instances in which Pausanias is a reliable observer (Habicht 1998: 28-63). His general survey of

Greek borders and borderlands never seems to be in opposition with the epigraphic evidence, and I believe that this outcome has much to do with his accurate perception of space, as well as his appreciation of the physical and political landscapes of Greece.

Pausanias's Border Informants

A next logical step is to ask how Pausanias was able to collect such reliable information on borders, especially given their low visibility. How does he know that the χωρίον called Petrosaka marked the borders between Megalopolis and Mantinea (8.12.4), or that the Kaphyatic rock was a boundary marker for the people of Orchomenos, Pheneos, and Kaphyas (8.13.6)? Here, I think, the answer is a simple one: local informants told him. I do not, however, believe that the informants were the same 'respectable local antiquarians', as Jones has named them, who guided and informed Pausanias at sanctuaries and cities (Hutton 2005: 27-28; Jones 2001). In the mountain passes of the Peloponnese, his most reliable informants were shepherds, woodcutters, charcoal burners, resin gatherers, and other locals living in the isolated cantons he describes. These locals knew the area and were the most capable of showing Pausanias where the borders of their polis were, pointing out the rocks, the ridges, and the imaginary political lines connecting them. These men are found in the epigraphic record, more specifically in the framework of border arbitration in which foreign arbitrators, unfamiliar with local topography, have to rely on shepherds as guides and witnesses. One of them is Ladikos, from Askyris, near Gonnoi:

> I know this territory (*chora*), which I have personally showed to the judges from the summit of Mt Nyseion and down this slope of the mountain to the ravine that the Kondaians made known to the judges. I have also heard from the elders that this place (*topos*) borders the territory of the Kondaians. Moreover, I myself know, from bringing my livestock to graze in this territory, that the Kondaians impose a right of way (*paragogion*) in this place (*IG* 9.2.521; Chandezon 2003: nos 18-19; Helly 1999: 100-101).

Such testimonies fit well with Pausanias's methods of investigation, which might explain why his geography of borders matches the epigraphic record. He used firsthand information when dealing with borders, first by crossing them himself, then by discussing them with the people who knew them best. Because the majority of Greek borders are simply delimited and not marked on the ground, their survival depends on oral transmission and local knowledge. The shepherds and charcoal burners gone, few people in the cities could name the local rocks and peaks, and subsequently point out the boundaries of the *chora*. This is supported by Pausanias's observation: 'In no land, which has been depopulated, is it easy to discover the truth about the boundaries [τῶν ὅρων, which may also be translated as 'borders']' (2.28.2). Still, this does not tell us why Pausanias asked them about borders in the first place. Why was he so interested in knowing where the boundaries were?

Pausanias's Interest in Borders

This keen interest in borders has been acknowledged before and explained in various ways. According to Frazer (1898: I.xxiii-xxiv), borders seemed to be given a prominent role because of Pausanias's method for describing territories on the famous 'radial plan'. On several occasions, when describing a region, Pausanias walks from the border of a given region or *polis* to its capital, describes the main monuments there, and then moves again to another border leading to another region/*polis*. The crossing of borders at one point of entry most often marks the transition between books (Hutton 2005: 78). However, although the radial plan is a dominant organizing principle for Pausanias, it is not systematically followed, and other principles were also at work, such as the description of *polis* territories among larger regions (Hutton 2005: 83-126). Hutton (2005: 110), who has recognized and most thoroughly studied the role of borders in the organization of Pausanias's narrative, compares his curiosity for borders with matters of geography. It seems clear that political borders in Pausanias function as landmarks, structuring the narrative and the geographical organization of his descriptions. However, there is a deeper interest beyond the structural role borders play in the composition of his books.

One could argue that borders interest Pausanias for being both stories and sights. When the borders are marked by a monument, they qualify as *theoremata* (sights). When the borders are not marked by one, as it is mostly the case, Pausanias can still use them as *logoi*, giving the occasion to narrate border issues and past conflicts, and subsequently to elaborate a historical, military, mythological, or religious digression about the *polis* he is about to describe. This scheme, however, is not systematically followed, because some borders are omitted and only half of them trigger a digression. However, the mention of borders has the potential of providing a connection with a mythical and historical *logos* that had so much appeal to the contemporary interest in the past. As being theoretically both *logoi* and *theoremata*, borders would then qualify as the 'remarkable' things that Pausanias has decided to describe in his agenda (1.39.3; Habicht 1998: 20-25). Can we then compare Pausanias's interest in borders with his (much better known) interest in deserted cities, collapsed temples, and missing statues? Can we explain Pausanias's renewed interest in borders as being part of his archaizing tendency, as analyzed by Arafat (1996: 1-42)? After all, at a time when Rome controls Greece, are not borders between *poleis* an archaizing trait? Given the fact that *poleis* are now embedded in the province of Achaia and administered by proconsuls dispatched by Rome, could borders be irrelevant? In other words, should we interpret Pausanias's interest in borders as a nostalgic reminder of a period that has ceased to exist?

This view has been defended by Alcock (1993). The survival of civic institutions into the Roman period would have been essentially formal in nature. The *poleis*, whose external affairs were now controlled by Rome, survived in an altered form, stripped of *eleutheria*. They were now 'dependent administrative districts' where citizens dealt with common affairs, local budgets, and the payment of tribute (Alcock 1993: 150-51).

In a reaction of pride and survival, Alcock argues, the Greek *polis* had to find ways to manifest its independence by defending its borders against its neighbors, which provides an explanation for the high number of border disputes in Roman Greece. Pausanias's interest in borders would be essentially ideological, a nostalgic reminder of an old-fashioned political organization (Alcock 1993: 119, 152; 1995: 335-36). 'Boundary maintenance ... played a major role in sustaining the social cohesion of a *polis*' writes Alcock (1993: 152), but borders were now 'illusory' (Alcock 1993: 128). So should we consider renewed border disputes in Roman Greece as a futile behavior by childish Greek *poleis* quarreling with much use of rhetoric under the patronizing and cynical eye of Rome, which pretended to be interested and respectful of old delimitations? Would this be another case of Greek *poleis* quarreling about the shade of a donkey, as Dion of Prusa would say (34.48-51)?

This view has been challenged in recent years, mainly by French historians and epigraphists. First, the presence of an external power limiting the external authority of *poleis* was nothing new in Roman Greece, as Macedon had ruled most Greek *poleis* since the end of the fourth century BC. Second, the examples of borders being transgressed by manifestations of supra-civic order are scarce, and some are already found in the Hellenistic period (Rousset 2008: 318-19). Third, the notion of *poleis* as 'administrative districts' does not take into account the complexity of Greek political identity under Roman rule (Brélaz 2008: 156). As a result, the acts of foreign policy between *poleis* have too often been interpreted as a means of building a *cultural identity* rather than a political phenomenon in its own right (Heller 2006: 369-72). Overall, Rousset argues that few elements disclose an unlimited calling into question of the civic territory's integrity; on the contrary, numerous inscriptions reveal that the Greek *poleis*, after Rome's arrival, continued to take care of their territorial sovereignty, which strongly continues to be defined by borders (Rousset 1994; 2008; Burton 2000; Brélaz 2008: 180; Fernoux 2009). In some cases, border disputes could escalate, which demonstrates that border issues are not futile (Brélaz 2008: 180-81). Borders also remain important because even under Roman rule they still separate territories with distinct legal and fiscal regimes. Throughout the empire, cities were able to keep their laws, lease their land and legally challenge their neighbors (Sommer 2015: 183). Federal structures, after having been perhaps dissolved following the destruction of Corinth in 146 BC, are re-established. Federal states, or *koina*, are attested in Thessaly, in Boeotia, Arcadia, Phokis, and Achaia (Cabanes 1998: 306-307). As a federation of *poleis*, *koina* had boundaries. In some cases, it seems that federal states enjoyed a certain level of authority that would have allowed them to arbitrate border conflicts. In 15 AD, the *synedrion* of the Thessalians carried out an arbitration operation on border issues between several poleis (*IG* 9.2.261; Cabanes 1998: 307). The current evidence suggests that *polis* boundaries still mark the limits of a polity in space and its ability to exercise some degree of political and legal authority. I would therefore favor the opinion—now well established among ancient historians—that borders remained an essential reality of Roman Greece and that their role was not illusory, nostalgic, or ideological. *Poleis* borders had a political, economic, and fiscal role in the construction of regional identity in the imperial period.

In this debate Pausanias's contribution is more valuable than originally thought. Hutton stressed that the borders Pausanias describes are in accordance with his time, and that his description is 'consistent with his desire to present an accurate portrayal of the present-day state of the antiquities of Greece' (Hutton 2005: 76). On several occasions, Pausanias reflects on changes that have affected border districts, thus providing a historical depth to his narrative. About Eleutherai, a contested border town since the late sixth century BC, Pausanias refers to past conflicts and tells us that the town is now part of Attica (1.38.8)—information we would be unable to gather from another source, especially since much of the material culture at Eleutherai is apparently Boeotian (Fachard 2013; Knodell *et al.* 2016). Pausanias also reveals historical details regarding Oropos (7.11.4-12.3), another historically challenged district on the Attic–Boeotian borders. Notwithstanding some possible chronological errors and omissions, the mention of such episodes demonstrates an interest in the modalities of the Roman conquest (Knoepfler 2004: 475-77). This may also suggest that Pausanias is well aware of Rome's impact on subordinate structures of political organization.

Pausanias's attitude to borders, beyond the geographical and descriptive level, is not a passive one. For example, he openly criticizes what he considers an unfair delimitation by Augustus of the borders between Messenia and Laconia, because they do not take into account old ethnic divisions of population minorities (Le Roy 2001: 235-37). By doing so, he openly stresses the importance of ethnicity and history as factors to take into account when arbitrating boundaries (Gengler 2005: 324-28; Luraghi 2011). Such passages suggest that border resolutions under Roman rule can still be a burning topic. Overall, it seems that Pausanias's interest in borders goes well beyond personal curiosity, a narrative tool, or his interest in human geography. By focusing on borders, he expresses a desire to also communicate an account of the geopolitics of Roman Greece in their historical context.

The Role of Borders in the Province and the Empire

Pausanias's interest in geopolitical boundaries is not isolated but seems to reflect a wider trend in the second century AD. Pausanias's time represents the culmination of a steady rise in border arbitrations after a first-century BC nadir (Rousset 1994) (Figure 7.6). While these numbers obviously depend on the (often imbalanced) available epigraphic evidence, the increase of border inscriptions under Roman rule throughout the first two centuries AD might reflect a growing importance of such territorial demarcations and new legal mechanisms for resolving them. This period also corresponds to a high number of boundary marks (Rousset 1994: 100). The number of border inscriptions in the second century AD is, of course, lower than in the third century BC, yet higher than in the Classical period, a time when civic independence and territorial integrity

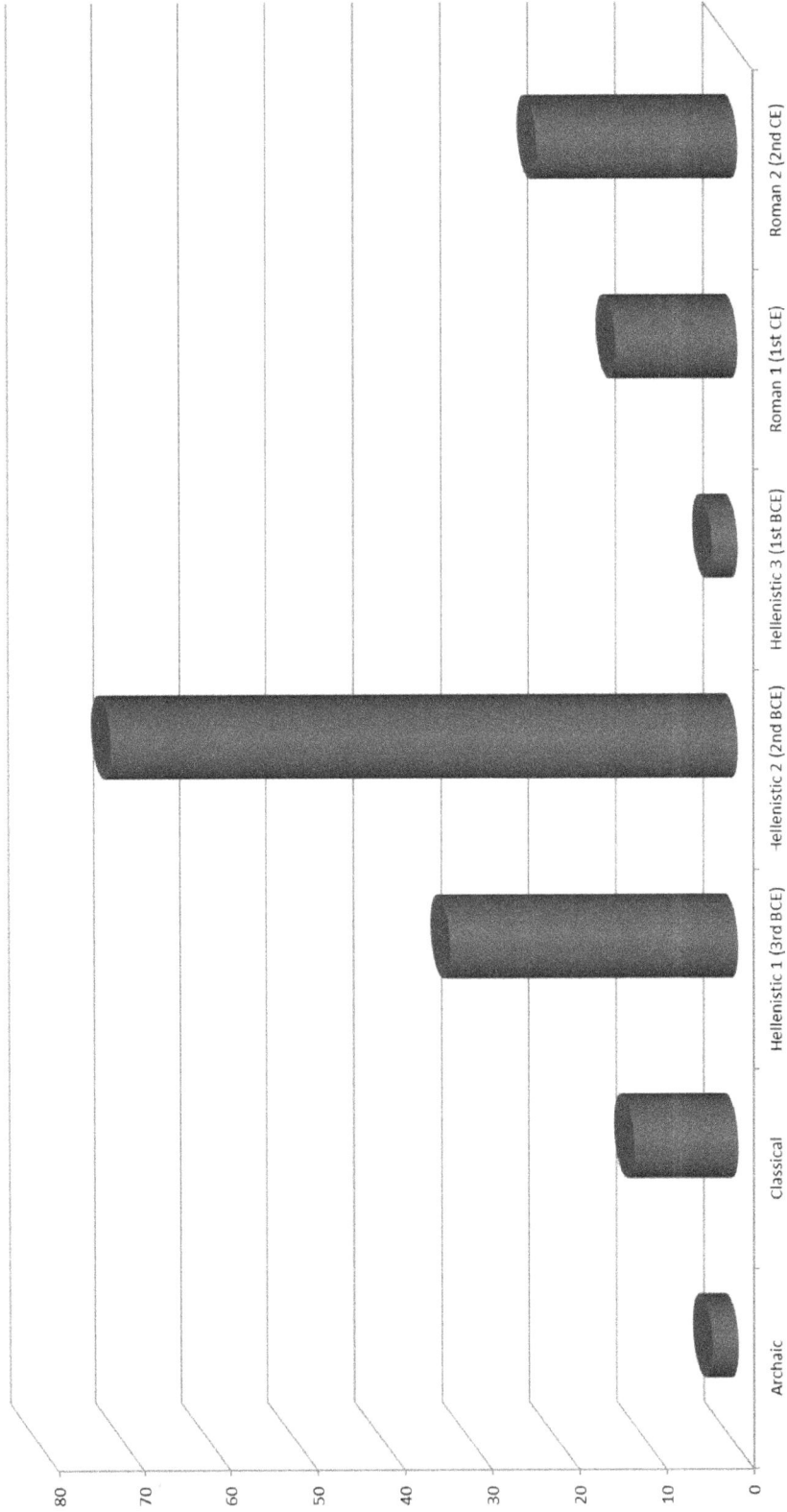

Figure 7.6 Graph showing the chronological distribution of border inscriptions (based on Rousset 1994).

reached their efflorescence. Again, this has much to say about the importance of the *polis* as a territorial unit for the administration of the province.

This importance of local boundaries does not seem to be peculiar to Greece, but part of a wider phenomenon throughout the Roman empire. At a global level, it has been argued that the most visible form of Roman ascendancy over the land is materialized by the remodeling of existing space through boundary marking and the operation of land registries (Jacques and Scheid 1990: 161-67). At a local level, however, issues related to the territorial administration of the provinces and the resolution of territorial disputes inside them are poorly known. Burton (2000: 196-97), whose seminal study offers the most insightful treatment of these territorial issues, has shown the ubiquity and importance of borders throughout the empire:

> The territory of the empire was not only administratively divided into provinces with clearly demarcated, if alterable, boundaries which defined the territorial limits of the legitimate powers of each provincial governor, but within each province each civic community, and most tribal ones, possessed fixed and publicly recognized territorial boundaries. Imperial estates and extra-territorial private estates also had formal boundaries which demarcated them from the territories of civic communities.

Burton demonstrates how borders were first needed in the fiscal sphere, as they represented the clearest framework for taxation. The Customs Law of Asia (Cottier *et al.* 2008) imposes import and export taxes at the borders of the province and refers to customs stations dispatched on the boundaries (11.26-28). Plutarch (*Moralia* 518E) expressed the annoyance felt when one faces custom officials searching baggage and property.

At the local level, boundaries between communities also played a role in taxation. This is made clear in a census return of 127 AD from the province of Arabia, where a widow called Babatha defines her property as within the boundaries (ἐν ὁρίοις) of the village of Maoza, which was administratively attached to the city of Petra (Burton 2000: 197). In Achaea, except for extraordinary levies, local communities were responsible for collecting tribute, although we lack precise information concerning various periods (Kallet-Marx 1995: 59-65; Alcock 1993: 19-24). Some *poleis* (Athens, Sparta, Elatea, etc.) and leagues seemingly enjoyed a preferential status, although it is unclear if (and when) they avoided taxation entirely. If some of them did, it seems logical to assume that their borders would then concretely separate the limits of taxation, and that exact position of cities with limited taxation might be increasingly important in relation to neighboring cities subjected to a different tax status. The *senatus consultum* of 170 BC in favor of Thisbe returns the land, harbors, revenues, and mountain pastures to the possession of the city (Sherk 1969: no. 2). The borders of the Thisbean *chora*, therefore, implicitly marked the spatial extent of the decision. Oropos was allowed to keep its revenues, including those originating from harbor customs, under the condition that they would be devoted to the sanctuary of Amphiaraeus. The Roman *publicani* tried to invalidate this decision, but the Senate confirmed Sylla's decision in 74/73 BC, preventing the *publicani* from taxing the Oropian territory (Fournier 2010: 603).

Without being explicitly stated, it seems logical to suggest that the borders of the Oropia might have acquired a renewed importance in the fiscal sphere (see Corbier 1991: 221-22). The current evidence for Achaea shows that boundary disputes could be related to pasture rights, as in the case opposing Orchomenos to Thisbe (Oliver and Clinton 1989: nos. 113-14); the control of a temple, as in the case of Artemis Limnatis between Messene and Sparta (Koursoumis 2014); or the delimitation of a territory to guarantee its territorial extension and seal the integration of former sacred land, as in the case of Delphi ca. 110 AD (Rousset 2002: 143-54). Throughout the empire, boundary disputes could be connected with the tax system, fishing rights, revenues, rights of pasturage, local customs duties, harbor rights, the implementation of exemptions, and the requisitioning of transport and supplies (Burton 2000).

The responsibility for resolving disputes generally belonged to the provincial governor, who could inspect the contentious border in person or delegate the matter. In some cases, specialists were hired to measure or mark resettled boundaries. Inscriptions of the imperial period mention various categories of land surveyors (Rousset 1994: 108-109), such as the χωρομέτρης who operated on the new delimitation of 78 AD between Sparta and Messene (*IG* V 1, 1431). In a famous border dispute opposing Delphi to its neighbors, Trajan dispatched C. Avidius Nigrinus to deal with the matter in person. This legate surveyed and inspected the border facing Antikyra, reviewed the testimonies of locals, and examined written documents that were presented to him as proofs (Rousset 2002: 150). Financial incentives were at stake, since the reaffirmation of Delphi's boundaries meant, among other things, that the city was confirmed in its right to exploit and control the sacred land. Reasons differed from city to city, but each one had concrete and direct advantages of having its borders formally recognized: 'Each city tended its territorial limits with great care, as its boundaries were of such great importance' (Corbier 1991: 221).

The evidence above further confirms that it would be a mistake to consider border disputes under Roman rule as futile, ideological, or illusory. The 'vulgate of the *Pax Romana*' (Heller 2006: 25) and Dion's 'Greek trifles' (38.38) have shaped a distorted view of the true importance of borders in a conquered Greece. Boundary disputes could be severe, implying violence and resulting in public disorder. Burton (2000) convincingly showed that authoritative border delimitations and demarcations in the provinces of the Roman empire were a matter of public authority and administration and were, therefore, important for the regulation of peaceful inter-community relations and taxations. Heller (2006: 25) made clear that, when dealing with border issues, Rome's central administration in the imperial period is anxious to 'evacuate the tensions that could harm the political and social order'. The increased number of inscriptions related to border conflicts and fiscal issues in the imperial period also reveals a frequent resort to imperial arbitration and an epigraphic habit of displaying such decisions (C. Brélaz, pers. comm.). In short, borders were necessary for a stable system of rule throughout the empire. Additionally, if we look at the distribution of border disputes and resolution throughout the empire, it seems that Achaea was not an especially turbulent province. Indeed, of the 88 examples of resolutions of territorial disputes by provincial governors and other imperial officials recorded by Burton (2000), only eight concern the province of Achaea. By comparison, Sardinia has three, Dalmatia 12. So local territorial disputes and their resolution are part of a wider phenomenon throughout the empire, not a characteristic of nostalgic Greek *poleis* fighting with rhetoric over the shade of a donkey.

Conclusions

Pausanias is well known for his fondness for artworks, temples, shrines, myths, and histories. However, his descriptive and interpretative methods are worth analyzing in detail, and Snodgrass (2001: 137) eloquently and soundly stressed that they make him 'one of us'. His agenda as a writer has been widely discussed in modern scholarship. John Cherry objectively and critically repositioned Pausanias in the genre of travel literature, and called to mind that the 'characteristic discourse of travel writing' was made of several interests 'overiding and binding together' (Cherry 2001: 249). Borders, boundaries, and the demarcation of territory should now firmly be counted among his broader interests in political and historical geography. Arguably, no other Greek author specifically locates and reports the position and nature of borders for so many regions of Greece, making Pausanias our richest written source about the conception of Greek political territory after inscriptions.

In the first place, borders play a crucial role in Pausanias's organizing scheme, with regional boundaries also serving as divisions between books and subsections in the text. They also serve as convenient introductions and conclusions when describing a *polis*, and are often used to prompt digressions in the narrative. Although he is far from exhaustive and systematic in his descriptions of borders he becomes more attentive in the Peloponnese, particularly in Arcadia. Here, his sparked interest in delimiting boundaries between *poleis* is topographical and descriptive, yet it is remarkable: his observation skills are at their most acute, and he has reached a new level of maturity in describing the landscape (Knoepfler 2004). Overall, his reasons for citing borders are varied (Table 7.2) and hard to categorize. They are mainly topographical-descriptive, but historical, mythological, political, geographical, and ethnic reasons are often intertwined, as in 4.1.1 (Laconia–Messenia). His attention to them thus signals their overall importance as real territorial landmarks when describing the landscape.

Moreover, Pausanias understands their geopolitical nature. In his description of Panopeus, Pausanias famously laments the lack of public monuments in the city, but nevertheless calls it a *polis*, because 'they have boundaries with their neighbors' (10.4.1— on this much-discussed passage see Franchi 2013). Panopeus stands, therefore, as an active *polis* operating in 'full interaction with neighboring polities' (*sensu* Cherry 1986: 24). Since the polis remained a fundamental cell of the empire (Jacques and Scheid 1990: 179), borders were essential for keeping these cells alive and functioning. The mention of borders and borderlands by Pausanias confirms both the local and global importance of borders in the public organization of Roman Achaea, something that Pausanias feels compelled to report, signaling a unity between city and territory, echoed by the border inscriptions of the first and second centuries AD (Rousset 2008).

The Greek world at large was an intricate mosaic of over a thousand *poleis* with individual and varied regional extents. Each polis was itself an imbrication of private, sacred, and public land (Papazarkadas 2011), sometimes jointly owned (Rousset 2013), marked on the ground when deemed necessary, but for the majority simply delimited. With the arrival of Rome, this complex system of land possession did not disappear. This territorial complexity was even increased with the advent of a global power remodeling space by establishing colonies (Rizakis 1996), modifying populations, reassigning disputed lands, developing imperial property, and imposing cadastral changes. Inside the borders of the *provincia*, these new layers had to fit or modify somehow the existing ones, but such a complex system could only function with the concept of clear borders and internal boundaries. Romans were well aware of this. Arguably, this territorial intelligence is one of the most striking aspects of their long-term domination of such a vast empire. Erasing and dramatically modifying local boundaries throughout the empire, especially those of *poleis*, would have resulted in chaos. On the contrary, by accepting, integrating, and managing the past and current borders around the Mediterranean, province after province, *polis* after *polis*, Rome was able to preserve a long-established territorial balance and order (in some cases several centuries old) and to adapt it to its 'global' organization. Parts of this fascinating process are echoed in Pausanias, who, I argue, captured much better than traditionally thought the true geopolitical importance of borders in the organization of Roman Greece.

Acknowledgments

I am immensely grateful to the editors of this volume for their patience and insightful corrections and suggestions, as well as to Tom Tartaron and Bob Chapman, who served as reviewers. This paper has benefited from the advice of Jack Davis and Peter van Dommelen and the review of Valentina di Napoli. Cédric Brélaz and Denis Rousset should be credited for closely reading and greatly improving this paper. I alone remain accountable for mistakes and imprecisions.

Endnotes

1. This can lead to problematic interpretations with compound words such as ΟΡΟΦΥΛΑΚΕΣ, only attested in inscriptions and without a breathing sign (Rousset 1994; Chankowski 2010: 347-59).
2. There is a vast bibliography on Attic *horoi*: for a broad approach, see Ober (1995); for mortgaged properties see Finley (1985), Lalonde (1991), and Ober (2006); and for *horoi* as deme markers, see Langdon (1985; 1988; 1999), Lalonde (2006), Papazarkadas (2011), and Fachard (2016).
3. These figures are imprecise. In the case of χωρίον, it is often difficult to know if the word refers to a village

(which would qualify as anthropic) or a region/district (which would qualify as natural only if it is uninhabited). I count 25 (certain) to 31 (probable) natural landmarks and 17 (certain) to 19 (probable) anthropic landmarks, with 11 unable to be determined. In both certain and probable cases, the natural landmarks predominate. Regarding inscriptions, I have used the numbers given by Rousset (1994), but categorizations are my own.

4. These Hermai were excavated in the early twentieth century but are now destroyed (Romaios 1950: 234; Papachatzis 1976: 305). They consisted of monticules of stones, terracotta figurines, and sherds, thrown there by the travelers thanking the divinity after concluding a safe journey (Jost 1985: 453-54).

About the Author

Sylvian Fachard was a Swiss National Science Foundation Senior Research Associate at the University of Geneva, and he has recently been appointed Andrew W. Mellon Professor of Classical Studies at the American School of Classical Studies at Athens. He co-directs the Mazi Archaeological Project in northwest Attica, Greece, and has directed excavation and publication projects in Eretria and in Argos. His monograph *La défense du territoire. Etude de la chôra et de ses fortifications, Eretria* (In Folio, 2012) was awarded the Georges Perrot Medal from the Académie des Inscriptions et Belles-Lettres de l'Institut de France. E-mail: sfachard@ascsa.edu.gr

Classical Authors and Texts

Dion of Prusa (Dio Chrysostom), *Discourses*.
Homer, *Iliad*.
Homer, *Odyssey*.
Pausanias, *Description of Greece*.

Plutarch, *Moralia*.
Siculus Flaccus, *De Condicionibus Agrorum*.
Thucydides, *The Peloponnesian War*.

Abbreviation

IG = *Inscriptiones Graecae*

References

Alcock, S.E.
  1993 *Graecia Capta: The Landscapes of Roman Greece*. Cambridge: Cambridge University Press.
  1995 Pausanias and the polis: use and abuse. In M.H. Hansen and K. Raaflaub (eds.), *Studies in the Ancient Greek Polis*, 326-44. Stuttgart: Steiner.
Arafat, K.W.
  1996 *Pausanias' Greece: Ancient Artists and Roman Rulers*. Cambridge: Cambridge University Press. https://doi.org/10.1017/CBO9780511470318
Aura Jorro, F., and F.R. Rodríguez Adrados (eds.)
  1999 *Diccionario griego-español* II. *Diccionario micénico* I. Madrid: Consejo Superior de Investigaciones Científicas
Beekes, R.S.P.
  2010 *Etymological Dictionary of Greek* II. Leiden Indo-European Etymological Dictionary Series 10.2. Leiden: Brill.

Bevan, A.
2010 Political geography and Palatial Crete. *Journal of Mediterranean Archaeology* 23: 27-54. https://doi.org/10.1558/jmea.v23i1.27

Brélaz, C.
2008 L'adieu aux armes: la défense de la cité grecque dans l'Empire romain pacifié. In C. Brélaz and P. Ducrey (eds.), *Sécurité collective et ordre public dans les sociétés anciennes*. Entretiens sur l'Antiquité Classique 54: 155-96. Genève: Fondation Hardt.

Burton, G.P.
2000 The resolution of territorial disputes in the provinces of the Roman empire. *Chiron* 30: 195-215.

Cabanes, P.
1998 Le monde grec européen et la Cyrénaïque. In C. Lepelley (ed.), *Rome et l'intégration de l'Empire: 44 av. J.-C.-260 ap. J.-C.*, 299-331. Paris: Presses universitaires de France.

Casevitz, M.
1993 Les mots de la frontière en grec. In Y. Roman (ed.), *La frontière. Séminaire de recherche sous la direction d'Yves Roman*. Travaux de la Maison de l'Orient 21: 17-24. Lyon: Maison de l'Orient méditerranéen.

Chadwick, J., and L. Baumbach
1963 The Mycenaean Greek vocabulary. *Glotta* 41: 157-271.

Chandezon, C.
2003 *L'élevage en Grèce, fin V*^{e}*-fin I*^{er} *siècle a.C. L'apport des sources épigraphiques*. Scripta Antiqua 5. Pessac, France: Ausonius.

Chankowski, A.S.
2010 *L'éphébie hellénistique: étude d'une institution civique dans les cités grecques des îles de la Mer Égée et de l'Asie Mineure*. Paris: de Boccard.

Chantraine, P.
1999 *Dictionnaire étymologique de la langue grecque. Histoire des mots*. 2nd edn. Paris: Klincksieck.

Cherry, J.F.
1986 Polities and palaces: some problems in Minoan state formation. In C. Renfrew and J.F. Cherry (eds.), *Peer Polity Interaction and Socio-Political Change*, 19-45. Cambridge: Cambridge University Press.
1987 Power in space: archaeological and geographical studies of the state. In J.M.E. Wagstaff (ed.), *Landscape and Culture: Geographical and Archaeological Perspectives*, 146-72. Oxford: Blackwell.
2001 Travel, nostalgia, and Pausanias' giant. In S.E. Alcock, J.F. Cherry and J. Elsner (eds.), *Pausanias: Travel and Memory in Roman Greece*, 33-52. New York: Oxford University Press.
2010 Sorting out Crete's prepalatial off-island interactions. In W.A. Parkinson and M.L. Galaty (eds.), *Archaic State Interaction: The Eastern Mediterranean in the Bronze Age*, 107-40. Santa Fe, New Mexico: School for Advanced Research Press.

Conolly, J., and M. Lake
2006 *Geographical Information Systems in Archaeology*. Cambridge: Cambridge University Press. https://doi.org/10.1017/CBO9780511807459

Corbier, M.
1991 City, territory and taxation. In J. Rich and A. Wallace-Hadrill (eds.), *City and Country in the Ancient World*. Leicester-Nottingham Studies in Ancient Society 2: 211-39. London and New York: Routledge. https://doi.org/10.4324/9780203418703_chapter_9

Cottier, M., M.H. Crawford, C.V. Crowther, J.-L. Ferrary, B.M. Levick, O. Salomies and M. Wörrle (eds.)
2008 *The Customs Law of Asia*. Oxford: Oxford University Press.

Fachard, S.
2013 Eleutherai as the gates to Boeotia. In C. Brélaz and S. Fachard (eds.), *Pratiques militaires et art de la guerre dans le monde grec antique. Etudes offertes à Pierre Ducrey à l'occasion de son 75ème anniversaire*, 81-106. Paris: Picard.

2016 Modeling the territories of Attic demes: a computational approach. In J. Bintliff and K. Rutter (eds.), *The Archaeology of Greece and Rome: Studies in Honor of Anthony Snodgrass*, 192-222. Edinburgh: Edinburgh University Press.

Fernoux, H.-L.
2009 Frontières civiques et maîtrise du territoire: un enjeu pour la cité grecque sous le Haut-Empire (Ier-IIIe siècle apr. J.-C.). In H. Bru, F. Kirbihler and S. Lebreton (eds.), *L'Asie Mineure dans l'Antiquité. Echanges, populations et territoire*, 135-64. Rennes, France: PU Rennes.

Finley, M.I.
1985 *Studies in Land and Credit in Ancient Athens, 500-200 B.C.: The Horos Inscriptions*. 2nd edn. New Brunswick, New Jersey: Transaction Publishsers.

Fournier, J.
2010 *Entre tutelle romaine et autonomie civique: l'administration judiciaire dans les provinces hellénophones de l'Empire romain, 129 av. J.-C-235 ap. J.-C.* Bibliothèque des écoles françaises d'Athènes et de Rome 341. Athens: Ecole française d'Athènes.

Franchi, E.
2013 Pausanias' mental maps und die Polis: 10.4.1 in context. *Ktema* 38: 323-40.

Frazer, J.G.
1898 *Pausanias' Description of Greece*. 6 vols. London: Macmillan.

Gengler, O.
2005 Héraclès, Tyndare et Hippocoon dans la description de Sparte par Pausanias: Mise en espace d'une tradition mythique. *Kernos* 18: 311-28. https://doi.org/10.4000/kernos.1545

Habicht, C.
1998 *Pausanias' Guide to Ancient Greece*. Sather Classical Lectures 50. Berkeley: University of California Press.

Heller, A.
2006 *'Les bêtises des Grecs': conflits et rivalités entre cités d'Asie et de Bithynie à l'époque romaine (129 a.C.–235 p.C.)*. Scripta antiqua 17. Bordeaux, France: Ausonius.

Helly, B.
1999 Modèle, de l'archéologie des cités à l'archéologie du paysage. In M. Brunet (ed.), *Territoires des cités grecques: actes de la table ronde internationale; 31 octobre - 3 novembre 1991*. Bulletin de correspondance hellénique supplément 34: 99-124. Athens: École Française d'Athènes.

Hutton, W.
2005 *Describing Greece: Landscape and Literature in the Periegesis of Pausanias*. Cambridge: Cambridge University Press.

Jacques, F., and J. Scheid
1990 *Rome et l'intégration de l'Empire: 44 av. J.-C. - 260 ap. J.-C.* Paris: Presses universitaires de France.

Jones, C.P.
2001 Pausanias and his guides. In S.E. Alcock, J.F. Cherry and J. Elsner (eds.), *Pausanias: Travel and Memory in Roman Greece*, 33-52. New York: Oxford University Press.

Jost, M.
1985 *Sanctuaires et cultes d'Arcadie*. Etudes péloponnésiennes 9. Paris: J. Vrin.
1998 *Pausanias. Description de la Grèce. VIII: l'Arcadie*. Translation and commentary by M. Jost. Paris: Les Belles Lettres.

Kallet-Marx, R.
1995 *Hegemony to Empire: The Development of the Roman Imperium in the East from 148 to 62 B.C.* Hellenistic Culture and Society 15. Berkeley: University of California Press.

Knodell, A.R.
2013 Small-World Networks and Mediterranean Dynamics in the Euboean Gulf: An Archaeology of Complexity in Late Bronze Age and Early Iron Age Greece. Unpublished PhD dissertation, Brown University, Providence, Rhode Island.

Knodell, A.R., S. Fachard and K. Papangeli
2016 The 2015 Mazi Archaeological Project:

regional survey in northwest Attica (Greece). *Antike Kunst* 59: 132-52.

Knoepfler, D.
2004 La découverte des *Histoires* de Polybe par Pausanias et la place du livre IX (Boiôtika) dans l'élaboration de la Périégèse. *Revue des Études Grecques* 117: 468-503. https://doi.org/10.3406/reg.2004.4589

Koursoumis, S.
2014 Revisiting Mount Taygetos: the sanctuary of Artemis Limnatis. *Annual of the British School at Athens* 109: 191-222. https://doi.org/10.1017/S0068245414000100

Koursoumis, S., and D. Kosmopoulos
2013 Ager Denthaliatis. Παλαιά και νέα ορόσημα στην κορυφογραμμή του Ταϋγετού. *Archaiologike Ephemeris* 152: 55-75.

Lalonde, G.V.
1991 Horoi. In G.V. Lalonde, M.K. Langdon and M.B. Walbank, *Inscriptions: Horoi, Poletai, Leases of Public Lands*. Athenian Agora 19: 5-51. Princeton, New Jersey: American School of Classical Studies at Athens.
2006 *IG* I³ 1055 B and the Boundary of Melite and Kollytos. *Hesperia* 75: 83-119. https://doi.org/10.2972/hesp.75.1.83

Langdon, M.K.
1985 The territorial basis of the Attic demes. *Symbolae Osloenses* 60: 5-15. https://doi.org/10.1080/00397678508590786
1988 The ZO/BA *horoi* at Vari in Attica. *Greek, Roman, and Byzantine Studies* 28: 75-81.
1999 Hymettiana III: the boundary markers of Alepovouni. *Hesperia* 68: 481-508. https://doi.org/10.2307/148412

Le Roy, C.
2001 Pausanias et la Laconie ou la recherche d'un équilibre. In D. Knoepfler and M. Piérart (eds.), *Editer, traduire, et commenter Pausanias en l'an 2000. Actes du colloque de Fribourg (18-22 septembre 1998) autour des deux éditions en cours de la Périégèse (Coll. des Universités de*

France - Fondazione Lorenzo Valla). Geneva: Droz.

Luraghi, N.
2011 *The Ancient Messenians: Constructions of Ethnicity and Memory*. Cambridge: Cambridge University Press.

Nordman, D.
1998 *Frontières de France: de l'espace au territoire: XVIe-XIXe siècle*. Paris: Gallimard.

Ober, J.
1995 Greek *horoi*: artifactual texts and the contingency of meaning. In D.B. Small (ed.), *Methods in the Mediterranean: Historical and Archaeological Views on Texts and Archaeology*, 91-123. Leiden: E.J. Brill.
2006 Solon and the *horoi*: facts on the ground in Archaic Athens. In J.H. Blok and A.P.M.H. Lardinois (eds.), *Solon of Athens: New Historical and Philological Approaches*, 441-56. Leiden: Brill.

Oliver, J.H., and K. Clinton
1989 *Greek Constitutions of Early Roman Emperors from Inscriptions and Papyri*. Memoirs of the American Philosophical Society 178. Philadelphia: American Philosophical Society.

Papachatzis, M.
1976 *Παυσανίου Ελλάδος Περιηγήσις, Βιβλίο 2. και 3. Κορινθιακά και Λακωνικά*. Athens: Ekdotiki Athinon.

Papazarkadas, N.
2011 *Sacred and Public Land in Ancient Athens*. Oxford: Oxford University Press. https://doi.org/10.1093/acprof:oso/9780199694006.001.0001

Rizakis, A.D.
1996 Les colonies romaines des côtes occidentales grecques: populations et territoires. *Dialogues d'histoire ancienne* 22: 255-324. https://doi.org/10.3406/dha.1996.2273

Romaios, K.A.
1950 Ερευνητική περιοδεία εις Κυνουρίαν. *Praktika* 1950: 234.

Rousset, D.
1994 Les frontières des cités grecques.

Premières réflexions à partir du recueil des documents épigraphiques. *Cahiers du Centre Gustave Glotz* 5: 97-126. https://doi.org/10.3406/ccgg.1994.1387

2002 *Le territoire de Delphes et la terre d'Apollon.* Bibliothèque des écoles françaises d'Athènes et de Rome 310. Athens: Ecole française d'Athènes.

2008 The city and its territory in the province of Achaea and 'Roman Greece'. *Harvard Studies in Classical Philology* 104: 303-37.

2013 Sacred property and public property in the Greek city. *Journal of Hellenic Studies* 133: 113-33. https://doi.org/10.1017/S0075426913000074

Rumford, C.

2006 Theorizing borders. *European Journal of Social Theory* 9: 155-69. https://doi.org/10.1177/1368431006063330

Sartre, M.

1979 Aspects religieux et économiques de la frontière dans les cités grecques. *Ktema* 4: 213-24.

Sherk, R.K.

1969 *Roman Documents from the Greek East: Senatus Consulta and Epistulae to the Age of Augustus.* Baltimore, Maryland: John Hopkins.

Snodgrass, A.M.

2001 Pausanias and the chest of Kypselos. In S.E. Alcock, J.F. Cherry and J. Elsner (eds.), *Pausanias: Travel and Memory in Roman Greece*, 127-41. New York: Oxford University Press.

Sommer, M.

2015 OIKOYMENH: *longue durée* perspectives on ancient Mediterranean 'globality'. In M. Pitts and M.J. Versluys (eds.), *Globalisation and the Roman World: World History, Connectivity and Material Culture*, 175-97. New York: Cambridge University Press.

Zizza, C.

2006 *Le iscrizioni nella Periegesi di Pausania. Commento ai testi epigrafici.* Studi e testi di storia antica diretti da Mauro Moggi 16. Pisa: Edizioni ETS.

8 Monumental Engagements: Cultural Interaction and Island Traditions in the West Mediterranean

Alexander Smith and Peter van Dommelen

Introduction

Archaeologists have long noted that single megaliths or standing stones, megalithic constructions like dolmens, and monumental architecture as massive as *nuraghi* and *talayots* are disproportionately common and variable on Mediterranean islands, and in particular in the western basin. Both the larger and the smaller islands boast their own types of megalithic or 'Cyclopean' architecture and monumental buildings, perhaps best exemplified by the *talayots* and *navetas* of the Balearic Islands. For a long time, their existence has been acknowledged in diffusionist terms as the odd results of somewhat secondary developments that occurred 'in the slipstream' of the great Childean transfer of civilization from east to west. In other words, the conventional assumption has long been that oriental architectural techniques and traditions of roughly Bronze Age date became somehow moored on the remote islands of the west Mediterranean. The radiocarbon revolution of the 1960s, however, and Renfrew's (1973) *Before Civilization* shattered this coherent picture, when it became clear that the Maltese 'temples' pre-dated the Sardinian *nuraghi* by the best part of a millennium, while the Corsican *turri* and Balearic *talayots* have since been shown to be of still later date (e.g., Cherry and Leppard 2014: 11-13).

In response, the specific local conditions of these places, i.e., that they are disproportionately found on islands, were foregrounded to explain the emergence of the unique monuments. John Evans's (1973) influential discussion of islands as 'laboratories of culture change' set up the new paradigm that has remained influential to this day (e.g., Kolb 2005; 2014). A remarkably explicit reworking of these ideas resulted in Lewthwaite's 'Island Filter Model', which attributed the distinct spread and nature of the Neolithization process in the west Mediterranean to the role of the islands (Lewthwaite 1986; Vicent García 1997). The implied assumption of this perspective is that islands are inherently isolated, and therefore that this regional context is perfect for observation and empirical analysis of how human cultures develop. Such a vantage point, while useful in its heuristic attempt at understanding aspects of first colonization and island biogeography, is rather limiting, however, when it comes to understanding cultural development, seafaring, and interconnectivity in prehistory and in historical epochs. In recent years, scholars have begun to argue against the inherent isolation of prehistoric islands (e.g., Broodbank 2000), arguing for a fundamentally different landscape of interaction, in which both insular and extra-insular factors played a role in the construction of island cultures and identities.

The west Mediterranean islands continue nevertheless to be seen as being at the mercy of isolation. As radiocarbon dating has dramatically increased our chronological understanding of extra-insular interactions in the past few decades, demonstrating in particular the separation of relative island chronologies for places like Sardinia, Corsica, and the Balearic Islands (Lull *et al.* 1999; Blake 2014), the specific operative chronological scales on each of these islands remain relatively rigid. These scales are predicated on a social evolutionist understanding of cultural progression that is as teleological as it is pessimistic, because this development is regarded as inexorably ending in the corruption or wholesale loss of 'pure' indigenous island culture due to external intervention, usually by imperial or colonial forces (e.g., Lilliu 1989). In this manner, the ideas first formulated by Evans can still be seen to underlie the ways that island chronologies of the west Mediterranean continue to depend on rigid and separate periodizations of 'pure' indigenous cultures, which are in turn based almost exclusively on the chronologies of monumental constructions and an isolationist vantage point (e.g., Kolb 2005: 171-72; cf. Lewthwaite 1990).

The consequences of this 'insular perspective' are widespread. It has, for instance, not only separated Sardinian from Balearic chronologies and developments, but has also isolated the islands' key monuments diachronically. The Sardinian *nuraghi* are first and foremost regarded as prehistoric Bronze Age monuments, just as the *talayots* of Mallorca and Menorca are seen as protohistoric monuments of the Iron Age. Because the former are conventionally dated to the sixteenth to ninth century BC, and the latter mostly between the ninth and sixth century BC, the two types of monuments remain broadly separate from each other in time (Guerrero Ayuso *et al.* 2002; Webster 2016); a rare exception is the Menorcan *talayot* of Cornia Nou that was constructed in the eleventh or tenth century BC (Anglada *et al.* 2014). The well sanctuaries on Sardinia that are conventionally ascribed to the turn of the second millennium BC are another case in point, as are the mid-first-millennium BC Mallorcan sanctuaries and megalithic *taula* precincts on Menorca; these later monuments are also routinely understood as representing a fairly particular point in their respective island cultural chronologies (Guerrero Ayuso *et al.* 2006). Precisely because the *nuraghi* and *talayots* represent the eponymous hallmarks of indigenous culture on their respective islands, the separation confirms the independence and unique character of both the monuments and the islands.

Monuments, especially when they are as huge and prominent as *nuraghi* and *talayots*, did not, however, cease to exist at the end of their notional cultural timeframes. Many, if not most, remained occupied or at least in some form of use well after these periods and, in that sense, most Sardinian and Balearic monuments certainly did co-exist and partook in similar or related historical processes.

Taking our cue from Cherry's (1981) insistence that, in order to understand the earliest colonization phases of islands, the archaeological evidence needs to be carefully and critically considered in relation to the specific circumstance of each island, we shift our attention toward the afterlife of monuments and examine their conditions with care. Just as Cherry (1985) showed that the early prehistoric islands of the east Mediterranean were hardly as much 'out of the stream' as assumed, we propose that the allegedly remote islands of the west Mediterranean had much more in common with each other during the first millennium BC than normally presumed. In this chapter, we argue for a broader understanding of monuments that encompasses both their conventional periods of 'original construction and use' and the later 'afterlives'. In this way, we contend, we may overcome the dichotomy that has come to divide the 'pure' indigenous monuments from their later 'derivative' phases of life, and we can begin to see connections that have hitherto remained overlooked. In what follows, we thus first describe and assess the afterlives of *nuraghi* and *talayots* on Sardinia and Menorca respectively (Figure 8.1), before comparing their trajectories in the regional contexts of their particular islands, in order to understand to what extent these 'later phases' may be understood as specific island phenomena or indeed as part of broader developments.

Afterlives of Monuments

The term 'afterlife of monuments' was first introduced and systematically used by Bradley (1993: 1) in his inspiring discussion of the ways in which monuments 'alter the earth'. He went on to note that 'the building of monuments imposes itself on human consciousness' by creating 'a new sense of place' through the material modification of the landscape, and that because of the simple fact that monuments tend to 'last for a very long time', they readily become integrated into later landscapes (Bradley 1993: 5). He also added that, as a corollary, monuments have frequently been subsumed in local perceptions of history and communal identities, to the extent that it is precisely the observation of a monument's afterlife that may offer significant clues to those perceptions. At the same time, however, monumental afterlives can be found across the globe in very different cultural contexts, and while the specifics necessarily vary in time and space, the phenomenon itself does not appear to be regionally specific (Bradley 1993: 5; cf. Alcock 2002: 28–32).

But what is the afterlife of a monument and, indeed, when was it? In archaeological terms, the straightforward answer is that once the monument was no longer used as originally intended and designed, regardless of whether there was a break in occupation or not, we are looking at its afterlife. Because so many monuments by their very nature survive over extended periods of time and go through many cycles of

Figure 8.1   Map of the west Mediterranean basin, showing the Balearic Islands and Sardinia, with the locations of the sites of Torre d'en Galmés and S'Urachi highlighted.

reuse and abandonment, it is usually more appropriate to speak of a series of distinct afterlives. From a historical, or more precisely culture-historical, perspective, however, a monument's afterlife begins when it continues to exist and to function past the monument's notional period of occupation—that is, when a Bronze Age burial mound is also used for interments in the Iron Age. Because most monuments are intimately associated with specific periods and cultures, as noted above, it is the latter definition that tends to prevail in much of the archaeological literature on monuments. It is this perspective, too, that is responsible for what has been termed an 'archaeological myopia' that registers only those cultural phases and archaeological remains that are expected at any given monument, and not later ones (Alcock 2002: 54; cf. Bradley 1993: 128-29). It is this perception that explains convoluted and paradoxical expressions like 'post-Nuragic use of a *nuraghe*' (Blake 1998: 60), because it assumes that a *nuraghe* 'properly belongs' to the Nuragic period alone, and that any later use was by definition out of place, if not out of time—even if the actual function and modes of occupation did not change at all (Blake 1998: 68).

In this chapter, we insist on the primacy of the archaeological focus, and we thus speak of the afterlives of monuments when we can observe tangible changes in the ways in which the monument was occupied and used. This may be portable material culture deposited within or distributed around the building, but it might also include modifications made to the fabric of the construction itself. Strictly speaking in archaeological terms, evidence of the continued importance of monuments can thus be continuous, fragmented, or non-existent, but even in cases where no later material evidence exists surrounding the monument, we still consider the monument's place in the landscape as a socially and ideologically relevant marker or beacon. The monument, as long as it remains unburied and somehow visible, however remotely, continues to form part of the physical landscape. As it thus remains integrated in the syntax of the cognitive landscape, we concur with Bradley's (1993: 129) conclusion that 'monuments and places worked together to direct and stimulate the experience of prehistoric people'.

People continued to create practices, traditions, and memories around monuments as centers of cultural focus, even in cases where the 'original' and later uses of a monument were clearly distinct and separate in time, or where there was little or no knowledge of its original significance (Rojas and Sergueenkova 2014). A case in point is the juxtaposition of a ninth-century AD Byzantine church with a second-millennium BC *nuraghe* at the site of Santa Sabina (Silanus) in central Sardinia, where the two monuments stand less than 50 m apart (Figure 8.2). While it is certainly the case that the wider area is rich in Nuragic-period remains, which most notably include two megalithic chamber tombs or *tombe di gigante* at a mere 200 m from Santa Sabina, and the well-sanctuary of Cherchizzo at just 400 m distance, it is equally evident that the single megalithic tower of the *nuraghe*, which today still stands tall to a height of just under 9 m, was by far the most visible element on the otherwise bleak and featureless *altopiano* of Abbasanta. It was thus the *nuraghe* that constituted the focal point in the landscape, which in all likelihood attracted the construction of the church

Figure 8.2   View of the Byzantine church and homonymous *nuraghe* of Santa Sabina (Silanus, Sardinia).

at this location, which in turn may have encouraged the expansion of the site into a monastic setting (Moravetti 1998: 533-38; Poli and Lambrocco 2002).

Sardinian and Balearic Afterlives

The case of Santa Sabina leaves us in little doubt that what is usually referred to as 'later reuse' of older monuments is not just accidental reoccupation but a far more subtle and complex process. The same point has been made by Rojas and Sergueenkova (2014) for Anatolia in the Classical period. At the same time, however, there is no shortage of situations defined by rather more straightforward instances of monumental reuse, such as that of megalithic *navetas* on Menorca or Sardinian *nuraghi* as sheep folds in recent centuries (e.g., Blake 1998: 65-67). On balance, therefore, it is the scale and measure of integration and engagement with the older monument that set apart the process we begin to distinguish at Santa Sabina.

This distinction between straightforward or occasional reuse and 'sustained engagement' with the monument may help to delve deeper into the monumental afterlives of *nuraghi* and *talayots* of the west Mediterranean islands. As the various examples already touched on in the foregoing readily demonstrate, it has not escaped archaeologists' attention that many monuments on the west Mediterranean islands have been reused or reoccupied at one point in time or another.

We are certainly not the first ones to draw attention to this phenomenon. A relatively well-documented and long-known example from Sardinia is the so-called 'Roman village' at *nuraghe* Su Nuraxi of Barumini, which was already highlighted by Lilliu (1955) in his original excavation report as 'Phase e, Punic-Roman period, post-Nuragic' of the originally Nuragic village surrounding the *nuraghe*. Even if Nuragic-style pottery continued to be a common occurrence in the houses of this period, their 'post-Nuragic' date was never questioned, because of the regular presence of clearly identifiable imported objects, such as two late fourth-century BC Black Figure Attic *lekythoi* and Punic coins of the fourth and third centuries BC. Lilliu's (1955: 416) characterization of this phase as 'several centuries of poor people's lives' at the monument underscores precisely our point that this 'afterlife' is not considered on its own terms and in its own context, which would be that of Punic and Roman republican Sardinia. Explicit investigation of the phenomenon is in fact a rather different matter, and the relatively rare instances of studies examining Punic or Roman-period occupation of 'prehistoric monuments' only underscore the 'archaeological myopia' already highlighted.

In Sardinia, the first systematic studies of monumental reuse were published by Lilliu (1990) and Pala (1990). Both articles primarily listed the rich archaeological documentation for the Roman-period occupation of *nuraghi*, Nuragic villages, and the occasional megalithic chamber tomb across Sardinia. Lilliu, moreover, added references to contemporary ancient authors, who reported amongst other things on local Sardinians living in *castra* or forts (Livy 41.12.5), which he quite plausibly suggests refers to *nuraghi* (Lilliu 1990: 416-19). Lilliu also goes beyond this description, when he posits that this reuse is not just accidental but on the contrary denotes the 'persistence' of 'ancient traditions' and long-standing ways of life of Sardinian communities into the Roman period (Lilliu 1990: 415, 446). Elsewhere, he has interpreted this persistence in terms of indigenous resistance against Roman rule (Lilliu 1971; 1988: 481). This particular theme has subsequently been taken up and elaborated by van Dommelen (1998; 2007). Blake (1998) has proposed a truly long-term perspective on monumental afterlives; she has not only drawn attention to the multiple afterlives of these monuments but also insists on the cultural differences between these phases and the need to examine each of them in its own right and in its own context. She argues that *nuraghi* and other monuments are best regarded as particular places that 'enable' new actions and interpretations because of their prominence and deep histories. As a result, throughout their histories '*nuraghi* have not only meant something different, they have *been* something different' (Blake 1998: 68, original emphasis).

On the Balearic Islands, the general perspective on the *talayots*' and other monuments' afterlives is somewhat different, even if there is a widespread, if implicit, assumption that most, if not all, monuments had extensive afterlives. On the one hand, cultural continuity is practically taken for granted for many sites on the islands of Mallorca and Menorca until the Roman conquest of 123 BC and the subsequent Roman occupation. It is at that point that a profound break in the islands' settlement and history is widely perceived to have occurred, one that signaled or caused a shift from the indigenous centers to the newly founded Roman towns (Salvà and Hernández-Gasch 2009: 311; López Mullor 2015: 139-40). There is, however, remarkably little empirical evidence on the ground for this shift. Roman occupation at sites like Palma or *Pollentia*, for instance, does not seem to begin until around the mid-first century BC (Orfila Pons *et al.* 2006: 135; 2008), while evidence of second-century BC Roman occupation has been attested at the Menorcan site of Sanisera (Contreras Rodrigo 1998; Contreras Rodrigo *et al.* 2006; Bravo Asensio and Contreras Rodrigo 2014), and by the small—but thoroughly Roman—fort site at Son Espases outside Palma de Mallorca (Estarellas Ordinas *et al.* 2014). All other historically known colonial sites are notoriously short of concrete remains of permanent Roman occupation before the first century BC. There is in fact no archaeological evidence whatsoever that supports a sharp and widespread break in settlement patterns on either of the islands, let alone the entire archipelago, in correlation with the conquest of 123 BC. This clearly begs the question of whether traditional chronologies and interpretations of Roman influence or Romanization distort or even thwart our understanding of the Balearic past by eclipsing the study of indigenous cultural or even spatial persistence.

On the other hand, even though the archaeological and historical evidence from the sixth to second centuries BC suggests that interaction with the outside world was limited, and that indigenous *talayots* and burial sites remained continuously in use, the surrounding colonial communities of Punic Ibiza, Iberian Spain, and Greek southern

France are nevertheless widely seen as exerting a strong influence over the islands. As a result, the *talayots* are commonly regarded as no longer 'truly indigenous' in these centuries, and they accordingly tend to be labeled 'protohistoric' (e.g., Guerrero Ayuso 1997).

The adoption of the term 'protohistory' is significant, because it assigns some agency to the 'persisting' indigenous inhabitants, while recognizing that they had begun to take part in an emerging colonial dialogue, and implying that, as a result, they had begun to partake in 'civilization' (Vanzetti 2004: 1-2). At the same time, there is also an assumption that the adoption of foreign elements and the engagement in broader economic and colonial networks inevitably resulted in a rapid loss of authenticity—as Lilliu assumed for Nuragic Sardinia (Lilliu 1989; see above). This emphasis on 'cultural purity' and its erosion as a result of external interaction underscores the prominence of culture history in the study of Balearic and Sardinian archaeology. It also frames arguments about—and our understanding of—the islands' past in terms of Greek, Phoenician, Carthaginian, and Roman histories, and imposes a teleological view of cultural development in the Mediterranean that only obfuscates indigenous agency, practices, and perceptions.

Microhistories

In order to go beyond brief observations and generic comments about monumental afterlives, we investigate two monumental afterlives in depth. Rather than arguing through case studies and examples, or outlining in exhaustive detail regional patterns of reoccupation and reuse, we take recourse to what historians have termed 'microhistories' to examine the afterlives of two particular monuments in Sardinia and on Menorca, as we aspire to do justice to the specific circumstances of these monuments and their historical conditions without losing sight of the broader issues at stake (Ginsburg 1993).

We first delve into the site of Torre d'en Galmés on the southern plain of the island of Menorca, which has been excavated extensively since the 1970s, in large part by the Museu de Menorca and subsequently by a team from Boston University between 2002 and 2014. Next, we turn to *nuraghe* S'Urachi in the lowlands around the Gulf of Oristano on the central western coast of Sardinia, where ongoing excavations by the Joukowsky Institute of Brown University and the *Comune* of San Vero Milis are targeting the afterlives of the monuments over the course of the first millennium BC. These two microhistories provide us with minute yet incisive vantage points on the importance of these monuments beyond their putative cultural 'lives', and highlight the adaptation of monuments to changing cultural or colonial scenarios that have historically been ignored.

Torre d'en Galmés, Menorca

As one of the largest and longest-surviving Talayotic sites on Menorca, Torre d'en Galmés, located in southeastern Menorca, offers a remarkable instance of persistence, external influence, and adaptation at and around indigenous settlements. This site remained occupied as it was in contact with the Punic world from the sixth century BC until well after Menorca had been incorporated into the Roman republic and subsequent empire in the first centuries BC/AD—even after the Roman settlements of *Mago*, *Iamo*, and *Sanisera* (near the modern towns of Mahon, Ciutadella, and Sanitja respectively) had been newly established on the Menorcan coast (Guerrero Ayuso *et al.* 2006).

The site of Torre d'en Galmés comprises three large *talayots* and a *taula* precinct that is best known for the bronze votive objects found there (Rosselló-Bordoy *et al.* 1974; Rosselló-Bordoy 1986). While research has long focused on these central monuments, the surrounding habitation spaces and other more modest remains of the site have been at the heart of the more recent excavations undertaken by the Museu de Menorca since the 1970s and by Boston University from 2002 to 2014 (Rosselló-Bordoy 1984; 1986; Pérez-Juez 2011). A pedestrian reconnaissance survey was also carried out in the immediate environs of the site by Alexander Smith in 2012 (Figure 8.4). The three *talayots* of Torre d'en Galmés are located in the northeastern portion of the archaeological site, according to its present delimitation, on what was once the site's center and its highest location (Figure 8.3, A). The *taula* complex is located immediately south of the central *talayot* (Figure 8.3, B), while domestic structures radiate slightly to the northeast and to a much greater extent south and westward down a sloping hill. These structures have yielded remains from the Late Talayotic into the Roman imperial period, and include in the southwest corner the so-called Cartailhac circle, which is the largest and one of the latest domestic structures (Figure 8.3, C).

The pedestrian survey investigated the fields immediately outside the modern site perimeter, and provided clear evidence that both settlement and many kinds of activities continued beyond the present site boundary. For the Roman period, pottery was recorded in 15 of the 29 fields investigated, equivalent to 49% of the total area covered. Amphora fragments dominated the assemblage recovered from find concentrations that extended southward in particular, in correspondence with some of the later domestic constructions (Figure 8.4, insert).

On Menorca, the so-called Late Talayotic or Post-Talayotic period, which is the sixth to second century BC and follows the Talayotic period 'proper', is not only denoted by external contacts but is also defined by widespread expansion and prosperity across the island. At Torre d'en Galmés, this phase witnessed maximal expansion of the settlement, as numerous dwellings were constructed (Pérez-Juez *et al.* 2007: 53). Throughout this time, the *talayot* nevertheless remained the central point of reference at the site, as it had been in previous centuries. Even the somewhat later *taula* complexes that were similarly maintained and used well into the Roman period were consistently constructed in proximity to a *talayot* (Figure 8.3).

Figure 8.3   Aerial view of Torre d'en Galmés with (A) three *talayot*s located in the northeast portion of the site, (B) the *taula* complex south of the central *talayot*, and the domestic area to the south and west of the central monumental area, with (C) the Cartailhac Circle representing the southwestern limit (satellite imagery courtesy of Google Earth, modified by A. Smith).

The persistence of site location is not a trivial matter, even if it may be easy to argue that the *talayot* offered a geographic advantage with its sweeping view of the surrounding landscape, or that the site had a proven record of adequate resources. Such arguments, however, do not address the question why the people of the Late Talayotic site continued to live at inland locations, despite a notable increase in off-island interactions on both Mallorca and Menorca. Coastal sites were extremely rare on both islands for this period, despite the increase in foreign imports. Even in the

Roman period, when coastal forts and towns were more common, most indigenous sites in the interior of the islands remained occupied.

This phenomenon is well illustrated by the survey results obtained around Torre d'en Galmés, where one single field of just 0.2 ha on the northern edge of the site yielded thousands of so-called Tarraconensis amphora sherds, datable to the first centuries BC and AD and of a type associated with the nearby Spanish mainland (Figure 8.4, A). Even if the heavy concentration of pottery in this field may have been the result of field clearances for cultivation, the presence and numbers of these amphorae nevertheless make it indisputably clear that Torre d'en Galmés hosted a significant Roman cultural presence between the third century BC and first century AD, i.e., before and after the Roman occupation of 123 BC. The claim that these finds denote Roman infantrymen or settled merchants is rather implausible, given the overall evidence for cultural continuity; it is therefore far more likely that the centuries around the turn of the millennium represent a further chapter in the site's indigenous history that involved widespread use of Roman material culture.

Since the survey results indicate that the site became larger and extended well beyond the three central *talayots* in precisely these centuries marked by Roman material culture, it is evident that settlement continuity is not just a hallmark of the protohistoric period but just as much a feature of the historical or Roman period. As is evident at Torre d'en Galmés, *talayots* and *taulas* retained their central role in indigenous settlements and similarly maintained their significance in the island landscape; it is thus quite plausible that they also signaled connections to the local past of the islands. Even if imported goods and raw materials became increasingly common in the new coastal settlements of the Balearic Islands after the Roman conquest, the much older indigenous sites in the interior continued to be occupied for several hundred years (Pérez-Juez 2011).

Domestic Monuments of Menorca

The houses at Torre d'en Galmés that represent the process of settlement expansion in the Post-Talayotic and Roman periods (sixth century BC to second century AD) not only signify the afterlives of this monumental complex, but also offer fascinating insights into the continuities and changes in Menorcan society throughout this period. These houses were built in the traditional megalithic style, mostly on a non-orthogonal or even circular plan, although quasi-orthogonal plans existed, too, since roughly the sixth century BC. While the former went out of use by the third to second century BC, the latter persisted until the first and second century AD; they also tend to be smaller (Pérez-Juez 2011: 122).

In Menorca, all these 'late' houses, including the quasi-orthogonal ones, included one or more internal columns. These usually consist of a single monolith as much as 2 m tall, which was topped by a massive and roughly rectangular cap stone, as if it were a giant capital (Figure 8.5). In smaller houses the column is often built up out of several drums. Unlike houses in Mallorca, those on Menorca generally included multiple columns that were placed in a circular pattern in the center of the dwelling. Even if

Figure 8.4   Aerial view of Torre d'en Galmés with the areas highlighted where Roman ceramics were recorded on the surface. The field adjacent to the letter A represents a field that was particularly full of Tarraconensis amphora sherds, an example of which can be seen on the right.

Figure 8.5   Top: the internal column of the Cartailhac Circle at Torre d'en Galmés. Bottom: a *taula* monument from Torralba d'en Salord. Note the structural similarities between the two.

House 2 at Torre d'en Galmés is one of the more modest constructions, it still boasted probably no fewer than five massive pillars, one of which still stands over 2 m tall and 1 m wide (Pérez-Juez 2011). Other houses, such as Circle 7 at Torre d'en Galmés, included a similarly large central space with at least four internal megalithic columns.

The magnificent Cartailhac Circle at Torre d'en Galmés offers clues for a fuller and more complex understanding of the cultural significance of these interior columns (Figure 8.5). At 375 sq m, Cartailhac is one of the largest structures at Torre d'en Galmés and is easily the largest house on the site. It features an external megalithic or 'Cyclopean' wall surrounding the house complex, a large outdoor area, and a 145 sq m house structure (Sintes Olives and Isbert Vaquer 2009: 254). It is also one of the latest constructions at Torre d'en Galmés, as it has been dated to the third century BC (Sintes Olives and Isbert Vaquer 2009: 256). While the excavators interpret the Cartailhac Circle as a domestic structure on the basis of clear evidence for domestic activities such as food consumption and metal production, it is striking how the shape of the internal columns strongly convey the impression of being in a *taula* (Sintes Olives and Isbert Vaquer 2009: 251; Figure 8.5).

The similarities between the supporting, internal columns of these houses and the earlier *taula*s are unmistakable, and even if they may not have served a ritual purpose in the houses, it is hard to escape the idea that these massive columns were not solely functional. It would thus appear plausible that these houses drew on specifically local architectural forms that referred to typically Menorcan monuments of an older tradition. Since they also tended to become bigger as the Late Talayotic period progressed, it does not seem far-fetched to interpret these colossal columns in terms of a hyper-representation of indigenous and past forms and traditions in response to external influences and pressures, including Roman military occupation. We thus suggest that these Post-Talayotic houses were perceived and shaped in reference to indigenous island identities that were reconstructed in the face of changing relationships with the outside world. These houses thus represent the afterlives of Menorcan monuments not only because they were built in close spatial contiguity, but also, and more significantly so, because they adopted and adapted older architectural traditions of the island and reworked these into new forms that were equally local and Menorcan.

We thus suggest that we are looking at a monumental afterlife that is not a straightforward consequence of external influences. Rather, it is one that was part of a set of diachronic engagements expressed on multiple levels within a not-so-isolated indigenous landscape, where older monuments were given new and evolving meanings as symbols of local identity.

S'Urachi, West Central Sardinia

In Sardinia, the ongoing excavations at *nuraghe* S'Urachi are systematically examining the 'afterlives' of the *nuraghe* across most of the first millennium BC. Since 2013, the S'Urachi Project has undertaken annual excavation campaigns to investigate in detail two areas immediately outside the outer defensive wall of the monument itself (Figure 8.6).

Figure 8.6 View of *nuraghe* S'Urachi (San Vero Milis, Sardinia).

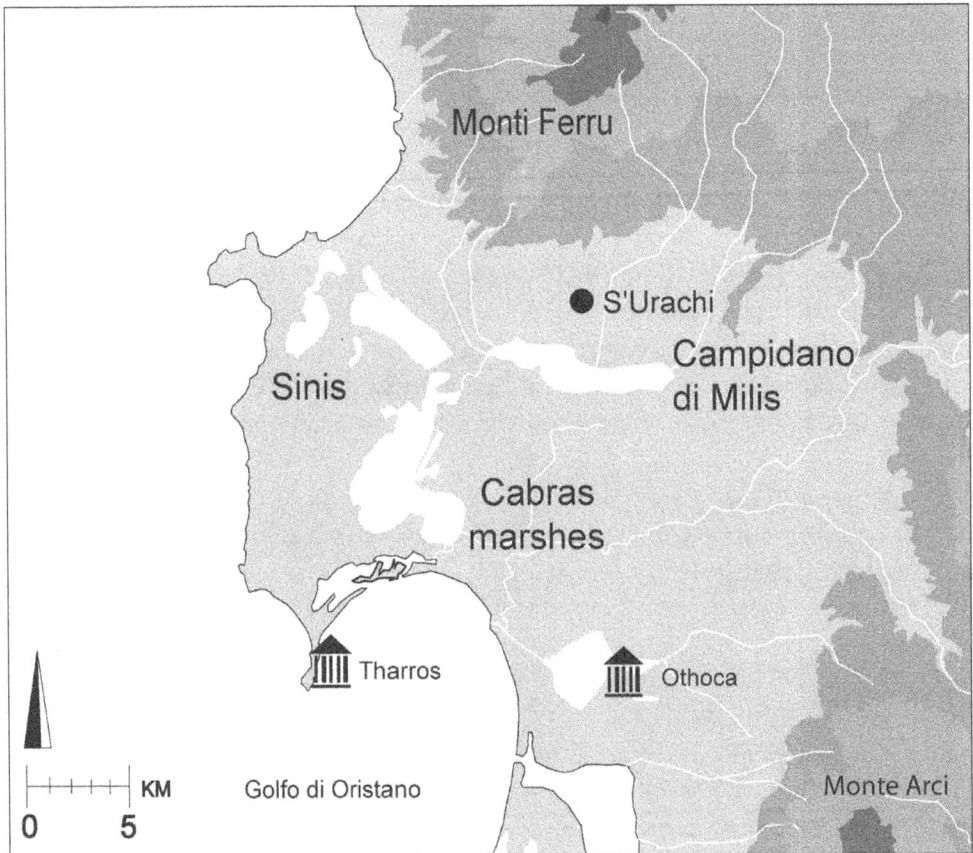

Figure 8.7 Location of *nuraghe* S'Urachi.

Nuraghe S'Urachi is situated in the lowlands of the *Campidano di Milis* between the Cabras salt marshes and the Gulf of Oristano to the south and the basalt slopes of the Monti Ferru to the north (Figure 8.7). The monumental core of the site consists of a large so-called complex *nuraghe* made up of a major central tower flanked by up to five lateral towers, all of which are surrounded by an outer defensive wall reinforced by ten towers. The entire complex measures about 42 m across and the exterior wall stands today up to 5 m tall (Stiglitz *et al.* 2015: 193-200; and see below, Figure 8.8).

In terms of our earlier discussion of monumental afterlives, the S'Urachi Project represents an attempt to overcome the 'archaeological myopia' that blurs *nuraghe* studies, as it specifically aims to bring into focus the Iron Age and Phoenician-Punic periods that have largely been overlooked thus far (van Dommelen and Roppa 2014). The excavations concentrate on two areas outside the *nuraghe* proper but immediately adjacent to the external defensive wall or *antemurale*, because work elsewhere has shown that both the later Iron Age and Roman occupation phases are mostly found in domestic structures surrounding the monument (as Lilliu already concluded in 1955). Because this spatial separation between the 'original' Bronze Age monument and the later 'reuse' phases in the village has only resulted in a further disconnect between the monument and its afterlives, the two excavation areas represent an attempt to reconnect these phases.

Although the excavations are still at an early stage, it has already become clear that most of the first millennium BC is represented in the two excavation areas, and that the sequences and contexts are as variable as they are complex. Overall, two major phases stand out that in conventional terms roughly cover the Archaic to Hellenistic periods (eighth/seventh to second century BC) and the late Punic period (second to first century BC). The Roman imperial period is so far only attested by stray finds from the top of the *nuraghe* (Stiglitz *et al.* 2015: 202).[1]

Area D, the southernmost of the two excavation areas, is defined by a remarkably rich and complex series of architectural remains that have engaged directly with the *nuraghe* in a variety of manners and at different moments in time, transforming it in more than one way. The oldest structures brought to light so far (2015) can broadly be ascribed to the later Archaic period, and, crucially, both engage directly with the *nuraghe*. One feature is a doorway through the outer defensive wall of the *nuraghe*, and the other a wall abutting a tower of the exterior *nuraghe* wall that defines a likely exterior courtyard (Figure 8.8, A and B). The presence of an entrance through this wall into the courtyard suggests that these two features may correspond to each other. Together, these features suggest that at this time, around the seventh or sixth century BC, the *nuraghe* itself was still frequently accessed, and possibly occupied; but the added complex of open and closed spaces had also fundamentally altered the use and presumably perception of the monument. While the added walls all appear to have been constructed in broadly Nuragic style and techniques, it is worth noting that the bulk of the portable material culture is overwhelmingly made up of Phoenician pottery, as is readily illustrated by two typically Phoenician tripod bowls found on the paved floor of the likely courtyard (Figure 8.8).

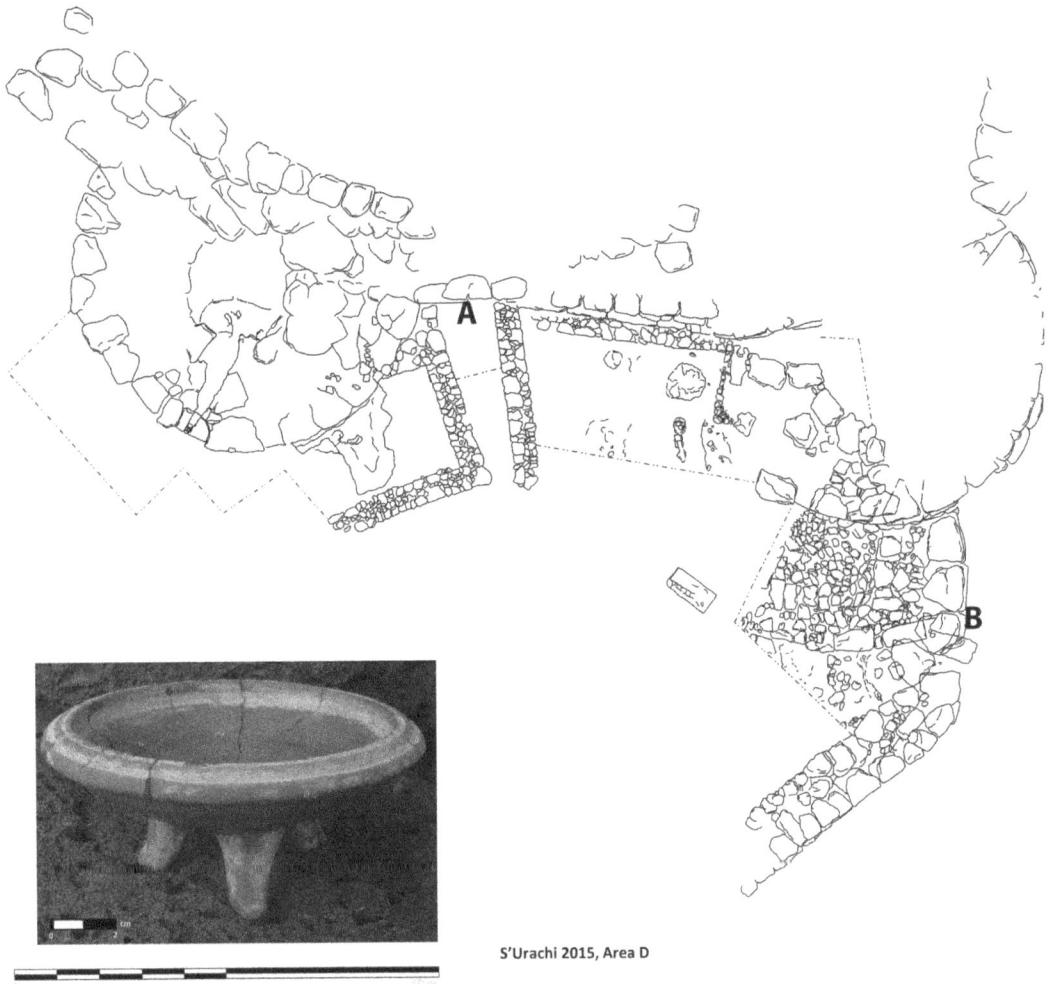

S'Urachi 2015, Area D

Figure 8.8   Plan of the southern sector of *nuraghe* S'Urachi (Area D), showing the location of the excavation areas discussed (A and B), and a Phoenician tripod bowl found on the paved floor of the likely courtyard (adjacent to wall B).

This area was drastically reorganized in the late second century BC, when a series of new rooms were built, one of which was partially constructed over one of the towers of the outer *nuraghe* wall (Figure 8.8, to the left of doorway A). The access to the doorway was also backfilled and blocked off entry to the *nuraghe*. This demonstrates unequivocally that by this time the *nuraghe* had ceased to function as an enclosed space, and suggests that it had perhaps begun to collapse. All earlier constructions were covered up and the floor level of the area was raised by more than a meter to create a platform for a number of parallel rooms that leaned against the upper part of the outer *nuraghe* wall. All in all, the appearance and functions of these spaces were fundamentally transformed. Poor preservation of these levels unfortunately means that we are unlikely to retrieve much information about these late Punic constructions.

An entirely different situation has come to light in Area E, which is situated just some 20 m along the outer defensive wall from Area D. Unlike the latter, Area E has turned out to be largely devoid of constructions, with just one corner of a room dated to the later Punic period. That does not mean that it was just empty space, as at some point in the Archaic period, possibly by the late seventh or early sixth century BC, the area was reorganized by constructing two stone embankments that created a roughly 5-m-wide ditch or channel, which suggests that the area mattered to the inhabitants of S'Urachi. Shortly afterward, however, they began to backfill the ditch with domestic trash from houses that are otherwise so far unknown.

Provisional as these results may be, they set out very clearly that S'Urachi's afterlife was manifold and multifaceted. Even if many details are yet to be clarified, the excavations demonstrate that the monument remained in use and occupied throughout the first millennium BC, and that over that period the forms and ways of using space changed substantially. During the earlier centuries of the first millennium BC, the *nuraghe* remained accessible through the outer defensive wall, but its spaces were extended and used in new ways, presumably quite differently from before. Several centuries afterward, in the later Punic period, the outer area was drastically reorganized, as floor levels were raised and entirely new buildings constructed; access to the interior of the *nuraghe* was no longer possible. As the portable material culture and faunal and organic remains indicate that some cultural traditions persisted, while new ones were adapted and constructed, it is evident that S'Urachi continued to be an important focus of social and economic life, and that it became integrated in its inhabitants' lives in a variety of ways.

Monumental Engagements

As our case studies have shown, architecture cannot be examined in isolation or in generic terms. The Talayotic and Nuragic monuments must be contextualized in the framework of daily life in all the various periods of occupation or use. Daily life includes the continued use of some monuments, such as the Menorcan *taula*, well beyond their times of construction. At the same time, monumental constructions cannot be understood only as persisting spaces of communal gathering or religious practice. They must also be contextualized for their role as domestic establishments in later periods, as in the case of S'Urachi. The monument can become a dwelling, a stable, or a number of different functional structures, and thus enter a new stage of meaning related to the local community and its construction of identity.

The continued use of a monument as a village center, dwelling, or even utilitarian space can be seen as more than simply a ruinous ghost, haunting the landscape. In their persistence of use and reconstructed local meaning in the landscape, monuments can serve as a continuous communal anchoring point. Their significance is not temporally isolated. They can be inspiring, grounding, or critical identity markers, even if they are not used in their original, intended capacity, as was the case at both Torre D'en Galmés and S'Urachi. Returning to what Blake (1998: 68) has noted, a monument can be generative of an indigenous identity, or make a connection to the landscape.

Blake (1998) also emphasizes that although modern archaeologists and historians consider such monuments as 'Nuragic', it was not always this way in the past. As the changing relationships with the *nuraghe* at S'Urachi show, there were episodes of both direct association with the heritage of the Nuragic people as well as disjuncture. Elsewhere in Sardinia, *nuraghi* remained a focal point for domestic and ritual purposes even during the later Roman period, but it is unclear and probably questionable whether there was a direct Nuragic association, as many sites were reused and re-purposed during this period (Blake 1998: 63-64). Blake (1998: 64) does not see this as 'passive ethno-cultural continuity' on the part of the Sardinians but emphasizes that they actively used these monuments to forge a new Sardo-Roman identity, and to (re) connect themselves with the past, even as or perhaps because they lived in a world that was politically and to some extent culturally Roman. As shown at Torre d'en Galmés, the continued centrality of *talayots* can similarly not be seen as a mere 'passive ethno-cultural continuity', but offers instead an instance of a quasi-political statement of the community's association with a local and older heritage, whether real or imagined, or an expression of communal cohesion and collective identity, if not both.

The meaning of monumental spaces and structures constantly shifts, and even if it is obvious that monuments retain some significance in the landscape long after their intended use, as is for instance evident at Santa Sabina, we must also understand that these sites and structures serve as a continuous stage for changing cultural significance. The meaning of a monument is malleable, and exploring the manner in which indigenous and colonial customs can shape their meaning is a step toward understanding the complexity and social construction of island traditions—not as points along a monolithic indigenous and subsequently colonial timeline, but from a microhistorical perspective on the intricacies of cultural change and modification in the wake of changing communal worldviews.

Conclusions

Our discussion of the monuments at Torre d'en Galmés and S'Urachi neatly underscores the fact that monumental places serve as both a witness to change as well as an inspiration of new traditions. The more we dig into the continuing roles and appearances of these monuments after their time of construction and period of initially intended use, the more we discover an increasingly complicated relationship with later communities. A recurring feature amidst all this complexity and variability, however, is what we would call an enduring and 'strong appeal' of these monuments that in many cases serves to generate or at least anchor local identities in subsequent periods.

A final element to consider is the role of the sea and the fact that we are talking about islands. The sea is never far away, even if for much of the past three or four millennia coastal settlement was relatively uncommon, including on a small island like Menorca. Even so, external influences can and did come to the islands, and obvious contrasts between insiders and outsiders were easily created. It is perhaps no coincidence that the island monuments are in all cases very much typically and distinctively local and that they remain so through time—even if their use and roles change, their 'strong appeal' and 'localness' continued to be recognized and indeed upheld. In other words, monuments never really died, as our discussion of Torre d'en Galmés and S'Urachi may have made clear. Later communities, including incoming people, forged a connection with these monuments, even as they redefined them, reusing or engaging with *nuraghi* as shrines or even burials sites, or funerary caves as houses, stables, and even apiaries; but they were and are always reintegrated into people's lives. We should therefore not think of islands as laboratories of cultural construction, but as proper social spaces in their own right, with distinct identities that are not so much isolated as local and integrative from islanders' perspectives—and these monuments play a key role in asserting, embodying, and 'nailing down' these local identities.

Acknowledgments

We thank the editors for their patience and the reviewers for their sound advice. We are also grateful for helpful feedback from Damià Ramis, Irene Riudavets, and Antoni Ferrer. We thank Amalia Pérez-Juez and Ricardo Elia, among the many other colleagues and students at Boston University, for their work and continued support of the presented research on Torre d'en Galmés. We are, finally, indebted to our friends and colleagues at S'Urachi, Alfonso Stiglitz, Andrea Roppa, and Damià Ramis in the first place, for the many discussions at and about the site that have contributed much to shaping our ideas and interpretations about the monument and its afterlives.

Endnote

1. Because the portable finds of this area had not yet been studied at the time of writing, all dates mentioned here are provisional. For more details, see the preliminary report by Stiglitz *et al.* (2015).

About the Authors

Alexander Smith is an Instructor at the College at Brockport's Anthropology Department and Delta College, as well as in the Art & Art History Department at the University of Rochester, New York. He has worked on Menorca since 2007, studying the indigenous Talayotic culture of the island, and since 2013 he has also worked on Sardinia as a survey and GIS specialist at the Nuragic site of S'Urachi. He works closely with the Memorial Art Gallery of Rochester, promoting classroom integration of museum resources and public archaeology. E-mail: alexander_smith@alumni.brown.edu

Peter van Dommelen is Director of the Joukowsky Institute of Archaeology and the Ancient World at Brown University, Rhode Island, where he is Joukowsky Family Professor of Archaeology and Professor of Anthropology. His research interests in colonialism and rural organization structure long-term fieldwork on the island of Sardinia. Recent publications have appeared in the *Journal of Roman Archaeology*, *Rivista di Studi Fenici* and the *Annual Review of Anthropology*, with A. Bernard Knapp, he has co-edited *The Cambridge Prehistory of the Bronze and Iron Age Mediterranean* (2014). He also serves as co-editor of the *Journal of Mediterranean Archaeology* and *World Archaeology*. E-mail: peter_van_dommelen@brown.edu

Classical Authors and Texts

Livy, *Ab Urbe Condita*.

References

Alcock, S.
  2002 *Archaeologies of the Greek Past. Landscape, Monuments and Memories*. Cambridge: Cambridge University Press.
Anglada, M., A. Ferrer, M. Plantalamor, D. Ramis, M. Van Strydonck and G. De Mulder
  2014 Chronological framework for the early Talayotic period in Menorca: the settlement of Cornia Nou. *Radiocarbon* 56: 411-24. https://doi.org/10.2458/56.16962
Blake, E.
  1998 Sardinia's nuraghi: four millennia of becoming. *World Archaeology* 30: 59-71. https://doi.org/10.1080/00438243.1998.9980397
  2014 Late Bronze Age Sardinia: acephalous cohesion. In A.B. Knapp and P. van Dommelen (eds.), *The Cambridge Prehistory of the Bronze and Iron Age Mediterranean*, 96-110. Cambridge: Cambridge University Press. https://doi.org/10.1017/cho9781139028387.009

Bradley, R.
  1993 *Altering the Earth: The Origins of Monuments in Britain and Continental Europe*. Monographs of the Society of Antiquaries of Scotland 8. Edinburgh: Society of Antiquaries of Scotland.
Bravo Asensio, C., and F. Contreras Rodrigo
  2014 Aproximación al estudio de la ciudad romana de Sanisera (Sanitja – Menorca). In M. Riera Rullan and J. Cardell (eds.), *V Jornades d'Arqueologia de les Illes Balears*, 189-98. Palma de Mallorca, Spain: Edicions Documenta Balear.
Broodbank, C.
  2000 *An Island Archaeology of the Early Cyclades*. Cambridge: Cambridge University Press.
Cherry, J.F.
  1981 Patterns and process in the earliest colonisation of the Mediterranean islands. *Proceedings of the Prehistoric Society* 47: 41-68. https://doi.org/10.1017/S0079497X00008859

1985 Islands out of the stream: isolation and interaction in early east Mediterranean insular prehistory. In A.B. Knapp and T. Stech (eds.), *Prehistoric Production and Exchange in the Aegean and East Mediterranean*. UCLA Institute of Archaeology Monograph 27: 12-29. Los Angeles: UCLA Institute of Archaeology.

Cherry, J.F., and T.P. Leppard
2014 A little history of Mediterranean island prehistory. In A.B. Knapp and P. van Dommelen (eds.), *The Cambridge Prehistory of the Bronze and Iron Age Mediterranean*, 10-24. Cambridge: Cambridge University Press. https://doi.org/10.1017/cho9781139028387.004

Contreras Rodrigo, F.
1998 Sanisera, ciudad romana de Menorca. Su origen. In C. Garrido (ed.), *La Mirada del pasado: Las culturas antiguas de las Illes Balears*, 303-305. Fornells, Spain: Edicions de turisme cultural.

Contreras Rodrigo, F., R. Müller and F.J. Valle de Tarzaga
2006 El asentamiento militar romano de Sanitja (123-45 a.C.): Una aproximación a su contexto histórico. *Mayurqa* 31: 231-50.

Estarellas Ordinas, M.M., J. Merino Santisteban and F. Torres Orell
2014 El jaciment Romà de Son Espases: L'organització de les estructures. In M. Riera Rullan and J. Cardell (eds.), *V Jornades d'Arqueologia de les Illes Balears*, 149-54. Palma de Mallorca, Spain: Edicions Documenta Balear.

Evans, J.
1973 Islands as laboratories of culture change. In C. Renfrew (ed.), *The Explanation of Culture Change: Models in Prehistory*, 517-20. London: Duckworth.

Ginsburg, C.
1993 Microhistory: two or three things that I know about it. *Critical Inquiry* 20: 10-35. https://doi.org/10.1086/448699

Guerrero Ayuso, V.
1997 *Colonización púnica de Mallorca: La documentación arqueológica y el contexto histórico*. Palma de Mallorca, Spain: Universitat de les Illes Balears.

Guerrero Ayuso, V.M., M. Calvo Trias and B. Salvà Simonet
2002 La cultura talayotica. Una sociedad de la edad del Hierro en la periferia de la colonización fenicia. *Complutum* 13: 221-58.

2006 *Historica de las islas Baleares 2. Mallorca y Menorca en la edad del hierro*. Palma de Mallorca: El Mundo.

Kolb, M.
2005 The genesis of monuments among the Mediterranean islands. In E. Blake and A.B. Knapp (eds.), *The Archaeology of Mediterranean Prehistory*. Blackwell Studies in Global Archaeology 6: 156-79. Malden, Massachusetts: Blackwell. https://doi.org/10.1002/9780470773536.ch7

2014 Monumentality among the Mediterranean isles. In J. Osborne (ed.), *Approaching Monumentality in Archaeology*. University of Buffalo, Institute for European and Mediterranean Archaeology Conference Proceedings 3: 153-80. Albany: State University of New York Press.

Lewthwaite, J.
1986 The transition to food production: a Mediterranean perspective. In M. Zvelebil (ed.), *Hunters in Transition: Mesolithic Societies of Temperate Eurasia and their Transition to Farming*, 53-66. Cambridge: Cambridge University Press.

1990 La strada del molo di Cagliari: l'esperienza di un archeologo di due estati in Sardegna (1976/77). *Quaderni Bolotanesi* 16: 83-103.

Lilliu, G.
1955 Il nuraghe di Barumini e la stratigrafia nuragica. *Studi Sardi* 12-13 (1952-1954): 90-469.

1971 *Costante resistenziale sarda*. Cagliari, Italy: Stef.

1988 *La civiltà dei Sardi dal Paleolitico all'età dei nuraghi.* 3rd edn. Turin: Nuova ERI.

1989 La Sardegna preistorica e le sue relazioni esterne. *Studi Sardi* 28 (1988-1989): 11-36.

1990 Sopravvivenze nuragiche in età romana. In A. Mastino (ed.), *L'Africa romana: atti del 7. Convegno di studio, 15-17 dicembre 1989*, 415-46. Sassari, Italy: Edizioni Gallizzi.

López Mullor, A.

2015 Les excavacions de la Mancomunitat de Catalunya a l'illa de Mallorca. In J. Rovira i Port and Á. Casanovas i Romeu (eds.), *La dècada prodigiosa 1914-1924. L'arqueologia catalana, un instrument vertebrador al servei de la Mancomunitat de Catalunya*, 127-44. Barcelona: Museu d'Arqueologia de Catalunya.

Lull, V., R. Micó, C. Rihuete and R. Risch

1999 *La Cova des Càrritx y la Cova des Mussol. Ideología y sociedad en la prehistoria de Menorca.* Barcelona: Consell Insular de Menorca.

Moravetti, A.

1998 *Ricerche archeologiche nel Marghine Planargia.* Sardegna Archeologica, Studi e Monumenti 5. Sassari, Italy: Carlo Delfino.

Orfila Pons, M., M.E. Chávez and M.Á. Cau

2006 Pollentia and the cities of the Balearic Islands. In L. Abad Casal, S. Keay and S. Ramallo Asensio (eds.), *Early Roman Towns in* Hispania Tarraconensis. Journal of Roman Archaeology Supplementary Series 62: 133-45. Portsmouth, Rhode Island: Journal of Roman Archaeology.

2008 Pollentia y las Baleares en época republicana. In J. Uroz, J.M. Noguera and F. Coarelli (eds.), *Iberia e Italia: Modelos romanos de integración territorial*, 43-66. Murcia, Spain: Tabularium.

Pala, P.

1990 Osservazioni preliminari per uno studio della riutilizzazione dei nuraghi in epoca romana. In A. Mastino (ed.), *L'Africa romana: atti del 7. Convegno*

di studio, 15-17 dicembre 1989, 549-56. Sassari, Italy: Edizioni Gallizzi.

Pérez-Juez, A.

2011 Excavaciones en la Casa 2 del yacimiento de Torre d'en Galmés, Alaior: Propuestas para el hábitat talayótico. In J. Gual Cerdó (ed.), *III Jornades d'Arqueologia de les Illes Balears*, 119-30. Mahón, Spain: Consell Insular de Menorca.

Pérez-Juez, A., J. Wiseman, P. Goldberg, J. Hansen, K. Mullen, M. Ostovich, C. Payne, S. Gornés, D. Cabanes, I. Euba, J. Vicente Morales, J. Morín and F.J. López Fraile

2007 El uso del espacio doméstico de una estructura del talayótico final: excavación de la Casa 2 del yacimiento de Torre d'en Galmés, Alayor 2003-2006. In *L'Arqueologia a Menorca: eina per al coneixement del passat*, 53-74. Mahón, Spain: Consell Insular de Menorca.

Poli, F., and G. Lambrocco

2002 La chiesa di Santa Sabina a Silanus, possibili percorsi di lettura. *Archivio Storico Sardo* 42: 27-85.

Renfrew, C.

1973 *Before Civilization: The Radiocarbon Revolution and Prehistoric Europe.* London: Jonathan Cape.

Rojas, F., and V. Sergueenkova

2014 Traces of Tarhuntas: Greek, Roman, and Byzantine interaction with Hittite monuments. *Journal of Mediterranean Archaeology* 27: 135-60. https://doi.org/10.1558/jmea.v27i2.135

Rosselló-Bordoy, G.

1984 Excavaciones arqueológicas en Torre d'en Gaumés (Alayor, Menorca). El recinto de taula y el sistema de recogida de aguas (campañas 1974, 1975 y 1977). *Noticiario Arqueológico Hispánico* 19: 103-97.

1986 *El poblado prehistórico de Torre d'en Gaumes (Alaior).* Palma de Mallorca: Institut d'Estudis Baleàrics.

Rosselló Bordoy, G., R. Sánchez Cuenca and P. De Montaner

1974 Imhotep, hijo de Ptah. *Mayurqa* 12: 123-42.

Salvà, B., and J. Hernández-Gasch
2009 Los espacios domésticos en las Islas Baleares durante las Edades del Bronce y del Hierro. De la sociedad naviforme a la talayótica. In M.C. Belarte (ed.), *L'espai domèstic i l'organització de la societat a la protohistòria de la Mediterrània occidental (Ier mil·lenni).* Arqueo Mediterrània 11: 299-321. Barcelona: Universitat de Barcelona and Institut Català d'Arqueologia Classica.

Sintes Olives, E., and F. Isbert Vaquer
2009 Investigación arqueológica y puesta en valor del recinto Cartailhac. *Patrimonio Cultural de España* 1: 251-60.

Stiglitz, A., E. Díes Cusí, D. Ramis, A. Roppa and P. van Dommelen
2015 Intorno al nuraghe: notizie preliminari sul Progetto S'Urachi (San Vero Milis, OR). *Quaderni della Soprintendenza Archeologica per le province di Cagliari e Oristano* 26: 191-218. http://www.quaderniarcheocaor.beniculturali.it/index.php/quaderni/article/view/254

van Dommelen, P.
1998 Punic persistence: colonialism and cultural identity in Roman Sardinia. In J. Berry and R. Laurence (eds.), *Cultural Identity in the Roman Empire*, 25-48. London: Routledge.
2007 Beyond resistance: Roman power and local traditions in Punic Sardinia. In P. van Dommelen and N. Terrenato (eds.), *Articulating Local Cultures: Power and Identity under the Expanding Roman Republic.* Journal of Roman Archaeology Supplementary Series 63: 55-70. Portsmouth, Rhode Island: Journal of Roman Archaeology.

van Dommelen, P., and A. Roppa
2014 Conclusioni: per una definizione dell'età del Ferro sarda. *Rivista di Studi Fenici* 41 (2013): 271-77.

Vanzetti, A.
2004 Risultati e problemi di alcune attuali prospettive di studio della centralizzazione e urbanizzazione di fase protostorica in Italia. In P. Attema (ed.), *Centralization, Early Urbanization and Colonization in First Millennium BC Italy and Greece* 1. *Italy.* Babesch Supplement Series 9: 1-28. Leuven: Peeters.

Vicent García, J.M.
1997 The Island Filter Model revisited. In M. Balmuth, A. Gilman and L. Prados-Torreira (eds.), *Encounters and Transformations: The Archaeology of Iberia in Transition.* Monographs in Mediterranean Archaeology 7: 1-13. Sheffield: Sheffield Academic Press.

Webster, G.
2016 *The Archaeology of Nuragic Sardinia.* Monographs in Mediterranean Archaeology 14. Sheffield: Equinox.

Part III

Comparative, Theoretical, and Disciplinary Concerns

Introduction to Part III: Comparative, Theoretical, and Disciplinary Concerns

Alex R. Knodell and Thomas P. Leppard

In this final section we expand outward, both geographically and conceptually. This is by far the longest and most diverse section of this volume, reflecting the eclecticism and range of John Cherry's career. The first four chapters in this section (by Broodbank, Fitzpatrick, Ryzewski, and Garrison) look beyond the Mediterranean, reflecting Cherry's own intellectual itinerance. Nevertheless, they also hearken back to themes that are interwoven in the foregoing papers. The latter three chapters (by Witmore, Knapp, and McKay) roam more widely through theoretical space, considering not only how we conceive of our data and where the locus of our interest in it lies, but also how types of data production (and retention) can structure interpretation and the construction of archaeological syntheses. In doing so, these chapters draw on John Cherry's longstanding insistence on the importance of a self-aware and reflexive approach to scholarship, especially concerning the archaeology of regions.

Broodbank and Fitzpatrick focus on island archaeology, following one of the hallmarks of Cherry's career. Broodbank asks the vital question, 'does island archaeology matter?', to which he provides, in the affirmative, a resounding explanation of why and how. His chapter's broad perspective on island environments and maritime theaters across the world builds upon the previous section of this volume by demonstrating the particular role Mediterranean islands have played in deep global history, especially in relation to mainlands. Fitzpatrick follows this theme to address how and in what terms a comparative island archaeology might be attempted. Such concerns reflect a growing interest in comparative archaeology and its utility in examining how trajectories of societal development are general or culturally specific (e.g., Smith *et al.* 2012; Kintigh *et al.* 2014). Fitzpatrick examines—following an early interest of Cherry (1981; 1990)—how islands may be ideal environments from which to begin a comparative approach, not least because of the geographic and physiographic conditions that characterize them.

Ryzewski's focus is on the past, present, and future of regional studies in Caribbean historical archaeology, providing a Cherry-esque report on the 'state of the field' for survey archaeology in the Caribbean. Ryzewski grapples with issues that have confronted other archaeologists as they seek to make the most of comparative perspectives, which sometimes involves transplanting methodologies from one context to another. She emphasizes the importance of flexibility in the face of environmental intransigence (fieldwalking in the Mediterranean and the Caribbean are very different propositions), but argues nonetheless that Caribbean regional archaeologies should develop a greater interest in landscape and non-site (or off-site) approaches. Methodologies of this sort, as Cherry (1983) has demonstrated, imply a responsibility to maintain a diachronic focus, and there are clear advantages of such *longue durée* perspectives in an environment where rigid periodization has been so significant.

Garrison also takes a comparative view using New World data, doing so through the lens of peer polity interaction (Renfrew and Cherry 1986). Noting the importance of the peer polity concept for Mayanists, Garrison examines how the wealth of new data generated since the 1980s (partly regional, partly textual) can be used to construct a revised model of interaction among Maya regional polities that combines the tenets of peer polity interaction with landscape ecology and spatial theory. The result is a powerful synthesis for understanding inter-state relations that also has implications beyond the Maya area. This underscores not only how New World and Old World archaeologies can engage in productive conversations on the same terms (see also Parkinson and Galaty 2007), but how broad models that are deliberately comparative can retain relevance and ultimately improve in light of evolving datasets.

The contributions by Witmore and Knapp orbit a common theoretical question: in regional approaches to social complexity, how much weight should be given to nonhuman agencies, and through what lens should these agencies be perceived? Witmore challenges how we conceive of complexity, suggesting that it cannot be understood only in reference to humans and their activity. Rather, he points to the wider world of things that constituted Classical Argos, showing how material agencies affected the organization and execution of statecraft. Witmore's thesis is relevant well beyond Argos, asking: how do networks of agencies come together to enable and constrain trajectories of complexity? Witmore performs vital work in forcing us to face, and potentially to defend, our definitions and preconceptions. Knapp, with a similar focus but a different perspective, also addresses how we consider materials and their agencies within human landscapes. Knapp uses materials from the Bronze Age smelting site of Politiko *Phorades* as a point of departure in considering the 'material turn'—drawing in part on the broader work of the 'new materialisms'—and approaches allied to it (e.g., Thomas 2015), exemplified by symmetrical archaeology (Olsen *et al.* 2012; Witmore 2014; Olsen and Witmore 2015). Knapp suggests that in the rush to understand the power of materials to constrain and to enable human action, we may have lost sight of underlying goals: how interested are we in explaining human processes without reference to humans, and has a deep, qualitative gulf between human and nonhuman agencies been glossed?

MacKay is similarly concerned with data—less how we theorize data, and more how their generation and curation drives (or limits) syntheses at a regional level. She highlights how digitization of data could have been expected to ease large-scale comparison and synthesis, yet this shows little sign of happening (see also Bevan 2015). This seems illustrative of a broader disjuncture between an interest in making comparisons and the functional, methodological limitations in doing so—a theme also considered by Ryzewski. MacKay remains optimistic, however, and digitization implies a degree of democratization beyond that associated with more traditional forms of publication and dissemination of data.

It is clear that several themes emerge from these disparate papers. In their divergence, we can track the varied concerns and themes of John Cherry's career—not only a concern with the regional archaeology of complex societies writ large, but with various aspects of the practice of archaeology that a regional perspective implies. Despite this range, there are nevertheless substantial areas of overlap. We explore these more substantively in the final, concluding chapter of this volume, but here note that these contributions are all concerned with the terms in which we understand material culture and how we can build larger, synthetic interpretations—either via embracing comparison in ecological and physiographic terms (Broodbank; Fitzpatrick) or sociopolitical models (Garrison), by understanding how to enact such comparison (Ryzewski; MacKay), or by revising, broadening, and critiquing our definitions of complexity and material worlds (Witmore; Knapp).

About the Authors

Alex R. Knodell is Assistant Professor of Classics and Co-Director of the Archaeology Program at Carleton College, Northfield, Minnesota. He currently co-directs the Mazi Archaeological Project (northwest Attica, Greece) and previously served as Field Director of the Brown University Petra Archaeological Project (Petra, Jordan). Other research interests include the development of complex societies in the Late Bronze Age and Early Iron Age Mediterranean, especially in relation to the Euboean Gulf of Greece. Recent articles have appeared in the *American Journal of Archaeology*, *Antike Kunst*, the *Journal of Archaeological Science*, the *Journal of Field Archaeology*, and *World Archaeology*. E-mail: aknodell@carleton.edu

Thomas P. Leppard is Renfrew Fellow in the McDonald Institute for Archaeological Research at the University of Cambridge. His research concerns the comparative archaeology of island societies in the Mediterranean, Caribbean, and Pacific, especially issues of colonization, mobility, and emergent social complexity. Recent articles on these subjects have appeared in *Human Ecology*, the *Cambridge Archaeological Journal*, *Current Anthropology*, the *Journal of Island and Coastal Archaeology*, the *Journal of Mediterranean Archaeology*, and *World Archaeology*. He currently conducts fieldwork in Micronesia and Sardinia. E-mail: tpl26@cam.ac.uk

References

Bevan, A.
2015 The data deluge. *Antiquity* 89: 1473-84. https://doi.org/10.15184/aqy.2015.102

Cherry, J.F.
1981 Pattern and process in the earliest colonization of the Mediterranean islands. *Proceedings of the Prehistoric Society* 47: 41-68. https://doi.org/10.1017/S0079497X00008859

1983 Frogs round the pond: perspectives in current archaeological survey projects in the Mediterranean region. In D. Keller and D. Rupp (eds.), *Archaeological Survey in the Mediterranean Area*. British Archaeological Reports, International Series 155: 375-416. Oxford: Archaeopress.

1990 The first colonisation of the Mediterranean islands: a review of recent research. *Journal of Mediterranean Archaeology* 3: 145-221.

Kintigh, K.W, J.H. Altschul, M.C. Beaudry, R.D. Drennan, A.P. Kinzig, T.A. Kohler, W.F. Limp, H.D.G. Maschner, W.K. Michener, T.R. Pauketat, P. Peregrine, J.A. Sabloff, T.J. Wilkinson, H.T. Wright and M.A. Zeder
2014 Grand challenges for archaeology. *Proceedings of the National Academy of Sciences* 111: 879-80. https://doi.org/10.1073/pnas.1324000111

Olsen, B., M. Shanks, T. Webmoor and C.L. Witmore
2012 *Archaeology: The Discipline of Things*. Berkeley: University of California Press. https://doi.org/10.1525/california/9780520274167.001.0001

Olsen, B., and C.L. Witmore
2015 Archaeology, symmetry, and the ontology of things: a response to critics. *Archaeological Dialogues* 22: 187-97. https://doi.org/10.1017/S1380203815000240

Parkinson, W.A., and M.L. Galaty
2007 Secondary states in perspective: an integrated approach to prehistoric state formation in the Aegean. *American Anthropologist* 109: 113-29. https://doi.org/10.1525/aa.2007.109.1.113

Renfrew, C., and J.F. Cherry (eds.)
1986 *Peer Polity Interaction and Socio-Political Change*. Cambridge: Cambridge University Press.

Smith, M.E., G.M. Feinman, R.D. Drennan, T. Earle and E. Morris
2012 Archaeology as a social science. *Proceedings of the National Academy of Sciences* 109: 7617-21. https://doi.org/10.1073/pnas.1201714109

Thomas, J.
2015 The future of archaeological theory. *Antiquity* 89: 1287-96. https://doi.org/10.15184/aqy.2015.183

Witmore, C.
2014 Archaeology and the New Materialisms. *Journal of Contemporary Archaeology* 1: 203-24. https://doi.org/10.1558/jca.v1i2.16661

9 Does Island Archaeology Matter?

Cyprian Broodbank

Introduction

Island archaeologists naturally tend to believe that their subject matters. Over the academic lifespan of many of us, however, the grounds on which this case has been built have shifted. When, during the 1970s and to a lesser extent the 1980s, island archaeology was a relatively young domain, justification and establishment seemed the paramount goals, and much effort went into demonstrating the wider relevance of the analysis of early island societies (e.g., Evans 1973; Keegan and Diamond 1987). Most of that brave new world was, if not lost, at least thrust into the background in the 1990s and the early years of our current millennium by a focus instead on cultural meanings, experiences, and consequences of insularity, inspired in part by post-modernism but stemming also from the rather two-dimensional, insufficiently compelling portraits of ancient island life that the preceding decades had bequeathed (e.g., Broodbank 2000: 6-35; Cherry 2004; Rainbird 2007).

Now, as we face a future of sharply growing competition for public as well as academic attention, and for resources within and beyond archaeology, island archaeology stands on potentially dangerously isolated ground. Its rising numbers of practitioners (positively marked by the success of the *Journal of Island and Coastal Archaeology*), its once salutary inward exploration of the many ways of being in an island world, and arguably the increasingly routinized range of questions asked of early island life, unintentionally but collectively point toward a self-imposed ghettoization. This chapter advocates a reversal of this trend. It argues that a good way to start is by taking a timely and critical look at whether, how, when, and why island archaeology's major findings about past island societies have mattered for the wider domain of archaeology and beyond—a lot, not so much, or barely at all? This question of the significance of past islands and islanders will be considered within three salient, if far from exclusive or all-embracing, frameworks: (1) the intrinsic; (2) the comparative sociopolitical; and (3) that of global deep history.

The Case for Intrinsic Importance

In a generous world this case would not need to be argued, for all distinctive classes of global environment and context ideally constitute equally valid areas of study in their own right. Island archaeology would in this regard take its place alongside the similarly self-defining archaeologies of, for example, arid zones, uplands, and deltas.

Given a long-established and manifest fascination with many facets of early island culture (and biology), particularly in the western intellectual tradition, the archaeology of islands could hold its head relatively high in such company. However, for reasons already alluded to, that generosity cannot be taken for granted. Fortunately, if we seek intrinsic reasons why the study of island pasts possesses a more convincing urgency today, several further possibilities do in fact present themselves.

The first involves contemporary identity politics and other uses and abuses of the past. Given the paucity of early island writing, and the variably reliable testimony over more than a few preceding generations of oral tradition and, equally, western ethnographies, it has long been recognized that island archaeology offers the best investigative avenue into most of the deeper past on most islands the world over. What deeper history is written about islands, and equally who writes it and from what internal or external perspective, is therefore vital for matters of identity today among island communities and nations such as those of the post-colonial Caribbean, Indian, and Pacific Oceans, and also the Mediterranean (Figure 9.1). And not only there; these sentences, it is impossible to resist noting, are written on the very day (23 June 2016) on which my own island went to the polls to decide whether or not it would remain in the European Union, with catastrophic results. The only caveat (of which Brexiteers might take note) is that the likely attention span accorded to such matters is pragmatically liable to vary immensely between more continental and insular audiences.

The second, and related, factor is geopolitics. One of the more unexpected and troubling features of the past and coming decades, when physical and ex-imperial geographies ostensibly have seemed likely to cede primacy to virtual ones, is the military and diplomatic resurgence of certain islands, often tiny, and even (in the South China Sea) freshly, strategically constructed. If we are to have any hope of addressing, let alone peacefully resolving, the fiercely contested claims over such islands and their extensive marine surroundings in existing theaters, and equally in the imminently emerging resource-rich island territories created by melting Arctic ice (Smith 2011), we will require the richest, most nuanced understanding possible of their long-term past if we are to begin to evaluate conflicting truth claims in the present and future.

Third, and most bleakly, islands, as in effect wrap-around coastal zones, are some of the places most immediately threatened by global warming (and by bitter irony also among those least responsible for its anthropogenic causes—with the exception of precociously industrial Britain, followed by Japan and recently others). Most vulnerable are low-lying atoll archipelagos, with entire island states, such as the Republics of Kiribati, the Marshall Islands, and Maldives, faced with extinction by inundation in the all-too-foreseeable future. Beyond the platitudes, hand-wringing, righteous (if largely impotent) indignation, chronically costly efforts at resistance, and growing talk of mass relocation, in order to contextualize the problem we will also need a far better, and archaeologically derived, knowledge of how, and how long, such island theaters have been occupied, and more generally of the overall place of islands in planet-wide patterns of occupation (or, just as crucially, failures of occupation) since at least the later Pleistocene.

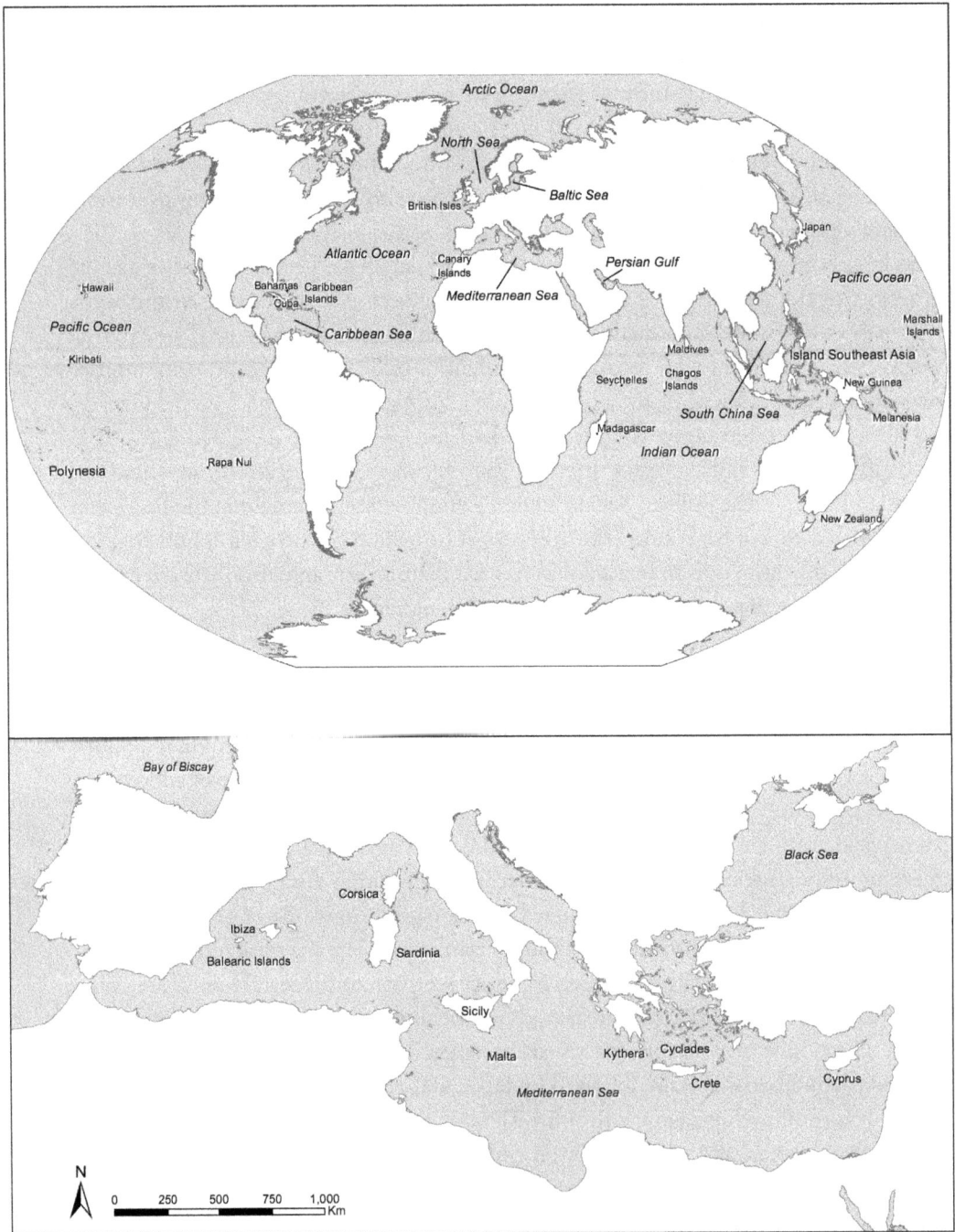

Figure 9.1 Top: world map showing oceans, seas, islands, and island groups mentioned in the text. Bottom: map of the Mediterranean sea with places mentioned in the text (maps by Evan Levine).

In summary, the intrinsic case for island archaeology as a means of improving our understanding of the long-term history and culture of islands and islanders can indeed be compellingly made for the present and future, yet most powerfully by being remade, too, in response to current challenges from far beyond archaeology itself.

The Case for the Utility of Comparative Sociopolitical Analysis

The classic formulation of this case, in the guise of the 'island laboratory' and the pious hope that detailed, bounded analysis of island sociopolitical formations such as Polynesian chiefdoms might result in a better understanding of archaeologically attested hierarchies elsewhere, has largely foundered in the face of several decades of withering criticism (e.g., Broodbank 2000: 6-35; see also Terrell *et al.* 1997; Boomert and Bright 2007; cf. Kirch 2007). Mainland archaeologists are not rushing to us to solve their burning questions, and frankly have never done so, at least not in ways that relate to the specifically insular status of our evidence. Much of the problem remains the extent to which island theaters really do furnish instructive analogs. Boundedness is a much less common attribute of island societies than was once believed, and when it does largely obtain (as in late pre-Contact Rapa Nui / Easter Island), the results are notoriously hard to translate and generalize. Equally, however, the spectacularly open radiation of languages and genes across Polynesia reflects a scenario more or less unmatched in the history of our planet since the peopling of the Americas: small, relatively homogenous and spatially focused initial populations, and a vast, suggestively structured emptiness into which to expand (Irwin 1992; Kirch 2010). The closest analogies for Polynesian expansion may well at some point be furnished by colonization of planetary and other bodies in outer, rather than earthly, space.

However, there are other ways in which islands might yet represent, in Terrell's words, 'good places to study the world' (Terrell 1986: 122). Leppard (2015) has recently explored which factors may, in otherwise diverse contexts, have prodded islanders down paths toward convergent solutions to recurring spatial problems. More generally, there is a persistent sense in which the writing of island archaeologies and histories tends to emphasize different qualities of human social, political, and economic association than those of more standard continental narratives, with less emphasis on vertical structures and territorial integrity, and more on flat hierarchies, horizontal networks, and self-ordering, fluid, open systems. These are, of course, qualities far from unique to, or universal in, island settings, but they do seem accentuated and accessible within such. Island archaeology, in this sense, is arguably peculiarly well-suited to offer antecedents for, and therefore insight into, the hyper-connected but un-centered world in which we live today.

The Role of Islands in Global Deep History

The two frameworks so far discussed have long been visible, in diverse guises, within island archaeological research agendas. Our third asks a simple question that so far island and other archaeologists have been curiously reluctant to address. To wit, as the shapes and trajectories of the deep, global history of our species become clearer, how much difference to its overall patterning has the existence of islands and their islanders in particular locations actually made, beyond their own internal dynamics, and especially during the deeper, primarily archaeologically accessible Holocene and late Pleistocene past that preceded many islands' manifest centrality over the past 500 or so years of global exploration and connectivity? In short, and bluntly, how important have islands and islanders been to long-term, cumulative world history? Not least as an inhabitant of one big island just off the coast of northwest Eurasia that mattered very little at this scale before the eighteenth century AD, and rapidly ceased to do so again from the later twentieth, it is apposite in ethical terms to stress that this question entails absolutely no positive or negative intrinsic valorization of island lives, either past or present. Nonetheless, from the perspective of the analysis of global history, the first, necessarily tentative answers are startling, instructive, and thought-provoking.

Islands and the Origins of Transoceanic Contacts

A useful starting point for this investigation is the world's three great oceans, their islands, and their surrounding rims. While the bringing together of the Atlantic has famously led the field of oceanic history as defined by the remit of the past few, globally decisive centuries (Crosby 1986; Reinhardt and Reinhartz 2006), it becomes clear once we go further back in time that—in the longer term—the Atlantic has proven the laggard in transoceanic contacts, in part due to the relative paucity, but above all the location, of its islands, the most remote of which remained empty until a few centuries ago. Despite some 6000 or more years of human activity in the Caribbean islands, and at least twice as long in continuous terms for some of the major islands off northwestern Europe's Atlantic façade, the first vestigial contacts across the ocean date to only a thousand years ago, in the form of Norse expansion. This was enabled by a locally recent adaption of the sailing technology developed several millennia earlier farther south (and apparently unknown in the Caribbean before 1492 AD), and it utilized the chain of stepping-stone islands across the Atlantic's narrowest, subpolar margin; as is well established, this expansion had no long-term impact, as measurable by any criterion, on people on either side of the ocean (Barrett 2003). Halfway from then to the present, when the 'Columbian moment', and its consequent momentous exchange, did take off, its initiation owed almost nothing to islands beyond the serendipity of first landfall in the Bahamas, and wider Caribbean consequences— save that the forms of exploitation inflicted on indigenous Canary islanders by west Mediterranean crusaders cum conquistadors-in-the-making during the fourteenth and especially the fifteenth century AD trialled strategies later unleashed on the New World's islanders (Mercer 1980; Fernández-Armesto 1982), strategies to which we return as ultimately of deeper ancestry. The Atlantic's early islanders were, in the final assessment, poorly placed to stitch their ocean and its populations together.

The Pacific, the most extensive island universe on the planet, ostensibly presents the opposite phenomenon in both geographical and human terms. The highly impressive later second millennium BC Lapita horticultural expansion in sailing canoes across major sea gaps into western Polynesia roughly coincides, after all, with the paddled canoes of Europe's Atlantic façade and Archaic Caribbean foragers on the other side of the Atlantic. Yet the best efforts to date the outermost points of Polynesian expansion to Rapa Nui, Hawaii, and New Zealand indicate landfalls there only in the centuries on either side of the turn of the second millennium AD, roughly in the same temporal window as the admittedly shorter Norse ventures across the north Atlantic (Wilmshurst *et al.* 2008; 2011; Athens *et al.* 2014). Slightly later again, and falling in Atlantic terms between the Norse and Columbian phases, are the increasingly secure indices of occasional Polynesian landfalls in mainland South America, which resulted in a westward spread back across Polynesia of the South American sweet potato and, it now seems, small amounts of human DNA in Rapa Nui, as well as the likely presence of Polynesian chickens in pre-Columbian Chile (Ballard *et al.* 2005; Storey *et al.* 2007; Thorsby 2012).

Two salient points stand out. Clearly, in the Pacific the first slight struts of an indirect transoceanic bridge and exchange were indeed effected by indigenous Pacific islanders rather than sailors from the continental rim, and decisively before the intrusion of western navigators. But equally, the scale of the impact at either end, albeit detectable, remains slight, and despite the great differences in the agents involved in the Pacific and Atlantic, in absolute terms the earliest trans-Pacific chronology only slightly pre-dates Columbus—and indeed Magellan. For all the Pacific's greater antiquity as an ocean full of islanders, the convergence of eastern Eurasia and the Americas across it, and the consequences of this, are barely older than the equivalent in the Atlantic.

In fact it is the Indian Ocean, until recently the least explored of the three, which appears to have led in transoceanic connections. One long-known hint of this likelihood is the Austronesian affiliation of Madagascan languages, although the antiquity of this transfer can only be fuzzily dated to the early centuries of the first millennium AD (Adelaar 1989; 1996). Recent research now pushes connections back between 1000 and 3000 years (see now Boivin *et al.* 2013). Admittedly, much of the earlier evidence pertains to circum- rather than transoceanic voyaging, especially in the northwestern sector between the Horn of Africa, southern Arabia, and the western edge of South Asia, extending the long-known Bronze Age connections between the civilizations of Sumer and the Indus Valley (Blench 2010; Fuller *et al.* 2011). However, reports from West Africa of banana phytoliths dating to the first millennium BC open up the prospect of direct connections between Island Southeast Asia and African landfall locations on the later Swahili coast (Lejju *et al.* 2006; but see Boivin *et al.* 2014)— perhaps providing antecedent context for the elusive linguistic transfer to Madagascar.

The apparent absence (or is it survival?) of Austronesian languages and bananas at intervening locations around the northern arc of the Indian Ocean provides a tantalizing argument for fairly direct, transoceanic transfer at least a thousand years before the equivalent in the Atlantic or Pacific. Frustratingly, while any such feats must owe much (as did the settlement of the Pacific) to the remarkable navigational prowess and technology encouraged by the great 'voyaging nursery' of Island Southeast Asia, the role that the islands in the midst of the Indian Ocean itself would have played remains uncertain, both due to their relative scarcity and the lack, so far, of any archaeological signs of passage. The most plausible islands to have more to reveal in this regard are the Maldive and Chagos archipelagoes, which form a midway chain, as well as possibly the Seychelles (Fitzpatrick and Callaghan 2008; Haour *et al.* 2016).

Islands of the Inner Seas

So far, we have seen strikingly little solid evidence that islands had much impact on overall global history until the last millennium or so before the present (albeit with a question mark hanging over the Indian Ocean). But the great oceans are not the only, and perhaps not the best, place to look. What of the world's smaller, and often inner, seas, especially those thickly studded with islands? Of course, these constitute far smaller theaters, but they are not necessarily parochial in their impact for all that— and not just because they tend to open onto larger masses of water into which the navigational and island life skills that they often fostered might subsequently expand (consider the Baltic, North Sea, and Mediterranean relative to the Atlantic, and much of the Southeast Asian maritime zone relative to the Indo-Pacific). Several such seas, in particular, potentially serve as maritime connecting zones between major terrestrial regions otherwise segregated or at best only circuitously linked (the Mediterranean, Caribbean, South China Sea, and wider Island Southeast Asian to western Melanesian zones come to mind). To what extent and how early did islands and islanders in such theaters transform wider dynamics around their perimeters?

The comparative archaeological analysis of the deep history of these inner seas remains a project in its infancy, and one largely ignored relative to comparisons across terrestrial space (see also Fitzpatrick, this volume). Its prosecution will be extremely challenging, not least due to gross inequalities in archaeological exploration, as well as survival and visibility, at least using traditional archaeological methods. Most lie in the tropical zones, with many of the key markers of circulation being in all likelihood perishable organic goods, crops, and foodstuffs that will require a full panoply of new bioarchaeological techniques to identify and fingerprint. In this sense, it may be some while before evidence is available in truly sufficient, comparable quantity. One major example of the type, however, lies within a more temperate zone characterized by excellent survival and high diagnosticity of abundant mineral-based (stone, pottery, and metal) materials, coupled with a long history of intensive archaeological investigation. This is the Mediterranean (Broodbank 2013; 2016).

The Mediterranean's islands occupy only some 4% of its land area, but an initial, and far from specious, impression would be that they have driven far more than 4% of its history. They punctuate the sea with highly variable density, but many are clearly very well situated to connect between the basin's major peninsulas, and a few indeed between its opposing rims. Equally, they have long been an explicit subject of island archaeological study, the foundations of which were largely laid by this volume's honorand (Cherry 1981; 1985; 1990; 2004). Yet can we establish more firmly how and when they became more than simply a parallel element of Mediterranean life, and began to serve as transformers and superchargers of it, well beyond the insular realm?

Of course, the presence of islands, as part of a convoluted land- and seascape of peninsulas and coasts, played a part in the set of affordances and inducements that stimulated the emergence of maritime activity in the Mediterranean in the first place, from its tentative Pleistocene beginnings onward (Broodbank 2006), as well as our ability to detect it, for example through movement of insular obsidian or other traces of early people on islands. Ultimately, without seafaring, it is hard to envisage the rise of the ancient Mediterranean in the manner we know it. This line of reasoning is, however, unsatisfactorily attenuated, and common to most island-rich theaters. Likewise, the maritime and coastwise spread of farming through the basin from the ninth to sixth millennium BC was also undoubtedly facilitated by the presence of islands, but not strictly dependent on this (Broodbank 2013). In this instance we can be quite precise; as Vigne (1992) long ago demonstrated, the arrival of farming on most of the major islands was part and parcel of wider mainstream (including mainland) processes, with no time-lag; but, equally, it is hard to point to a case where the peopling of an island by farmers fundamentally altered the onward process. This is especially so since the collapse of Lewthwaite's once intriguing 'Tyrrhenian filter' model, whereby Sardinia and Corsica stripped down the agricultural package that was passed further west (e.g., Lewthwaite 1986; cf. Zeder 2008). In a similar way, the first farmers on the Strait of Sicily's islands do not seem to have immediately brought farming to adjacent regions of coastal North Africa (while the Strait of Gibraltar manifestly did see such transfers: Broodbank 2013: 201-12). Even the precociously early Pre-Pottery Neolithic of Cyprus is without agreed, identifiable onward consequence; like the subsequent Neolithic settlement of Crete, it may have been a 'spur' event rather than a link in a chain (Vigne *et al.* 2012; Vigne 2013; Manning 2015).

It is with the third and second millennia BC (broadly the Bronze Age, plus a Copper Age in the west during the earlier millennium) that we see indisputable and specific indications of island societies transforming wider Mediterranean dynamics (Broodbank 2013). The most spectacular example is the second millennium BC palace-centered society of Minoan Crete, whose various external relations of trade, cultural affiliation, and arguably political hegemony had a profound impact upon other, smaller Aegean islands as well as the Aegean mainland—indeed, without Crete it remains hard to imagine Mycenae and its contemporaries emerging at the time, and in the form, that they did (Broodbank 2004; see also Manning, this volume). Toward the end of the second millennium BC, decentered, mercantile urban entities on Cyprus pioneered a rather different, and precocious, role in the transition away from palatial economies in the east Mediterranean, and also drove the expansion of direct voyaging between the eastern, center, and possibly western Mediterranean (Sherratt and Sherratt 1993; Sherratt 2003). It is slowly becoming clear that contemporary Sardinia played a similarly active connecting role in the center and west (Broodbank 2013: 475-77, 491-94; Blake 2014). However, modest forerunners of these largely big-island drivers can be detected at least as far back as the third millennium BC, and arguably the later fourth, not least in island clusters like the Early Bronze Age Cyclades, which facilitated communications and exchange within the Aegean (Renfrew 1972: 440-75; Broodbank 2000).

At a variety of Mediterranean scales, from intra-basin to inter-basin, the cumulative peopling of islands large and (increasingly) small, and the creation of networks centered on them, eventually turned the Mediterranean inside out: from a world of mainland coasts with the islands at their margins, to a situation in which peopled islands created new insular centers that acted back, sometimes decisively, on mainland history (e.g., Knappett and Nikolakopoulou 2014). Interestingly, the higher stakes created by a more connected Mediterranean could make island societies potentially more vulnerable as well as more powerful—witness the ending of 'temple' society on Malta during the later third millennium BC under conditions of rapidly increasing, possibly involuntary off-island engagement (Malone and Stoddart 2013), while Kythera during the mid- to late second millennium BC illustrates how a single island could slip over the cusp from centrality to victimhood with startling ease (Broodbank *et al.* 2005). Moreover, the same distance-busting technologies—primarily large, fast, longboat canoes and then sailing ships (Broodbank 2010)—could alternately promote or threaten island ways of life. The adoption of sailing ships, for example, seems to have been fundamental to the expansions of three large islands (first Crete and then Cyprus and Sardinia), but disastrous for the hitherto canoe-based societies of smaller islands in the Aegean at the end of the third millennium BC, in the central Mediterranean by the mid- to late second millennium BC, and in the Balearics at the start of the first millennium BC (e.g., Broodbank 2013: 353-54, 373-75, 416-17).

The Iron Age Mediterranean (early to mid-first millennium BC) witnessed three particularly significant island developments, two directly relevant to the present theme, and the third to the wider history of the exploitation of islands. First, and as a culmination of the growth of island networks during the Bronze Age, the pan-Mediterranean expansion of connectivity traditionally attributed to the Phoenicians, which effectively brought the Mediterranean into being as (more or less) an interactive whole, relied heavily on island nodes—both at its extremities (Tyre and Cadiz) and its intervening points: Cyprus, Crete, Sicily and offshore islets, Malta, Sardinia, and Ibiza (Aubet 2001). While attractive stretches of mainland coast were also targeted (most famously at Carthage), islands had clearly by now become one of the locational templates for the diverse mobile, maritime actors who were stitching this network together. Given that the first major intra-Mediterranean empires of the mid-first millennium BC, those of Punic Carthage and Classical Athens (based in almost-insular Attica), emerged from the politicization of regional segments of such networks, it is perhaps unsurprising that these empires were fundamentally insular in their composition, and the battles that won and lost them primarily maritime ones—from Sardinia, Sicily, and the Balearics in the Punic instance to the Aegean thalassocracy of Athens (Broodbank 2013: 578-83, 606-607; Morris 2009). This makes a telling contrast to the notable resistance on the part of Mediterranean islands (most notably Cyprus) to incorporation by the earlier, external, terrestrially-based empires of the Bronze and Iron Age Near East, and may go some way to explain the new prominence of islands in the strategic thinking of Persia, their late heir and a contemporary of both Athens and Carthage (Broodbank 2013: 583-84). Meanwhile, turning to our third development, the incorporation of islands by larger extractive polities, especially hitherto under-inhabited islands such as Ibiza, encouraged a ruthless new variant on an older theme, one up until then islander-driven, of small-island economic specialization, namely the realization of islands as ideal locations for cash-cropping by servile or otherwise dependent labor, for large-scale export to overseas consumers (Horden and Purcell 2000: 224-30; Goméz Bellard 2008).

To summarize, islands provide mainstream, parallel histories within the Mediterranean from the spread of farming onward, and by the third and more obviously second millennium BC certain of their societies began to reshape overall Mediterranean dynamics in crucial respects, a phenomenon that intensified and diversified in the ensuing first millennium BC. A Mediterranean history without islands has therefore been a nonsensical concept for some 5000 years. This implies a far greater depth to the antiquity of islanders as historical actors on the wider stage than we have witnessed elsewhere among the larger oceans.

Other Mediterraneans?

To what extent are the Mediterranean's island societies uniquely precocious in this regard? Comparison is hampered, as noted already, by a variety of factors. In several cases, the theaters or numbers of islands are too small to encourage comparison—for example, Bahrain and Gotland probably accelerated connections within the early Persian Gulf and Baltic, respectively, but quite how early, and decisively, is hard to gauge (Boivin and Fuller 2009; see also Rainbird 2007: 114-38). The most likely other candidates for islands that refashioned wider history from an early date must be those of the South China Sea, Island Southeast Asia, and western Melanesia (where, interestingly, the importance of isthmian routes, primarily at Kra, as well as straits, such as those of Malacca and Torres, also mirror on a grander scale the conditions at Mediterranean Corinth and Messina, respectively) (Sherratt 2006). Even at lower Pleistocene sea-levels, islands almost certainly played a role in the remarkably early peopling of Australia (Kealy *et al.* 2015), though, equally, tiny examples in the Torres Strait later helped to filter out any transfer of horticulture southward from New Guinea

(Harris 1995). We have already identified this zone as the nursery for voyaging across the Indian as well as Pacific Oceans. But unfortunately, due to the largely organic—and therefore under-detected—nature of so much of the evidence, and the paucity of targeted research on issues parallel to those long analyzed in the Mediterranean, this is a deep island history that largely remains to be explored. Are there, for example, antecedents to the island trader states of later times in Southeast Asia, as is hinted on the mainland Kra isthmus by excavations at Khao Sam Kaeo (Murillo-Barroso *et al.* 2010; Bellina *et al.* 2014)? Before the inception of the convenient tracer of Chinese porcelain (the equivalent to the ceramic trade wares of the Mediterranean), how extensive were exchange networks across this region, especially in organic preciosities such as bird of paradise feathers, spices (now detected at the Roman port of Berenice in the Red Sea, across the Indian Ocean [Sidebotham 2011]), and even *trepang* (sea cucumbers), whose harvesting by island Macassar traders for a Chinese market had breached the coast of hunter-gatherer Australia at least several centuries before the advent of western navigators (Clark and May 2013)? And last but not least, where did the distinctive East Asian sailing technologies first emerge and diversify into seacraft as different as Chinese junks, Polynesian outrigger canoes, and the hybrid vessels captured in the art of Borobudur (Anderson 2010)? In the lower reaches and deltas of the Chinese Yellow River and the Yangtze (compare farther west the key roles played in this respect by the Nile, and also at Mesopotamia's confluence with the Persian Gulf) or in the tangled sea world of islands further south?

This leaves one major candidate for potential comparison. The Caribbean and its surrounds—including the long continental rim from Florida to the Orinoco delta, as well as the island-poor expanse of the Gulf of Mexico—has long been described as a Mediterranean of the Americas (e.g., Collier 1964; Brotherston 1992: 10). In loose geographical terms the term is apposite, despite such substantial differences as the Caribbean's long, open oceanic interface with the Atlantic, in that both are situated between three major continental zones with, in each case, the middle zone (Mesoamerica and the Near East) evolving into an early hub of cities, states, and empires. But with a fine resolution on early developments in the Mediterranean itself, and a specific focus on islands, how helpful actually is this comparison, and from what period might it begin to make sense? In the Caribbean islands, the challenges of preservation and recovery in the tropical zone again apply, but recent years have seen a major surge in state-of-the-art research (Fitzpatrick 2015; see also Hofman *et al.* 2008; Keegan *et al.* 2013) that goes a long way toward addressing this question, with somewhat intriguing results.

Starting with the Caribbean before 1492 AD, island archaeology reveals some 6000 or more years of human activity in the region, the last 2000 pre-Columbian years of which have left a dense archaeological record of horticultural expansion, settlement, and interaction, and the latter half of this span also of increasing social complexity (Fitzpatrick 2015). What is striking, however, is the fact that despite greatly improved knowledge of the sectors of the continental rim from which island populations originated, and increasingly rich analyses of the dynamic, interactive networks that drew islanders and occasionally mainlanders together (Hofman *et al.* 2007; 2014), there remains to this day obdurately little indication that the existence of peopled Caribbean islands made a substantial external difference to the historical dynamics of the surrounding world, either in terms of islands acting back decisively upon the continental rim, or connections between regions of that rim via intervening islands. Thus, before 1492 AD, the trajectories of (1) the Yucatan and greater Mesoamerica, (2) the northern parts of South America, and (3) Florida plus the broader southeastern part of North America remained essentially separate, or at least not connected via their island intermediaries. Unlike the Mediterranean islands' early role as 'tremplins des civilisations' (Laviosa-Zambotti's memorable words, cited in Guilaine 1994: 428), Caribbean islands remained relatively peripheral to overall American pre-Columbian dynamics.

If this observation holds good, the question must be: why? One likely factor is geographical configuration. In both the Mediterranean and Caribbean, the overall distribution of islands certainly does favor transfer between otherwise widely separate sectors of the continental rim. But while, in the former, mainland and island configurations render such transmissions relatively short and direct, the immensely long, linear, slender island arcs of the Caribbean would progressively filter out far more. Maritime scale is a second factor, in the context of the distance-shrinking sailing vessels that spread across the Mediterranean from the third to first millennium BC but which remained unknown in a consequently far larger (in terms of experienced space) pre-Columbian Caribbean (Broodbank 2010; Fitzpatrick 2013). Order of magnitude differences in the time elapsed, especially since the spread in each theater of agriculturalists, may also be relevant. The Spanish arrival in the Caribbean islands came after horticultural societies had been established there for only some 2000 years, equivalent to a date variably between 6500 and 3000 BC for most Mediterranean island agriculturalists and thereby to a broad, mainly Neolithic time-range that terminates decisively before any islanders had begun to shape wider Mediterranean history. Had Columbus and his successors not truncated indigenous history, it is quite plausible that at least some more fully Mediterranean dynamics might have emerged over time in the Caribbean islands and their surroundings too. Equally, the relationship between Mesoamerica and, say, Cuba might have come to more closely resemble that between Bronze Age Egypt or Mesopotamia, on the one hand, and Minoan Crete on the other.

Such tantalizing counter-factualism aside, however, should we not be struck by the speed with which the Caribbean *after* Columbus did begin to look radically more Mediterranean in terms of its islands' dynamics? Within a few generations of 1492 AD, and with most of the native population dead from disease, exploitation, and direct or indirect violence, the Caribbean islands had sprouted new fortified coastal nodes, slave economies, cash-cropping plantations, traders, pirates, and a suite of external engagements all around the continental perimeter and far beyond (Armstrong 2014; Hofman *et al.* 2014; Ryzewski and Cherry 2015). But this swift behavioral Mediterraneanization was surely the result of the export of an ancient model of island centrality and exploitation—a distinctive way of thinking about islands—that had originated and been refined on the opposite side of the Atlantic, in the Mediterranean itself (and already exported, as noted above, to the unfortunate isles of the Canaries and others in the 'Mediterranean Atlantic'), rather than the culmination of some indigenous, long-term dynamic. The export of that extremely effective, but in many ways also pathological, model to the Caribbean islands, furthermore, might be seen as only the first major step in its subsequent globalization during the ensuing few centuries before the present.

Conclusion

All of this prompts two parting thoughts. First, of course, it serves to confirm further the genuinely unusual centrality of islands to deep Mediterranean history. Several reasons for this have already been made apparent. The islands of the Mediterranean are numerous, often strategically located for interconnections, and attractive for extraction and exploitation from the days of obsidian procurement to the cash cropping of later antiquity and beyond—all within a geographical scale negotiable by early paddled canoes and then shrunk further by sail technology. But one final decisive and, for island archaeologists, somewhat ironic factor also stands out. The boundaries between the insular and non-insular in the Mediterranean are exceptionally blurred and easily surmountable, with its true islands in effect a wrap-around intensification of a wider coast-rich condition common to much of the basin (for example, Sicily, which comprises some 25% of all Mediterranean insular space is only just an island; the Peloponnese, at potentially another 35%, was only just not, despite the etymology of its name—the Isle of Pelops). Mediterranean islands therefore readily became quintessences, hyper-expressions, of the qualities and affordances of their surrounding basin in a manner that, if not unique (mainland and insular Southeast Asia again come to mind), does appear to be rare on a global scale. In short, perhaps Mediterranean islands mattered so much from so far back in part because they were only just spatially insular, and culturally very negotiably so.

Second, do we need to rethink the aims of a comparative island archaeology? So far, most work in this vein has been process-driven and ahistorical, in the sense that the island theaters compared lacked any direct relations with each other; the implicit assumption has been that the qualities of islands and potentials of insularity are widely shared, if not indeed universal to island life. This agenda remains entirely valid, and important, at many levels, but it would also be immensely enriched by a historical sense of the potential distinctiveness of deep island histories and concepts of insularity in different theaters, and of the intersections and relatedness of these over the past few centuries of global convergence (see also Fitzpatrick, this volume). If we can achieve this aim, island archaeology will stand more secure than ever in its contribution to the deep history of humanity.

Acknowledgments

This paper has evolved from one first trialled at a meeting of the SAA in Honolulu in 2013, which was quite understandably critically received in some quarters. So much so, in fact, that I was glad to have a ticket off Oahu for two hours later, and on to a four-day trip around the Big Island in the peerless company of this volume's honorand. It was a memorable time of free-wheeling island archaeology, the fruitless pursuit of honeycreepers and unreciprocated conversations with nenes, of encounters with volcanoes, torrential rain, sea turtles, indifferent lodgings, and outstanding dinners. Returning to the prototype of this paper, there was clearly, as John used to put it of my PhD chapters, room for improvement, and I trust that this version makes a better case. It is an enormous pleasure and honor to be dedicating it to my former supervisor, long-term mentor, and good friend—a man who loves islands as much as I do, but who also taught me how to think about them rigorously and creatively. Few have captured the raw astonishment of unanticipated discovery better than Keats in his famous lines on Cortez, 'when with eagle eyes / He star'd at the Pacific—and all his men / Look'd at each other with a wild surmise— / Silent, upon a peak in Darien'. My personal archaeological Pacific (in more ways than one, as would soon transpire), was the early writing of John Cherry, and I cannot thank him enough for the example he has always set of what archaeology can and should be: intellectually vibrant, ambitiously comparative, optimistic as to its remit, open-minded to all fields and disciplines, and above all exciting in its practice as well as vision. Finally, my warmest thanks go to this volume's editors, Alex Knodell and Tom Leppard, and to Bernard Knapp as series editor, for their all-but-infinite patience, to Tom for further last-minute assistance, and to Roger Blench, Scott Fitzpatrick, Corinne Hofman, and Alessandro Vanzetti for recent and challenging conversations about islands that have greatly honed my thinking.

About the Author

Cyprian Broodbank is Disney Professor of Archaeology at the University of Cambridge, where he is also Head of the Department of Archaeology and Director of the McDonald Institute for Archaeological Research. Broadly interested in island archaeology and Mediterranean prehistory, he co-directs the Kythera Island Project and is author of *An Island Archaeology of the Early Cyclades* (Cambridge University Press, 2000), winner of the James Wiseman book award from the Archaeological Institute of America, and *The Making of the Middle Sea: A History of the Mediterranean from the Beginning to the Emergence of the Classical World* (Thames and Hudson, 2013), which won the Wolfson History Prize in 2014. E-mail: cb122@cam.ac.uk

References

Adelaar, K.A.

1989 Malay influence on Malgasy: linguistic and culture-historical implications. *Oceanic Linguistics* 28: 1-46. https://doi.org/10.2307/3622973

1996 Malgasy culture history: some linguistic evidence. In J. Reade (ed.), *The Indian Ocean in Antiquity*, 487-500. London: Kegan Paul International and the British Museum.

Anderson, A.

2010 The origins and development of seafaring: towards a global approach. In A. Anderson, J.H. Barrett and K. Boyle (eds.), *The Global Origins and Development of Seafaring*, 3-16. Cambridge: McDonald Institute for Archaeological Research.

Armstrong, D.V.

2014 New directions in Caribbean historical archaeology. In W.F. Keegan, C.L. Hofman and R. Rodríguez Ramos (eds.), *The Oxford Handbook of Caribbean Archaeology*, 525-41. Oxford: Oxford University Press.

Athens, J.S., T.M. Rieth and T.S. Dye

2014 A palaeoenvironmental and archaeological model-based estimate for the colonisation of Hawai'i. *American Antiquity* 79: 144-55. https://doi.org/10.7183/0002-7316.79.1.144

Aubet, M.E.

2001 *The Phoenicians and the West: Politics, Colonies and Trade.* Cambridge: Cambridge University Press.

Ballard, C., P. Brown, R.M. Bourke and T. Harwood (eds.)

2005 *The Sweet Potato in Oceania: A Reappraisal.* Ethnology Monographs 19 / Oceania Monographs 56. Sydney and Pittsburgh: Oceania Publications.

Barrett, J.H. (ed.)

2003 *Contact, Continuity and Collapse: The Norse Colonization of the North Atlantic.* Turnhout, Belgium: Brepols.

Bellina, B., P. Silapanth, B. Chaisuwan, C. Thongcharoenchaikit, J. Allen, V. Bernard, B.

Borell, P. Bouvet, C. Castillo, L. Dussubieux, J. Malakie LaClair, S. Srikanlaya, S. Peronnet and T.O. Pryce

2014 The development of coastal polities in the upper Thai-Malay peninsula in the late 1st millennium BCE. In N. Revire and S.A. Murphy (eds.), *Before Siam: Essays in Art and Archaeology*, 69-89. Bangkok: River Books and The Siam Society.

Blake, E.

2014 Late Bronze Age Sardinia: acephalous cohesion. In A.B. Knapp and P. van Dommelen (eds.), *The Cambridge Prehistory of the Bronze and Iron Age Mediterranean*, 96-108. New York: Cambridge University Press. https://doi.org/10.1017/cho9781139028387.009

Blench, R.M.

2010 Evidence for the Austronesian voyages in the Indian Ocean. In A. Anderson, J.H. Barrett and K. Boyle (eds.), *The Global Origins and Development of Seafaring*, 239-48. Cambridge: McDonald Institute for Archaeological Research.

Boivin, N., A. Crowther, R. Helm and D.Q. Fuller

2013 East Africa and Madagascar in the Indian Ocean world. *Journal of World Prehistory* 26: 213-81. https://doi.org/10.1007/s10963-013-9067-4

Boivin, N., A. Crowther, M. Prendergast and D.Q. Fuller

2014 Indian Ocean food globalisation and Africa. *African Archaeological Review* 31: 547-81. https://doi.org/10.1007/s10437-014-9173-4

Boivin, N., and D.Q. Fuller

2009 Shell middens, ships and seeds: exploring coastal subsistence, maritime trade and the dispersal of domesticates in and around the ancient Arabian Peninsula. *Journal of World Prehistory* 22: 113-80. https://doi.org/10.1007/s10963-009-9018-2

Boomert, A., and A. Bright
2007 Island archaeology: in search of a new horizon. *Island Studies Journal* 2: 3-26.

Broodbank, C.
2000 *An Island Archaeology of the Early Cyclades.* Cambridge: Cambridge University Press.
2004 Minoanisation. *Proceedings of the Cambridge Philological Society* 50: 46-91. https://doi.org/10.1017/S006867350000105X
2006 The origins and early development of Mediterranean maritime activity. *Journal of Mediterranean Archaeology* 19: 199-230. https://doi.org/10.1558//jmea.2006.v19i2.199
2010 'Ships a-sail from over the rim of the sea': Voyaging, sailing and the making of Mediterranean societies, c. 3500-500 BC. In A. Anderson, J.H. Barrett and K. Boyle (eds.), *The Global Origins and Development of Seafaring*, 249-64. Cambridge: McDonald Institute for Archaeological Research.
2013 *The Making of the Middle Sea: A History of the Mediterranean from the Beginning to the Emergence of the Classical World.* London: Thames and Hudson.
2016 The transmitting sea: a Mediterranean perspective. In E. Kiriatzi and C. Knappett (eds.), *Human Mobility and Technological Transfer in the Prehistoric Mediterranean*, 18-30. Cambridge: Cambridge University Press. https://doi.org/10.1017/9781316536063.003

Broodbank, C., E. Kiriatzi and J.B. Rutter
2005 From pharaoh's feet to the slave-women of Pylos? The history and cultural dynamics of Kythera in the Third Palace period. In A. Dakouri-Hild and S. Sherratt (eds.), *Autochthon: Studies Presented to Oliver Dickinson on the Occasion of his Retirement.* British Archaeological Reports, International Series 1433: 70-96. Oxford: Archaeopress.

Brotherston, G.
1992 *Book of the Fourth World: Reading the Native Americas through their Literature.* Cambridge: Cambridge University Press.

Cherry, J.F.
1981 Pattern and process in the earliest colonization of the Mediterranean islands. *Proceedings of the Prehistoric Society* 47: 41-86. https://doi.org/10.1017/S0079497X00008859
1985 Islands out of the stream: isolation and interaction in early east Mediterranean prehistory. In A.B. Knapp and T. Stech (eds.), *Prehistoric Production and Exchange in the Aegean and East Mediterranean.* UCLA Institute of Archaeology Monograph 27: 12-29. Los Angeles: UCLA.
1990 The first colonisation of the Mediterranean islands: a review of recent research. *Journal of Mediterranean Archaeology* 3: 145-221.
2004 Mediterranean island prehistory: what's different and what's new? In S. Fitzpatrick (ed.), *Voyages of Discovery: The Archaeology of Islands*, 233-48. Westport, Connecticut: Praeger.

Clark, M., and S.K. May (eds.)
2013 *Macassan History and Heritage: Journeys, Encounters and Influences.* Canberra: Australian National University Press.

Collier, A.
1964 The American Mediterranean. In R.C. West (ed.), *Handbook of Middle American Indians* I. *Natural Environment and Early Cultures*, 122-42. Austin: University of Texas Press.

Crosby, A.W.
1986 *Ecological Imperialism: The Biological Expansion of Europe, 900-1900.* Cambridge: Cambridge University Press.

Evans, J.D.
1973 Islands as laboratories for the study of cultural process. In C. Renfrew (ed.), *The Explanation of Culture Change: Models in Prehistory*, 517-20. London: Duckworth.

Fernández-Armesto, F.
1982 *The Canary Islands after the Conquest:*

The Making of a Colonial Society in the Early Sixteenth Century. Oxford: Oxford University Press.

Fitzpatrick, S.M.
2013 Seafaring capabilities in the pre-Columbian Caribbean. *Journal of Maritime Archaeology* 8: 101-38. https://doi.org/10.1007/s11457-013-9110-8
2015 The pre-Columbian Caribbean: colonization, population dispersal, and island adaptations. *Paleoamerica* 1: 305-31. https://doi.org/10.1179/2055557115Y.0000000010

Fitzpatrick, S.M., and R. Callaghan
2008 Seafaring simulations and the origins of prehistoric settlers to Madagascar. In G. Clark, F. Leach and S. O'Connor (eds.), *Islands of Inquiry: Colonisation, Seafaring and the Archaeology of Maritime Landscapes.* Special issue of *Terra Australis* 29: 47-58.

Fuller, D.Q., N. Boivin, T. Hoogervorst and R. Allaby
2011 Across the Indian Ocean: the prehistoric movement of plants and animals. *Antiquity* 85: 544-58. https://doi.org/10.1017/S0003598X00067934

Gómez Bellard, C.
2008 Ibiza: the making of new landscapes. In P. van Dommelen and C. Gómez Bellard (eds.), *Rural Landscapes of the Punic World*, 44-75. London: Equinox.

Guilaine, J.
1994 *La Mer Partagée: la Méditerranée avant l'Ecriture, 7000-2000 avant Jésus-Christ.* Paris: Hachette.

Haour, A., A. Christie and S. Jaufur
2016 Tracking the cowrie shell: excavations in the Maldives, 2016. *Nyame Akuma* 85.

Harris, D.
1995 Early agriculture in New Guinea and the Torres Strait divide. *Antiquity* 69: 848-54. https://doi.org/10.1017/S0003598X00082387

Hofman C.L., A.J. Bright, A. Boomert and S. Knippenberg
2007 Island rhythms: the web of social relationships and interaction networks in the pre-Columbian Lesser Antilles. *Latin American Antiquity* 18: 243-68. https://doi.org/10.2307/25478180

Hofman, C.L., M.L.P. Hoogland and A.L. van Gijn (eds.)
2008 *Crossing the Borders: New Methods and Techniques in the Study of Archaeological Materials from the Caribbean.* Tuscaloosa: University of Alabama Press.

Hofman, C.L., A. Mol, M.L.P. Hoogland and R. Valcárel Rojas
2014 Stage of encounter: migration, mobility and interaction in the pre-colonial and early colonial Caribbean. *World Archaeology* 46: 590-609. https://doi.org/10.1080/00438243.2014.925820

Horden, P., and N. Purcell
2000 *The Corrupting Sea: A Study of Mediterranean History.* Oxford: Blackwell.

Irwin, G.
1992 *The Prehistoric Exploration and Colonisation of the Pacific.* Cambridge: Cambridge University Press. https://doi.org/10.1017/CBO9780511518225

Kealy, S., J. Louys and S. O'Connor
2015 Islands under the sea: a review of early modern human dispersal routes and migration hypotheses through Wallacea. *Journal of Island and Coastal Archaeology* 11: 364-84. https://doi.org/10.1080/15564894.2015.1119218

Keegan, W.F., and J. Diamond
1987 Colonization of islands by humans: a biogeographical perspective. *Advances in Archaeological Method and Theory* 10: 49-92. https://doi.org/10.1016/B978-0-12-003110-8.50005-0

Keegan, W.F., C.L. Hofman and R. Rodríguez Ramos (eds.)
2013 *The Oxford Handbook of Caribbean Archaeology.* Oxford: Oxford University Press.

Kirch, P.V.
2007 Hawaii as a model system for human ecodynamics. *American Anthropologist* 109: 8-26. https://doi.org/10.1525/aa.2007.109.1.8
2010 *On the Road of the Winds: An Archaeological History of the Pacific Islands before European Contact.* Berkeley: University of California Press.

Knappett, C., and I. Nikolakopoulou
2014 Inside out? Materiality and connectivity in the Aegean archipelago. In A.B. Knapp and P. van Dommelen (eds.), *The Cambridge Prehistory of the Bronze and Iron Age Mediterranean*, 25-39. New York: Cambridge University Press. https://doi.org/10.1017/cho9781139028387.005

Lejju, B.J., P. Robertshaw and D. Taylor
2006 Africa's earliest bananas? *Journal of Archaeological Science* 33: 102-13. https://doi.org/10.1016/j.jas.2005.06.015

Leppard, T.P.
2015 Adaptive responses to demographic fragility: mitigating stochastic effects in early island colonization. *Human Ecology* 43: 721-34. https://doi.org/10.1007/s10745-015-9779-4

Lewthwaite, J.
1986 The transition to food production: the Mediterranean perspective. In M. Zvelebil (ed.), *Hunters in Transition*, 53-66. Cambridge: Cambridge University Press.

Malone, C., and S. Stoddart
2013 Ritual failure and the temple collapse of prehistoric Malta. In V.G. Koutrafouri and J. Sanders (eds.), *Ritual Collapse: Archaeological Perspectives*, 63-84. Leiden: Sidestone Press.

Manning, S.W.
2015 Temporal placement and context of Cypro-PPNA activity on Cyprus. *Eurasian Prehistory* 11: 9-28.

Mercer, J.
1980 *Canary Islanders: The Prehistory, Conquest and Survival*. London: Bellow Publishing.

Morris, I.
2009 The Greater Athenian state. In I. Morris and W. Scheidel (eds.), *The Dynamics of Ancient Empires*, 99-177. Oxford: Oxford University Press.

Murillo-Barroso, M., T.O. Pryce, B. Bellina and M. Martinón-Torres
2010 Khao Sam Kaeo – an archaeometallurgical crossroads for trans-Asiatic technological traditions. *Journal of Archaeological Science* 37: 1761-72. https://doi.org/10.1016/j.jas.2010.01.036

Rainbird, P.
2007 *The Archaeology of Islands*. Cambridge: Cambridge University Press. https://doi.org/10.1017/CBO9780511619007

Reinhardt, S.G., and D. Reinhartz (eds.)
2006 *Transatlantic History*. College Station: Texas A&M University Press.

Renfrew, C.
1972 *The Emergence of Civilisation: The Cyclades and the Aegean in the Third Millennium BC*. London: Methuen.

Ryzewski, K., and J.F. Cherry
2015 Struggles of a sugar society: surveying plantation-era Montserrat, 1650–1850. *International Journal of Historical Archaeology* 19: 356-83. https://doi.org/10.1007/s10761-015-0292-7

Sherratt, A.
2006 Portages: a simple but powerful idea in understanding human history. In C. Westerdahl (ed.), *The Significance of Portages*. British Archaeological Reports, International Series 1499: 1-13. Oxford: Archaeopress.

Sherratt, S.
2003 The Mediterranean economy: 'globalization' at the end of the second millennium BCE. In W.G. Dever and S. Gitin (eds.), *Symbiosis, Symbolism, and the Power of the Past: Canaan, Ancient Israel, and Their Neighbors from the Late Bronze Age through Roman Palestina*, 37-62. Winona Lake, Indiana: Eisenbrauns.

Sherratt, S., and A. Sherratt
1993 The growth of the Mediterranean economy in the early first millennium BC. *World Archaeology* 24: 361-78. https://doi.org/10.1080/00438243.1993.9980214

Sidebotham, S.E.
2011 *Berenike and the Ancient Maritime Spice Route*. Berkeley: University of California Press. https://doi.org/10.1525/california/9780520244306.001.0001

Smith, L.C.

2011 Agents of change in the New North. *Eurasian Geography and Economics* 52: 30-55. https://doi.org/10.2747/1539-7216.52.1.30

Storey, A.A., J.M. Ramírez, D. Quiroz, D.V. Burley, D.J. Addison, R. Walter, A. Anderson, T.L. Hunt, J.S. Athens, L. Huynen and E.A. Matisoo-Smith

2007 Radiocarbon and DNA evidence for a pre-Columbian introduction of Polynesian chickens to Chile. *Proceedings of the National Academy of Sciences* 104: 10335-39. https://doi.org/10.1073/pnas.0703993104

Terrell, J.E.

1986 *Prehistory in the Pacific Islands: A Study of Variation in Language, Customs, and Human Biology.* Cambridge: Cambridge University Press.

Terrell, J.E., T.L. Hunt and C. Gosden

1997 Human diversity and the myth of the primitive isolate. *Current Anthropology* 38: 155-95. https://doi.org/10.1086/204604

Thorsby, E.

2012 The Polynesian gene pool: an early contribution by Amerindians to Easter Island. *Philosophical Transactions of the Royal Society B* 367: 812-19. https://doi.org/10.1098/rstb.2011.0319

Vigne, J.-D.

1992 The large 'true' Mediterranean islands as a model for the Holocene human impact on the European vertebrate fauna? Recent data and new reflections. In N. Benecke (ed.), *The Holocene History of the European Vertebrate Faunas*, 295-322. Rahden, Germany: Marie Leidorf.

2013 The origins of mammals on the Mediterranean islands as an indicator of early voyaging. *Eurasian Prehistory* 10: 45-56.

Vigne, J.-D., F. Briois, A. Zazzo, G. Willcox, T. Cucchi, S. Thiébault, I. Carrère, Y. Franel, R. Touquet, C. Martin, C. Moreau, C. Comby and J. Guilaine

2012 First wave of cultivators spread to Cyprus at least 10,600 y ago. *Proceedings of the National Academy of Sciences* 109: 8445-49. https://doi.org/10.1073/pnas.1201693109

Wilmshurst, J.M., A. Anderson, T.F.G. Higham and T.H. Worthy

2008 Dating the late prehistoric dispersal of Polynesians to New Zealand using the commensal Pacific rat. *Proceedings of the National Academy of Sciences* 105: 7676-80. https://doi.org/10.1073/pnas.0801507105

Wilmshurst, J.M., T.L. Hunt and A. Anderson

2011 High-precision radiocarbon dating shows recent and rapid initial human colonization of East Polynesia. *Proceedings of the National Academy of Sciences* 108: 1815-20. https://doi.org/10.1073/pnas.1015876108

Zeder, M.

2008 Domestication and early agriculture in the Mediterranean basin: origins, diffusion, and impact. *Proceedings of the National Academy of Sciences* 105: 11597-604. https://doi.org/10.1073/pnas.0801317105

10 Islands in the Comparative Stream: The Importance of Inter-Island Analogies to Archaeological Discourse

Scott M. Fitzpatrick

> My own experience has been that the tools I need for my trade are paper, tobacco, food, and a little whisky. (William Faulkner)

Introduction

Island archaeology as a subfield of study has garnered significant scholarly attention over the last few decades (also Broodbank, this volume). It has been argued, however, that this is a false distinction and that islands—as far as humans are concerned—are really no different than other kinds of landmasses. Almost two decades ago, Rainbird (1999) maintained that the very notion of islands being considered different by anthropologists and archaeologists was rooted in western concepts that privileged (biased) assumptions of isolation and remoteness, and that this had manifested itself in literature: there are many examples that highlight or expound on these concepts, including Daniel Defoe's *Robinson Crusoe* (1790), Jules Verne's *The Mysterious Island* (1874), and Paul Theroux's *The Happy Isles of Oceania* (1992). There really is no question that islands historically have been conceptualized as different, and sometimes erroneously so, by laymen and scholars alike.

In addition, Rainbird (1999) and others (e.g., Boomert and Bright 2007) have criticized island archaeology for both its earlier emphasis on islands constituting 'cultural laboratories' and its use of biogeographical principles in attempting to explain the variables that may have influenced how islands were colonized (Keegan and Diamond 1987). While this concept of islands as 'laboratories' has shed explanatory power over time and is no longer considered a perfectly appropriate means to examine populations cross-culturally (Broodbank, this volume), there is—for a number of reasons—merit in analyzing island populations differently, not least of which is that islands can be considered 'model systems' ecologically (Vitousek 2002), and that, as a corollary of such ecological processes, they are suitable for examining a host of issues relating to human colonization (Kirch 2007). I return to this point later.

I contend that islands are inherently different types of space with regard to a series of factors. The very fact that most islands around the world were settled relatively late (e.g., Gamble 2013) points to certain social and technological issues (or even thresholds) that must be overcome to ensure both successful travel and colonization (e.g., suitable watercraft, seafaring and navigational skills, translocation of plants and animals). In addition, humans are by their very nature not good swimmers—and given the sheer distances involved to settle most islands, it is easy to see why they can be conceived of in terms of differing demands on dispersal capacity. So if island archaeology can be distinguished separately in its own right, then we can move beyond singular case studies and begin to compare them both within and outside of major island regions.

The abstract for a paper Cherry (1981) published nearly 35 years ago highlights the relevant questions and makes suggestions about a possible way forward:

> When and how were the Mediterranean islands first settled? Has insularity itself—the special characteristics of islands everywhere—acted as a constraint on the manner and rate of their colonization by man? If so, is it possible for archaeologists to make use of ecological and biogeographical models which have been developed to account for the abundance and diversity of animals and plants on islands of varying size and remoteness? … As a reflection of personal research interests, I emphasize the east Mediterranean evidence, but there are useful insights to be gleaned, I believe, by comparing what we find there with the pattern for the islands of the west.

A subsequent, seminal paper by Keegan and Diamond (1987) provided what was really the first major attempt to examine comparatively the colonization of islands from a biogeographical perspective. The authors were 'interested in questions of when, how, and why preindustrial human populations reached oceanic islands and what happened to the populations after arrival', and they concluded that 'biogeographical principles can be used to identify significant patterns in the spatial distributions of insular cultures' (Keegan and Diamond 1987: 50, 82). While some may take issue with this observation, especially given that humans are good at circumventing many of the impediments to island colonization that confront colonizing species (e.g., winds, currents, acquiring water and other resources in impoverished or marginal environments), biogeography still seems to offer one reasonable approach to explore, so long as human ingenuity is recognized as playing a potential role.

Broodbank has noted that '[a]nother hardy aspect is the suggestion that island groups are ideal places to construct comparative experiments in adaptation and differentiation among discrete island populations that share an original common culture' (Broodbank 2000: 27). This was a concept derived from Evans (1977), but it testifies to the now long-held belief that island-to-island comparisons (and across regions or subregions) are worth exploring. It was only eight years previous to the publication of Broodbank's book that I had had the opportunity, as an undergraduate, to first conduct archaeological fieldwork on an island. The experiences I had working on Barbados in the southeastern Caribbean were pivotal, in the sense that it was all

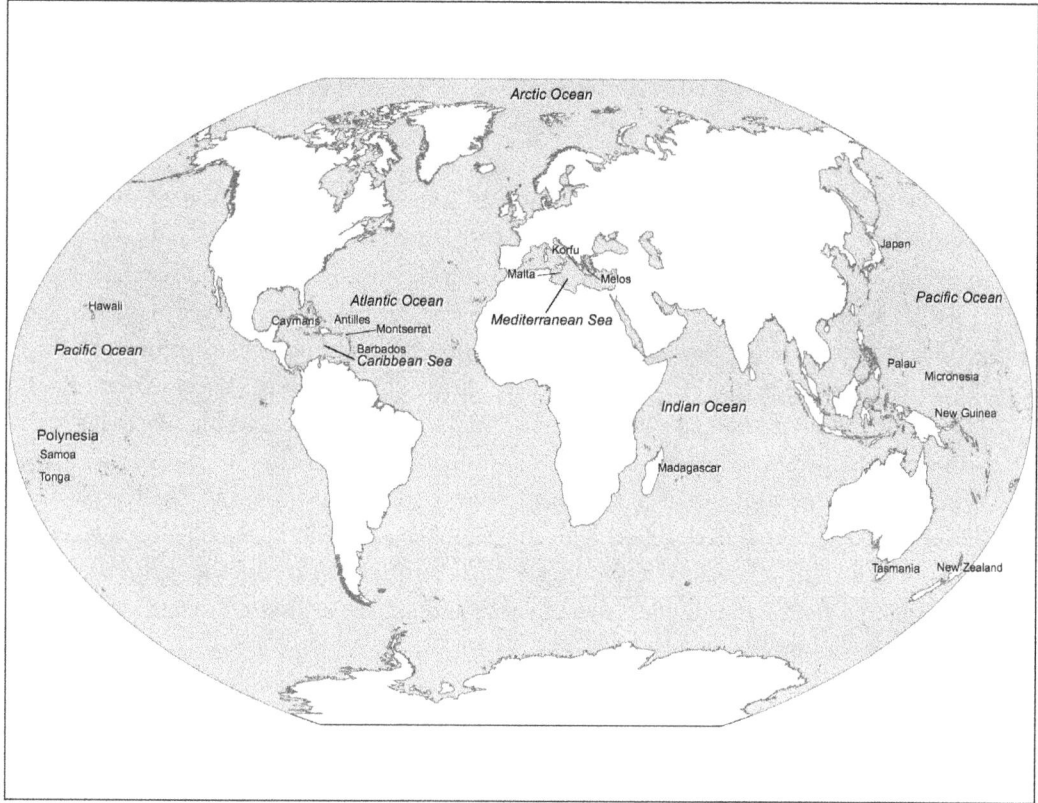

Figure 10.1   World map showing oceans, seas, islands, and island groups mentioned in the text (map by Evan Levine).

very new and interesting to me (the only other place to which I had flown prior to that was Hawaii the previous year) (Figure 10.1). Visiting, in a short period of time, a Pacific archipelago and a Caribbean island with significantly different cultural histories piqued my curiosity regarding addressing the comparative questions that Cherry had framed in his 1981 paper on the Mediterranean (and which have been amplified by others since, including many of his protégés).

This brings us to a larger body of issues regarding how comparative island archaeology has developed and deepened, and how it has been useful (if we agree that it has; Broodbank, this volume). What have we learned from talking to each other? Has there actually been substantive benefit from getting people in the same room and talking about these larger issues? What has not moved forward? Are the gulfs between data and tradition perhaps sometimes too great to allow for meaningful comparison?

The Subfield of Island and Coastal Archaeology

I have written a number of papers highlighting what I and others believe are core constituents of the subfield of island archaeology (see, for example, chapters in Fitzpatrick

2004). In a recent review (Fitzpatrick *et al.* 2015), my colleagues and I outlined 13 of these issues: (1) the antiquity of coastal adaptations and maritime dispersals; (2) variation in marine or coastal productivity; (3) development of specialized maritime technologies and capabilities; (4) underwater archaeology and drowned terrestrial landscapes; (5) cultural responses to insularity, isolation, and circumscription; (6) cultural contacts and historical processes; (7) human impacts and historical ecology in island and coastal ecosystems; (8) conservation and management of island and coastal sites; (9) the expanding methodological toolkit available to coastal and island archaeologists; (10) aquatic or maritime influences on symbolic expression (e.g., art, ornaments, etc.); (11) contributions to biogeography and ecology; (12) philosophical dilemmas on islands as units of analysis; and (13) islands as case studies for understanding human diasporas.

While it is not necessary here to review each and every one, I would like to highlight those constituents that seem especially conducive to conducting a comparative island archaeology (in addition, it is relevant to stress there are some that Cherry has been especially influential in developing or highlighting, and that have helped answer some of the questions related to developing island comparisons across the world's seas and oceans). To do this, I provide a few insights and analogies that tie in with the general theme of the current volume.

In terms of scholarly approaches to archaeological research, much has been made—after Archilocus—of the fox and the hedgehog (see Preface, this volume): the hedgehog, whose life's work is built around a single great idea, and the fox, who works instead with multiple concepts. While not disagreeing with the metaphor's structure, I wonder if this may mask other equally important (animalistic?) dichotomous analogies with which we can frame aspects of the honorand's career that have influenced research agendas in island archaeology. First, I outline the areas of study particularly amenable to approaching islands in a comparative framework; I then address Cherry's contributions in the context of these areas of study.

A Comparative Island Archaeology

There have been various scholarly attempts to examine and compare the manifestations of island life from different theoretical and methodological perspectives. While these have often focused on how geography, economics, politics, tourism, and colonialism have affected the development of and interaction between small island states and other places (e.g., Baldacchino 2007), much less attention has been given to how islands might be compared archaeologically, especially between regions.

There are of course some exceptions. These include Sahlins's (1955) benchmark essay, in which he argued that the construction of the famous *moai* of Rapa Nui (Easter Island) was a case of 'esoteric efflorescence'—essentially, that the limited resources available in a very circumscribed and remote environment led Polynesians to create increasingly larger stone statues in competitive displays of status and power. Renfrew

(1984), 30 years later, suggested a similar phenomenon for the 'temples' found on Malta (see also Bonanno *et al.* 1990), in effect adopting Sahlins's principles to identify what he surmised were key features of islands and island societies. Mitchell (2004), in the first major comparative examination of African islands, addresses several themes worth investigating, including human impacts and ecological transformations, the pivotal role of islands in trade internationally, and the use of biogeography to analyze possible correlations such as dates of colonization and size or distance from the mainland, *vis-à-vis* Keegan and Diamond (1987). More recently, Leppard (2014b) argued that there were similar dynamics in the colonization process for islands in the Caribbean, Mediterranean, and Pacific wherein colonizing 'bursts' occurred during preferable climatic regimes; he also argued that certain environmental conditions (e.g., smaller land area) led to demographic pressures in ways that were different from continental landmasses. These and many other studies of islands around the world have provided a strong foundation for identifying features of islands that may be similar or unique and that have indeed enriched how we think of island societies in the past. With all of these issues in mind, then, what phenomena or analytical units might be the most useful or conducive to explore in terms of comparing islands in prehistory?

There are several arenas of investigation that have been examined previously and/ or should be increasingly emphasized to help broaden the comparative scope of island archaeology. These are: (1) the development of seafaring and navigational (wayfinding) strategies; (2) the influence of environmental conditions (e.g., winds, currents) on colonization and dispersal; (3) biogeographic principles; (4) human responses to insularity and remoteness; (5) historical ecology and human impacts; and (6) the initiation of trade and exchange behaviors for reasons alternate to those that might be seen on continental landmasses.

Many of these areas of study have already been examined by scholars as fundamental aspects of island archaeology within itself (Fitzpatrick 2004; Erlandson and Fitzpatrick 2006; Fitzpatrick *et al.* 2015), and as such do not require reiterating at length. Nonetheless, it is worthwhile to address the basic premises of each and how Cherry's contributions have played a role in the intellectual development of these integral pieces. Let me begin with six realms of study that I believe are the most critical to constructing a comparative framework for the study of islands archaeologically, and then move on to the honorand's particular influence in two of them.

The Development of Seafaring and Navigational (Wayfinding) Strategies

It is an obvious point that the colonization of islands by humans could not have occurred without some type of watercraft (Anderson *et al.* 2010; but see Anderson 2017 for discussion of potential dispersal in Wallacea by humans with limited or no watercraft). For directed voyages that required a return trip, a suite of navigational or wayfinding strategies also had to be developed to enhance or ensure success, with improvements in watercraft construction allowing seafarers more effectively to manage oceanographic and anemological (wind-related) effects.

The Mediterranean (Broodbank 2006), North Atlantic (Barrett 2010; Van de Noort 2011), and Pacific (Finney 1985; Irwin 1992; 2008; Lewis 1994; Anderson 2008) are the best-known and studied regions in which sophisticated voyaging techniques were implemented. These included the sail used with a single hull and keel (e.g., Mediterranean, North Atlantic) or outrigger configuration (Indo-Pacific) coupled with landscape and/or celestial navigation, recognizing intrinsic variability between traditions of such navigation. In the Caribbean, Amerindians seemed to have used dugout canoes exclusively without the sail or stabilization techniques such as the outrigger; these vessels were nonetheless perfectly suitable for travel between the islands and some surrounding mainland areas, given the prevailing winds and currents (Fitzpatrick 2013) and archipelagic configuration (Keegan and Diamond 1987: 60-61).

While the antiquity of seafaring is still debated, it is relatively clear that the crossing of larger water gaps was preceded by nearshore maritime adaptations that eventually advanced to encompass movements across greater distances. The reasons for this advance may conceivably have included population pressure and the stimulus to seek out new resources or habitable land. In essence, examining the structure of how seafaring strategies evolved through time and the social and natural mechanisms that led to their development in the world's largest seas and oceans might make a particularly amenable topic for comparison.

The Influence of Environmental Conditions on Colonization and Dispersal

Related to seafaring—requisite for the prehistoric colonization of islands—is a suite of environmental conditions to which voyagers had to respond and manage. Efficiency in prediction, management, and response allowed them to traverse larger bodies of water, locate islands, and then presumably (though perhaps not in all cases), return to points of origin. In many respects, the archaeological record plainly illustrates that humans were able successfully to circumvent or breach many of the environmental obstacles they confronted through trial and error in watercraft construction and wayfinding (Irwin 1992).

While there are many parallels between major island theaters in terms of the social and environmental mechanisms used to facilitate travel (e.g., Leppard 2015), it is also worth exploring differences related to how seafarers adapted to changes in prevailing and seasonal or annual winds (e.g., El Niño or Madden-Julian Oscillations), currents, and other natural processes that would have affected movement. In the Caribbean, archaeological and ethnohistoric evidence suggests that only dugout canoes were used (posing the question of why peoples living in one of the world's largest seas never developed more sophisticated techniques such as the sail, despite many of the Antilles having been visited and/or settled for thousands of years; see also Broodbank, this volume). In this case, I have argued that prevailing currents and winds—both of which predominantly move westward across the Caribbean Sea—facilitated mobility in certain directions, particularly between South America and the northern Antilles (Fitzpatrick 2013), but also restricted it, a model supported by computer simulations of seafaring (Callaghan 2001). These oceanographic and anemological effects might also explain (1) the chronological disparity seen in the late colonization of islands (post-600 AD) such as Jamaica and the Bahamian archipelago, (2) the lag in settlement of much of the southern Lesser Antilles compared to the northern part of the subduction arc (ca. 1 AD for the former and ca. 3000 BC for the latter), and (3) the absence of any prehistoric settlement on the Caymans (Scudder and Quitmyer 1998).

The disparity of approximately two millennia between the settlement of east and west Polynesia is also intriguing, with a number of mechanisms (social, technological, environmental) being used to explain why Lapita groups were unable to settle islands further east than Sāmoa. It is likely that a number of physiological factors resulted in this pattern of colonization. Anderson *et al.* (2006), for example, have argued that increased prevalence and intensity of El Niño during the Late Holocene—in which winds shift eastward, making downwind sailing easier—may have spurred voyaging; central to this argument is the assumption that maritime technologies at this time did not permit windward sailing, thus limiting eastward movement until episodic westerlies (as occurs with El Niño) were present. Montenegro *et al.* (2014) used computer simulations of seafaring combined with 'ease of eastward' travel estimates based on land distribution and wind pattern analysis to attempt to determine the potential role of environmental factors. They demonstrated that voyages east of west Polynesia (Sāmoa, Tonga), which was the limit of the initial Lapita colonization horizon, would have been more challenging, given significantly longer distances involved when land distribution was considered. Ultimately, it may have been the development of the double-hulled canoe, coupled with enhanced knowledge of celestial and other navigational or wayfinding techniques, that allowed for greater numbers of people and provisions to be transported over more remote distances, once prevailing and episodic environmental factors (i.e., winds and currents) became more familiar and controllable (Montenegro *et al.* 2016).

Biogeographical Principles

The equilibrium theory of island biogeography, first synthesized by MacArthur and Wilson (1963; 1967) for nonhuman species, predicted that islands which were larger and in closer proximity to other landmasses (such as continents) would have greater species richness, and that the success of colonization would be dependent on island size and the degree of remoteness. Naturally, this became an appealing concept for archaeologists working on islands who were interested in explaining the variables that may have influenced how or when some were colonized before others (e.g., Held 1989; Fitzhugh and Hunt 1997; Terrell 1997; Giovas 2006).

Keegan and Diamond (1987) were the first to examine different island regions from a biogeographical perspective, illustrating the potential for using the theory in comparative island archaeology. In their analysis, they postulated that: (1) islands closer to other landmasses (particularly on the scale of continents) would be colonized before those farther away; (2) larger islands would be colonized earlier than smaller ones; (3) islands would be colonized by either the peoples closest to them or by those with the easiest access (taking winds and currents into consideration); and (4) peoples that were more technologically advanced (i.e., with more highly developed seafaring skills) would colonize islands, and those farther away, before less technologically advanced peoples (Keegan and Diamond 1987: 52). However, they noted numerous paradoxes in these assumptions, including the relatively late colonization of Madagascar (ca. 1 AD) by Austronesian-speaking groups who probably originated from somewhere in Indonesia. This was despite Madagascar's close proximity to the African continent—one of many curious island colonization patterns (see also Broodbank, this volume).

To explore the underlying reasons why these patterns may have emerged on a global scale, Keegan and Diamond examined more closely the area, distance, and configurational effects of islands, the different phases of colonization that would likely emerge as humans reached pristine islands for the first time (niche shifts, beachhead bottlenecks, degradation of island environments), and life history strategies (e.g., K-versus r-selected, tramps versus supertramps) that may have enabled success. Based on these results, Keegan and Diamond suggested that biogeographical applications to archaeology were useful in that they seemed to indicate that many of the same parameters that influenced the colonization of islands by plants and nonhuman animals could also be applied to *Homo sapiens*.

While new research on the antiquity of island colonization by humans suggests that island biogeographical principles do not provide immutable rules for explaining how and why different patterns of prehistoric population dispersals and settlements emerged, it is clear that they can and do provide a useful framework for developing models that can be refined and used comparatively. As Keegan and Diamond (1987: 81) noted: 'This emphasis on general patterns prompts worldwide comparisons of human colonization, and comparisons of human colonization with related problems for plants and animals, which help to focus attention on the intellectual issues that archaeological investigations can address'.

Human Responses to Insularity and Remoteness

In what ways might human populations living on islands have developed specifically in cultural and biological terms in response to aquatic perimeters and relative distance to other islands or mainland areas? This issue has been explored most frequently in the Pacific; this is perhaps unsurprising, given the ocean's sheer scale and unusual physiographic configuration. While Pacific islanders were and are arguably some of the world's most proficient and prolific traditional seafarers, the enormity of the Pacific exacerbated the inherent challenges that voyagers faced when voyaging between islands. As Fitzpatrick and Anderson (2008) noted, there were many cases where isolation was a real phenomenon, as Rapa Nui, Palau, Tasmania, and the so-called 'Mystery Islands' (Anderson 2001) clearly demonstrate.

In other parts of the world, the issue of remoteness and isolation has played less of a role in explaining how islanders adapted to their environment and in discussing levels of interaction that may have occurred with other groups (although for a nuanced view see Robb 2001). The comparatively smaller size of the Caribbean, Mediterranean, and North Atlantic—with the latter two in particular having well-documented and sophisticated seafaring traditions—is a likely reason, perhaps suggesting that raw distance was less of a factor in delineating how social networks developed; but this should not be given *a priori*, and should be subject to interrogation. Part of the problem lies in what is, for archaeology, essentially a 'seafaring paradox'; we only see material culture if there were in fact successful landfalls, represented in the archaeological record by the presence of sites, artifacts, burials, and translocated plants and animals. As a result of this paradox in identifying the tangible evidence for seafaring, any unsuccessful voyages, of which there must have been many, will be intrinsically archaeologically inconspicuous. Instead, we are left to rely on oral traditions, historical accounts, or historical analogies that nonetheless hint at the difficulties voyagers have had through the centuries, difficulties that ultimately led to failed, disastrous, or aborted ventures. The thousands of known shipwrecks worldwide (Ruppé and Barstad 2002)—the result of natural catastrophes, accidents, and conflict—supply grim testimony of the extent of seafaring calamities.

Regardless of this paradox and arguments either against isolation in island contexts or (near) universal interaction, there are clear cases in the Pacific of remoteness playing a role in how societies developed through time. Conversely, in the Caribbean, there has been much greater emphasis on the interconnected nature of prehistoric island populations (Hofman *et al.* 2008), although, as noted previously, there are still curious chronological disparities across the Lesser Antilles, despite their close proximity to many other and much larger islands (Fitzpatrick 2006). Could this be explained by the prevailing winds and currents (Callaghan 2001; 2008; Fitzpatrick 2013) that encouraged contact with some islands but limited it for others, or perhaps as purposeful avoidance due to various social or natural processes?

The point recalls one made by Anderson (2004): boats are not passive platforms that ensure successful travel at will, and not everyone in an island population will have the necessary skills in constructing boats, developing navigational skills, and so on. There are myriad factors that affect a positive outcome when traveling across larger bodies of water that are, by comparison, of much less concern or completely absent as regards terrestrial environments: winds, currents (and episodic variations in their duration and intensity), inclement weather—including squalls or major storms (e.g., typhoons, hurricanes), issues with boat performance and maintenance, navigational hazards, and other problems. It is these technological and social variables that—in being applicable to a broad array of prehistoric island and coastal situations—provide a foundation for a comparative examination of how and why remoteness is such an important structuring factor for human behavior in (and thereby the archaeological record of) island regions.

Historical Ecology and Human Impacts

Of the facets of island archaeology, island historical ecology (sometimes referred to as human ecodynamics) has probably had the greatest influence in distinguishing islands from other types of landmasses, both biologically and culturally. Historical ecology as a transdisciplinary approach (combining data derived from anthropological, archaeological, paleoecological, historical, and biological studies) focuses on correlating chronological, spatial, and social incongruencies to examine how landscapes have been affected or altered by humans. One of the primary constituents of historical ecology is the recognition that there are few places on earth that humans have not dramatically influenced, both directly and indirectly (e.g., Crumley 1994; Kirch and Hunt 1997; Balée 1998; Jackson *et al.* 2001; Butzer 2005; Fitzpatrick and Keegan 2007; Rick and Erlandson 2008; Braje *et al.* 2017). Balée (2006: 76) outlines the major premises of historical ecology: (1) nearly all environments on earth have in some way been affected by humans; (2) there is no genetic basis for humans to have decreased or increased the diversity of species and other environmental structures; (3) the disturbance of landscapes differs between societies depending on various political, cultural, and socioeconomic criteria; and (4) the interaction of humans and their environments across time and space can be studied in an integrated manner.

While the notion that islands are ideal 'cultural laboratories' (Kirch 1980; Fitzhugh and Hunt 1997) to study issues surrounding isolation and remoteness (and the influence of these parameters on human societies) has been de-emphasized in recent years, with the tenets of historical ecology borne in mind, islands can alternatively—and perhaps more appropriately—be conceived of as 'model systems' (Vitousek 2002; Kirch 2007). This approach, which emphasizes the boundedness and separation of islands that were completely devoid of human presence for much of their evolutionary history, can facilitate our understanding of how various kinds of ecological systems operate before and after *Homo sapiens* arrived. A key premise of historical ecology or human ecodynamics is the concept that humans and their behavior cannot be decoupled from the environment. In essence, one affects the other, and in terms of islands these processes—which include the corollary landscape modification (Bevan and Conolly 2011)—are likely to be more visible, given remote islands' ecological fragility and long-term disassociation with humans.

Archaeologists working on islands, often in conjunction with other scientists, have used a historical ecology approach to draw attention to the need to incorporate a diverse dataset that includes palaeoecological, archaeological, anthropological, and historical evidence. In part, this field of study recognizes that the environments observed on islands historically or in the present are not truly representative of the biological diversity present prior to human contact. As such, both pre-colonization and archaeological data are critical to establishing baselines for settlement that can be used to discern the degree to which humans may have transformed or otherwise impacted island ecologies, with these data critical for implementing conservation measures (e.g., see Rick and Erlandson 2008; Leppard 2014a).

Initiation of Trade and Exchange Behaviors

The development of trade and exchange systems within and between islands and archipelagoes—and in some cases between these and mainlands—was and always will be a fundamental of island life. While the movement and exchange of both perishable and non-perishable items is clearly not unique to islands, they take on a different meaning when one considers the patchiness of various island resources and the ways in which commodities derived from these resources were moved, acquired, and used.

The archaeological record is replete with examples of materials transported to other locations, materials which were not easily accessible and whose acquisition required long-distance travel and some level of social intercourse, often negotiation. Prized lithic materials, such as obsidian, offer advantageous routes into considering trade and exchange. Numerous cases worldwide testify to the importance—derived from its isomorphic structure and hence predictable fracture properties—of obsidian (White *et al.* 2006; Kuzmin and Glascock 2007; Reepmeyer *et al.* 2012; Stevenson *et al.* 2013; Torrence *et al.* 2013; Freund and Batist 2014; Vella 2016). Talasea obsidian found in the province of West New Britain in Papua New Guinea was exchanged with communities in the western Pacific hundreds of kilometers away from its source, particularly during the Lapita era, ca. 3000–2000 BP. The island of Kozu, 50 km offshore from Tokyo, was visited precociously early (25,000-20,000 BP) to obtain obsidian, as was Melos, over 100 km away from the Greek mainland, at ca. 11,000 BP (Erlandson 2001: 311). These latter two examples are important because they demonstrate early indirect evidence of seafaring, but with the primary goal of obtaining obsidian, rather than actually settling the islands.

In the Pacific, numerous atolls were settled by humans beginning as early as 2000 BP, and, given the lack of volcanic materials and clay for producing pottery, many initiated exchange relationships with populations on 'high' (i.e., geologically young oceanic) islands to acquire these resources, as well as to obtain timber for making canoes. The *sawei* exchange in Micronesia, which involved a flotilla of atoll-dwellers visiting Yap in a tributary relationship (Fitzpatrick 2008), is one excellent example among many others. As regards smaller island populations generally, these exchange behaviors often derive from biological and cultural necessity, both to find suitable marriage partners and as a buffer against catastrophes such as extended drought, typhoons or other tropical storms, and periods of lower food yield. This is often termed the 'rescue effect' and was critical to ensuring long-term survivability by being able to rely on adjacent island communities in times of stress (Keegan and Diamond 1987).

Cherry's Island Archaeology

John Cherry has been instrumental in the development of island archaeology, trained students to continue this work, and provided an enriched understanding of island cultures that has reached significantly beyond the boundaries of both *terra firma* and the Mediterranean. The six aspects of island archaeology outlined above are those that I feel are critical for facilitating comparisons between the world's seas and oceans in terms of prehistoric colonization, settlement patterns, sociopolitical development, and other cultural processes. In the spirit of this volume, I provide two animalistic dichotomies (apart from the fox and the hedgehog), that, in my view, can be used to highlight some of Cherry's more notable contributions to island archaeology as a subfield of study.

Human Impacts and Historical Ecology: The Rat and the Octopus

As noted previously, islands can serve as model systems (Kirch 2007; Vitousek 2002) to investigate the effects that humans can have on islands. This is amply demonstrated in a Pacific folk tale involving a rat and an octopus, described by Anderson (2009: 1503):

> [T]he rat refuses to share food with the land crab and when they go sailing the land crab chews a hole in the boat and walks along the sea floor, leaving the rat to drown. But the rat prevails upon an octopus to carry him ashore on its head. As it does so, the rat chews the hair off the octopus's head and then skips ashore, jeers at his bald benefactor, and arranges to have him killed and eaten. This widespread story acknowledges, in sly self-awareness by Pacific Islanders, the consequences of human arrival in the islands of Remote Oceania.

In many regards, Cherry's efforts to examine islands within and between regions have been pivotal in that he laid the groundwork for archaeologists to develop or 'make use of ecological models ... to account for the abundance and diversity of animals and plants on islands of varying size and remoteness' (Cherry 1981: 41). A historical ecology framework, which has guided many archaeologists over the last 20 years, is becoming increasingly useful for identifying long-term changes to island environments by humans. By collating disparate lines of evidence—archaeological, anthropological, historical, palaeoecological, and modern biological studies—to answer questions about the degree of impact on what were once pristine environments, archaeologists working in different island regions have begun to forge a much better understanding of long-term human-mediated ecodynamics (e.g., Fitzpatrick and Keegan 2007; Kirch 2007; Rick and Erlandson 2008).

An Expanding Methodological Toolkit: The Tortoise and the Hare

Cherry's career is somewhat reminiscent of the competition between unequal partners where ingenuity and persistence are employed to overcome innate advantage, in the sense that his scholarly pursuits for many years dealt with the Mediterranean, where he refined and developed new modes of approaching island settlement through an archaeological lens. He is, of course, primarily recognized for his research there, though in recent years he has moved to another large sea, the Caribbean, applying many of the same elements of a methodological and theoretical toolkit refined in one island region and now transferred to another. In this sense he is a tortoise, whose deliberate methodical consistency has paid major dividends from a comparative island archaeological framework. In particular, Cherry's fieldwork on the volcanically active island of Montserrat—fieldwork which combines targeted surveys, high resolution mapping, and risk assessment to archaeological sites (Cherry *et al.* 2012; Ryzewski and Cherry 2012)—is a carryover from strategies practiced in the Mediterranean and brought into an area where these types of research designs were virtually unknown (see also Ryzewski, this volume). That he and his research group have included both prehistoric and historic sites in his inventory is especially noteworthy, as this has rarely been done in the Caribbean. It is also a testament to how Cherry has bridged the gap between data and tradition, for few Caribbean archaeologists up until relatively recently had actually worked on islands outside their area, leading to a degree of intellectual insularity that was and still is frustratingly painful with which to deal.

Some Final Thoughts

Island archaeology is a dynamic and growing subfield of study that encompasses a broad range of interests, scientific pursuits, and goals (Evans 1977; Cherry 1981; 2004; Rainbird 1999; 2007; Broodbank 2000; Anderson 2004; Fitzpatrick 2004; Renfrew 2004; Boomert and Bright 2007; Fitzpatrick *et al.* 2015). While a number of scholars over the last few decades have made significant contributions to island archaeology, few beyond John Cherry have had such a prolific career, spanning more than one major aquatic realm. It is quite clear that Cherry's influence in the Mediterranean and Caribbean has had a lasting impact on not only my own scholarship, but also on a new generation of young scholars, an impact which seems likely to continue for some time.

Acknowledgments

I thank Thomas Leppard and Alex Knodell for the kind invitation to participate in the event honoring John's career and John for inspiring my own. My only regret is that I did not have as many opportunities as I would have liked to discuss with him the issues brought up in this chapter, ideally over a bourbon or three. But I'm sure Faulkner would have approved of what has transpired already.

About the Author

Scott M. Fitzpatrick is Professor in the Department of Anthropology and Associate Director of the Museum of Natural and Cultural History at the University of Oregon. He is an archaeologist who specializes in the prehistory and historical ecology of island and coastal regions, particularly the Pacific and Caribbean. Much of his research focuses on colonization events, seafaring, adaptations to smaller islands, exchange, and human impacts on ancient environments. He has published several books and more than 100 journal articles and book chapters, and is the founding co-editor of the *Journal of Island and Coastal Archaeology*, an associate editor for *Archaeology in Oceania*, and serves on the editorial boards for the *Caribbean Journal of Science* and the *Journal of Archaeological Science: Reports*. E-mail: smfitzpa@uoregon.edu

References

Anderson, A.
2001   No meat on that beautiful shore: the prehistoric abandonment of subtropical Polynesian islands. *International Journal of Osteoarchaeology* 11: 14-23. https://doi.org/10.1002/oa.542
2008   Traditionalism, interaction, and long-distance seafaring in Polynesia. *Journal of Island and Coastal Archaeology* 3: 240-50. https://doi.org/10.1080/15564890802340000
2004   Islands of ambivalence. In S.M. Fitzpatrick (ed.), *Voyages of Discovery: The Archaeology of Islands*, 251-74. Westport, Connecticut: Praeger.
2009   The rat and the octopus: initial human colonization and the prehistoric introduction of domestic animals to Remote Oceania. *Biological Invasions* 11: 1503-19. https://doi.org/10.1007/s10530-008-9403-2
2017   Ecological Contingency Accounts for Earliest Seagoing in the Western Pacific Ocean. *Journal of Island and Coastal Archaeology*. Online: http://dx.doi.org/10.1080/15564894.2016.1277286

Anderson, A., J.H. Barrett and K.V. Boyle (eds.)
2010   *The Global Origins and Development of Seafaring*. Cambridge: McDonald Institute for Archeological Research.

Anderson, A., J. Chappell, M. Gagan and R. Grove
2006   Prehistoric maritime migration in the Pacific islands: an hypothesis of ENSO forcing. *The Holocene* 16: 1-6. https://doi.org/10.1191/0959683606hl901ft

Baldacchino, G. (ed.)
2007   *A World of Islands: An Island Studies Reader*. Charlottetown, Canada: Institute of Island Studies.

Balée, W.
1998   (ed.) *Advances in Historical Ecology.* New York: Columbia University Press.
2006   The research program of historical ecology. *Annual Review of Anthropology* 35: 75-98. https://doi.org/10.1146/annurev.anthro.35.081705.123231

Barrett, J.H.
2010   Rounding up the usual suspects: causation and the Viking Age diaspora. In A. Anderson, J.H. Barrett and K.V. Boyle (eds.), *The Global Origins and Development of Seafaring*, 289-302. Cambridge: McDonald Institute for Archaeological Research.

Bevan, A., and J. Conolly
2011   Terraced fields and Mediterranean landscape structure: an analytical case study from Antikythera, Greece. *Ecological Modelling* 222: 1303-14. https://doi.org/10.1016/j.ecolmodel.2010.12.016

Bonanno, A., T. Gouder, C. Malone and S. Stoddart
1990   Monuments in an island society: the Maltese context. *World Archaeology* 22: 190-205. https://doi.org/10.1080/00438243.1990.9980140

Boomert, A., and A.J. Bright
2007   Island archaeology: in search of a new horizon. *Island Studies Journal* 2: 3-26.

Braje, T.J., T.P Leppard, S.M. Fitzpatrick and J.M. Erlandson
2017   Archaeology, historical ecology and anthropogenic island ecosystems. *Environmental Conservation* 44: 286-97. https://doi.org/10.1017/S0376892917000261

Broodbank, C.
2000   *An Island Archaeology of the Early*

Cyclades. Cambridge: Cambridge University Press.

2006 The origins and early development of Mediterranean maritime activity. *Journal of Mediterranean Archaeology* 19: 199-230.

Butzer, K.

2005 Environmental history in the Mediterranean world: cross-disciplinary investigation of cause-and-effect for degradation and soil erosion. *Journal of Archaeological Science* 32: 1773-1800. https://doi.org/10.1016/j.jas.2005.06.001

Callaghan, R.T.

2001 Ceramic Age seafaring and interaction potential in the Antilles: a computer simulation. *Current Anthropology* 42: 308-13. https://doi.org/10.1086/320012

2008 On the question of the absence of Archaic Age sites on Jamaica. *Journal of Island and Coastal Archaeology* 3: 54-71. https://doi.org/10.1080/15564890801928615

Cherry, J.F.

1981 Pattern and process in the earliest colonization of the Mediterranean Islands. *Proceedings of the Prehistoric Society* 47: 41-68. https://doi.org/10.1017/S0079497X00008859

2004 Mediterranean island prehistory: what's different and what's new. In S.M. Fitzpatrick (ed.), *Voyages of Discovery: The Archaeology of Islands*, 233-48. Westport, Connecticut: Praeger.

Cherry, J.F., K. Ryzewski and T.P. Leppard

2012 Multi-period landscape survey and site risk assessment on Montserrat, West Indies. *Journal of Island and Coastal Archaeology* 7: 282-302. https://doi.org/10.1080/15564894.2011.611857

Crumley, C.L. (ed.)

1994 *Historical Ecology: Cultural Knowledge and Changing Landscapes*. Santa Fe, New Mexico: School of American Research Press.

Erlandson, J.M.

2001 The archaeology of aquatic adaptations: paradigms for a new millennium. *Journal of Archaeological Research* 9: 287-350. https://doi.org/10.1023/A:1013062712695

Erlandson, J.M., and S.M. Fitzpatrick

2006 Oceans, islands, and coasts: current perspectives on the role of the sea in human prehistory. *Journal of Island and Coastal Archaeology* 1: 5-32. https://doi.org/10.1080/15564890600639504

Evans, J.D.

1977 Island archaeology in the Mediterranean: problems and opportunities. *World Archaeology* 9: 12-26. https://doi.org/10.1080/00438243.1977.9979682

Finney, B.R.

1985 Anomalous westerlies, El Niño, and the colonization of Polynesia. *American Anthropologist* 87: 9-26. https://doi.org/10.1525/aa.1985.87.1.02a00030

Fitzhugh, B., and T.L. Hunt

1997 Introduction. Islands as laboratories: archaeological research in comparative perspective. *Human Ecology* 25: 379-83. https://doi.org/10.1023/A:1021867425111

Fitzpatrick, S.M.

2004 (ed.) *Voyages of Discovery: The Archaeology of Islands*. Westport, Connecticut: Praeger.

2006 A critical approach to ^{14}C dating in the Caribbean: using chronometric hygiene to evaluate chronological control and prehistoric settlement. *Latin American Antiquity* 17: 389-418.

2008 Maritime interregional interaction in Micronesia: deciphering multigroup contacts and exchange systems through time. *Journal of Anthropological Archaeology* 27: 131-47. https://doi.org/10.1016/j.jaa.2007.12.002

2013 Seafaring capabilities in the pre-Columbian Caribbean. *Journal of Maritime Archaeology* 8: 101-38. https://doi.org/10.1007/s11457-013-9110-8

Fitzpatrick, S.M., and A. Anderson

2008 Islands of isolation: archaeology and the power of aquatic perimeters. *Jour-*

nal of Island and Coastal Archaeology 3: 4-16. https://doi.org/10.1080/15564890801983941

Fitzpatrick, S.M., and W.F. Keegan
2007   Human impacts and adaptations in the Caribbean Islands: an historical ecology approach. *Earth and Environmental Science Transactions of the Royal Society of Edinburgh* 98: 29-45. https://doi.org/10.1017/S1755691007000096

Fitzpatrick, S.M., T.C. Rick and J.M. Erlandson
2015   Recent progress, trends, and developments in island and coastal archaeology. *Journal of Island and Coastal Archaeology* 10: 1-25. https://doi.org/10.1080/15564894.2015.1029361

Freund, K.P., and Z. Batist
2014   Sardinian obsidian circulation and early maritime navigation in the Neolithic as shown through social network analysis. *Journal of Island and Coastal Archaeology* 9: 364-80. https://doi.org/10.1080/15564894.2014.881937

Gamble, C.
2013   *Settling the Earth: The Archaeology of Deep Human History*. Cambridge: Cambridge University Press. https://doi.org/10.1017/CBO9781139003933

Giovas, C.M.
2006   No pig atoll: island biogeography and the extirpation of a Polynesian domesticate. *Asian Perspectives* 45: 69-95. https://doi.org/10.1353/asi.2006.0004

Held, S.O.
1989   Colonization cycles on Cyprus: the biogeographic and paleontological foundations of early Prehistoric settlement. *Report of the Department of Antiquities of Cyprus*: 7-28.

Hofman, C.L., A.J. Bright, M.L. Hoogland and W.F. Keegan
2008   Attractive ideas, desirable goods: examining the Late Ceramic Age relationships between Greater and Lesser Antillean societies. *Journal of Island and Coastal Archaeology* 3: 17-34. https://doi.org/10.1080/15564890801984097

Irwin, G.
1992   *The Prehistoric Exploration and Colonisation of the Pacific*. Cambridge: Cambridge University Press. https://doi.org/10.1017/CBO9780511518225
2008   Pacific seascapes, canoe performance, and a review of Lapita voyaging with regard to theories of migration. *Asian Perspectives* 47: 12-27. https://doi.org/10.1353/asi.2008.0002

Jackson, J.B., M.X. Kirby, W.H. Berger, K.A. Bjorndal, L.W. Botsford, B.J. Bourque, R.H. Bradbury, R. Cooke, J.M. Erlandson, J.A. Estes and T.P. Hughes
2001   Historical overfishing and the recent collapse of coastal ecosystems. *Science* 293: 629-37. https://doi.org/10.1126/science.1059199

Keegan, W.F., and J.M. Diamond
1987   Colonization of islands by humans: a biogeographical perspective. *Advances in Archaeological Method and Theory* 10: 49-92. https://doi.org/10.1016/B978-0-12-003110-8.50005-0

Kirch, P.V.
1980   Polynesian prehistory: cultural adaptation in island ecosystems. *American Scientist* 68: 39-48.
2007   Hawaii as a model system for human ecodynamics. *American Anthropologist* 109: 8-26. https://doi.org/10.1525/aa.2007.109.1.8

Kirch, P.V., and T.L. Hunt (eds.)
1997   *Historical Ecology in the Pacific*. New Haven, Connecticut: Yale University Press.

Kuzmin, Y.V., and M.D. Glascock
2007   Two islands in the ocean: prehistoric obsidian exchange between Sakhalin and Hokkaido, Northeast Asia. *Journal of Island and Coastal Archaeology* 2: 99-120. https://doi.org/10.1080/15564890701273765

Leppard, T.P.
2014a Modeling the impacts of Mediterranean island colonization by Archaic Hominins: the likelihood of an insular Lower Palaeolithic. *Journal of Mediterranean Archaeology* 27: 231-

54. https://doi.org/10.1558/jmea.v27i2.231

2014b Similarity and diversity in the prehistoric colonization of islands and coasts by food-producing communities. *Journal of Island and Coastal Archaeology* 9: 1-15. https://doi.org/10.1080/15564894.2013.848957

2015 Passive dispersal versus strategic dispersal in island colonization by hominins. *Current Anthropology* 56: 590-95. https://doi.org/10.1086/682325

Lewis, D.

1994 *We, the Navigators: The Ancient Art of Landfinding in the Pacific.* Honolulu: University of Hawaii Press.

MacArthur, R.H., and E.O. Wilson

1963 An equilibrium theory of insular zoogeography. *Evolution* 17: 373-87. https://doi.org/10.1111/j.1558-5646.1963.tb03295.x

1967 *The Theory of Island Biogeography.* Princeton, New Jersey: Princeton University Press.

Mitchell, P.

2004 Towards a comparative archaeology of Africa's islands. *Journal of African Archaeology* 2: 229-50. https://doi.org/10.3213/1612-1651-10029

Montenegro, A., R.T. Callaghan and S.M. Fitzpatrick

2014 From west to east: environmental influences on the rate and pathways of Polynesian colonization. *The Holocene* 24: 242-56. https://doi.org/10.1177/0959683613517402

2016 Using seafaring simulations and shortest-hop trajectories to model the prehistoric colonization of Remote Oceania. *Proceedings of the National Academy of Sciences* 113: 12685-90.

Rainbird, P.

1999 Islands out of time: towards a critique of island archaeology. *Journal of Mediterranean Archaeology* 12: 216-34. https://doi.org/10.1558/jmea.v12i2.29971

2007 *The Archaeology of Islands.* Cambridge: Cambridge University Press. https://doi.org/10.1017/CBO9780511619007

Reepmeyer, C., G. Clark and P. Sheppard

2012 Obsidian source use in Tongan prehistory: new results and implications. *Journal of Island and Coastal Archaeology* 7: 255-71. https://doi.org/10.1080/15564894.2011.611858

Renfrew, C.

1984 *Approaches to Social Archaeology.* Edinburgh: University of Edinburgh Press.

2004 Islands out of time? Towards an analytical framework. In S.M. Fitzpatrick (ed.), *Voyages of Discovery: The Archaeology of Islands,* 275-94. Westport, Connecticut: Praeger.

Rick, T.C., and J.M. Erlandson (eds.)

2008 *Human Impacts on Ancient Marine Ecosystems: A Global Perspective.* Berkeley: University of California Press.

Robb, J.

2001 Island identities: ritual, travel, and the creation of difference in prehistoric Malta. *European Journal of Archaeology* 4: 175-202.

Ruppé, C.V., and J.F. Barstad (eds.)

2002 *International Handbook of Underwater Archaeology.* New York: Kluwer Academic / Plenum Publishers.

Ryzewski, K., and J.F. Cherry

2012 Communities and archaeology under the Soufrière Hills volcano on Montserrat, West Indies. *Journal of Field Archaeology* 37: 316-27. https://doi.org/10.1179/0093469012Z.00000000028

Sahlins, M.

1955 Esoteric efflorescence in Easter Island. *American Anthropologist* 57: 1045-52. https://doi.org/10.1525/aa.1955.57.5.02a00150

Scudder, S.J., and I. Quitmyer

1998 Evaluation of evidence for pre-Columbian human occupation at Great Cave, Cayman Brac, Cayman Islands. *Caribbean Journal of Science* 34: 41-49.

Stevenson, C.M., T.N. Ladefoged, S. Haoa, O. Chadwick and C. Puleston

2013 Prehistoric obsidian exchange on Rapa Nui. *Journal of Island and Coastal*

Archaeology 8: 108-21. https://doi.org/
10.1080/15564894.2012.745457

Terrell, J.E.

1997 The postponed agenda: archaeology and human biogeography in the twenty-first century. *Human Ecology* 25: 419-36. https://doi.org/10.1023/A:1021871526019

Torrence, R., S. Kelloway and P. White

2013 Stemmed tools, social interaction, and voyaging in early-mid Holocene Papua New Guinea. *Journal of Island and Coastal Archaeology* 8: 278-310. https://doi.org/10.1080/15564894.2012.761300

Van de Noort, R.

2011 *North Sea Archaeologies: A Maritime Biography, 10,000 BC to AD 1500.* Oxford: Oxford University Press.

Vella, C.

2016 Manipulated connectivity in island isolation: Maltese prehistoric stone tool technology and procurement strategies across the fourth and third millennia BC. *Journal of Island and Coastal Archaeology* 11: 344-63. https://doi.org/10.1080/15564894.2015.1135838

Vitousek, P.M.

2002 Oceanic islands as model systems for ecological studies. *Journal of Biogeography* 29: 573-82. https://doi.org/10.1046/j.1365-2699.2002.00707.x

White, J.P., H. Jacobsen, V. Kewibu and T. Doelman

2006 Obsidian traffic in the southeast Papuan Islands. *Journal of Island and Coastal Archaeology* 1: 101-108. https://doi.org/10.1080/15564890600583579

11 A Thorny Endeavor: Historical Archaeology and Diachronic, Regional Landscape Survey in the Caribbean Lesser Antilles

Krysta Ryzewski

Introduction

The Caribbean of interest to historical archaeologists, spanning the past ca. 525 years, is a multicultural and interconnected region that remains largely defined in research practice by the past colonial associations of particular islands and island groups. By virtue of common language, citizenship, or interest, practitioners routinely cluster islands into analytical groupings that sustain historical affiliations with European imperial systems. The result is scholarship that relies upon a foundation of European colonialism in both the past and present definitions of Caribbean cultural geographies (e.g., the British, French, or Dutch West Indies, among others: see Hofman *et al.* 2014: 591). Furthermore, major differences between languages, pedagogies, and legal systems exist among these island groupings, and these directly affect traditions of archaeological training, methodological practice, and heritage management policies (Siegel 2011; Siegel and Righter 2011). While Euro-colonial affiliations remain pragmatic for geopolitical and historical discussions, they perhaps unintentionally limit an understanding of the Caribbean region's fluidity, posing a challenge to archaeologists who wish to examine issues of locality, mobility, and cultural transformations on and between islands during the historic period (Hauser and Kelly 2009). By imposing colonial-era cartographic boundaries onto the spaces of the Caribbean in general and the Lesser Antilles in particular, the roles that topography, connectivity, or, in some cases, actual historical relationships played in shaping the multi-cultural practices of the region may be obscured (Figure 11.1).

Multi-method archaeological survey approaches offer opportunities for historical archaeologists to extend scopes of inquiry across modern boundaries in the Lesser Antilles. These methods accommodate diachronic perspectives, which are necessary for documenting multiple communities and cultures within individual islands, and they produce robust data for conducting intra- and inter-island landscape comparisons in

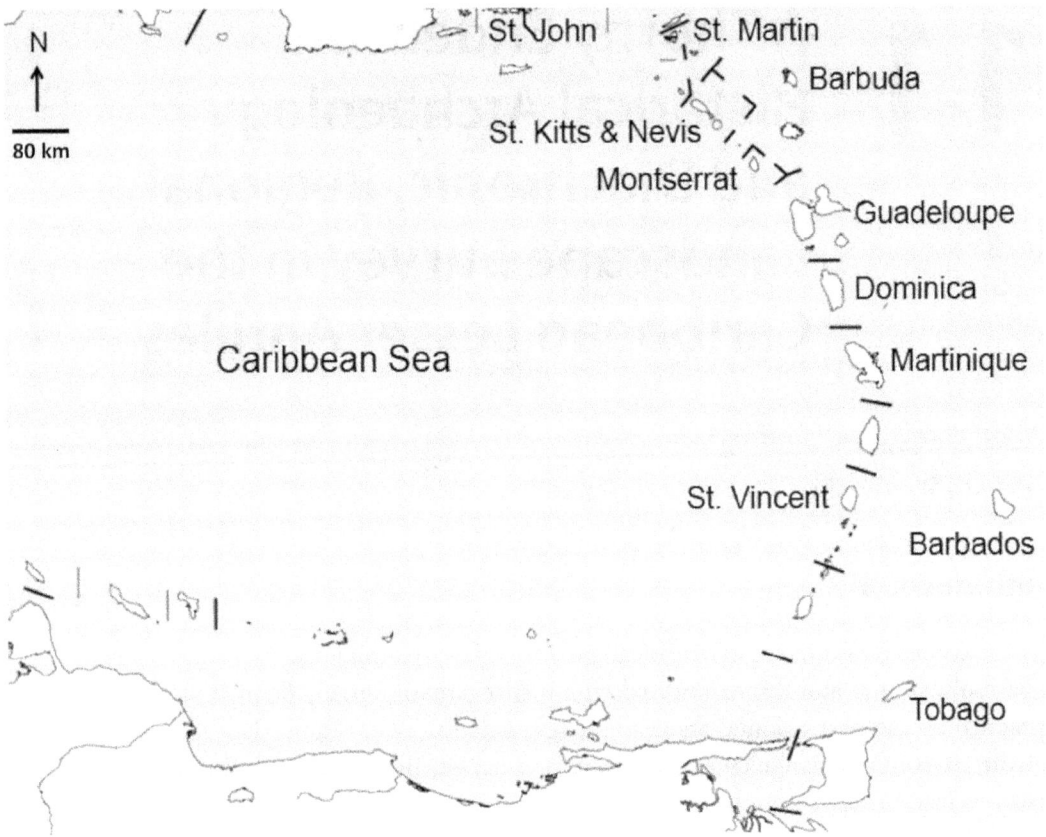

Figure 11.1   Map of the Lesser Antilles region of the Caribbean with labels for several of the islands discussed
in the text (Wikicommons, modified by K. Ryzewski).

ways that operate outside of colonial constructs and beyond predominant emphases
on single-sited archaeology.

Archaeology in the Caribbean developed relatively late in comparison to
counterparts in North America, Mesoamerica, and the Mediterranean. In each of
these traditions different approaches to survey dominate the practice of landscape
archaeology. In North America and Mesoamerica survey methods are integrated into
regional research frameworks and commonly include prospection via 'full coverage'
remote sensing or shovel test pit-based data collection; by contrast, Mediterranean
approaches to regional landscapes emerged from a tradition of intensive pedestrian
survey, which affords high-resolution data collection within smaller areas and may
have the potential to produce diachronic and comparative results (Alcock and Cherry
2004; Knodell and Leppard, this volume; see Opitz *et al.* 2015 for longer discussion
on geographically-divergent survey traditions). Caribbean survey practices do not
fit comfortably within either of these traditions. Although archaeological survey
in various guises has been employed across the area, especially in cultural resource
management operations, multi-period, regional survey does not exist in the Caribbean

as a standard component of archaeological research practice for prehistoric or historical archaeologists. Most historical archaeological studies that are microregional or island-wide in scope involve limited systematic field-walking or remote sensing, and are instead focused on locating sites identified from historical maps, archival documents, or standing remains. Recent research on the islands of St. John and Montserrat, however, is gradually changing the methodological course of historical landscape archaeology. Studies of both have used targeted and systematic survey techniques to substantially revise earlier site inventories that were compiled from visible remains, historic maps, and limited pedestrian reconnaissance (Ausherman 1982; Armstrong 2003: 82; Miles and Munby 2006; Cherry and Ryzewski 2011; Cherry *et al.* 2012; Cherry *et al.* 2015). These recent surveys have effectively demonstrated how multi-method, systematic approaches to island landscapes have the potential to yield an exponential increase in the location and analysis of anthropogenic features and less prominent settlements in areas within and beyond the plantation estates that dominated island economies for much of the historic period.

The following discussion highlights contributions from and challenges for survey approaches in the historical archaeology of the Caribbean Lesser Antilles. A brief history of the application of survey in Lesser Antillean archaeology emphasizes the state of divergence and diversity in the region's methodological approaches. Based on these and other examples, two challenges, environment and scale, are identified as two of the potential reasons limiting the widespread adoption of survey. A selection of case studies is foregrounded, with the intention of introducing the range of approaches and objectives associated with multi-method survey in recent scholarship of the historic period. The discussion concludes with reflections on emergent issues and future directions for the next generation of landscape archaeology and survey methodologies in Caribbean historical archaeology.

History of Survey in the Lesser Antilles

Survey has long been a tool for inventorying cultural resources and identifying research sites on many islands in the Lesser Antilles. As an approach for understanding various aspects of land use, settlement patterns, and island ecosystems, survey strategies have tended to encompass quite different reconnaissance and recovery techniques. Additionally, truly diachronic survey, encompassing both prehistoric and historic-period remains, is a rarity in the region.

Systematic survey approaches were first employed in the Lesser Antilles during the 1970s and quickly gained traction across the region, inspiring several island-wide landscape studies and inventories during the mid-1980s. Most, if not all, of the earliest surveys, including those on St. Kitts (Allaire 1974; Goodwin 1979) and Dominica (Petitjean-Roget 1978), focused on identifying prehistoric settlement patterns and cultural ecologies of the islands (see also Barbotin 1970; Dethlefsen *et al.* 1982; and earlier work by de Jong 1947). On St. Kitts, Goodwin (1979) first adapted survey approaches to facilitate the navigation of formidable mountainous terrain and dense tropical vegetation by narrowing his focus to the systematic assessment of remains in proximity to drainage systems (i.e., gullies), which archaeologists traversed between coastal outlets and upper-elevation, inland terrain. Similar topography-driven methods were later adopted by Wilson (1991) in his prehistoric settlement survey of Nevis and Cherry and Ryzewski in their first phase of diachronic survey on Montserrat (Cherry *et al.* 2012).

Several island-wide landscape surveys were conducted during the 1980s. These included Drewett and Harris's (1991) archaeological survey of Barbados, Haviser's surveys of the Dutch islands (St. Eustatius: Haviser 1985b; Saba: Haviser 1985a; St. Martin: Haviser 1988), Wilson's (1991) comparative settlement study on Nevis, and Watters and Scaglion's (1980) transect-based surveys of Barbuda and Montserrat (see also Barka 1985; 1993; Handler 1989). While the stated aim of these studies was to inventory or examine island-wide settlement patterning over time, none of the studies involved comprehensive documentation of historic-period landscapes as part of their research objectives. At best, the locations of major historic sites and their most visible standing remains were briefly noted.

It is important to appreciate that these early island-wide studies were accomplished prior to the advent or accessibility of geolocational technologies (e.g., GPS, GIS, remote sensing). Surveyors faced major difficulties in working with outdated maps, locating start and end points of survey transects, using compasses in poor visibility conditions, and placing sites located in dense forest conditions on maps post-survey (Watters and Scaglion 1980: 340; Haviser 1985b: 67). Nevertheless, these first-generation scholars of Caribbean landscape archaeology are to be credited for pioneering multi-stage sampling designs and transect survey approaches that informed subsequent scholarship.

By the late 1990s and early 2000s, access to GPS, GIS, and remote sensing technologies transformed Caribbean survey from exclusively pedestrian-based reconnaissance to multi-method, hybrid mapping and recovery initiatives. With these advances came a florescence of landscape-based studies, with the majority focused on prehistoric land-use and multi-period occupations during the pre-Columbian era (e.g., the regional Windward Islands survey: Bradford 2001; Carriacou: Kaye *et al.* 2003; St. Vincent: Callaghan 2007; Dominica: Shearn 2015; Guadeloupe: Stouvenot and Casagrande 2015). It was during this period that historical archaeologists gradually began to incorporate survey into research programs on a more routine basis. Delle's (1994) groundbreaking study of historic settlement patterns on St. Eustatius utilized the systematic, comparative, and multi-method landscape analyses that he also employed on Jamaica (Delle 1998; 2002; 2014). His work established the foundation for similar surveys across the Lesser Antilles, including on Tobago (Clement 1995; 1997), Saba (Espersen 2009), St. John (Armstrong 2003; Armstrong *et al.* 2007; 2009), Nevis (Meniketti 2004; 2016), Barbados (Finch *et al.* 2013; Bergman and Smith 2014), and Dominica (Hauser 2015b). By the turn of the twenty-first century, the relatively small number of landscape-focused studies in historical archaeology were transforming conceptions of island ecosystems and colonial relationships by documenting how populations utilized the spaces in between and beyond the bounds of plantation estates, as with the study of provision gardens for enslaved laborers located in the remote interior mountainous region of Montserrat (Pulsipher 1994; Pulsipher and Goodwin 1999).

Parallel to the emergence of landscape archaeology and multi-method survey techniques over the past three decades has been the growth of cultural resource management (CRM) in the Lesser Antilles, especially in the French and Dutch West Indies (Bérard and Stouvenot 2011; Kelly 2014; Haviser and Hofman 2015). In the French West Indies, for example, these efforts include numerous government-sponsored surveys conducted either as microregional assessments (on land and underwater) or thematic surveys (e.g., military remains, indigo plantations, lime kiln industries) under the supervision of the *Service Régional d'Archéologie* in Guadeloupe, Martinique, and Guyane (SRA), the *Institut National de Recherches Archéologiques Préventives* (INRAP), and the *Carte Archéologique Nationale*, among other entities (Verrand 2004; Verrand and Vidal 2004; Kelly 2014: 20-21). As a result of these intensive CRM-based surveys, there exists a fairly robust, decades-old gray literature, based mainly on pedestrian survey projects and located in local French and Dutch West Indian archival repositories.

This brief and partial summary of survey approaches in the Lesser Antilles demonstrates the diversity of orientations shaping the region's landscape archaeology and illustrates the upward trajectory of multi-method survey projects in terms of both quantity and specificity. As a primary research focus in historical archaeology, diachronic, regional survey and other landscape approaches are hardly standard or well-developed components of archaeological practice. However, there now exists a handful of long-term research projects entirely devoted to landscape archaeology, such as the Survey and Landscape Archaeology on Montserrat project, the *Mission Sud-Dominique*, and the Archaeological Survey of Colonial Dominica; these projects either partly or entirely focus on the historic period, using multi-method survey techniques and comparative, multi-sited analyses (Cherry *et al*. 2015; Hauser 2015a; 2015b; Shearn 2015: 201).

Environment and Scale

There are two factors that I argue account for the relatively slow incorporation of survey approaches into Lesser Antillean historical archaeology, as well as the sheer variety of techniques and related research orientations that currently exist across the region: environment and scale.

The most obvious challenge to conducting Caribbean survey is undoubtedly the merciless environmental conditions—extreme heat, dense vegetation, thorny plants, and poisonous animals (Figure 11.2). From St. John to Barbados, descriptions of these conditions often appear as disclaimers at the start of field reports, and every Caribbean archaeologist has their own horror story involving a harrowing encounter

Figure 11.2   An example of survey conditions in the Lesser Antilles; thick vegetation, thorny plants, and poisonous animals require clearing in order to locate and photograph archaeological features. Windmill tower clearance at Lower Waterworks Estate, Montserrat, showing John Cherry (background) and Samantha Ellens (foreground).

with dangerous plants or animals (see Armstrong 2003: 86; Espersen 2009: 16). These conditions do pose real limitations for conducting targeted and systematic pedestrian survey; crawling on hands and knees, scrambling up rock faces, and macheteing through brush on extensive tract surveys are certainly more common occurrences than intensive fieldwalking across open plow zones or controlled, gridded surface collection. It is not productive or, in many cases, possible to conduct the sort of pedestrian survey that our Mediterranean colleagues enjoy. As the examples in the following section demonstrate, survey in the Caribbean should be considered a different but no less robust species of systematic recovery.

The second major challenge to the current state of survey projects is that the region and the research within it are challenged by issues of scale, both temporal span and geographic scope (on scale and regional comparability see Hauser and Kelly 2009). Part of this issue attends to the fact that the vast majority of archaeological research either stops or starts at the misleadingly momentous 'Columbian divide'—1492 AD or thereabouts. Two distinct traditions of scholarly research dominate and fracture Caribbean archaeology: Pre-Columbian archaeology, focused especially on the peopling of the islands, subsequent large-scale population movements, and regional interaction spheres; and Post-Columbian historical archaeological studies, largely oriented toward the experience of European colonization and the growth of plantation-based economies and labor systems—these studies are most commonly accessed through the lens of individual sites (Rouse 1986; 1992; Keegan 2004; for applications of survey of prehistoric landscapes see Crock and Petersen 2004; de Waal 2006; Hofman and Bright 2010; Hofman and Hoogland 2012; Fitzpatrick 2013; Shearn 2015).

For historical archaeologists, the Columbian divide eclipses and understates what was actually a very uneven period of European colonization, one that occurred over the course of a century or more in less hospitable places like Montserrat and Dominica, colonized in 1632 and 1763 AD respectively. Here, the issue of pace is overlooked, both in regards to the pace that capitalism, colonial hierarchies, and industries became inscribed on the landscape, and to the pace at which indigenous populations responded to the arrival of Europeans and enslaved Africans. The Columbian divide also fails to recognize continuities in pottery and lithic traditions, exchange networks, and other Island Carib/Kalinago practices that may have been adopted by and integrated into post-Columbian communities (Hofman *et al.* 2014; Ryzewski and Cherry 2015).

Even more problematic is that these self-imposed temporal limits further reinforce uncritical assumptions about island settlement patterns over time. Some scholars have gone so far as to assert, based on the absence of early records or high visibility early colonial sites, that the islands were *completely empty* at the time of European arrival. This story is one that perpetuates the prevailing myth of indigenous disappearance and discounts the inter-island mobility that facilitated Carib resilience into modern times (Reid 2009). It is recounted in the histories of St. Eustatius, Nevis, Montserrat, and Dominica, and even in archaeological publications—most notably Robert Evans's chapter in the 1968 IACA proceedings, 'The lack of archaeology in Dominica', which concluded that Dominica was a mere stepping stone to more favorable islands because its mountainous environment offered minimal prospects for long-term settlement (Evans 1968; cited in Shearn 2015: 201). This assertion has since been totally disproven (Honeychurch 1997; Lenik 2012; Shearn 2015).

A major contribution of survey-based archaeology is its ability to produce diachronic data that spans the entire human occupational history of a site, region, or island. This sort of data is especially valuable in island settings, where groups often settled in the same strategic locations and drew repeatedly upon similar resource bases over the course of millennia, resulting in the presence of multi-period archaeological sites (Figure 11.3). During survey or excavation of these multi-period sites it is often impossible to ignore the presence of materials outside of a particular timeframe. Such is the case at the Valentine Ghaut site on Montserrat, where a Late Ceramic period settlement (ca. 1000 AD) was later reoccupied in the seventeenth and nineteenth centuries (Bocancea *et al.* 2013; Rothenberg *et al.* 2016).

Finally, in terms of temporal scale, projects that are truly diachronic in scale and scope, meaning survey-based research that seeks to identify all traces of human

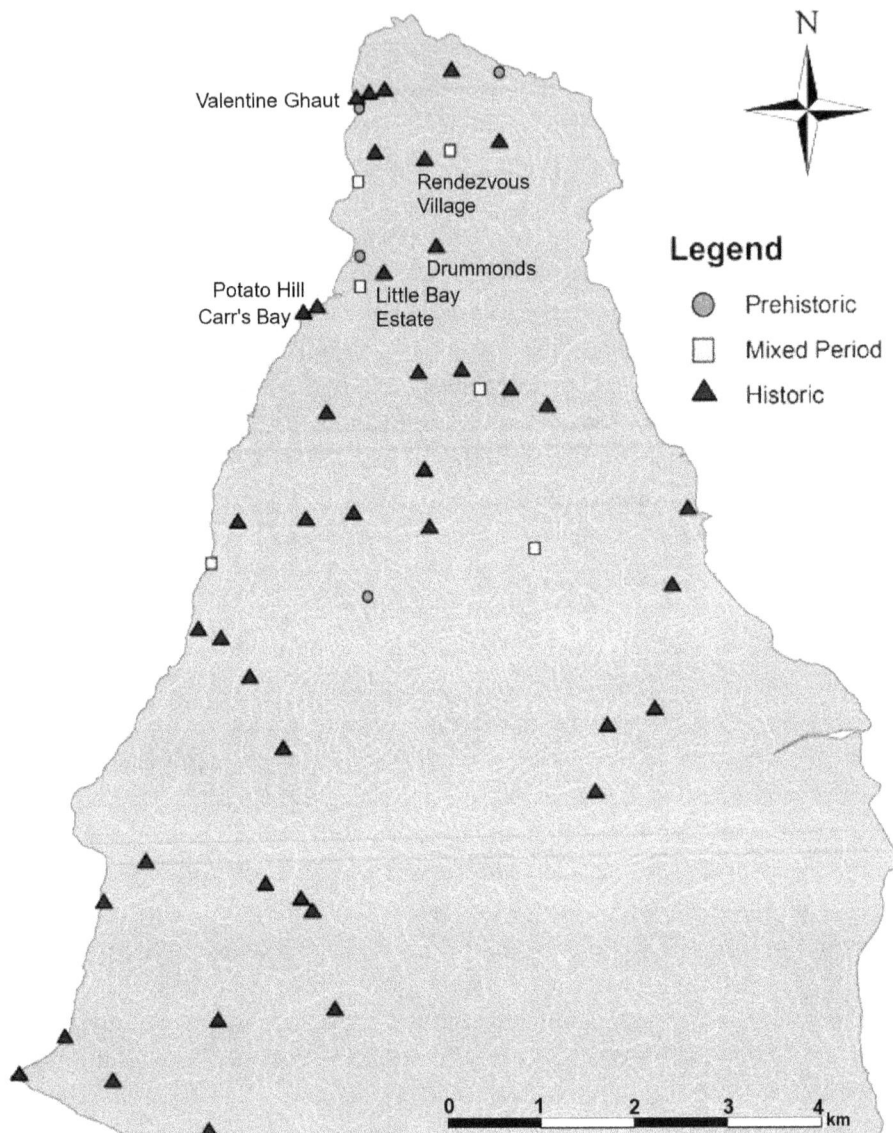

Figure 11.3   Ages and locations of archaeological sites in the non-exclusion zone of Montserrat identified and documented during the SLAM project's pedestrian surveys between 2010 and 2016 (map by B. Doucet).

activity on the islands over the course of their ca. 6000 year history, remain altogether uncommon within Caribbean archaeology. Although landscape approaches have the potential to augment the complementary research goals shared on both sides of the Columbian divide, such as interests in inter- and intra-island exchange and kinship networks, there are few examples that attempt to integrate them. The Survey and Landscape Archaeology on Montserrat (SLAM) is one of the few current research projects in the Caribbean that involves prehistorians and historical archaeologists in equal measure in its design. While the SLAM project employs a broad diachronic approach that is suited to address assumptions perpetuated by the Columbian divide, the following examples demonstrate how some historical archaeologists in the region are also framing their research in diachronic time spans in their survey-based investigations of island settlement patterns. In these more truncated diachronic approaches, historical archaeological studies tend to encompass either centuries of a shorter horizon, a particular cultural group, or multiple generations.

Diachronic Survey and Landscape Studies in Lesser Antillean Historical Archaeology: Some Examples

Over the past 25 years, historical archaeology in the Caribbean has matured into a decidedly multi-scalar, microregional, and multi-sited research program (Delle 1994; Hauser 2009; Kelly and Bérard 2014; Ryzewski and Cherry 2015). Interested in how capitalism and European colonization transformed island landscapes, and how both locality and regionality were experienced by island residents, especially enslaved Africans and others whose histories were undocumented, the first landscape studies in historical archaeology either focused on or began with plantation estates as the primary unit of study (Hauser 2009: 5; see also Armstrong 1990; Pulsipher 1991; Pulsipher and Goodwin 1999; Farnsworth 2001). Gradually, historical archaeologists have utilized multi-method survey approaches to successfully move away from earlier single-site-based studies and to extend the analytical gaze beyond the industrial core of plantation estates. The methods and contributions, several of which are summarized below, consider the broader landscapes of production and dwelling, including slave villages, provisions gardens, road systems, caves, environmental management practices, communication networks, and inter-visible settlements. There also exists a growing number of landscape-based studies that do not begin with the plantation, but instead aim to recover information about the spaces and people who lived, worked, and congregated in-between estates. These examples illustrate the diversity of survey methods in Lesser Antillean historical archaeology, and how they facilitate both nuanced understandings of island landscapes and regional comparative analyses.

St. John

Armstrong's landscape study, during the late 1990s, of the East End Community on St John set the standard for the systematic survey of marginal historic communities in the Lesser Antilles. Armstrong's (2003) work combined tax records, historic maps, and survey in an effort to chart the cultural and economic changes in the Danish West Indies that coincided with a 150-year period of land ownership by free, black island residents beginning in the late eighteenth century, well before emancipation. With 30 archaeologists split into three crews, a team conducted an intensive survey in the inhospitable East End terrain, walking transects at five-meter intervals parallel to the hill slopes (Armstrong 2003: 87). Their survey identified 50 individual house sites with associated activity areas, as well as terrace systems, wells, stone walls, and other features, which they mapped using a differential GPS and later GIS (Armstrong 2001). The results of the East End survey relocated a community who lived in the remote outskirts of St. John from the eighteenth through the early twentieth centuries, but still remained connected with global circulations of goods and people through their own maritime activities (cf. Bennet *et al.* 2000 on landscape archaeology of Ottoman Greece). A 'venue of freedom', the archaeology of the East End community, viewed diachronically, provides an important case study about the gradual process of economic transition during the period of estate consolidation and emancipation on St. John (Armstrong 2003: 94).

Dominica

Recent work by Mark Hauser (2015a; 2015b) as part of the Archaeological Survey of Colonial Dominica (ASCD) demonstrates the contributions of pedestrian survey approaches in detecting local variability in settlement patterning, land use, and social differentiation, through the comparative analysis of four plantation settlements and their surrounding landscapes within the island's Portsmouth microregion. Focused on the archaeological horizon that corresponds with the height of Dominica's sugar industry, between the 1770s and 1810 AD, Hauser's research operates from a more truncated and focused diachronic perspective that spans multiple generations. Even within this 40-year time frame, which is considerably shorter than some of the multi-century diachronic approaches practiced on nearby islands, the ASCD surveys have successfully recorded the extent to which the construction of new industrial outbuildings built to accommodate sugar production mobilized significant and subtle changes in land use on sugar estates. The emergent patterned variation of these changes, or discontinuities, and the distinctive arrangements of space between estates are comparable between the four estates in terms of property size, population density, landscape features, and material culture (Hauser 2015a: 612). Building from multi-sited comparisons between the estates, Hauser examined how planters intentionally created 'blind spots' that allowed them to articulate power by covertly observing and controlling movement, as well as socioeconomic and racial hierarchies across the regional landscape (Hauser 2015a: 144; cf. Delle 1998; 2014). Planters achieved such control by manipulating lines of sight across the region, by the strategic placement of structures, and by positioning structures at points that facilitated long-distance auditory networks between estates. This work reflects an increasing consideration among historical archaeologists of regional analysis as a means of articulating relationships between archaeological sites and the people who once inhabited them (Hauser 2009: 3).

Montserrat

One component of the work under way as part of the Survey and Landscape Archaeology on Montserrat project uses an iterative process between extensive-tract pedestrian survey, airborne LiDAR analysis, and GIS in the densely forested Centre Hills region in order to examine the high-elevation plantation landscapes and the

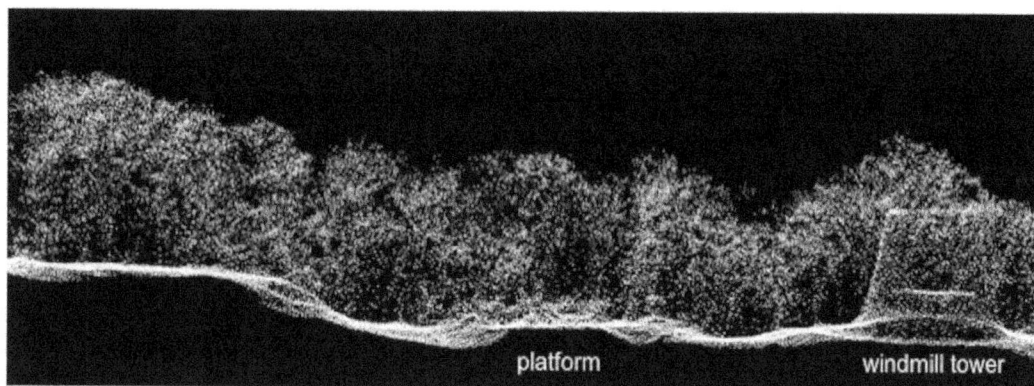

Figure 11.4   Three-dimensional cross-section of the Fairy Walk Estate (1763) in the dense vegetation of the Centre Hills region of Montserrat, rendered from airborne LiDAR point cloud data (image by A. Zissis, modified by K. Ryzewski).

broader context of industrial production and slavery on the island. This iterative survey technique has enabled the location and documentation of the central facilities and surrounding landscapes of multiple eighteenth-century sugar plantations, including the previously unknown Fairy Walk estate (Figure 11.4).

The combination of airborne LiDAR and GIS analysis also assisted in the remote mapping of the Bugby Hole Estate, which was missed by two earlier transect and inventory surveys (Watters and Scaglion 1980; Miles and Munby 2006). The site is now permanently situated in the volcanic exclusion zone and can only be studied using remote sensing technologies.

A second example of multi-method survey on Montserrat is the location of an unidentified marginal community on the outskirts of plantation life, atop Potato Hill. The site of Potato Hill is situated on a prominent elongated knoll that runs east–west and divides Little Bay from Carr's Bay on the northwest coast of Montserrat. Within this northernmost microregion of the island, since 2010 SLAM project surveys have identified and recorded 13 historic-period sites located beyond central industrial or residential areas of known plantation sites. In addition to Potato Hill, the nearby sites of Drummonds and Rendezvous Village also produced surface artifactual evidence of modest settlements, apparently occupied for generations by non-elite communities who would have contributed to the plantation economy in various capacities (Cherry *et al.* 2012). The sites of Potato Hill, Drummonds, and Rendezvous Village each occupy isolated hilltops, with commanding views of the water, neighboring mountains, and valleys. Potato Hill, with its relatively flat summit, steep slopes, and (at the western end) vertical sea-cliff, was both attractive for settlement and defensively advantageous; it also had access to water sources from the small ghauts that run down to the bays to the north and south and the water catchment system on the top of the hill (Ryzewski and Cherry 2016). Here, land clearance afforded archaeologists the rare opportunity to complete a gridded survey with 100% collection of surface finds. Distribution maps of the finds

Figure 11.5   Feature 298 atop Potato Hill was originally located by the presence of artifact surface scatter during the area's 2013 gridded surface survey. Shovel testing in 2013 (STPs 3 and 4 on the map) located the western edge of a stone building foundation, which was further excavated during the 2015 and 2016 SLAM field seasons, revealing an early colonial multi-room domestic structure with remains dating from the seventeenth and eighteenth centuries. Excavation locations from 2015 are outlined in white, and from 2016 are in black (image collected and modified by B. Doucet, M. Pihokker, and K. Ryzewski 2016).

aided in locating four domestic structures on the hilltop, two of which are currently under excavation (Figure 11.5; cf. Finch *et al.* 2013).

Archaeological remains confirm that Potato Hill was home to a small long-term or repeatedly-occupied community between the seventeenth and nineteenth century AD, over the course of 150 years. Nestled between three plantation estates, two bays, and a military outpost, all active during the peak period of eighteenth-century sugar production, Potato Hill must be understood within a broader landscape context, which can only be done through employing a multi-sited, multi-method strategy.

French West Indies

Kelly (2009: 80) rightly contends that because most research in the region has been conducted in the Anglophone Caribbean, historical archaeologists have embraced uncritical assumptions about the 'nature and scale of context' in ways that structure the English colonial world as the foundational framework when conducting comparative analyses. As a result, differences between European imperial policies and initiatives are difficult to examine archaeologically. To address this disparity, Kelly's recent survey and excavation work on estates in Martinique and Guadeloupe employs a cross-colonial, multi-island regional comparative perspective that contrasts artifact data collected during surface surveys and excavations on the French islands with those recovered from British territories, in this case Jamaica. Comparisons between the slave villages at the sites of Habitation Grande Pointe and Habitation La Mahaudière in Guadeloupe noted the rarity of eighteenth-century material culture and a marked increase in artifact density during the nineteenth century. Inter-island comparisons between the Guadeloupe data and the assemblage recovered from the site of Habitation Crève Coeur on Martinique noted similar artifact patterning, with artifact densities and the appearance of European goods (especially glass and ceramics) increasing after the turn of the nineteenth century (Kelly 2009: 80). Extending the analysis from the French islands of Guadeloupe and Martinique regionally, it appears that French Caribbean artifact distribution patterns, especially during the eighteenth century, contrasted significantly with those observed in Anglophone contexts, such as on the Seville Estate on Jamaica, where diverse earlier artifact assemblages were recovered from surface surveys (Armstrong 1990; Kelly and Bérard 2014).

Such innovative, cross-cultural comparative research, rooted in controlled survey methods, demonstrates how material differences contributed to quite different colonial experiences in French and British territories. Viewed diachronically, these findings also contribute to understanding how distinct creole cultures later developed across the region (Kelly 2009: 90).

St. Vincent

There remains a longer conversation to be had elsewhere about the involvement of survey in rescue-based and CRM work in the region. Some of the most exciting multi-period finds in the region were recovered from recent CRM initiatives, most notably at the Argyle site in St. Vincent, a small Carib/Kalinago coastal village occupied in the late sixteenth to early seventeenth century, just prior to European arrival (Poerschmann and Meyer 2008; Hofman and Hoogland 2011; Hofman *et al.* 2014). At Argyle, Leiden University's Caribbean Research Group uncovered European materials comingled with indigenous objects from the Greater and Lesser Antilles, suggesting that mixtures of cultural influences were already present at the time of European arrival. Finds included an indigenous coarse earthenware pottery vessel inlaid with European glass beads and pig teeth (Hofman *et al.* 2014: fig. 6). The research at Argyle is optimally poised to question the assumptions of indigenous disappearance during the initial period of European settlement and divisions in archaeological practice that are perpetuated by the Columbian divide.

The surveys summarized here, and a number of others, both terrestrial and underwater, have produced significant multi-scalar and truncated diachronic results that are contributing to nuanced understandings of landscapes of colonialism, industry, exploitation, and multiculturalism in the Lesser Antilles (e.g., Barka 1985; Delvoye 1994; Clement 1997; Espersen 2009; Farmer 2011; Leshikar-Denton 2013; Bergman and Smith 2014; Meniketti 2016).

Discussion and Conclusions

Over 30 years ago, John F. Cherry encouraged his colleagues across the Mediterranean region to synthesize and compare data collected during archaeological survey projects (Cherry 1983). His objective was to stimulate new interregional research questions in ways that would engage the challenge of conducting multi-scalar and multi-temporal research across an incredibly diverse cultural and ecological landscape. The issue of comparability between survey datasets has persisted for two decades after Cherry's initial call, but it is now a central focus of landscape archaeology in the Mediterranean (Alcock and Cherry 2004; Knodell and Leppard, this volume). If the decades-long timeframe that Mediterranean archaeologists took to grapple with issues of scale, comparability, and interregional questions is any indication, it will be some time before Caribbean archaeology comes to terms with similar issues that it now faces. Major challenges concerning the same issues of scale and comparability lie ahead for survey archaeology in the Caribbean, whether they arise on projects that are prehistoric, historical, or multi-period in scope. In historical archaeology, major comparative databases, such as the Digital Archaeological Archive of Comparative Slavery (DAACS), are emerging as invaluable resources for data organization and dissemination. However, though immensely useful for scholars conducting single-sited or comparative studies involving places associated with slavery (usually plantation estates), this and other database resources tend to unintentionally reinforce the Columbian divide in their exclusion of prehistoric remains, and they continue to alienate pedestrian survey from other fieldwork practices in their primary concern with historic-period excavated materials, rather than artifacts and landscape data collected during pedestrian or remote-sensing surveys.

As argued elsewhere (Cherry *et al.* 2015), there is not, nor should there be, a one-size-fits-all approach to survey in the Lesser Antilles. There is ample room in the area to involve approaches that are well-suited to consider islands, microregions, households, and sometimes even individuals as units of comparative analysis. In historical archaeology, multi-method survey and the appropriate inter- and intra-island comparisons of results provide the means for producing data that will integrate and articulate local experiences with global processes in ways that will encourage regional conversations about mobility, creolization, colonialism, and heritage.

Assisted by advances in technologies over the past few decades, survey in the Caribbean continues to develop as a multi-method, hybrid technique that is, as Kelly (2009: 80) contends, ready to challenge the assumptions of scale and context tied to the region's colonial affiliations. Nevertheless, diachronic survey in the historical archaeology of the Lesser Antilles remains a small but growing practice. The community of scholars who are incorporating integrative landscape approaches into their work is demonstrating how plantation boundaries did not necessarily define community boundaries. They are examining how and why activities took place at out-of-bounds, liminal, and less visible places, including provision grounds, markets, free settlements, military outposts, and indigenous sites. Archaeologists working on both sides of the Columbian divide share similar aims in understanding processes of interaction, migration, and mobility (Curet and Hauser 2011; Hofman *et al.* 2014: 592; Kelly and Bérard 2014). Survey in the Lesser Antilles has proven its potential to take island archaeologists beyond the physical boundaries of the site, beyond the temporal boundaries of a particular period of interest, and eventually should move research beyond the camps entrenched on either side of the Columbian divide.

Acknowledgments

Special thanks to Alex Knodell and Tom Leppard for including a Caribbean historical archaeological perspective in this volume and in the preceding conference in honor of John Cherry. I am grateful to several Caribbean archaeology colleagues who shared resources and ideas with me from their own current survey work during the drafting of this chapter, including Benoit Bérard, Christian Stouvenot, and Mark Hauser. I am most indebted to John Cherry; on Montserrat we owe all of the accomplishments of our landscape-based research to the decades of experience from the Mediterranean that he has successfully transferred to the Caribbean, transforming new fields of practice in the process. Although most of the publications from Montserrat that I cite here are works I co-authored with John, I take full credit for any errors or omissions. Ongoing fieldwork by the SLAM project on Montserrat is supported by funding from the National Endowment for the Humanities, Collaborative Research Grant (#RZ51674-14).

About the Author

Krysta Ryzewski is Associate Professor of Anthropology at Wayne State University in Detroit, where she co-leads the Anthropology of the City initiative. As a historical archaeologist, her research focuses on relationships of disruptive social and environmental pressures in urban North America (Detroit) and in the Caribbean (Montserrat). Her research has been featured in *Science Magazine*, and funded by the National Endowment of the Humanities, National Science Foundation, National Geographic Society, and the Wenner-Gren Foundation. Recent articles have appeared in the *International Journal of Historical Archaeology*, the *Journal of Archaeological Science*, and the *Journal of Contemporary Archaeology*. E-mail: krysta.ryzewski@wayne.edu

References

Alcock, S.E., and J.F. Cherry (eds.)
2004   *Side-by-Side Survey: Comparative Regional Studies in the Mediterranean World.* Oxford: Oxbow Books.

Allaire, L.
1974   An archaeological reconnaissance of St. Kitts, Leeward Islands. In *Proceedings of the Fifth International Congress for the Study of Pre-Columbian Cultures of the Lesser Antilles*, 158-61. St. John's, Antigua: Antigua Archaeological Society.

Armstrong, D.V.
1990   *The Old Village and the Great House: An Archaeological and Historical Examination of Drax Hall Plantation, St. Ann's Bay, Jamaica.* Champaign: University of Illinois Press.
2001   A venue for autonomy: archaeology of a changing cultural landscape, the East End community, St. John, Virgin Islands. In P. Farnsworth (ed.), *Island Lives: Historical Archaeologies of the Caribbean*, 142-64. Tuscaloosa: University of Alabama Press.
2003   *Creole Transformation: From Slavery to Freedom. Historical Archaeology of the East End community, St. John, Virgin Islands.* Tallahassee: University Press Florida.

Armstrong, D.V., M.W. Hauser, D.W. Knight and S. Lenik
2009   Variation in venues of slavery and freedom: interpreting the late eighteenth-century landscape of St. John, Danish West Indies using archaeological GIS. *International Journal of Historical Archaeology* 13: 94-111. https://doi.org/10.1007/s10761-008-0066-6

Armstrong, D.V., M.W. Hauser, S. Lenik and K. Wild
2007   Estate consolidation, land use, and ownership: a GIS archaeological landscape survey of St. John, Danish West Indies (1780-1800) with a particular focus on Annaberg Plantation. In B. Reid (ed.), *Proceedings of the Twenty-First Congress of the International*

Association for Caribbean Archaeology, 69-80. St. Augustine, Trinidad: University of the West Indies.

Ausherman, B. (ed.)
1982   *St. John Sites Report, 1981-1982.* St. Thomas, United States Virgin Islands: Division of Archaeology and Historic Preservation.

Barbotin, M.F.
1970   Les sites archéologiques de Marie-Galante (Guadeloupe). In *Proceedings of the Third Congress of the International Association for Caribbean Archaeology*, 27-44. St. George's, Grenada: Grenada Historical Society.

Barka, N.
1985   *Archaeology of St. Eustatius, Netherlands Antilles: An Interim Report on the 1981-1984 Seasons.* St. Eustatius Archaeological Research Series 1. Williamsburg, Virgina: College of William and Mary.
1993   *Archaeological Survey of Sites and Buildings, St. Maarten, Netherlands Antilles* I. St. Maarten Archaeological Research Series 3. Williamsburg, Virginia: College of William and Mary.

Bennet, J., J.L. Davis and F. Zarinebaf-Shahr
2000   Pylos Regional Archaeological Project, Part III: Sir William Gell's itinerary in the Pylia and regional landscapes in the Morea in the Second Ottoman Period. *Hesperia* 69: 343-80. https://doi.org/10.2307/148401

Bérard, B., and C. Stouvenot
2011   French West Indies. In P. Siegel and E. Righter (eds.), *Protecting Heritage in the Caribbean*, 80-89. Tuscaloosa: University of Alabama Press.

Bergman, S., and F.H. Smith
2014   The spaces in between: archaeological investigations at St. Nicholas Abbey sugar plantation. In K. Kelly and B. Bérard (eds.), *Bitasion: Archéologie des Habitations-Plantations des Petites Antilles*, 127-46. Leiden: Sidestone Press.

Bocancea, E., K. Ryzewski and J.F. Cherry
2013 *Report on the Survey and Excavations at Valentine Ghaut, Montserrat 2010-2013*. Olveston, Montserrat: Montserrat National Trust.
Bradford, M.A.C.
2001 Caribbean Perspectives on Settlement Patterns: The Windward Island Study. Unpublished PhD dissertation, University of Iowa, Iowa City, Iowa.
Callaghan, R.T.
2007 Prehistoric settlement patterns on St. Vincent, West Indies. *Caribbean Journal of Science* 43: 11-22. https://doi.org/10.18475/cjos.v43i1.a3
Cherry, J.F.
1983 Frogs round the pond: perspectives in current archaeological survey projects in the Mediterranean region. In D. Keller and D. Rupp (eds.), *Archaeological Survey in the Mediterranean Area*. British Archaeological Reports, International Series 155: 375-416. Oxford: Archaeopress.
Cherry, J.F., and K. Ryzewski
2011 Archaeology at risk, archaeology of risk: diachronic land-use, settlement, and volcanic activity on Montserrat. In B. Bérard (ed.), *Proceedings of the Twenty-Fourth Congress of the International Association of Caribbean Archaeologists*, 408-20. Fort de France, Martinique: Université de Antilles et de la Guyane.
Cherry, J.F., K. Ryzewski and T.P. Leppard
2012 Multi-period landscape survey and site risk assessment on Montserrat, West Indies. *Journal of Island and Coastal Archaeology* 7: 282-302. https://doi.org/10.1080/15564894.2011.611857
Cherry, J.F., K. Ryzewski, T.P. Leppard and E. Bocancea
2015 Diachronic, multi-scalar landscape archaeology on Montserrat: opportunities and challenges. In L. de Olmo (ed.), *Proceedings of the Twenty-Fifth Congress of the International Association of Caribbean Archaeology*, 395-

413. San Juan, Puerto Rico: Instituto de Cultura Puertorriqeña.
Clement, C.O.
1995 Landscapes and Plantations on Tobago: A Regional Perspective. Unpublished PhD dissertation, University of Florida, Gainesville, Florida.
1997 Settlement patterning on the British Caribbean island of Tobago. *Historical Archaeology* 31: 93-106. https://doi.org/10.1007/BF03373605
Crock, J.G., and J.B. Petersen
2004 Inter-island exchange, settlement hierarchy, and a Taino-related chiefdom on the Anguilla Bank, Northern Lesser Antilles. In A. Delpuech and C.L. Hofman (eds.), *Late Ceramic Age Societies in the Eastern Caribbean*, 139-58. Oxford: Archaeopress.
Curet, A.L., and M.W. Hauser (eds.)
2011 *Islands at the Crossroads: Migration, Seafaring, and Interaction in the Caribbean*. Tuscaloosa: University of Alabama Press.
de Jong, J.J.P.B.
1947 *Archaeological Material from Saba and St. Eustatius, Lesser Antilles*. Leiden: Leiden University Press.
de Waal, M.S.
2006 Pre-Columbian Social Organisation and Interaction Interpreted through the Study of Settlement Patterns: An Archaeological Case Study of the Pointe des Châteaux, La Désirade and Les Îles de lat Petite Terre Micro-Region, Guadeloupe, FWI. Unpublished PhD dissertation, Leiden University, Leiden.
Delle, J.A.
1994 The settlement pattern of sugar plantations on St. Eustatius. In D.W. Linebaugh and C.G. Robinson (eds.), *Spatial Patterning in Historical Archaeology: Selected Studies of Settlement*, 33-61. Williamsburg, Virginia: William and Mary Center for Archaeological Research.
1998 *An Archaeology of Social Space: Analyzing Coffee Plantations in Jamaica's Blue*

Mountains. New York: Plenum Press. https://doi.org/10.1007/978-1-4757-9159-4

2002 Power and landscape: spatial dynamics in early nineteenth century Jamaica. In M.O. Donovan (ed.), *The Dynamics of Power.* Center for Archaeological Investigations Occasional Paper 30: 341-61. Carbondale: Southern Illinois University.

2014 *The Colonial Caribbean: Landscapes of Power in the Plantation System.* Cambridge: Cambridge University Press.

Delvoye, L.

1994 A reconnaissance of Corre Corre Bay, St. Eustatius. In A. Versteeg (ed.), *Between St. Eustatius and the Guianas: Contributions to Caribbean Archaeology,* 43-52. Oranjestad: St. Eustatius Historical Foundation.

Dethlefsen, E., S.J. Gluckman, R.D. Mathewson and N.F. Barka

1982 Archaeology on St. Eustatius: the Pompeii of the New World. *Archaeology* 35: 8-15.

Drewet, P.L., and M.H. Harris

1991 The archaeological survey of Barbados 1985-86. In L.S. Robinson (ed.), *Proceedings of the Twelfth Congress of the International Association of Caribbean Archaeology,* 175-202. Fort de France, Martinique: Université de Antilles et de la Guyane.

Espersen, R.

2009 From Folklore to Folk History: Contextualizing Settlement at Palmetto Point, Saba, Dutch Caribbean. Unpublished MA Thesis, Leiden University, Leiden.

Evans, R.C.

1968 The lack of archeology on Dominica. In *Proceedings of the Second International Congress for the Study of the Pre-Columbian Cultures of the Lesser Antilles,* 93-102. Bridgetown, Barbados: Barbados Museum and Historical Society.

Farmer, K.

2011 Barbados. In P.E. Siegel and E. Righter

(eds.), *Protecting Heritage in the Caribbean,* 112-24. Tuscaloosa: University of Alabama Press.

Farnsworth, P. (ed.)

2001 *Island Lives: Historical Archaeologies of the Caribbean.* Tuscaloosa: University of Alabama.

Finch, J., D.V. Armstrong, E. Blinkhorn and D. Barker

2013 Surveying Caribbean cultural landscapes: Mount Plantation, Barbados, and its global connections. *Internet Archaeology* 35. https://doi.org/10.11141/ia.35.5

Fitzpatrick, S.M.

2013 The southward route hypothesis. In W.F. Keegan, C.L. Hofman and R. Rodríguez Ramos (eds.), *The Oxford Handbook of Caribbean Archaeology,* 198-205. Oxford: Oxford University Press. https://doi.org/10.1093/oxfordhb/9780195392302.013.0068

Goodwin, C.

1979 Prehistoric Cultural Ecology of St. Kitts, West Indies: A Case Study in Island Archaeology. Unpublished PhD Dissertation, Arizona State University, Tempe, Arizona.

Handler, J.S.

1989 *Searching for a Slave Cemetery in Barbados, West Indies: A Bioarchaeological and Ethnohistorical Investigation.* Center for Archaeological Investigations Research Paper 59. Carbondale: Southern Illinois University.

Hauser, M.W.

2009 Scale, locality and the Caribbean historical archaeology. *International Journal of Historical Archaeology* 13: 3-11. https://doi.org/10.1007/s10761-008-0068-4

2015a Blind spots in empire: plantation landscapes in early colonial Dominica (1763-1807). In L.W. Marshall (ed.), *The Archaeology of Slavery: A Comparative Approach to Captivity and Coercion,* 143-65. Carbondale: Southern Illinois University.

2015b The infrastructure of nature's island:

settlements, networks and economy of two plantations in colonial Dominica. *International Journal of Historical Archaeology*, 19: 601-22. https://doi.org/10.1007/s10761-015-0300-y

Hauser, M.W., and K.G. Kelly (eds.)
2009   *Centering the Caribbean: Landscapes and Scale in Caribbean Historical Archaeology.* Special issue of *International Journal of Historical Archaeology* 13(1).

Haviser, J.B.
1985a   *An Archaeological Survey of Saba, Netherlands Antilles, Phase 1.* Reports of the Archaeological and Anthropological Institute of the Netherlands Antilles 3. Willemstad, Curaçao: Archaeological and Anthropological Institute of the Netherlands Antilles

1985b   An inventory of prehistoric resources on St. Eustatius, Netherlands Antilles. In *Proceedings of the Tenth Congress of the International Association of Caribbean Archaeology*, 61-82. Fort de France, Martinique: Université de Antilles et de la Guyane.

1988   *An Archaeological Survey of St. Martin-St. Maarten.* Reports of the Archaeological-Anthropological Institute of the Netherlands Antilles 7. Willemstad, Curaçao: Archaeological and Anthropological Institute of the Netherlands Antilles

Haviser, J.B., and C.L. Hofman
2015   A review of archaeological research in the Dutch Caribbean. In C.L. Hofman and J.B. Haviser (eds.), *Managing Our Past into the Future: Archaeological Heritage Management in the Dutch Caribbean*, 37-71. Leiden: Sidestone Press.

Hofman, C.L., and A.J. Bright
2010   Towards a pan-Caribbean perspective of pre-colonial mobility and exchange: preface to a special volume of the Journal of Caribbean Archaeology. In C.L. Hofman and A.J. Bright (eds.), *Mobility and exchange from a Pan-Caribbean perspective.* Special issue 3 of *Journal of Caribbean Archaeology* 9: i-iii.

Hofman, C.L., and M.L.P. Hoogland
2011   Unraveling the multi-scale networks of mobility and exchange in the pre-colonial circum-Caribbean. In C.L. Hofman and A. van Duijvenbode (eds.), *Communities in Contact: Essays in Archaeology, Ethnohistory and Ethnography of the Amerindian circum-Caribbean*, 15-43. Leiden: Sidestone Press.

2012   Caribbean encounters: rescue excavations at the early colonial Island Carib site of Argyle, St. Vincent. In C. Bakels and H. Kamermans (eds.), *The Fifth Decade.* Analecta Praehistorica Leidensia 43/44: 63-76. Leiden: Faculty of Archaeology.

Hofman, C.L., A. Mol, M.L.P. Hoogland and R. Valcarcel Rojas
2014   Stages of encounters: migration, mobility and interaction in the pre-colonial and early colonial Caribbean. *World Archaeology* 46: 590-609. https://doi.org/10.1080/00438243.2014.925820

Honeychurch, L.
1997   Crossroads in the Caribbean: a site of encounter and exchange on *Dominica. World Archaeology* 28: 291-304. https://doi.org/10.1080/00438243.1997.9980349

Kaye, Q., M. Kappers and S.M. Fitzpatrick
2003   Archaeological survey of Carriacou, West Indies. In C.T. Maria and M.A. Garcia Arevalo (eds.), *Proceedings of the Twentieth Congress of the International Association of Caribbean Archaeology*, 391-98. Santo Domingo, Dominican Republic: Museo del Hombre Dominicano.

Keegan, W.F.
2004   Islands of chaos. In A. Delpuech and C.L. Hofman (eds.), *Late Ceramic Age Societies in the Eastern Caribbean.* British Archaeological Reports, International Series 1273: 33-44. Oxford: Archaeopress.

Kelly, K.G.
2009   Where is the French Caribbean?

French colonial archaeology in the English lake. *International Journal of Historical Archaeology* 13: 80-93. https://doi.org/10.1007/s10761-008-0069-3

2014 Archaeology, plantations, and slavery in the French West Indies. In K.G. Kelly and B. Bérard (eds.), *Bitasion: Archéologie des Habitations-Plantations des Petites Antilles*, 17-32. Leiden: Sidestone Press.

Kelly, K.G., and B. Bérard (eds.)
2014 *Bitasion: Archéologie des Habitations-Plantations des Petites Antilles*. Leiden: Sidestone Press.

Lenik, S.
2012 Carib as colonial category: comparing ethnohistoric and archaeological evidence from Dominica, West Indies. *Ethnohistory* 59: 79-107. https://doi.org/10.1215/00141801-1435401

Leshikar-Denton, M.E.
2013 Problems and progress in the Caribbean. In C.V. Ruppe and J.F. Barstad (eds.). *International Handbook of Underwater Archaeology*, 279-98. New York: Springer.

Meniketti, M.G.
2004 The Historical Archaeology of Nevis, West Indies: Capitalism, Environment, and the Evolution of the Caribbean Colonial Landscape, 1625-1833. Unpublished PhD dissertation, Michigan State University, East Lansing, Michigan.

2016 *Sugar Cane Capitalism and Environmental Transformation: An Archaeology of Colonial Nevis, West Indies*. Tuscaloosa: University of Alabama Press.

Miles, D., and J. Munby
2006 Montserrat before the volcano: a survey of plantations prior to the 1995 eruptions. *Landscapes* 7: 48-69. https://doi.org/10.1179/lan.2006.7.2.48

Opitz, R.S., K. Ryzewski, J.F. Cherry and B. Moloney
2015 Using airborne LiDAR survey to explore historic-era archaeological landscapes of Montserrat in the eastern Caribbean. *Journal of Field Archaeology* 40: 523-41. https://doi.org/10.1179/2042458215Y.0000000016

Petitjean-Roget, H.
1978 Archaeological reconnaissance in the island of Dominica (West Indies). In *Proceedings from the Seventh International Congress for the Study of Pre-Columbian Civilizations of the Lesser Antilles*, 81-97. Montreal: Centre de Recherches Caraïbes, Université de Montréal.

Poerschmann, M., and J. Meyer
2008 *Argyle International Airport Project Environmental Impact Assessment*. Kingstown, St. Vincent: Government of Saint Vincent and the Grenadines and International Airport Development Company.

Pulsipher, L.M.
1991 Galways Plantation, Montserrat. In H.J. Viola and C. Margolis (eds.), *Seeds of Change: A Quincentennial Commemoration*, 139-60. Washington, DC: Smithsonian Institution Press.

1994 The landscapes and ideational roles of Caribbean slave gardens. In N.F. Miller and K.L. Gleason (eds.), *The Archaeology of Garden and Field*, 202-22. Philadelphia: University of Pennsylvania.

Pulsipher L.M., and C.M. Goodwin
1999 'Here where the old time people be': reconstructing the landscapes of the slavery and post-slavery era on Montserrat, West Indies. In J.B. Haviser (ed.), *African Sites Archaeology in the Caribbean*, 9-37. Kingston, Jamaica: Ian Randle.

Reid, B.
2009 *Myths and Realities of Caribbean History*. Tuscaloosa: University of Alabama Press.

Rothenberg, M.A., B. Doucet, J.F. Cherry and K. Ryzewski
2016 *Survey and Landscape Archaeology on Montserrat: Report on 2016 Survey Operations*. Olveston, Montserrat: Montserrat National Trust.

Rouse, I.B.

1986 *Migrations in Prehistory: Inferring Population Movement from Cultural Remains.* New Haven, Connecticut: Yale University Press.

1992 *The Tainos: Rise and Decline of the People who Greeted Columbus.* New Haven, Connecticut: Yale University Press.

Ryzewski, K., and J.F. Cherry

2015 Struggles of a sugar society: surveying plantation-era Montserrat, 1650-1850. *International Journal of Historical Archaeology* 19: 356-83. https://doi.org/10.1007/s10761-015-0292-7

2016 Surveying a long-term settlement on Potato Hill, Montserrat. In L. Bates, J.M. Chenoweth and J.A. Delle (eds.), *Archaeologies of Slavery and Freedom in the Caribbean: Exploring the Places in Between*, 258-308. Gainesville: University of Florida Press.

Shearn, I.

2015 Investigating pre-Columbian settlement patterns in Dominica using a three-tiered survey strategy. In L. de Olmo (ed.), *Proceedings of the Twenty-Fifth Congress of the International Association for Caribbean Archaeology*, 199-225. San Juan, Puerto Rico: Instituto de Cultura Puertorriqeña.

Siegel, P.E.

2011 Protecting heritage in the Caribbean. In P.E. Siegel and E. Righter (eds.), *Protecting Heritage in the Caribbean*, 152-62. Tuscaloosa: University of Alabama Press.

Siegel, P.E., and E. Righter (eds.)

2011 *Protecting Heritage in the Caribbean.* Tuscaloosa: University of Alabama Press.

Stouvenot, C., and F. Casagrande

2015 Recherche des occupations pré-colombiennes dans les hauteurs de Capesterre-Belle-Eau (Guadeloupe): résultats préliminaires. Paper presented at the Twenty-Sixth Congess of the International Association for Caribbean Archaeology, Maho, St. Maarten / St. Martin.

Verrand, L.

2004 Fortifications militaires de Martinique, 1635-1845. In K.G. Kelly (ed.), *Historical Archaeology in the French Caribbean*. Special issue 1 of *Journal of Caribbean Archaeology* 5: 11-28.

Verrand, L., and N. Vidal

2004 Les fours a chaux de Martinique. In K.G. Kelly (ed.), *Historical Archaeology in the French Caribbean*. Special issue 1 of *Journal of Caribbean Archaeology* 5: 29-46.

Watters, D.R., and R. Scaglion

1980 Utility of a transect survey technique in Caribbean prehistoric studies: applications on Barbuda and Montserrat. In S.M. Lewenstein (ed.), *Proceedings of the Eighth International Congress for the Study of Pre-Columbian Cultures of the Lesser Antilles*. St. Kitts, 338-47. Tempe: Arizona State University.

Wilson, S.M.

1991 The prehistoric settlement survey of Nevis: 1984-1988. In E.N. Ayubi and J.B. Haviser (eds.), *Proceedings of the Thirteenth Congress of the International Associaton for Caribbean Archaeology*, 269-79. Willemstad, Curaçao: Archaeological and Anthropological Institute of the Netherlands Antilles.

12 Embedded Heterarchies of the Maya: Political Structure and Interactions Inspired by Peer Polity Interaction

Thomas G. Garrison

Introduction

Many Mayanists first became familiar with the work of John Cherry with his landmark volume on peer polity interaction, co-edited with Colin Renfrew (Renfrew and Cherry 1986). In his case study of Minoan state formation, Cherry (1986: 45) concludes by stating: 'Peer polity interaction, in short, may be an abstract concept, seemingly far removed from the archaeological record itself, but it has the virtue of encouraging detailed factual research stimulated by fresh questions'. This statement rings true for the case of the ancient Maya, even more so with the near-complete decipherment of their ancient hieroglyphic script since the time of the original peer polity model. This chapter focuses on new ways of understanding Maya polities from both a structural and behavioral standpoint. To understand the structure of Maya political territories an analytical framework of embedded heterarchies is proposed, while behavior is explained through the application of concepts derived from landscape ecology theory to this structure. Focus is given to the highest level of the analytical hierarchy: alliances, which are temporary macropolitical formations in which political territories occasionally participate. The case study focuses on the Three Rivers region of northeast Guatemala and northwest Belize and its fluctuating interaction with broader alliances initiated outside of that region. Inspired by Cherry's (1986) analysis of Minoan peer polities, this chapter seeks to provide new directions in studying Maya politics through the presentation of a new model for understanding their structures and interactions. Additionally, it is hoped that some of the concepts introduced here may be valuable for looking at other peer polity civilizations. The original model was designed to account for the full range of interactions between autonomous political units, including imitation and emulation, warfare, competition, and the exchange of material goods and information (Renfrew 1986: 1). The analytical hierarchy proposed here takes into account more explicitly the relationship of political units to their regional environmental conditions as well as interactions involving more than two autonomous polities, some of which work in tandem for varying periods of time.

The Settlement and Physiographic Hierarchies in the Structure of Maya Political Territories

Since the turn of the millennium, there have been arguments suggesting that ancient Maya political organization was heterarchical in nature (Scarborough *et al.* 2003; Becker 2004). A more likely scenario is that there were heterarchical aspects to ancient Maya society that were embedded within an overall hierarchical framework. In considering the hierarchical aspects of this structure, there are two types of hierarchy with which the Maya archaeologist must contend. The first hierarchy is the *settlement hierarchy*, which encompasses the range of site types found within a study region. Garrison and Dunning (2009: 526-33) define the structural components of political territories hierarchically based on archaeological data, but have tried to incorporate Maya concepts of social organization into the typology. In this model, political territories are composed of a capital, minor centers, household groups, and temporary settlements. Statistical analysis of settlement data suggests that there may be up to seven levels in Maya settlement hierarchies, but there have not been enough intensive investigations of multiple levels of settlement in a single region to confirm or deny this larger number of divisions (Garrison 2007: 265-75). The second hierarchy that must be considered is a *physiographic hierarchy*, which is composed of progressively greater units of environmental analysis that geographers and ecologists use to study the natural landscape of the Maya area. The ancient Maya, like most societies, were intimately aware of their environmental surroundings, and political territories implemented different adaptive strategies depending on their specific settings. Consequently, it is without question that the geographical context of settlements contributed to the variability seen in Maya sociopolitical organization (Dunning *et al.* 1998). In turn, the severe, oftentimes coordinated engineering of the natural landscape by the ancient Maya (Scarborough 2000) means that the physiography itself was influenced by culture.

In order to best understand Maya sociopolitical structure, I propose an *analytical hierarchy* based on theories developed by David L. Clarke (1972; 1977; 1979) concerning levels of organization, incorporating aspects of both the settlement and physiographic hierarchies. The proposed analytical hierarchy is designed to consider peer polities in their environmental contexts. This provides a framework for conceptualizing different scales of analysis within particular civilizations. The analytical hierarchy does not contain any explanatory power in and of itself. For the case of the Maya, I propose using concepts based on landscape ecology to examine the specific structure, interactions, and changes within the analytical hierarchy. These ideas were originally proposed to explain heterarchical dynamics within tropical forest landscapes (Fedick 1996); the ecological concepts provide a mechanism for an explanation of cultural dynamics within the context of the analytical hierarchy. The heterarchical origin of the explanatory concepts is appropriate since the model is centered on the idea that individual units of equal status within the analytical hierarchy interact with one another in what are essentially embedded heterarchical networks. From a comparative perspective, alternate concepts may be chosen to explain dynamics within an analytical hierarchy proposed for a different civilization. For example, models derived from network theory seem appropriate for driving explanatory power in the case of the Aegean islands (e.g., Broodbank 2000). For the Maya, who exhibit heterarchical tendencies at various levels of society, explanation is most powerful when applying ideas from landscape ecology. The rest of this chapter presents the proposed model and examines the case of political alliances as a way to demonstrate its utility.

Perceiving the Maya Area: A New Analytical Hierarchy

How scholars perceive divisions in the Maya area greatly affects their interpretations of cultural processes. In the early twentieth century the Maya area was perceived as consisting of an Old Empire in the south and a New Empire in the north (Morley 1946). During the 1960s through the 1980s archaeologists noted regional variations in the Maya area, ranging from architectural styles to ceramic sphere divisions (Ashmore 1981). In the 1990s and 2000s, distinct regions were recognized based on the distribution of elite titles mentioned in the hieroglyphic texts (Stuart 1993; Jackson 2005). These examples serve to illustrate that how we perceive the Maya area (or any other civilization under investigation) affects the questions that we can address archaeologically.

Here, Clarke's (1979) concept of a nested hierarchy of analytical units for the archaeology of space and settlement provides the fundamental structure for the analysis of settlement patterns in the Maya area. More powerful technological tools for spatial analysis, like Geographic Information Systems (GIS), allow for a reassessment of Clarke's largely theoretical work on spatial analysis from the 1970s. The analytical hierarchy proposed here is derived from geographical (physiographic hierarchy) and archaeological (settlement hierarchy) interpretations, which are intertwined to begin with, and supplemented with the controlled use of epigraphic, ethnohistoric, and ethnographic data. Some of the hierarchical divisions build on the previous work of other scholars, while others represent new divisions designed to facilitate interpretation at smaller scales of analysis. From narrowest to broadest, the divisions proposed for analysis are: the area, the territory, the adaptive region, and the alliance. All four are briefly defined here, with some covered more extensively in print elsewhere (Dunning *et al.* 1998; Garrison 2007; Garrison and Dunning 2009).

Areas

The minimal units of spatial analysis in the analytical hierarchy are *areas*, which represent the constituent components of a political *territory* (see below). Areas can be analyzed independently or as a representative portion of the total territory, and are a combination of settlement and microenvironmental components. For example, a minor center located on a *bajo* (seasonal swamp) island would be an area of analysis that would incorporate the site as well as the different vegetation classes found in relation to the site. Another example of an area is the intersite area between two sites. An intersite area is a large tract of land made up of diverse terrain and vegetation types, which correlate with different forms of ancient settlement remains associated with rural peripheries (Garrison 2007: 101-108).

Areas can overlap depending on the archaeological questions being addressed. For example, a small site within an intersite area can be considered an area in and of itself. Areas can also be defined by minor physiographic constraints: a group of small islands within a single *bajo* could be considered an area for analysis. The area concept is flexible, so that researchers can divide up territories into many configurations that will help to see the whole picture from multiple perspectives. In Clarke's (1972; 1979) terms this would facilitate the creation of different models to test and compare. More than any other category in this hierarchy the area concept is a tool, applied subjectively by the researcher, to facilitate the analysis of a complex and diverse settlement system. Figure 12.1 depicts the areas defined for the San Bartolo-Xultun territory, including the 25 sq km intersite area (Garrison 2007).

Territories

The *territory* is the most crucial level in the analysis of settlement because it represents the largest stable independent sociopolitical organization of the ancient Maya (Garrison and Dunning 2009). The term is used here to describe the basic city-state political unit of the Maya, including a capital and its hinterland population. Many other terms, among them *polities*, *realms*, *regional states*, and *provinces* have been used as labels for similar concepts (Lucero 1999). *Territory* is preferred here because it implies the existence of boundaries, which I believe existed, at least in the densely populated southern lowlands. A territory represents the sum of its constituent areas both in terms of microenvironmental and settlement diversity. The boundaries of the territory are determined by microenvironmental boundaries, physiographic province boundaries, and local physiographic features such as deep arroyos, rivers, and *bajos*. The placement of these boundaries is based on the spatial relationships between territorial capitals. Once two adjacent capitals have been identified, the most appropriate territorial boundary can be hypothesized based on the physiography, rather than the more arbitrary use of Thiessen polygon lines at the halfway point between two sites (Hammond 1974; Mathews 1991). Territories may be studied in terms of internal dynamics or external interactions. External analysis of territories requires looking at larger scales of the analytical hierarchy.

Adaptive regions

Adaptive regions are 'areas within the greater Maya Lowlands that have environmental characteristics distinct from adjoining areas' (Dunning *et al.* 1998: 87). Their boundaries are determined by their constituent physiographic provinces. Adaptive regions also define some degree of regional cultural affiliation. Sites within an adaptive region are

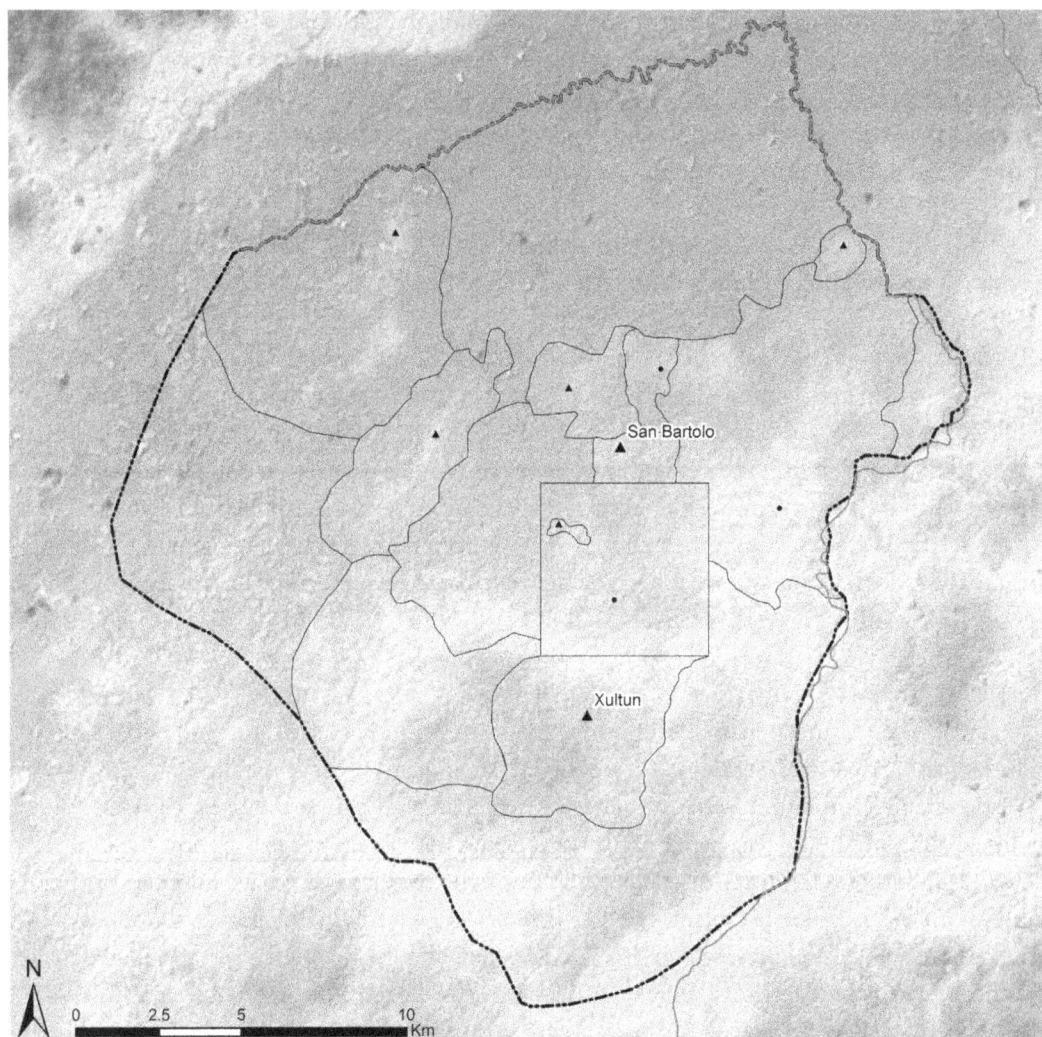

Figure 12.1 Map of the San Bartolo-Xultun territory showing constituent areas drawn with natural hypothesized boundaries; the square in the center shows the study area of the inter-site survey.

all faced with subsisting in a shared environment. Maya living in an adaptive region requiring the successful exploitation of *bajo* resources had a different perception of their environment than other Maya groups living in an adaptive region made up of lacustrine watersheds. The shared communal perception of environment and subsistence strategies internal to the adaptive regions fostered localized cultural affiliation even if two territories were in political conflict. Figure 12.2 shows the known political territories of the Three Rivers adaptive region and their hypothesized boundaries.

Alliances
There were times, especially during the Classic Period, when Maya territories would ally themselves in larger groups expanding beyond adaptive regional boundaries. These

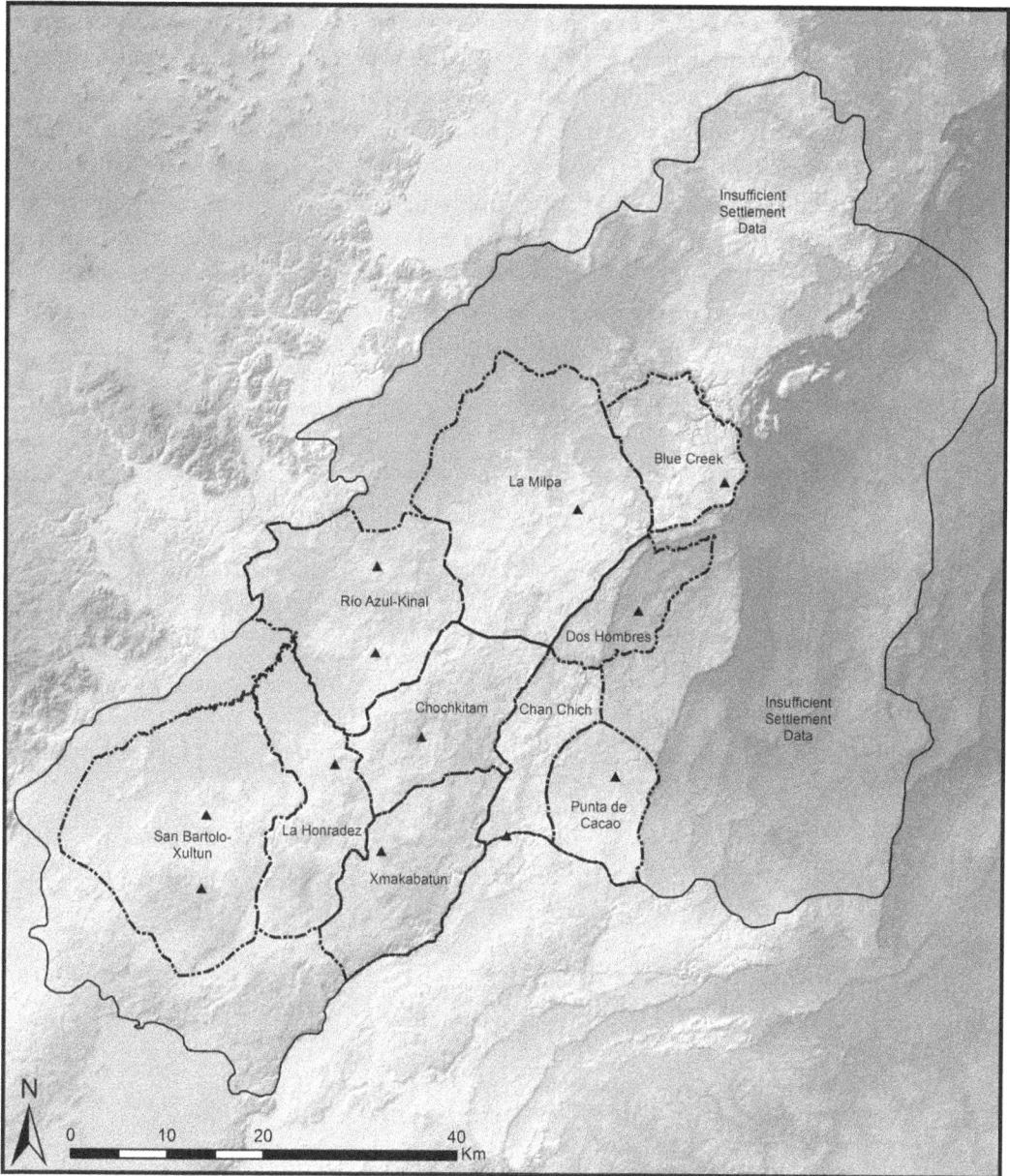

Figure 12.2   The Three Rivers adaptive region, including its Late Classic political territories and their hypothesized boundaries.

macropolitical organizations have most recently been called overkingships (Martin and Grube 2008). Nevertheless, even during these times of unity, the fundamental political organization of the Maya was at the level of the territory. Even though there were often explicit statements of subordination (Martin and Grube 2008: 18-21), there was always a sense of territorial autonomy, and when these macropolitical structures fell apart the constituent components would return to their normal local territorial interests (and this recognition probably has broader, cross-cultural relevance). For this reason, it seems appropriate to refer to units of broader political affiliation as *alliances*, while acknowledging that these were not always equal partnerships. Alliances were inherently unstable because they were simply an extension of elite political networks (Martin and Grube 2008: 20) rather than a broader form of affiliation that may have affected more classes in the local sociopolitical hierarchy. Figure 12.3 shows the Northern Plateau, Southern Plateau, and Three Rivers adaptive regions, which played prominent roles in the Tikal Alliance discussed below.

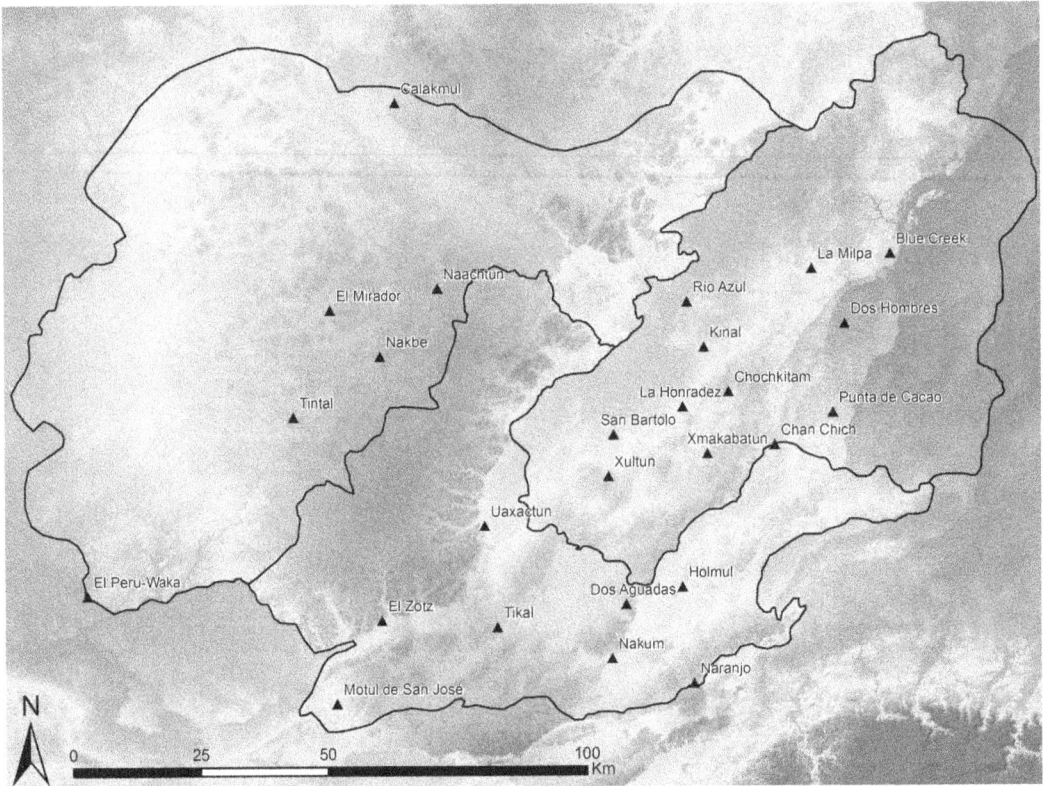

Figure 12.3 The Northern Plateau, Southern Plateau, and Three Rivers adaptive regions, including major sites.

Landscape Ecology Theory as an Explanatory Tool

The proposed analytical hierarchy defines the framework for looking at interactions and changes between Maya sociopolitical units at different scales, but does not hold any explanatory power for studying these processes in and of itself. Scott Fedick (1996), borrowing concepts from landscape ecology to explain spatial heterogeneity in the Maya landscape, has interpreted the landscape of the Maya as a managed mosaic of diverse resources. Here landscape ecology, as a heterachically oriented theory, is used to explain dynamics within the proposed analytical hierarchy. Given that the Maya incorporated both forms of sociopolitical organization into their settlement it is appropriate to combine hierarchy and heterarchy theories to explain change. The concepts introduced here may be appropriate in comparative cases, but alternate theoretical constructs, such as those introduced by network theory, may be more appropriately applied to analytical hierarchies developed for other civilizations.

Landscape ecology is concerned with structure, function, and change in the heterogeneous natural landscape. The *structure* is the composition of all resources that make up the landscape. *Function* represents interactions in the environment, and *change* is seen as the environmental and human-induced changes that affect the structure and function (Fedick 1996: 336). These concepts can be applied to the different levels of the analytical hierarchy presented above, but with a greater emphasis on sociopolitical structures and interaction.

The structure of any given level in the hierarchy is equivalent to the sum of all of the units in the next-lowest scale in the hierarchy. For example, the structure of a territory is equivalent to the total size and composition of all of its areas (as defined above). In the broadest application of this principle, the structure of the entire Maya area is defined by the 31 adaptive regions of which it is composed (Figure 12.4; Dunning *et al.* 1998; Garrison 2007: 26-30). The structure concept of landscape ecology provides a theoretical link between the proposed hierarchical divisions, which are based on Clarke's work, and the more heterachically oriented landscape ecology theory.

Function within the proposed analytical hierarchy represents the various cultural interactions that took place which allowed the Maya to sustain themselves. This includes the heterarchical interactions between units within the same level in the hierarchy, as well as peaceful transactions made between units in a hierarchical relationship. An example of this latter form of transaction would be a ritually reciprocated tribute payment in which the elites receiving tribute provide ritual nourishment to their subjects. Theories of the heterogeneity of landscape argue against a higher-level bureaucracy as a form of organization, because in this type of environment adaptation occurs at the local level, based on the suite of resources available (Fedick 1996: 338-42). This does not have to be true. The vast majority of recognized transactions were conducted in a heterarchical fashion, especially among hinterland populations that represented a significant portion of the total populace. The concept of function can incorporate both heterarchical and hierarchical interactions as long as they do not alter the *structure* of the entities involved

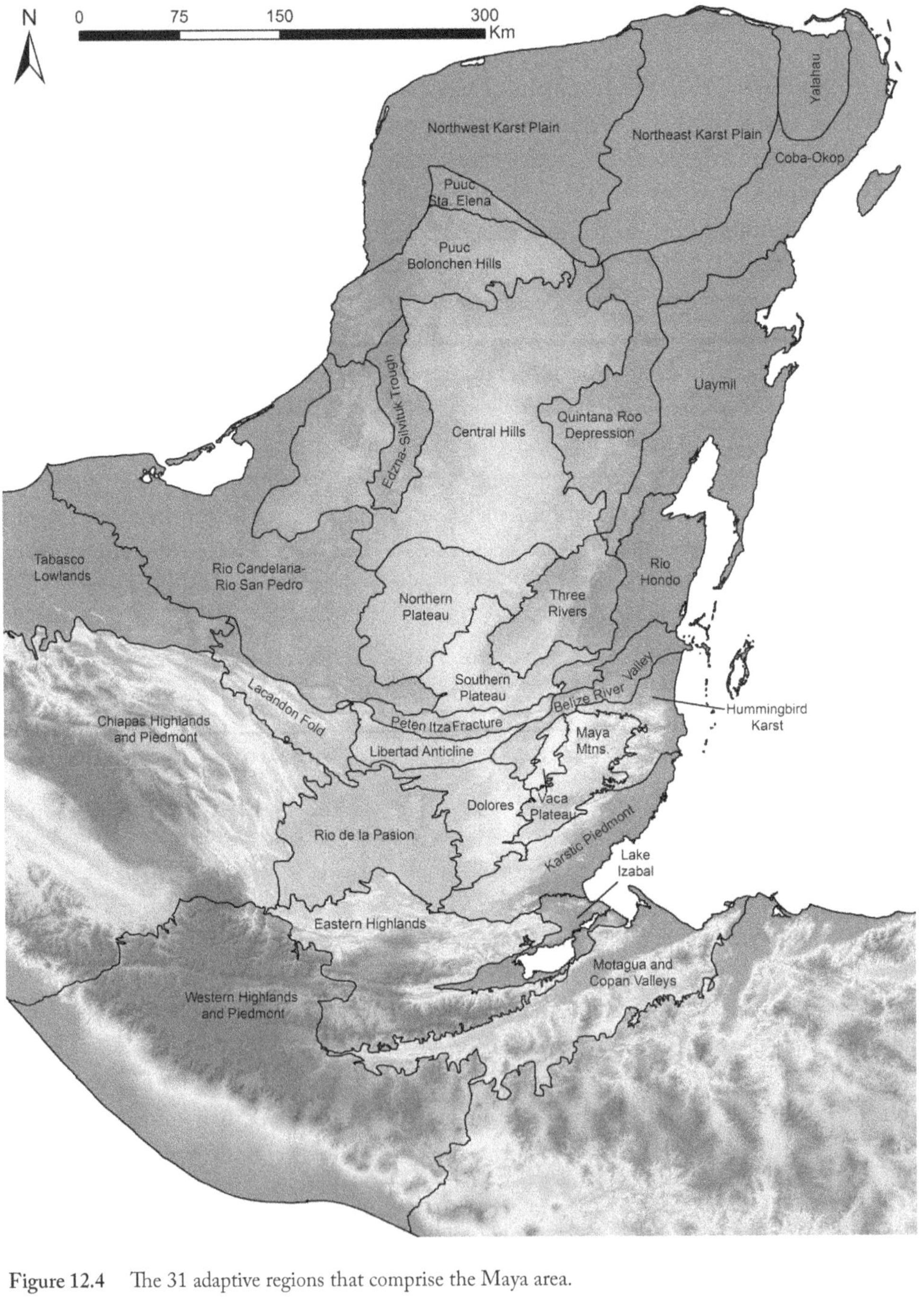

Figure 12.4   The 31 adaptive regions that comprise the Maya area.

in the interaction. This concept is most analogous to the interactions proposed in the original peer polity model (Renfrew and Cherry 1986).

Change is what happens when the structure of the hierarchy is altered. Alterations in the structure also cause changes in patterns of interaction as defined by the function concept. Change can refer to both environmental and anthropogenic changes that affect the structure of the analytical hierarchy. Examples of environmental change are: drought, deforestation, erosion, El Niño events, or increased seasonality. Some of these environmental changes are actually anthropogenic (i.e., deforestation) or are natural processes accelerated by humans (i.e., erosion); but, because they represent changes to the physical environment, they are classified under environmental change. Anthropogenic changes to the *structure* of the settlement hierarchy often relate more to political events that *change* the relationships manifested within the hierarchy. Examples of these changes are: warfare, accessions of charismatic leaders, exogamous marriages, changing tribute patterns, changing trade routes, and entrance into an alliance.

Change is reflected in major shifts in Maya settlement patterns. These shifts have been detected archaeologically by identifying ceramic associations with building phases and spatial distributions of architecture (Haviland 1963; Willey *et al.* 1965; Puleston 1983; Ford 1986). The concept of change, as defined in landscape ecology theory, provides a mechanism to explain settlement alterations. Change is almost always multicausal, but major factors can be isolated to categorize the type of change occurring at any given time, at any scale. Once these changes are isolated, patterns may be detected by examining categories of change through time and space.

The Embedded Heterarchy Model: A Hierarchical Approach

The analytical framework of areas, territories, adaptive regions, and alliances was originally designed to place data from a survey (2002–2005) of the San Bartolo-Xultun intersite area in a regional context (Garrison 2007). This analytical hierarchy incorporates many scales of analysis with multiple entities from one level joining together to form a single entity at a higher level. The territory, or regional polity, is the fundamental building block of the Maya area, and there is evidence that this was always the case during the Classic Period, even during moments of broader political alliance.

A lattice-like exchange network (Demarest 1989; 2004) subsumed under the control of a large center is here defined as an *embedded heterarchy*. At the most basic level, embedded heterarchies were the sustaining force of every territory in the Maya area. The hinterland population harvested resources from throughout the territory, providing for each other through local exchange networks in addition to supplying the population of the territorial capital. The local network is embedded within the otherwise hierarchical relationship between capital and hinterland. An embedded heterarchy also existed among the territorial elites within the same adaptive region. This heterarchy manifested itself in shared elite material culture as well as in the exchange of ideas resulting from a common perception of local regional environmental

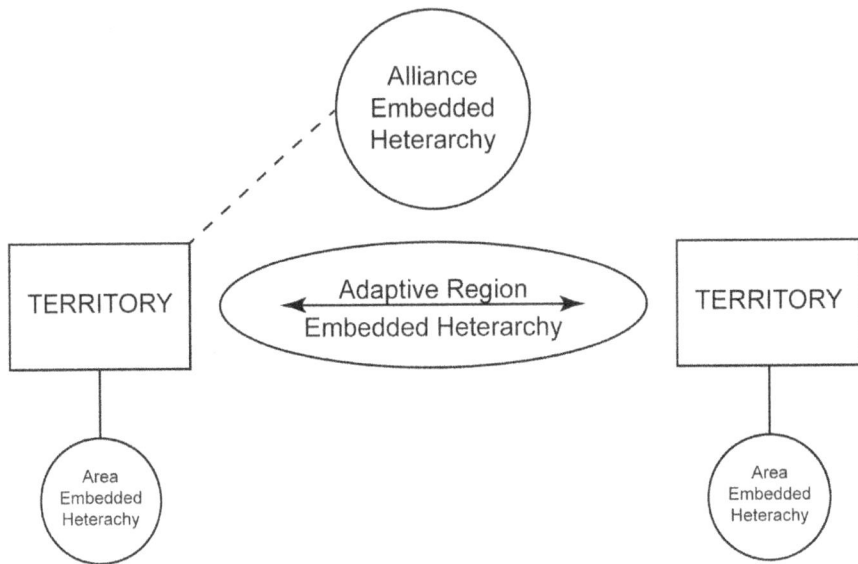

Figure 12.5   Schematic of the Embedded Heterarchy Model.

diversity. Ideational exchange is evinced not only in texts and iconography, but also in site planning principles (Ashmore 1986; 1989; 1991; 1992; Ashmore and Sabloff 2002; Houk 1996; 2003). These exchanges highlight regional idiosyncrasies in sociopolitical organization as well as ideological variability. During the periods of large alliances, interregional groups of territories made up an embedded heterarchy whose interactions contributed to a sense of shared affiliation with the larger alliance. Other territories chose to maintain their independent status. The organizational principles of the embedded heterarchy model are diagrammed in Figure 12.5.

Embedded heterarchies were a critical part of the structure of a naturally hierarchical system. The complexity of this form of organization requires a theoretical model that can account for both the hierarchical and heterarchical aspects of Maya sociopolitical structures. Here, the heterarchically based landscape ecology theory is considered to be embedded within an analytical hierarchy of settlement units derived from Clarke's (1979) concept of a nested hierarchical model for archaeological taxonomy. The landscape ecology concepts of structure, function, and change are used to explain order in the analytical hierarchy. The change concept is particularly important for tracking spatial and temporal variability as well as providing a mechanism for explaining major shifts in settlement through time. The conflation of these two approaches created 'hierarchically nested heterarchies'. I have simplified this term, instead calling it the embedded heterarchy model. As Cherry (1986) intended with his application of peer polity interaction to the Minoan case study, the goal here is to stimulate new research by reconsidering the structure and interactions of Maya political territories. The rest of this paper will be used to elaborate the embedded heterarchy model at the alliance level of the analytical hierarchy.

Maya Alliances

During various periods in the history of the Maya lowlands, numerous territories would group together in alliances. A capital could be in control of its own territory while at the same time be joined to another territorial capital during periods of alliance. For example, Early Classic Caracol was allied with Tikal at first, but displayed an act of political independence when the ruler of Caracol joined with Calakmul to attack his former ally (Martin 2001; 2005a). Alliances were formed between members of the ruling elite of each territory; therefore, it is prudent to examine the nature of Maya political interactions from the perspective of the territory. Territorial rulers interacted with the elites of other independent territories in the course of geopolitical developments across the Maya lowlands.

Two of the most important studies of Maya politics that postdate the decipherment have been those of Demarest (1992) and of Martin and Grube (2008). Demarest (1992) convincingly argues that Maya elites were involved in economic exchanges to acquire the paraphernalia necessary to perform the rituals of the 'theatre state'. Drawing analogies from Southeast Asia, he argues that control was maintained over subordinate populations through the performance of ideology, which could only be done by the elites. He uses this ideological basis for power to argue that the Maya organized themselves into politically unstable galactic polities that pulsated in and out of brief periods of hegemonic expansion.

Martin and Grube (2008) express the same arguments regarding hegemony as Demarest, but through hieroglyphic decipherment have identified two major powers that seem to have dominated most periods of expansion. These are what they call the superstates of Tikal and Calakmul, although they do concede that there were lesser hegemonies in other regions as well. In Martin and Grube's view, certain rulers of major centers became 'overkings' of other rulers at smaller centers so that the dominant ruler could then act through an established local dynasty to accomplish sociopolitical goals. Importantly, it is noted that during periods of hegemonic expansion there 'was not an acquisition of territory *per se*, but rather an extension of [the] elite networks' (Martin and Grube 2008: 20). This is similar to Demarest's (1992) arguments that elite exchange was crucial to political control. There also seems to be a clear difference between sites that willingly entered into alliance through statements of subordination or fealty versus those that were violently conquered by members of an alliance. Violence does not appear to have been used as a coercive tool to force cooperation. Rather, as in the case of Calakmul's conquest of Tikal in 562 AD, military aggression seems to have been a tool for total suppression rather than an instigator of collaboration.

Both works point to the inherent instability of the pulsating galactic polity or superstates, with Demarest (1992: 156) going as far as to argue that the Maya 'existed in a state of dynamic instability'. Marcus (1993: 134), in another landmark paper, likewise refers to large regional states that 'do not seem to have been long-term stable units'. Still, it is unfair to characterize all Maya politics as unstable. Instead, the major issue concerns the appropriate scale at which to analyze Maya politics. If we focus our efforts on the broadest expansions of political entities in the history of the lowlands, then the Maya political system appears to be extremely unstable, with only brief periods of hegemonic unification. If, however, we focus on the territory system as being the default form of organization, then the Maya political system appears to be extremely stable, with almost all of these entities lasting from 300 to over 700 years.

This inherent instability of the so-called hegemonies is why I refer to them as alliances. These alliances were temporary moments of broader unity that interrupted the otherwise stable geopolitical situation of independent territories. During times of expansion the overking of the expanding territory may have had a degree of control over a subordinate territorial capital, but the fundamental relationship was still heterarchical, being based on mutual benefits through economic and ideological exchange. In this sense the territorial ruler that initiates an alliance may be considered a 'first among equals' rather than a *de facto* overlord. The overkings did not possess the military power to keep all of their allied territories physically subdued, so a degree of diplomacy was necessary for these macropolitical alliances to exist. It is the removal of hierarchy that distinguishes the alliance from all previous models, whether they be hegemonies, regional states, or galactic polities. This sort of heterarchical relationship amongst united territories is thus better encompassed by the term 'alliance'.

The territories of the Three Rivers region (San Bartolo-Xultun, Río Azul-Kinal, La Milpa, Blue Creek) were participants in the Classic Period Tikal alliance. What follows is an examination of this alliance within the framework of the Embedded Heterarchy Model, with a particular focus on the relationships of these territories to Tikal. Other regions are touched upon, but space does not permit a full treatment of all of Tikal's complex political interactions.

Structure, Function, and Change in the Tikal Alliance

In this broadest, macroregional level of settlement analysis many of the most frequently discussed facets of Maya civilization (kingship, warfare, foreign relations, exchange) take on a prominent role. However, beneath this macrolevel there were complex interrelationships and hierarchies that were extremely important at more localized scales of activity.

During the Middle Preclassic (1000–400 BC) and the beginning of the Late Preclassic (400 BC–200 AD), Tikal was similar to many other early settlements in the Maya lowlands. The pioneer populations settled on the *bajo*/wetland margins as well as on the nearby high terrain. Most exchanges were interdependent with some degree of socioeconomic differentiation beginning to emerge in the early Late Preclassic. A similar pattern was definitely occurring at San Bartolo and almost certainly among other early members of the future Tikal Alliance.

This was in stark contrast to the developments occurring contemporaneously in the Mirador Basin to the north. Nakbe was a major Middle Preclassic settlement, with

El Mirador succeeding as the greatest Preclassic power in the lowlands. El Mirador developed broad exchange networks throughout the Maya lowlands and highlands and beyond. Taube (2003) has noted that lowland Chicanel sphere ceramics (dating to the Late Preclassic) have been found in both the Merchant's Barrio (Rattray 1987) and the Pyramid of the Sun (Smith 1987) excavations at the great central Mexican power of Teotihuacan. El Mirador seems to be the most likely exchange partner to provide these early ceramics to the Teotihuacanos simply based on the monumentality of the site, which dwarfs other Late Preclassic settlements.

In other areas of the lowlands the institution of Maya kingship, described by the word *ajaw*, emerged during the Late Preclassic, as evidenced at San Bartolo (Saturno *et al.* 2006). Formal settlement hierarchies developed in some areas to create the first political territories. Sites like Tikal, San Bartolo, and probably Naranjo and Caracol were capitals of these territories. At an interregional level these capitals would have been involved in heterarchical exchange networks, most likely independent of El Mirador. The structure of the southern Maya lowlands on the eve of the Late Preclassic to Early Classic transition (200–300 AD) was one of two different political situations, which involved separate types of functions. On the one hand there was the vast Late Preclassic metropolis of El Mirador and its broad pan-Mesoamerican exchange network to the north, while on the other hand there were the small independent territories involved in interregional exchanges to the south.

The Late Preclassic to Early Classic transition witnessed a total reconfiguration of Maya lowland settlement and, therefore, political and exchange networks. Environmental degradation as well as possible climatic disturbances had catastrophic effects on the burgeoning Late Preclassic populations (Dunning 1995; Dunning *et al.* 2002). In the immense territory occupied by El Mirador and its satellite centers the stress was too much to overcome and the entire settlement network was abandoned (Hansen *et al.* 2002). In the independent territories to the south some areas reacted by shifting the capital to a nearby locale, as with the San Bartolo to Xultun shift and the consolidation of the settlement network at Holmul (Estrada-Belli 2010). At other sites, such as Tikal (Harrison 1999) and Blue Creek (Guderjan *et al.* 2003), the Late Preclassic to Early Classic transition was smooth and involved continuous growth. With the lowland populations nucleated at select centers, the stage was set for one of the greatest changes in the history of the Maya lowlands.

The 378 AD *entrada* of Sihyaj K'ahk' and a contingent of Teotihuacanos sent by Spearthrower Owl cemented the shift in power in the lowlands to Tikal (Stuart 2000). The overarching goal of this Early Classic (300–600 AD) *entrada* may have been to consolidate the lowland exchange networks in order to provide a reliable source of royal and ritual paraphernalia to the Teotihuacan court. Taube (2003: 313) notes that the Teotihuacan elites had 'a deep interest and understanding of the accoutrements and symbolism of Maya kingship' and that they 'were aware of the symbolism and rituals of Maya royal ancestor veneration'. The dissolution of the El Mirador exchange network would have caused a crisis at Teotihuacan, which used elite trade goods from the Maya lowlands in their own rituals. Sihyaj K'ahk' may have been sent to the Maya area to re-establish relations with the most strategically located settlement in terms of economics and to consolidate trade networks around this site.

For the Maya, the *entrada* represented the introduction of a new form of political organization superimposed on their preexisting system of territorial divine kingship. Sihyaj K'ahk' installed new *ajawob* in some territories himself, while many other dynasties were formally established in the decades following the *entrada*. Many of these dynastic founders either came from or were endorsed by Tikal. In this sense Tikal formed a far-reaching alliance with numerous centers located strategically either near resource concentrations or on critical junctures of exchange corridors, especially riverine systems. While numerous sites were members of the Early Classic Tikal Alliance, it seems that there was some degree of mutual respect and interdependence among the allies, arguing against a demonstrably hierarchical system of macropolitical organization. As I have argued throughout this chapter, Maya alliances were temporary moments of broader unity that interrupted the otherwise stable geopolitical situation of independent territories. Following the Teotihuacan *entrada* there was a broad alliance of sites connected to Tikal, with a general interest in the economic distribution of the trappings of Maya royal costume and ritual associated with the state (Demarest 1992).

Cowgill (1992: 96) speculates that commercial success, particularly in obsidian working, was an important factor in the formation of Teotihuacan during its Patlachique Phase (150–1 BC). He also argues that during the subsequent Tzacualli Phase (1–150 AD) the Teotihuacan elites consolidated the Basin of Mexico through a combination of military threat, ideological promotion, and economic rewards (Cowgill 1992: 97). It was this strategy of consolidation that Sihyaj K'ahk' introduced into the lowland Maya political economy, but only as a means to create a reliable provider of elite material culture to the Teotihuacan capital.

To the north of the Tikal Alliance, the Snake Kingdom (*Kaan*) elites, based first at Dzibanche and later at Calakmul (Martin 2005b), nurtured their own territorial control. They lay in wait, devising a strategy to break up the emerging exchange networks. The result of Calakmul's dissatisfaction was to develop a military strategy that mimicked the Tikal Alliance's strategy of unifying independent territories toward a single cause. The difference with Calakmul was that the major goal was the disruption of the Tikal Alliance, and specifically the Tikal dynasty, rather than gaining access to any complex long-distance exchange network. Calakmul did not attempt to establish strong ties with Teotihuacan, following the defeat of Tikal. In fact, Teotihuacan itself seems to have gone into a period of major turmoil and decline just decades after Tikal's defeat by Calakmul, if not sooner. The members of the Calakmul Alliance that fought against Tikal retained their own territorial independence, with some sites, such as Naranjo, breaking free from Calakmul following Tikal's defeat.

The first half of the Late Classic (600–800 AD) saw a return to small independent territory status for most of the former members of the Early Classic Tikal Alliance. While sites engaged in intense warfare, and possibly civil war in the Pasión region to the southwest, sites in the Three Rivers region concentrated on interaction with more local territories. At these sites there was still continuous royal ritual, as evidenced by stelae dedications at Xultun, but in general the territories of the Three Rivers region distanced themselves from the broader geopolitical conflicts occurring in the west. The interactions that took place amongst these sites resulted in a unified strategy to cope with the political fallout of the dissolution of the Tikal Alliance. The Three Rivers region capitals constructed large plazas where they could assemble the entire hinterland population of their territories while at the same time prohibiting the performance of many major rituals outside the capital. It seems likely that other regionally defined political strategies also would have emerged during this time (see Laporte 2004 for an example from the Dolores region).

During the eighth and early ninth centuries AD, Tikal was restored to power under the leadership of a succession of charismatic leaders who were also impressive military strategists. Tikal's recovery and the subsequent reunification of a similar—but different—Tikal Alliance coincided with a population explosion throughout the lowlands. Many new sites grew into formidable centers in and of themselves. Examples from the Three Rivers region include Chan Chich and Dos Hombres, the latter of which may have had its own emblem glyph (Adams *et al.* 2004). Iconographically, there was a renaissance of imagery related to Teotihuacan, although this may have been as much a reference to the Early Classic Tikal Alliance as it was to the great central Mexican metropolis, which had long since collapsed. The Late Classic represents the apogee of the state rituals practiced by Maya elites. The new Tikal Alliance facilitated the distribution of the necessary accoutrements among allies, rather than trying to export to central Mexico.

Nevertheless, even this resurgence of Tikal and its allies came to an end in the Terminal Classic (800–900 AD). It is possible that population pressure eventually surpassed the carrying capacity of the land in some areas, a situation that may have been compounded by localized periods of extended drought. As some of the royal courts of the Tikal Alliance began to succumb in the Terminal Classic, this created a snowball effect that culminated in the total cessation of elite activity in the southern lowlands. While opportunistic lineages tried to pick up the pieces in some minor centers, these attempts were short-lived, leaving only a series of squatter populations that clung on until the eleventh century AD, when the lowlands were almost completely abandoned, with a few notable exceptions.

Discussion and Conclusions

The Embedded Heterarchy Model proposed in this chapter is inspired by Cherry's (1986) goal of stimulating new research questions based on a new perception of the structure and interactions of ancient political units, in this case those of the ancient Maya. Critical to this model is the issue of scale. The use of scales of analysis facilitates the interpretation of cultural phenomena within their spatio-temporal context, without denying the interrelatedness of all scales to ancient Maya civilization as a whole. Transitional periods such as the Late Preclassic to Early Classic or the Late Classic to Terminal Classic were particularly transcendental events that affected all scales in the analytical hierarchy. The territory, of all of the scales of analysis, was the building block of Maya sociopolitical organization from the Late Preclassic onward. There were brief periods of broad political alliances that have led some to argue that Maya politics were inherently unstable (Demarest 1992), but on closer scrutiny this seems more a matter of perspective.

While here applied to the case of the Maya, I suggest that a similar approach could be applicable to other cases that broadly fall under Renfrew and Cherry's (1986) definition of peer polities and their operation as regionally constituted units of complex societies. Scales of analysis in archaeological interpretation allow certain cultural phenomena to be contained within their appropriate level of influence. For example, a military defeat for a territorial polity may not have demonstrably affected the day-to-day agricultural activities of a Maya farmer, but it would have been devastating to the ruling elite residing in the capital. We might ask whether the complex histories and political interactions recorded in the epigraphic record really matter when examining the humble remains of intersite archaeology. Similarly, while subsistence strategies are obviously important to the population as a whole, the Maya elite were mostly concerned with the performance of ritual to perpetuate their states. If the archaeologist is addressing issues of dynastic legitimacy and hierarchical social organization, then preference needs to be given to analysis of the political economy and exchange networks. Identifying appropriate scales of analysis facilitates a holistic approach to the study of ancient Maya culture, which consisted of numerous classes that were part of the same cultural tradition (Willey 1956). However, despite the shared worldview of these different levels of society, the everyday interests and challenges for members of each social class surely differed. Ideally archaeologists will use scalar systems of analysis, similar to the one used here, so that they may study multiple aspects of civilization without overemphasizing any single cultural phenomenon.

Transitional periods are the key moments for studying processes that affect numerous scales of analysis. Processes of change occurred during transitional periods that led to the reorganization of the sociopolitical order. Once major patterns of change are identified they may then be integrated with identified spatial trends to build a model that best reflects the available data. In the Maya area transitional processes did not occur uniformly across time and space, a fact demonstrated by a broad look at the Late Classic to Terminal Classic transition (Demarest *et al.* 2004). In the present study, there are notable variations during transitional periods at both large and small spatial scales. For example, in the case studies used here the effects of the Late Classic to Terminal Classic transition varied according to time and space. During this transition, the San Bartolo-Xultun intersite area was abandoned, but elite culture continued to thrive at Xultun until 889 AD. In contrast, other sites of the Three Rivers adaptive region seem to have been abandoned by 850 AD, while the power of the second Tikal Alliance was waning as early as 800 AD. This variation covers nearly a century of time and thousands of square kilometers of space.

Looking at different spatial scales and temporal trends is one of the ways in which archaeologists can reconcile culture history with cultural process. Gordon Willey (1980) believed that culture history and processualism were not antithetical approaches to archaeology, a view that is shared here. This is particularly relevant to the Maya, where some of the ideas of the New Archaeology were difficult to apply to complex societies (Sabloff 1983). Much of the nature of Maya civilization is best explained through culture history, while the analysis of cultural transitions is best facilitated by a processual approach. Stated another way, the processes that take place at transitional periods are what drive the cultural history of ancient Maya civilization. The Embedded Heterarchy Model presented in this study is able to explain cultural process while remaining faithful to known historical events. Just as with peer polity interaction (Renfrew and Cherry 1986), it is hoped that this model represents a middle ground and will initiate new discussions and arguments regarding ancient political structure and interaction. The combination of a well-reasoned analytical hierarchy derived from environmental and cultural information with a relevant theoretical approach (in this case landscape ecology) should be a broadly applicable way to study complex societies and peer polities.

Acknowledgments

I would like to thank John Cherry for his mentorship and collegiality during my time spent as a postdoc at Brown University between 2007 and 2012. Great thanks to Alex Knodell and Tom Leppard for not only organizing this volume, but also challenging me to rethink old ideas and continue to think broadly in archaeology. Much of this research was done during my time as a graduate student at Harvard University, and was supported by a John G. Owens Fellowship and a Harvard Dissertation Completion Fellowship. Any factual errors are mine alone.

About the Author

Thomas G. Garrison is Assistant Professor of Anthropology at Ithaca College. His research focuses on the archaeology of the ancient Maya civilization and remote sensing applications in archaeology. He currently directs the Proyecto Arqueológico El Zotz, in Guatemala, as well as the Maya Aerial Technology Survey. He is co-author of *Temple of the Night Sun: A Royal Tomb at El Diablo, Guatemala* (Mesoweb Press, 2015), and has recently published articles on Maya settlement patterns, human–environmental interaction, and remote sensing in *Advances in Archaeological Practice*, the *Journal of Field Archaeology*, the *Journal of Archaeological Science*, the *International*

Journal of Remote Sensing, and *Latin American Antiquity.* E-mail: tgarrison1@ithaca.edu

References

Adams, R.E.W., H.R. Robichaux, F. Valdez, Jr., B.A. Houk and R. Mathews
  2004 Transformations, periodicity, and urban development in the Three Rivers Region. In A.A. Demarest, P.M. Rice and D.S. Rice (eds.), *The Terminal Classic in the Maya Lowlands: Collapse, Transition, and Transformations,* 324-41. Boulder: University Press of Colorado.

Ashmore, W.A.
  1981 *Lowland Maya Settlement Patterns.* Albuquerque: University of New Mexico Press.
  1986 Peten cosmology in the Maya southeast: an analysis of architecture and settlement patterns at Classic Quirigua. In P.A. Urban and E.M. Schortman (eds.), *The Southeast Maya Periphery,* 35-49. Austin: University of Texas Press.
  1989 Construction and cosmology: politics and ideology in lowland Maya settlement patterns. In W.F. Hanks and D.S. Rice (eds.), *Word and Image in Maya Culture: Explorations in Language, Writing, and Representation,* 271-86. Salt Lake City: University of Utah Press.
  1991 Site-planning principles and concepts of directionality among the ancient Maya. *Latin American Antiquity* 2: 199-226. https://doi.org/10.2307/972169
  1992 Deciphering Maya architectural plans. In E.C. Danien and R.J. Sharer (eds.), *New Theories on the Ancient Maya.* University Museum Monograph 77: 173-84. Philadelphia: University of Pennsylvania.

Ashmore, W.A., and J.A. Sabloff
  2002 Spatial order and Maya civic plans. *Latin American Antiquity* 13: 201-16. https://doi.org/10.2307/971914

Becker, M.J.
  2004 Maya heterarchy as inferred from Classic-period plaza plans. *Ancient Mesoamerica* 15: 127-38. https://doi.org/10.1017/S0956536104151079

Broodbank, C.
  2000 *An Island Archaeology of the Early Cyclades.* Cambridge: Cambridge University Press.

Cherry, J.F.
  1986 Polities and palaces: some problems in Minoan state formation. In C. Renfrew and J.F. Cherry (eds.), *Peer Polity Interaction and Socio-Political Change,* 19-46. Cambridge: Cambridge University Press.

Clarke, D.L.
  1972 A provisional model of an Iron Age society and its settlement system. In D.L. Clarke (ed.), *Models in Archaeology,* 801-69. London: Methuen.
  1977 Spatial information in archaeology. In D.L. Clarke (ed.), *Spatial Archaeology,* 1-32. New York: Academic Press.
  1979 Towards analytical archaeology: new directions in the interpretive thinking of British archaeologists. In D.L. Clarke (ed.), *Analytical Archaeologist,* 145-79. New York: Academic Press.

Cowgill, D.
  1992 Toward a political history of Teotihuacan. In A.A. Demarest and G.W. Conrad (eds.), *Ideology and Pre-Columbian Civilizations,* 87-114. Santa Fe, New Mexico: School of American Research Press.

Demarest, A.A.
  1989 The Olmec and the rise of civilization in eastern Mesoamerica. In R.J. Sharer and D.C. Grove (eds.), *Regional Perspectives on the Olmec,* 303-44. Cambridge: Cambridge University Press.
  1992 Ideology in ancient Maya cultural evolution: the dynamics of galactic

polities. In A.A. Demarest and G.W. Conrad (eds.), *Ideology and Pre-Columbian Civilizations*, 135-58. Santa Fe, New Mexico: School of American Research Press.

2004 *Ancient Maya: The Rise and Fall of a Rainforest Civilization*. Cambridge: Cambridge University Press.

Demarest, A.A., P.M. Rice and D.S. Rice

2004 *The Terminal Classic in the Maya Lowlands: Collapse, Transition, and Transformation*. Boulder: University Press of Colorado.

Dunning, N.P.

1995 Coming together at the temple mountain: environment, subsistence and the emergence of lowland Maya segmentary states. In N. Grube (ed.), *The Emergence of Lowland Maya Civilization: The Transition from the Preclassic to the Early Classic*. Acta Mesoamericana 8: 61-70. München, Germany: Verlag Anton Saurwein.

Dunning, N., T. Beach, P. Farrell and S. Luzzadder-Beach

1998 Prehispanic agrosystems and adaptive regions in the Maya lowlands. *Culture & Agriculture* 20: 87-101. https://doi. org/10.1525/cag.1998.20.2-3.87

Dunning, N.P., S. Luzzadder-Beach, T. Beach, J.G. Jones, V. Scarborough and T.P. Culbert

2002 Arising from the *bajos*: the evolution of a neotropical landscape and the rise of Maya civilization. *Annals of the Association of American Geographers* 92: 267-83. https://doi.org/ 10.1111/1467-8306.00290

Estrada-Belli, F.

2010 *The First Maya Civilization: Ritual and Power Before the Classic Period*. London and New York: Routledge.

Fedick, S.L.

1996 Conclusion. In S.L. Fedick (ed.), *The Managed Mosaic: Ancient Maya Agriculture and Resource Use*, 335-47. Salt Lake City: University of Utah Press.

Ford, A.

1986 *Population Growth and Social Complexity: An Examination of Settlement and Environment in the Central Maya Lowlands*. Anthropological Research Papers 35. Phoenix: Arizona State University.

Garrison, T.G.

2007 Ancient Maya Territories, Adaptive Regions, and Alliances: Contextualizing the San Bartolo-Xultun Intersite Survey. Unpublished PhD dissertation, Harvard University, Cambridge, Massachusetts.

Garrison, T.G., and N.P. Dunning

2009 Settlement, environment, and politics in the San Bartolo-Xultun territory, El Peten, Guatemala. *Latin American Antiquity* 20: 525-52. https://doi. org/10.1017/S1045663500002868

Guderjan, T.H., J. Baker and R.J. Lichtenstein

2003 Environmental and cultural diversity at Blue Creek. In V.L. Scarborough, F. Valdez, Jr., and N. Dunning (eds.), *Heterarchy, Political Economy, and the Ancient Maya: The Three Rivers Region of the East-Central Yucatán Peninsula*, 77-91. Tucson: University of Arizona Press.

Hammond, N.

1974 Preclassic to Postclassic in northern Belize. *Antiquity* 48: 177-89. https:// doi.org/10.1017/S0003598X00057860

Hansen, R.D., S. Bozarth, J. Jacob, D. Wahl and T. Schreiner

2002 Climatic and environmental variability in the rise of Maya civilization: a preliminary perspective from the northern Peten. *Ancient Mesoamerica* 13: 273-95. https://doi.org/10.1017/ S0956536102132093

Harrison, P.D.

1999 *The Lords of Tikal: Rulers of an Ancient Maya City*. London: Thames and Hudson.

Haviland, W.A.

1963 Excavation of Small Structures in the Northeast Quadrant of Tikal, Guatemala. Unpublished PhD Dissertation, University of Pennsylvania, Philadelphia, Pennsylvania.

Houk, B.A.

1996 The Archaeology of Site Planning: An Example from the Maya Site of Dos Hombres, Belize. Unpublished PhD Dissertation, University of Texas, Austin, Texas.

2003 The ties that bind: site planning in the Three Rivers region. In V.L. Scarborough, F. Valdez, Jr. and N. Dunning (eds.), *Heterarchy, Political Economy, and the Ancient Maya: The Three Rivers Region of the East-Central Yucatán Peninsula*, 52-63. Tucson: University of Arizona Press.

Jackson, S.E.

2005 Deciphering Classic Maya Political Hierarchy: Epigraphic, Archaeological, and Ethnohistoric Perspectives on the Courtly Elite. Unpublished PhD Dissertation, Harvard University, Cambridge, Massachusetts.

Laporte, J.P.

2004 Terminal Classic settlement and polity in the Mopan Valley, Petén, Guatemala. In A.A. Demarest, P.M. Rice and D.S. Rice (eds.), *The Terminal Classic in the Maya Lowlands: Collapse, Transition, and Transformations*, 195-230. Boulder: University Press of Colorado.

Lucero, L.

1999 Classic lowland Maya political organization: a review. *Journal of World Prehistory* 13: 211-63. https://doi.org/10.1023/A:1022337629210

Marcus, J.

1993 Ancient Maya political organization. In J.A. Sabloff and J.S. Henderson (eds.), *Lowland Maya Civilization in the Eighth Century A.D.*, 111-83. Washington, DC: Dumbarton Oaks Research Library and Collection.

Martin, S.

2001 Unmasking 'Double Bird', ruler of Tikal. *Precolumbian Art Research Institute Journal* 2(1): 7-12.

2005a Caracol Altar 21 revisited: more data on Double Bird and Tikal's wars of the mid-sixth century. *Precolumbian Art Research Institute Journal* 6(1): 1-9.

2005b Of snakes and bats: shifting identities at Calakmul. *Precolumbian Art Research Institute Journal* 6(2): 5-15.

Martin, S., and N. Grube

2008 *Chronicle of the Maya Kings and Queens: Deciphering the Dynasties of the Ancient Maya*. 2nd edn. New York: Thames and Hudson.

Mathews, P.

1991 Classic Maya emblem glyphs. In T.P. Culbert (ed.), *Classic Maya Political History: Hieroglyphic and Archaeological Evidence*, 19-29. Cambridge: Cambridge University Press.

Morley, S.G.

1946 *The Ancient Maya*. Stanford: Stanford University Press.

Puleston, D.E.

1983 *The Settlement Survey of Tikal*. Tikal Report 13. Philadelphia: University Museum.

Rattray, E.

1987 Los barrios foráneos de Teotihuacan. In E. McClung de Tapia and E.C. Rattray, *Teotihuacan: Nuevos datos, nuevas síntesis, nuevos problemas*, 243-73. Mexico City: UNAM.

Renfrew, C.

1986 Introduction: peer polity interaction and socio-political change. In C. Renfrew and J.F. Cherry (eds.), *Peer Polity Interaction and Socio-Political Change*, 1-18. Cambridge: Cambridge University Press.

Renfrew, C., and J.F. Cherry

1986 *Peer Polity Interaction and Socio-political Change*. Cambridge: Cambridge University Press.

Sabloff, J.A.

1983 Classic Maya settlement pattern studies: past problems, future prospects. In E.Z. Vogt and R.M. Leventhal (eds.), *Prehistoric Settlement Patterns: Essays in Honor of Gordon R. Willey*, 413-22. Albuquerque: University of New Mexico Press.

Saturno, W.A., D. Stuart and B. Beltrán
2006 Early Maya writing at San Bartolo, Guatemala. *Science* 311: 1281-83. https://doi.org/10.1126/science.1121745

Scarborough, V.L.
2000 Resilience, resource use, and socioeconomic organization: a Mesoamerican pathway. In G. Bawden and R. Reycraft (eds.), *Natural Disaster and the Archaeology of Human Response*, 195-212. Albuquerque: University of New Mexico Press.

Scarborough, V.L., F. Valdez, Jr. and N. Dunning
2003 *Heterarchy, Political Economy, and the Ancient Maya: The Three Rivers Region of the East-Central Yucatán Peninsula*. Tucson: University of Arizona Press.

Smith, R.E.
1987 *A Ceramic Sequence from the Pyramid of the Sun, Teotihuacan, Mexico*. Papers of the Peabody Museum of Archaeology and Ethnology 74. Cambridge, Massachusetts: Harvard University.

Stuart, D.
1993 Historical inscriptions and the Maya collapse. In J.A. Sabloff and J.S. Henderson (eds.), *Lowland Maya Civilization in the Eighth Century A.D.*, 321-54. Washington, DC: Dumbarton Oaks Research Library and Collection.

2000 'The arrival of strangers': Teotihuacan and Tollan in Classic Maya history. In D. Carrasco, L. Jones and S. Session (eds.), *Mesoamerica's Classic Heritage: From Teotihuacan to the Aztecs*, 465-513. Boulder: University Press of Colorado.

Taube, K.A.
2003 Tetitla and the Maya presence at Teotihuacan. In G.E. Braswell (ed.), *The Maya and Teotihuacan: Reinterpreting Early Classic Interaction*, 273-314. Austin: University of Texas Press.

Willey, G.R.
1956 The structure of ancient Maya society: evidence from the southern lowlands. *American Anthropologist* 58: 777-82. https://doi.org/10.1525/aa.1956.58.5.02a00020

1980 Towards a holistic view of Maya civilization. *Man* 15: 249-66. https://doi.org/10.2307/2801670

Willey, G.R., W.R. Bullard, Jr., J.B. Glass and J.C. Gifford
1965 *Prehistoric Maya Settlement Patterns in the Belize Valley*. Papers of the Peabody Museum of Archaeology and Ethnology 54. Cambridge, Massachusetts: Harvard University.

13 Complexities and Emergence: The Case of Argos

Christopher Witmore

Revealing Complexities

When Gordon Childe situated massive changes in human styles of living in terms of 'revolution' (Childe 1950), he embraced the wrong term. The notion of 'revelation' lends more to understanding formational differences within various human complexities. Revelation, irrespective of any theological overtones, relates to the way in which the naively-given background comes to be understood in a different way. What was latent is now revealed, now manifest; or, in Heideggerian terms, 'unconcealed'. Insofar as the discussion of formative complexities is concerned one may tease out a key implication: that the conditions under which changes occur and the features that are given in those moments are different from the qualities extant things lend to later situations or the definitions they come to acquire. What emerges as the sanctuary of the cow-eyed goddess, the Argive Heraion, may have been defined originally by its proximity to the buried dead at Prosymna, and the nearby spring, known today as *Vraserka* (the Slavic toponym means 'the place with waters'), only later to be revealed as a meeting place on the threshold of common territories and a locus for competition between communities (compare de Polignac 1995; Hall 1995; Antonaccio 1999: 93-96; Kõiv 2003: 299-304). Whatever its trajectory, because of the lag-time that goes with things acquiring definition—into their maturation—one should be wary of regarding the formation of what archaeologists often call *complexities* in Kantian terms; that is, in terms of humans exerting their powers of will in devising an elaborate and intricate system. This also means that revelation, which relies on the relevance of particular things *for* humans, belongs to a subset of a larger process of *emergence*, which is open to all entities, whether human or nonhuman.

It is often assumed, with the emergence of complexities, that the initiative comes from humans seeking to consolidate power in order to legitimize present circumstances; the designs and ideologies of headmen and chiefs or kings and aristocrats are presumed to precede any form of material expression. Of course, farmers transform obligations into material entities, such as berms around plots, and leaders play a role in rendering legal bonds concrete and visible, as roads or enveloping walls; certainly, form requires creative expression, but these constructs never appear in a vacuum. The world is always already saturated with a bewildering diversity of entities ready to lend themselves to endeavors conditioned by various modes of life. Emergence is as much a reflection of the propensity of terraces to outlive their makers or to offer unpredicted qualities in different scenarios as it is an expression of humans who make sense of things after coming to experience them in a different way. If we only define the Argive Heraion in terms of its trajectory toward a presumed end, a *telos*, which provides the supposed rationale for why it was envisioned, then we not only miss how complexities might have turned out otherwise, but also how such locales and monuments may operate differently in other situations.[1] We treat such things as intermediaries to something else, rather than grasping them in their own terms; that is, understanding things, whether terraces or rock-cut voids, in themselves (Olsen 2010; Olsen and Witmore 2015).

Complexity is taken to refer to composite differentiation, intricacy, involved nature, or structure (see, for example, Cilliers 1998; within archaeology, Kohring and Wynne-Jones 2007). The diversity and heterogeneity of a state or social entity is reduced to a litany of generic features that can be identified across comparable situations. Morris (2009: 520) has offered a concise definition: 'cultural complexity is *the scale of practices (settlement, energy capture, monument-building, inequality and heterogeneity, and communication) characterizing societies*' (emphasis in original). If we take a complex, heterogeneous assemblage such as the Argive *polis* (city-state) to be a composite of various functioning components—that is, to be an aggregate of smaller pieces—then we tend to lose sight of its status as an entity that exceeds the sum of its parts (also see DeLanda 2006; 2016; Harman 2009). I seek here to maintain symmetry in both directions; that is, toward the unified whole and the autonomous components. Returned to self-rule at the turn of the third century BC, Argos, as a *polis*, integrates monuments, temples, and infrastructures as elements of renewed democratic statecraft. Argos also reveals them in different ways; these components not only constitute the *polis* as an object, but the *polis* also constitutes its own elements. 'At whatever point we fix our gaze, entities are assembled from other entities: they can be viewed as unified things when seen from the outside, yet they are always pieced together from a vast armada of autonomous components' (Harman 2010: 172).[2] The *polis* is both more and less than an aggregate of smaller parts. This is, indeed, how the *politeia* was understood: 'sometimes multiple and heterogeneous … and sometimes a unified entity' (Vernant 2006: 252). *Politeia* was both the state and the citizen body as a whole. It is as this sociopolitical entity that we encounter the *polis*, which, as Aristotle contended (*Politics* 1253a.19-20), was necessarily prior to the *oikos* (both the house and the household) and its individual citizens; the whole is prior to its parts. Argos as a *polis* retroactively defined its components. From an analytical angle, one should not view the relationship between the *polis*, its citizens, and their *oikoi* as a nested hierarchy; rather, these are different entities with different properties and different rapports. As a sociopolitical entity, as a 'thing' (Witmore 2014: 4; Olsen and Witmore 2015: 191; cf. Harman 2013), the Argive *polis* possesses a reality irreducible to any of its components or to any of the relations into which it may enter (this is an important consideration for a different understanding of complexity, which will be developed in the following). These components—*oikoi* and *polis*-dwellers—are also autonomous and possess excesses irreducible to the greater assemblage that was the *polis*. Thus, all these things retain legitimacy as and at different levels of analysis.

My aspirations in this chapter are twofold. First, I aim to explore the conditions that make the *polis* possible, through the example of Argos after the turn of the third century BC, when, in the wake of intense strife, Argive statecraft had come to be experienced as a curatorial proposition (Figure 13.1). These conditions are based somewhat loosely on the ability of the *polis* to collect, accommodate, and sustain crowds, as well as to facilitate their kinetics. These conditions are admittedly mingled, as aspects cross-cut each other in various ways. While far from exhaustive, they rely as much on infrastructures, media, enacted practices of design, and the repetitive acts necessary for strengthening the psychopolitical commitment of *polis*-dwellers as on broad ideological or political processes. The maintenance of key elements after 300 BC lends itself to the endeavor of understanding the components of a fully developed Argive *polis*.

Second, this exploration offers some oblique perspective on how the *polis* withstands structural changes in its components. Despite many trials and tribulations, which led to transformation in its constituent parts, Argos, once it had emerged, continued to persist as an autonomous *polis*. Treating the *polis* as a thing, or what DeLanda (2006; 2016) has defined as a heterogeneous assemblage that exceeds its components, reveals much about the question of emergence and how archaeologists might approach issues of complexity, state formation, and interaction while respecting this heterogeneity. Admittedly, this endeavor is speculative. It also resists the lure of serving empirical truths against mythological illusions. Thus, this essay works with a range of things, archaeological—objects excavated—and literary: the texts of Aristotle, and those of others well removed from the third century BC, including Plutarch and Pausanias.

Unlike many archaeological studies of social complexity, this paper does not begin with an apparent stage, formative toward a known *telos* (cf. Snodgrass 1986). Such approaches are fundamental to understanding the development of sociopolitical complexity; yet, set within a scheme of formation along the presumed course of history, they run the risk of locking the things they address into an inevitable trajectory where the end is known and their definition is determined by appealing to this outside moment. This mode of explanation situates the *polis* as a *resultant*, rather than an *emergent*, entity (this distinction is discussed below). The trajectory is not inevitable. The *polis*, even with its many forms, is only one of other possibilities. Alternative community assemblages were obscured in mimetic repetition of political form in Greece in the eighth century BC. Moreover, long-term understandings of complexities do not require a timeline for their orientation—indeed, we might envision complementary approaches to resultant explanations. Sometimes one may dig deep amid specific circumstances, and these may provide another angle on questions of emergence.

Before proceeding, we may note two further contrasts with respect to how archaeologists have come to understand 'sociopolitical' or 'systemic' complexity. First, the notion of complexity is often considered with respect to various 'scales', as in 'zoom'

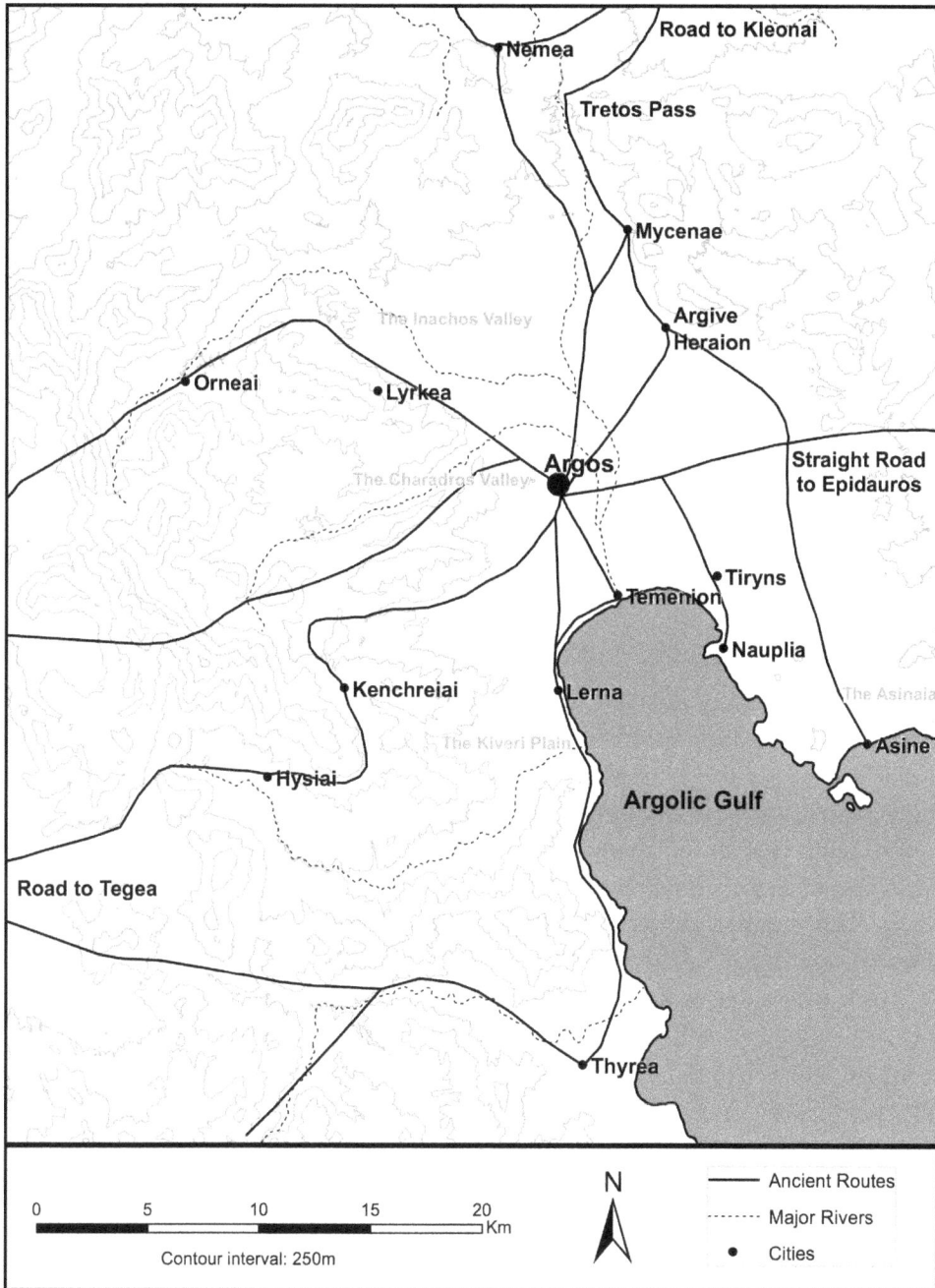

Figure 13.1   Map of the Argolid with sites mentioned in the text (map by Evan Levine).

relative to proportions flattened as a map, or on a screen, or the geographical extent of particular entities. Rather than approach the city-state *a priori* at different scales, one may consider the *polis* as an entity that operates in a range of situations, both small and large. Among the ancients, the *polis* was recognized as an entity that reared and harbored; that is, a 'complex' that provided a safe interior for those who dwelt within. Among other capacities, the *polis* was known as an entity that acts, that arbitrates, that forms alliances, and that goes to war.

Second, complexity, when understood ecologically, should be formulated in the plural. In the language of systems theory, the environment of a system will necessarily be more complex than that system (in that it contains other systems); systems must operate to reduce their complexity relative to their environments. Only complexity, according to Luhmann, 'can reduce complexity'. Here, Luhmann's (1989: 144-45) definition of complexity is revealing:

> A state of affairs is complex when it arises out of so many elements that these can only be related to one another selectively. Therefore complexity always presupposes, both operatively as well as in observation, a reduction procedure that establishes a model of selecting relations and provisionally excludes, as mere possibilities, (i.e. potentializes) other possibilities of connecting elements together.

This consistent need to reduce complexity situates simplicity as a future prospect, one that was never in the past; complexity is not acquired, for it is already there. Hence, it is appropriate to speak of *complexities*. Complexities, moreover, are not exclusive to humans-among-themselves, for they are the lot of other things. Insofar as the *polis* is concerned, we are dealing with agrarian complexities. At once fatherland, mother, and nurse (Isocrates, *Panegyricus* 4.25), the *polis* provides a hospitable environment and encompasses its interrelation, and here etymologies are informative.

The Latin root of the English word 'complex', *complexus*, denotes 'encompassing', 'encircling', and 'embracing'. From this angle the *polis* can be understood as an *encapsulating totality*. This meaning allows one to hold the tendency to understand complexities in terms of connectivity and composite differentiation in symmetry to its wider effects. (Network theory, incidentally, embraces this twentieth-century spatial grammar and deploys it as an operative principle in a world where point-to-point movement was the exception rather than the rule [Latour 2009].) I will maintain this semantic valence in approaching the Argive polis—one may even think of the Argive *complex*. Yet, as the word *polis* carries a similar range of meaning, this is somewhat redundant. The Indo-European base, shared with the Sanskrit *pur*, comes from the root *pri*, which means 'to fill' (Chantraine 1968: 926). The Greek words *pímplimi* and *plétho* and the Latin words *plenus* and *pleo* echo this meaning—'to fill full', 'to be full' or 'to become full'. The Greek *polus* and *pléthos* and the Latin *plebs* and *populus* refer to the 'many', the 'throng', the 'crowd', the 'multitude'. The relation of these words lends to *polis* the connotation of 'being filled up with many'.

Complexus derives from the Latin root *com*, in the sense of 'together', 'in combination' or 'union', and *plex* or ply, from *plekein* or *plicare*, 'to fold'. Here we may note a meaning, which allows us to understand how things from one time may be enrolled in another, of how agencies from the deep past may play a role in subsequent formations, or of how forms recur in the shape that societies take. The streets of Classical Argos orient streets of the Hellenistic city (Marchetti 2000; 2013). The space of protection in the old Aspis, according to Plutarch (32.1), would come to provide a secure bastion during the assault by Pyrrhus of Epirus centuries later. All complexities simultaneously draw on things whether old or young, ancient or recent. These things offer their qualities to subsequent situations even though they may come to be revealed in a different way.

Argos, Agrarian Complexities

Around the common hearth begins the collection of crowds. It is no coincidence that the communal flame of Argos was known as the fire of Phoroneus. Son of the first legendary king of Argos, born of the very land through which coursed his father, the river Inachos, a contender with Prometheus for the bringer of fire to humans, within the figure of Phoroneus the Argives recognized the close relationship between the taming of fire and the founding of the commons (Pausanias 2.19.5; also see Piérart 1993; on the sociology of the hearth following Vitruvius, see Sloterdijk 2014: 217-28). Phoroneus was the first to bring the Argives together in a *koinon*, together as a community in cohabitation, for—prior to that time—they had lived apart in hereditary isolation (Pausanias 2.15.5).[3] Around this fire, which the Argives kept burning, the community was collectively bound. Divinely sparked, the fire of Phoroneus served to remind all citizens of a pre-*polis* background, when living apart in scattered families was overturned through the leadership of an entrepreneurial king of divine lineage—a mode of living apart that was to be disabled by the manifest presence of the *polis*. Located as it was in the heart of the agora and at the crossroads of the plain, the fire was centered within spaces of gathering (Figure 13.2). Open areas for lingering, for mixing, disposed to chance interactions, near architectures set aside for sanctioned assembly—the old, straight-tiered theater, the hypostyle hall—the common ground of the agora was the place of the *agon*, the place of assembly and debate (*agora* and *agon* share a common root *ag*, to 'drive' or 'lead' [see Larmour 1999: 26-55; also Barker 2009]). Here it was difficult to remain aloof. It hardly matters, as far as later Argive self-definition (at the turn of the third century BC) was concerned, that these open spaces appeared after the expansion of earlier Argive communities in the tenth and ninth centuries BC (Piérart and Touchais 1996: 21-30). Whatever the intentions of their original designers, once the marshy ground was drained it was laid open to future possibilities, and these spaces offered their form to the collection of crowds among, other things.

Such spaces take on new meaning when one considers how an important condition for any democratic *polis* is an effect of what Sloterdijk (2005: 944) has defined as 'waiting power'—the facility to wait and to facilitate others in waiting. A democratic

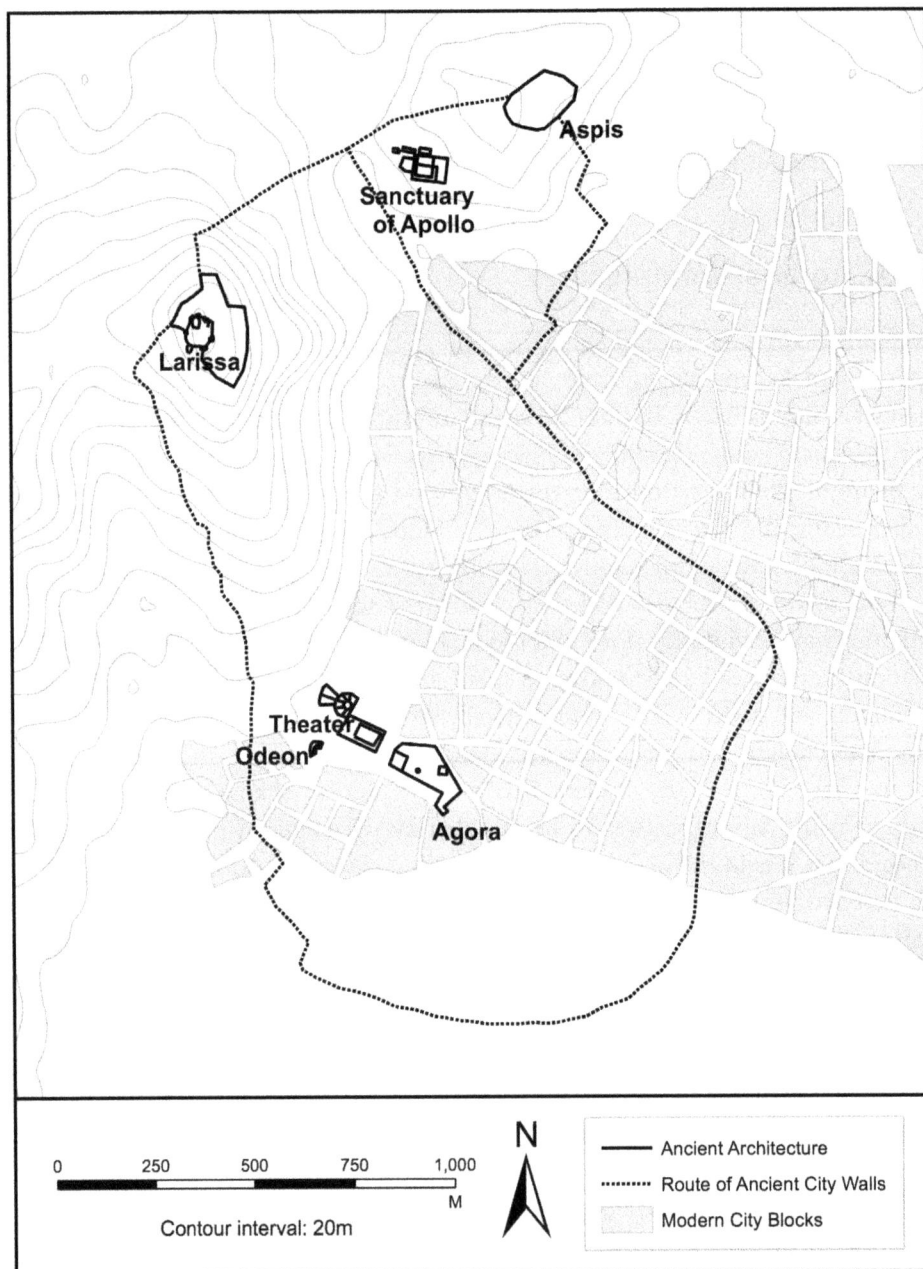

Figure 13.2 Map of the Argive *asty* (map by Evan Levine).

polis needed specific areas of assembly and gathering, dates and times for meetings, and a guarantee that key matters of concern could be raised, and all these features were tied to the condition of waiting. Areas for prolonged hesitation and postponed consideration, protracted controversy, anticipated debate, and accommodated dissent; dedicated space for a diverse assembly among men, a public assembly (the *aliaia* [*heliaia*]), where common concerns, given importance in a council of chosen peers (the *bola* [*boule*]),[4] were aired for those present to hear—these were necessary spatial conditions for any democratic *polis*. Indeed, democratic *poleis* worked hard to preserve the right that an issue could be raised, and decisions of the *polis* could transpire, in a public forum.

Such shared spaces also lent themselves to the collection of pride-engendering architectures and esteem-inducing objects of the Argive past. One need not have strayed far from the shared warmth of Phoroneus's fire to find some of the most venerated monuments and memorials. In the nearby sanctuary of Apollo Lykeios a monument portrayed an event wherein a wolf attacked a bull outside Argos at a time when Danaus sought refuge (Plutarch 32.4-5; Pausanias 2.19.3-4). Having interpreted the event correctly as an omen, Danaus made his vows to Apollo Lykeios and won the kingdom of Argos by force. The association with the wolf was fundamental to Apollo, protector of the city, and thus to Argos (outwardly, this special relationship of Argos, Apollo, and wolf was mobilized in the 'Wolf A' coinage of the *polis*, which dates to the late fourth through mid-third centuries BC [see Gershenson 1992: 8]).

The gods, and their veiled prompts, factored greatly in matters of democratic statecraft. Participation in common festivals was an important attribute of building sound citizens. To participate with and among other members of a community was about seeing and being seen. But this was not only an issue of being among other *polis*-dwellers; it was also about being revealed as a productive member before the *polis*, manifest within its people, its constructed forms, including revered monuments, and the gods, who bestowed favor upon Argos.

Protectors of communal solidarity, regulators of community action, the efficacy of settled gods extended beyond their venerated houses and sanctuaries. Decisions made within the assemblies were conditioned to a major degree by oracles and prophecy, by gods and their messengers, which showed devotion to those who in turn were devoted to the *polis*. This had a calming effect in the decision-making apparatus, for others were always present to contest, to offer a different interpretation, to keep in check major decisions of Argos, by respecting what they held to be messages from the gods, who shared in the successes and failures of the *polis*. (Here, it should be noted that these observations concern the self-definition of the Argive *polis*, and as such concentrate on what are considered to be religious, not historical, truths [see Luhmann 2013: 178].)

Accommodating citizens required spaces to be made hospitable for life. Houses, maintained and augmented over generations, sheltered Argive families, 'companions of the cupboard', and their labors' companions—horses, oxen, or goats for milk—within a shared, protective envelope, in close proximity as neighbors. Within the community enclosure one found water from many wells (Strabo 8.6.7), stores for fruits from many fields, wood for the many hearth fires, and a multitude of others with whom to share one's burdens in both friendship and rivalry, in collaboration and competition. Not everyone need have lived within the urban sphere of the *asty* to be accommodated. As a psychopolitical dimension to having a guaranteed accommodation within, every citizen must have believed that the best chance for an *oikos* to exist was within the communal sphere of protection, provided by the *polis*, against the shared outside.

The common fire, spaces for assembly, abodes for the gods, exhibitions of esteemed objects, many households, were all situated within a large circle of protection, as both territory and walls. Lending form and longevity to the community, Argive walls carried the practical and symbolic weight of group solidarity. There was much to beautifully wrought walls; a lure for feeling, they were as much about psychology as containment. Bearing esteem-inducing effects for the *polis*, well-fit walls of polygonal masonry, such the new ramparts on the Aspis, signaled the power of what any outside threat confronted from within. Bearing a strange inconsistency between roughened limestone surfaces and flawlessly aligned seams, every block was poised to its neighbor with utmost complementary precision (Figure 13.3). Each was unique, perhaps signaling the motley composition of citizenry enclosed behind it. This carefully executed dressing reinforced civic pride for those who lived behind shared walls, those who lived by shared laws. Conspicuous walls carried the double dimension of community and security.

Here one should note that the construction of more encompassing walls arose in a plain of contrasts, a land saturated with walled ruins and the stories put to them. Overt

Figure 13.3   Remnants of polygonal walling on the Aspis (photograph by Chistopher Witmore)

disparities with monumental walls, those believed to have sheltered the residences of past kings and their entourages in exclusive interiors, were seen at Tiryns, at Mycenae, and in Argos on the Aspis and perhaps on the Larisa, or elsewhere. Disparities with and comparisons to these prominent, yet less-encompassing, bastions were open to a community focused on collective security behind their own unique walls.

Building and sustaining good citizens, and upholding *polis* order, required other forms of participation. Shared struggle in warfare further annealed the Argive sense of commonality, and among the shared responsibilities of citizens was that of bearing arms. For this, good citizens of a *polis* had to be disarmed with respect to each other (Aristotle, *Politics* 1252b-1253a; Sloterdijk 2005). Competition, friendship, and the accommodation of dissent filled this gap. The location of a racetrack in the agora, perhaps present from the Classical period, reinforced the heart of the city as the locus of the competition amongst men, as with the *agon* of speaking.

Security rested upon an inclusive community, undivided amongst men of proper birth. In Argos, membership was reinforced by an imagined commonality: the three old Dorian tribes (*phylai*): the *Dymanes, Hylleis*, and *Pamphylai*, joined later by a fourth, the *Hyrnathioi* (for epigraphic evidence, see Kritzas 1979). These *phylai* served as commons for groups of *phratries*, twelve to each *phyle*, and to these were given names related to the heroes of local traditions (Piérart and Touchais 1996: 42, 62). The memory of these tribal forms was both a source of legitimacy and an acknowledgment of the common effort to come together. Participation within them was tied to the maintenance of a shared political and ethnic identity. One should not ignore the fact that such an inclusive community within an agrarian society rested upon radical inequalities that existed between citizens and others: foreigners, females, workers, slaves, or tenants. Whether or not these inequities were observed, they eluded self-descriptions of the Argive *polis*, which comforted itself with an image of naturalized disparities; thus were vested interests ignored, injustices disregarded, and acts of violence obscured (Luhmann 2013: 175-83).

Participation also took the form of offices. In order to douse as many citizens as possible in the waters of commonality and contribution (and in order to permanently delay would-be tyrants), Argos limited representative officials to six-month terms (*Politics* 1308a.15-24; inscriptions confirm these half-year terms, see Kritzas 2003: 58; also Robinson 2011: 15). This rapid turnover in magistracies resulted in the continual reproduction of expertise where carefully defined tasks were distributed into various offices, including the Council (*bola*), the *Damiogoi*, the Generals (*stratagoi*), the *Polemarchs*, the 'Eighty' (*ogdoekonta*), and the 'Six-Hundred' (*hexakosioi*). Only witnesses from the tribes and treaty negotiators were exempt from abbreviated tenures (see Kritzas 2003: 58). Common law and guarantees through institutionalized dispute resolution among peers constituted another condition. To be *apolis*, city-less, was akin to Homer's tribeless, lawless, and heartless (*aphritor, athemistos, anestios*) man (*Politics* 1253a.5).

Another key facet of Argive 'waiting power' (as in the ability to postpone consideration) rested on effective communication (Sloterdijk 2005: 949). Otherwisefleeting words had to be captured if they were to be effectively projected into the political domain and beyond. To be a good democratic citizen one had to engage with those aspects of *polis* culture, inscribed for posterity. In Argos, spoken words were given a prolonged presence as inscribed bronze plaques.

According to Thucydides (5.47.11), the temple of Apollo was used as a repository for the official archives of Argos. Affixed by iron nails to the temple of Apollo Lykeios,[5] these plaques existed within a milieu, both public and sacred, within the agora. Over the course of decades, the proliferation of these plaques led to a situation where, by the third century BC, they covered large portions of the temple. Plaques, many sized to fit within the space of two open hands, covered architraves, triglyphs, metopes, and even portions of the drip edge in the cornice.[6] While nearly every inscribed enactment of the Argive state in the previous two centuries began or ended with ἁλιαίαι ἔδοξε τελείαι (*aliaiai edoxe teleiai*), 'decreed by [i.e., seemed good to] the assembly,' a stamp that eventually became synonymous with the council and the people—ἔδοξε τᾶι βουλᾶι καὶ τῶι δάμωι (*edoxe tai boulai toi damoi*) (Robinson 2011: 10)—the presence of these inscriptions outside of the realm of legible engagement placed literate observers in the position of spectator rather than participant (des Courtils 1981: 609). This observation does not foreclose on the legibility of displays at lower levels of the temple (to the extent that the possibility for perusal occurred on a passing whim). Still, by shifting plaques up toward the eaves they were moved out of a setting that afforded opportunity-to-be-read-in-passing, and into a state of being present under the watchful eyes of the ever-vigilant Apollo, in the city's most venerated sanctuary (Thucydides 5.47.11; Pausanias 2.19.3). Here, the power of these plaques was further strengthened. It is also of consequence that a surfeit of bronze messages extending up and over the whole of the entablature would seem to have overwhelmed observers, literate or otherwise. Whether an engagement with the text was direct or vicarious (i.e., read to illiterate citizens by literate ones) is no more and no less important than this relationship with the exhibition space.

A democratic *polis* contained old messages that were coextensive with all citizens, those present and those still to come. The importance with which Argos regarded the mnemonic reservoirs of the *polis* was manifest in its use of stone chests (*petroi*) covered by heavy slabs (weighing as much as 1.5 tons) for the safe deposits of inscribed bronze straps. Left in a storehouse of a treasury under the protection of the goddess of organization, Pallas (Athena), these *chalkeons telamonas* (the latter term carries connotations of bearing or supporting) held records of land leases, money loans, and deposits. Pierced and fastened together by bronze wires in some cases, many were organized in groups within chests that were themselves numbered (Kritzas 2006). Acts necessary for maintaining the *polis*, whose revenues were drawn principally from sacred and public lands (*hiera kai damosia chora*), required archival repositories where financial transactions may be known. Notwithstanding their value as surrogates for what was loaned, such archival consistency was not so much an issue of transparency now, but for transparency in the future, should financial records become an issue at a later date.[7] So effective were these bronze straps within their persistent capsules that they stubbornly bore their messages for more than two millennia before strangers sorted through them. For Argive citizens, these messages were further secured under the protection of Pallas, who safeguarded the *polis*.

The agora, the common domain, was saturated with images of the territorial form. From this exhibition center—the heart of Argos—the *polis* emanated outwards. Here, roads both radiate and converge. The road to Lyrkea and Orneai, the road to Mycenae, Nemea, and Kleonai, to the Heraion, the straight road to Epidaurus with its offshoots to Nauplia and Asine, the road to Kenchreai, Lerna, and Thyrea, and the road to Tememion, the Argive port—their destinations were known, and as such they manifested the most distant extents of the *chora* within. (It should be stated that roads are necessary for the normal kinetics of a *polis*, which must provide for repetitive movements and means of association between open spaces, rooms for dwelling, places for labor, areas for commerce, and tracts for deriving food, water, clothing, shade, and well-being. As infrastructure, they lend form to future lives by stubbornly orienting and organizing.)

From the Larisa, with its temples to Athena and Zeus, the whole of the plain is available for circumspection. As the verdict will remain unsettled, I would suggest that there were large portions of unencumbered plain, broken by no more than berms, allowing for open visibility. This openness was a reflection of labor investment in maintaining fields, in watching plants grow, in observing fellow agrarians, companions in labor, or horses. The unobstructed view was a criterion for protection, according to Aristotle (*Politics* 7.5.2.1327a; also see de Polignac 1995: 34); this openness also allows the high-walled enclosure of the community to be seen seeing others. The combination of conspicuous walls and open vistas occasioned the 'revelation of [*polis*] power before itself', with its far-reaching sight (Sloterdijk 2014: 265-66). For the *polis* to be defined from within is not to foreclose on other orientations, but it does underline the close connection between infrastructure, form, and organization (also see Vernant 2006: 248). A protected enclosure of shared walls within another protected enclosure of shared territorial borders, the *polis* encompassed both walled space and the surrounding lands; it extended itself over *asty* and *chora*.

The *chora* is the territory, the domain of activity encompassed by the *polis*. Argos is the plain; such is the meaning of the name (there is debate over the extent of Argos's control over the plain in earlier periods [compare de Polignac 1995; Hall 1995]). And yet, in addition to the Argive plain, its *chora* also encompassed the valleys of the Inachos and Charadros and of Akhladokampos, the plains of Kiveri and of the Thyreatis to the south and the Asinaia to the east, the district of Berbati, and north of the Tretos Pass (Tomlinson 1972: 7-14). Thus the domain of activity incorporated more than the *agros*, tilled land. Land for herds and herdsmen—the toponym *Euboia*, the mountain above the Heraion, suggests its utility of purpose: good for cows. There was land for forests and woodcutters, coastline for inshore fishers, and more. There is a thorough enmeshment of *polis*-dwellers with their *chora*. The union of the self with a patch of ground was redefined by the *polis* (with the aid of contrived legitimization in myth), for wherever one broke earth, watched plants grow, and harvested, it was within the sphere of community protection.

The *polis* was a form of political dwelling whose territorial extent was determined by the size of the population—both humans and their partners in agriculture or their living wealth, their styles of living—and its relations with different forms of land and with other *poleis* with whom it shared borders. With respect to the extent of one's property, 'ideal' conditions called for a restrained liberalism—enough to live freely without lack.[8] Such is the dream where scarcity reigns. Walled space, however, is only so large. There is only so much prime land to go around. Even in the plain, the moisture content of soils determined the best areas for particular crops.[9] Thus the *polis* has to find ways to alleviate tensions that naturalized associations failed to mollify. The population of Argos was distributed throughout its territory within *komai*—documentary evidence suggests there were dozens of these dependent settlements (see Kritzas 2003: 58). Shifts in the distribution of property through expansion and confiscation may have been among the modes of compromise.

It was in situations of strife, both internal and external, that Argive statecraft was revealed as tenuous and in need of protection. In the wake of the attack by Pyrrhus of Epirus (272 BC), a point when even the *polis* itself had come, arguably, to be experienced as a curatorial proposition, these features were exaggerated.

Pursued by Areus, king of Sparta, Pyrrhus came to Argos to fight on behalf of Aristeas in a feud with Aristippus, friend to Pyrrhus's rival Antigonas Gonatas, king of Macedon. Allowed through the walls by Aristeas, Pyrrhus inverted the agora into a space of battle. There, according to Plutarch, Pyrrhus confronted the wolf monument in the sanctuary of Apollo Lykeios, the very emblem of Argos, as a portent of his impending doom, which soon followed. Girard's (1989) thesis of the scapegoat resonates with Pyrrhus's death. Even if he was not the object of shared violence in Girard's (1989) sense, the outcome was in service to the *polis*. As sacrificial victim, Pyrrhus was subsumed to that familiar schema where common membership is founded, where community solidarity is renewed, through the shared murder (also see Sloterdijk 2014: 176-79). An enemy at first, a powerful king no less, turned scapegoat at last. And around the scapegoat Argos converged; a pyre was constructed in the center of the agora and, here, in shared warmth, Argives gathered (Pausanias 2.21.4). Through a collective expulsion, with cathartic results, the Argive sense of community was maintained.

Just as the nocturnal expulsion of Pleistarchus, brother to Cassander, was believed to have been effected by none other than Apollo, Argives would come to regard the old woman who struck Pyrrhus with a roof tile as none other than Demeter herself (Pausanias 1.13.8). Argos, despite its repeated hardships, had not been forgotten by the gods, and this, again, holds a pyschopolitical dimension. Inwardly, such justificatory stories further strengthen the Argive community's sense of integrity. Outwardly, the *polis* appears to be upheld through divine sanction, protection, and sustenance. The on-going maintenance of the *polis* would memorialize Pyrrhus's failed hopes as another common trial of the Argives. Yet another shared struggle was to be translated into the monumental and displayed as part of the self-exhibition of shared achievements. A monument of white marble, carved with elephants and other instruments of warfare, was set up where the body of Pyrrhus was burned, adjacent to a mound containing the head of the Gorgon, Medusa. The bones were interred on the spot where he fell, in the sanctuary of Demeter. His shield was placed above the doorway of this sanctuary (Pausanias 2.21.4-5). These objects added to the expositions of the Argive past, along with the shield of Diomedes and the Palladian from Troy stolen by none other than Odysseus and Diomedes, or so the Argives claimed (against rival claims by Athens, Sparta, and Rome, among others [see Nilsson 1992: 435-36]). As such objects are indifferent to the old myths of shared association and common origin that will be iteratively connected to them, Argives must continue to participate in the revelation of the *polis* before itself, just as others had done before, and in such ways new self-definitions emerge.

Argos, Emergence and Endurance

Looking at the conditions that make the Argive *polis* possible is a necessary prelude to thinking about questions of emergence and endurance. In this chapter I have said very little about the nature of interaction between the Argive *polis* and other sociopolitical entities (Renfrew and Cherry 1986), or about issues of connectivity which other authors have addressed in this volume. Instead, my purpose has been to explore how Argos as a sociopolitical entity self-defines. A study of this kind does not provide an antithesis in the context of this volume, but a complement, for it offers another angle on sociopolitical complexities. We may now make some brief observations with regard to emergence.

Archaeological approaches to social complexity often follow two basic angles on emergence: (1) the new and novel arises from the old and outmoded; (2) the composite and intricate forms from the simple and austere (although see Kohring and Wynne-Jones 2007). This mode of explanation tends to regard the object of study as *resultant*, rather than *emergent*. As a resultant entity, the *polis* is reduced to an amalgam of simpler forms and its components are regarded as means to a known end. Emergence, however, suggests that there is no direct route to the *polis*, and when situated in the interplay of pre-*polis* entities of the eighth century BC the outcomes are open-ended—counterfactual alternatives to the *polis* existed. The *polis*, even with its many forms, is only one of other possibilities. Rather than begin with a pre-*polis* background, I have chosen to undertake a case study at the turn of the third century BC, when the Argive *polis* was revealed as losable and in need of curation and care; at that time particular features were exaggerated and different self-definitions emerged.

By emergence—'to come forth into view'—I am not speaking of the morphogenetic history that lies outside of things. Indeed, things rarely retain their 'histories' (see Olsen

2010; Olivier 2011), and this is an important factor that allows emergence to occur, for to reveal is also to obscure, and in offering their diverse qualities to new situations former associations for things fall by the wayside. Emergence is not derivative of processes, which are taken to be at the root of all historical change (compare Gosden and Malafouris 2015). Actual things and their interactions, I suggest, contribute to genuine emergence. Here, the question is not so much at what level this is viewed, but how to situate a given entity without reducing it to its components or its effects. No matter at what level we address them, all things are gatherings, assemblages, and therefore complexities. Even the smallest of the individual limestone blocks within the polygonal walls of the Aspis is a co-realization of limestone, form in relation to other forms, the purpose that is the pride-infused wall, and skilled stonemasons with hammers and chisels. Indeed, complexities, such as the *polis*, emerge through mergers between actual entities. And, once the *polis* emerges, once it is revealed as such, it retroactively defines the entities and interactions that contributed to its coming into existence. It is, moreover, also enduring enough to be a factor in historical explanations (cf. DeLanda 2011: 391).

As we have seen, the *polis* was both a large, autonomous thing and an assemblage of heterogeneous parts, each of which also possessed dignity as things-in-themselves. Because the *polis* exceeded its components, changes could occur within those components without necessarily changing the *polis* as a whole. The Argive *polis* was remarkably stable. Despite the loss of democracy, with the institution of oligarchies (power plays such as these are often regarded as central to understanding changes in complexities; see Kohring and Wynne-Jones 2007) the *polis* continued to exist. Argos weathered the loss of the archive of Pallas. It endured changes in the distribution of land, at times to the exclusion of other independent farmers. Indeed, it is only in recent years that a systematic survey has been undertaken in the hinterland of Argos, and the things found in the course of this work reveal a dramatic shift in the distribution of sites and settlements during the Roman Period (James *et al.* 2016).[10] With shifts in land settlement patterns, archaeologists routinely infer transformations in social complexities (Cherry 1984)—rightly so, as the psychopolitical realities of Roman Argos were different. One may ponder, however, even after the formerly open, straight-tiered theater offered its design to an enclosed odeon at some point in the first century AD, or after the hypostyle hall lent its form to a bath complex two centuries later, whether the *polis* continued to persist. In the face of such overt changes, the Argive *polis* seems to have continued to accommodate *polis*-dwellers as a self-governing entity over its territory. By that time the *polis* had been repeatedly revealed as a mode of political dwelling that could cope with such changes (recall, in Luhmann's [1989] terms, such changes indicated a reduction of complexity), and herein lay its effectiveness.

Archaeological explanation of long-term change requires an understanding of both persistence and transformation. While the long-term need not be revealed along a timeline, this chapter has foregone long-term explanation in order to address issues of complexity and maintenance within the *polis* at a critical moment. While this endeavor would seem to be at variance with long-term explanation, its novelty of purpose lies in reconsidering how we understand complexities. We may now offer a slightly reformulated definition of complexity: something is complex if it is able to weather changes in any of its components without it affecting the whole. With this definition I do not mean to imply that transformative entities lack complexity; rather, I would suggest that the quality and maintenance of stability should be taken into account, as should the excess that undergirds its persistence as a sociopolitical entity. Key institutions eventually broke down; the curation of pride-infused objects inevitably ceased; walls ultimately lost their charm; in due course, the gods were evicted, bronze plaques were melted down, and monuments emerged as quarries— death came to all *polei*s in their own time (cf. Hansen 2006). There were, of course, many avenues to destruction, and thereby emergence. Raze city walls and exile the population; take away the *chora*; submit to outside rule so that responsibility for the welfare of inhabitants rests elsewhere—when *necessary* features of an entity were subverted, new complexities were revealed. By that time, another political form had emerged and all the components were retroactively defined. Former components of the *polis* had become different things.

Dealing with the self-definition of sociopolitical entities such as the Argive *polis* is a speculative exercise; one that here rests predominantly on historical sources of information. For something to be revealed, humans must comprise a major component, and it is history that tells us what happened to Argive *polis*-dwellers. The foregoing narrative should be assessed from the angle of its limitations. Ruined walls, abandoned rooms, erstwhile delimited spaces; rubbish, detritus, bits of ceramic or lithics on plowed surfaces—all hold idiosyncratic memories of their own pasts. What they may lack in terms of historical specificity they make up for in other ways. If one conceives of that struggle to understand humble things, to open oneself to their propensities (spatial and otherwise), to what potentials they offer, rather than foregrounding what ends they may, or may not, come to, as among the most fundamental of archaeological aspirations, then one may consider themselves to follow that path so well maintained by the archaeologist deservedly celebrated in this volume.

Endnotes

1. Other situations may result through interactions with other things—a farmhouse is transformed into a sheepfold, a quarry, a ruin, or the rectilinear foundation is eventually buried under alluvium.
2. The point is that while a storage building or monument may exist prior to or apart from third-century BC Argos, what constitutes an explicit element for a complex system such as a *polis* does not pre-date the complex system that constitutes or constructs it. Argos retroactively defines its components in a different way. They come to act as nested elements of a complexity with respect to a *polis*.
3. It is worth noting that Pausanias uses the term *synagon*, living together, rather than *synoikismos*, living together in the common house.
4. On Argive democracy in the late fourth to early third century BC, see Piérart (2000). Not everyone agrees with a probouleutic sequence wherein issues were weighed by the *bola* before they were aired in the *aliaia* (see, for example, Leppin 1999, as discussed by Robinson 2011: 15-18).

5. Here, I will take some liberties with respect to the specificity of the blocks for the sake of the narrative. In lieu of excavation of the temple, des Courtils (1981: 610) rightly leaves open the question as to what kind of building these blocks may have belonged: '*portique ou temple*'.

6. Architectural blocks found in the French excavations of the agora contain impressions, nails, and nail holes, which suggest that the size of the plaques ranged between a height of 5 to 10 cm and width between 10 and 25 cm (Roux 1953; des Courtils 1981).

7. Here I am establishing a contrast to Kritzas's argument that the archive was meant to provide absolute transparency (Kritzas 2003: 55; a point echoed by Robinson 2011: 15). If transparency were indeed the objective, the straps would be better displayed in public areas, such as the agora, rather than placed in stone, bronze, or terracotta containers and sealed under massive stone lids.

8. Indeed, such matters, without agrarian informants or new documentary evidence, will remain as formulated ideals for which Aristotle provides testimony: the size of land was best envisioned as a combination of *sophrónos* and *eleftheríos*—temperance and unrestraint (*Politics* 1265a).

9. At the dawn of the nineteenth century AD the drier parts of the Argive plain were covered in cereals; areas with more moisture, in cotton and vines; and the marshy areas near the sea, in rice and *kalambokki* (maize) (see Lehmann 1937).

10. This survey is not in the Argive plain, where Hellenistic surfaces are buried in many areas under alluvium (Zangger 1993), but rather in the upland area of the Inachos river valley.

Acknowledgments

This article has benefited from conversations with Sue Alcock, John Cherry, Bruce Clarke, Sylvian Fachard, Graham Harman, David Larmour, Don Lavigne, Justin Miller, Laurent Olivier, Bjørnar Olsen, and Michael Shanks. I would like to thank Alex Knodell and Tom Leppard for the kind invitation to participate in the workshop and this volume. Alex Knodell, Tom Leppard, Tom Tartaron, and Bob Chapman read an earlier version of this article and offered valuable comments, which helped to improve it—for this I am grateful. Finally, I am indebted to Evan Levine for his assistance with the figures.

About the Author

Christopher Witmore is Associate Professor of Archaeology and Classics at Texas Tech University. His research engages objects, land, and ecology in Greece over the very long term. Co-author of *Archaeology: The Discipline of Things* (2012), and co-editor of *Archaeology in the Making* (2013), he was recently the Donnelley Family Fellow at the National Humanities Center and is currently working on the book *Old Lands: A Chorography of the Eastern Morea*. E-mail: christopher.witmore@ttu.edu

Classical Authors and Texts

Aristotle, *The Politics*.
Isocrates, *Panegyricus*.
Pausanias, *Description of Greece*.

Plutarch, *The Parallel Lives: The Life of Pyrrhus*.
Strabo, *Geography*.
Thucydides, *The Peloponnesian War*.

References

Antonaccio, C.M.
1999   Placing the past: the Bronze Age in the cultic topography of Early Greece. In S.E. Alcock and R. Osborne (eds.), *Placing the Gods: Sanctuaries and Sacred Space in Ancient Greece*, 79-104. Oxford: Clarendon Press.

Barker, E.
2009   *Entering the Agon*. Oxford: Oxford University Press. https://doi.org/10.1093/acprof:oso/9780199542710.001.0001

Chantraine, P.
1968   *Dictionnaire Étymologique de la Langue Grecque Histoire des Mots*. Paris: Éditions Klincksieck.

Cherry, J.F.
1984   The emergence of the state in the Prehistoric Aegean. *Proceedings of the Cambridge Philological Society* 30: 18-48. https://doi.org/10.1017/S0068673500004600

Childe, V.G.
1950   The urban revolution. *Town Planning Review* 21: 3-17. https://doi.org/10.3828/tpr.21.1.k853061t614q42qh

Cilliers, P.
1998   *Complexity and Postmodernism: Understanding Complex Systems*. London and New York: Routledge.

de Polignac, F.
1995   *Cults, Territory, and the Origins of the Greek City-State*. Trans. J. Lloyd. Chicago: University of Chicago Press.

DeLanda, M.
2006   *A New Philosophy of Society: Assemblage Theory and Social Complexity*. New York: Continuum.

2011   Emergence, causality and realism. In L. Bryant, N. Srnicek and G. Harman (eds.), *The Speculative Turn: Continental Materialism and Realism*, 381-92. Melbourne: re.press.

2016   *Assemblage Theory*. Edinburgh: Edinburgh University Press.

des Courtils, J.
1981   Note de topographie argienne. *Bulletin de correspondance hellénique* 105: 607-10. https://doi.org/10.3406/bch.1981.4797

Gershenson, D.E.
1992   *Apollo the Wolf God*. Journal of Indo-European Studies Monograph 8. Washington, DC: Institute for the Study of Man.

Girard, R.
1989   *The Scapegoat*. Trans. Y. Freccero. Baltimore: Johns Hopkins University Press.

Gosden, C., and L. Malafouris
2015   Process archaeology (P-Arch). *World Archaeology* 47: 701-17. https://doi.org/10.1080/00438243.2015.1078741

Hall, J.M.
1995   How Argive was the 'Argive' Heraion? The political and cultic geography of the Argive Plain, 900-400 B.C. *American Journal of Archaeology* 99: 577-613. https://doi.org/10.2307/506184

Hansen, M.H.
2006   *Polis: An Introduction to the Ancient Greek City-State*. Oxford: Oxford University Press.

Harman, G.
2009   DeLanda's ontology: assemblage and realism. *Contemporary Philosophy Review* 41: 367-83. https://doi.org/10.1007/s11007-008-9084-7

2010   *Towards Speculative Realism: Essays and Lectures*. Winchester, United Kingdom: Zero Books.

2013   *Bells and Whistles: More Speculative Realism*. Winchester, United Kingdom: Zero Books

James, S., D. Nakassis, S. Gallimore and W. Caraher
2016   The Western Argolid Regional Project: results of the 2015 season. Paper presented at the Annual Meeting of the Archaeological Institute of America, San Francisco.

Kohring, S., and S. Wynne-Jones
2007   *Socialising Complexity: Structure, Interaction and Power in Archaeological Discourse*. Oxford: Oxbow Books.

Kõiv, M.
2003 *Ancient Tradition and Early Greek History: The Origins of States in Early-Archaic Sparta, Argos and Corinth.* Tallinn: Avita Publishers.

Kritzas, C.
1979 Κατάλογος πεσόντων απο το Άργος. In *Στήλη: Τόμος εις Μνήμην Νικολάου Κοντολέοντος*, 497-510. Athens: Association of Friends of Nicholas Kontoleon.
2003 Literacy and society. *Kodai: Journal of Ancient History* 13-14: 53-60.
2006 Nouvelles inscriptions d'Argos: les archives des comptes du Trésor sacré. *Comptes rendus des séances de l'Académie des Inscriptions et Belles-Lettres* 150: 397-434.

Larmour, D.H.J.
1999 *Stage and Stadium: Drama and Athletics in Ancient Greece.* Hildesheim, Germany: Weidmann.

Latour B.
2009 Spheres and networks: two ways to reinterpret globalization. *Harvard Design Magazine* 30: 138-44.

Lehmann, H.
1937 *Argolis* I. *Landeskunde der Ebene von Argos und ihrer Randgebiete.* Athens: Deutsches Archaologisches Institut.

Leppin, H.
1999 Argos: Eine griechische Demokratie des fünften Jahrhunderts v. Chr. *Ktema* 24: 297-312.

Luhmann, N.
1989 *Ecological Communication.* Trans. J. Bednarz. Chicago: University of Chicago Press.
2013 *Theory of Society* II. Trans. R. Barrett. Stanford. Stanford University Press.

Marchetti, P.
2000 Recherches sur les mythes et la topographie d'Argos, V. Quelques mises au point sur les rues d'Argos. A propos de deux ouvrages recents. *Bulletin de correspondence hellénique* 124: 273-89. https://doi.org/10.3406/bch.2000.7264
2013 Argos: la ville en ses remparts. In

D. Mulliez (ed.), Στα βήματα του *Wilhelm Vollgraff: Εκατό χρόνια αρχαιολογικής δραστηριότητας στο Άργος / Sur les pas de Wilhelm Vollgraff: Cent ans d'activités archéologiques à Argos.* Recherches franco-helléniques 4: 317-34. Athens: École française d'Athènes.

Morris, I.
2009 Cultural complexity. In C. Gosden, B. Cunliffe and R.A. Joyce (eds.), *The Oxford Handbook of Archaeology*, 519-54. Oxford: Oxford University Press. https://doi.org/10.1093/oxfordhb/9780199271016.013.0018

Nilsson, M.P.
1992 *Geschichte der Griechischen Religion* I. München: Beck.

Olivier, L.
2011 *The Dark Abyss of Time: Archaeology and Memory.* Lanham, Maryland: AltaMira Press.

Olsen, B.
2010 *In Defense of Things: Archaeology and the Ontology of Objects.* Lanham, Maryland: AltaMira Press.

Olsen, B., and C. Witmore
2015 Archaeology, symmetry, and the ontology of things: a response to critics. *Archaeological Dialogues* 22: 187-97. https://doi.org/10.1017/S1380203815000240

Piérart, M.
1993 De l'endroit où l'on abritait quelques statues d'Argos et de la vraie nature du feu de Phoroneus: une note critique. *Bulletin de correspondance hellenique* 117: 609-13.
2000 Argos: un autre democratie. In P. Flensted-Jensen, T.H. Nielsen and L. Rubinstein (eds.), *Polis & Politics: Studies in Ancient Greek History*, 297-314. Copenhagen: Museum Tusculanum Press.

Piérart, M., and G. Touchais
1996 *Argos: Une ville grecque de 6000 ans.* Paris: CNRS Editions. https://doi.org/10.4000/books.editionscnrs.3841

Renfrew, C., and J.F. Cherry

1986 *Peer Polity Interaction and Socio-Political Change*. Cambridge: Cambridge University Press.

Robinson, E.W.

2011 *Democracy Beyond Athens: Popular Government in the Greek Classical Age*. Cambridge: Cambridge University Press. https://doi.org/10.1017/CBO9780511977527

Roux, G.

1953 Deux études d'archéologie péloponnésienne. *Bulletin de correspondance hellénique* 77: 116-38. https://doi.org/10.3406/bch.1953.2443

Sloterdijk, P.

2005 Atmospheric politics. In B. Latour and P. Weibel (eds.), *Making Things Public: Atmospheres of Democracy*, 944-51. Cambridge, Massachusetts: MIT Press.

2014 *Spheres* II. *Globes, Macrospherology*. Trans. W. Hoban. South Pasadena, California: Semiotext(e).

Snodgrass, A.M.

1986 Interaction by design: the Greek city state. In C. Renfrew and J.F. Cherry (eds.), *Peer Polity Interaction and Socio-Political Change*, 47-59. Cambridge: Cambridge University Press.

Tomlinson, R.A.

1972 *Argos and the Argolid: From the End of the Bronze Age to the Roman Occupation*. Ithaca, New York: Cornell University Press.

Vernant, J-P.

2006 *Myth and Thought among the Greeks*. Trans. J. Lloyd and J. Fort. Brooklyn: Zone Books.

Witmore, C.

2014 Archaeology and the New Materialisms. *Journal of Contemporary Archaeology* 1: 203-24. https://doi.org/10.1558/jca.v1i2.16661

Zangger, E.

1993 *The Geoarchaeology of the Argolid*. Argolis 2. Berlin: Mann.

14 The Way Things Are…

A. Bernard Knapp

> When archaeologists resort to model making, the 'structural system' … is ultimately represented by a set of material lifeless things; … Am I making my point? Ideas are more important than things; creative imagination is deeply entangled with the formulation of verbal concepts; archaeologists need to appreciate that the material objects revealed by their excavations are not 'things in themselves', nor are they just artefacts—things made by men—they are representations of ideas.
>
> (Leach 1977: 166, 167)

Introduction

With the foregoing words, penned over 35 years ago, the Cambridge social anthropologist Edmund Leach castigated the archaeological discipline at a conference entitled *Archaeology and Anthropology: Areas of Mutual Interest* (Spriggs 1977). Today, by contrast, I think most archaeologists and anthropologists would agree, to differing extents and for different reasons, with the notion that material objects *are* 'things in themselves' rather than just 'representations of ideas', and that people and social life depend on things, or indeed *are* things. At the very least, archaeologists of most persuasions seem to accept that objects are integral to human action, not just the backdrop to it (Gosden and Marshall 1999: 169).

Archaeological research increasingly focuses on the inescapable 'entanglement' of humans and things, of subjects and objects, of mind and matter (Hodder 2011: 155; 2012). *The Social Life of Things* (Appadurai 1986; see also Hoskins 1998) was the first work that sought to highlight multiple ways in which 'things', like people, have active social lives, even biographies (for the sake of clarity, Kopytoff's [1986] now-famous article in that volume was concerned not with 'things' as such, but rather with how their exchange might help in investigating the concept of commodification). Whilst Joy (2009: 540-45) has traced subsequent, archaeological applications of object biographies, as well as their potentials and limitations, Tilley (2006: 10, original emphasis) had already argued that 'if things have their own biographies, it is but a short step to consider these things as having their own agency and actively having *effects* in relation to persons'. Such 'effects' might better be seen as 'affordances' (Knappett 2005; after Gibson 1977), which refers to an object's potential—or a landscape's usages—as defined by their *relational* material properties.

In Knappett's (2011: 63) example, a door may afford an opening to many people, but not to a child who cannot reach its handle. One of Keane's (2014: S315-16) examples of affordance is a wooden chair, which may afford sitting but also the possibility of use as a stepladder, a paperweight, a hat hook or, ultimately, as firewood. Crucially, the notion of affordance is indeterminate and relational. The material features of the chair afford its use for sitting, standing, or hanging your hat, but it is a human agent who decides which feature s/he wants, and for what purpose. Keane's essay is actually concerned with Eastern Orthodox icons, which have all the characteristics we associate with material objects: shape, size, weight, and solidity. He stresses (Keane 2014: S317):

> The material properties of the icons and all that surrounds them, including the places in which they are to be found and the actions people perform toward and with them, serve as affordances for further actions and reflections on them.

Elsewhere, Tilley (2007: 19) maintained that if we interpret 'agency' as providing affordances for living and acting in the world, as well as constraints for thought and action, then objects and landscapes may well 'influence forms of perception and activity, but they do not determine thought and action' (Tilley 2010: 29).

In a recent paper, Given (n.d.) has embraced the notion of material agency, arguing that the slag resulting from smelting copper ores on Cyprus plays an active role in material and social worlds. He examines Iron Age to Late Roman slag and slag heaps known from regional archaeological survey across the island, arguing for 'the elaborate entanglement that connected slag with other materials, humans and the environment'. In his view, '[a]ncient metallurgy is constituted by the lively roles of materials and processes, by dramas and biographies, and by ongoing flows of materials and identities' (Given n.d.). Here I take slag and some other archaeometallurgical things known from excavations at a Late Bronze Age (LBA) Cypriot site as my point of departure. I consider a range of archaeometallurgical materials, critically examining various notions related to their agency or cultural biography (and that of objects and things more generally).

My own position stems from concerns about the usefulness of approaches that so ardently embrace material or object agency. At least occasionally, it seems that 'the way things are' depends on who is examining them, what they are seeking to prove, and with which trends in social theory they seek to align themselves. Instead, we need to separate some of the chaff of materiality from the wheat of archaeological materials and material practices. There is no question that archaeology must focus not just on people but also on the material world that surrounds and often drives them, or flows with them. But we need to consider very carefully if, and to what extent, a thing-oriented approach may enhance or impoverish our understanding of human activity in the past, and our attempts to reconstruct or explain it. Ideally, we need to move on from a perspective that opposes people and ideas versus materials and material things to one that embraces and explores their mutual emergence (compare Witmore, this volume), even if not a common 'agency' (Lindstrøm 2015).

People and Things

Although it is preferable to distinguish between 'objects' (implies a perceiving subject), 'artifacts' (implies human intervention), and 'things' (neutral, ambiguous) (Knappett 2008; 2011: 175; van der Leeuw 2008: 222-23), in this study I slip back and forth in their usage, as their definition *per se* is not my concern. The relations between things (objects, artifacts) and people permeate both archaeological and social theory today: from agency (Dobres and Robb 2000), phenomenology (Ingold 2000), and object agency (Gosden 2005; Knappett and Malafouris 2008) to materiality and material agency (Meskell 2005; Miller 2005; Tilley *et al.* 2006), the cognitive life of things (Malafouris and Renfrew 2010), Actor Network Theory (ANT) (Latour 2005: Knappett 2008; 2011; van Oyen 2015), human–thing entanglements (Hodder 2011; 2012; Hodder and Mol 2015), and symmetrical archaeology (Shanks 2007; Webmoor and Witmore 2008; Olsen 2012b; Olsen *et al.* 2012; Webmoor 2013). Witmore (2014) discusses most of these approaches under the rubric of the 'new materialisms'.

The concept of 'materiality', which critiques the notion of separate material and cultural domains, and seeks to accommodate the material form of things (Hicks 2010: 74), focuses not just on object agency (e.g., Gosden 2005; Knappett and Malafouris 2008) but also and increasingly on networks and 'meshworks' (e.g., Ingold 2007; Robb 2010; Knappett 2011). Materiality basically focuses on the physical property of things and how that impacts on people (Jones and Boivin 2012: 3); it is now widely used to explore relationships between people and things, but in particular what things 'do' or what they 'are' (van der Veen 2014: 199). With respect to the social life of material things, Webmoor and Witmore (2008: 53) contend that: 'Something fundamental and potent is at work with the "social", but our [archaeological] explanations have come to be cloaked in a shroud of secrecy with regard to what the social is'. I would counter that, however one regards the social, many scholars seem to have some concept of what they mean by 'materiality', yet archaeological case study encounters with materiality remain few and their interpretations difficult to sustain.

Human–thing interaction may be seen in diverse ways: object and human biographies, making and exchanging things, communities or ecologies of practice, making places or contexts of social action (Tilley 2006; Witmore 2014). Robb (2013: 661) suggests that many of these factors 'foreground the causal potential for action in the mutually constitutive relationship between humans and material things'. If early attempts to assess the active role of material things tended to emphasize the social over the material, or production over consumption, the inevitable reaction was to argue that archaeologists had to 'take things more seriously' (Webmoor 2007), that things are not just material agents to be coveted, valued, owned, exchanged, feared, or fetishized, but rather '[things] are us' or can become us (Webmoor and Whitmore 2008). Thus we should not be focusing on what objects were made to be but instead on what they can be made to become (Gosden 2005: 208, citing Thomas 1991).

Concerning ANT (Latour 2005), Knappett (2008: 141-42) considers it to represent an approach to social phenomena whose aim is to decenter the human subject and to overcome any assumed ontological primacy of people by adopting some level of impartiality in social analysis. Such impartiality purportedly enables the focus to fall on things as well as on people, and at the same time shifts the focus onto relations between diverse elements in sociomaterial 'ensembles'.

Symmetrical archaeology, in turn, rejects any approach that might be seen as modernist in a Cartesian sense, and tends to value and essentialize things in and of themselves (Pluciennik 2013: 157). A symmetrical orientation seeks to place people and things on an equal footing (Thomas 2015: 24), and advocates an agnosticism with respect to the players in any social or technical analysis: it has proved to be influential as well as controversial, especially in acknowledging the possibility of non-anthropocentric agency in social and material practices (Webmoor 2013: 112; Olsen and Witmore 2015). As the main protagonists complain: '[A]cademic study has consistently privileged the human and cultural over the material-thing world … We are arguing for a symmetrical treatment of maker and material in the processes of making' (Olsen *et al.* 2012: 189). In this view, '[s]ymmetry involves an extended concern that includes how things exist, act, and affect one another apart from any human relations, whether or not this interaction eventually also affects human life' (Olsen *et al.* 2012: 13). Human agents are inseparable from and must always be engaged with the 'world of things' (Olsen *et al.* 2012: 159). As Witmore (2014: 204) says, 'things are things'; in a more expansive mood, Olsen and Witmore (2015: 191, original emphasis) state: 'Within a symmetrical approach, *every being in the world can equally be seen as a differentiated thing*; that is, farmers, centaurs, ruined temples, the goddess Athena, plowed furrows, earthworms and cisterns are equally individual and differentiated entities or units that cannot be broken into their parts'.

Thomas (2015: 24) notes that there is a 'growing tension' between the notion that archaeology must become a 'discipline of things' and a belief that archaeologists should not have to apologize for their concern with people in a social context (see also Fowles 2010: 23). Ingold (2012) complains that symmetrical archaeology fails to consider what living in the world might be like from a nonhuman perspective. Barrett (2014: 72), in turn, points out that in treating things as agents, and all materials as constituting 'entities', symmetrical archaeology has missed a crucial distinction between living and nonliving matter. Accordingly, it fails to investigate the 'distinctive features of human biology' that contribute to different kinds of humanity under diverse material and historical conditions. In Barrett's (2014: 65-66) view, human life must be distinguished from the physicality of nonhuman things, and archaeologists should focus on the ways that 'different qualities of humanness have been constituted in the symbiotic relationships between *Homo sapiens* and other living and non-living things'. Olsen and Witmore (2015: 189-90), on the defensive, claim that Barrett has only presented a classic case of 'purification', one again dissecting the world into two utterly opposed realms, life itself and 'base matter', where inanimate objects are 'secondary being(s)'.

Ingold (2007: 2-3, 9, 10) earlier had acknowledged that things are 'active constituents of a world-in-formation', but not because they are imbued with agency (similarly

Lindstrøm 2015: 229). He wants to step back from the materiality of objects and focus on the properties of materials, and he remains quite critical of works on materiality (as a concept) and material culture as opposed to the actual 'materials' of things, or non-things. In Ingold's perspective, it is the capacity, purpose, and especially the properties of a material that define an object. The discussions he criticizes are not about the 'tangible stuff' of craftsmen and producers but rather are concerned with 'the abstract ruminations of philosophers and [social and cultural] theorists'. He complains that such works are 'expounded in a language of grotesque impenetrability' in the context of other 'unfathomable qualities' such as agency, intentionality, sociality, spatiality, and embodiment, amongst others. He asks (Ingold 2007: 3, original emphasis): 'What academic perversion leads us to speak not of *materials and their properties* but of *the materiality of objects?*' In fact, Ingold's paper itself is not far removed from such unfathomable 'ruminations', albeit ostensibly concerned to present the 'empirical' angle by examining rocks, bone/horn, skin, wool, hair, air, water, etc. (similarly in Ingold's [2014] caustic response to Witmore 2014).

Like Ingold, others have turned to the nonhuman, organic, or inorganic world to consider agency and/or intentionality. At least one archaeologist has recently pondered the materiality of plants (van der Veen 2014), whilst an anthropologist evaluates the (relational) material agency of water (Strang 2014; cf. Normark 2015). All this leads down a somewhat slippery slope to a sweeping critique of 'anthropocentricity', which implies that the archaeological study of cultures need have no reference to humans, whether agents, individuals, subjects, or collectivities, but instead must focus on the nexus amongst things (Nativ 2014). Latour (2005: 70) too critiques anthropocentrism, arguing that instead we need to recognize that humans and things are equally involved in any action that takes place in the world (Thomas 2015: 24). In my view, such critiques should facilitate a focus on interactions *amongst* humans, other living beings, and things, each with their own particular affordances.

Robb (2010: 514) declares that '[u]nderstanding forms of agency different from our own is perhaps the most difficult challenge we face as prehistoric anthropologists'. Indeed, archaeologists have become divided in their thinking about material agency, some embracing a view that such agency involves a nearly autonomous intentionality, agenda, and range of action (e.g., Olsen 2003; 2012b; Webmoor and Witmore 2008; Olsen *et al.* 2012), others adopting a (more moderate) stance that stresses how material objects embody and incorporate intra-human relations and thus have the capacity to affect the way people act (e.g., Gosden and Marshall 1999; Meskell 2004). Pauketat's recent review (*Cambridge Archaeological Journal* 25 [2015]: 909-11) of four key volumes representative of the 'ontological turn' in archaeology deftly points out that this turn involves moving away from 'representational' approaches (e.g., agency, ideology, society) toward 'relational' theories, i.e., those that embrace '… the kinds, dimensions and implications of relationships themselves'.

In the view of Knappett and Malafouris (2008), material agency is not concerned with changing the locus of agency from humans to materials, but rather with considering materials as critical in examining processes of agency. Lindstrøm (2015) presents a much more sweeping if less focused critique of symmetrical archaeologists' use of the term 'agency'; he maintains that it becomes logically meaningless if applied to anything that moves or has some effect on its surroundings. In his view, 'only animals and humans have agency proper' (Lindstrøm 2015: 227). I am more inclined to the view of Robb (2010: 494): '[A]gency is fundamentally material … because material things mediate and form the context for relationships between people, and because people form important relations with material things'. If we define 'agency' as a capacity to act or be acted upon, then it is possible to pursue discussions of the agentive capacities of objects, landscapes, animals, plants, air, water, and so on. As Strang (2014: 166-67) argues in her paper on water and agency, 'whether human groups succeed in taming a river or not, it remains "a force to be reckoned with"'. In considering the capacity of water to carve a river bank, and the ability of rock to resist, we might therefore imagine (with Ingold) that the intrinsic agency of material things is located in their particular physical properties, and that these and their agentive capacities exist independently of human interpretation of them. We might *equally* say, however, that these properties make things 'good to think with'. Accepting that things have agentive capacities does not obviate human agency in manipulating or managing the material world.

In discussing the 'material-cultural turn' in archaeology and anthropology, Hicks (2010) elaborates on the many ways that archaeologists and anthropologists differ in their attitudes and approaches to material culture studies, materiality and materials. As a field of study, archaeology has (almost) always been concerned with the study of people in the past *through their material remains*. Witmore (2014: 204), however, claims otherwise: '[A]rchaeology has shed its old definition as the study of the human past through its material remains in favor of a more befitting self-definition as the discipline of things, as an "ecology of practices" that approaches the world with care and in wonder', which in turn 'enables us to think of an archaeology without the Past'. Shouldn't archaeology be concerned with materials and things in both the present and 'the Past'? No matter how much we might agree that archaeology is all about things, it is still about human beings as well, and not just people classified by materialists as another class of (living) thing (Edgeworth 2014: 227).

Being neither a philosopher nor a rhetorician, I do not propose to take up the **intellectual challenge of** reconciling the relationship between matter and meaning. Indeed, why would I, now that every new issue of, e.g., *Norwegian Archaeological Review*, *Archaeological Dialogues*, or the *Journal of Contemporary Archaeology* publishes point and counterpoint on symmetrical archaeology? I would say, however, that there is a great deal of philosophical inflation in this entire arena of discussion, which art theorists would label as 'post-critical' (e.g., Foster 2015). 'Criticality', necessarily, requires someone to assume a certain distance, or detachment, and to remind those leading the discussion that we are not always all on the same side, at least not all of the time. Consequently, I persist in the view that agency or intentionality are best applied to matter by a thinking (i.e., human) subject. Those who feel otherwise need to develop much more explicitly—much more critically—their philosophical ruminations about how and why the complex nexus of humans, things, animals, plants, etc. that we deem to be 'social' is not initiated by people.

The Biography and Materiality of Things

The basic idea behind a cultural biography of things is that objects are constantly transformed through time and space, that the transformations of people and objects are closely bound up with each other, and that the meanings of objects change and are renegotiated throughout an object's life (Gosden and Marshall 1999: 169-70). Biographical approaches to material culture critique any binary distinction between people and things, and argue instead that they are intermingled and mutually constructed in social life (Dakouri-Held 2013: 312; see also Kopytoff 1986: 90). In terms of their biographies, objects may be either 'lived' (derived from social actions) or 'inscribed' (a consequence of their design) (Marshall 2008: 63-65; Joy 2009: 545), what Robb (2004; 2010: 505) terms 'extended' artifacts. Objects are the intentional products of human action or design, but they may 'act' as agents that direct human use and maintenance (Gosden and Marshall 1999: 173-74). Based on its lived or inscribed social life, the aura with which an object is imbued is at least in part what loads an object with agency (Burström 2014: 67).

Moreover, the impact of an object's agency is not only dependent on its biography, but also is increasingly seen as resulting from its material characteristics. Indeed, the capacity of acting must inhere in part in the material in question (Knappett 2011: 173). Even if, however, an object's materiality is regarded as agentive in itself, its meaning remains ambiguous, resisting some possibilities whilst affording others. In pre-modern contexts, the material itself—its physical, chemical, tactile, and visual properties—must always have been an essential part of an object's biography, the very core of its 'thingness', which went some way in determining its social value (Panagiotopoulos 2013: 149).

Materials not only have properties, which are objective or at least measurable, but also qualities, which are subjective, i.e., imposed by human agents (Pye 1968: 47, as noted by Panagiotopoulos 2013: 149, and, negatively, by Ingold 2007: 14). The (apparent) fact that many elites in the LBA eastern Mediterranean preferred objects made of ivory rather than cheaper and more common bone, or selected exotic lapis lazuli cylinder seals in a context (Bronze Age Aegean palace at Thebes) where such objects were not related to their normal (sealing) function, suggests that the authenticity of the material rather than the external appearance of the object—i.e., the qualities, not the properties of the material—is what was important (Panagiotopoulos 2013: 163-65). If we turn to examine another set of decidedly non-elite, archaeometallurgical materials and things, what can we say about their 'properties' and 'qualities', their materiality and biographies?

Archaeometallurgical Things

As argued above, if we are to accept the basic concepts associated with object biography or material agency, we must also consider the extent to which thing-oriented approaches enhance or impoverish archaeological understanding of, and attempts to reconstruct or explain, past human activity. In what follows, looking through the lens provided by some unusual things, I assess some of the prevalent views discussed above on material agency, considering whether they obscure or illuminate attempts to nuance our understanding of the material and behavioural past.

According to Olsen *et al.* (2012: 66, original emphasis), 'postexcavation work with the material is still a material encounter qualitatively comparable to those experienced during fieldwork', and an immediate familiarity with such material that has been cleaned, examined, and analyzed is 'indispensable for a *discipline* of things' and '*increases* the potential meaningfulness of things'. Here I discuss various cleaned, examined, and analyzed things from excavations at a Bronze Age archaeometallurgical site on Cyprus, and consider how—or if—we might assess them with respect to their biographic or agential meanings.

The Sydney Cyprus Survey Project and Politiko *Phorades*

Slag is glorious ... Slag *is* the flow. (Given n.d.)

During the course of the Sydney Cyprus Survey Project (Given and Knapp 2003), an intensive field survey conducted in the northern foothills of the Troodos mountain range (Figure 14.1), our geomorphologist observed some slag and furnace material eroding from the bank of a dry creek bed, material that proved to be unprecedented in Cypriot archaeology and archaeometallurgy. Once anointed a 'site', Politiko *Phorades* was excavated over three field seasons (1997, 1998, 2000) and is now interpreted as a small copper-smelting workshop (Knapp 2003; Knapp and Kassianidou 2008). Radiocarbon dates, stratified pottery and the geological setting all place *Phorades* in an early phase of the LBA (ca. 1650–1500 BC).

Although the stratigraphy of the slag heap at *Phorades* proved to be complex, geomorphological input helped us to untangle the differing natural and anthropogenic forces (agencies?) that resulted in the site's formation. The excavations showed that the metalworkers used river channel deposits to construct an artificial bank, a flat working platform within which we uncovered a stone-lined cavity holding several tuyère fragments, and around which were several almost complete tuyères (Figure 14.2). This cavity was somehow related to the smelting process, perhaps a tapping pit. The slag produced was piled against the creek's bank, and eventually formed a small heap.

The 3.5 tons of slag fragments excavated at *Phorades* differ in type and shape from all other known slags excavated on Cyprus, e.g., from Middle Bronze Age Alambra *Mouttes* (Gale *et al.* 1996: 389-90, 414) and Pyrgos *Mavrorachi* (Giardino 2000: 21), and from LBA Apliki *Karamallos* (Muhly 1989: 306) and Kition (Tylecote 1982: 89). This slag was homogeneous, very dense, and magnetic. Given (n.d.) describes slag in general as follows: '[S]lag has a very real and powerful materiality that compels us to feel its properties'. As he maintains, slag is 'good to think with' and 'forces us to engage with the materiality and sensuality of the whole production process, before, during and after the actual smelting'. He discusses phenomenologically if not poetically the

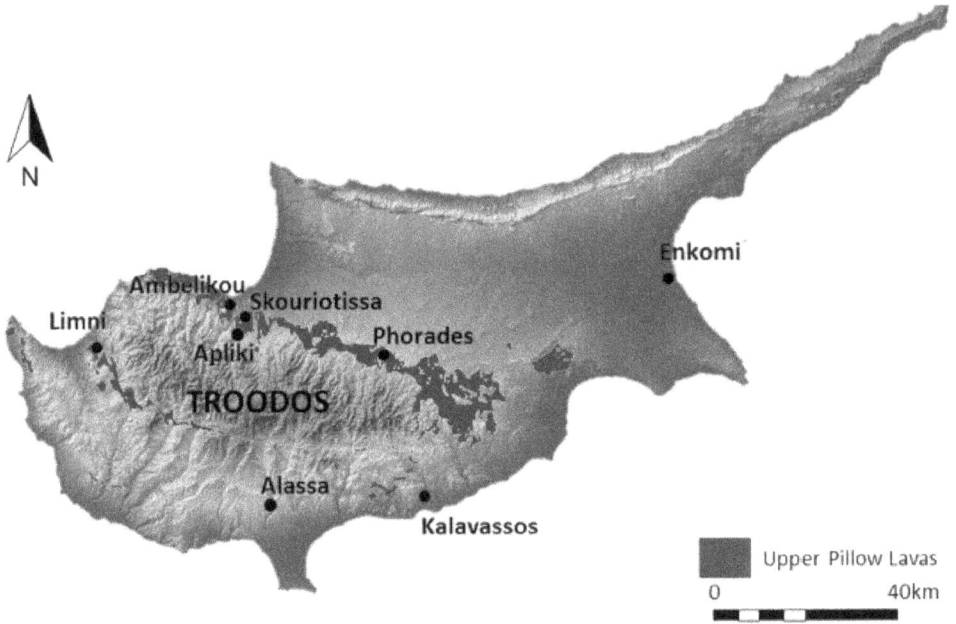

Figure 14.1   Map of Cyprus showing Upper Pillow Lava formations and the location of Politiko *Phorades* (map produced by A. Agapiou with digital data provided by the Cyprus Geological Survey; courtesy of Vasiliki Kassianidou).

Figure 14.2   Stone-lined cavity (black arrow) and tuyères (white arrows) from Politiko *Phorades* (photograph by Paul Duffy).

sounds, smells, and entanglements of slag, always linking his narrative to material and documentary evidence. And, although I would not agree that a slag cake has an 'ongoing life', it does have an *after*life (see further below). Moreover, when Given describes slag's 'materiality', he is at times gratifyingly explicit, at other times indulgently lyrical:

> The materiality of slag encompasses the geological and hydrological processes that produced the ore and flux, the compressed air forced through the bellows, the soil in which the *Pinus brutia* grew to supply the charcoal, the river that lay down the sediment which formed the clay for the furnace lining.
> ... In the materiality of the slag lives the interaction with the heat and charcoal and flux in the furnace, the running slag meeting the surfaces of the pit, blows from the hammer in the hands of the worker, the scratching of the sharp chipped stones under the threshing sledge.

Back at *Phorades*, bulk chemical analysis (using X-ray fluorescence) of the slags revealed high percentages of iron oxides. Within the slag matrix, microanalysis revealed not only tiny prills, but also a small fragment of matte, silver-blue in color (Figure 14.3).

In other words, after a range of post-excavation analytical work, we were able to determine that the metal produced in the smelter at *Phorades* was matte, the result of an intermediate step in the production of copper metal. Matte has always proved quite rare in excavations of archaeometallurgical sites (Graziadio 2014 lists some examples). In order to produce copper metal (perhaps in the form of an oxhide ingot), matte had

c. 1 cm

Figure 14.3   A small piece of silver-blue matte from *Phorades*: 73.5% copper, 2.6% iron and 23.9% sulphur (courtesy of Vasiliki Kassianidou).

to undergo a series of further transformations, each of which would produce a different type of slag. With the exception of one slag sample—which contained matte as well as black copper (another intermediate product with a high percentage of copper)—among those analyzed, all others represent primary smelting slags. In other words, it would seem that only this initial stage in the process of producing copper metal took place at *Phorades*.

Whilst the presence of matte is a clear indicator that *Phorades* was a primary smelting workshop, how should we understand its biography? How might we define its aura or determine what loads it with agency—if it has any? According to Olsen *et al.* (2012: 201-203, original emphasis), archaeologists need to recognize that things make a difference and play some role in their own formation: indeed, 'respecting the integrity and otherness of things includes their right *not* to be meaningful', and 'the thing is mostly significant for what it *is*'. So, following that view, should we conclude that the matte has no meaning other than its matte-ness? Given (n.d.) suggests that matte, along with slag, and the smell of the smelting process, were all part of the 'generative process', reflecting the 'rhythms of material and human collaboration'. Similarly, Doonan *et al.* (2012: 56) see the smelting process at the Cypriot site of Maroni *Vournes* as an unfolding 'choreographed drama', an 'olfactory encounter' that embedded itself in the memories of the community and heightened their sense of identity and place. For some, then, matte certainly does exude an aura, into which you may read whatever you wish.

Whilst the relevant literature suggests that an object's agency is dependent on its biography, increasingly it is also seen as resulting from the material itself—its physical, chemical, tactile, and visual properties. When it comes to matte, we know its chemical makeup, and we can see and feel a 'cold' piece of silvery-blue metal, but how do we determine its biography or assess its agency?

Had the metallurgical process gone as planned, the matte would have been transformed into another thing, a copper oxhide ingot (not, then, as Given n.d., sees copper—'an absence, a removal, a biography cut short'). Clearly oxhide ingots have biographies (if not some agency) when they were not themselves transformed into other things—copper or bronze statuettes, stands, weapons, jewellery, and so on. I would accept the notion that, depending on their context, oxhide ingots—especially those that crossed cultural borders—have compelling biographies well worth pursuing (e.g., those found on Sardinia in hoards, cult sites, and Nuragic villages, perhaps in workshops—Blake 2014: 101-102). I would also entertain the notion that such ingots might be assigned some agency, or at least 'mutability' (Panagiotopoulos 2013: 167-68). I am less confident, however, that we can establish a biography for or discuss the agency of our small piece of matte, or for that matter of various other things recovered in the excavations at *Phorades*.

During the excavations, for example, we recovered more than 6000 fragments of coarsely made furnace rims, walls, and bases (Hein *et al.* 2007: 146-47). Some fingerprint impressions on these fragments, most often where the wall joins the base, show that the furnaces were designed and made—by human agents—to stand alone. Although I see no biographies for these furnaces, Given (n.d.) embeds in his discussion of the 'sounds of slag' the 'throbbing roar of the furnace', the human engagement with what is happening inside the furnace, and the building and stoking of furnaces within (Iron Age) slag heaps. And, of course, if one views metallurgy as a continual interaction between materials, heat, and human practices (Deleuze and Guattari 1987: 404-15), or as an 'unbroken contrapuntal coupling of a gestural dance with a modulation of the material' (Ingold 2012: 434) (both cited in Given n.d.), you could no doubt concoct a furnace-based biography (tracing the materials, construction, use, and dismantling to remove matte and slag; then its role in the site formation process, its excavation, and afterlife). In my view, however, furnaces only *afford* the smelting of metal and the ultimate transformation of that metal into something (an oxhide ingot) whose biography might be traced.

Both the matte and the furnace(s), however, might be seen from another perspective. Hahn and Weiss (2013: 4) suggest that new meanings emerge for a thing/object whose use came to an end during its 'first *life-span*' (the afterlife being its 'second life'). Pondering the meanings of these things in the 'here-now' as opposed to the 'there-then' (Knappett 2013: 39), we might consider them as waste, or we might think about how they produce new meanings after being discarded or left behind. Given's (n.d.) view is that slag cakes, at least, 'have lives of their own, which continue to unfold and develop millennia after they were first tapped out of their furnaces in molten form'. That may be so, but how we value such things in archaeology is clear: the matte and slag from *Phorades*, as well as the furnaces that were left to decay, had become worthless to those who made or produced them. For archaeologists, however, these things have become valuable for interpretation, as the matte is virtually unique in the history of archaeometallurgical research on Cyprus (there are matte inclusions within conglomerate slags at Maroni *Vournes*: Doonan *et al.* 2012: 54). Moreover, most of the (fragmentary) objects previously identified as 'furnaces' were most likely casting pits, or hearths in which crucibles, used either for refining or melting metal, were heated (Kassianidou 2012: 103; for the purported furnaces, see Dikaios 1969–71, I: 22, 58; Tylecote 1982: 92; Stech *et al.* 1985: 388-90).

The excavations at *Phorades* also produced other things abandoned after their first life-span: e.g., 50 almost complete tuyères and up to 600 tuyère fragments belonging to three different types; cylindrical, double-walled (unique on Cyprus), and elbow (one example) (Figure 14.4). When the nozzles of these objects are preserved, they are slagged and highly vitrified. Detailed chemical, mineralogical, and petrographic analyses of the furnaces and tuyères from *Phorades* (Hein and Kilikoglou 2007; Hein *et al.* 2007) demonstrate that the people who conducted the smelting operations had made these objects from local, heat-resistant clays, to withstand temperatures up to 1200° C.

In the view of Olsen *et al.* (2012: 186, 189), we cannot explain adequately the meanings of things by subordinating them to their maker's intentions, or, for that

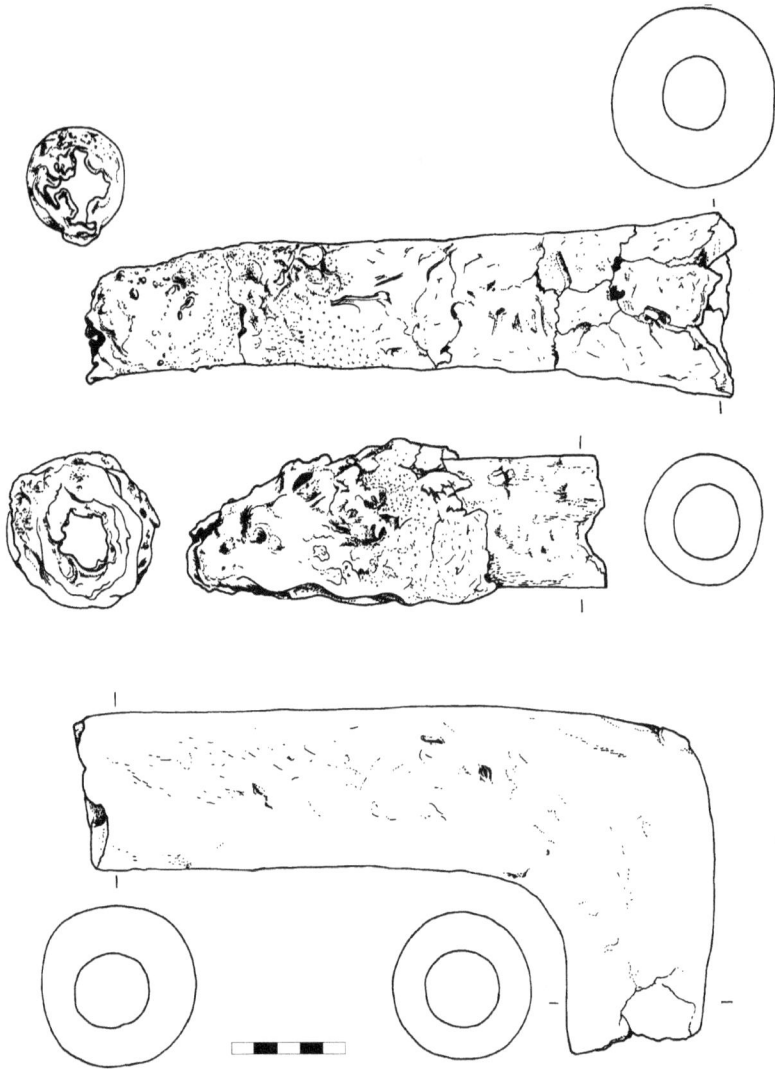

Figure 14.4   Three types of tuyères from Politiko *Phorades*: cylindrical, double-walled, and elbow (drawn by Glynnis Fawkes).

matter, to economic necessity. They lament the loss of the meaning and integrity of the actual materials or the 'raw materiality' of objects, of subsuming the issue of how things get made within their social, 'extramaterial' aspects. I would suggest, on the contrary, that in the myriad analyses carried out on these archaeometallurgical things (e.g., Kassianidou 1999; 2011; Hein *et al.* 2007; Hein and Kilikoglou 2007; 2011), we have come to the fullest possible terms with their basic material essence, i.e., their 'raw materiality'. Moreover, we have already proceeded to consider the obvious entanglements between these objects and their maker, or their context(s) of production, use, or consumption (Knapp 2003; Knapp and Kassianidou 2008). Surely we have not subordinated materiality to the will of a maker or the nature of the social structure? We now understand that *Phorades* was a primary smelting workshop, and we know from other archaeometallurgical evidence found in the coastal towns of LBA Cyprus (Knapp 2012: 17-18; Kassianidou 2013) that further, secondary smelting and refining processes were carried out in those centers, where the matte or black copper became transformed into standardized (oxhide) ingots that were distributed and consumed, within and beyond the island.

The materials excavated at *Phorades* enabled us to reconstruct the activities that once occurred at the site. The concentrations of broken tuyères and furnace fragments, the large quantities of slag, and a suite of archaeometallurgical analyses all show that *Phorades* was a primary smelting workshop. Once the operation was shut down, all those things left behind (the slag, the broken installations, and metallurgical detritus) no longer had any use. Like Knappett's (2013) Bronze Age Aegean sealings, these things had only a temporary existence and their durable 'imprint' evokes both presence and absence, loss and discovery, past and present.

With object biographies, or object 'itineraries' (Hahn and Weiss 2013), the perceived beginning and ending of an object may be difficult to pinpoint, but their transformation (e.g., the matte that would have become part of an oxhide ingot, or ultimately a metal artifact) is often more evident. New things thus emerge from the remodeling of other things, and objects that have been buried, lost, discarded, or left behind gain new relevance upon their rediscovery (Hahn and Weiss 2013: 7-8). Many objects pass through long periods of stasis before their transformation, but in the case of the matte, slag, tuyères, and furnace remains from *Phorades*, can we say that these things initiated the transformation? I would suggest instead that these recently recovered objects have been re-evaluated, or redefined in a new (archaeological) context. It is now possible to make more informed statements about the production and circulation of copper metal, and its transformation into other, intermediate (ingots) or ultimate objects and things (weapons, stands, statuettes), much the same as Joy (2009: 546-52) has done for a British Iron Age bronze mirror. The end result is that we have been able to reconstruct in more convincing detail the smelting technology at work during the mid-second millennium BC on Cyprus, and the likely community setting in which that technology, and those transformations, were carried out (Knapp 2003).

Conclusions

When we say, metaphorically, that something, or 'some thing', makes us sad, or happy, or melancholy, we do not mean that it does so intentionally (Depner 2013: 86). If we say a building 'impresses' us, it is we that have such an impression (Lindstrøm 2015: 216). Some things, however, clearly are more than just charged with memory and meaning, and it is crucial to examine individual objects in order to comprehend better their material characteristics, their material existence.

Olsen (2012a: 100) makes the crucial point that we need to overcome the artificial separation between data, methodology, and theory, all too common in the archaeology of Cyprus and the eastern Mediterranean. And we must we must explore the common ground where theory interacts with and is infused by data, thus no longer separating the 'what' from the 'how' of material things. Ever since Kopytoff's (1986) initial study, archaeologists and material-culture specialists have engaged the biography concept in diverse and intriguing ways. Some would say that such studies have tended to overplay an object's agency (Hoskins 2006: 75; Fontijn 2013: 187), or to see it through a theoretical veneer that infuses an object with human agency or colors its perception with some other quality of human life (Fontijn 2013: 192).

Do things have lives of their own that people cannot predict or control? Perhaps, with some things, as that is *the way things are*. The loss or depletion or decay of some things, or the invention and adoption of other things, may have unforeseen effects. It all depends on how you want to see these things. You might, for example, choose to view the onset of the Neolithic and the turn to a more settled way of living as a time when human life and human culture became increasingly material, when people began to accumulate more material things, newly domesticated animals, recently cultivated crops. Alternatively, you could choose to view this as a time when the ever-increasing accumulation of material things forced people to become more sedentary (Hodder 2014: 28). To my way of thinking, that would be tantamount to saying that the intensified production of copper in Late Bronze Age Cyprus forced its makers to exchange it, or to make more, new, and different things.

For Given (n.d.), slag has a rich and continuing biography—in its modern-day use for village and vineyard terrace walls, threshing floors, paving of country roads, and the manufacture of cement. Its materiality ('the *slagness* of slag') is portrayed as the transformations—the 'flows and fluxes'—it undergoes, from the collecting of ores, additives, and charcoal to the tapping out of the molten mixture, to the hardness of the end product. This strikes me, however, as an Ingoldian type of materiality that rejects the notion of form imposed by human intention onto an inert lump of 'raw material' and instead proposes a 'contrapuntal coupling of a gestural dance with a modulation of the material' (Ingold 2012: 434), what Given glosses as 'ongoing flux and form-taking activity'. In my view, using Ingold's own terms, this portrays slag in 'a language of grotesque impenetrability' proposing 'unfathomable qualities' that make materiality as opaque as Ingold's (2007: 2–3, fig. 1) stone.

Acknowledgments

I am grateful to the editors for inviting me to be involved in this volume honoring a long-term colleague and friend, one who has always appreciated a critical glance at archaeological views that seem either too traditional, or too radical. I also thank the editors for attempting to make this study 'conform' to the rest of the volume: Thomas Leppard in particular made some comments about a 'thing-oriented approach' that

I have woven into this study. My thanks also go to another long-term colleague and collaborator, Michael Given, who provided not only invaluable comments on an earlier version of this paper, but also a draft of his forthcoming paper, which came at a crucial point in my deliberations about just where my arguments in this chapter might go; without his engaging and original ideas, they might have gone nowhere.

About the Author

A. Bernard Knapp is Emeritus Professor of Mediterranean Archaeology in Archaeology, Department of Humanities, at the University of Glasgow, and Honorary Research Fellow at the Cyprus American Archaeological Research Institute. He co-edits the *Journal of Mediterranean Archaeology* with John F. Cherry and Peter van Dommelen and is the general editor of the series *Monographs in Mediterranean Archaeology* (Equinox). He is the author or editor of several books including, most recently, *The Cambridge Prehistory of the Bronze and Iron Age Mediterranean* (Cambridge University Press, 2014), co-edited with Peter van Dommelen, and, co-authored with Stella Demesticha, *Mediterranean Connections: Maritime Transport Containers and Seaborne Trade in the Bronze and Early Iron Ages* (Routledge, 2017). E-mail: Bernard.Knapp@glasgow.ac.uk

References

Appadurai, A. (ed.)
  1986 *The Social Life of Things: Commodities in Cultural Perspective.* Cambridge: Cambridge University Press.
Barrett, J.C.
  2014 The material constitution of humanness. *Archaeological Dialogues* 21: 65-74. https://doi.org/10.1017/S1380203814000105
Blake, E.
  2014 Late Bronze Age Sardinia: acephalous cohesion. In A.B. Knapp and P. van Dommelen (eds.), *The Cambridge Prehistory of the Bronze and Iron Age Mediterranean*, 96-108. New York: Cambridge University Press. https://doi.org/10.1017/cho9781139028387.009
Burström, N.M.
  2014 Things in the eye of the beholder: a humanistic perspective on archaeological object biographies. *Norwegian Archaeological Review* 47: 65-82.

https://doi.org/10.1080/00293652.2014.909877
Dakouri-Held, A.
  2013 Craft and sensory play in Late Bronze Age Boeotia. In J. Day (ed.), *Making Senses of the Past: Toward a Sensory Archaeology.* Center for Archaeological Investigations, Southern Illinois University Carbondale, Occasional Paper 40: 310-34. Carbondale and Edwardsville: Southern Illinois University.
Deleuze, G., and F. Guattari
  1987 *A Thousand Plateaus: Capitalism and Schizophrenia.* Trans. B. Massumi. London: Continuum.
Depner, A.
  2013 Worthless things? On the difference between devaluing and sorting out things. In H.P. Hahn and H. Weiss (eds.), *Mobility, Meaning and Transformations of Things: Shifting Contexts*

of Material Culture through Time and Space, 78-90. Oxford: Oxbow Books.

Dikaios, P.
1969–71 *Enkomi: Excavations 1948-1958*. 3 vols. Mainz-am-Rhein: Philip von Zabern.

Dobres, M.-A., and J. Robb (eds.)
2000 *Agency in Archaeology*. London and New York: Routledge.

Doonan, R.C.P., G. Cadogan and D. Sewell
2012 Standing on ceremony: the metallurgical finds from Maroni *Vournes*, Cyprus. In V. Kassianidou and G. Papasavvas (eds.), *Eastern Mediterranean Metallurgy and Metalwork in the Second Millennium BC*, 48-57. Oxford: Oxbow Books.

Edgeworth, M.
2014 Material and cognitive dimensions of archaeological evidence. *Journal of Contemporary Archaeology* 1: 225-27. https://doi.org/10.1558/jca.v1i2.26673

Fontijn, D.
2013 Epilogue. Cultural biographies and itineraries of things: second thoughts. In H.P. Hahn and H. Weiss (eds.), *Mobility, Meaning and Transformations of Things: Shifting Contexts of Material Culture through Time and Space*, 183-95. Oxford: Oxbow Books.

Foster, H.
2015 *Bad New Days: Art, Criticism, Emergency*. London: Verso Books.

Fowles, S.
2010 People without things. In M. Bille, F. Hastrup and T.K. Sørenson (eds.), *An Anthropology of Absence: Materialities of Transcendence and Loss*, 23-41. London: Springer. https://doi.org/10.1007/978-1-4419-5529-6_2

Gale, N.H., Z.A. Stos-Gale and W. Fasnacht
1996 Copper and copper working at Alambra. In J.E. Coleman, J.A. Barlow, M.K. Mogelonsky and K.W. Scharr, *Alambra: A Middle Bronze Age Site in Cyprus. Investigations by Cornell University, 1974-1984*. Studies in Mediterranean Archaeology 118: 359-426. Jonsered: Paul Åström's Förlag.

Giardino, C.
2000 Prehistoric copper activity at Pyrgos. *Report of the Department of Antiquities, Cyprus*: 19-32.

Gibson, J.J.
1977 The theory of affordances. In R. Shaw and J. Bransford (eds.), *Perceiving, Acting, and Knowing: Toward an Ecological Psychology*, 67-82. Hillsdale, New Jersey: Erlbaum.

Given, M.
n.d. Island of slag: the materiality, monumentality and biography of copper slag on Cyprus. In L.C. Nevett and J. Whitley (eds.), *An Age of Experiment: Classical Archaeology Transformed 1976-2014*, Cambridge: McDonald Institute for Archaeological Research (in press).

Given, M., and A.B. Knapp
2003 *The Sydney Cyprus Survey Project: Social Approaches to Regional Archaeological Survey*. Monumenta Archaeologica 21. Los Angeles: Cotsen Institute of Archaeology.

Gosden, C.
2005 What do objects want? *Journal of Archaeological Method and Theory* 12: 193-211. https://doi.org/10.1007/s10816-005-6928-x

Gosden, C., and Y. Marshall
1999 The cultural biography of objects. *World Archaeology* 31: 169-78. https://doi.org/10.1080/00438243.1999.9980439

Graziadio, G.
2014 The oxhide ingots production in the eastern Mediterranean. *Egitto e Vicono Oriente* 37: 5-25.

Hahn, H.P., and H. Weiss
2013 Introduction: biographies, travels and itineraries of things. In H.P. Hahn and H. Weiss (eds.), *Mobility, Meaning and Transformations of Things: Shifting Contexts of Material Culture through Time and Space*, 1-13. Oxford: Oxbow Books.

Hein, A., and V. Kilikoglou
2007 Modeling of thermal behavior of ancient metallurgical ceramics. *Journal of the American Ceramic Society*

90: 878-84. https://doi.org/10.1111/j.1551-2916.2006.01466.x

2011 Technological aspects of Bronze Age metallurgical ceramics in the eastern Mediterranean. In P.P. Betancourt and S.C. Ferrence (eds.), *Metallurgy: Understanding How, Learning Why. Studies in Honor of James D. Muhly*, 181-87. Philadelphia: Institute for Aegean Prehistory Press.

Hein, A., V. Kilikoglou and V. Kassianidou

2007 Chemical and mineralogical examination of metallurgical ceramics from a Late Bronze Age copper smelting site in Cyprus. *Journal of Archaeological Science* 34: 141-54. https://doi.org/10.1016/j.jas.2006.04.005

Hicks, D.

2010 The material-cultural turn: event and effect. In D. Hicks and M.C. Beaudry (eds.), *The Oxford Handbook of Material Culture Studies*, 25-98. Oxford: Oxford University Press.

Hodder, I.

2011 Human-thing entanglement: towards an integrated archaeological perspective. *Journal of the Royal Anthropological Institute* 17: 154-77. https://doi.org/10.1111/j.1467-9655.2010.01674.x

2012 *Entangled: An Archaeology of the Relationships between Humans and Things*. Oxford: Wiley-Blackwell. https://doi.org/10.1002/9781118241912

2014 The entanglements of humans and things: a long-term view. *New Literary History* 45: 19-36. https://doi.org/10.1353/nlh.2014.0005

Hodder, I., and A. Mol

2015 Network analysis and entanglement. *Journal of Archaeological Method and Theory* 23: 1-29.

Hoskins, J.

1998 *Biographical Objects: How Things Tell the Stories of People's Lives*. London and New York: Routledge.

2006 Agency, biography and objects. In C. Tilley, W. Keane, S. Küchler, M. Rowlands and P. Spyer (eds), *Hand-*

book of Material Culture, 74-84. London: Sage. https://doi.org/10.4135/9781848607972.n6

Ingold, T.

2000 *The Perception of the Environment: Essays in Livelihood, Dwelling and Skill*. London and New York: Routledge. https://doi.org/10.4324/9780203466025

2007 Materials against materiality. *Archaeological Dialogues* 14: 1-15. https://doi.org/10.1017/S1380203807002127

2012 Toward an ecology of materials. *Annual Review of Anthropology* 41: 427-42. https://doi.org/10.1146/annurev-anthro-081309-145920

2014 Is there life amidst the ruins? *Journal of Contemporary Archaeology* 1: 231-35. https://doi.org/10.1558/jca.v1i2.26675

Jones, A.M., and N. Boivin

2012 The malice of inanimate objects: material agency. In D. Hicks and M.C. Beaudry (eds.), *The Oxford Handbook of Material Culture Studies*, 333-51. Oxford: Oxford University Press.

Joy, J.

2009 Reinvigorating object biography: reproducing the drama of object lives. *World Archaeology* 41: 540-56. https://doi.org/10.1080/00438240903345530

Kassianidou, V.

1999 Bronze Age copper smelting technology in Cyprus—the evidence from Politico *Phorades*. In S.M.M. Young, A.M. Pollard, P. Budd and R.A. Ixer (eds.), *Metals in Antiquity*. British Archaeological Reports, International Series 792: 91-97. Oxford: Archaeopress.

2011 Blowing the wind of change: the introduction of bellows in Late Bronze Age Cyprus. In P.P. Betancourt and S.C. Ferrence (eds.), *Metallurgy: Understanding How, Learning Why. Studies in Honor of James D. Muhly*, 41-47. Philadelphia: Institute for Aegean Prehistory Press.

2012 Metallurgy and metalwork in Enkomi:

the early phases. In V. Kassianidou and G. Papasavvas (eds.), *Eastern Mediterranean Metallurgy and Metalwork in the Second Millennium BC*, 94-106. Oxford: Oxbow Books.

2013 The production and trade of Cypriot copper in the Late Bronze Age: an analysis of the evidence. *Pasiphae* 7: 133-46.

Keane, W.

2014 Rotting bodies: the clash of stances toward materiality and its ethical affordances. In *The Anthropology of Christianity: Unity, Diversity, New Directions.* Supplement 10 to *Current Anthropology* 55: S312-21. https://doi.org/10.1086/678290

Knapp, A.B.

2003 The archaeology of community on Bronze Age Cyprus: Politiko *Phorades* in context. *American Journal of Archaeology* 107: 559-80. https://doi.org/10.3764/aja.107.4.559

2012 Metallurgical production and trade on Bronze Age Cyprus: views and variations. In V. Kassianidou and G. Papasavvas (eds.), *Eastern Mediterranean Metallurgy and Metalwork in the Second Millennium BC*, 14-25. Oxford: Oxbow Books.

Knapp, A.B., and V. Kassianidou

2008 The archaeology of Late Bronze Age copper production: Politiko *Phorades* on Cyprus. In Ü. Yalçin (ed.), *Anatolian Metal* IV. *Frühe Rohstoffgewinnung in Anatolien und seinen Nachbarländern.* Die Anschnitt, Beiheft 21. Veröffentlichungen aus dem Deutschen Bergbau-Museum 157: 135-47. Bochum: Deutsches Bergbau-Museum.

Knappett, C.

2005 *Thinking Through Material Culture: An Interdisciplinary Perspective.* Philadelphia: University of Pennsylvania Press. https://doi.org/10.9783/9780812202496

2008 The neglected networks of material agency: artefacts, pictures and texts.

In C. Knappett and L. Malafouris (eds.), *Material Agency: Towards a Non-Anthropocentric Approach*, 139-56. New York: Springer. https://doi.org/10.9783/9780812202496

2011 *An Archaeology of Interaction: Network Perspectives on Material Culture and Society.* Oxford: Oxford University Press. https://doi.org/10.1093/acprof:osobl/9780199215454.001.0001

2013 Imprints as punctuations of material itineraries. In H.P. Hahn and H. Weiss (eds.), *Mobility, Meaning and Transformations of Things: Shifting Contexts of Material Culture through Time and Space*, 37-49. Oxford: Oxbow Books.

Knappett, C., and L. Malafouris (eds.)

2008 *Material Agency: Towards a Non-Anthropocentric Approach.* New York: Springer.

Kopytoff, I.

1986 The cultural biography of things: commoditization as process. In A. Appadurai (ed.), *The Social Life of Things: Commodities in Cultural Perspective*, 64-91. Cambridge: Cambridge University Press. https://doi.org/10.1017/cbo9780511819582.004

Latour, B.

2005 *Reassembling the Social: An Introduction to Actor-Network-Theory.* Oxford: Oxford University Press.

Leach, E.

1977 A view from the bridge. In M. Spriggs (ed.), *Archaeology and Anthropology: Areas of Mutual Interest.* British Archaeological Reports, Supplementary Series 19: 161-76. Oxford: British Archaeological Reports.

Lindstrøm, T.C.

2015 Agency 'in itself': a discussion of inanimate, animal and human agency. *Archaeological Dialogues* 22: 207-38. https://doi.org/10.1017/S1380203815000264

Malafouris, L., and C. Renfrew (eds.)

2010 *The Cognitive Life of Things: Recasting the Boundaries of the Mind.* Cambridge:

McDonald Institute for Archaeological Research.

Marshall, Y.
2008   The social lives of lived and inscribed objects: a Lapita perspective. *Journal of the Polynesian Society* 117: 59-101.

Meskell, L.
2004   *Object Worlds in Ancient Egypt*. Oxford: Berg.
2005   (ed.) *Archaeologies of Materiality*. Oxford: Blackwell.

Miller, D. (ed.)
2005   *Materiality*. Durham, North Carolina: Duke University Press.

Muhly, J.D.
1989   The organisation of the copper industry in Late Bronze Age Cyprus. In E.J. Peltenburg (ed.), *Early Society in Cyprus*, 298-314. Edinburgh: Edinburgh University Press.

Nativ, A.
2014   Anthropocentricity and the archaeological record: towards a sociology of things. *Norwegian Archaeological Review* 47: 180-95. https://doi.org/1 0.1080/00293652.2014.957235

Normark, J.
2015   Going against the flow: reaction to Veronica Strang. *Archaeological Dialogues* 22: 199-206. https://doi.org/ 10.1017/S1380203815000252

Olsen, B.
2003   Material culture after text: re-membering things. *Norwegian Archaeological Review* 36: 87-104. https://doi. org/10.1080/00293650310000650
2012a Archaeological theory, Christmas port and red herrings: reply to comments. *Current Swedish Archaeology* 20: 95-106.
2012b Symmetrical archaeology. In I. Hodder (ed.), *Archaeological Theory Today*, 208-28. 2nd edn. Cambridge: Polity.

Olsen, B., M. Shanks, T. Webmoor and C. Witmore
2012   *Archaeology: The Discipline of Things*. Berkeley: University of California Press. https://doi.org/10.1525/california/9780520274167.001.0001

Olsen, B., and C. Witmore
2015   Archaeology, symmetry and the ontology of things. A response to critics. *Archaeological Dialogues* 22: 187-97.   https://doi.org/10.1017/ S1380203815000240

Panagiotopoulos, D.
2013   Material versus design: a transcultural approach to the two contrasting properties of things. *Transcultural Studies* 2013(1): 145-76. Online: http://journals.ub.uni-heidelberg.de/index.php/transcultural/issue/view/1306.

Pauketat, T.R.
2015   Review of I. Hodder, *Entangled: An Archaeology of the Relationships between Humans and Things* (Malden, Massachusetts, Wiley-Blackwell, 2012); L. Malafouris, *How Things Shape the Mind: A Theory of Material Engagement* (Cambridge, Massachusetts: MIT Press, 2013); B. Olsen, M. Shanks, T. Webmoor and C. Witmore, *Archaeology: The Discipline of Things* (Berkeley: University of California Press, 2012); and P. Graves-Brown, R. Harrison and A. Piccini (eds.), *The Oxford Handbook of the Archaeology of the Contemporary World* (Oxford: Oxford University Press, 2013). *Cambridge Archaeological Journal* 25: 909-11.

Pluciennik, M.
2013   Escaping from the pen? *Archaeological Dialogues* 20: 155-59. https://doi. org/10.1017/S1380203813000202

Pye, D.
1968   *The Nature and Art of Workmanship*. Cambridge: Cambridge University Press.

Robb, J.
2004   The extended artifact and the monumental economy: a methodology for material agency. In E. Demarrais, C. Gosden and C. Renfew (eds.), *Rethinking Materiality: The Engagement of Mind with the Material World*, 131-39. Cambridge: McDonald Institute for Archaeological Research.
2010   Beyond agency. *World Archaeology* 42:

493-520. https://doi.org/10.1080/004 38243.2010.520856

2013 Material culture, landscapes of action, and emergent causation: a new model for the origins of the European Neolithic. *Current Anthropology* 54: 657-83. https://doi.org/10.1086/673859

Shanks, M.
2007 Symmetrical archaeology. *World Archaeology* 39: 589-96. https://doi.org/10.1080/00438240701679676

Spriggs, M. (ed.)
1977 *Archaeology and Anthropology: Areas of Mutual Interest*. British Archaeological Reports, Supplementary Series 19. Oxford: British Archaeological Reports.

Stech, T., R. Maddin and J.D. Muhly
1985 Copper production at Kition in the Late Bronze Age. In V. Karageorghis and M. Demas, *Excavations at Kition* V.1: 388-402. Nicosia: Department of Antiquities.

Strang, V.
2014 Fluid consistencies: material relationality in human engagements with water. *Archaeological Dialogues* 21: 133-50. https://doi.org/10.1017/S1380203814000130

Thomas, J.
2015 Why 'the death of archaeological theory'? In C. Hillerdal and J. Siapkas (eds.), *Debating Archaeological Empiricism: The Ambiguity of Material Evidence*, 11-31. London and New York: Routledge.

Thomas, N.
1991 *Entangled Objects: Exchange, Material Culture and Colonialism in the Pacific*. Cambridge, Massachusetts: Harvard University Press.

Tilley, C.
2006 Theoretical perspectives: objectification. In C. Tilley, W. Keane, S. Kuechler-Fogden, M. Rowlands and P. Spyer (eds.), *Handbook of Material Culture*, 7-11. London: Sage.

2007 Materiality in materials. *Archaeological Dialogues* 14: 16-20. https://doi.org/10.1017/S1380203807002139

2010 *Interpreting Landscapes: Geologies, Topographies, Identities*. Explorations in Landscape Phenomenology 3. Walnut Creek, California: Left Coast Press.

Tilley, C., W. Keane, S. Kuechler-Fogden, M. Rowlands and P. Spyer (eds.)
2006 *Handbook of Material Culture*. London: Sage.

Tylecote, R.F.
1982 The Late Bronze Age: copper and bronze metallurgy at Enkomi and Kition. In J.D. Muhly, R. Maddin and V. Karageorghis (eds.), *Early Metallurgy in Cyprus, 4000-500 BC*, 81-103. Nicosia: Pierides Foundation.

van der Leeuw, S.
2008 Agency, networks, past and future. In C. Knappett and L. Malafouris (eds.), *Material Agency: Towards a Non-Anthropocentric Approach*, 217-47. New York: Springer. https://doi.org/10.1007/978-0-387-74711-8_12

van der Veen, M.
2014 The materiality of plants: plant-people entanglements. *World Archaeology* 46: 799-812. https://doi.org/10.1080/00438243.2014.953710

van Oyen, A.
2015 Actor-network theory's take on archaeological types: becoming, material agency and historical explanation. *Cambridge Archaeological Journal* 25: 63-78. https://doi.org/10.1017/S0959774314000705

Webmoor, T.
2007 What about 'one more turn after the social' in archaeological reasoning? Taking things seriously. *World Archaeology* 39: 547-62. https://doi.org/10.1080/00438240701679619

2013 Symmetry, SIS, archaeology. In P. Graves-Brown, R. Harrison and A. Piccini (eds.), *The Oxford Handbook of the Archaeology of the Contemporary World*, 105-20. Oxford: Oxford University Press.

Webmoor, T., and C. Witmore

2008 Things are us! A commentary on human/things relations under the banner of a 'social' archaeology. *Norwegian Archaeological Review* 41: 53-70. https://doi.org/10.1080/00293650701698423

Witmore, C.

2014 Archaeology and the New Materialisms. *Journal of Contemporary Archaeology* 1: 203-24. https://doi.org/10.1558/jca.v1i2.16661

15 Tradition and Divide in Archaeological Publication

Camilla MacKay

Introduction

Over the course of many years, John Cherry has provided some of the most comprehensive and influential assessments of survey archaeology and the state of the field from the 1980s to the present. While his article 'Frogs round the pond' (Cherry 1983) naturally only touches on the use of computers, data from Mediterranean surveys even then held the promise of considering larger regional questions through the computer-based integration and analysis of multiple datasets. Twenty years later, Cherry predicted that the use of online data from archaeological surveys would expand these possibilities: 'The likely next stage—though it may require some convergence or agreement about standards of data presentation—is the possibility of conducting meta-searches of numerous Web-based survey databases' (Cherry 2003: 153). But while it is indisputable that the affordances offered by technology have changed and enhanced research questions in archaeology (see Knodell and Leppard, this volume), the possibilities of digital publication of archaeological survey data have not translated into the widespread adoption—or even more crucially use—of wholly digital publications. Comparisons are for the most part only possible in the same way they have always been, through narrative accounts and catalogs. Consider the nature of this publication: the medium and form is in essentials hardly different than it would have been decades ago. The same is true of the dissemination of results of archaeological fieldwork. While the complexity of certain types of archaeological data, like excavation data, may make online publication of meaningful data difficult, even relatively simple survey data are either not at all or not consistently published online, and the type of regional cross-pollination of information that digital publication might facilitate is still lacking.

The intractably conservative (because of self-imposed and externally imposed constraints on its authors) field of scholarly publishing has meant that the sharing predicted and encouraged by Cherry is still in the future. Because of this, there must be greater consideration to the ways in which technology and online dissemination can partner with traditional models of publishing to encourage sharing of information in order to improve understanding of the regional approaches to society and complexity that are the subject both of Cherry's work and this volume.

Digital Scholarship, Digital Publication, and the Humanities

For years, there have been predictions of the gradual demise of the book, yet books remain a predominant mode of communication in the humanities and social sciences. Concomitant are predictions of multimodal digital scholarship eclipsing the limitations of print and print-imitative digital publishing. An example is the digital replacement of print journals that mimic a print volume/issue method of publication, which is largely unnecessary in the digital work but ingrained in existing processes and built-in digital publishing platforms. Yet there is very little sign of digital-only scholarship superseding traditional media. While books from North American and European university and academic presses are now often available as e-books (if not simultaneously with print), there is no diminution in the availability of print, and the turn to print-on-demand by many presses has made print books even more available and more long-lived. Predictions about the role of reuse of data in the archaeology of the future through their online publication are like the assumptions of the death of print monographs a decade ago: they have not materialized.

The data collected in the course of field projects today are not in and of themselves problems: rather, the problem lies, if it exists, in the publication of data that allows reuse and in whether anyone wants to reuse that data. Scholars in the humanities and social sciences are deeply wedded to the long-form narrative (e.g., Elliott 2015), and, in archaeology, to the curated catalog, which is antithetical to the unordered presentation of data. As Manovich writes in *The Language of New Media*, data

> do not tell stories; they do not have a beginning or end; in fact, they do not have any development, thematically, formally, or otherwise that would organize their elements into a sequence. Instead, they are collections of individual items, with every item possessing the same significance as any other. (Manovich 2002: 218)

Moreover, he adds, 'database and narrative are natural enemies' (Manovich 2002: 225). An additional complication is that it is hard to use someone else's data. Even with carefully curated metadata, there is no standardization, and with many publications, there is no way of downloading, manipulating, and effectively reusing raw data. The possibilities for capturing data digitally undoubtedly enhance the research questions of practitioners, but there is only so much querying of static online databases anyone wants to do or can do; there is only a return to the recording of the data and the interpretation and bias that accompanies that process, and contextualization is crucial (Rabinowitz and Sedikova 2011; Faniel *et al.* 2013). Self-consciousness of the limitations of archaeological data by its practitioners must also play a role, since archaeologists must be aware of the fallacies that may lie in too close scrutiny of archaeological data because of limitations in its collection (although Moore and Richards [2015: 35] point out: 'Such cultural reluctance is not new to archaeology; yet these issues have not precluded the sharing of data in the past, but have simply constrained the scale of dissemination').

Why has online publication and reuse of archaeological data not significantly advanced? Why is digital publication of data either not done, or if so, why can these data not join the conversation? Why can excavation and survey monographs and the synthetic articles of, for example, the *Journal of Mediterranean Archaeology*, not live side by side with digital data-driven publishing that is, crucially, used and cited within academic scholarly communication?

Experiments that have sought to support complex digital presentation of scholarly inquiry (i.e., digital scholarship, enabled by tools or digital formats and inseparable from its digital format) in an academic environment have often disappeared. Critical considerations of these projects in the humanities are all too rare, but a few recent assessments address the reasons for failures. In the 1990s, Project Gutenberg was an early attempt to create a prestigious platform for digitally enhanced publications in history, but it evolved to become an attempt at an economically sustainable model for digital publishing and thus into little more than a digital platform for traditional books. It was not sustainable, partly because there was little desire then (as now) to read them online (Seaman and Graham 2012). Another, in which archaeology and classics played a large role, was Project Bamboo (2008–2012), an expensive multi-institutional and multi-national project intended to be a 'cyberinfrastructure initiative for the arts and humanities' (projectbamboo.org): that is, a means of providing shareable tools and services, including those that would enable the interoperability and sharing of data. But the scholars, technologists, and librarians involved never came to a common ground, and the project was never even comprehensively defined. A major difficulty was that the scholars were never engaged in so-called solutions to problems they did not really perceive or believe in (Dombrowski 2014).

Several recent initiatives in digital publication in the humanities (some of which have yet to begin publishing) acknowledge the necessity of having a print surrogate of digital editions, with the result that many of the publications themselves are essentially digital replications of print books, although with the very important feature that they are all open access. These include the newly formed Lever Press of the Oberlin Group of liberal arts college libraries (www.leverpress.org), the highly publicized new Amherst College Press (acpress.amherst.edu), California Classical Studies (calclassicalstudies.org), and Dickinson College Commentaries (dcc.dickinson.edu). The expanded possibilities of digital scholarship beyond open access, and in particular integration of data that is too voluminous or difficult to publish in traditional media, may remain challenging because of real and perceived failures like those of projects such as Project Gutenberg and Project Bamboo, or the failure of digital presses like Rice University Press (Moody 2013) or Anvil Academic (http://www.clir.org/initiatives-partnerships/anvil-academic-publishing).

Individual publications of archaeological data, like the projects discussed above, have been no more successful. In *Side by Side Survey* (Gates *et al.* 2004), which includes a catalog of online publications of survey data, Gates, Alcock, and Cherry already sounded a note of pessimism about the long-term potential for websites and the lack of digital publication of archaeological survey data: 'The number of websites, Mediterranean-wide, is apparently quite modest—certainly fewer than we had supposed might exist—and, despite much casual talk about "web publishing", very few of them in fact present data at the level of detail that would be standard in a printed final publication' (Gates *et al.* 2004: 243). Despite their acknowledgment of the ephemerality of the sites, it is nevertheless somewhat surprising how many sites have disappeared, and even disappeared completely. In December 2015, only one fifth of the sites listed in 2003 (11 of 55) either still existed or redirected in a way that made it easy to discover the new site. In many cases, the 2003 sites belonged to scholars who were still active in the field in 2015, but who had essentially abandoned these online platforms. Sometimes, the site was updated to point to a synthetic print publication that was intended to supersede the more raw data originally available. These trends concerning the ephemerality of websites extend well outside archaeological scholarship. Consider the widely publicized recent study that found that 50% of Supreme Court web citations no longer return either any page, or the correct information on a live link (Zittrain *et al.* 2014).

Online Digital Repositories

Are solutions to be found in the relatively new online repositories of archaeological publications and archaeological data, which provide long-term and stable platforms and curated content? The Archaeology Data Service (archaeologydataservice.ac.uk/), for example, which stores records for a number of archaeological projects, has existed since 1996. But Archaeological Data Service archives are often downloadable content such as reports; the material either cannot be read online, or is difficult to use online: for example, images may not be easily consulted with the text. A more recent project is tDAR, the Digital Archaeological Record (tdar.org), which is a repository of largely North American data, yet tDAR in particular is not an open access publication site, but rather an archive, and one can easily find oneself browsing metadata for datasets and reports for which no access is available. These are just two of the numerous projects that have been developed, either for single projects, or as software available for any projects, to capture and manage digital data, but primary goals of tDar and the Archaeology Data Service are the archiving and publication of data. Other tools available that encompass a broader lifecycle of archaeological data starting at discovery, such as ARK (ark.lparchaeology. com), may have an online publication component, but long-term preservation and presentation of data is often dependent on personal initiative and institutional support, and one can expect the same lack of stability seen in the websites of the early 2000s.

A sophisticated recent entry to the field is Open Context, a project of the Alexandria Archive. Open Context is an attempt in part to turn data publication into real publication, with components of the traditional scholarly communication model like peer review, an expectation that archaeologists will need expert guidance and leadership in the mechanics of digital publishing—like with print publishing— and with an emphasis on facilitating reuse of data. Projects can present data including reports, images, catalogs, and GIS data, all of which are readable and searchable online. Importantly, all the data are open access; the site is intended for publication of data, and not simply its preservation. Crucially, data are also archived by the California Digital Library. Open Context moves from the organization and curation of the data to the design and publication of the data, and acknowledges the role of context and narrative.

Because it is open access and because it has existed for several years, citations of Open Context projects may provide some information as to the acceptance and reuse of archaeological data from a curated data publication platform. Google Scholar indexes citations to Open Context URLs, thus showing mention of Open Context as a whole, but also citations to projects published from Open Context. A search in late 2015 yielded 118 scholarly works citing Open Context, following the removal of duplicates, Twitter archives, and webpages that linked to Open Context. These works included articles, books, chapters, dissertations, theses, and white papers. Of these, the majority (64%) mentioned Open Context in the service of something else: usually a footnote mentioning its existence, and many of these articles were not about archaeology at all but rather about digital scholarship and digital publishing. Twenty-five (21%) were articles *about* Open Context itself, not about its projects and data, and 22 of these were authored or co-authored by its editors-in-chief, Sarah Whitcher Kansa and Eric Kansa. Three Google citations actually were Open Context projects, specifically documents providing reports on field projects published on Open Context. Finally, 15 articles (a rather low 13%) cited archaeological data published through Open Context. The number is not very high (even if the method of measurement through Google Scholar is likewise not very accurate), but I think it is nonetheless a sign of at least moderate success: the site is providing access to projects and data that are being recognized and, most importantly, cited in a scholarly context. Yet none of those articles and dissertations delve into the data: what are cited are the narratives of the projects.

The practice of citation itself is one of the points of resistance to the reuse of digital data, and perhaps a reason for the lack of citations of specific material from Open Context. Citations of data in the print-centered world produce anxiety. One need only look as far as the citation guidelines for the very series in which this volume is published, where at the time of publication only one example was provided for a web publication, which was listed like a monograph with a single author and distinct title. The reality of data authorship and web access is of course much more complex and variable. As Borgman (2015: 251-52) suggests, even when data would better be cited, authors find print publications to use as proxies for the data contained within. Given the short lives of most web publications, this is no wonder. Yet the greater problem is making data reusable by actually publishing it openly in the first place. As Borgman (2015: 268) writes:

> Data citation is a solution for a poorly defined problem. Mapping bibliographic citation to data citation on the grounds that publications and data deserve equal status is misguided. Making data discoverable is the real problem at hand. Publications are, and will remain, the stars and planets of the scientific universe. Methods to assign credit only need to shine enough light on data that they cease to be dark matter.

While in theory the use, comparison, and aggregation of archaeological data predicted by Cherry could be accomplished through a single site like Open Context, with its attention to metadata, the projects published therein are disparate and largely unrelated. Interest in comparative, cross-regional archaeology, evinced by scholars like Cherry and the contributors to this volume, is dependent on narrative interpretation and arguments.

Archaeological projects now are gathering more and more data in digital form, but even when openly available online, substantive reuse of these data remains elusive in the scholarly communications ecosystem. Cherry's prediction of sharing survey data in the relatively early years of presentation of archaeological data online was logical then as now, but it is still in the future, as emphasis on publishing archaeological fieldwork remains traditional. Scholarly publishing, despite economic and practical incentives for new formats and new modes of dissemination, remains almost intractably consistent and conservative; academia continues to resist fully digitally enabled publication, despite the sense it makes within such a data-driven field as archaeology, and publishers fear loss of income with more open formats of digital publication. There are many reasons for this: the importance of narrative interpretation as a primary mode of communication and the domination of the monograph as a form of scholarship in the humanities; the alleged conservatism of tenure and promotion committees, despite institutional and society-level acknowledgment of the validity of rigorous digital scholarship, like the January 2016 College Art Association and Society of Architectural Historians guidelines for evaluation of digital scholarship (College Art Association and the Society of Architectural Historians 2016); or the lack of logical place within the structure of scholarly communication for born-digital scholarship (e.g., MacKay 2014). Interpretation of archaeological fieldwork remains the most essential part of publication.

Preservation and robust curation of archaeological data online may become more necessary as granting agencies increasingly either require data management plans, or those that already require data management plans move beyond accepting mere promises of data backups (e.g., in the US, government agencies like the National Science Foundation). But until there is a way that data and narrative are more closely aligned in openly available repositories, let alone published in consistent ways, the situation will not markedly improve. Moreover, scholars in the humanities in particular are unused to paying for the right to publish their material; paying for publication can feel like vanity publishing, but storage and publication of data, especially through a fee-based external archaeological repository that might ensure the stability that the local institutional website does not, is unlikely to be widely adopted until this culture changes.

A Note on Linked Data

Linked data, whereby data from disparate online sites or repositories can be collected and reused based on machine-readable metadata, may someday provide possibilities for richer searching and aggregation of data. The potentials of linked data are dependent on the rigorous use of controlled vocabularies and metadata schemas (ontologies), and while certain concepts and areas in linked data are well-established (for example, international conventions for identifying authors, like the Virtual International Authority File [viaf.org]), conventions for identifying abstruse and disparate archaeological finds, are, with some examples, not. There are competing examples of controlled identifiers and ontologies, especially for abstruse data; and in the case of survey data, it is hard to imagine being able to identify. In general, examples of linked data benefiting the end user are still rare, though some sites show its promise. Some well-defined sources, like Pleiades (pleiades.stoa.org), which provides stable identifiers for places of importance in the ancient Mediterranean, have enabled the collection of linked data through use of the Pleiades vocabulary. The online project OCRE (Online Coins of the Roman Empire; numismatics.org/ocre) aggregates examples of coins through the use of controlled numismatic identifiers created from a standard print reference work, *Roman Imperial Coinage*. While the number of repositories that publish coins following these standards such that they can be included in the OCRE database is limited, they are large and influential (e.g., the American Numismatics Society and the British Museum), and thus one can imagine more widespread adoption in order to facilitate discovery of coins from smaller collections.

Nonetheless, enhancement of scholarly communications and scholarly publication through linked data is still some way in the future, and can best be envisioned for closely controlled fields with widespread adherence to the same standards. Roman coins have long been extremely well known and well classified: OCRE is truly useful in that it collects information like photographs of coins from online databases that make use of shared vocabulary. Other types of archaeological data, like pottery, are messier, and especially in the case of survey archaeology, where identification of surface finds can be tentative. Given different methods of recording data, the different interests of specialists on projects, and the local variability of pottery production, linked data seems more likely to be useful in an environment like numismatics (see, for example, Kansa 2014 on ambivalence about linked data and the use of the complicated CIDOC-CRM ontology).

Were there a widespread commitment to publishing open archaeological data through platforms like Open Context, however, linked data might be a way to discover certain types of well-defined data (that from temporal periods or geographical areas) based on shared vocabularies.

A Case for Open Access

While solutions to several of the problems noted above are unlikely to appear anytime soon, there is at least one more immediate means for ameliorating the sharing of archaeological interpretation and data: a commitment on the part of authors to open access dissemination of their publications through trusted, open-access institutional and subject repositories (for long-term preservation, not the potentially ephemeral social networking sites like Academia.edu, although these are good for discovery). This is especially important for archaeological publications, because of the prevalence of monographs for publications of individual projects. Publishers, authors, and funders have grappled with the business models of journal publishing and a majority of publishers of toll-access journals now allow some form of open-access dissemination of the intellectual content of articles (see sherpa.ac.uk/romeo/). The number of fully open-access journals likewise continues to grow (doaj.org). National and private granting agencies too are pushing the issue with open-access requirements for grant-funded research. But books are a different model. There is a general lack of advocacy for open access by authors, accompanied by uncertainty concerning the balance necessary for the coexistence of open access to scholarship and a market for scholarly monographs. This means that methods for sharing data are still far from robust. Advocacy and understanding on the part of authors therefore must grow. Archaeologists often work in countries with far fewer resources than those of their home institutions. Moreover, open access represents an 'ethical imperative of equal access to knowledge … and it seems especially significant as we seek to build truly global scholarly communities' (Elliott 2015). While open access to research may be emerging too slowly, interest in open access will continue to grow as authors rethink the form of publication and the benefits of reaching a wider audience.

In conjunction with online presentation of archaeological data, open digital access to a synthetic long-form publication will drive use of the archive through embedded links. Consider the difficulty of typing in a long, number-filled URL of the sort Open Context uses. Yet when archaeological data is published online, were authors to include links to their own data in those still-essential synthetic publications, and to make those publications openly available, it is more likely that the links will be followed, and the more likely that those links may lead to exploration of additional data.

It seems increasingly unrealistic to envision a substantial change in the near future in humanities and social sciences scholarship, despite concern for declining revenues at presses, predictions that the 'digital native' generation will prefer digital publication (they in fact like reading books in print, as many surveys have now documented), and new possibilities for digitally enhanced publication. Yet even if the essentially narrative monograph and article persist, discovery of scholarship is increasingly important and increasingly conducted (almost exclusively) online. A greater connection between narrative publication in archaeology and the data can enhance the possibility of serendipitous discovery—and use—of broader and deeper (and just plain more) data than is possible through print publication. Adaptation of the traditional model of publishing to link to permanent, durable, and stable open archives of data, like those long available through the ADS or more recently through Open Context, can help advance scholarly inquiry in archaeology—or can at least speed the process.

Open access to the traditional narratives and catalogs may not facilitate the type of interactive experience with archaeological data predicted by John Cherry, but it can help to better facilitate the transfer of knowledge as academic authors and scholarly publishing move very gradually toward the possibilities offered by digital publication and the promise of meaningful comparisons that elucidate examination of regional approaches to the archaeological record.

Acknowledgments

I thank John Cherry for his guidance and mentorship as an advisor, and for the pleasure, renewed when researching this paper, of reading his always lucid and elegant scholarship. I am also grateful to Alex Knodell and Tom Leppard for the opportunity to participate in this conference and publication.

About the Author

Camilla MacKay is Director of Research and Instructional Services and Scholarly Communications Librarian at Bryn Mawr College. She has participated in fieldwork most recently in Greece as a member of the Eastern Boeotia Archaeological Project. Her research interests include medieval and post-medieval pottery and the intersection of digital and print scholarly publications, inspired in part by serving as one of the senior editors of the open access journal *Bryn Mawr Classical Review*. E-mail: cmackay@ brynmawr.edu

References

Borgman, C.L.
  2015 *Big Data, Little Data, No Data: Scholarship in the Networked World*. Cambridge, Massachusetts: MIT Press.

Cherry, J.F.
  1983 Frogs round the pond: perspectives on current archaeological survey projects in the Mediterranean region. In D.R. Keller and D.W. Rupp (eds.), *Archaeological Survey in the Mediterranean Area*. British Archaeological Reports, International Series 155: 375-415. Oxford: British Archaeological Reports.
  2003 Archaeology beyond the site: regional survey and its future. In J.K. Papadopoulos and R.M. Leventhal (eds.), *Theory and Practice in Mediterranean Archaeology: Old World and New World*

Perspectives. Cotsen Advanced Seminars 1: 137-59. Los Angeles: Cotsen Institute of Archaeology.

College Art Association and the Society of Architectural Historians
  2016 *Guidelines for the Evaluation of Digital Scholarship in Art and Architectural History*. Online: http://www.collegeart.org/pdf/evaluating-digital-scholarship-in-art-and-architectural-history.pdf

Dombrowski, Q.
  2014 What ever happened to Project Bamboo? *Literary and Linguistic Computing* 29: 326-39. https://doi.org/10.1093/llc/fqu026

Elliott, M.A.
  2015 The future of the monograph in the digital era: a report to the Andrew W.

Mellon Foundation. *Journal of Electronic Publishing* 18(4). Online edition: https://doi.org/10.3998/3336451.0018.407

Faniel, I., E. Kansa, S.W. Kansa, J. Barrera-Gomez, and E. Yakel
2013   The challenges of digging data: a study of context in archaeological data reuse. In *Proceedings of the 13th ACM/IEEE-CS Joint Conference on Digital Libraries*, 295-304. New York: ACM. https://doi.org/10.1145/2467696.2467712

Gates, J.E., S.E. Alcock and J.F. Cherry
2004   Internet resources for Mediterranean regional survey projects: a preliminary listing. In S.E. Alcock and J.F. Cherry (eds.), *Side-by-Side Survey: Comparative Regional Studies in the Mediterranean World*, 243-51. Oxford: Oxbow Books.

Kansa, E.
2014   Open Context and linked data. *ISAW Papers* 7.10. Online: http://dlib.nyu.edu/awdl/isaw/isaw-papers/7/kansa/

MacKay, C.
2014   Book Reviews and digital scholarship. *Journal of Electronic Publishing* 17(3). Online: https://doi.org/10.3998/3336451.0017.305

Manovich, L.
2002   *The Language of New Media*. Cambridge, Massachusetts: MIT Press.

Moody, F.
2013   Rice University Press: nascentis fame. *Journal of Electronic Publishing* 16(1). Online: https://doi.org/10.3998/3336451.0016.102

Moore, R., and J. Richards
2015   Here today, gone tomorrow: open access, open data and digital preservation. In A.T. Wilson and B. Edwards (eds.), *Open Source Archaeology: Ethics and Practice*. Berlin and Boston: De Gruyter. https://doi.org/10.1515/9783110440171-004

Rabinowitz, A., and L. Sedikova
2011   On whose authority? Interpretation, narrative, and fragmentation in digital publishing. In J. Erszebet, F. Redo and V. Szeverenyi (eds.), *On the Road to Reconstructing the Past: Computer Applications and Quantitative Methods in Archaeology (CAA)*, 134-40. Budapest: Archaeolingua.

Seaman, J.T., Jr., and M.B.W. Graham
2012   Sustainability and the scholarly enterprise: a history of Gutenberg-e. *Journal of Scholarly Publishing* 43: 257-93. https://doi.org/10.3138/jsp.43.3.257

Zittrain, J.L., K. Albert and L. Lessig
2014   Perma: scoping and addressing the problem of link and reference rot in legal citations. *Harvard Law Review Forum* 127(165): 165-88. https://doi.org/10.1017/s1472669614000255

16 Retrospect and Prospect in Regional Archaeology

Thomas P. Leppard and Alex R. Knodell

Introduction

In this concluding chapter we examine some common themes in the foregoing papers and assess how coherent 'regional approaches' are when viewed comparatively and diachronically. In this vein, we also highlight areas of disagreement or difference between the individual chapters. Under the banner of retrospect, areas of conceptual overlap include: (1) common concerns about how to integrate wider material environments into archaeological narratives without ceding too much ground either to determinism or to an anthropocentric position; (2) interpretative interests in data-generation and integration; and (3) explicit concern with how complex societies—especially 'states'—function and interrelate. Areas more divergent include: (1) approaches to scale and what constitutes 'regional' archaeology and (2) the extent to which it is possible to make comparative generalizations between different contexts.

We then turn to prospect, a topic on which the honorand of this volume has repeatedly mused (Cherry and Renfrew 1986; Cherry 2003; 2004). Knowing what we do about the current practice of archaeology, its technological trajectories over the last couple of decades, and the training and research foci of its practitioners, what future patterns might we sketch (see Kintigh *et al.* 2014)? We suggest that there exist reasons to be both optimistic and pessimistic, not least related to the capacity of material, geological, and biological approaches to extract more and better data from archaeological landscapes, even as a variety of forces threaten these landscapes. In terms of bodies of theory deployed to make sense of these burgeoning data, we explore what developing theories of regional archaeology might look like. We stress—reiterating our earlier discussion (Knodell and Leppard, this volume)—a need above all for diversity in regional approaches to the study of complex societies, although this requires individual practitioners to be both increasingly specific in the presentation of their work and engaged with literature beyond their particular specializations.

Convergent Themes

The previous chapters of this volume all examine the archaeology of complex societies, but range substantially in time, space, and approach. In which areas, then, does tacit consensus between the varied approaches adopted here occur? All of these contributions are concerned at some level with regional archaeology as (broadly) described in the introductory chapter (Knodell and Leppard, this volume). We detect in several of them, moreover, shared interests in the relationship between human and nonhuman agents and forces. These latter vary widely, from things to central places to landscapes to dynamic climates. While such matters are rarely treated together, we find a common interest in approaching material things and physical environments from increasingly critical perspectives, especially in establishing a middle ground between determinism and agency. The operation and maintenance of complex societies is another common thread throughout the volume, although (perhaps surprisingly) there is rather less about issues of emergence or state formation (but see especially Manning, this volume). We see increasing interest—here and across the discipline as a whole—in tracing explicit connections between territory and polity in how complex societies construct and maintain social power and authority. The explicit integration of multiple scales of analysis is a shared attribute of several of the preceding papers, and is crucial to what we consider the most meaningful regional approaches to society and complexity.

Materials and Environments between Determinism and Agency

Many of the papers in this volume betray a deep concern with the nonhuman material world. Here we note the (at least implicit) presence of a conceptual middle ground which lies between the extremes of environmental determinism and the reification of humans as the only actors in an otherwise mute landscape. In particular, it is clear that both the 'new materialisms' (see papers by Witmore, Knapp) and the resurgent interest in environmental dynamism (papers by Manning, Garrison, Fitzpatrick) in both Old and New World archaeology have impacted regional archaeology and studies of social complexity.

In Broodbank's and Fitzpatrick's approaches to island environments (echoed by Smith and van Dommelen), an underlying assumption is that different types of configuration of the physical world pose fundamentally similar types of problems to humans. Building on their own and others' previous work (Evans 1973; 1977; Cherry 1981; 1984; Keegan and Diamond 1987; Broodbank 2000; 2013; Fitzpatrick *et al.* 2007; Fitzpatrick and Anderson 2008; Cherry and Leppard 2014), they note how island environments often share regularities in terms of biophysical systems: how their biotas are organized; their responsiveness to climatic and oceanographic dynamism; and their often-comparable geologies and pedologies. Broodbank and Fitzpatrick both suggest that the regularities of geographic organization that islands and archipelagoes represent may have driven the adoption of similar strategies—of subsistence configuration, of movement and exchange, and of sociopolitical organization—in otherwise dissimilar contexts. Fitzpatrick, with a more explicitly ecological focus, addresses comparable processes in the horticulturalist colonization of the tropical and subtropical insular Caribbean and Pacific. Broodbank ranges more widely, exploring the potential of and inherent limitations in searching for frames of reference for the Mediterranean, highlighting the utility of the later prehistoric archaeology of Indonesia, Malaysia, and potentially the Indian Ocean as a source of viable comparanda. He cautions against unnecessary haste in the bid to compare and contrast, however, and explores in detail just how rare the Mediterranean situation might be.

While Fitzpatrick and Broodbank address the relationship between islands and cultural systems, the significance of their work extends well beyond island archaeology. Implicit in their papers is the challenge that, if comparable types of environmental organization can drive convergent adaptations (such as similar types of subsistence or resource-acquisition strategies in island contexts), then more complex adaptive outcomes (such as social, spatial, and political organization) may also emerge and converge. This underlying assumption is also evident, albeit expressed differently, in Manning's paper. Manning, in exploring how dynamism in climate systems may be translated into variable effects depending on landscape context, similarly operates under the assumption that certain classes of nonhuman material process (in this instance, the establishment of the Late Holocene climate regime and the heterogeneous changes that implies) provide the context for human action and frame trajectories of social development. Manning also highlights how structural change in material conditions is unlikely simply to drive macro-scale social change in a simple linear relationship. At the same time he stresses that seeking to explain change within appropriate and coherent timeframes—with broader reference to social and environmental process—is vital. We should be cautious, then, in regarding attempts to explain correspondence in temporal patterning between climatic and social processes. For example, the breakdown of the Old Kingdom in Egypt, the disappearance of the Early Helladic II 'Corridor Houses' in the Aegean, and wider upheavals across southwest Asia around 2200 BC are likely influenced by, but cannot be fully explained as a simple outcome of, Holocene climatic wobbles (Weninger *et al.* 2009). Clearly we should expect a relationship, but the effects of large-scale environmental change are mediated in various ways. It may be that large-scale social change is a final outcome, but the intervening socioecological processes are complex.

We see a number of strengths to this approach, which is not in and of itself fundamentally novel, but charts a safe course between determinist and constructivist extremes. In particular, we should stress that this perspective—which conceives of total material and social environments as the context in which human action occurs—avoids the dangers of a framework in which humans only respond to environmental dynamism. In Broodbank's, Fitzpatrick's, and Manning's papers, humans do not respond to the machinations of the environment in that they form part of it, their own actions driving—perhaps more than any other species—changes in wider biophysical systems (see also Garrison, this volume). In this sense these papers endorse a Historical Ecology framework (e.g., Crumley 1994; Butzer 2005; Fitzpatrick and Keegan 2007), but one that is enriched by human agency and the variability of human responses to adversity (e.g., Bevan *et al.* 2013).

In general, we might see notions of constraint and opportunity, rather than determinacy, as more productive means of understanding the relationship between human agency and the materials within which it is embedded. This point is reiterated by Garrison in his consideration of the appropriate scales and angles of analysis for territories of Classic Maya city states, inspired by Renfrew and Cherry's peer polity interaction (Renfrew and Cherry 1986). For Garrison, the ecological context of the Classic Maya does not determine trajectories of development or even modes of interaction (Dunning *et al.* 2004), but acknowledging the environmental parallels in the Maya area suggests both appropriate scales of analysis as well as common challenges faced by Maya polities, with levels of political integration (territories versus alliances, in Garrison's terms) relating to physiographic organization.

How, if at all, do discussions of environmental context and human agency speak to the 'new materialisms', or at least to implicitly allied approaches grouped under the banner of the 'material turn' (Thomas 2015)? Witmore is concerned with the material conditions for the operation of the Greek *polis* that was Classical Argos, albeit working within a very different intellectual tradition than the ones described above, and less concerned with ecology and environment (see Latour 2005; Sloterdijk 2005; Witmore 2007; Webmoor and Witmore 2008). Nevertheless, we see shared interests in (rightly) advocating for the role of the nonhuman. Witmore addresses the extent to which the total material environment of Argos—both as produced by humans, and generative of itself—framed and delimited human action and, thereby, social and political functions. This is not enormously distinct from the position we sketched in the preceding paragraphs. Witmore is keen to move away from an exclusively human agency and toward a more widely distributed agency, and this has the salutary effect of accentuating that human activity can be frustrated or enabled in its goals by material conditions. Knapp, despite questioning the extent to which interest in human behavior has been diluted in 'new materialist' and allied approaches, finds common ground with Witmore in recognizing a dynamic role for material things and physical environments in enabling and limiting human activity. Sekedat echoes this in his discussion of the constitution of landscapes of action, necessarily involving human and nonhuman agency. While not all of the papers in this volume explicitly engage with current theoretical debates concerning the relationships between humans and material worlds, there nonetheless seems to be a consensus that materials, environments, and their human relationships should be understood as neither determinants of human action nor passive recipients of it, but rather as framing *and* defining landscapes of human choice.

The Operation and Maintenance of Social Complexity

Many of the papers in this volume (including those by Galaty, Bennet, Parkinson, Sekedat, Garrison, Fachard, and Manning) deal with the archaeology of states and of empires. A common theme is the importance of grasping not only how states construct and maintain different sorts of power, but also how such power is expressed across the territory of a political entity (such a theme is not surprising in this volume—see Cherry 1983; 1986; 1987).

Several papers address the nature of the states that appeared in the Aegean in the Middle and Late Bronze Age (2000–1050 BC). Manning deals explicitly with the emergence of these states and types of explanation that have been mobilized to account for this emergence. After unpacking—and nuancing—broad-brush periodization and associated implications about causation in the later third millennium, he considers Cretan trajectories from hierarchies to states and formalized modes of governance, explaining how diverse sets of imagery, behavior, and material culture were co-opted and utilized in Aegean elite contexts. Bennet, similarly, pays close attention to the deployment of materials and symbols by elites within and outside of the palace to articulate and maintain ideologies of power. In exploring the notable absence of ruler imagery in the otherwise richly decorated palaces, Bennet suggests that this absence is in fact an index of how the palatial elite conducted the administration of the palace and the wider state. Both papers examine elite Bronze Age Aegean ideology via its referent materials, used both to differentiate and to unify within regionally distinct polities, which nonetheless shared certain island-wide or cross-regional characteristics.

The focus of Bennet on how individual palaces mobilized symbolic as well as actual capital prompts a question that has recently been addressed in synthetic studies of the economic operation of Mycenaean palaces (Nakassis *et al*. 2011; Parkinson *et al*. 2013; Nakassis *et al*. 2016): to what extent can we generalize about the 'palatial' in contrast to individual palatial systems, mainly the best-known examples of Pylos and Knossos? Clearly, the problem of generalizing about the degree of what we might call structural parallelism between the Late Helladic centers (as well as between Protopalatial centers on Crete) has been considered before (Killen 2007), but ongoing work at several centers has not yet forced a resolution. Newer data from the second-tier sites at Eleon in Boeotia and Iklaina in Messenia (Burke *et al*. 2013; Cosmopoulos 2015), as well as recent discoveries at Aghios Vassileos in Laconia, further underscore that, while certain aspects of palatial administration seem to be widespread (not least Linear B), there is substantial variability in physical layout and distribution of activities within and around major Mycenaean sites. The concern must be that a corollary of this is that talking in terms of 'Mycenaean'—or, indeed, 'Minoan'—strategies may be a bridge too far, and Bennet is surely correct to emphasize the partial nature of the evidence and the importance of interpretive conservatism. More generally, the nature of the research undertaken at the major centers necessarily means that previous palatial iterations, with their potential variability, are obscured by the final phase of construction.

If the modes in which palatial elites attempted to legitimize and maintain their regimes of power differed subtly from site to site, we might also speculate whether the nature of the breakdown of these regimes also differed. There has been an understandable tendency to seek unifying explanations for the Late Helladic 'collapse', especially as the final breakdowns of these complex systems seem to occur, more or less, within a century of one another. We touch on the issue of emergence and collapse below, but here we simply note that seeking monocausal explanations may not necessarily be the most efficient route (see Knapp and Manning 2016). One of us (Knodell 2013) has previously suggested that thinking in terms of the network durability of Mycenaean states may be a useful way to model and explain their rapid breakdown (or, from an alternative perspective, why they failed to be more than a transient phenomenon). More or less durable forms of spatial control, or different means of conceptualizing the space in which the palace exerted forms of authority (see Glatz 2009 regarding the case of Late Bronze Age Anatolia), might account for the slightly differing longevity of 'palatial' systems in different parts of the Aegean at different times.

Systems of power and their maintenance are also a major focus for Sekedat and Galaty. Both papers are concerned with the acquisition and deployment of high-value or high-status goods in elite contexts. Sekedat's main interest is in how the procurement of certain types of materials by the Roman state (in this case, marble) can be examined from a regional perspective, how this can be understood to have driven what we might call integrative processes, and how such an approach can contribute to wider debates on the nature of the imperial economy. Galaty, in contrast, follows Cherry (2010) in addressing how eastern Mediterranean exotica were consumed in Minoan and Mycenaean contexts (again hinting at variability in regimes of value across the second millennium Aegean and eastern Mediterranean). Here we detect echoes of a broader and burgeoning interest in the construction of value in the ancient world (Papadopoulos and Urton 2012). In terms of the Late Bronze Age Aegean, Galaty's approach arguably represents a conceptual compromise (anticipated by Cherry 1986) to the often revisited debate of local emergent process versus external stimulus (Manning 2008; this volume; Legarra Herrero 2016). We suggest that such contextual approaches to systems of power and value, based on the acquisition and deployment of exotic goods in new, regionally specific contexts, have resonance well beyond the geographical and chronological contexts they describe.

In historical periods we have the obvious benefit of textual sources to aid interpretations and explanations of political interactions on a regional scale. Fachard brings multiple types of data to bear on the issue of how Classical and Hellenistic *poleis* demarcated discrete, if small, territories. He stresses how the capacity to maintain and articulate a coherent border—via monuments, memorialization, and reiterated action (see Alcock 2003)—was emblematic of political and administrative independence, albeit in the context of Roman hegemony. Sekedat explores parallel dissonances between the local and the imperial. In case studies from the New World, Garrison moves beyond models of peer polity interaction to examine actual territorial relationships based on archaeological and—significantly—textual data, noting the impact of the decipherment of the Maya script on studies of political relationships; Ryzewski reflects on the impact that the variety of historical documents available to historical archaeologists has had on the archaeology of the Caribbean. These latter two papers, while concerned with area-specific agendas, again reinforce lessons for Mediterranean archaeologists about the importance of triangulating on research problems from multiple sources of data and theory.

In terms of drawing wider lessons, we might wonder how peer polity (Renfrew and Cherry 1986) models are improved or obviated by differing types and quantities of data available to archaeologists interested in complex societies. As a potentially crude but perhaps productive comparison based on textual accounts, we note that Maya elites and the administrative classes of ancient Greek *poleis* seem extremely interested in their peers, Minoan and Mycenaean palatial states much less so. This may be a function of the evidence—there are no Linear B stelae recording boundaries or deeds of named rulers, for example (Bennet, this volume). However, the absence of evidence here may in fact be quite good evidence for absence. There is a general sense in which at least the Bronze Age palaces of Pylos and Knossos seem resolutely focused on internal territorial operations and less on boundaries, whereas for Classical Athens and Tikal the concern is in part reversed. Such differences conceivably derive from differing conceptions of governance and space in small peer polities (e.g., Smith 2003). Why such differing conceptions emerge, and the functional reasons for their emergence in terms of how states operate, may be fruitful venues for future work based on more direct comparison.

Points of Dissonance

While the chapters of this volume share much background and consensus on several issues, not least those described above, certain points of dissonance have also emerged. We see this as somewhat inevitable, considering the breadth of material and the specializations represented here, but far from problematic. Rather, these divergences provide fruitful grounds for discussion concerning the central themes of this volume, in particular regarding issues of scale and approaches to cross-cultural relevance or comparison.

Scales of Analysis and Regional Archaeology

There are differences in how the papers in this volume—all concerned generally with regional approaches to society and complexity—deploy or endorse (tacitly or explicitly) bodies of theory as they relate to the appropriate scale at which to undertake regional archaeology. While there is clearly widespread interest in multi-scalar analysis, approaches remain multifarious. For much of its history, regional archaeology has tended to shy away from widespread endorsements of theoretical schools or positions, beyond broadly adhering to an agenda of defining patterns in the distribution of material culture and interpreting the significance of such patterns *vis-à-vis* the organization of human societies (Knodell and Leppard, this volume). More explicit efforts to set an agenda, for example oriented around archaeologies of landscape (e.g., Knapp and Ashmore 1999), settlement pattern studies (Kowalewski 2008), or regional settlement demography (Drennan *et al.* 2015), have generally been made with the acknowledgment that there is no need for one theoretical agenda to preclude another.

The foregoing papers cover the gamut from settlement hierarchies (distribution, function, political organization) to symmetrical archaeology, with historical ecological and landscape approaches in between, not to mention Alfred Gell. We argue that such divergence in ways of dealing with the problem of archaeology above the level of the site is unequivocally healthy and, considering the variety of intellectual veins which have flowed into 'regional archaeology' (definitions of which vary widely between practitioners), largely unavoidable. We also note that the foregoing contributions endorse a degree of flexibility in approaches to and definitions of scale; none is irreducibly wedded to a scale-specific credo. This range also glosses the fact that a working definition of *region* does not emerge from reading these papers in tandem. As we note in the introduction to this volume, 'region' can be used to describe spatial entities from a small, microgeographical area to a polity and its associated structures and beyond.

While we stress the positive aspects of such a range, as it also brings out the multiple scales on which complex societies operate, there remains a nagging question concerning whether or not we are all doing the same thing. Here Parkinson's paper is instructive. Parkinson highlights what he describes as the historical schizophrenia of European archaeology, torn as it is between, on the one hand, grand syntheses and, on the other, chronologies and interpretations built on relatively few sites (something that Childe 1925 and Renfrew 1972 have in common). Parkinson, recognizing this contradiction as an inherent weakness (although it may also be a weakness inherent to many world archaeologies), suggests that the tradition of intensive microregional study bridges the divide between the local and the continental (*contra* Blanton 2001). In this conception, a multi-scalar approach is the most efficient way to build a robust understanding of dynamism in the spatial organization of human societies, and this is echoed in papers by Sekedat, Garrison, and Ryzewski, among others. Other contributions exist at more extreme points on the spatial spectrum: Broodbank's focus is substantially wider, Witmore's more restricted. This raises the question of the appropriate scale, or scales, of analysis at which to understand how polities and systems of polities form and operate. This is inevitably context-dependent, but this dependency surely has implications for comparability, a topic to which we turn below.

A more specific focus on Blanton's (2001) notion of 'Mediterranean myopia' may be instructive. The charge leveled at Mediterranean archaeologists working at a regional level is that a methodological myopia—an intensive focus on a very small study area or microregion—restricts an appreciation of the broader picture. Presumably, whether or not Mediterraneanists are myopic is dependent on the scale of the systems in which they are interested. Not all ancient polities operated on a scale comparable to the Oaxacan state, even if assessments of the size of the Monte Alban polity are accurate (Blanton *et al.* 1999); it is also not clear that studying the extent of an entity is (necessarily) preferable to focusing on a subset of it. These points relate to appropriate scales and hierarchies of sampling—again, no new theme to the contributors of this volume and to its honorand (Cherry *et al.* 1978). Primary determinants of method should be (1) what it is that we wish to know and (2) how secure we would like our inferences to be. For example, in seeking to understand the long-term settlement dynamics of a small island, a hierarchical sampling strategy which covers that island seems intrinsically appropriate (Cherry 1982); a more detailed focus on the expansion and contraction of a site or a polity over its long history requires a more focused lens (e.g., van Dommelen and Roppa 2012; Whitelaw 2014).

The scale of 'Mediterranean-style' surveys may, then, be fundamentally appropriate to the nature of the objects under study. That granted, the reason for the scale and methodological intensity adopted should arguably be made more explicit in the Mediterranean. One of the shared strengths of Garrison's, Ryzewksi's, Parkinson's, and Sekedat's papers is their articulation of why the scale of analysis adopted is so important. These papers also have the advantage that the regional scale projects on which they draw are question-led, beyond the usual appeal to settlement dynamics over the *longue durée*. More generally, and happily, the 'great divide' (Renfrew 1980) largely fails to materialize between and amongst the papers in this volume, pointing a way forward for continued engagement through divergent paths.

Seeking Comparison: Side-by-Side, or Back to Front?

Many of the papers presented here endorse a comparative perspective. In anthropological archaeology, comparative approaches have received substantial attention as a coherent intellectual enterprise, especially in the context of the functioning of states and political organizations. This, of course, is in part the intellectual tradition in which the peer polity concept is embedded, and the utility of comparison in elucidating the extent to which we can generalize about human social and spatial organization continues to be explored (Smith 2012). It has been emphasized, however, that how and on what terms comparison is attempted is a determinant of how useful an exercise this may be (e.g., Yoffee 2005: 193-94; Cherry and Davis 2007: 126). Given the nature of the papers in this volume, the specifics of comparison are infrequently explored in detail, nor is direct comparison an explicit aim of all of the papers. Nevertheless, the mechanics of comparison still require attention. We focus here on Galaty's and MacKay's papers as a means of illustrating this point.

MacKay's paper reviews what, in some terms, seems to have been a shortfall in the regional archaeology of the Mediterranean. As intensive pedestrian surveys blossomed across the Mediterranean between 1980 and 2000, the rich potential for a basin-wide diachronic dataset—through which generalized trends and localized exceptions might be accessed quantitatively—was recognized (e.g., Alcock and Cherry 2004). A functional aspect of this project involved the availability of the huge datasets generated by survey projects, and here MacKay highlights the more or less general failure of electronic databases with associated metadata to emerge in a useful and widespread fashion. Her argument addresses what might be considered a wider problem discussed at various points in this volume: comparing the results of survey projects. The limitations inherent in this sort of undertaking were already made explicit by Given (2004), and it is not clear that we can advance his conclusions, excepting that we can note, with MacKay, mild surprise that such a desirable agenda has not been further advanced. In the probable continued absence of the direct means to compare surveys 'side-by-side', we argue that the approach adopted by, e.g., Bevan and Conolly (2013) may represent best practice, emphasizing the explicit acknowledgment of the route taken from data to interpretation, and relative strengths and weaknesses therein.

The Mediterranean region is not alone in its struggles of comparing results between projects. Access to and comparison between large digital datasets is not widely facilitated in archaeology in general, and the medium itself seems to possess severe structural problems in terms of curation and consultation (Bevan 2015). Nevertheless, some successful examples do exist, especially when it comes to electronic databases of archaeological sites (e.g., the Electronic Atlas of Ancient Maya Sites, the Digital Archaeological Atlas of the Holy Land, the MAGIS [Mediterranean Archaeology GIS] project). These are far from comprehensive, however, and are updated only to varying degrees. Moreover, they provide limited information about sites and survey boundaries, and no information 'beyond the site'. The large-scale benefits are clear, but these resources have relatively little specialized use for regional archaeologists.

On a related point, several papers in this volume—including Galaty, Broodbank, and Smith and van Dommelen—rely to differing extents on comparison, not between datasets, but between archaeologically or ethnographically known societies (or both) to illuminate some aspect of these societies. Broodbank and Smith and van Dommelen couch the intellectual basis for the comparisons they undertake in prevailing physiographic organization (i.e., insularity and attendant ecological or even social properties); Galaty, working with ethnographic data, bases his comparison between ethnohistoric Albanian village societies and the Bronze Age Aegean in terms of the apparent willingness, in both contexts, to embrace and refigure exotic import goods. Few of these papers explicitly address the nature of how inferences from such comparison can be rendered more robust, but focusing on shared conditions, as these chapters do, is surely the most productive way to build good analogical arguments (Wylie 1982). If we wish to make claims about human behavior and why this changes over time in different cultural circumstances, then interesting outcomes lie down a path of detailed and thoughtful comparison. Here, Cherry's own fieldwork odyssey across the Atlantic is instructive (Cherry *et al.* 2012). What is to be gained by, and what are the risks of, moving into new but structurally parallel fields of research? One vital and obvious immediate return is the clarity that such immersion brings to any attempts at comparison, surely an improvement on armchair attempts at moving to new research areas; it is also to be suspected that one way to overcome certain interpretive gulfs is to see, as it were, how the other half lives. As the foregoing papers make clear, the basis for and nature of the comparison is likely to affect the usefulness of the outcome. Nevertheless, there is much to be gained from thoughtful, critical, and properly contextualized comparative frameworks, both in terms of method and in terms of interpretations relevant to the trajectories of complex societies.

Prospects and Concerns

Scrying the innards of these papers, and recognizing that predicting the future tends to have a low rate of success, what might we hope for in regional archaeology to come? Our hope here is less to prescribe and more to conjecture where current trajectories might take us, based on the foregoing papers and our own reviews here and in the introductory chapter of the volume.

Before moving on to an attempt to extrapolate from current trends, we note some concerns that necessarily constrain and promote certain research agendas. The archaeological record is, in some senses, a finite resource, and our capacity to access it is at risk from a series of angles. Most obviously and in most high-profile fashion, the continuing destruction of sites and monuments is problematic, via any agency (non-state actors and insurgent organizations, populations habituated to looting, environmental degradation, development, etc.), especially considering that these activities tend to cluster in certain parts of the world. Both the material stuff and research contexts of regional archaeology are increasingly threatened as the archaeological record falls between the crosshairs of political, religious, and ethnic contestation. The development of policy concerning regional archaeological practice also affects how we interpret our data, and varies considerably throughout the world. The organization of permit systems, the relationship between cultural resource management and academic archaeology, funding structures, and prevailing political climates all profoundly impact the practice of archaeology, and increasing variability in how nation states approach these issues only complicates the sort of comparative approach advocated here.

With such concerns in mind, what might we expect from regional archaeology in the short- to medium-term? As described in our introduction to this volume, technological change has already had a profound impact on archaeological research at a variety of scales, especially the regional scale and beyond. In particular, the increasing availability of remotely operated vehicles—whether the now ubiquitous and affordable aerial drones, or the less affordable but increasingly common unmanned submersibles—has the potential to transform radically how fieldwork is carried out. At a gross level, regional archaeologists are necessarily interested in spatial patterns that are difficult to observe or access from a pedestrian perspective. Small fragments of cultural material distributed across large and varied spaces, or alternatively large, anthropogenic landforms that are expressed only very subtly as slight variation against a background (for example, Roman roads or plowed-out burial tumuli), are intrinsically obscure. The rise of platforms—at increasingly low cost—for technologies such as aerial photography or more advanced imaging technologies, more adept at recognizing large-scale anthropic landforms and landscapes, holds much promise. We predict that this will have a somewhat democratizing effect on the field, not unlike the early days of the 'new wave' of archaeological survey in the Mediterranean, circumventing the requirement for hefty grants and bearing implications for junior scholars in terms of richer, diverse datasets from which to approach new research questions. An attendant question is: has the sophistication of our research questions kept pace with the sophistication of our technology? We might wonder whether, in the rush to embrace the novel, we are really generating fresh insights into how humans behaved and organized themselves in the past, and how this changed (some might, after all, fairly venture that the questions raised in this volume are not so different than those posed some decades ago). Nevertheless, the range of applications of new technologies outside of more traditional archaeological research and into issues of managing and sustaining cultural resources is surely reason to be cautiously optimistic. In general, we would imagine that the broadening use of low-cost technologies in regional archaeology will continue to expand datasets and open up hitherto unimagined vistas.

What of the now venerable concerns of regional archaeological research? And how do they specify on what basis such research happens? We would like to consider here the relationship between the methodologies of regional archaeology and specific types of questions asked by regional archaeologists. The importance of a diachronic approach has been an essential assumption of most practitioners of survey or pedestrian archaeology in the Mediterranean, although it is often less so beyond that region, for a variety of reasons. As research programs advance, however, it has become clear that greater methodological flexibility may be required in order to focus on types of data that are inherently less visible in the standard type of approach. An obvious example involves the debate regarding Lower and Middle Palaeolithic sites on Mediterranean islands (e.g., Leppard 2014; Runnels 2014). If resolving this debate is in part dependent on generating more data, then strategies of recovery tailored to the problem (i.e., identifying and targeting landscape niches that are likely to have been the focus of any archaic hominin activity) are vital. This high-resolution focus by specialists on certain types of material culture in certain types of places inevitably involves losses from a diachronic perspective. Trade-offs like this are probably necessary in other research contexts, including the unresolved debate regarding 'off-site' material (e.g., Caraher *et al.* 2006), but also other themes discussed in the foregoing, such as, for instance, the emergence and operation of the Minoan palaces (cf. Schoep *et al.* 2012; Manning, this volume). Our point is not that this is inherently negative, nor inherently positive; rather it is simply that, to the extent that research is question-led rather than data generation-led, a diachronic perspective will not always remain the norm, and this should be embraced under the banner of methodological diversity.

Serendipity in the process of archaeological discovery—the chance site, the unlooked-for technological innovation—has been a favorite theme of John Cherry throughout his career (see Davis, this volume). New discoveries—whether island Mesolithics or hitherto unexplored political centers—clearly inform and impact how archaeology is undertaken, and these tend to be at the level of the site (as Parkinson recognizes in his chapter). The relevant question, then, is from what direction might we expect the unexpected? We have already hinted at one, in the form of newer survey technologies, but the archaeological sciences—and perhaps especially burgeoning work on stable isotopes and archaeogenetics—already have a clear, if under-recognized, capacity to set research agendas (Killick and Goldberg 2009), and they hold more promise than ever in addressing regional-scale research questions. Other surprises may be geographical: the northern shore of the Mediterranean can be argued to have been thoroughly explored; the Maghreb, much less so. There are few areas of the planet untouched by regional archaeology, but there are areas—temporal, as well as spatial— where this work has not clustered. Philosophically we should be optimistic that what data we have are more or less representative, but we can only become more sure of this as research expands into areas that have not formed the traditional focus of regional archaeological projects. Central Asia, Siberia, sub-Saharan Africa, and the Canadian Arctic (interestingly, areas remote from initial emergence of 'pristine' states) are not as well-represented in the survey literature. We would hazard that those areas that have witnessed the most intense exploration at the regional level—specifically, the northern Mediterranean, parts of southwest Asia, and Mesoamerica—have fewer novelties in store in terms of newly discovered sites, but further fieldwork and re-analysis of settlement pattern data, with new questions and techniques, will continue to be a fruitful way forward, as will comparisons within and between traditionally distinct cultural areas and archaeological sub-disciplines.

The prospects for regional archaeology, then, within and beyond the Mediterranean, surely relate to the extent that time-honored archaeological questions—concerning nomadism and sedentism, state formation, human–environmental interaction, material worlds, collapse—are tackled from newer methodological and theoretical angles, especially through technological and scientific innovations, while recognizing the operational constraints of policy and wider political contexts. These are themes explored by the papers in this volume by senior and junior scholars who have helped and are helping to define and further the field in these terms. In the final analysis, it is appropriate—and clearly no coincidence—that these themes characterize John Cherry's career, which has always focused on research questions of first-order importance, specified flexibly and clearly, and approached using a varied methodological and theoretical toolkit that does not foreclose on interpretation but rather pushes and cajoles into new horizons of exploration.

Acknowledgments

Bernard Knapp, Tom Tartaron, and Bob Chapman read drafts of this chapter, and we are very grateful for their considered and constructive comments. As students of this volume's honorand, we owe as much to him as do other contributors. We enthusiastically echo here previous comments by our more illustrious forebears regarding unfailing intellectual and moral support, an infectious sense of excitement about and the importance of immersion in our field, teaching and supervision of the highest quality, and a profound understanding of the best proportion of carrot versus stick. On a more personal note, neither of us can really imagine how we might have embarked on a career in this field, let alone how we might have completed our graduate studies, without John Cherry's unfailing support, his willingness to exaggerate our virtues to anyone who would listen, and his steadfast friendship expressed, as it has been, in myriad ways. We take this opportunity to thank him deeply for all that he has done for us, and hope this book serves as some small symbol of our gratitude.

About the Authors

Thomas P. Leppard is Renfrew Fellow in the McDonald Institute for Archaeological Research at the University of Cambridge. His research concerns the comparative archaeology of island societies in the Mediterranean, Caribbean, and Pacific, especially issues of colonization, mobility, and emergent social complexity. Recent articles on these subjects have appeared in *Human Ecology*, the *Cambridge Archaeological Journal*, *Current Anthropology*, the *Journal of Island and Coastal Archaeology*, the *Journal of Mediterranean Archaeology*, and *World Archaeology*. He currently conducts fieldwork in Micronesia and Sardinia. E-mail: tpl26@cam.ac.uk

Alex R. Knodell is Assistant Professor of Classics and Co-Director of the Archaeology Program at Carleton College, Northfield, Minnesota. He currently co-directs the Mazi Archaeological Project (northwest Attica, Greece) and previously served as Field Director of the Brown University Petra Archaeological Project (Petra, Jordan). Other research interests include the development of complex societies in the Late Bronze Age and Early Iron Age Mediterranean, especially in relation to the Euboean Gulf of Greece. Recent articles have appeared in the *American Journal of Archaeology*, *Antike Kunst*, the *Journal of Archaeological Science*, the *Journal of Field Archaeology*, and *World Archaeology*. E-mail: aknodell@carleton.edu

References

Alcock, S.E.
2003 *Archaeologies of the Greek Past: Landscapes, Monuments, and Memories.* Cambridge: Cambridge University Press.

Alcock, S.E., and J.F. Cherry (eds.)
2004 *Side-by-Side Survey: Comparative Regional Studies in the Mediterranean World.* Oxford: Oxbow Books.

Bevan, A.
2015 The data deluge. *Antiquity* 89: 1473-84. https://doi.org/10.15184/aqy.2015.102

Bevan, A., and J. Conolly
2013 *Mediterranean Islands, Fragile Communities and Persistent Landscapes: Antikythera in Long-Term Perspective.* Cambridge: Cambridge University Press. https://doi.org/10.1017/CBO9781139519748

Bevan, A., J. Conolly, S. Colledge, C. Frederick, C. Palmer, R. Siddall and A. Stellatou
2013 The long-term ecology of agricultural terraces and enclosed fields from Antikythera, Greece. *Human Ecology* 41: 255-72. https://doi.org/10.1007/s10745-012-9552-x

Blanton, R.
2001 Mediterranean myopia. *Antiquity* 75: 627-69. https://doi.org/10.1017/S0003598X00088918

Blanton, R., G. Feinman, S. Kowalewski and L. Nicholas

1999 *Ancient Oaxaca*. Cambridge: Cambridge University Press. https://doi.org/10.1017/CBO9780511607844

Broodbank, C.

2000 *An Island Archaeology of the Early Cyclades*. Cambridge: Cambridge University Press.

2013 *The Making of the Middle Sea: A History of the Mediterranean from the Beginning to the Emergence of the Classical World*. London: Thames and Hudson.

Burke, B., B. Burns, A. Charami and O. Kyriazi

2013 Eastern Boeotia Archaeological Project: preliminary report on excavations 2011-2013. *Teiresias* 43(2): 9-25.

Butzer, K.

2005 Environmental history in the Mediterranean world: cross-disciplinary investigation of cause-and-effect for degradation and soil erosion. *Journal of Archaeological Science* 32: 1773-1800. https://doi.org/10.1016/j.jas.2005.06.001

Caraher, W.R., D. Nakassis and D. Pettegrew

2006 Siteless survey and intensive data collection in an artifact-rich environment: case studies from the Eastern Corinthia, Greece. *Journal of Mediterranean Archaeology* 19: 7-43. https://doi.org/10.1558/jmea.2006.19.1.7

Cherry, J.F.

1981 Pattern and process in the earliest colonization of the Mediterranean islands. *Proceedings of the Prehistoric Society* 47: 41-86. https://doi.org/10.1017/S0079497X00008859

1982 A preliminary definition of site distribution on Melos. In C. Renfrew and M. Wagstaff (eds.), *An Island Polity: The Archaeology of Exploitation in Melos*, 10-23. Cambridge: Cambridge University Press.

1983 Evolution, revolution, and the origins of complex societies in Minoan Crete. In O. Kryszkowska and L. Nixon (eds.), *Minoan Society: Proceed-*

ings of the Cambridge Colloquium 1981, 33-45. Bristol: Bristol Classical Press.

1984 The initial colonization of the west Mediterranean islands in the light of island biogeography and palaeogeography. In W. Waldren, R. Chapman, J. Lewthwaite and R.-C. Kennard (eds.), *The Deya Conference of Prehistory: Early Settlement in the Western Mediterranean Islands and Peripheral Areas*. British Archaeological Reports, International Series 229: 7-28. Oxford: Oxbow Books.

1986 Palaces and polities: some problems in Minoan state formation. In C. Renfrew and J.F. Cherry (eds.), *Peer Polity Interaction and Socio-Political Change*, 19-45. Cambridge: Cambridge University Press.

1987 Power in space: archaeological and geographical studies of the state. In J.M.E. Wagstaff (ed.), *Landscape and Culture: Geographical and Archaeological Perspectives*, 146-72. Oxford: Blackwell.

2003 Archaeology beyond the site: regional survey and its future. In J.K. Papadopoulos and R.M. Leventhal (eds.), *Theory and Practice in Mediterranean Archaeology: Old and New World Perspectives*. Cotsen Advanced Seminars 1: 137-60, Los Angeles: Cotsen Institute of Archaeology.

2004 Mediterranean island prehistory: what's different and what's new? In S. Fitzpatrick (ed.), *Voyages of Discovery: The Archaeology of Islands*, 233-48. Westport, Connecticut: Praeger.

2010 Sorting out Crete's off-island prepalatial interactions. In W. Parkinson and M. Galaty (eds.), *Archaic State Interaction: The Eastern Mediterranean in the Bronze Age*, 107-40. Santa Fe, New Mexico: School For Advanced Research Press.

Cherry, J.F., and J.L. Davis

2007 An archaeological homily. In M. Galaty and W. Parkinson (eds.), *Rethinking Mycenaean Palaces II:*

Revised and Expanded Second Edition. Monograph 60: 118-27. Los Angeles: Cotsen Institute of Archaeology.

Cherry, J.F., C. Gamble and S. Shennan (eds.)
1978 *Sampling in Contemporary British Archaeology.* British Archaeological Reports, British Series 50. Oxford: British Archaeological Reports.

Cherry, J.F., and T.P. Leppard
2014 A little history of Mediterranean island prehistory. In A.B. Knapp and P. van Dommelen (eds.), *The Cambridge Prehistory of the Bronze and Iron Age Mediterranean*, 10-24. New York: Cambridge University Press. https://doi.org/10.1017/cho9781139028387.004

Cherry, J.F., and C. Renfrew
1986 Epilogue and prospect. In C. Renfrew and J.F. Cherry (eds.), *Peer Polity Interaction and Socio-Political Change*, 149-58. Cambridge: Cambridge University Press.

Cherry, J.F., K. Ryzewski and T.P. Leppard
2012 Multi-period landscape survey and site risk assessment on Montserrat, West Indies. *Journal of Island and Coastal Archaeology* 7: 282-302. https://doi.org/10.1080/15564894.2011.611857

Childe, V.G.
1925 *The Dawn of European Civilisation.* London: Kegan Paul.

Cosmopoulos, M.
2015 A Mycenaean open-air cult place in Iklaina. *Journal of Ancient Egyptian Interconnections* 7: 41-49.

Crumley, C.L. (ed.)
1994 *Historical Ecology: Cultural Knowledge and Changing Landscapes.* Advanced Seminar Series 5. Santa Fe, New Mexico: School for Advanced Research Press.

Drennan, R.D., C.A. Berrey and C.E. Peterson
2015 *Regional Settlement Demography in Archaeology.* New York: Eliot Werner Publications.

Dunning, N.P., S. Luzzadder-Beach, T. Beach, J.G. Jones, V. Scarborough and T.P. Culbert
2004 Arising from the *bajos*: the evolution of a neotropical landscape and the rise of Maya civilization. *Annals of the Association of American Geographers* 92: 267-83. https://doi.org/10.1111/1467-8306.00290

Evans, J.D.
1973 Islands as laboratories of cultural change. In C. Renfrew (ed.), *The Explanation of Culture Change: Models in Prehistory*, 517-20. London: Duckworth.
1977 Island archaeology in the Mediterranean: problems and opportunities. *World Archaeology* 9: 12-26. https://doi.org/10.1080/00438243.1977.9979682

Fitzpatrick, S.M., and A. Anderson
2008 Islands of isolation: archaeology and the power of aquatic perimeters. *Journal of Island and Coastal Archaeology* 3: 4-16. https://doi.org/10.1080/15564890801983941

Fitzpatrick, S.M., J. Erlandson, A. Anderson and P.V. Kirch
2007 Straw boats and the proverbial sea: a response to 'Island archaeology: in search of a new horizon'. *Island Studies Journal* 2: 229-38.

Fitzpatrick, S.M., and W.F. Keegan
2007 Human impacts and adaptations in the Caribbean islands: an historical ecology approach. *Transactions of the Royal Society of Edinburgh* 98: 29-45. https://doi.org/10.1017/s1755691007000096

Given, M.
2004 Mapping and manuring: can we compare sherd density figures? In S.E. Alcock and J.F. Cherry (eds.), *Side-by-Side Survey: Comparative Regional Studies in the Mediterranean World*, 13-21. Oxford: Oxbow Books.

Glatz, C.
2009 Empire as network: spheres of material interaction in Late Bronze Age Anatolia. *Journal of Anthropological Archaeology* 28: 127-41. https://doi.org/10.1016/j.jaa.2008.10.003

Keegan, W.F., and J. Diamond
1987 Colonization of islands by humans: a biogeographical perspective. *Advances in Archaeological Method and Theory* 10: 49-92. https://doi.org/10.1016/B978-0-12-003110-8.50005-0

Killen, J.T.
2007 Critique: a view from the tablets. In M. Galaty and W. Parkinson (eds.), *Rethinking Mycenaean Palaces II: Revised and Expanded Second Edition.* Monograph 60: 114-17. Los Angeles: Cotsen Institute of Archaeology.

Killick, D., and P. Goldberg
2009 A quiet crisis in American archaeology. *SAA Archaeological Record* 9(1): 6-10, 40.

Kintigh, K., J. Altschul, M. Beaudry, R. Drennan, A. Kinzig, T. Kohler, F.W. Limp, H. Maschner, W. Michener, T. Pauketat, P. Peregrine, J. Sabloff, T. Wilkinson, H. Wright and M. Zeder
2014 Grand challenges for archaeology. *American Antiquity* 79: 5-24. https://doi.org/10.7183/0002-7316.79.1.5

Knapp, A.B., and W.A. Ashmore
1999 Archaeological landscapes: constructed, conceptualized, ideational. In W.A. Ashmore and A.B. Knapp (eds.), *Archaeologies of Landscape: Contemporary Perspectives*, 3-30. Malden, Massachusetts: Blackwell.

Knapp, A.B., and S. Manning
2016 Crisis in context: the end of the Late Bronze Age in the Eastern Mediterranean. *American Journal of Archaeology* 120: 99-149. https://doi.org/10.3764/aja.120.1.0099

Knodell, A.R.
2013 Small-World Networks and Mediterranean Dynamics in the Euboean Gulf: An Archaeology of Complexity in Late Bronze Age and Early Iron Age Greece. Unpublished PhD dissertation, Brown University, Providence, Rhode Island.

Kowalewski, S.
2008 Regional settlement pattern studies. *Journal of Archaeological Research* 16: 225-85. https://doi.org/10.1007/s10814-008-9020-8

Latour, B.
2005 From Realpolitik to Dingpolitik. In B. Latour and P. Weibel (eds.), *Making Things Public*, 14-44. Cambridge, Massachusetts: MIT Press.

Legarra Herrero, B.
2016 Primary state formation processes on Bronze Age Crete: a social approach to change in early complex societies. *Cambridge Archaeological Journal* 26: 349-67. https://doi.org/10.1017/S0959774315000529

Leppard, T.P.
2014 Modeling the impacts of Mediterranean island colonization by archaic hominins: the likelihood of an insular Lower Palaeolithic. *Journal of Mediterranean Archaeology* 27: 231-54. https://doi.org/10.1558/jmea.v27i2.231

Manning, S.
2008 Protopalatial Crete: formation of the palaces. In C. Shelmerdine (ed.), *The Cambridge Companion the Aegean Bronze Age*, 105-20. Cambridge: Cambridge University Press. https://doi.org/10.1017/CCOL9780521814447.005

Nakassis, D., M.L. Galaty and W.A. Parkinson (eds.)
2016 Discussion and debate. Reciprocity in Aegean palatial societies: gifts, debt, and the foundations of economic exchange. *Journal of Mediterranean Archaeology* 29: 61-132. https://doi.org/10.1558/jmea.v29i1.31013

Nakassis, D., W.A. Parkinson and M.L. Galaty
2011 Redistributive economies from a theoretical and cross-cultural perspective. *American Journal of Archaeology* 115: 177-84. https://doi.org/10.3764/aja.115.2.177

Papadopoulos, J.K., and G. Urton
2012 *The Construction of Value in the Ancient World*. Los Angeles: Cotsen Institute of Archaeology.

Parkinson, W., D. Nakassis and M. Galaty (eds.)
2013 Crafts, specialists, and markets in Mycenaean Greece. *American Journal*

of Archaeology 117: 413-59. https://doi.org/10.3764/aja.117.3.0413

Renfrew, C.
1972 *The Emergence of Civilisation: The Cyclades and the Aegean in the Third Millennium BC.* London: Methuen.
1980 The great tradition versus the great divide: archaeology as anthropology? *American Journal of Archaeology* 84: 287-98. https://doi.org/10.2307/504703

Renfrew, C., and J.F. Cherry
1986 *Peer Polity Interaction and Socio-Political Change.* Cambridge: Cambridge University Press.

Runnels, C.
2014 Early Palaeolithic on the Greek islands? *Journal of Mediterranean Archaeology* 27: 211-30. https://doi.org/10.1558/jmea.v27i2.211

Schoep, I., P. Tomkins and J. Driessen
2012 *Back to the Beginning: Reassessing Social and Political Complexity on Crete during the Early and Middle Bronze Age.* Oxford: Oxbow Books.

Sloterdijk, P.
2005 Atmospheric politics. In B. Latour and P. Weibel (eds.), *Making Things Public*, 944-51. Cambridge, Massachusetts: Massachusetts Institute of Technology Press.

Smith, A.T.
2003 *The Political Landscape: Constellations of Authority in Early Complex Polities.* Berkeley: University of California Press.

Smith, M.E. (ed.)
2012 *The Comparative Archaeology of Early Complex Societies.* Cambridge: Cambridge University Press.

Thomas, J.
2015 The future of archaeological theory. *Antiquity* 89: 1287-96. https://doi.org/10.15184/aqy.2015.183

van Dommelen, P., and A. Roppa
2012 Rural settlement and land use in Punic and Roman republican Sardinia. *Journal of Roman Archaeology* 25: 49-68. https://doi.org/10.1017/S1047759400001136

Webmoor, T., and C. Witmore
2008 Things are us! A commentary on human/things relations under the banner of a 'social' archaeology. *Norwegian Archaeology Review* 41: 53-70. https://doi.org/10.1080/00293650701698423

Weninger, B., L. Clare, E.J. Rohling, O. Bar-Yosef, U. Böhner, M. Budja, M. Bundschuh, A. Feurdean, H.-G. Gebel, O. Jöris, J. Linstädter, P. Mayewski, T. Mühlenbruch, A. Reingruber, G. Rollefson, D. Schyle, L. Thissen, H. Todorova and C. Zielhofer
2009 The impact of rapid climate change on prehistoric societies during the Holocene in the Eastern Mediterranean. *Documenta Praehistorica* 36: 7-59. https://doi.org/10.4312/dp.36.2

Whitelaw, T.M.
2014 Political formations in prehistoric Crete. *Bulletin of the Institute of Classical Studies* 57: 143-44.

Witmore, C.
2007 Symmetrical archaeology: excerpts of a manifesto. *World Archaeology* 39: 546-62. https://doi.org/10.1080/00438240701679411

Wylie, A.
1982 An analogy by any other name is just as analogical: a commentary on the Gould-Watson dialogue. *Journal of Anthropological Archaeology* 1: 382-401. https://doi.org/10.1016/0278-4165(82)90003-4

Yoffee, N.
2005 *Myths of the Archaic State: Evolution of the Earliest Cities, States, and Civilizations.* Cambridge: Cambridge University Press. https://doi.org/10.1017/CBO9780511489662

Afterword: My Life with John Cherry

Jack L. Davis

In early January 2008, over a winter's dinner in the Palmer House in Chicago, Sue Alcock brought up the concept of 'serendipity', the topic of a forthcoming lecture she had been invited to offer Darwin College, Cambridge. Sue challenged John Cherry and me to come up with good examples of serendipity in archaeology, but I remember being singularly unhelpful: I couldn't think of anything other than the usual boilerplate that archaeologists toss around, about the luck of so-and-so in making his or her big unexpected discovery, particularly when in pursuit of an entirely different objective. But subsequently it occurred to me that in my own professional life there have been many other kinds of serendipitous events, and particularly in my relationship with John Cherry. Here I offer a few long-term reflections on my life with John as a postscript, a reminiscence perhaps made especially appropriate in that many of the characters I mention appear elsewhere in this volume, even more so since our lives have been closely linked since very early on in our respective careers.

Part 1: The American School of Classical Studies at Athens, 1975

At some point in my second year as a student at the American School of Classical Studies at Athens (ASCSA), while writing my PhD dissertation about Aghia Irini, it occurred to me that, if that settlement had been a pivotal node in Aegean exchange in the later Bronze Age, then one should find evidence for contact between Kea and Attica on the adjacent mainland. Because there was little relevant published information, I turned to antiquities collections in the foreign schools for inspiration and confirmation—I hoped. While I was studying sherds from Brauron at the ASCSA, a young American woman waltzed in. She stuck out her hand to shake mine and announced: 'I'm Robin Torrence. Pleased to meet you. Why don't you come over to the British School and meet my boyfriend, John Cherry?'

Part 2: Melos, 1978

Several years later, I had finished my dissertation (John was still working on his—not to dwell on that…). Jack Caskey had cancelled the field season at Aghia Irini. While on vacation in Nauplion I received a message at my hotel: 'A Mr. Cherry rang for you from Melos. You are to get in touch with him urgently.' When I reached John, the message was 'Professor Renfrew wants you to come to Melos immediately. There has been a problem, and he needs you to join the team. It will be fun! We can study the Late Cycladic I pottery together.' So, off I went. Vacation cancelled. John and I began our first collaboration together with Callum Macfarlane. There was merriment too: a trouncing by the local Melian football team, in which much blood was shed—by us, not them.

First Interlude

Later in 1978 John and I decided to highlight Cycladic prehistory at the annual meetings of the AIA in Vancouver; that workshop resulted in our first edited book, which appeared in the following year: *Papers in Cycladic Prehistory*. Having weighed the merits of the then recently published *Thera and the Aegean World II* (literally, at 4.8 kg on his kitchen scales), Paul Halstead in *Antiquity* described *Papers* as bantam-weight—a compliment, I think. Joint appearances at conferences soon became so regular that some colleagues took to introducing us as Chavis and Derry.

At some point we concocted plans for a regional study of Kea, as a foil to the Melos survey, and by autumn 1981 the stage was set. Then disaster struck: our permit request for summer 1982 was denied by KAS (the Central Archaeological Council of the Greek Ministry of Culture).

Part 3: Kea and the Nemea Valley, 1982–1989

The Kea permit denial seemed a heavy blow at the time, but the cloud had a silver lining. Jim Wright discovered our misfortune. He was organizing the Nemea Valley Archaeological Project (NVAP) and wanted us to join him. John and I thus found ourselves at the heart of the largest interdisciplinary studies program yet launched on the Greek mainland.

But by the time NVAP was officially constituted in 1984 we had enjoyed a reversal of fortune and were able to survey northwest Kea in 1983 (with team leaders Cathy Morgan, John Bennet, Sophia Voutsaki, and Todd Whitelaw—all then still graduate students). At Nemea we would refine methods and implement (with variable success) the first infield collection of primary survey data on a laptop—the incredible EPSON-PX8.

Second Interlude

As John and I became closer friends, Sheffield, Southampton, then Cambridge became more and more a part of my life and Chicago part of his. Cyprian Broodbank came on the scene in Cambridge, Nemea, and even Chicago. Separated by an ocean,

John and I corresponded constantly, and in the earlier 1980s we discovered email. We knew in theory that it was possible to transmit electronic messages over a mainframe computer, although we didn't know anyone who had done it. Eventually we achieved some success in transmitting e-mails between Chicago and Cambridge. John and I were in Chicago sending, Robin was in Cambridge on the receiving end. After hours of disappointment, Robin rang on the phone to report success: 'Mr. Watson, come here. I want to see you.'

Part 4: On the Road, 1989

Sue Alcock had shown a certain promise as a fieldwalker at Nemea in 1984; in 1986 she returned to Nemea to organize surface collection of the entire city-state center of Phlious. Then, as NVAP wound down, in 1989 we began to discuss what to do next. That talk resulted in Sue, John, his daughter Ceridwen, and me taking a road trip to Pylos at the end of the summer. John and I drove the long way via Monemvasia, and over Taygetos to Kalamata, while Sue, in the back seat, entertained Ceridwen with stories of two dogs, Dolfur and Dalneenah, and of Fred the Fish, who self-immolated in a volcano. In Monemvasia we stayed in a newly remodeled *hammam*. The owner had a niece who, he said, was studying archaeology, and he asked us to leave our addresses. I received that very piece of paper in a note from his niece, Tania Valamoti, now one of the foremost paleobotanists in Europe, just weeks before the conference in December 2015 that was the basis for this volume. That road-trip was the genesis of the Pylos Regional Archaeological Project.

Part 5: Pylos and Albania, 1994

At PRAP we began to pick up a third generation of students, including Mike Galaty, a Bennet student at Wisconsin, and thus a Cherry grandson. We cross-pollinated Bill Parkinson—after being my undergraduate anthropology student in Chicago he became John's graduate student in Ann Arbor. At the end of PRAP's field season, Shari Stocker, Charles Watkinson, Bill Alexander, John, and I embarked on another road trip: to Albania to help negotiate an arranged marriage for Bill. That excursion resulted in MRAP and DRAP and, I once dared to hope, the end of archaeological acronyms ending in AP.

My Life with John

Collaborations continued, and, on the whole, it would seem that my life with John has evolved as a concatenation of serendipitous events set in motion by that first handshake with Robin Torrence 40 years ago. In addition to John's many successes and scholarly achievements, which this volume reflects, the most remarkable consequence in my eyes has been the many durable friendships John and I have gained, none more lasting than our own. We have been each other's best man and remain best friends to this day.

At my wedding John quoted Homer. I conclude instead with a passage sometimes attributed to Aristotle (*Magna Moralia* 1213a.13-24):

> A friend is a second self, so that our consciousness of a friend's existence … makes us more fully conscious of our own existence.

John Cherry (left) and Jack Davis (right) during the Nemea Valley Archaeological Project (courtesy of the Department of Classics, University of Cincinnati).

About the Author

Jack L. Davis is Carl W. Blegen Professor of Greek Archaeology in the Department of Classics at the University of Cincinnati and former Director of the American School of Classical Studies at Athens. He has co-directed regional archaeological survey projects in Greece on Keos, in the Nemea Valley, and in Messenia, as well as excavations and regional studies in Albania. He currently co-directs excavations at the Palace of Nestor at Pylos. His recent books include *Between Venice and Istanbul: Colonial Landscapes in Early Modern Greece* (American School of Classical Studies at Athens, 2007), co-edited with Siriol Davies, and *Philhellenism, Philanthropy, or Political Convenience* (American School of Classical Studies at Athens, 2013), co-edited with Natalia Natalia Vogeikoff-Brogan. E-mail: davijk@ucmail.uc.edu

Index

Figures in *italics*; n refers to note; t refers to table.

www.ingramcontent.com/pod-product-compliance
Lightning Source LLC
Chambersburg PA
CBHW081427270326
41932CB00019B/3119